Lecture Notes in Computer Science 2635

Edited by G. Goos, J. Hartmanis, and J. van Leeuwen

Springer
Berlin
Heidelberg
New York
Hong Kong
London
Milan
Paris
Tokyo

Olaf Owe Stein Krogdahl Tom Lyche (Eds.)

From Object-Orientation to Formal Methods

Essays in Memory of Ole-Johan Dahl

Volume Editors

Olaf Owe
Stein Krogdahl
University of Oslo
Department of Informatics
P.O. Box 1080, 0316 Oslo, Norway
E-mail: {olaf,stein.krogdahl}@ifi.uio.no

Tom Lyche
University of Oslo
Institute of Informatics and CMA
P.O. Box 1053, Blindern, 0316 Oslo, Norway
E-mail: tom@ifi.uio.no

The illustration appearing on the cover of this book is the work of Daniel Rozenberg (DADARA).

Library of Congress Control Number: 2004103001

CR Subject Classification (1998): D.2, D.3, D.1, F.3, F.4

ISSN 0302-9743
ISBN 3-540-21366-X Springer-Verlag Berlin Heidelberg New York

Springer-Verlag is a part of Springer Science+Business Media

springeronline.com

Printed in Germany

Typesetting: Camera-ready by author, data conversion by Boller Mediendesign
Printed on acid-free paper SPIN: 10992401 06/3142 5 4 3 2 1 0

Ole-Johan Dahl

Preface

After Ole-Johan's retirement at the beginning of the new millennium, some of us had thought and talked about making a "Festschrift" in his honor. When Donald Knuth took the initiative by sending us the first contribution, the process began to roll! In early 2002 an editing group was formed, including Kristen Nygaard, who had known Ole-Johan since their student days, and with whom he had developed the Simula language. Then we invited a number of prominent researchers familiar with Ole-Johan to submit contributions for a book honoring Ole-Johan on the occasion of his 70th birthday. Invitees included several members of the IFIP 2.3 working group, a forum that Ole-Johan treasured and enjoyed participating in throughout his career. In spite of the short deadline, the response to the invitations was overwhelmingly positive.

The original idea was to complete the book rather quickly to make it a gift he could read and enjoy, because by then he had had cancer for three years, and his health was gradually deteriorating. Kristen had been regularly visiting Ole-Johan, who was in the hospital at that time, and they were working on their Turing award speech. Ole-Johan was gratified to hear about the contributions to this book, but modestly expressed the feeling that there was no special need to undertake a book project on his behalf. Peacefully accepting his destiny, Ole-Johan died on June 29, 2002. Kristen, who was 5 years older than Ole-Johan, was still very active. Quite surprisingly, he died 6 weeks later of a sudden heart attack. During this short period, Norway lost its two greatest computer scientists.

We are grateful to all who helped with the book, especially all the contributors and the anonymous referees. Credit is due to Ellef Gjelstad, who helped with the preparation of the manuscript.

University of Oslo
December 2003

Olaf Owe,
Stein Krogdahl,
Tom Lyche

Table of Contents

A Biography of Ole-Johan Dahl

Olaf Owe, Stein Krogdahl, and Tom Lyche

Department of Informatics, University of Oslo

On 12 October 1931, Ole-Johan Dahl was born to the family of a ship captain in Mandal, the southernmost city of Norway. In 1952, three years after beginning his studies at the University of Oslo, he was introduced to computers at the Norwegian Defense Research Establishment (NDRE) where he fulfilled his military service obligation. Jan V. Garwick was responsible for the field of mathematical analysis and calculations, and Ole-Johan was placed in the "computing room" led by Garwick's assistant, Kristen Nygaard. It is quite likely that, in this setting, Garwick, Nygaard and Dahl were the first in Norway to develop programs on "large" digital computers. In the years to come, NDRE cultivated a scientific collaboration with the pioneering computer group at the University of Manchester and the electronics company Ferranti. As a result of this tie, NDRE got the first version of Ferranti's Mercury computer in 1957.

Ole-Johan's next project was to develop and implement a "high level" language for numerical computation, called MAC (Mercury Automatic Coding). While Kristen changed focus to the area of operations research in the mid-1950s, Ole-Johan became Garwick's main collaborator. Together they formed the first real programming group in Norway.

In 1958, Ole-Johan completed the Candidatus Realium degree at the University of Oslo in mathematics. His thesis entitled "Multiple Index Countings on the Ferranti Mercury Computer" [94], was formally in the area of numerical analysis, but actually in computer science and programming, a field that had not yet emerged. In fact, he was one of the first to acquire a relevant and modern education in computer science.

In 1960 Kristen had become research director at the Norwegian Computing Center (NCC). He decided to make an attempt solve two main problems in operations research, namely, *the lack of concepts and language for description and communication about large and complex systems*, and *the lack of a specialized programming language for simulation tasks.* Realizing that he could not do this by himself, he looked to Ole-Johan, a specialist in programming language, as the obvious collaborator.

They started working together in 1961, and in 1963 Ole-Johan joined Kristen full-time at NCC. Together they created the Simula 1 language (1961-1965) and Simula 67 (1965-1968), introducing the concepts of class, subclass and inheritance, virtual binding of operations, and dynamic creation of objects. The Simula concept of quasi-parallelism reflected that objects may in principle be independent processes running in parallel. Implicit forms of information hiding, through the subclass mechanism, were later also complemented by explicit forms of information hiding.

O. Owe et al. (Eds.): From OO to FM (Dahl Festschrift), LNCS 2635, pp. 1–7, 2004.

These concepts, which constitute what today is called object-orientation, have greatly influenced modern programming languages, programming methodology and modeling languages, including UML. The class related concepts in Simula were clearly ahead of their time; it took some 20 years until they gained understanding and popularity. Languages such as Smalltalk, Beta, C++, Eiffel, Java, and C#, have directly adopted Simula's fundamental concepts about objects and classes. Object-orientation is today the dominant style of programming, description, and modeling.

To quote Bjarne Stoustrup: "Simula isn't just an innovative programming language. From the beginning it came with a philosophy of design based on modeling that has had impact far beyond the realm of programming and programming languages." The object-oriented philosophy also underlies the modern use of windows and the graphical interfaces that we all use.

How could Ole-Johan and Kristen, at such an early stage, design a language with all the mechanisms that today form the "object-oriented" paradigm for system development? An important part of the answer is obviously that they were extraordinary talented researchers in the field, and with rather different perspectives and personalities, which frequently led to confrontations and heated discussions. There is a famous story illustrating their style of working: A new employee at NCC came worriedly running down to the receptionist and cried out: "We must do something! There are two men fighting upstairs in front of the blackboard." The receptionist listened for a moment, and replied: "No don't worry. It is just Kristen and Ole-Johan discussing Simula!"

In addition, it was probably very fortunate that they first designed a language for simulation (Simula 1), and later generalized the concepts in a general purpose language (Simula 67). Ole-Johan has expressed it this way: "A reason for this may be that in developing a complicated simulation model it is useful to decompose it in terms of 'objects', and to have an explicit mapping from external objects to program constructs. A natural way of developing real systems is not much different." Kristen emphasized that an essential motivation behind Simula was system description, and the need for a language to model real world concepts.

The final recognition of Ole-Johan and Kristen as the founders of object orientation has been established through two prestigious awards, both given during their last year of life: In November 2001, they were awarded the IEEE John von Neumann Medal "for the introduction of the concepts underlying object-oriented programming through the design and implementation of Simula 67," and in February 2002, they were given the A. M. Turing Award by the ACM "for ideas fundamental to the emergence of object-oriented programming, through their design of the programming languages Simula 1 and Simula 67" [tribute].

Earlier, in June 2000, they were awarded Honorary Fellowships for "their originating of object technology concepts" by the Object Management Group, the main international standardization organization within object-orientation. In August 2000 they were appointed Commanders of the Order of Saint Olav by the King of Norway (one of the highest national awards), and in 1999 they became the first to receive the Rosing Honorary Prize, awarded by the Norwegian Data Association for exceptional professional achievements. Both were elected members of the Norwegian Academy of Science. Ole-Johan was also a member of IFIP Working Group 2.3 and of Academia Europaea, and he received an honorary doctorate from the University of Lund, Sweden.

A characteristic of Ole-Johan as a researcher was his quest for simplicity, elegance, and purity rather than ad hoc solutions with their associated exceptions and compromises. This is reflected in the class concept of Simula. From an educational point of view, its elegance, generality and simplicity make Simula well suited for teaching object orientation.

We include below a version of the last paper Ole-Johan wrote [36][1], which provides a detailed summary of the research leading up to Simula, as well as afterthoughts and viewpoints of its cultural impact. Other sources of information on the development of Simula are [23], and more recently [Hol94, Kro03, Bös03].

Research at the University of Oslo

In 1968 Ole-Johan was invited to be a full professor to create the discipline of computer science at the University of Oslo. He spent enormous efforts building up a curriculum in computer science in the late 1960s, writing textbooks at night while teaching during the day, and supervising up to 20 graduate students at a time. For 10 years from 1968 he was the only professor in computer science in Oslo. For many years, he had only one lecturer and a few research assistants helping him. The courses he designed met the highest international standards of the time and for many years to come. Most of the courses were offered for 20 years or more with only minor changes; some are still being taught.

After beginning his career at the university, Ole-Johan deliberately stopped working on further development of Simula as such. In his new position he felt that it was essential to build up computer science to be an accepted academic discipline, and establish a theoretical foundation for basic concepts of computer science and programming languages. He made important advances in programming methodology, introducing techniques for program structuring and conceptual modeling, based on the experiences of the design and implementation of Simula. Early works in this direction include the papers [1, 4, 10, 13, 14, 16, 17, 63] with his work on *Hierarchical Program Structures* as the best known and most influential.

Inspired by Tony Hoare's logic for program reasoning [Hoa69], he continued research in the area of program architecture, programming and specification languages, as well as verification methods and techniques. Most of this work is related to the area of formal methods, where the idea is to use mathematical methods to specify, develop and reason about programs. Because of his computer science background and education, his theoretical work was accompanied by concern for practical relevance and usefulness. Exploiting the advantages of both, he advocated combined use of top-down development and bottom-up development.

[1] References labeled with numbers refer to the bibliography of Ole-Johan.

This led to research on abstract data types, a concept inspired by the class concept of Simula and Tony Hoare's paper entitled *Proof of correctness of data representation* [Hoa72]. In particular, Ole-Johan focused on generator induction, inspired by the work of John Guttag and Jim Horning, subtyping, inspired by Simula's subclass mechanism and by the work on order sorted algebra, and integration of applicative and imperative class-based reasoning. Based on mechanizable evaluation and reasoning, he developed a theory for "constructive" types and subtypes centered around a long term project, called Abstraction Building, Education Language (ABEL), which served as a research testbed and source of student projects [5, 21, 25, 26, 33, 34, 43, 44, 46, 53], and resulted in several dr. scient theses supervised by Ole-Johan [Owe80, Nos84, Mel86, Lys91].

Ole-Johan was teaching formal methods, and their practical use for 30 years. He believed that computer science students should know the principles of program reasoning, and that this would make them better programmers even without performing detailed verification. The course work has resulted in the book, *Verifiable Programming* [5], which includes much of his own research and results. He supervised a large number of students, ten of whom became university professors.

Formal Methods, Object-Orientation, and Concurrency

Work towards the understanding and formalization of what is now called object-orientation, was carried out already in the early 1970s [15, 18], and with the thesis of Arne Wang, one of Ole-Johan's first students [Wan74].

Ole-Johan's early approach to reasoning about object-oriented systems builds on the idea of limiting direct access to attributes of an object from outside, either disallowing all remote variable access or allowing access to some variables (seen as an abbreviation for implicit read and write operations). This means that one can give local invariants in a class and prove that the class invariant is established and maintained by looking at the text of the class itself and possibly superclasses. When subclassing is restricted so that super-invariants are respected, reasoning about objects can be done without looking at the global state space: Hoare style reasoning can be done locally in each class.

Early on it was recognized that this kind of class-based reasoning was fruitful for the Monitor concept of Hoare [Hoa74] and for aspects of operating systems concerning process control. The co-routine and monitor papers were part of this research direction [15, 18, 19, 20, 21, 29, 35, 64] and the thesis of Stein Gjessing, who had been supervised by Ole-Johan [Gje83].

In contrast to those object-oriented approaches where "everything is an object", Ole-Johan believed in object classes side by side with data types. Ole-Johan's view was that objects should reflect mutable data structures, handled by references, and data types should reflect immutable, but copyable, data [28]. This called for user defined data types. In ABEL, a functional sublanguage was defined for definition of abstract data types, whereas classes were defined in an imperative style. Thus Ole-Johan considered functional programming as a complement to object-oriented programming rather than a competitor.

According to the original ideas of Simula, an object would in general have its own activity, as well as data and procedures. Objects with activity were reflecting "independent processes", and objects without activity (but still with data and procedures) were called passive. In Simula 67 these ideas were realized by allowing objects to be co-routines, the natural way at that time to imitate concurrent processes and a useful simulation mechanism. In today's world a natural adaptation would be to let objects be concurrent processes, and one would obtain a distributed system by a set of objects running in parallel and interacting by remote method calls (only). This is the approach taken in Ole-Johan's later works. See for instance [26, 36].

Ole-Johan's work on abstract specification of concurrent objects by means of histories presents a techniques for "black box" interface specification of process classes. The abstract state of a concurrent object is represented by its communication history, i.e., the trace of all visible communication events involving the object, such as method calls. As the abstract state at any given time is reflected by a finite history, Ole-Johan developed specification techniques based on finite traces, and a central idea was to use right-append as a trace generator in order to describe new actions in terms of the current history, thereby avoiding recursive process definitions as found e.g. in CSP. Reasoning about concurrent objects in terms of such histories is compositional and integrates well with object-orientation. Ole-Johan developed a style of history specification where specifications of a certain form can easily be refined into an imperative object-oriented implementation. The use of histories was initiated in the early 1970s and remained an important research topic for him throughout the 1990s [21, 22, 26, 41, 58]. When he retired, Ole-Johan was writing a book on concurrency based on research in connection with a course on concurrency and process control [69, 54].

The above principles for object-oriented programming, specification, and reasoning, constitute what we may call "the Dahl School." A further introduction is given in the paper by Johnsen and Owe in this volume.

International Visits

Due to Ole-Johan, several prominent researchers visited Oslo. In particular we mention the one year stay of Donald Knuth from Stanford University in 1972 to 1973. Knuth had a great impact on the computer science development in Oslo at an early and crucial period in time.

Knuth, who immediately understood the benefits of the Simula ideas, gave up work on his own simulation language (SOL), and became a supporter of Simula. He could have made Simula quite well-known by teaching it at Stanford, but when asking for a inexpensive compiler for academic use at Stanford, he was unfortunately turned down by NCC (despite the strong arguments of both Kristen and Ole-Johan, who fully understood the importance of this opportunity).

In the late 1970s Reiji Nakajima, a post doc at that time, made a one year visit to Oslo, which led to a number of interesting discussions around abstract data types and ABEL. In the early 80s, Neelam Soundarajan visited Oslo for a year, working together with Ole-Johan on reasoning with histories. Ole-Johan enjoyed this cooperation very much, appreciating Neelam's clarity. Neelam came for a second year in the early 1990s. Zhenjia Lei, University of Xi'an also visited Ole-Johan, which resulted in a return visit by Ole-Johan in Xi'an in the mid-1990s. Apart from this visit, Ole-Johan had only one sabbatical leave during his career, which was spent at Stanford University in the late 1970s.

Ole-Johan also enjoyed the many shorter visits by a large number of scientists, including Tony Hoare, Hans Langmaack, Dines Bjørner, Eugene Kindler, Cliff Jones, Manfred Broy, David Luckham, Jean-Pierre Jouannaud, Pierre Lescanne, and Willem-Paul de Roever, most of whom also enjoyed music evenings and dinners in Ole-Johan's home.

Personal Interests

Ole-Johan was a music lover and an excellent amateur pianist. In fact, he was one of the best "prima vista" amateur pianists in Norway. He knew the world of classical music well, and that of chamber music in particular. Much of his free time was filled by music, and he was a central member of the Board of Oslo Quartet Association and a driving force behind the yearly chamber music courses at the Nansen School in Lillehammer. He regularly arranged house concerts at the department, often playing together with visitors who happened to be musicians, or with his wife or daughter.

In addition he enjoyed and excelled in many kinds of games including chess and bridge, and spent much time as a student pursuing these interests. At conferences he was known for his skills in classical billiards (3 balls) in addition to the piano. A personal bibliography is written by his wife [Dah03].

References

[Bös03] Laszlo Böszörmenyi, Stefan Podlipnig: People behind Informatics: In memory of Ole-Johan Dahl, Edsger W. Dijkstra and Kristen Nygaard. Book written for the memorial exhibition at the international conferences JMLC 2003 and EuroPar 2003, Institute of Information Technology, University of Klagenfurt, Austria, August 2003. `http://www-itec.uni-klu.ac.at/~laszlo/Memorial/memorial_exhibition.htm`

[Dah03] Tove Dahl: A brief biography of Ole-Johan Dahl. 2003. In [Bös03].

[Gje83] Stein Gjessing: Aspects of Semantics and Verification of Monitors, dr. philos. thesis, Department of Informatics, University of Oslo, 1983.

[Hoa69] C. A. R. Hoare: An axiomatic basis for computer programming. *Comm. ACM* 12 (1969), pp. 576–580.

[Hoa72] C. A. R. Hoare: Proof of the Correctness of Data Representations. *Acta Informatica*, vol. 1, 1972, pp. 271–281.

[Hoa74] C. A. R. Hoare: Monitors: an Operating System Structuring Concept. *Comm. ACM* 17(10)(1974), pp. 549-557.

[Hol94] Jan Rune Holmevik: Compiling Simula: A Historical Study of Technological Genesis. *IEEE Annals of the History of Computing*, Vol. 16 no. 4, 1994.

[Kro03] Stein Krogdahl: The birth of Simula. In the final proceedings of HiNC 1, Trondheim, June 2003. IFIP. To appear.

[Lys91] Olav Lysne: term rewriting. dr. scient. thesis, Department of Informatics, University of Oslo, 1991.

[Mel86] Sigurd Meldal: On Hierarchical Abstraction and Partial Correctness of Concurrent Structures. dr. scient. thesis, Department of Informatics, University of Oslo, 1986.

[Nos84] Decision Algorithms for Program Verification. Dr. scient. thesis, Department of Informatics, University of Oslo, 1984.

[Owe80] Olaf Owe: A specification technique with idealization. Dr. scient. thesis, Department of Informatics, University of Oslo, 1980.

[Wan74] Arne Wang: Generalized Types in High-Level Programming Languages. Research Report in Informatics no. 1, 1974, cand. real. thesis. Department of Mathematics, University of Oslo.

[tribute] The Department's page of tribute: http://www.ifi.uio.no/adminf/tribute.html with links to Ole-Johan's and Kristen's own homepages (Kristen's is more rich on information). For Kristen there is a memorial page at `http://www.ifi.uio.no/in_memoriam_kristen/` See also `http://www.jot.fm/issues/issue_2002_09/eulogy`

A Bibliography of Ole-Johan Dahl

Olaf Owe, Stein Krogdahl, and Tom Lyche

Department of Informatics, University of Oslo

This bibliography is based on information collected by Berit Strange, from the Library of the Department of Informatics, University of Oslo. Ole-Johan's homepage www.ifi.uio.no/~olejohan/ contains links to some papers.

Books

1. *Structured Programming.* O.-J. Dahl, E.W. Dijkstra, C.A.R. Hoare. Academic Press, London, 1972. (220 pages). Also as: *A.P.I.C. Studies in Data Processing* no. 8. ISBN 0-12-200550-3, 0-12-200556-2
2. *SIMULA begin.* G.M. Birtwistle, O.-J. Dahl, B. Myhrhaug and K. Nygaard. Auerbach Publishers Inc, 1973 (391 pages) ISBN 91-44-06211-7. 2. edition published by Studentlitteratur, Stockholm & Chartwell-Bratt Ltd, England, 1973
3. *Syntaks og semantikk i programmeringssprk (Syntax and Semantics in Programming Languages).* O.-J. Dahl. Studentlitteratur, Lund, Sweden, 1972 (103 pages) ISBN 91-44-07111-6 (In Norwegian)
4. *Algoritmer og datastrukturer (Algorithms and Data Structures).* O.-J. Dahl and Dag Belsnes. Studentlitteratur, Lund, Sweden, 1973 (170 pages) ISBN 91-44-06991-x (In Norwegian)
5. *Verifiable Programming.* O.-J. Dahl. Prentice Hall (International series in computer science), New York, 1992, revised edition 1993 (269 pages) ISBN 0-13-951062-1

Papers in Proceedings, Journals, and Books

6. Automatisk koding – et prosjekt ved forsvarets forskningsinstitutt [English: Automatic coding – a project at the Norwegian Research Defense Establishment]. O.-J. Dahl. (In Norwegian) *In: Proceedings of NordSAM*, May 1959, Karlskrona. (The Nordic Symposium on Application of Mathematical Machines) Carl-Erik Frberg and Yngve Rollof (eds.), 1959, pages 135-141.
7. Litt om symbolbruken i Algol [English: A Note on the Use of Symbols in Algol]. O.-J. Dahl. *In: BIT* (Nordic Journal of Information Processing) 2(1962) no. 1, pages 7-8. (In Norwegian)
8. SIMULA – a Language for Describing Discrete Event Systems. K. Nygaard and O.-J. Dahl. *In: Proceedings of the IFIP Conference, 1965.* Vol. 2, Spartan Books, Washington, D.C.; Macmillan, New York, pages 554-555.
9. SIMULA – an ALGOL-Based Simulation Language. O.-J. Dahl and K. Nygaard. *In: Communications of the ACM* 9(1966), pages 671-682.

O. Owe et al. (Eds.): From OO to FM (Dahl Festschrift), LNCS 2635, pp. 8–14, 2004.

10. Discrete Event Simulation Languages. O.-J. Dahl. *In: Programming Languages.* G. Genuys (ed). NATO Advanced Study Department. Academic Press, 1968, pages 349-395.
11. Class and Subclass Declarations. O.-J. Dahl and K. Nygaard. *In: Simulation Programming Languages,* J.N. Buxton (ed.), Proceedings of the IFIP working conference on simulation programming languages, Oslo, May 1967, North-Holland, Amsterdam, 1968, pages 158-174.
12. Some Features of the SIMULA 67 Language. O.-J. Dahl, B. Myhrhaug and K. Nygaard. *In: Digest of the Second Conference on Application of Simulation,* Dec. 1968, New York, IEEE (cat no. 68C60-SIM) pages 29-32.
13. Decomposition and Classification in Programming Languages. O.-J. Dahl. *In: Linguaggi nella societ e nella tecnica, Convegno promosso dalla Ing. C. Olivetti & C., S. p. A. per il centenario della nascita di Camillo Olivetti,* Milano, 1970. (Saggi di cultura contemporanea 87) pages 371-383.
14. Programming Languages as Tools for the Formulation of Concepts. O.-J. Dahl. *In: Proceedings of the 15th Scandinavian Congress*, Oslo 1968, K.E. Aubert and W. Ljunggren (eds.). *Lecture notes in Mathematics* no. 118, Springer, 1970, pages 18-29.
15. Coroutine Sequencing in a Block Structured Environment. Arne Wang and O.-J. Dahl. *In: BIT* 11(1971) pages 425-449.
16. Hierarchical Program Structures. O.-J. Dahl and C.A.R. Hoare. *In: Structured Programming.* Academic Press, 1972, pages 175-220 (see [1] above)
17. Programming Discipline. O.-J. Dahl. *In: Proceedings of the 1974 CERN School of Computing,* Godysund, Aug. 1974. CERN Report 74-23, Geneva, pages 426-435.
18. An Approach to Correctness Proofs of Semicoroutines. O.-J. Dahl. *In: Mathematical Foundations of Computer Science,* 3rd Symposium, Jadwisin near Warsaw, 17-22 jun, 1974. *LNCS* no. 28, Springer, 1975, pages 157-174.
19. Analysis of an Algorithm for Priority Queue Administration. A. Jonassen and O.-J. Dahl. *In: BIT* 15(1975) no. 4, pages 409-422.
20. A Model for Controlling a Network of Processors and Storage Units. O.-J. Dahl. *In: Thorie des algorithmes, des langages et de la programmation: Textes des exposs du sminaire organis par l'Institut du Recherche d'Informatique et d'Automatique (IRIA), Rocquencourt, Octobre 1974.* M. Nivat (ed.). IRIA, Rocquencour, France, 1975, pages 83-94. ISBN 2-7261-0120-8
21. Can program proving be made practical? O.-J. Dahl. *In: Les fondements de la programmation,* M. Amirchahy and D. Nel (eds.). IRIA, Le Chesnay, France (Text in English.) pages 57-114. ISBN 2726101844
22. Time Sequences as a Tool for Describing Program Behaviour. O.-J. Dahl. *In: Abstract Software Specifications, January 22–February 2, 1979, Copenhagen Winter School,* D. Bjrner (ed.). *LNCS* no. 86, Springer 1979, pages 274-290.
23. The Development of the Simula Languages (Chapter IX: SIMULA Session). K. Nygaard and O.-J. Dahl. *In: History of Programming Languages.*

Richard L. Wexelblat (ed.), Academic Press, New York, 1981, pages 439-493.
Also in: ACM Sigplan History of Programming Languages Conference, June, 1978. *ACM Sigplan Notices* 13(1978) no. 8, pages 245-272.

24. Object Oriented Specification. O.-J. Dahl. *In: Research Directions in Object-Oriented Programming,* Bruce Shriver and Peter Wegner (eds.), MIT Press, Cambridge, 1987, pages 561-576.
(Presented at the Object-Oriented Programming Workshop, June, 1986.)
25. Generator induction in order sorted algebra. O. Owe & O.-J. Dahl. *In: Formal Aspects of Computing* 3(1991) pages 2-20.
26. Formal Development with ABEL. O.-J. Dahl and O. Owe. *In: Proceedings of Formal Software Development Methods.* VDM '91, Oct. 1991. *LNCS* no. 552, Springer, 1991, pages 320-362.
27. Object Orientation and Formal Techniques (extended abstract). O.-J. Dahl. *In: VDM '90 VDM and Z – Formal Methods in Software Development. LNCS* no. 428, Springer, 1992, pages 1-11.
28. Value Types and Object Classes. O.-J. Dahl. *In: ASU Newsletter* 20(1992) no. 1, pages 8-20.
29. Monitors Revisited. O.-J. Dahl. *In: A classical Mind: Essays in Honour of C.A.R. Hoare.* A.W. Roscoe (ed.). Prentice Hall, 1994, pages 93-103.
30. Relating a Simulation Model to an Applicative Specification. O.-J. Dahl. *In: Modelling and Simulation: Proceedings ESM, Praha, 1995,* M. Snorek, M. Sujansky, A. Verbraeck (eds.) Society for Computer Simulation International, 1995, pages 633-638.
31. *Recent Trends in Data Type Specification: 11th Workshop on Specification of Abstract Data Types jointly with the 8th COMPASS Workshop, Oslo, Norway, September 19-23, 1995, Selected papers.* Magne Haveraaen, O. Owe, O.-J. Dahl (eds.). *LNCS* no. 1130, Springer, 1996, (550 pages) ISBN 3-540-61629-2
32. Data Access Safety and Storage Economy in Programming Languages. O.-J. Dahl. (8 pages) 23rd ASU Conference, August 1997, Stara Lesna, Slovakia. *ASU Newsletter* vol. 24, no. 2, Feb. 1998.
33. On Introducing Higher Order Functions in ABEL. O.-J. Dahl and Bjrn Kristoffersen. *In: Nordic Journal of Computing* 5(1998) pages 50-69.
34. Subtyping and Constructive Specification. O.-J. Dahl, O. Owe, Tore J. Bastiansen. *In: Nordic Journal of Computing* 5(1998) pages 19-49.
35. A Note on Monitor Versions: an Essay in the Honour of C.A.R. Hoare. O.-J. Dahl. *In: Millennial Perspectives in Computer Science* (Proceeding of the 1999 Oxford-Microsoft Symposium in Honour of Sir Tony Hoare). Jim Davis, Bill Roscoe and Jim Woodcock (eds.). PALGRAVE, in the series Cornerstones of Computing, 2000, pages 91-98.
36. The Roots of Object Orientation: the Simula Language. O.-J. Dahl. *In: Software Pioneers: Contribution to Software Engineering.* Manfred Broy, Ernst Denert (eds.), Springer Verlag, 2002. pages 78-90. (Talk given at conference in Bonn, June 2001) ISBN 3-540-43081-4

Reports from University of Oslo

Early reports are from Department of Mathematics, section D (for numerical analysis and computer science). Later reports are from Department of Informatics (IFI), which was formed in 1978. Reports marked by a star (*) represent early versions or revisions of papers mentioned above.

Research Reports

37. Analysis of an Algorithm for Priority Queue Administration. Arne Jonassen and O.-J. Dahl. Research Report in Informatics no. 3, 1975 (68 pages) ISBN 82-553-0203-4 *
38. An Approach to Correctness Proofs of Semicoroutines. O.-J. Dahl. Research Report in Informatics no. 13, 1977 (20 pages) ISBN 82-90230-00-1 *
39. Can Program Proving be Made Practical? O.-J. Dahl. Research Report in Informatics no. 33, 1978 (57 pages) Lectures presented at the EEC-CREST course on Programming Foundations, Toulouse 1977 (revised May 1978). ISBN 82-90230-26-5 *
40. Time Sequences as a Tool for Describing Program Behaviour. O.-J. Dahl. Research Report no. 48, 1979 (17 pages) ISBN 82-90230-43-5 *
41. Partial Correctness Semantics of Communicating Sequential Processes. Neelam Soundararajan and O.-J. Dahl. Research Report no. 66, 1982 (29 pages) ISBN 82-90230-62-1
42. Notes on a LIFO Disciplined Simplex Algorithm. O.-J. Dahl. Research Report no. 79, 1984 (7 pages) ISBN 82-90230-76-1
43. Logic of Programming and Specification. O.-J. Dahl. Research Report no. 84, 1984 (48 pages) ISBN 82-90230-83-4
44. A Presentation of the Specification and Verification Project ABEL. O.-J. Dahl and O. Owe. Research Report no. 90, 1984 (9 pages) ISBN 82-90230-89-3. Also in the proceedings of the 3. Verification Workshop, Watsonville, CA, Feb. 1985.
45. Specification and Reasoning about Discrete Simulation Models: A Case Study. O.-J. Dahl. Research Report no. 94, 1985 (10 pages) ISBN 82-90230-93-1. Lecure at the IMACS World Congress on System Simulation and Scientific Computation, Oslo, Aug. 1985.
46. Preliminary Report on the Specification and Programming Language ABEL. O.-J. Dahl, Dag F. Langmyhr, O. Owe. Research Report no. 106, 1986 (86 pages) ISBN 82-7368-006-1
47. Object Oriented Specification. O.-J. Dahl. Research Report no. 108, 1987 (18 pages) ISBN 82-7368-009-6 *
48. Generator Induction in Order Sorted Algebras. O.-J. Dahl and O. Owe. Research Report no. 122, 1989 (17 pages) ISBN 82-7368-027-4 *
49. Object Orientation and Formal Techniques (extended abstracts). O.-J. Dahl. Research Report no. 138, 1990 (11 pages) ISBN 82-7368-044-4 *
50. Formal Development with ABEL. O.-J. Dahl and O. Owe. Research Report no. 159, 1991 (43 pages) ISBN 82-7368-066-5 *

51. Value Types and Object Classes. O.-J. Dahl. Talk presented at the 25 years SIMULA 67 Anniversary Conferences, Nordwijkerhout 11-12 June, 1992 and Oslo 22 June. Research Report no. 170, 1992 (13 pages) ISBN 82-7368-079-7 *
52. Monitors Revisited. O.-J. Dahl. Research Report no. 175, 1993 (12 pages) ISBN 82-7368-084-3 *
53. Co- and Contravariance in Functional Subtypes: Contribution to IFIP WG 2.3, June 1994. O.-J. Dahl. Research Report no. 191, 1994 (7 pages) ISBN 82-7368-101-7
54. Hoare-style Parallel Programming: Foils for a student course, IN305. O.-J. Dahl. Research Report no. 192, 1994 ISBN 82-7368-102-5
55. On the Use of Subtypes in ABEL. O.-J. Dahl and O. Owe. Revised version. Research Report no. 206, 1995 (20 pages) ISBN 82-7368-117-3 *
56. On Introducing Higher Order Functions in ABEL. O.-J. Dahl and Bjrn Kristoffersen. Research Report no. 210, 1995 (18 pages) ISBN 82-7368-123-8 *
57. Subtyping and Constructive Specification. O.-J. Dahl, O. Owe and Tore J. Bastiansen. Research Report no. 228, 1996 (38 pages) ISBN 82-7368-142-4 *
58. Formal Methods and the RM-ODP. O.-J. Dahl and O. Owe. Research Report no. 261, 1998 (17 pages) ISBN 82-7368-192-0

Compendiums and Lecture Notes

59. Kompendium til DB-2 (maskinsprk og operasjonssytem). O.-J. Dahl. Dept. of Mathematics, 1969 (48 pages) (In Norwegian).
60. Listestrukturer: Ch. 7 from Compendium Ikke-numeriske metoder. O.-J. Dahl. Dept. of Mathematics, 1970 (46 pages) (In Norwegian).
61. Forelesninger i DB 2. O.-J. Dahl & co. 2. edition, Dept. of Mathematics, 1971 (171 pages) (In Norwegian).
62. Top-Down Parsers Expressed in a High-Level Language. O.-J. Dahl. Dept. of Mathematics, 1972 (12 pages).
63. Hierarchical Program Structures. O.-J. Dahl. Lecture Note no. 6, Dept. of Mathematics, 1973 (57 pages). The predecessor of [1].
64. Two Lectures for the Graduate Course: Parallel Programming and Operating Systems. O.-J. Dahl and C.A.R. Hoare. Lecture Note no. 7, Dept. of Mathematics, 1973 (15 pages).
65. Runtime organisasjon for SIMULA/ALGOL. O.-J. Dahl. Compendium 11. Dept. of Informatics, 1980 (36 pages) (In Norwegian).
66. Stochastiske simuleringsmodeller. O.-J. Dahl. (36 pages) Compendium 13, Dept. of Informatics (In Norwegian).
67. Program Specification and Verification Techniques. O.-J. Dahl. Part I, 1988, Part II and III 1990. Compendium 42, Dept. of Informatics (153 pages).
68. Substitusjonssystemer. O.-J. Dahl. Lecture notes (12 pages) Aug. 1989 (In Norwegian)

69. Parallell programmering (Parallel Programming). O.-J. Dahl. Compendium 45, Dept. of Informatics (69 pages), Revised Aug. 1995 (In Norwegian). Kompendium 46, Aug. 1996 (In Norwegian).
70. Stochastic Simulation Modelling. O.-J. Dahl. Compendium 69, Dept. of Informatics, April 1996 (36 pages).

Reports from the Norwegian Computing Center (NCC), Oslo

71. Preliminary Presentation of the Simula Language and some Examples of Network Descriptions. O.-J. Dahl and K. Nygaard. NCC Doc., May 18th 1963.
72. SIMSCRIPT Implementation. Vic Bell and O.-J. Dahl. NCC Doc. (31 pages), Nov. 1963.
73. The SIMULA Storage Allocation Scheme. O.-J. Dahl. NCC Doc. 162, Nov. 1963 (9 pages)
74. SIMULA Status Report. O.-J. Dahl. NCC Doc. 1.1, 1964 (10 pages)
75. The SIMULA Data Structures. O.-J. Dahl. NCC Doc. March 1964 (23 pages)
76. The SIMULA Language: Specifications 17 March 1964. O.-J. Dahl and K. Nygaard. NCC Doc. March, 1964 (30 pages)
77. The SIMULA Project: Technical Progress Report 1. O.-J. Dahl and K. Nygaard. NCC Doc. July 1, 1964 (7 pages)
78. SIMULA status report. O.-J. Dahl. NCC Doc. 1.10, 1964 (24 pages)
79. SIMULA – A Language for Programming and Description of Discrete Event Systems: Introduction and User's Manual. O.-J. Dahl and K. Nygaard. NCC Publ. no. 11, May 1965 (103 pages). Revised versions: 1966. III, 108 pages. 5th ed. NCC, 1967 (124 pages)
80. Basic Concepts of SIMULA – an ALGOL Based Simulation Language. O.-J. Dahl and K. Nygaard. NCC Doc., 1965 (17 pages)
81. SIMULA, an ALGOL Based Simulation Language. O.-J. Dahl and K. Nygaard. NCC Doc., April 1966 (26 pages) *
82. Discrete Event Simulation Languages: Lectures Delivered at the NATO Summer School, Villard-de-Lans, Sept. 1966. O.-J. Dahl. NCC Doc., 1966 (63 pages) *
83. SIMULA: Simula Tracing System. O.-J. Dahl, B. Myhrhaug and K. Nygaard. NCC Doc., 1966.
84. Class and Subclass Declarations. O.-J. Dahl and K. Nygaard. NCC Publ. no. 93, (Presented at IFIP Working Conference on Simulation Languages, Lysebu, Oslo, May 1967). March 1967 (17 pages) *
85. SIMULA 67 Common Base Proposal. O.-J. Dahl and K. Nygaard. NCC Doc., May 1967 (10 pages)
86. Proposals for Consideration by the SIMULA 67 Common Base Conference. O.-J. Dahl and K. Nygaard. NCC Doc., June 1967.
87. SIMULA 67 Common Base Definition. O.-J. Dahl and K. Nygaard. NCC Doc., June 1967 (31 pages).

88. SIMULA 67 Common Base Language. O.-J. Dahl, B. Myhrhaug, K. Nygaard. NCC Publ. S-2, 1968 (141 pages).
Revised editions: (1970, 145 pages, SIMULA information: NCC Publ. S-22). (1982, 127 pages, NCC Publ. no. 725). (1984, 172 pages, NCC Publ. no. 743). ISBN 82-539-0225-5 [1]
89. Some Uses of the External Class Concept in SIMULA 67. O.-J. Dahl, B. Myhrhaug, K. Nygaard. NCC Doc., 1968. (Presented at the NATO sponsored conference on Software Engineering, Garmisch, Germany, October 1968)
90. SIMULA 67 – Basic Information. O.-J. Dahl and K. Nygaard. NCC Publ. no. S-3, 1968 (12 pages).
91. SIMULA 67 – Implementation Guide. O.-J. Dahl, B. Myhrhaug. NCC Publ. no. S-9, 1969. Rev. March 1973, NCC Publ. no. S-47 (146 pages).
92. The Development of the SIMULA Languages. K. Nygaard and O.-J. Dahl. NCC Doc. (Publication 603), 1978 (28 pages) ISBN 82-539-0072-4 (Note: includes a bibliography.) *

Reports from the Norwegian Defense Research Establishment (NDRE), Kjeller, Norway

93. An Automatic Coding Scheme for the Ferranti MERCURY Computer. O.-J. Dahl. NDRE Report IR-F-286, 1956.
94. Multiple Index Countings on the Ferranti MERCURY Computer. O.-J. Dahl. Norwegian Defense Research Establishment, 1957. (NDRE Report 23) & Cand real thesis, University of Oslo, Dept. of Mathematics, 1957.
95. Programmer's Handbook for the Ferranti MERCURY Computer Frederic at the Norwegian Defense Research Establishment. O.-J. Dahl, Jan V. Garwick. NDRE. 2. edition published by Merkantile Trykkeri, Oslo, 1958. 3. edition, NDRE, 1962 (117 pages).
96. Mac Bulletin I. O.-J. Dahl. NDRE report (S-15), 1960 (10 pages)[2]
97. Mac Bulletin II. O.-J. Dahl. NDRE report (S-17), 1960 (3 pages)
98. Mac Bulletin V: Macros. O.-J. Dahl NDRE report (S-57), 1963 (13 pages)

Video Recorded Talks

99. ACM SIGPLAN History of Programming Languages Conference, January 1978, Los Angeles. SIMULA Session. Speakers: Nygaard and Dahl. 1 videotape (VHS) (60 min), ACM, 1980.
100. The talk given at Software Pioneers Conference, Bonn, June 2001 (supplied with the book [36] above).
101. Introduction to SIMULA (talk given in Norwegian), to be available through the department homepage: http://www.ifi.uio.no/.

---

[1] All versions of the common base language definition assume knowledge of Algol 60. A final and complete version of the SIMULA 67 language definition without this assumption is found in: Standard SIMULA, as approved by the SIMULA Standards Group Aug. 26, 1986. (176 pages) ISBN 91-7162-234-9.

[2] MAC was an acronym for MERCURY Automatic Coding, a high level programming language for the MERCURY computer, and a compiler.

The Birth of Object Orientation: the Simula Languages*

Ole-Johan Dahl

Abstract. The development of the programming languages Simula I and Simula 67 is briefly described. An attempt is made also to explain the cultural impact of the languages, in particular the object oriented aspects.

1 Introduction

In 1962 Kristen Nygaard, KN, initiated a project for the development of a discrete event simulation language, to be called Simula. At the time KN was the director of research at the Norwegian Computing Center, NCC, (a semi-governmental institution). KN also served as the administrative leader for the duration of the project. This required much creative manipulation in an environment that outside the NCC was largely hostile. The language development proper was a result of a close cooperation between KN and the author, OJD, whereas implementation considerations were mainly the responsibility of the latter.

We were both fostered at the Norwegian Defence Research Establishment in the pioneering group headed by Jan V. Garwick, the father of Computer Science in Norway. But our backgrounds were nevertheless quite different. KN had done Monte Carlo computations calibrating uranium rods for a nuclear reactor and later operations research on military systems. OJD had developed basic software together with Garwick and designed and implemented a high level programming language. Our difference in background probably accounts for some of the success of the Simula project.

The present paper mainly deals with language issues, including some thoughts on their possible cultural impact, especially on later programming languages. For other aspects of the project the reader is referred to [30].

Two language versions were defined and implemented. The first one, later called Simula I, was developed under a contract by UNIVAC. (UNIVAC wanted us to provide also a Fortran-based version, but that was abandoned because the block structure turned out to be essential to our approach.) It was up and running by the end of 1964. The second version, Simula 67, was sponsored by the NCC itself. It is a generalization and refinement of the former, fairly ambitious, intended mainly as a general purpose programming language, but with simulation capabilities.

* An almost identical version of this paper has been published in *Software pioneers*, Springer, 2002.

O. Owe et al. (Eds.): From OO to FM (Dahl Festschrift), LNCS 2635, pp. 15–25, 2004.

2 Simula I

It was decided at an early stage that our language should be based on a well known one. Algol 60 was chosen for the following main reasons:

- the block structure,
- good programming security,
- European patriotism.

We realised that in order to profit from block structure in simulation models it would be necessary to break out of the strict LIFO regime of block instances in Algol. Thus, a new storage management system was developed based on a list structured free store, [3]. Then a useful simulation language could be defined by adding a few special purpose mechanisms to Algol 60:

- A procedure-like **activity** declaration giving rise to so called “processes”. Processes could range from record-like data structures to block structured programs executing in a coroutine-like fashion, [35], [9], over a simulated system time.
- Explicit process pointers for dynamic naming and referencing. (The pointers were indirect through list forming “element” records.)
- A mechanism for accessing, from the outside, quantities local to the outermost block level of processes, designed so that the access security inherent in Algol would be maintained (the **inspect** construct).
- A few run time mechanisms for the scheduling and sequencing of processes in system time, such as *hold*(...), suspending the calling process for a specified amount of system time.

The following skeleton example could be a small fragment of a road traffic simulation. It is taken from the Simula I manual, [4], but slightly extended. It may serve to indicate the flavour of the language.

```
SIMULA begin activity Car;
               begin real X0, T0, V;
                  real procedure X; X := X0+V*(time−T0);
                  procedure newV(Vnew); real Vnew;
                     begin X0 := X; T0 := time; V := Vnew end;
                  Car behaviour: ......; hold(<travel time>); ......
               end of Car;
               activityPolice;
               begin ......; inspect <process> when Car do
                  if X <is within city> and V>50 then
                     begin newV(50); <give fine> end; ......
               end of Police;
               main program: <initialise>; hold(<simulation period>)
end of simulation model;
```

The example shows that the idea of data objects with associated operators was under way already in 1965. According to a comment in [4] it was a pity that the variable attributes of a *Car* process could not be hidden away in a subblock. It would have required the accessing procedures to be hidden similarly.

New processes would be generated explicitly. For programming security reasons, however, process deletions had to be implicit, in our implementation through reference counts and a last resort garbage collector. The bulk of the implementation effort therefore consisted in writing a new run time system for the Algol system provided by UNIVAC; the compiler extensions, on the other hand, were minimal. The "block prefix" **SIMULA** served to introduce the Simula I additions to Algol. Consequently any Algol program not containing that keyword would execute normally on our compiler. That was an important consideration in those days.

A paper on Simula I was published in CACM 1966, [5]. It was also the main topic of lectures given by OJD at the NATO Summer School at Vilard-de-Lans the same year. The lectures were written up and published as a chapter of [6].

The language was used for simulation purposes as well as for teaching at several locations at home and abroad, also within the UNIVAC organization. A modified version was used for Burroughs computers. This was through the advocacy of Don Knuth and J. McNeley, the authors of SOL, another Algol-like simulation language.

3 Simula 67

In spite of the success of Simula I as a practical tool it became increasingly clear that the activity/process concepts, if stripped from all references to simulated time, would be useful for programming and system design in general. If possible the special purpose simulation facilities should be definable within the new language. Also the list processing facilities of Simula I would be useful, although we felt that the referencing mechanism should be simplified.

At the Vilard-de-Lans Summer School Tony Hoare had put forth a proposal for "record handling" with record classes and subclasses, as well as record references restricted to, or "qualified by", a given class or subclass by declaration. Attribute accessing was by dot notation, see [19], as well as [17] and [18].

We chose the terms "class" and "objects" of classes for our new Simula. The notion of subclass was especially appealing to us, since we had seen many cases of objects belonging to different classes having common properties. It would be useful to collect the common properties in a separate class, say C to be specialised differently for different purposes, possibly in different programs. The solution came with the idea of class prefixing: using C as a prefix to another class, the latter would be taken to be a subclass of C inheriting all properties of C.

Technically the subclass would be seen as "concatenated" class in which the parameter parts, the block heads, and the block tails of the two classes were juxtaposed (The block tail of the prefixing class could be separated into initial actions and final actions, that of the prefixed class sandwiched between them.) The attributes of a compound object would be accessible by dot notation down to the prefix level of the qualifying class of the reference used. Access to deeper levels could be achieved by class discrimination as in Simula I.

The breakthrough happened in January of 1967. An IFIP sponsored working conference on simulation languages had been approved to take place in Oslo in May. There followed some hectic winter months during which our new concepts were explored and tested. A paper was ready just in time for advance distribution to the invitees, [7]. The new language was to be called Simula 67, [8]. The paper occurring in the proceedings was mended by the addition of "virtual" specifications, see below.

One way of using a class, which appeared important to us, was to collect concepts in the form of classes, procedures, etc under a single hat. The resulting construct could be understood as a kind of "application language" defined on top of the basic one. It would typically be used as a prefix to an in-line block making up the application program.

We illustrate this idea by showing a simplified version of a *SIMULATION* class defining the simulation oriented mechanisms used in our Simula I example.

```
class SIMULATION;
begin class process;
        begin real EventTime, NextEvent; ...... end;
        ref(process) current;
        comment current points to the currently operating process.
                    It is the head of the "time list" of scheduled ones,
                    sorted with respect to nondecreasing EventTimes;
        real procedure time; time := current.EventTime;
        procedure hold(deltaT); real deltaT;
        begin current.EventTime := time+deltaT;
              if time ≥ current.NextEvent.EventTime then
              begin ref(process)P; P :- current; current :- P.NextEvent;
                    <move P to the right position in the time list>;
              resume(current) end end of hold;
        ......
end of SIMULATION;
```

```
SIMULATION begin
  process class Car;
  begin real X0, T0, V;
        real procedure X; X := X0+V*(time-T0);
        procedure newV(Vnew); real Vnew;
          begin X0 := X; T0 := time; V := Vnew end;
        Car behaviour: ......; hold(<travel time>); ......
  end of Car;
```

```
  process Police;
  begin ......; inspect <process> when Car do
          if X <is within city> and V > 50 then
             begin newV(50); <give fine> end; ......
  end of Police;
  main program: <initialise>; hold(<simulation period>)
end of simulation model;
```

Thus, the "block prefix" of Simula I is now an ordinary class declared within the new language, and the special purpose **activity** declarator is replaced by *process* **class**.

We chose to introduce a special set of operators for references, in order to make it clear that the item in question is a reference, not (the contents of) the referenced object. The *resume* operator is a basic coroutine call, defined for the whole language.

Notice that the class *SIMULATION* is completely self-contained. If some necessary initializing operations were added, it could be separately compiled and then used repeatedly in later programs. In actual fact a somewhat more elaborate class is predefined in Simula 67, providing an application language for simulation modelling. That class is itself prefixed by one containing mechanisms for the management of circular lists.

It is fair to say that Simula 67 invites to bottom up program design, especially through the possibility of separate compilation of classes. As a last minute extension, however, we introduced a top down oriented mechanism through a concept of "virtual procedures".

In general attribute identifiers may be redeclared in subclasses, as is the case of inner blocks. The identity of an attribute is determined by the prefix level of the accessing occurrence, or, if the access is remote, by the class qualifying the object reference in question. In this way any ambiguity of identifier binding is resolved textually, i.e at compile time; we call it static binding.

On the other hand, if a procedure P is specified as **virtual** in a class C the binding scheme is semi-dynamic. Any call for P occurring in C or in any subclass of C will bind to that declaration of P which occurs at the innermost prefix level of the actual object containing such a declaration (and similarly for remote accesses). Thus, the body of the procedure P may, at the prefix level of C, be postponed to occur in any subclass of C. It may even be replaced by more appropriate ones in further subclasses.

This binding scheme is dynamic in the sense that it depends on the class membership of the actual object. But there is nevertheless a degree of compiler control; the access can be implemented as indirect through a table produced by the compiler for C and for each of its subclasses.

As a concrete example the "fine giving" operation of the above example could be formalised as a virtual procedure, as follows: Redefine the head of the prefixed block as a subclass *RoadTraffic* of *SIMULATION*. In addition to the classes *Car* and *Police* declarations introduce the following specification:

virtual procedure *Fine*(*cr*); **ref**(*Car*)*cr*;

If appropriate the *RoadTraffic* class may be separately compiled. Using that class as a block prefix at some later time, a suitable fining procedure can be defined in that block head.

There is an alternative more implementation oriented view of virtual procedures. As mentioned in connection with Simula I, deletion of objects would have to be implicit (in Simula 67 by garbage collector alone). But then there is a danger of flooding the memory with useless data, especially if there are implicit pointers between block instances. In Algol 60 there must be a pointer from a procedure activation back to its caller in order to implement procedure parameters and parameters "called by name". Such pointers from objects back to their generating block instance would have been destructive. So, it was decided that parameters to objects must be called by "value" (including object references). The absence of procedure parameters, however, was felt to be a nuisance. Fortunately the virtual procedure mechanism provided a solution to the dilemma: a virtual procedure can be seen as a parameter, where the actual parameter is a procedure residing safely within the object itself, at an appropriate prefix level. There is the additional advantage that the procedure has direct access to attributes of the object containing it.

Similar considerations led to forbidding class prefixing across block levels. Fortunately this would not prevent the use of separately compiled, "external" classes. Since there is no reference to nonlocal quantities in such a class, it can be called in as an external one at any block level of a user program.

4 Language Finalisation and Distribution

A couple of weeks after the IFIP Conference a private "Simula Common Base Conference" was organised, attended by several interested persons. The objective was to agree on the definition of a common core language. We made a proposal to the CBC to extend the language by "class-like" types giving rise to permanently named objects, directly accessed, thus extending the Algol variable concept. The proposal was prudently voted down, as not sufficiently worked through. However, a Pascal-like **while** statement was added, and the virtual mechanism was slightly revised.

A "Simula Standards Group", SSG, was established, to consist of representatives from the NCC and various implementation groups. 5 compilers were implemented initially. It was decided that the NCC would propose mechanisms for text handling, I/O, and file handling. Our good colleague Bjørn Myhrhaug of the NCC gave three alternatives for text handling and I/O. The ones chosen by the SSG would have required class-like types in order to be definable within the Common Base.

The class concept as it was formulated originally, was too permissive for the purpose of developing large systems. There was no means of enforcing a programming discipline protecting local class invariants (such as those expressed verbally for the *Simulation* class example). This was pointed out by Jacob Palme of the Swedish defence research institute. He proposed hiding mechanisms for protecting variable attributes from unauthorised updating. The proposal was approved by the SSG as the last addition ever to the language. The authors toyed with the idea of class-like types for some time, but it was never implemented.

The first compilers were operative already in 1969, three for Control Data computers. Then came implementations for UNIVAC and IBM machines. The general distribution of the compilers was, however, greatly hampered by the high prices asked for the compilers by the NCC, very unwisely enforced by the NTNF (Norwegian Council for Scientific and Technical Research) stating that programming languages only had a 3-5 years lifetime and thus had to provide profits within this time span. However, a nice compiler for the DEC 10 system, implemented by a Swedish team in the early 1970's, contributed considerably to the spreading of the language. Lectures by OJD at NATO Summer Schools, as well as a chapter in [9] must have made the new concepts better known in academic circles.

The most important new concept of Simula 67 is surely the idea of data structures with associated operators (and with or without own actions), called *objects*. There is an important difference, except in trivial cases, between

- *the inside view* of an object, understood in terms of local variables, possibly initialising operations establishing an invariant, and implemented procedures operating on the variables maintaining the invariant, and
- *the outside view*, as presented by the remotely accessible procedures, including some generating mechanism, dealing with more "abstract" entities.

This difference, as indicated by the *Car* example in Simula I, and the associated comments, underlies much of our program designs from an early time on, although not usually conscious and certainly not explicitly formulated. (There is e.g an intended invariant of any *Car* object vaguely stating that its current position X is the right one in view of the past history of the object.)

It was Tony Hoare who finally expressed mathematically the relationship of the two views in terms of an "abstraction function", see [20]. He also expressed requirements for the concrete operations to correctly represent the corresponding abstract ones. Clearly, in order to enforce the use of abstract object views, read access to variable attributes would also have to be prevented.

5 Cultural Impact

The main impact of Simula 67 has turned out to be the very wide acceptance of many of its basic concepts: objects, but usually without own actions, classes, inheritance, and virtuals, often the default or only way of binding "methods", (as well as pointers and dynamic object generation).

There is universal use of the term "object orientation", OO. Although no standard definition exists, some or all of the above ideas enter into the OO paradigm of system development. There is a large flora of OO languages around for programming and system specification. Conferences on the theory and practice of OO are held regularly. The importance of the OO paradigm today is such that one must assume something similar would have come about also without the Simula effort. The fact remains, however, that the OO principle was introduced in the mid 60's through these languages.

Simula 67 had an immediate success as a simulation language, and was, for instance extensively used in the design of VLSI chips, e.g. at INTEL. As a general programming language, its impact was enhanced by lectures at NATO Summer Schools given by OJD, materialized as a chapter in a book on structured programming, [9]. The latter has influenced research on the use of abstract data types, e.g., the CLU language, [29], as well as research on monitors and operating system design, [21].

A major new impact area opened with the introduction of workstations and personal computers. Alan Kay and his team at Xerox PARC developed Smalltalk, [15], an interactive language building upon Simula's objects, classes and inheritance. It is oriented towards organising the cooperation between a user and her/his personal computer.

An important step was the integration of OO with a graphical user interfaces, leading the way to the Macintosh Operating System, and then to Windows.

In the larger workstation field, Lisp was (and in some places still is) an important language, spawning dialects such as MACLISP, [16], at MIT, and InterLisp at Xerox PARC. Both got OO facilities, MACLISP through ZetaLisp introducing also multiple inheritance, [2], and InterLisp through LOOPS (Lisp Object-Oriented Programming System). The object-oriented component of the merged effort, CommonLisp, is called CLOS (Common Lisp Object System), [24].

With the general acceptance of object-orientation, object-oriented databases started to appear in the 1980's. The demand for software reuse also pushed OO tools, and in the 1990's OO tools for system design and development became dominant in that field. UML (Unified Modeling Language), [1], is very much used, and CORBA (Common Object Request Broker Architecture), is a widely accepted tool for interfacing OO systems. The Microsoft Component Object Model, COM, [27], is an important common basis for programming languages such as C♯, as well as other tools.

A large number of OO programming languages have appeared. We list below some of the more interesting or better known languages, in addition to those mentioned above.

- BETA is a compilable language built around a single abstraction mechanism, that of patterns, which can be specialised to classes, singular objects, types, as well as procedures. It was developed from the later 1970's by KN and colleagues in Denmark, [25], [26].
- Bjarne Stroustrup extended the Unix-related language C with several Simula-inspired mechanisms. The language, called C++, has been much used and has contributed importantly to the dissemination of the OO ideas, [33]. Since C is fairly close to machine code, security aspects are not the best. As a result, complex systems may be difficult to implement correctly. C++ has been revised and extended, e.g. by multiple inheritance.
- Eiffel, [28], is an OO programming language designed by Bertrand Meyer in the 1980's, well known and quite widely used. It has pre- and post-conditions and invariants.

- SELF, [34], is an OO language exploring and using object cloning instead of object generation from a class declaration.
- JAVA, [22], is a recent Simula-, Beta-, and C++-inspired language, owing much of its popularity to its integration with the Internet. Its syntax is unfortunately rather close to that of C++ and thus C (but with secure pointers). It contains Beta-like singular objects and nested classes, but not general block structure. Parallel, "multi-threaded", execution is introduced, but outside compiler control. As a result, much of the programming security otherwise inherent in the language is lost. The synchronisation mechanisms invite to inefficient programming and do not facilitate good control of process sequencing, see [14].

The authors believed that the use of class declarations for the definition of "application languages" as natural extensions of a basic one would be of special importance in practice. However, although various kinds of packages or modules are defined for many languages, they are not consequences of a general class declaration as in Simula 67.

The coroutine-like sequencing of Simula has not caught on as a general purpose programming tool. A natural development, however, would have been objects as concurrent processes, e.g. as in COM.

One may fairly ask how it could happen that a team of two working in the periphery of Europe could hit on programming principles of lasting importance. No doubt a bit of good luck was involved. We were designing a language for simulation modelling, and such models are most easily conceived of in terms of cooperating objects. Our approach, however, was general enough to be applicable to many aspects of system development.

KN oriented his activities for some years to trade union work, as well as system development and description, see [23]. In 1976 he turned back to programming language design, see BETA above. In [32] he introduced new constructs for OO layered distributed systems.

OJD has been professor of Informatics at Oslo University for the period 1968–1999, developing curricula including OO programming. He has explored the concept of time sequences to reason about concurrent systems, [10], [11]. In [13] he applies techniques, such as Hoare logic and Guttag-Horning axiomatisation of types and subtypes, [31], to the specification and proof of programs, including OO ones. See also [12].

Of the Simula authors especially KN has been consistently promoting the OO paradigm for system development.

Acknowledgments

The author is greatly indebted to Kristen Nygaard for helping to explain the impact of object orientation in various areas of programming and system work. Also Olaf Owe has contributed.

References

1. G. Booch, J. Rumbaugh, I. Jacobson: *The Unified Modeling Language User Guide.* Addison-Wesley, 1998.
2. H. Cannon: *Flavors, A Non-Hierarchical Approach to Object-Oriented Programming.* Draft 1982.
3. O.-J. Dahl: *The Simula Storage Allocation Scheme.* NCC Doc. 162, 1963.
4. O.-J. Dahl, K. Nygaard: *SIMULA – A language for programming and description of discrete event systems. Introduction and user's manual.* NCC Publ. no. 11, 1965.
5. O.-J. Dahl, K. Nygaard: SIMULA – an ALGOL-based Simulation Language. *CACM 9(9),* 671–678, 1966.
6. O.-J. Dahl: Discrete Event Simulation Languages. In F. Genuys, ed.: *Programming Languages.* Academic Press, pp 349–394, 1968.
7. O.-J. Dahl, K. Nygaard: Class and Subclass Declarations. In J. Buxton, ed.: *Simulation Programming Languages.* Proceedings from the IFIP Working Conference in Oslo, May 1967. North Holland, 1968.
8. O.-J. Dahl, B. Myhrhaug, K. Nygaard: *SIMULA 67 Common Base Language.* Norwegian Computing Center 1968.
9. O.-J. Dahl, C.A.R. Hoare: Hierarchical Program Structures. In O.-J. Dahl, E.W. Dijkstra, C.A.R. Hoare: *Structured Programming.* Academic Press 1972, pp. 175–220.
10. O.-J. Dahl: Can Program Proving be Made Practical? In M. Amirchahy, D. Neel: *Les Fondements de la Programmation.* IRIA 1977, pp. 57–114.
11. O.-J. Dahl: Time Sequences as a Tool for Describing Process Behaviour. In D. Bjørner, ed.: *Abstract Software Specifications, LNCS 86,* pp. 273-290.
12. O.-J. Dahl, O. Owe: Formal Development with ABEL. In *VDM91, LNCS 552,* pp. 320–363.
13. O.-J. Dahl: *Verifiable Programming*, Hoare Series, Prentice Hall 1992.
14. O.-J. Dahl: A Note on Monitor Versions. In *Proceedings of Symposium in the Honour of C.A.R. Hoare at his resignation from the University of Oxford.* Oxford University 1999. Also available at www.ifi.uio.no/~olejohan. (Department of Informatics, University of Oslo).
15. A. Goldberg, D. Robson: *Smalltalk-80: The Language and its Implementation.* Addison Wesley, 1984.
16. B.S. Greenberg: *The Multics MACLISP Compiler. The Basic Hackery – a Tutorial.* MIT Press 1977, 1988, 1996.
17. C.A.R. Hoare: Record Handling. In *ALGOL Bulletin no. 21.* 1965.
18. C.A.R. Hoare: Further Thoughts on Record Handling. In *ALGOL Bulletin no. 23.* 1966.
19. C.A.R. Hoare: Record Handling. In F. Genuys, ed.: *Programming Languages.* Academic Press, pp 291–346, 1968.
20. C.A.R. Hoare: Proof of the Correctness of Data Representations. *Acta Informatica*, vol. 1, 1972.
21. C.A.R. Hoare: Monitors: an Operating System Structuring Concept. *Comm. ACM* 17(10)(1974), pp. 549-557.
22. J. Gosling, Bill Joy, G. Steele: *The Java Language Specification.* Java(tm) Series, Addison-Wesley 1989.
23. P. Håndlykken, K. Nygaard: The DELTA System Description Language: Motivation, Main Concepts and Experience from use. In: Software Engineering Environments (ed. H. Hünke), GMD, North-Holland, 1981.

24. S.E. Keene: *Object-Oriented Programming in COMMON LISP-A Programmer's Guide to CLOS.* Addison-Wesley 1989.
25. B.B. Kristensen, O.L. Madsen, B. Møller-Pedersen, K. Nygaard: Abstraction Mechanisms in the BETA Programming Language. *Proceedings of the Tenth ACM Symposium on Principles of Programming Languages.* Austin, Texas, 1983.
26. O.L. Madsen, B. Møller-Pedersen, K. Nygaard: *Object Oriented Programming in the BETA Programming Language.* Addison-Wesley/ACM Press 1993.
27. R.C. Martin: *Design Principles and Design Patterns.* Microsoft, http://www.objectmentor.com/.
28. B. Meyer: *Eiffel: The Language.* Prentice Hall 1992.
29. B. Liskov, A. Snyder, R. Atkinson, C. Schaffert: Abstraction Mechanisms in CLU. *Comm. ACM 20:8* (1977), PP. 564-576.
30. K. Nygaard, O.-J. Dahl: SIMULA Session. In R. Wexelblatt, ed.: *History of Programming Languages.* ACM 1981.
31. O. Owe, O.-J. Dahl: Generator Induction in Order Sorted Algebras. *Formal Aspects of Computing* (1991), 3:2–20.
32. K. Nygaard: GOODS to Appear on the Stage. *Proceedings of the 11th European Conference on Object-Oriented Programming.* Springer 1997
33. B. Stroustrup: *The C++ Programming Language.* Addison-Wesley 1986.
34. D. Ungar, R.B. Smith: SELF: The Power of Simplicity. In *SIGPLAN Notices 22(12),* 1987.
35. A. Wang, O.-J. Dahl: Coroutine Sequencing in a Block Structured Environment. In *BIT 11* 425–449, 1971.

An Algebraic Theory of Actors and Its Application to a Simple Object-Based Language

Gul Agha and Prasanna Thati

University of Illinois at Urbana-Champaign, USA
{agha,thati}@cs.uiuc.edu
http://osl.cs.uiuc.edu/

1 Introduction

The development of Simula by Ole-Johan Dahl and Kristen Nygaard introduced a number of important programming language concepts – *object* which supports modularity in programming through encapsulation of data and procedures, the concept of *class* which organizes behavior and supports Abstract Data Types, and the concept *inheritance* which provides subtyping relations and reuse [6]. Peter Wegner terms programming languages which use objects as *object-based languages*, and reserves the term object-oriented languages for languages which also support classes and inheritance [58].

Concurrency provides a natural model for the execution of objects: in fact, Simula uses co-routines to simulate a simple form of concurrency in a sequential execution environment. The resulting execution is tightly synchronized and, while this execution model is appropriate for simulations which use a global virtual clock, it is not an adequate model for distributed systems. The Actor Model unifies the notion of objects with concurrency; an actor is a concurrent object which operates asynchronously and interacts with other actors by sending asynchronous messages [2].

Many models for concurrent and distributed computation have been developed. An early and influential model is *Petri Nets* developed by Carl Adam Petri [44]. In the Petri Net model, there are two kinds of elements – nodes and tokens. Nodes are connected to other nodes by fixed (static) links. Tokens are passed between nodes using these links. The behavior of each node is governed by reactive rules which are triggered based on the presence of tokens at the nodes.

Another popular model of concurrency is based on communicating processes. Two exponents of this sort of model are Robin Milner who defined the *Calculus of Communicating Systems (CCS)* [38], and Tony Hoare who defined the programming language, *Communicating Sequential Processes (CSP)* [20]. In both these systems, asynchronous processes have a fixed communication topology (processes which can communicate with each other are statically determined) and the communication is synchronous – i.e. a message exchange involves an explicit handshake between the sender and the receiver.

In contrast to these models, the notion of actors is very flexible. In the earliest formulation of the Actor Model, an actor was defined by Carl Hewitt as an

O. Owe et al. (Eds.): From OO to FM (Dahl Festschrift), LNCS 2635, pp. 26–57, 2004.

autonomous agent which has intentions, resources, contain message monitors and a scheduler [19]. Later work by Hewitt and his associates developed a more abstract model of parallelism based on causal relations between asynchronous events at different actors – where an event represents the sending or receiving of a message [10, 16]. The formulation of the Actor Model that most people refer to is based on the transition system in Agha [1]. In particular, this formulation provides a basis for the operational semantics developed in [3].

The Actor Model is more flexible than Petri Nets, CCS or CSP. Petri Nets have been generalized to Colored Petri Nets which allow tokens to carry data. It is possible to encode actor computations in this more general model by interpreting actor behaviors although it is not clear how useful such an encoding is [42].

In fact, the work on actors inspired Robin Milner to develop the π-calculus [41], a model which is more general than CCS. As Milner reports: "... the pure λ-calculus is built with just two kinds of things: terms and variables. Can we achieve the same economy for a process calculus? Carl Hewitt, with his Actor Model, responded to this challenge a long ago; he declared that a value, an operator on values, and a process should all be the same kind of thing: an *actor*. This goal impressed me, because it implies a homogeneity and completeness of expression .... But it was long before I could see how to attain the goal in terms of an algebraic calculus .... So, in the spirit of Hewitt, our first step is to demand that all things denoted by terms or accessed by names–values, registers, operators, processes, objects–are all the same kind of thing; they should *all* be processes. Thereafter we regard access-by-name as the raw material of computation ...." [39].

The π-calculus allows names to be communicable – thus capturing an essential aspect of actors which provides it greater flexibility. However, there are number of differences between the two models that are caused by differing goals and ontological commitments. The goal of explicitly modeling distributed systems has motivated the development of actors, while the goal of providing an algebraic formulation has been central to work on π-calculus. As a consequence, the Actor Model uses asynchronous communication which is natural in distributed systems, while the π-calculus uses synchronous communication which results in a simpler algebra. As in object-based systems, each actor has a distinct identity which is bound to a unique name which does not change. By contrast, in the π-calculus, different processes can have the same name, and these names can disappear.

This paper develops a formal calculus for actors by imposing suitable type restrictions on the π-calculus. Our aim is to gain a better understanding of the implications of the different ontological commitments of the Actor Model. We present a typed variant of π-calculus, called Aπ, which is an accurate representation of the Actor Model, and we investigate a basic theory of process equivalence in Aπ. We then illustrate how Aπ can be used to provide formal semantics for actor-based concurrent programming languages. The Actor Model has served as the basis of a number of object-based languages [4, 59]. Since our aim is to investigate the effects of only the basic ontological commitments of the Actor

Model, we focus our presentation on a simple actor-based language which was first defined in [1].

Following is the layout of the rest of this paper. In Section 2, we give a brief and informal description of the Actor Model, and in Section 3, we describe a simple actor language (SAL). In Section 4, we present the calculus $A\pi$, and in Section 5, we investigate a basic theory of process equivalence in $A\pi$. In Section 6, we provide a formal semantics for SAL by translating its programs to $A\pi$. In Section 7, we conclude the paper with an overview of several other research directions that have been pursued on the basic Actor Model over the last two decades.

2 The Actor Model

A computational system in the Actor Model, called a *configuration*, consists of a collection of concurrently executing actors and a collection of messages in transit [1]. Each actor has a unique name (the *uniqueness* property) and a behavior, and communicates with other actors via asynchronous messages. Actors are reactive in nature, i.e. they execute only in response to messages received. An actor's behavior is deterministic in that its response to a message is uniquely determined by the message contents. Message delivery in the Actor Model is fair [10]. The delivery of a message can only be delayed for a finite but unbounded amount of time.

An actor can perform three basic actions on receiving a message (see Figure 1): (a) create a finite number of actors with universally fresh names, (b) send a finite number of messages, and (c) assume a new behavior. Furthermore, all actions performed on receiving a message are concurrent; there is no ordering between any two of them. The following observations are in order here. First, actors are persistent in that they do not disappear after processing a message (the *persistence* property). Second, actors cannot be created with well known names or names received in a message (the *freshness* property).

The description of a configuration also defines an interface between the configuration and its environment, which constrains interactions between the two. An interface is a set of names ρ, called the *receptionist* set, that contains names of all the actors in the configuration that are visible to the environment. The only way an environment can effect the actors in a configuration is by sending messages to the receptionists of the configuration; the non-receptionist actors are all hidden from the environment. Note that uniqueness of actor names automatically prevents the environment from receiving messages in configuration that are targeted to the receptionists, because to receive such messages the environment should have an actor with the same name as that of a receptionist. The receptionist set may evolve during interactions, as the messages that the configuration sends to the environment may contain names of actors are not currently in the receptionist set.

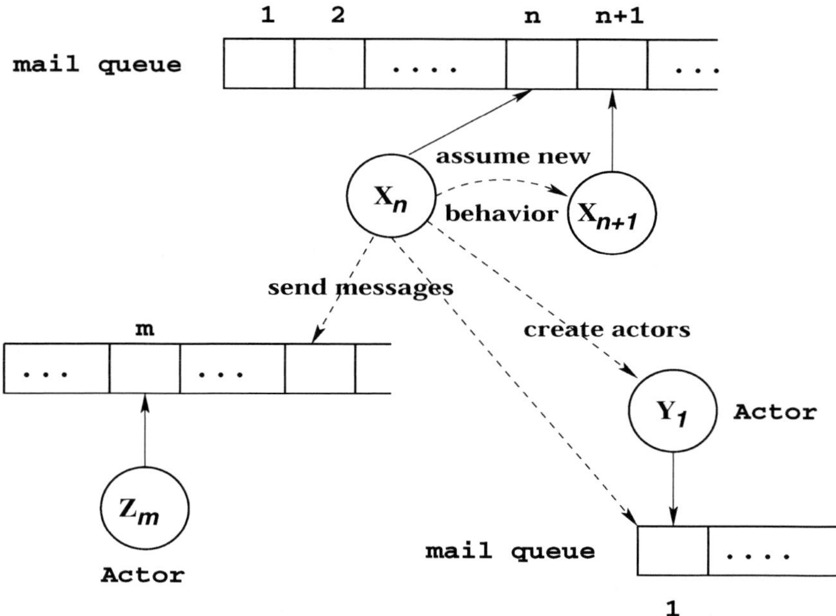

Fig. 1. A diagram illustrating computation in an actor system.

3 A Simple Actor Language (SAL)

A SAL program consists of a sequence of behavior definitions followed by a single (top level) command.

$$Pgm ::= BDef_1 \ \ \ldots \ \ BDef_n \ \ Com$$

The behavior definitions are templates for actor behaviors. The top level command creates an initial collection of actors and messages, and specifies the interface of the configuration to its environment.

3.1 Expressions

Three types of primitive values - booleans, integers and names - are presumed. There are literals for boolean and integer constants, but none for names. Primitive operations include $\wedge, \vee, \neg$ on booleans, $+, -, *, =$ on integers. Expressions always evaluate to values of one of the primitive types. An expression may contain identifiers which may be bound by formal parameters of the behavior definition in which the expression occurs (see behavior definitions in Section 3.3). Identifiers are lexically scoped in SAL. We let e range over the syntactic domain of expressions, and u, v, w, x, y, z over actor names.

3.2 Commands

Following is the syntax for SAL commands.

Com ::=	**send** $[e_1, ..., e_n]$ **to** x	**(message send)**
	become $B(e_1, ..., e_n)$	**(new behavior)**
	let $x_1 =$ **[recep] new** $B_1(e_1, ..., e_{i_1})$,	
	$\ldots\ x_k =$ **[recep] new** $B_k(e_1, ..., e_{i_k})$	
	in *Com*	**(actor creations)**
	if e **then** *Com₁* **else** *Com₂*	**(conditional)**
	case x **of** $(y_1 : Com_1, \ldots, y_n : Com_n)$	**(name matching)**
	$Com_1 \parallel Com_2$	**(composition)**

Message send: Expressions e_1 to e_n are evaluated, and a message containing the resulting tuple of values is sent to actor x. A message send is asynchronous: execution of the command does not involve actual delivery of the message.

New behavior: This specifies a new behavior for the actor which is executing the command. The identifier B should be bound by a behavior definition (see behavior definitions in Section 3.3). Expressions e_1 to e_n are evaluated and the results are bound to the parameters in the acquaintance list of B. The resulting closure is the new behavior of the actor. A `become` command cannot occur in the top level command of an actor program, because the top level command specifies the initial system configuration and not the behavior of a single actor.

Actor creations: Actors with the specified behaviors are created. The identifiers $x_1, \ldots, x_n$, which are all required to be distinct, denote names of the actors, and the command *Com* is executed under the scope of these identifiers. In the top level command of a program, the identifiers can be optionally tagged with the qualifier `recep`. The corresponding actors will be receptionists of the program configuration, and can thus receive messages from the environment; all the other actors are (at least initially) private to the configuration. The set of receptionists can of course expand during the execution, as messages containing the names of non-receptionists are sent to the environment.

While the scope of the identifiers declared as receptionists is the entire top level command, the scope of the others is only the `let` command. Because actor names are unique, a name can not be declared as a receptionist more than once in the entire top level command. An actor creates new actors with universally fresh names, and these names must be communicated before they can be used by any actor other than the creator. This freshness property would be violated if any of the new actors is declared as a receptionist. Therefore, the `recep` qualifier can not be used in behavior definitions.

Conditional: The expression e should evaluate to a boolean. If the result is true, command Com_1 is executed, else Com_2 is executed.

Name matching: The name x is matched against the names $y_1, \ldots, y_n$. If there is a match, the command corresponding to one of the matches is non-deterministically chosen and executed. If there is no match, then there is no further execution of the command. Note that the mismatch capability on names is not available, i.e. it is not possible to take an action based on the failure of a match.

Composition: The two composed commands are executed concurrently.

A couple of observations are in order here. First, there is no notion of sequential composition of commands. This is because all the actions an actor performs on receiving a message, other than the evaluation order dependencies imposed by the semantics, are concurrent. Second, message passing in SAL is analogous to *call-by-value* parameter passing; expressions in a `send` command are first evaluated and a message is created with the resulting values. Alternately, we can think of a *call-by-need* message passing scheme. But both the mechanisms are semantically equivalent because expressions do not involve recursions and hence their evaluations always terminate.

3.3 Behavior Definitions

The syntax of behavior definitions is as follows.

$BDef$ ::= **def** $\langle$*beh name*$\rangle$($\langle$*acquaintence list*$\rangle$)[$\langle$*input list*$\rangle$]
Com
end def

The identifier $\langle$*beh name*$\rangle$ is bound to an abstraction and the scope of this binding is the entire program. The identifiers in acquaintance list are formal parameters of this abstraction, and their scope is the body *Com*. These parameters are bound during a behavior instantiation, and the resulting closure is an actor behavior. The identifiers in input list are formal parameters of this behavior, and their scope is the body *Com*. They are bound at the receipt of a message. The acquaintance and input lists contain all the free identifiers in *Com*. The reserved identifier *self* can be used in *Com* as a reference to the actor which has (an instance of) the behavior being defined. The execution of *Com* should always result in the execution of at most a single `become` command, else the behavior definition is said to be erroneous. This property is guaranteed statically by requiring that in any concurrent composition of commands, at most one of the commands contains a `become`. If the execution of *Com* does not result in the execution of a `become`, then the corresponding actor is assumed to take on a '*sink*' behavior that simply ignores all the messages it receives.

3.4 An Example

SAL is not equipped with high-level control flow structures such as recursion and iteration. However, such structures can be encoded as patterns of message passing [18]. The following implementation of the factorial function (adapted from [1]) shows how recursion can be encoded. The example also illustrates *continuation passing style* of programming common in actor systems.

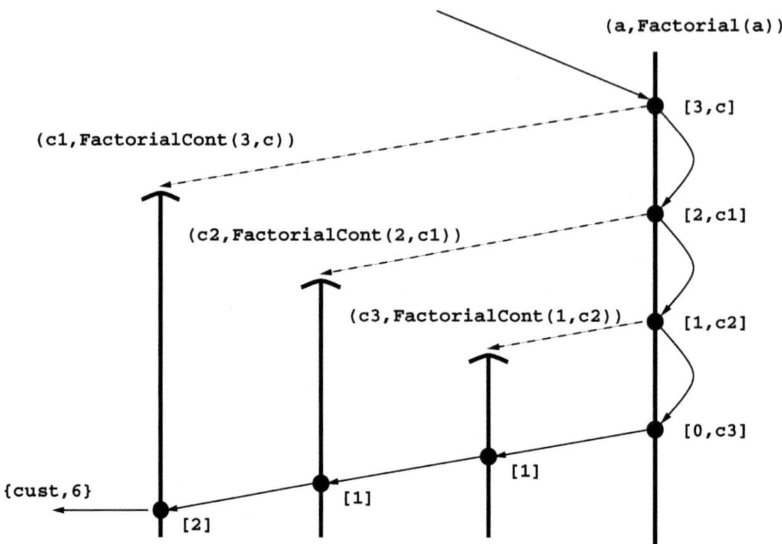

Fig. 2. A diagram illustrating computation of factorial 3, whose result is to be sent back to the actor c. The vertical lines denote time lines of actors. An arrow to the top of a time line denotes an actor creation. Other arrows denote messages.

def *Factorial* ()[*val,cust*]
  become *Factorial* () ||
  if $val = 0$
    then send [1] to *cust*
    else let $cont =$ **new** *FactorialCont* (*val,cust*)
        in send [$val - 1$, *cont*] **to** *self*
end def

def *FactorialCont* (*val,cust*)[*arg*]
  send [$val * arg$] **to** *cust*
end def

A request to factorial actor includes a positive integer n and the actor name *cust* to which the result has to be sent. On receiving a message the actor creates a continuation actor *cont* and sends itself a message with contents $n - 1$ and *cont*. The continuation actor has n and *cust* as its acquaintances. Eventually a chain of continuation actors will be created each knowing the name of the next in the chain (see Figure 2). On receiving a message with an integer, the behavior of each continuation actor is to multiply the integer with the one it remembers and send the reply to its customer. The program can be proved correct by a simple induction on n. Note that since the factorial actor is stateless, it can process different factorial requests concurrently, without affecting the result of a factorial evaluation.

Following is a top level command that creates a factorial actor that is also a receptionist and sends a message with value 5 to it.

let x = [**recep**] **new** *Factorial*()
in send [5] **to** x

4 The Calculus Aπ

The Actor Model and π-calculus have served as the basis of a large body of research on concurrency. In this section, we represent the Actor Model as a typed asynchronous π-calculus [7, 21], called Aπ. The type system imposes a certain discipline on the use of names to capture actor properties such as uniqueness, freshness and persistence. This embedding of the Actor Model in π-calculus not only provides a direct basis for comparison between the two models, but also enables us to apply concepts and techniques developed for π-calculus to the Actor Model. As an illustration of how the theory of behavioral equivalences for π-calculus can be adapted to the Actor Model, we develop a theory of *may* testing for Aπ in Section 5. In the interest of space and simplicity, we skip the proofs of all the propositions we state. In fact, the proofs are variations of the ones presented in [53, 54].

4.1 Syntax

We assume an infinite set of names $\mathcal{N}$, and let $u, v, w, x, y, z, \ldots$ range over $\mathcal{N}$. The set of configurations, ranged over by P, Q, R, is defined by the following grammar.

$$
\begin{aligned}
P := \ & 0 \ \mid \ x(y).P \ \mid \ \overline{x}y \ \mid \ (\nu x)P \ \mid \ P_1|P_2 \\
& \mid \ \texttt{case}\ x\ \texttt{of}\ (y_1 : P_1, \ldots, y_n : P_n) \ \mid \ B\langle \tilde{x}; \tilde{y} \rangle
\end{aligned}
$$

The order of precedence among the constructs is the order in which they are listed. The reader may note that, as in the π-calculus, only names are assumed to be primitive in Aπ. As we will see in Section 6, datatypes such as booleans and integers, and operations on them, can be encoded as Aπ processes. These encodings are similar to those for π-calculus [40]; the differences arise mainly due to the typing constraints imposed by Aπ.

Following is the intended interpretation of Aπ terms as actor configurations. The *nil* term 0, represents an empty configuration. The output term $\overline{x}y$, represents a configuration with a single message targeted to x and with contents y. We call x the *subject* of the output term. Note that unlike in SAL, where tuples of arbitrary length can be communicated, only a single name can be communicated per message in Aπ. As we will explain in Section 4.3, *polyadic* communication (communication of tuples of arbitrary length) can be encoded in Aπ, although only after relaxing the persistence property. The input term $x(y).P$ represents

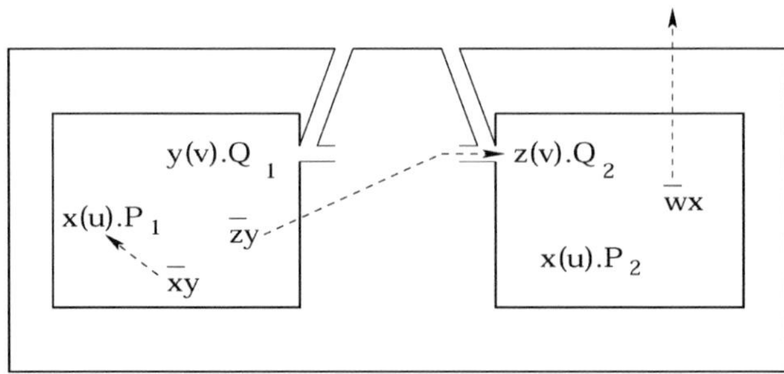

Fig. 3. A visualization of the Aπ term $R = (\nu x)(x(u).P_1|y(v).Q_1|\overline{x}y|\overline{z}y) \mid (\nu x)(x(u).P_2|z(v).Q_2|\overline{w}x)$. A box around subterms indicates a restriction operator. An outlet next to an actor inside the box indicates that the actor is a receptionist for the configuration.

a configuration with an actor x whose behavior is $(y)P$. The parameter y constitutes the formal parameter list of the behavior $(y)P$, and binds all the free occurrences of y in P. The actor x can receive an arbitrary name z and substitute it for y in the definition of P, and then behave like $P\{z/y\}$ (see below for the definition of substitution). We call x the subject of the input term.

The restricted process $(\nu x)P$ is the same as P, except that x is no longer a receptionist of P. All free occurrence of x in P are bound by the restriction. Thus, the receptionists of a configuration P, are simply those actors whose names are not bound by a restriction. The composition $P_1|P_2$ is a configuration containing all the actors and messages in P_1 and P_2. The configuration $\texttt{case}\ x\ \texttt{of}\ (y_1 : P_1, \ldots, y_n : P_n)$ behaves like P_i if $x = y_i$, and like 0 if $x \neq y_i$ for $1 \leq i \leq n$. If more than one branch is true, one of them is non-deterministically chosen. Note that this construct does not provide mismatch capability on names, i.e. it does not allow us to take an action based on the failure of a match. Thus, this construct is much like the `case` construct of SAL.

The term $B\langle\tilde{u};\tilde{v}\rangle$ is a behavior instantiation. The identifier B has a single defining equation of the form $B \stackrel{def}{=} (\tilde{x};\tilde{y})x_1(z).P$, where $\tilde{x}$ is a tuple of distinct names of length 1 or 2, and x_1 denotes the first component of $\tilde{x}$. This definition, like a behavior definition in SAL, provides a template for an actor behavior. The tuples $\tilde{x}$ and $\tilde{y}$ together contain exactly the free names in $x_1(z).P$, and constitute the acquaintance list of the behavior definition. The reason behind the constraint on length of $\tilde{x}$ will be clear in Section 4.2. For an instantiation $B\langle\tilde{u};\tilde{v}\rangle$, we assume $len(\tilde{u}) = len(\tilde{x})$, and $len(\tilde{v}) = len(\tilde{y})$. In the case where $\tilde{v}$ is the empty tuple, we write $B\langle\tilde{u}\rangle$ as a shorthand for $B\langle\tilde{u};\rangle$.

For example, the configuration

$$R = (\nu x)(x(u).P_1|y(v).Q_1|\overline{x}y|\overline{z}y) \mid (\nu x)(x(u).P_2|z(v).Q_2|\overline{w}x)$$

is a composition of two sub-configurations (see Figure 3). The first consists of two actors x and y, a message targeted to x, and a message targeted to an actor

z that is external to the sub-configuration. The actor y is a receptionist, while x is hidden. The second sub-configuration, also contains two actors x and z, and a message targeted to an external actor w. Note that although the name x is used to denote two different actors, the uniqueness property of actor names is not violated in R because the scopes of the two restrictions of x do not intersect. The actors y and z are receptionists of the configuration R.

The reader may note that we use the `case` construct and recursive definitions instead of the standard match ($[x = y]P$) and replication ($!P$) operators of π-calculus. We have chosen these constructs mainly because they are more convenient in expressing actor systems. However, both these constructs can be encoded using the match and replication operators. For instance, the reader can find an encoding of recursive definitions using the standard π-calculus constructs in [40].

Before presenting the type system, a few notational conventions are in order. For a tuple $\tilde{x}$, we denote the set of names occurring in $\tilde{x}$ by $\{\tilde{x}\}$. We denote the result of appending $\tilde{y}$ to $\tilde{x}$ by $\tilde{x}, \tilde{y}$. We assume the variable $\hat{z}$ ranges over $\{\emptyset, \{z\}\}$. By $\tilde{x}, \hat{z}$ we mean $\tilde{x}, z$ if $\hat{z} = \{z\}$, and $\tilde{x}$ otherwise. By $(\nu\hat{z})P$ we mean $(\nu z)P$ if $\hat{z} = \{z\}$, and P otherwise. We define the functions for free names, bound names and names, $fn(.)$, $bn(.)$ and $n(.)$, of a process as expected. As usual, we do not distinguish between alpha-equivalent processes, i.e. between processes that differ only in the use of bound names. A name substitution is a function on names that is almost always the identity. We write $\{\tilde{y}/\tilde{x}\}$ to denote a substitution that maps x_i to y_i and is identity on all other names, and let σ range over substitutions. We denote the result of simultaneous substitution of y_i for x_i in P by $P\{\tilde{y}/\tilde{x}\}$. As usual, we define substitution on processes only modulo alpha-equivalence, with the usual renaming of bound names to avoid captures.

4.2 Type System

Not all terms represent actor configurations. For example, the term $x(u).P|x(v).Q$ violates the uniqueness property of actor names, as it contains two actors with name x. The term $x(u).(u(v).P|x(v).Q)$ violates the freshness property because it creates an actor with name u that is received in a message. Uniqueness of actor names and freshness of names of newly created actors, capture essential aspects of object identity. We enforce such constraints by imposing a type system.

Enforcing all actor properties directly in Aπ results in a language that is too weak to express certain communication patterns. For example, consider expressing polyadic communication in Aπ, where tuples of arbitrary length can be communicated. Since communication in Aπ is monadic, both the sending and receiving actors have to exchange each component of the tuple one at a time, and delay the processing of other messages until all the arguments are transfered. But on the other hand, the persistence property implies that both the actors are always ready to process any message targeted to them. We therefore relax the persistence requirement, so that instead of assuming a new behavior immediately after receiving a message, an actor can wait until certain synchronization conditions are met before processing the next message. Specifically, we allow an actor to assume a series of fresh names, one at a time, and resume the old name at a later point. Basically, the synchronization task is delegated from one new name to another until the last one releases the actor after the synchronization conditions are met.

We assume $\bot, * \notin \mathcal{N}$, and for $X \subset \mathcal{N}$ define $X^* = X \cup \{\bot, *\}$. For $f : X \rightarrow X^*$, we define $f^* : X^* \rightarrow X^*$ as $f^*(x) = f(x)$ for $x \in X$ and $f^*(\bot) = f^*(*) = \bot$. A typing judgment is of the form $\rho; f \vdash P$, where ρ is the receptionist set of P, and $f : \rho \rightarrow \rho^*$ is a temporary name mapping function that relates actors in P to the temporary names they have currently assumes. Specifically

- $f(x) = \bot$ means that x is a regular actor name and not a temporary one,
- $f(x) = *$ means x is the temporary name of an actor with a private name (bound by a restriction), and
- $f(x) = y \notin \{\bot, *\}$ means that actor y has assumed the temporary name x.

The function f has the following properties. For all $x, y \in \rho$,

- $f(x) \neq x$: This holds for obvious reasons.
- $f(x) = f(y) \notin \{\bot, *\}$ implies $x = y$: This holds because an actor cannot assume more than one temporary name at the same time.
- $f^*(f(x)) = \bot$: This holds because temporary names are not like regular actor names in that they themselves cannot temporarily assume new names, but can only delegate their capability of releasing the original actor to new names.

We define a few functions and relations on the temporary name mapping functions, that will be useful in defining the type rules.

Definition 1. *Let $f_1 : \rho_1 \rightarrow \rho_1^*$ and $f_2 : \rho_2 \rightarrow \rho_2^*$.*

1. *We define $f_1 \oplus f_2 : \rho_1 \cup \rho_2 \rightarrow (\rho_1 \cup \rho_2)^*$ as*

$$(f_1 \oplus f_2)(x) = \begin{cases} f_1(x) \text{ if } x \in \rho_1, \text{ and } f_1(x) \neq \bot \text{ or } x \notin \rho_2 \\ f_2(x) \text{ otherwise} \end{cases}$$

Note that $\oplus$ is associative.

2. *If $\rho \subset \rho_1$ we define $f|\rho : \rho \rightarrow \rho^*$ as*

$$(f|\rho)(x) = \begin{cases} * & \text{if } f(x) \in \rho_1 - \rho \\ f(x) & \text{otherwise} \end{cases}$$

3. *We say f_1 and f_2 are compatible if $f = f_1 \oplus f_2$ has following properties: $f = f_2 \oplus f_1$, and for all $x, y \in \rho_1 \cup \rho_2$, $f(x) \neq x$, $f^*(f(x)) = \bot$, and $f(x) = f(y) \notin \{\bot, *\}$ implies $x = y$.* □

Definition 2. *For a tuple $\tilde{x}$, we define $ch(\tilde{x}) : \{\tilde{x}\} \rightarrow \{\tilde{x}\}^*$ as $ch(\epsilon) = \{\}$, and if $len(\tilde{x}) = n$, $ch(\tilde{x})(x_i) = x_{i+1}$ for $1 \leq i < n$ and $ch(\tilde{x})(x_n) = \bot$.* □

$$NIL\text{: } \emptyset; \{\} \vdash 0 \qquad\qquad MSG\text{: } \emptyset; \{\} \vdash \overline{x}y$$

$$ACT\text{: } \frac{\rho; f \vdash P}{\{x\} \cup \hat{z}; ch(x, \hat{z}) \vdash x(y).P} \text{ if } \begin{array}{l} \rho - \{x\} = \hat{z},\ y \notin \rho, \text{ and} \\ f = \begin{cases} ch(x, \hat{z}) \text{ if } x \in \rho \\ ch(\epsilon, \hat{z}) \text{ otherwise} \end{cases} \end{array}$$

$$CASE\text{: } \frac{\forall 1 \leq i \leq n \ \ \rho_i; f_i \vdash P_i}{(\cup_i \rho_i); (f_1 \oplus f_2 \oplus \ldots \oplus f_n) \vdash \texttt{case}\ x\ \texttt{of}\ (y_1 : P_1, \ldots, y_n : P_n)}$$
$$\text{if } f_i \text{ are mutually compatible}$$

$$COMP\text{: } \frac{\rho_1; f_1 \vdash P_1 \qquad \rho_2; f_2 \vdash P_2}{\rho_1 \cup \rho_2; f_1 \oplus f_2 \vdash P_1 | P_2} \text{ if } \ \rho_1 \cap \rho_2 = \phi$$

$$RES\text{: } \frac{\rho; f \vdash P}{\rho - \{x\}; f|(\rho - \{x\}) \vdash (\nu x)P}$$

$$INST\text{: } \{\tilde{x}\}; ch(\tilde{x}) \vdash B\langle \tilde{x}; \tilde{y} \rangle \text{ if } len(\tilde{x}) = 2 \text{ implies } x_1 \neq x_2$$

Table 1. Type rules for Aπ.

The type rules are shown in Table 1. Rules *NIL* and *MSG* are obvious. In the *ACT* rule, if $\hat{z} = \{z\}$ then actor z has assumed temporary name x. The condition $y \notin \rho$ ensures that actors are not created with names received in a message. This is what is commonly referred to as the *locality* property in the π-calculus literature [35] [1]. The conditions $y \notin \rho$ and $\rho - \{x\} = \hat{z}$ together guarantee the freshness property by ensuring that new actors are created with fresh names. Note that it is possible for x to be a regular name, i.e. $\rho - \{x\} = \emptyset$, and disappear after receiving some message, i.e. $x \notin \rho$. We interpret this as the actor x having assumed a *sink* behavior, i.e. that it simply consumes all the messages that it now receives. With this interpretation the intended persistence property is not violated. Note that a similar interpretation was adopted to account for the case where the body of a SAL behavior definition does not execute a `become` command (see Section 3.3).

The compatibility check in *CASE* rule prevents errors such as: two actors, each in a different branch, assuming the same temporary name; or, the same actor assumes different temporary names in different branches. The *COMP* rule guarantees the uniqueness property by ensuring that the two composed configurations do not contain actors with the same name. In the *RES* rule, f is updated so that if x has assumed a temporary name y in P, then y's role as a temporary name is remembered but x is forgotten. The *INST* rule states that if $len(\tilde{x}) = 2$, then $B\langle \tilde{x}; \tilde{y} \rangle$ denotes a configuration containing a single actor x_2 that has assumed temporary name x_1.

[1] In the context of π-calculus, the locality constraint stipulates that a processes can not receive a name and listen to it; the constraint is enforced by the simple syntactic rule that in a term $x(y).P$, the name y can not occur as the subject of an input.

Type checking a term involves checking the accompanying behavior definitions. For *INST* rule to be sound, for every definition $B \stackrel{def}{=} (\tilde{x};\tilde{y})x_1(z).P$ and substitution $\sigma = \{\tilde{u},\tilde{v}/\tilde{x},\tilde{y}\}$ that is one-to-one on $\{\tilde{x}\}$, the judgment $\{\tilde{u}\}; ch(\tilde{u}) \vdash (x_1(z).P)\sigma$ should be derivable. From Lemma 1, it follows that this constraint is satisfied if $\{\tilde{x}\}; ch(\tilde{x}) \vdash x_1(z).P$ is derivable. Thus, a term is well-typed only if for each accompanying behavior definition $B \stackrel{def}{=} (\tilde{x};\tilde{y})x_1(z).P$, the judgment $\{\tilde{x}\}; ch(\tilde{x}) \vdash x_1(z).P$ is derivable.

The following theorem states a soundness property of the type system.

Theorem 1. *If $\rho; f \vdash P$ then $\rho \subset fn(P)$, and for all $x, y \in \rho$, $f(x) \neq x$, $f^*(f(x)) = \bot$, and $f(x) = f(y) \notin \{\bot, *\}$ implies $x = y$. Furthermore, if $\rho'; f' \vdash P$ then $\rho = \rho'$ and $f = f'$.* □

Not all substitutions on a term P yield terms. A substitution σ may identify distinct actor names in P, and therefore violate the uniqueness property. But, if σ renames different actors in P to different names, then $P\sigma$ will be well typed. This is formally stated in Lemma 1, where we have used the following notation. For a set of names X, $\sigma(X)$ denotes the set obtained by applying the substitution σ to each element of X. Further, if σ is a substitution which is one-to-one on X, $f\sigma : \sigma(X) \rightarrow \sigma(X)^*$ is defined as $f\sigma(\sigma(x)) = \sigma(f(x))$, where $\sigma(\bot) = \bot$ and $\sigma(*) = *$.

Lemma 1. *If $\rho; f \vdash P$ and σ is one-to-one on ρ then $\sigma(\rho); f\sigma \vdash P\sigma$.* □

A consequence of Lemma 1 is that the type system respects alpha-equivalence, i.e. if P_1 and P_2 are alpha-equivalent, then $\rho; f \vdash P_1$ if and only if $\rho; f \vdash P_2$. For a well-typed term P, we define $rcp(P) = \rho$ if $\rho; f \vdash P$ for some f.

4.3 Operational Semantics

We specify the operational semantics of $A\pi$ using a labeled transition system (see Table 2). The rules are obtained by simple modifications to the usual rules for asynchronous π-calculus [7]. The modifications simply account for the use of `case` construct and recursive definitions instead of the standard match and replication operators.

The transition system is defined modulo alpha-equivalence on processes, i.e. alpha-equivalent processes are declared to the same transitions. The symmetric versions of *COM*, *CLOSE*, and *PAR*, where the roles of P_1 and P_2 are interchanged, are not shown. Transition labels, which are also called actions, can be of five forms: τ (a silent action), $\overline{x}y$ (free output of a message with target x and content y), $\overline{x}(y)$ (bound output), xy (free input of a message), and $x(y)$ (bound input). We denote the set of all visible (non-τ) actions by $\mathcal{L}$, let α range over $\mathcal{L}$, and let β range over all the actions.

The interpretation of these rules in terms of the Actor Model, is as follows. The *INP* rule represents the receipt of a message by an actor, and the *OUT* rule represents the emission of a message. The *BINP* rule is used to infer bound

$$INP \quad x(y).P \xrightarrow{xz} P\{z/y\} \qquad\qquad BINP \; \frac{P \xrightarrow{xy} P'}{P \xrightarrow{x(y)} P'} \; y \notin fn(P)$$

$$OUT \quad \overline{x}y \xrightarrow{\overline{x}y} 0$$

$$RES \; \frac{P \xrightarrow{\alpha} P'}{(\nu y)P \xrightarrow{\alpha} (\nu y)P'} \; y \notin n(\alpha) \qquad\qquad OPEN \; \frac{P \xrightarrow{\overline{x}y} P'}{(\nu y)P \xrightarrow{\overline{x}(y)} P'} \; x \neq y$$

$$PAR \; \frac{P_1 \xrightarrow{\alpha} P_1'}{P_1|P_2 \xrightarrow{\alpha} P_1'|P_2} \; bn(\alpha) \cap fn(P_2) = \emptyset \qquad\qquad COM \; \frac{P_1 \xrightarrow{\overline{x}y} P_1' \quad P_2 \xrightarrow{xy} P_2'}{P_1|P_2 \xrightarrow{\tau} P_1'|P_2'}$$

$$CLOSE \; \frac{P_1 \xrightarrow{\overline{x}(y)} P_1' \quad P_2 \xrightarrow{xy} P_2'}{P_1|P_2 \xrightarrow{\tau} (\nu y)(P_1'|P_2')} \; y \notin fn(P_2)$$

$$BRNCH \; \texttt{case}\ x\ \textbf{of}\ (y_1 : P_1, \ldots, y_n : P_n) \xrightarrow{\tau} P_i \;\; \texttt{if}\ x = y_i$$

$$BEHV \; \frac{(x_1(z).P)\{(\tilde{u}, \tilde{v})/(\tilde{x}, \tilde{y})\} \xrightarrow{\alpha} P'}{B\langle \tilde{u}; \tilde{v}\rangle \xrightarrow{\alpha} P'} \; B \stackrel{def}{=} (\tilde{x}; \tilde{y})x_1(z).P$$

Table 2. A labeled transition system for Aπ.

inputs, i.e. receipt of messages that contain actor names that were previously unknown to the receiving configuration. The *RES* rule states that an action α performed by P can also be performed by $(\nu x)P$, provided x does not occur in α. This condition disallows the emission of a message which contains the name of a hidden actor in the configuration (a non-receptionist), and prevents confusing a received name with the name of a hidden actor. The *OPEN* rule accounts for the former type of actions, while the latter can be accounted for by an alpha-conversion of the recepient $(\nu x)P$ to a term $(\nu y)P\{y/x\}$, where y does not occur in α, and then applying the *RES* rule. Note that in the *OPEN* rule, the hidden actor name that is being emitted is bound in the output action, but is no longer bound by a restriction in the transition target. Thus, the actor which was hidden in the transition source, becomes a receptionist in the target. The side condition of the *OPEN* rule prevents the emission of messages that are targeted to the hidden actor.

The *PAR* rule captures the concurrent composition of configurations. The side condition of the rule prevents erroneous inferences of bound inputs and outputs. For example, if P_1 performs a bound input $x(y)$, and $y \in fn(P_2)$, then the entire configuration $P_1|P_2$ can *not* perform the bound input $x(y)$ as it already 'knows' the name y. Similarly, it would be erroneous to allow bound outputs of P_1 with the output argument occuring free in P_2; such behavior would confuse the name of a previously hidden actor with the name of another actor.

The *COM* rule is used to infer the communication of a receptionist name between two composed configurations. The *CLOSE* rule is used to infer the communication of non-receptionist names between the configurations. The side condition prevents confusion of the private name that is communicated, with other names in the recipient P_2. Note that the transition target has a top-level restriction of the communicated name; thus the actor whose name is communicated (internally) is still a non-receptionist in the transition target.

The *BRNCH* and *BEHV* rules are self explanatory. The following theorem states that the type system respects the transition rules.

Theorem 2. *If P is well-typed and $P \xrightarrow{\alpha} P'$ then P' is well-typed.*

Since well-typed terms are closed under transitions, it follows that actor properties are preserved during a computation. However, note that the source and the target of a transition need not have the same typing judgment. Specifically, both the receptionist set and the function that relates actors to the temporary names they have assumed, may change. For instance the receptionist set changes when the name of a hidden actor is emitted to the environment, or an actor disappears after receiving a message. (The reader may recall that the latter case is interpreted as the actor assuming a sink behavior.) Similarly, the temporary name map function changes when an actor with a temporary name re-assumes its original name.

Example 1 (polyadic communication). We show how the ability to temporarily assume a fresh name can be used to encode polyadic communication in Aπ. Suppose that the subject of a polyadic receive is not a temporary name. In particular, in the encoding below, x cannot be a temporary name. The idea behind translation is to let x temporarily assume a fresh name z which is used to receive all the arguments without any interference from other messages, and re-assume x after the receipt. For fresh u, z we have

$$\begin{aligned}
\lfloor \overline{x}\langle y_1, \ldots, y_n\rangle \rfloor &= (\nu u)(\overline{x}u \mid S_1\langle u; y_1, \ldots, y_n\rangle) \\
S_i &\stackrel{def}{=} (u; y_i, \ldots, y_n)u(z).(\overline{z}y_i \mid S_{i+1}\langle u; y_{i+1}, \ldots, y_n\rangle) \quad 1 \le i < n \\
S_n &\stackrel{def}{=} (u; y_n)u(z).\overline{z}y_n \\
\lfloor x(y_1, \ldots, y_n).P \rfloor &= x(u).(\nu z)(\overline{u}z \mid R_1\langle z, \hat{x}; u, \tilde{a}\rangle) \\
R_i &\stackrel{def}{=} (z, \hat{x}; u, \tilde{a})z(y_i).(\overline{u}z \mid R_{i+1}\langle z, \hat{x}; u, \tilde{a}\rangle) \quad 1 \le i < n \\
R_n &\stackrel{def}{=} (z, \hat{x}; u, \tilde{a})z(y_n).(\overline{u}z \mid \lfloor P \rfloor)
\end{aligned}$$

where $\tilde{a} = fn(x(y_1, \ldots, y_n).P) - \{x\}$, and $\hat{x} = \{x\}$ if for some ρ, f, we have $\rho \cup \{x\}; f \vdash \lfloor P \rfloor$, and $\hat{x} = \emptyset$ otherwise. □

Before we proceed any further, a few definitions and notational conventions are in order. The functions $fn(.)$, $bn(.)$ and $n(.)$ are defined on $\mathcal{L}$ as expected. As a uniform notation for free and bound actions we adopt the following convention from [7]: $(\emptyset)\overline{x}y = \overline{x}y$, $(\{y\})\overline{x}y = \overline{x}(y)$, and similarly for input actions. We define a complementation function on $\mathcal{L}$ as $\overline{(\hat{y})xy} = (\hat{y})\overline{x}y$, $\overline{(\hat{y})\overline{x}y} = (\hat{y})xy$. The variables s, r, t are assumed to range over $\mathcal{L}^*$. The functions $fn(.)$, $bn(.)$, $n(.)$, and complementation on $\mathcal{L}$ are extended to $\mathcal{L}^*$ the obvious way. Elements in $\mathcal{L}^*$ are called traces. Alpha-equivalence over traces is defined as expected, and alpha-equivalent traces are not distinguished. The relation $\Longrightarrow$ denotes the reflexive transitive closure of $\xrightarrow{\tau}$, and $\xRightarrow{\beta}$ denotes $\Longrightarrow\xrightarrow{\beta}\Longrightarrow$. For $s = l.s'$, $P \xrightarrow{l}\xrightarrow{s'} Q$ is compactly written as $P \xrightarrow{s} Q$, and similarly $P \xRightarrow{l}\xRightarrow{s'} Q$ as $P \xRightarrow{s} Q$. The assertion, $P \xRightarrow{s} P'$ for some P', is written as $P \xRightarrow{s}$, and similarly $P \xrightarrow{s}$ and $P \xrightarrow{\tau}$.

Not every trace produced by the transition system corresponds to an actor computation. For instance, we have

$$(\nu x)(x(u).P|\overline{x}x|\overline{y}x) \xrightarrow{\overline{y}(x)} x(u).P|\overline{x}x \xrightarrow{\overline{x}x}$$

But the message $\overline{x}x$ is not observable; due to the uniqueness property of actor names, there can never be an actor named x in the environment. To account for this, we define for any set of names ρ, the notion of a ρ-well-formed trace such that only ρ-well-formed traces can be exhibited by an actor configuration with ρ as its initial receptionist set.

Definition 3. *For a set of names ρ and trace s we define $rcp(\rho, s)$ inductively as*

$$rcp(\rho, \epsilon) = \rho \qquad rcp(\rho, s.(\hat{y})xy) = rcp(\rho, s) \qquad rcp(\rho, s.(\hat{y})\overline{x}y) = rcp(\rho, s) \cup \hat{y}$$

We say s is ρ-well-formed if $s = s_1.(\hat{y})\overline{x}y.s_2$ implies $x \notin rcp(\rho, s_1)$. We say s is well-formed if it is $\emptyset$-well-formed. □

The following lemma captures our intuition.

Lemma 2. *Let $P|Q$ be a well-typed $A\pi$ term with $rcp(P) = \rho_1$ and $rcp(Q) = \rho_2$. Then $P|Q \Longrightarrow$ can be unzipped into $P \xRightarrow{s}$ and $Q \xRightarrow{\overline{s}}$ such that s is ρ_1-well-formed and $\overline{s}$ is ρ_2-well-formed.* □

For convenience, since we work only modulo alpha-equivalence on traces, we adopt the following hygiene condition. Whenever we are interested in ρ-well-formed traces, we will only consider traces s such that if $s = s_1.\alpha.s_2$, then $(\rho \cup n(s_1) \cup fn(\alpha)) \cap bn(\alpha.s_2) = \emptyset$.

The transition sequences are further constrained by a fairness requirement which requires messages to be eventually delivered, if they can be. For example, the following transition sequences are unfair.

$$\begin{aligned} Diverge\langle x\rangle|\overline{x}u|y(v).\overline{v}v|\overline{y}v &\xrightarrow{\tau} Diverge\langle x\rangle|\overline{x}u|y(v).\overline{v}v|\overline{y}v \\ &\xrightarrow{\tau} Diverge\langle x\rangle|\overline{x}u|y(v).\overline{v}v|\overline{y}v \\ &\xrightarrow{\tau} \cdots \end{aligned}$$

$$\text{where } Diverge \stackrel{def}{=} (x)x(u).(\overline{x}u \mid Diverge\langle x\rangle)$$

In every transition above, the message $\overline{x}y$ is delivered to its target; but the message $\overline{y}v$ is never delivered.

Fairness in actors requires that the delivery of a message is not delayed infinitely long; but it can be delayed for any finite number of steps. Thus, only infinite transition sequences can be unfair. However, note that our fairness constraint does *not* require that *every* message is eventually delivered to its target. Because we have relaxed the persistence property, an actor may disappear during a computation, after which all the message targeted to it become permanently disabled. Thus, the fairness criteria only requires that there is no message that is infinitely often enabled, but not delivered. This is consistent with our convention that an actor that disappears is assumed to take on a *sink* behavior.

The fairness requirement can be enforced by defining a predicate on sequences of transitions as described in [48] such that only fair sequences satisfy the predicate. However, we do not pursue this any further in this paper, as fairness does not effect the theory we are concerned with. The reader is referred to Section 5.4 for further discussion.

4.4 Discussion

There has been considerable research on actor semantics in the past two decades. We set Aπ in the context of some of the salient work. A significant fraction of the research has been in formal semantics for high level concurrent programming languages based on the Actor Model, e.g. [3, 13] where a core functional language is extended with actor coordination primitives. The main aim of these works has been to design concurrent languages that could be useful in practice. Accordingly, the languages assume high-level computational notions as primitives, and are embellished with type systems that guarantee useful properties in object-based settings. In contrast, Aπ is a basic calculus that makes only the ontological commitments inherent in the Actor Model, thus giving us a simpler framework for further theoretical investigations. In Section 6, we show how Aπ can be used to give a translational semantics for SAL.

In [48, 49], actors are modeled in rewriting logic which is often considered as a universal model of concurrency [33, 36]. An actor system is modeled as a specific rewrite theory, and established techniques are used to derive the semantics of the specification and prove its properties. In a larger context, this effort belongs to a collection of works that have demonstrated that rewriting logic provides a good basis to unify many different concurrency theories. For example, we have also a rewrite theory formulation of the π-calculus [52]. In comparison, Aπ establishes a connection between two models of concurrency that is deeper than is immediately available from representing the two models in a unified basis. Specifically, the theory that we have developed in Section 5, can be seen as a more elaborate investigation of the relationship between two specific rewrite theories, and provides a formal connection that helps in adapting and transferring results in one theory to the other.

There are several calculi that are inspired by the Actor Model and the π-calculus [15, 22, 45]. But these are neither entirely faithful to the Actor Model, nor directly comparable to the π-calculus. For example, they are either equipped with primitives intrinsic to neither of the models [15, 22], or they ignore actor properties such as uniqueness and persistence [45]. These works are primarily intended for investigation of object-oriented concepts.

5 A Theory of May Testing for Aπ

Central to any process calculus is the notion of behavioral equivalence which is concerned with the question of when two processes are equal. Typically, a notion of success is defined, and two processes are considered equivalent if they have the same success properties in all contexts. Depending on the chosen notion of context and success one gets a variety of equivalences [8, 12, 46].

The *may testing* equivalence is one such instance [17, 12], where the context consists of an observing process that runs in parallel and interacts with the process being tested, and success is defined as the observer signaling a special event. The possible non-determinism in execution leads to at least two possibilities for the definition of equivalence. In may testing, a process is said to pass a test proposed by an observer, if there exists *at least one* run that leads to a success. By viewing a success as something bad happening, may testing can be used for reasoning about *safety* properties. An alternate definition, where a process is said to pass a test if *every* run leads to a success, is called the *must testing* equivalence. By viewing a success as something good happening, must testing can be used for reasoning about *liveness* properties. In this paper, we will be develop only with the theory may testing for Aπ.

Context-based behavioral equalities like may testing suffer from the need for universal quantification over all possible contexts; such quantification makes it very hard to prove equalities directly from the definition. One solution is to find an alternate characterization of the equivalence which involves only the processes being compared. We provide an alternate characterization of may testing in Aπ that is *trace* based and directly builds on the known characterization for asynchronous π-calculus.

5.1 A Generalized May Preorder

As in any typed calculus, may testing in Aπ takes typing into account; an observer O can be used to test a configuration P only if $P|O$ is well-typed. Note that $P|O$ is well-typed only if $rcp(P) \cap rcp(O) = \emptyset$. Thus, O can be used to test the equivalence between P and Q only if $rcp(O) \cap (rcp(P) \cup rcp(Q)) = \emptyset$.

The uniqueness property of actor names naturally leads to a generalized version of may testing, where the equivalence $\simeq_\rho$ is tagged with a parameter ρ. All possible observers O that do not listen on names in ρ, i.e. $rcp(O) \cap \rho = \emptyset$, are used for deciding $\simeq_\rho$. Of course, for processes P and Q to be compared with $\simeq_\rho$, it has to be the case that $rcp(P), rcp(Q) \subset \rho$.

Definition 4 (may testing). *Observers are processes that can emit a special message $\overline{\mu}\mu$. We let O range over the set of observers. We say O accepts a trace s if $O \stackrel{\overline{s}.\overline{\mu}\mu}{\Longrightarrow}$. For P, O, we say P $\underline{\text{may}}$ O if $P|O \stackrel{\overline{\mu}\mu}{\Longrightarrow}$. For ρ such that*

(L1)	$s_1.(\hat{y})s_2$	$\prec$	$s_1.(\hat{y})xy.s_2$	if $(\hat{y})s_2 \neq \bot$
(L2)	$s_1.(\hat{y})(\alpha.xy.s_2)$	$\prec$	$s_1.(\hat{y})xy.\alpha.s_2$	if $(\hat{y})(\alpha.xy.s_2) \neq \bot$
(L3)	$s_1.(\hat{y})s_2$	$\prec$	$s_1.(\hat{y})xy.\overline{x}y.s_2$	if $(\hat{y})s_2 \neq \bot$
(L4)	$s_1.\overline{x}w.(s_2\{w/y\})$	$\prec$	$s_1.\overline{x}(y).s_2$	

Table 3. A preorder relation on traces.

$rcp(P), rcp(Q) \subset \rho$, we say $P \sqsubset\!\!\!\sim_\rho Q$, if for every O such that $rcp(O) \cap \rho = \emptyset$, P may O implies Q may O. We say $P \simeq_\rho Q$ if $P \sqsubset\!\!\!\sim_\rho Q$ and $Q \sqsubset\!\!\!\sim_\rho P$. □

The relation $\sqsubset\!\!\!\sim_\rho$ is a preorder, i.e. reflexive and transitive, and $\simeq_\rho$ is an equivalence relation. Further, note that the larger the parameter ρ, the smaller the observer set that is used to decide $\sqsubset\!\!\!\sim_\rho$. Hence if $\rho_1 \subset \rho_2$, we have $P \sqsubset\!\!\!\sim_{\rho_1} Q$ implies $P \sqsubset\!\!\!\sim_{\rho_2} Q$. However, $P \sqsubset\!\!\!\sim_{\rho_2} Q$ need not imply $P \sqsubset\!\!\!\sim_{\rho_1} Q$. For instance, $0 \simeq_{\{x\}} \overline{x}x$, but only $0 \sqsubset\!\!\!\sim_\emptyset \overline{x}x$ and $\overline{x}x \not\sqsubset\!\!\!\sim_\emptyset 0$. Similarly, $\overline{x}x \simeq_{\{x,y\}} \overline{y}y$, but $\overline{x}x \not\sqsubset\!\!\!\sim_\emptyset \overline{y}y$ and $\overline{y}y \not\sqsubset\!\!\!\sim_\emptyset \overline{x}x$. However, $P \sqsubset\!\!\!\sim_{\rho_2} Q$ implies $P \sqsubset\!\!\!\sim_{\rho_1} Q$ if $fn(P) \cup fn(Q) \subset \rho_1$.

Theorem 3. *Let $\rho_1 \subset \rho_2$. Then $P \sqsubset\!\!\!\sim_{\rho_1} Q$ implies $P \sqsubset\!\!\!\sim_{\rho_2} Q$. Furthermore, if $fn(P) \cup fn(Q) \subset \rho_1$ then $P \sqsubset\!\!\!\sim_{\rho_2} Q$ implies $P \sqsubset\!\!\!\sim_{\rho_1} Q$.* □

5.2 An Alternate Characterization of May Testing

We now build on the trace-based characterization of may testing for asynchronous π-calculus presented in [7] to obtain a characterization of may testing in Aπ. Following is a summary of the alternate characterization of may testing in asynchronous π-calculus. To account for asynchrony, the trace semantics is modified using a trace preorder $\preceq$ that is defined as the reflexive transitive closure of the laws shown in Table 3, where the notation $(\hat{y})\cdot$ is extended to traces as follows.

$$(\hat{y})s = \begin{cases} s & \text{if } \hat{y} = \emptyset \text{ or } y \notin fn(s) \\ s_1.x(y).s_2 & \text{if } \hat{y} = \{y\} \text{ and there are } s_1, s_2, x \text{ s.t.} \\ & \quad s = s_1.xy.s_2 \text{ and } y \notin fn(s_1) \cup \{x\} \\ \bot & \text{otherwise} \end{cases}$$

The expression $(\hat{y})s$ returns $\bot$, if $\hat{y} = \{y\}$ and y is used in s before it is received for the first time, i.e. the first free occurrence of y in s is *not* as the argument of an input. Otherwise, the expression returns the trace s with the first such free input changed to a bound input. The (unparameterized) may preorder $\sqsubset\!\!\!\sim$ in asynchronous π-calculus (which corresponds to $\sqsubset\!\!\!\sim_\emptyset$ in our setting) is then characterized as: $P \sqsubset\!\!\!\sim Q$ if and only if $P \stackrel{s}{\Longrightarrow}$ implies $Q \stackrel{r}{\Longrightarrow}$ for some $r \preceq s$.

The intuition behind the preorder is that if an observer accepts a trace s, then it also accepts any trace $r \preceq s$. Laws *L1-L3* capture asynchrony, and *L4* captures the inability to mismatch names. Laws *L1* and *L2* state that an observer cannot force inputs on the process being tested. Since outputs are asynchronous, the actions following an output in a trace exhibited by an observer need not be causally dependent on the output. Hence the observer's outputs can be delayed until a causally dependent action (*L2*), or dropped if there are no such actions (*L1*). Law *L3* states that an observer can consume its own outputs unless there are subsequent actions that depend on the output. Law *L4* states that without mismatch an observer cannot discriminate bound names from free names, and hence can receive any name in place of a bound name. The intuition behind the trace preorder is formalized in the following lemma that is proved in [7] for asynchronous π-calculus.

Lemma 3. *If* $P \stackrel{\bar{s}}{\Longrightarrow}$, *then* $r \preceq s$ *implies* $P \stackrel{\bar{r}}{\Longrightarrow}$. □

We note that, the lemma above also holds for Aπ with very simple modifications to the proof.

Actor properties such as uniqueness and freshness "weaken" may equivalence in Aπ, in comparison to asynchronous π-calculus. Specifically, the type system of Aπ reduces the number of observers that can be used to test actor configurations. For example, the following two processes are distinguishable in asynchronous π-calculus, but equivalent in Aπ:

$$P = (\nu x)(x(z).0|\overline{x}x|\overline{y}x) \qquad\qquad Q = (\nu x)(x(z).0|\overline{y}x)$$

The observer $O = y(z).z(w).\overline{\mu}\mu$ can distinguish P and Q in asynchronous π-calculus, but is not a valid Aπ term as it violates the freshness property (*ACT* rule of Table 1). In fact, no Aπ term can distinguish P and Q, because the message $\overline{x}x$ is not observable.

The following alternate preorder on configurations characterizes the may preorder in Aπ.

Definition 5. *We say* $P \ll_\rho Q$, *if for every ρ-well-formed trace s,* $P \stackrel{s}{\Longrightarrow}$ *implies there is* $r \preceq s$ *such that* $Q \stackrel{r}{\Longrightarrow}$. □

To prove the characterization, we define an observer $O(s)$ for a well-formed trace s, such that P $\underline{may}$ $O(s)$ implies $P \stackrel{r}{\Longrightarrow}$ for some $r \preceq s$.

Definition 6 (canonical observer). *For a well-formed trace s, we define an observer*

$$O(s) = (\nu\tilde{x}, z)(|_{y_i \in \chi} Proxy(s, y_i, z) \mid O'(s, z)), \text{ where } z \text{ fresh}$$

$\{\tilde{x}\}$ = *set of names occurring as argument of bound input actions in s*
χ = *set of names occuring as subject of output actions in s*

$O'(\epsilon, z) \stackrel{\triangle}{=} \overline{\mu}\mu$
$O'((\hat{v})uv.s, z) \stackrel{\triangle}{=} \overline{u}v|O'(s, z)$

$$O'(\overline{u}v.s, z) \triangleq z(w_1, w_2).\texttt{case } w_1 \texttt{ of } (u : \texttt{case } w_2 \texttt{ of } (v : O'(s, z))) \quad w_1, w_2 \textit{ fresh}$$
$$O'(\overline{u}(v).s, z) \triangleq z(w, v).\texttt{case } w \texttt{ of } (u : O'(s, z)) \quad w \textit{ fresh}$$

$$Proxy(\epsilon, y, z) \triangleq 0$$
$$Proxy((\hat{v})uv.s, y, z) \triangleq Proxy(s, y, z)$$
$$Proxy((\hat{v})\overline{u}v.s, y, z) \triangleq \begin{cases} y(w).(\overline{z}\langle y, w\rangle \mid Proxy(s, y, z)) \ \ w \textit{ fresh} & \textit{if } u = y \\ Proxy(s, y, z) & \textit{otherwise} \end{cases}$$

In the above, $\triangleq$ *is used for macro definitions. The reader may verify that* $\chi - \{\tilde{x}\}; f \vdash O(s)$ *where* f *maps every name in its domain to* $\bot$. *Further, if* s *is* ρ*-well-formed we have* $rcp(O(s)) \cap \rho = \emptyset$, *because the set of names occurring as subject of output actions in a* ρ*-well-formed trace is disjoint from* ρ. □

The observer $O(s)$ consists of a collection of proxies and a central matcher. There is one forwarding proxy for each external name that a configuration sends a message to while exhibiting s. The proxies forward messages to the matcher which analyzes the contents. This forwarding mechanism (which is not necessary for the construction of canonical observers in the corresponding proof for asynchronous π-calculus), is essential for Aπ because of uniqueness of actor names. Further, note that the forwarding mechanism uses polyadic communication, whose encoding was shown in Section 4.3. The following lemma formalizes our intention behind the construction of $O(s)$.

Lemma 4. *For a well-formed trace* s, $O(s) \stackrel{\overline{r}.\overline{\mu}\mu}{\Longrightarrow}$ *implies* $r \preceq s$. □

The following theorem, which establishes the alternate characterization of may preorder in Aπ, can be proved easily using Lemmas 2, 3, and 4.

Theorem 4. $P \sqsubset\!\!\!\sim_\rho Q$ *if and only if* $P \ll_\rho Q$. □

5.3 Some Axioms for May Testing

Table 4 lists some inference rules besides the reflexivity and transitivity rules, and some axioms for $\sqsubset\!\!\!\sim_\rho$. For an index set $I = \{1, \ldots, n\}$, we use the macro $\sum_{i\in I} P_i$ to denote, $(\nu u)(\texttt{case } u \texttt{ of } (u : P_1, \ldots, u : P_n))$ for u fresh if $I \neq \emptyset$, and 0 otherwise. For an index set that is a singleton, we omit I and simply write $\sum P$ instead of $\sum_{i\in I} P$. We let the variable G range over processes of form $\sum_{i\in I} P_i$. We write $\sum_{i\in I} P_i + \sum_{j\in J} P_j$ to denote $\sum_{k\in I\uplus J} P_k$. We write $\sqsubseteq$ as a shorthand for $\sqsubseteq_\emptyset$, and $=$ for $=_\emptyset$.

Axioms *A1* to *A17* are self explanatory. We note that they also hold in asynchronous π-calculus [7]. But axiom *A18* is unique to Aπ. It captures the fact that a message targeted to an internal actor in a configuration, cannot escape to the environment. The axiom states that there are only two ways such a message can be handled in the next transition step: it can be consumed internally or delayed for later. The axiom also allows for dropping of the message permanently, which is useful when the message target no longer exists (it may have disappeared

I1	if $P \sqsubseteq_\rho Q$ and $rcp(R) \cap \rho = \emptyset$, then $(\nu x)P \sqsubseteq_{\rho-\{x\}} (\nu x)Q$, $P\|R \sqsubseteq_\rho Q\|R$.
I2	if for each $z \in fn(P,Q)$ $P\{z/y\} \sqsubseteq_\rho Q\{z/y\}$ then $x(y).P \sqsubseteq_\rho x(y).Q$
I3	if for each $i \in I$ $P_i \sqsubseteq_\rho \sum_{j\in J} Q_{ij}$ then $\sum_{i\in I} P_i \sqsubseteq_\rho \sum_{i\in I, j\in J} Q_{ij}$
I4	if $\rho_1 \subset \rho_2$ and $P \sqsubseteq_{\rho_1} Q$ then $P \sqsubseteq_{\rho_2} Q$.

A1	$G + G = G$	*A3*	$P\|0 = P$	*A5*	$(P\|Q)\|R = P\|(Q\|R)$
A2	$G \sqsubseteq G + G'$	*A4*	$P\|Q = Q\|P$		

A6	$(\nu x)(\sum_{i\in I} P_i) = \sum_{i\in I} (\nu x)P_i$	
A7	$(\nu x)(P\|Q) = P\|(\nu x)Q$	$x \notin n(P)$
A8	$(\nu x)(\overline{x}y\|\alpha.P) = \alpha.(\nu x)(\overline{x}y\|P)$	$x \notin n(\alpha)$
A9	$(\nu x)(\overline{x}y\|x(z).P) = (\nu x)(P\{y/z\})$	
A10	$(\nu x)(y(z).P) = \begin{cases} y(z).(\nu x)P & \text{if } x \neq y, x \neq z \\ 0 & \text{if } x = y \end{cases}$	
A11	$\overline{x}y\| \sum_{i\in I} P_i = \sum_{i\in I} (\overline{x}y\|P_i)$	$I \neq \emptyset$
A12	$\alpha. \sum_{i\in I} P_i = \sum_{i\in I} \alpha.P_i$	$I \neq \emptyset$
A13	$P = \sum P$	
A14	$x(y).(\overline{u}v\|P) \sqsubseteq \overline{u}v\|x(y).P$	$y \neq u, y \neq v$
A15	$P\{y/z\} \sqsubseteq \overline{x}y\|x(z).P$	
A16	$x(y).(\overline{x}y\|P) \sqsubseteq P$	$y \notin n(P)$
A17	$(\nu x)P \sqsubseteq P\{y/x\}$	
A18	If $x \in \rho$, $w \neq x$ and $w \neq y$, then	

$$\overline{x}y|z(w).P \sqsubseteq_\rho \sum z(w).(\overline{x}y|P) + \sum z(w).P + \sum Q$$

$$\text{where } Q = \begin{cases} P\{y/w\} & \text{if } x = z \\ 0 & \text{otherwise} \end{cases}$$

Table 4. Inference rules and axioms for $\overset{\sqsubset}{\sim}_\rho$ in Aπ.

during the computation). As an application of this axiom, if $x \in \rho$, we can prove $\overline{x}y \sqsubseteq_\rho 0$ as follows. For w fresh,

$$\begin{array}{rll} \overline{x}y & \sqsubseteq_\rho \overline{x}y|(\nu w)(w(w).0) & (A3, A10, I1) \\ & \sqsubseteq_\rho (\nu w)(\overline{x}y|w(w).0) & (A7) \\ & \sqsubseteq_\rho (\nu w)(\sum w(w).0 + \sum w(w).\overline{x}y + \sum 0) & (A18, I1) \\ & \sqsubseteq_\rho \sum(\nu w)(w(w).0) + \sum(\nu w)w(w).\overline{x}y + \sum(\nu w)0 & (A6) \\ & \sqsubseteq_\rho 0 & (A1, A10, A13, I3) \end{array}$$

Inference rules *I1* and *I3* are self explanatory, while *I4* is motivated by Theorem 3. We illustrate *I1* through some examples. First, using $\overline{x}y \sqsubseteq_{\{x\}} 0$ (proved above) and *I1*, we get $(\nu x)\overline{x}y \sqsubseteq (\nu x)0$, and by axiom *A17* we have $(\nu x)0 \sqsubseteq 0$.

Therefore, $(\nu x)\overline{x}y \sqsubseteq 0$. Note the use of the ability to contract the parameter ρ of the may preorder after applying a restriction. Second, the following example illustrates the necessity of the side condition $rcp(R) \cap \rho = \emptyset$ for composition: $\overline{x}y \mathrel{\overset{\sqsubset}{\sim}}_{\{x\}} 0$ but not $\overline{x}y|x(y).\overline{y}y \mathrel{\overset{\sqsubset}{\sim}}_{\{x\}} x(y).\overline{y}y$, for the LHS can satisfy the observer $y(u).\overline{\mu}\mu$ and the RHS can not.

Note that the inference rules are generalizations of rules for asynchronous π-calculus presented in [7], in order to handle parameterization of the may preorder. In fact, the rules for asynchronous π-calculus can be obtained by setting $\rho = \emptyset$ in *I1, I2* and *I3*. Rule *I4* is unique to the parameterized may preorder.

The soundness of rules *I1-I4* can be easily proved directly from Definition 4. Soundness of the axioms is easy to check. For *A1-A17*, whenever $P \sqsubseteq Q$, we have $P \overset{s}{\Longrightarrow}$, implies $Q \overset{r}{\Longrightarrow}$ such that $r \preceq s$. For *A18* , both LHS and RHS exhibit the same ρ-well-formed traces. The reader can verify that *A18* would also be sound as an equality.

5.4 Discussion

The alternate characterization of may testing for Aπ turns out to be the same as that for L$\pi_=$ which we presented in [54]. L$\pi_=$ is a version of asynchronous π-calculus with match operator and the locality constraint (see Section 4.2 for a discussion on locality). This shows that of all the constraints enforced by the type system of Aπ, only locality and uniqueness (which is taken care of by parameterization of the may preorder) has an effect on may testing.

In Section, 4.3, we claimed that the fairness property of the Actor Model does not affect the theory we have presented. The justification is simple. May testing is concerned only with the occurrence of an event after a finite computation, while fairness affects only infinite computations. An interesting consequence of fairness, however, is that must equivalence [17] implies may equivalence, which was shown for a specific actor-based language in [3]. It can be shown by a similar argument that this result holds in Aπ also.

There has been a significant amount of research on notions of equivalence and semantic models for actors, including asynchronous bisimulation [15], testing equivalences [3], event diagrams [10], and interaction paths [50]. We have not only related may testing [3] to the interaction paths model [50], but also related our characterizations to that of asynchronous π-calculus and its variants.

6 Formal Semantics of SAL

Aπ can serve as the basis for actor based concurrent programming languages. As an illustration, we give a formal semantics for SAL by translating its programs into Aπ. The translation can be exploited to apply the characterizations established in Section 5 to reason about programs in SAL.

In Sections 6.1 and 6.2, we show how booleans, natural numbers and operations on them can be represented as processes in Aπ. These data types, along with names, are assumed as primitive in SAL. Of course, this exercise is not entirely necessary, and in fact, a better strategy may be to directly consider an extended version of Aπ with basic data types. The characterizations for Aπ can be adapted in a straightforward manner to the extended calculus. We have chosen the other approach here, mainly to illustrate that the type system of Aπ does not reduce the expressive power of the calculus. In Sections 6.3-6.5, we present the translation of SAL expressions, commands and behavior definitions. SAL expressions and commands are translated into Aπ terms, and their evaluation is modeled as computation in these terms. SAL behavior definitions are translated into recursive definitions in Aπ.

6.1 Booleans

Booleans are encoded as configurations with a single actor that is also a receptionist. In the following, $\underline{T}$ defines the receptionist behavior for *true*, and $\underline{F}$ for *false*.

$$\underline{T} \stackrel{def}{=} (x)x(u,v,c).\overline{c}u$$

$$\underline{F} \stackrel{def}{=} (x)x(u,v,c).\overline{c}v$$

The behaviors accept messages containing three names, of which the last name is assumed to be the customer name (see Section 4.3 for an encoding of polyadic communication). The behavior $\underline{T}$ replies back to the customer with the first name, while $\underline{F}$ replies back with the second name.

The negation function can be encoded as follows

$$Not \stackrel{def}{=} (x)x(u,c).(\nu v,y,z)(\overline{u}\langle y,z,v\rangle \mid v(w).\texttt{case}\ w\ \texttt{of}(y:\underline{F}\langle v\rangle, z:\underline{T}\langle v\rangle))$$

$Not(x)$ can be thought of as the function *not* available at name x. Evaluation of the function is initiated by sending a message containing a value and a customer name, to x. The customer eventually receives the negation of the value sent. The reader may verify that

$$Not\langle x\rangle \mid \underline{F}\langle u\rangle \mid \overline{x}\langle u,c\rangle \stackrel{\overline{c}(v)}{\Longrightarrow} \underline{T}\langle v\rangle$$

Following is the encoding of boolean *and*

$$\begin{aligned} And \stackrel{def}{=} (x)x(u,v,c).(\nu y,z_1,z_2)(&\overline{u}\langle z_1,z_2,y\rangle \mid \overline{v}\langle z_1,z_2,y\rangle \mid \\ & y(w_1).y(w_2).(\overline{c}y \mid \\ & \quad \texttt{case}\ w_1\ \texttt{of}\ (\\ & \quad\quad z_1 : \texttt{case}\ w_2\ \texttt{of}\ (z_1 : \underline{T}\langle y\rangle, z_2 : \underline{F}\langle y\rangle), \\ & \quad\quad z_2 : \underline{F}\langle y\rangle\ ))) \end{aligned}$$

The reader may verify the following

$$And\langle x\rangle \mid \underline{T}\langle u\rangle \mid \underline{F}\langle v\rangle \mid \overline{x}\langle u,v,c\rangle \stackrel{\overline{c}(y)}{\Longrightarrow} \underline{F}\langle y\rangle$$

The reader may also verify that for each behavior B defined above $\{x\};\{x \mapsto \bot\} \vdash B\langle x\rangle$.

6.2 Natural Numbers

Natural numbers are built from the constructors 0 and S. Accordingly, we define the following two behaviors.

$$Zero \stackrel{def}{=} (x)x(u,v,c).\overline{c}\langle u,x\rangle$$
$$Succ \stackrel{def}{=} (x,y)x(u,v,c).\overline{c}\langle v,y\rangle$$

With these, natural numbers can be encoded as follows.

$$\underline{0}(x) \triangleq Zero\langle x\rangle$$
$$\underline{S^{n+1}0}(x) \triangleq (\nu y)(Succ\langle x,y\rangle \mid \underline{S^n 0}(y))$$

The number S^n0 is encoded as a sequence of $n+1$ actors each pointing to the next, and the last one pointing to itself. The first n actors have the behavior *Succ* and the last has behavior *Zero*. Only the first actor is the receptionist to the entire configuration. As in our encoding for booleans, both the behaviors accept messages with three names, the last of which is assumed to denote the customer. The behavior *Succ* replies back to the customer with the second name and the name of next actor in the sequence, while *Zero* replies back with the first name and its own name.

We only show the encoding of the addition operation, and hope the reader is convinced that it is possible to encode the others. Our aim is to define a behavior *Add* such that

$$Add\langle x\rangle \mid \underline{S^n0}(u) \mid \underline{S^m0}(v) \mid \overline{x}\langle u,v,c\rangle \stackrel{\overline{c}(w)}{\Longrightarrow} \underline{S^{n+m}0}(w)$$

We first define a behavior *AddTo* such that

$$AddTo\langle x\rangle \mid (\nu u)(\underline{S^n0}(u) \mid \overline{x}\langle u,v,c\rangle) \mid \underline{S^m0}(v) \Longrightarrow \quad (\nu u)(\underline{S^{n+m}0}(u) \mid \overline{c}u)$$

We will then use *AddTo* to define *Add*.

$$\begin{aligned} AddTo \stackrel{def}{=} (x)x(u_1,u_2,c).(\nu y_1,y_2,w)(&\overline{u_2}\langle y_1,y_2,w\rangle \mid \\ & w(z_1,z_2).\texttt{case}\ z_1\ \texttt{of}\ (\\ &\quad y_1 : \overline{c}u_1, \\ &\quad y_2 : (\nu v)(Succ\langle v,u_1\rangle \mid \overline{x}\langle v,z_2,c\rangle \mid AddTo\langle x\rangle))) \end{aligned}$$

We are now ready to define *Add*.

$$\begin{aligned} Add \stackrel{def}{=} (x)x(u,v,c).(\nu y,z,w)(&AddTo\langle y\rangle \mid \underline{0}(w) \mid \overline{y}\langle w,u,z\rangle \mid \\ & z(w).(\nu y)(AddTo\langle y\rangle \mid \overline{y}\langle w,v,c\rangle)) \end{aligned}$$

Lemma 5. $Add\langle x\rangle \mid \underline{S^n0}(u) \mid \underline{S^m0}(v) \mid \overline{x}\langle u,v,c\rangle \stackrel{\overline{c}(w)}{\Longrightarrow} \underline{S^{n+m}0}(w)$

The reader may verify that for a natural number N, and each behavior B defined above, $\{x\};\{x \mapsto \bot\} \vdash \underline{N}(x)$, and $\{x\};\{x \mapsto \bot\} \vdash B\langle x\rangle$. This encoding of natural numbers can be extended to integers in a fairly straightforward manner (for example, by using tags to indicate the sign).

6.3 Expressions

Now that we have a representation of the basic constituents of expressions - namely, booleans, integers, and names - what remains is the representation of dependencies between the evaluation of subexpressions of an expression.

The translation of an expression takes as an argument, the name of a customer to which the result of the expression's evaluation is to be sent. An identifier expression x is translated as

$$\lfloor x \rfloor c = \overline{c}x$$

A constant (boolean or integer) expression e is translated as

$$\lfloor e \rfloor c = (\nu y)(\underline{e}\langle y \rangle \mid \overline{c}y)$$

where $\underline{e}$ is the encoding of the constant e. For an $n-$ary operator Op, the expression $Op(e_1, ..., e_n)$ is encoded as

$$\lfloor Op(e_1, \ldots, e_n) \rfloor c = (\nu y_1, \ldots, y_{n+1}, z)(Marshal(y_1, \ldots, y_{n+1}, z) \mid \\ \lfloor e_1 \rfloor y_1 \mid \ldots \mid \lfloor e_n \rfloor y_n \mid \overline{y_{n+1}}c \mid \underline{Op}\langle z \rangle)$$

where $\underline{Op}$ is the encoding of operator Op, and z, y_i are fresh. The expressions e_1 to e_n are concurrently evaluated. The configuration $Marshal(y_1, \ldots, y_{n+1}, z)$ marshals their results and the customer name into a single tuple, and forwards it to an internal actor that implements Op. The marshaling configuration is defined as

$$Marshal(y_1, \ldots, y_n, c) = (\nu u)(R\langle y_1, u \rangle \mid \ldots \mid R\langle y_n, u \rangle \mid S_1\langle u, y_1, \ldots, y_n, c \rangle)$$

where

$$R \stackrel{def}{=} (x, y)\ x(u).\overline{y}\langle u, x \rangle$$

$$\begin{aligned} S_i \stackrel{def}{=} & (x, y_i, \ldots, y_n, v_1, \ldots, v_{i-1}, c) \\ & \quad x(v_i, w).\texttt{case}\ w\ \texttt{of}\ (\\ & \qquad y_i : S_{i+1}\langle x, y_{i+1}, \ldots, y_n, v_1, \ldots, v_i, c \rangle \\ & \qquad y_{i+1} \cdots y_n : S_i\langle x, y_i, \ldots, y_n, v_1, \ldots, v_{i-1}, c \rangle \mid \overline{x}\langle v_i, w \rangle) \\ & \qquad\qquad \text{for } 1 \leq i < n \end{aligned}$$

$$S_n \stackrel{def}{=} (x, v_1, \ldots, v_{n-1}, c)\ x(v_n, w).\overline{c}\langle v_1, \ldots, v_n \rangle$$

By structural induction on an expression e and name x, it is easy to show that $\emptyset; \{\} \vdash \lfloor e \rfloor x$.

6.4 Commands

Although the Actor Model stipulates that the actions an actor performs on receiving a message are all concurrent, execution of SAL commands may involve sequentiality. For example, expressions need to be evaluated before the results are used to send messages or instantiate a behavior. This sequentiality is represented as communication patterns in the Aπ configurations that encode these commands. The translation of a command takes as an argument, the name of the SAL actor which executes the command. In the following, we assume that the names introduced during the translation are all fresh.

Message send: We use the *Marshal* configuration to marshal the results of expression evaluations into a polyadic message to the target.

$$[\![\textbf{send } [e_1, \ldots, e_n] \textbf{ to } z]\!]x = (\nu y_1, \ldots, y_n)(Marshal(y_1, \ldots, y_n, z) \mid [\![e_1]\!]y_1 \mid \ldots \mid [\![e_n]\!]y_n)$$

New behavior: We use an actor's ability to temporarily assume a new name to wait for the results of expression evaluations before assuming the new behavior.

$$[\![\textbf{become } B(e_1, \ldots, e_n)]\!]x = (\nu y_1, \ldots, y_n, z)([\![e_1]\!]y_1 \mid \ldots \mid [\![e_n]\!]y_n \mid Marshal\langle y_1, \ldots, y_n, z\rangle \mid z(u_1, \ldots, u_n).\underline{B}\langle x, u_1, \ldots, u_n\rangle)$$

where $\underline{B}$ is the Aπ behavior definition that is the translation of the SAL behavior definition B (see Section 6.5).

Actor creation: The identifiers in the `let` command are used as names for the new actors. If not tagged by the `recep` qualifier, these names are bound by a restriction. The actors are created at the beginning of command execution, but they assume a temporary name until their behavior is determined.

$$\begin{aligned}[\![\textbf{let } & y_1 = [\textbf{recep}] \textbf{ new } B_1(e_1, \ldots, e_{i_1}), \\ \ldots\ & y_k = [\textbf{recep}] \textbf{ new } B_k(e_1, \ldots, e_{i_k}) \textbf{ in } Com]\!]x = \\ & (\nu \tilde{y})([\![\textbf{become } B_1(e_1, \ldots, e_{i_1})]\!]y_1 \mid \ldots \mid \\ & [\![\textbf{become } B_k(e_1, \ldots, e_{i_k})]\!]y_k \mid [\![Com]\!]x)\end{aligned}$$

where $\tilde{y}$ consists of all y_i which have not been qualified with `recep`.

Conditional: We use a temporary actor that waits for the outcome of the test before executing the appropriate command.

$$\begin{aligned}[\![\textbf{if } e \textbf{ then } Com_1 \textbf{ else } Com_2]\!]x = \\ (\nu u)([\![e]\!]u \mid u(z).(\nu v_1, v_2)(\overline{z}\langle v_1, v_2, u\rangle \mid \\ u(w).\texttt{case } w \texttt{ of } (v_1 : [\![Com]\!]x, v_2 : [\![Com]\!]x))\end{aligned}$$

Name matching: The translation simply uses the `case` construct of Aπ.

$$\begin{aligned}[\![\textbf{case } z \textbf{ of}(y_1 : Com_1, \ldots, y_n : Com_n)]\!]x = \\ \texttt{case } z \texttt{ of } (y_1 : [\![Com_1]\!]x, \ldots, y_n : [\![Com_n]\!]x)\end{aligned}$$

Concurrent Composition: The translation of a concurrent composition is just the composition of individual translations.

$$[\![Com_1 \mid\mid Com_2]\!]x = [\![Com_1]\!]x \mid [\![Com_2]\!]x$$

This completes the translation of commands. Let *Com* be a command such that in any of its subcommands that is a concurrent composition, at most one of the composed commands contains a `become`. Further, assume that a name is declared as a receptionist at most once, and that `let` constructs with receptionist declarations are not nested under other `let` or conditional constructs. Let x be a fresh name. Then by structural induction on *Com*, we can show that $\{x, \tilde{y}\}; f \vdash \lfloor Com \rfloor x$ if *Com* contains a `become`, and $\{\tilde{y}\}; f \vdash \lfloor Com \rfloor x$ otherwise, where $\tilde{y}$ is the set of all names declared as receptionists in *Com*, and f is a function that maps all names in its domain to $\bot$.

6.5 Behavior Definitions

Behavior definitions in SAL are translated to behavior definitions in Aπ as follows

$$\lfloor \mathbf{def}\ B(\tilde{u})[\tilde{v}]\ \ Com\ \ \mathbf{end\ def} \rfloor \ = \ \underline{B} \stackrel{def}{=} (self; \tilde{u}) self(\tilde{v}).\lfloor Com \rfloor self$$

Note that the implicitly available reference *self* in a SAL behavior definition becomes explicit in the acquaintance list after translation. Since the body of a behavior definition does not contain receptionist declarations, it follows that $\{self\}; \{self \mapsto \bot\} \vdash self(\tilde{v}).\lfloor Com \rfloor self$. So the RHS is well-typed.

We have completed the translation of various syntactic domains in SAL, and are ready to present the overall translation of a SAL program. Recall that a SAL program consists of a sequence of behavior definitions and a single top level command. Following is the translation.

$$\lfloor BDef_1\ \ ...\ \ BDef_n\ \ Com \rfloor = \lfloor BDef_1 \rfloor\ \ \ldots\ \ \lfloor BDef_n \rfloor\ \ \lfloor Com \rfloor x$$

where x is fresh. Since the top level command cannot contain a `become`, its translation does not use the argument x supplied. Indeed, $\{\tilde{y}\}; f \vdash \lfloor Com \rfloor x$, where $\{\tilde{y}\}$ is the set of all names declared as receptionists in *Com*, and f maps all names in $\{\tilde{y}\}$ to $\bot$.

6.6 Discussion

The translation we have given, can in principle be exploited to use the testing theory developed for Aπ, to reason about SAL programs. Note that the characterization of may-testing for Aπ applies unchanged to SAL. This is because the set of experiments possible in SAL have the same distinguishing power as the experiments in Aπ. Specifically, the canonical observers constructed for Aπ in Section 5, are also expressible in SAL. Further, it follows immediately from Lemma 4 and Theorem 4 that these observers have all the distinguishing power, i.e. are sufficient to decide $\underset{\sim}{\sqsubset}_\rho$ in Aπ.

Although, SAL is a very simple language, it can be enriched with higher level programming constructs without altering the characterization. This is corroborated by the work in [34], where a high level actor language is translated to a more basic kernel language (similar to SAL) in such a way that the source and its translation exhibit the same set of traces.

Translational semantics for actor languages similar to SAL has been previously attempted. In [11] a simple actor language is translated into linear logic formulae, and computations are modeled as deductions in the logic. In [29] an actor-based object-oriented language is translated into HACL extended with records [28]. These translations provide a firm foundation for further semantic investigations. However, to reap the benefits of these translations, one still has to explicitly characterize actor properties such as locality and uniqueness in the underlying formal system, and identify the changes to the theory due to them. For instance, the asynchronous π-calculus can be seen as the underlying system of our translation, whereas only Aπ terms correspond to SAL programs, and the characterization of may testing for Aπ is very different from that for asynchronous π-calculus.

7 Research Directions

In this paper, we have focused only on the semantic aspects of the Actor Model, while much of the actor research over the last two decades has been on languages and systems.

Actor programming has been effective in combining benefits of object style encapsulation with the concurrency of real-world systems. The autonomy of actors frees a programmer from the burden of explicitly managing threads and synchronizing them. In fact, the autonomy of actors also facilitates mobility. Over the years, many implementations of the Actor Model have been done [9, 55, 59]. In fact, the numerous agent languages currently being developed typically follow the Actor Model [32, 23]. The Actor Model has also been used for efficient parallel computation [24, 26, 27, 51]. Actor languages and systems currently being developed include SALSA for web computing [56], Ptolemy II for embedded systems [30], and ActorFoundry for distributed computing [43].

An important area of active research in the Actor Model is the use of *computational reflection* [31]. The execution environment of an actor application can be represented as a collection of actors called *meta-actors*. These meta-actors constitute the middleware which mediates the interaction of the actor application and the underlying operating systems and networks. In order to customize fault-tolerance, security, synchronization and other types of interaction properties, meta-actors may be customized (see, for example, [5, 47]). Moreover, the meta-actor model supports the ability to express dynamic coordination policies as executable synchronization constraints between actors: the constraints may be enforced by customizing the meta-actors during execution [14]. An operational semantics of such reflective systems is developed in [57] and a rewriting model has been proposed in [37].

The use of meta-actors supports a separation of design concerns which is now popularly known as *aspect-oriented programming* [25]. The development of aspect-oriented programming will enable the reuse of interaction protocols and functional behavior of an object. The separation of the concurrent interaction protocols from the sequential behavior of actors is another step in the revolution in programming that was instigated by Dahl and Nygaard when they developed the idea of separating the interface of an object from its representation.

8 Acknowledgments

The research described in here has been supported in part by DARPA under contracts F33615-01-C-1907 and F30602-00-2-0586, and by ONR under contract N00014-02-1-0715. Part of the work described in here is a sequel to the research done in collaboration with Reza Ziaei, whom we would like to thank. We also thank Carolyn Talcott for useful discussions and comments.

References

[1] G. Agha. *Actors: A Model of Concurrent Computation in Distributed Systems.* MIT Press, 1986.

[2] G. Agha. Concurrent Object-Oriented Programming. *Communications of the ACM*, 33(9):125–141, September 1990.

[3] G. Agha, I. Mason, S. Smith, and C. Talcott. A Foundation for Actor Computation. *Journal of Functional Programming*, 1996.

[4] G. Agha, P. Wegner, and A. Yonezawa (editors). Proceedings of the ACM SIGPLAN workshop on object-based concurrent programming. Special issue of SIGPLAN Notices.

[5] M. Astley, D. Sturman, and G. Agha. Customizable middleware for modular distributed software. *CACM*, 44(5):99–107, 2001.

[6] G.M. Birtwistle, O-J. Dahl, B. Myhrhaug, and K. Nygaard. *Simula Begin.* Van Nostrand Reinhold, New York, 1973.

[7] M. Boreale, R. de Nicola, and R. Pugliese. Trace and testing equivalence on asynchronous processes. *Information and Computation*, 172(2):139–164, 2002.

[8] M. Boreale and D. Sangiorgi. Some congruence properties for π-calculus bisimilarities. In *Theoretical Computer Science 198*, 1998.

[9] J. P. Briot. Acttalk: A framework for object-oriented concurrent programming - design and experience. In *Object-based parallel and distributed computing II - Proceedings of the* 2nd *France-Japan workshop*, 1999.

[10] W.D. Clinger. *Foundations of Actor Semantics.* PhD thesis, Massachusetts Institute of Technology, AI Laboratory, 1981.

[11] J. Darlington and Y. K. Guo. Formalizing actors in linear logic. In *International Conference on Object-Oriented Information Systems*, pages 37–53. Springer-Verlag, 1994.

[12] R. de Nicola and M. Hennesy. Testing equivalence for processes. *Theoretical Computer Science*, 34:83–133, 1984.

[13] F.Dagnat, M.Pantel, M.Colin, and P.Sall. Typing concurrent objects and actors. In *L'Objet – Mthodes formelles pour les objets (L'OBJET)*, volume 6, pages 83–106, 2000.

[14] S. Frolund. *Coordinating Distributed Objects: An Actor-Based Approach for Synchronization.* MIT Press, November 1996.

[15] M. Gaspari and G. Zavattaro. An Algebra of Actors. In *Formal Methods for Open Object Based Systems*, 1999.

[16] I. Greif. Semantics of communicating parallel processes. Technical Report 154, MIT, Project MAC, 1975.

[17] M. Hennessy. *Algebraic Theory of Processes.* MIT Press, 1988.

[18] C. Hewitt. Viewing Control Structures as Patterns of Message Passing. *Journal of Artificial Intelligence*, 8(3):323–364, September 1977.

[19] C. Hewitt, P. Bishop, and R. Steiger. A Universal Modular Actor Formalism for Artificial Intelligence. In *International Joint Conference on Artificial Intelligence*, pages 235–245, 1973.

[20] C.A.R. Hoare. *Communication Sequential Processes.* Prentice Hall, 1985.

[21] K. Honda and M. Tokoro. An Object Calculus for Asynchronous Communication. In *Fifth European Conference on Object-Oriented Programming*, July 1991. LNCS 512, 1991.

[22] J-L.Colao, M.Pantel, and P.Sall. Analyse de linarit par typage dans un calcul d'acteurs primitifs. In *Actes des Journes Francophones des Langages Applicatifs (JFLA)*, 1997.

[23] N. Jamali, P. Thati, and G. Agha. An actor based architecture for customizing and controlling agent ensembles. *IEEE Intelligent Systems*, 14(2), 1999.

[24] L.V. Kale and S. Krishnan. CHARM++: A portable concurrent object oriented system based on C++. In *Proceedings of the Conference on Object Oriented Programming Systems, Languages and Applications*, 1993.

[25] G. Kiczales, J. Lamping, A. Mendhekar, C. Maeda, C.V. Lopes, J.M. Loingtier, and J. Irwin. Aspect oriented programming. In *Proceedings of the European Conference on Object-Oriented Programming (ECOOP).* Springer Verlag, 1997. LNCS 1241.

[26] W. Kim. *ThAL: An Actor System for Efficient and Scalable Concurrent Computing.* PhD thesis, University of Illinois at Urbana Champaign, 1997.

[27] W. Kim and G. Agha. Efficient support of location transparency in concurrent object-oriented programming languages. In *Proceedings of SuperComputing*, 1995.

[28] N. Kobayashi and A. Yonezawa. Higher-order concurrent linear logic programming. In *Theory and Practice of Parallel Programming*, pages 137–166, 1994.

[29] N. Kobayashi and A. Yonezawa. Towards foundations of concurrent object-oriented programming – types and language design. *Theory and Practice of Object Systems*, 1(4), 1995.

[30] E. Lee, S. Neuendorffer, and M. Wirthlin. Actor-oriented design of embedded hardware and software systems. In *Journal of circuits, systems, and computers*, 2002.

[31] P. Maes. *Computational Reflection.* PhD thesis, Vrije University, Brussels, Belgium, 1987. Technical Report 87-2.

[32] P. Maes. Intelligent software: Easing the burdens that computers put on people. In *IEEE Expert, special issue on intelligent agents*, 1996.

[33] N. Martí-Oliet and J. Meseguer. Rewriting logic as a logical and semantic framework, 1993.

[34] I.A. Mason and C.Talcott. A semantically sound actor translation. In *ICALP 97*, pages 369–378, 1997. LNCS 1256.

[35] M. Merro and D. Sangiorgi. On Asynchrony in Name-Passing Calculi. In *Proceeding of ICALP '98.* Springer-Verlag, 1998. LNCS 1443.

[36] J. Meseguer. Rewriting Logic as a Unified Model of Concurrency. Technical Report SRI-CSI-90-02, SRI International, Computer Science Laboratory, February 1990.

[37] J. Meseguer and C. Talcott. Semantic models for distributed object reflection. In *Proceedings of the European Conference on Object-Oriented Programming*, pages 1–36, 2002.

[38] R. Milner. *Communication and Concurrency.* Prentice Hall, 1989.

[39] R. Milner. Interactions, turing award lecture. *Communications of the ACM*, 36(1):79–97, January 1993.

[40] R. Milner. *Communicating and Mobile Systems: the π-calculus.* Cambridge University Press, 1999.

[41] R. Milner, J. Parrow, and D. Walker. A calculus of mobile processes (Parts I and II). *Information and Computation*, 100:1–77, 1992.

[42] S. Miriyala, G. Agha, and Y.Sami. Visulatizing actor programs using predicate transition nets. *Journal of Visual Programming*, 1992.

[43] Open Systems Laboratory. The Actor Foundry: A Java based actor programming language. Available for download at http://www-osl.cs.uiuc.edu/foundry.

[44] J.L. Peterson. Petri nets. *Comput. Survey*, Sept. 1977.

[45] A. Ravara and V. Vasconcelos. Typing non-uniform concurrent objects. In *CONCUR*, pages 474–488, 2000. LNCS 1877.

[46] R.Milner and D. Sangiorgi. Barbed bisimulation. In *Proceedings of* 19th *International Colloquium on Automata, Languages and Programming (ICALP '92).* Springer Verlag, 1992. LNCS 623.

[47] D. Sturman and G. Agha. A protocol description language for cutomizing semantics. In *Proceedings of symposium on reliable distributed systems*, pages 148–157, 1994.

[48] C. Talcott. An Actor Rewriting Theory. In *Electronic Notes in Theoretical Computer Science 5*, 1996.

[49] C. Talcott. Interaction Semantics for Components of Distributed Systems. In E.Najm and J.B. Stefani, editors, *Formal Methods for Open Object Based Distributed Systems.* Chapman & Hall, 1996.

[50] C. Talcott. Composable semantic models for actor theories. *Higher-Order and Symbolic Computation*, 11(3), 1998.

[51] K. Taura, S. Matsuoka, and A. Yonezawa. An efficient implementation scheme of concurrent object-oriented languages on stock multicomputers. In *Symposium on principles and practice of parallel programming (PPOPP)*, pages 218–228, 1993.

[52] P. Thati, K. Sen, and N. Martí-Oliet. An executable specification of asynchronous pi-calculus semantics and may testing in maude 2.0. In 4th *International Workshop on Rewriting Logic and its Applications*, September 2002.

[53] P. Thati, R. Ziaei, and G. Agha. A theory of may testing for actors. In *Formal Methods for Open Object-based Distributed Systems*, March 2002.

[54] P. Thati, R. Ziaei, and G. Agha. A theory of may testing for asynchronous calculi with locality and no name matching. In *Proceedings of the* 9th *International Conference on Algebraic Methodology and Software Technology.* Springer Verlag, September 2002. LNCS 2422.

[55] C. Tomlinson, W. Kim, M. Schevel, V. Singh, B. Will, and G. Agha. Rosette: An object-oriented concurrent system architecture. *Sigplan Notices*, 24(4):91–93, 1989.

[56] C. Varela and G. Agha. Programming dynamically reconfigurable open systems with SALSA. *SIGPLAN Notices*, 36(12):20–34, 2001.

[57] N. Venkatasubramanian, C. Talcott, and G. Agha. A formal model for reasoning about adaptive QoS-enabled middleware. In *Formal Methods Europe (FME)*, 2001.

[58] P. Wegner. Dimensions of object-based language design. In *Proceedings of the Conference on Object-Oriented Programming, Systems, Languages, and Applications (OOPSLA)*, pages 168–182, 1987.

[59] A. Yonezawa. *ABCL: An Object-Oriented Concurrent System.* MIT Press, 1990.

Towards Posit & Prove Calculi for Requirements Engineering and Software Design

In Honour of the Memory of Professor Ole–Johan Dahl

Dines Bjørner

Computer Science and Engineering (CSE)
Informatics and Mathematical Modelling (IMM)
Building 322, Richard Petersens Plads
Technical University of Denmark (DTU)
DK–2800 Kgs.Lyngby, Denmark
db@imm.dtu.dk
http://www.imm.dtu.dk/~db/

Abstract. Some facts: Before software and computing systems can be developed, their requirements must be reasonably well understood. Before requirements can be finalised the application domain, as it is, must be fairly well understood. Some opinions: In today's software and computing systems development very little, if anything is done, we claim, to establish fair understandings of the domain. It simply does not suffice, we further claim, to record assumptions about the domain when recording requirements. Far more radical theories of application domains must be at hand before requirements development is even attempted. In another ("earlier") paper [6] we advocate(d) a strong rôle for domain engineering. We there argued that domain descriptions are far more stable than are requirements prescriptions for support of one or another set of domain activities. In the present paper we shall argue, that once, given extensive domain descriptions, it is comparatively faster to establish trustworthy and stable requirements than it is today. And we shall further, presently, argue that once we have a sufficient (varietal) collection of domain specific, ie. related, albeit distinct, requirements, we can develop far more reusable software components than using current approaches. In this contribution we shall thus reason, at a meta-level, about two major phases of software engineering: Requirements engineering, and software design. We shall suggest a number of requirements engineering and software design concerns, stages and steps

The paper represents work in progress. It is based on presentations of *"topics for discussion"* at the IFIP Working Group 2.3. Such presentations are necessarily of "work in progress" — with the aim of the presentation being to solicit comments. Hence the paper ("necessarily") is not presenting "final" results.

O. Owe et al. (Eds.): From OO to FM (Dahl Festschrift), LNCS 2635, pp. 58–82, 2004.

1 Introduction

Our concern, in the present and in most of our work in the last almost 30 years, has been that of trying to come to grips with principles and techniques for software development.

The present paper sketches some such principles and techniques for some of the stages within the phases of requirements engineering and software design.

Our lecture notes, [7], the reader will find a rather comprehensive treatment of these and "most other related" software engineering issues!

1.1 Itemised Summary

Some facts:

- Before software and computing systems can be developed, their requirements must be reasonably well understood.
- Before requirements can be finalised the application domain, as it is, must be fairly well understood.

Some opinions:

- In today's software and computing systems development very little, if anything is done, we claim, to establish fair understandings of the domain.
- It simply does not suffice, we further claim, to record assumptions about the domain when recording requirements.
- Far more radical theories of application domains must be at hand before requirements development is even attempted.

In another ("earlier") paper [6] we advocate(d) a strong rôle for domain engineering.

- We there argued that domain descriptions are far more stable than are requirements prescriptions for support of one or another set of domain activities.
- In the present paper we shall argue, that once, given extensive domain descriptions, it is comparatively faster to establish trustworthy and stable requirements than it is today.
- And we shall further, presently, argue that once we have a sufficient (varietal) collection of domain specific, ie. related, albeit distinct, requirements, we can develop far more reusable software components than using current approaches.

In this contribution we shall thus reason, at a meta-level, about two major phases of software engineering:

- Requirements engineering, and
- software design.

We shall suggest a number of requirements engineering and software design concerns, stages and steps, notably, for

- requirements:
  - Domain requirements,
  - interface requirements, and
  - machine requirements.
- Specifically:
  - Domain requirements projection,
  - determination,
  - extension, and
  - initialisation.
- And Software Design:
  - Architecture design, and
  - component determination and design.

1.2 Claimed, 'Preliminary' Contributions

We claim that this paper reports on two kinds of methodological contributions: The "posit & prove calculation" principles of projection, determination, extension and initialisation; and the principle of the stepwise "posit & prove calculation" of software architecture design.

2 Requirements Engineering

2.1 Delineation of Requirements

From [23] we quote: *"Requirements engineering must address the contextual goals why a software is needed, the functionalities the software has to accomplish to achieve those goals, and the constraints restricting how the software accomplishing those functions is to be designed and implemented. Such goals, functions and constraints have to be mapped to precise specifications of software behaviour; their evolution over time and across software families has to be coped with as well [29]."*

We shall, in this paper, not cover the pragmatics of why software is needed, and we shall, in this paper, exclude "the mapping to precise software specifications" as we believe this is a task of the first stages of software design — as will be illustrated in this paper.

2.2 Requirements Acquisition

The process of requirements acquisition will also not be dealt with here. We assume that proper such techniques, if available, will be used. For example [16, 8, 18, 9, 15, 28, 20, 14, 10, 17, 25, 24, 26, 19, 27]. That is: We assume that somehow or other we have some, however roughly, but consistently expressed itemised set of requirements. We admit, readily, that to achieve this is a major feat. The domain requirements techniques soon to be outlined in this paper may help "parameterise" the referenced requirements acquisition techniques.

2.3 On the Avaliability of Domain Models

It is a thesis of this paper that it makes only very little sense to embark on requirements engineering before one has a fair bit of understanding of the application domain. Granted that one may feel compelled to develop both "simultaneously", or that one ought expect that others have developed the domain descriptions (including formal theories) "long time beforehand." Yes, indeed, just as control engineers can rely on Newton's laws and more than three hundred years of creating improved understanding of the domain of Newtonian physics: The "mechanical" world as we see it daily, so software engineers ought be able, sooner or later, to rely on elsewhere developed models of — usually man–made — application domains. Since that is not yet the situation we shall in software engineering have to make the first attempts at creating such domain–wide descriptions — hoping that eventually the domain specific professions will have reseachers with sufficient computing science education to hone and further develop such models.

2.4 Domain Requirements

It is also a thesis of this paper that a major, perhaps the most important aspects of requirements be systematically developed on the basis of domain descriptions. This 'thesis' thus undercuts much of current requirements engineerings' paradigms, it seems.

By a domain requirements we shall understand those requirements (for a computing system) which are expressed solely by using terms of the application domain (in addition to ordinary language terms). Thus a domain requirements must not contain terms that designate the machine, the computing system, the hardware + software to be deviced.

How do we go about doing this?

There seems to be two orthogonal approaches. In one we follow the domain facets outlined above. In the other we apply a number of "operators", to wit:

- projection, determination, extension, and initialisation,

to domain required facets. We treat the latter first:

Facet-Neutral Domain Requirements:

- Projections:
  Well, first we ask for which parts of the domain we, the client, wish computing support. Usually we must rely on our domain model to cover far more than just those parts. Hence we establish the first bits of domain requirements by *projecting* those parts of both the informal and the formal descriptions onto — ie., to become — the domain requirements.
- Determinations:
  Then we look at those projected parts: If they contain undesired looseness or non–determinism, or if parts, like types, are just sorts for which we now

wish to state more — not implementation, but "contents" — details, then we remove such looseness, such non–determinacy, such sorts, etc. This we call *determination.*
- Extensions:
Certain functionalities can be spoken of in the domain but to carry them out by humans have either been too dangerous, too tedious, uneconomical, or otherwise infeasible. With computing these functionalities may now be feasible. And, although they, in a sense "belong" to the domain, we first introduce them while creating the domain requirements. We call this *domain extension.* The distinction, thus is purely pragmatic.
- Initialisations:
In describing a domain, such as we for example described the "space" of all time tables, we must, for each specific time table, designate the "space" of all its points of departures and arrivals. If our requirements involve these departure and arrival points (airports, railway stations, bus depots, harbours), then sooner or later one has to initialise the computing system (database) to reflect all these many entities. Hence we need to establish requirements for how to *initialise* the computing system, how to maintain and update it, how to vet (ie., contextually check) the input data, etc.

There may be other domain–to–requirements "conversion" steps. We shall, in this paper, only speak of these.

In doing the above we may iterate between the four (or more) domain–to–requirements "conversion" steps.

We now illustrate what may be going on here. But first we need to tak an aside: To bring "an entire" domain model"! That is, the next section ("A Domain Intrinsics Model") does not belong to the requirements modelling phase of development, but to the domain modelling phase of development.

A Domain Intrinsics Model: We wish to illustrate the concepts of projection, determination, extension and initialisation of a domain requirements from a domain. We will therefore postulate a domain. We choose a very simple domain. That of a traffic time table, say flight time table. In the domain you could, in "ye olde days" hold such a time table in your hand, you could browse it, you could look up a special flight, you could tear pages out of it, etc. There is no end as to what you can do to such a time table. So we will just postulate a sort, TT, of time tables. Airline customers, in general only wish to inquire a time table (so we will here omit treatment of more or less "malicious" or destructive acts). But you could still count the number of digits "7" in the time table, and other such ridiculous things. So we postulate a broadest variety of inquiry functions that apply to time tables and yield values. Specifically designated airline staff may, however, in addition to what a client can do, update the time table, but, recalling human behaviours, all we can ascertain for sure is that update functions apply to time tables and yield two things: Another, replacement time table and a result such as: *"your update succeeded"*, or *"your update did not succeed"*, etc. In essence this is all we can say for sure about the domain of time table creations and uses.

```
scheme TI_TBL_0 =
   class
      type
         TT, VAL, RES
         QU = TT → VAL
         UP = TT → TT × RES
      value
         client_0: TT → VAL, client(tt) ≡ let q:QU in q(tt) end
         staff_0: TT → TT × RES, staff(tt) ≡ let u:UP in u(tt) end
         timtbl_0: TT → Unit
         timtbl(tt) ≡
            (let v = client_0(tt) in timtbl_0(tt) end)
            ⌈⌉
            (let (tt′,r) = staff_0(tt) in timtbl_0(tt′) end)
   end
```

The system function is here seen as a never ending process, hence the type **Unit.** It internal non–deterministically alternates between "serving" the clients and the staff. Either of these two internal non–deterministically chooses from a possibly very large set of queries, respectively updates.

We now return from our domain modelling detour. In the next four sections we illustrate a number of domain requirements steps. There are other such steps ('fitting', etc.) which we will leave un–explained.

Projections: In this case we have defined such a simple, ie., small domain, so we decide to project all of it onto the domain requirements:

```
scheme TI_TBL_1 = TI_TBL_0
```

Determinations: Now we make more explicit a number of things: Time tables record, for each flight number, a journey: a sequence of two or more airport visits, each designated by a time of arrival, the airport name and a time of departure.

```
scheme TI_TBL_2 =
   extend TI_TBL_1 with
      class
         type
            Fn, T, An
            JR′ = (T × An × T)*
            JR = {| jr:JR′ • len jr ≥ 2 ∧ ... |}
            TT = Fn →m JR
      end
```

where we omit (...) to express further wellformedness constraints on journies.

Then we determine the kinds of queries and updates that may take place:

```
scheme TI_TBL_3 =
  extend TI_TBL_2 with
    class
      type
        Query == mk_brow() | mk_jour(fn:Fn)
        Update == mk_inst(fn:Fn,jr:JR) | mk_delt(fn:Fn)
        VAL = TT
        RES == ok | not_ok
      value
        Mq: Query → QU
        Mq(qu) ≡
          case qu of
            mk_brow() →
              λtt:TT•tt,
            mk_jour(fn)
              → λtt:TT • if fn ∈ dom tt then [fn↦tt(fn)] else [] end
          end

        Mu: Update → UP
        Mu(up) ≡
          case qu of
            mk_inst(fn,jr) →
              λtt:TT • if fn ∈ dom tt then (tt,not_ok) else (tt ∪ [fn↦jr],ok) end,
            mk_delt(fn) →
              λtt:TT • if fn ∈ dom tt then (tt \ {fn},ok) else (tt,not_ok) end
          end
    end
```

And finally we redefine the client and staff functions:

```
scheme TI_TBL_4 =
  extend TI_TBL_3 with
    class
      value
        client_4: TT → VAL, client_4(tt) ≡ let q:Query in (Mq(q))(tt) end
        staff_4: TT → TT × RES, staff_4(tt) ≡ let u:Update in (Mu(u))(tt) end
    end
```

The timtbl function remains "basically" unchanged!

```
scheme TI_TBL_5 =
  extend TI_TBL_4 with
    class
      value
        timtbl_5: TT → Unit
        timtbl_5(tt) ≡
          (let v = client_4(tt) in timtbl_5(tt) end)
          ⊓
          (let (tt′,r) = staff_4(tt) in timtbl_5(tt′) end)
    end
```

Extensions: Suppose a client wishes, querying the time table, to find a connection betwen two airports with no more than n shift of aircrafts. For $n = 0, n = 1$ or $n = 2$ this may not be difficult to do *"in the domain"*: A few 3M Post it's a human can perhaps do it in some reasonable time for $n = 1$ or $n = 2$. But what about for $n = 5$. Exponential growth in possibilities makes this an infeasible query *"in the domain"*. But perhaps not using computers. (The example is, perhaps a bit contrived.)

```
scheme TI_TBL_6 =
  extend TI_TBL_5 with
    class
      type
        Query == ... | mk_conn(fa:An,ta:An,n:Nat)
        VAL = TT | CNS
        CNS = (JR*)-set
      value
        Mq(q) ≡
          case q of
            ...
            mk_conn(fa,ta,n) → λtt:TT • ...
          end
    end
```

where we leave it to the reader to define the "connections" function!

Initialisations: We remind the reader that this and the immediate three

Initialisation here means: From a given input of flight journies to create an initial time table (ie., an initial database). Ongoing changes to time tables have been provided for through the insert and delete operations — already defined. In their definition, however, we skirted an issue which is paramount also in initialisation: Namely that of vetting the data: That is, checking that a journey flies non–cyclically between existing airports, that flight times are commensurate with flight distances and type of aircraft (jet, supersonic or turbo–prop), that at all airports planes touch down and take off at most every n minutes, where n could be 2, but is otherwise an airport parameter. To check some of these things information about airports and air space is required.

```
scheme TI_TBL_7 =
  extend TI_TBL_6 with
    class
      type
        Init_inp = (Fn × JR)-set
        AP = An →m Airport
        AS = (An × An) →m AirCorridor-set
        Number, Length
```

```
    value
        obs_RunWays: Airport → Number
        obs_Distance: AirCorridor → Length
        ...
end
```

We leave it to the imagination, skills and stamina of the reader to complete the details! Our points has been made: 'Initialisation', suddenly uncovers a need for enlarging the domain descriptions, and *"there is much more to initialisation than meets the eye."*[1]

Facet-Oriented Domain Requirements: We may be able to make a distinction between "intended" and un–intended inconsistencies and "intended" and unintended conflicts. The "intended" ones are due to inherent properties of the domain. The un–intended ones are due to misinterpretations by the domain recorders or, are "real enough," but can be resolved through negotiation between stake–holders — thus entailing aspects of business process re–engineering — before requirements capture has started.

We thus assume, for brevity of exposition, that un–intended inconsistencies and un–intended conflicts have been thus resolved, and that otherwise "separately" expressed perspectives have been properly integrated (ie. ameliorated).

A major aspect of domain requirements is that of establishing contractual relationships between the human or support technology 'agents' in the environment of the "software, ie., the system–to–be", and the software 'agents'. As a result of a properly completed and integrated domain modelling of support technologies, management & organisation, rules & regulations, and human behaviour, we have thus identified domain inherent inconsistencies and conflicts. They appear as a form of non–determinism. These forms of non–determinism typically need either be made deterministic, as in domain requirements determination, or be made part of a contract assumed to be enforced by the environment: Namely a contract that says: *"The environment will promise (cum guarantee) that the inconsistency or the conflict will not 'show up'!"*

These contractual relationships express assumptions about the interaction behaviour — to be further explored as part of the next topic: 'Interface Requirements'. If the environment side of the combined system of the "software, ie., the system–to–be" does not honour these contractual relationships, then the "software, ie., the system–to–be" cannot be guaranteed to act as intended!

We thus relegate treatment of some facet–oriented domain requirements to the requirements capture and modelling stage of interface requirements.

Towards a Calculus of Domain Requirements: We have sketched a "posit & prove calculus" for deriving domain requirements. So far we have identified

[1] Reasonable C code for the input of directed graphs is usually twice the "size" of similarly reasonable C code for their topological sorting!

four operations in this "posit & prove calculus": Projection, determination, extension and initialisation. In each derivation step the operation takes two arguments. One argument is the domain requirements developed so far. The other argument is the concerns of that step of derivation: What is, and what is not to be projected, what is and what is not to be determined, what is and what is not to be extended, respectively what is and what is not to be initialised, etc. The "proof" part of the "posit & prove calculus" is a conventional proof of correctness between the two arguments.

We have still to further develop: Identify possibly additional domain requirements derivation operators, and to research and provide further principles and detailed techniques also for already identified derivation operations.

It seems that the sequence of applying these derivators is as suggested above, but is that "for sure?".

2.5 Interface Requirements

By an interface requirements we shall understand those requirements (for a computing system) which concern very explicitly the "things" 'shared' between the domain and the machine: In the domain we say that these "things" are the observable phenomena: the information, the functions, and/or the events of, or in, the domain, In the machine we say that they are the data, the actions, and/or the interrupts and/or the occurrence of inputs and outputs of the machine. By 'sharing' we mean that the latter shall model, or be harmonised with, the former. There are other interface aspects — such as "translates" into "bulk" input/output, etc.

But we shall thus illustrate just the first two aspects of 'sharing'.

External Vs. Internal 'Agent' Behaviours: The objectives of this step of requirements development is the harmonisation of external and internal 'agent' behaviours.

One the side of the environment there are the 'agents', say the human users, of the "software–to–be". On the side of the "software–to–be" there is, say, the software 'agents' (ie. the processes) that interact with environment 'agents'. Harmonisation is now the act of securing, through proper requirements capture negotiations, as well as through proper interaction dialogue and "vetting" protocols, that the two kinds of 'agents' live up to mutually agreed expectations.

Other than this brief explication we shall not treat this area of requirements engineering further in the present paper.

GUIs and Databases: Assume that a database records the data which reflects the topology of some air traffic net, or that records the contents of a time table, and assume that some graphical user interface (GUI) windows represent the interface between man and machine such that items (fields) of the GUI are indeed "windows" into the underlying database. We prescribe and model, as an interface requirements, such GUIs and databases, the latter in terms of a relational, say an `SQL`, database.

type
  Nm, Rn, An, Txt
  GUI = Nm $\overrightarrow{m}$ Item
  Item = Txt × Imag
  Imag = Icon | Curt | Tabl | Wind
  Icon == mk_Icon(val:Val)
  Curt == mk_Curt(vall:Val*)
  Tabl == mk_Tabl(rn:Rn,tbl:TPL-**set**)
  Wind == mk_Wind(gui:GUI)

Observe how the "content" values of icons and curtains are allowed to be any values, as now defined:

Val = VAL | REF | GUI
VAL = mk_Intg(i:Intg) | mk_Bool(b:**Bool**) | mk_Text(txt:**Text**) | mk_Char(c:**Char**)

RDB = Rn $\overrightarrow{m}$ TPL-**set**
TPL = An $\overrightarrow{m}$ VAL
REF == mk_Ref(rn:Rn,an:An,sel:(An $\overrightarrow{m}$ OVL))
OVL == nil | mk_Val(val:VAL)

Icons effectively designate a system operator or user definable constant or variable value, or a value that "mirrors" that found in a relation column satisfying an optional value (OVL). Similar for curtains and tables. Tables more directly reflect relation tuples (TPL). GUIs (Windows) are defined recursively.

If, for example, the names space values of Nm, Rn, and An, and the chosen constant texts Txt, suitably mirror names and phenomena of the domain, then we may be on our way to satisfying a "classical" user interface requirement, namely that *"the system should be user friendly"*.

For a specific interface requirements there now remains the task of relating all shared phenomena and data to one another via the GUI. In a sense this amounts to mapping concrete types onto primarily relations, and entities of these (phenomena and data) onto the icons, curtains, and tables.

2.6 Machine Requirements

By machine requirements we understand those requirements which are exclusively related to characteristics of the hardware to be deployed (and, in cases even designed) and the evolving software. That is, machine requirements are, in a sense, independent of the specific "details" of the domain and interface requirements, ie., "considers" these only with a "large grained" view.

Performance Issues: Performance has to do with consumption of computing system resources:. Besides time and (storage) space, there are such things as number of terminals, the choice of the right kind of processeing units, data communication bandwidth, etc.

Time and Space: Time and (storage) space usually are singled out for particular treatment. Designated functions of the domain and interface requirements are mandated to execute, when applied, within stated time (usually upper) bounds. This includes reaction times to user interaction. And designated domain information are likewise mandated to occupy, when stored, given (stated) quantities of locations.

Dependabilities: Dependability is an "ility" "defined" in terms of many other "ilities". We single out a few as we shall later demonstrate their possible discharge in the component software system design.

Availability: There might be situations where a domain description or a domain (or interface) requirements prescription define a function whose execution, on behalf of a user, when applied, is of such long duration that the system, to other users, appear unavailable.

In the examle of the time table system, such may be the case when the *air travel connections* function searchers for connections: The computation, with possible "zillions" of database (cum disk) accesses, "grinds" on "forever".

Accessability: There might be situations where a domain description or a domain (or interface) requirements prescription may give the impression that certain users are potentially denied access to the system.

In the example of the time table system, such may be the case when the time table process non–deterministically chooses between "listening" to requests (queries) from clients and (updates) from staff. The semantics of both the internal ($\sqcap$) and the external ($\square$) non–deterministic operators are such as to not guarantee fair treatment.

Other Dependabilities: We omit treatment of the reliability, fault tolerance, robustness, safety, and security "ilities".

Discussion: We refrain from attempting to formalise the machine requirements of availablity and accessability — for the simple reason that whichever way we today may know how to formalise them, we do not yet know of a systematic way of transforming these requirements into, ie., of "posit & prove calculating" their implementations.

This is clearly an area for much research.

Maintainabilities: Computing systems have to be maintained: For a number of reasons. We single out one and characterise this and other maintenance issues.

Adaptability: We say that a computing system is adaptable (not adaptive), wrt. change of "soft" and "hard" functionalities, when change of software or hardware "parts" only involves "local" adaptations.

"Locality", obviously, is our hedge. Not having defined it we have said little, if anything. The idea is that whatever changes have to be made in order to accomodate replacement hardware or replacement software, such changes are to be made in one place: One is able, a priori, to designate these places to within, say, a line, a paragraph, or, at most, a page of documentation.

We shall discuss adaptability further when we later tackle component software design issues.

Performability: A computing system satisfies a performability requirements, wrt. change (usually improvement) of "soft" and "hard" performance issues [time, space], when such change only involves "local" changes.

Correctability: A computing system is correctable (not necessarily correct), wrt. debugging "soft" and "hard" bugs, when such change only involves "local" corrections.

Preventability: A computing system has its failure modes being preventable (not necessarily prevented), wrt. "soft" and "hard" bugs, when regular tests can forestall error modes. For hardware, preventive maintenance is an old "profession". Rerunning standard, accumulative test suites, whenever other forms of maintenance has been carried out, may be one way of carrying out preventive maintenance?

Portabilities: By portability we understand the ability of software to be deployed on different computing systems platforms: From legacy operating systems to, and between such systems as (Microsoft's) `Windows`, `Unix` and `Linux`.

One can distinguish between the computing systems platform on which it may be requirements mandated that development shall take place — in contrast to the computing systems platforms on which it may be requirements mandated that execution and maintenance shall take place. Etcetera.

2.7 Feature Interaction Inconsistency and Conflict Analysis

One thing is to "dream" up "zillions" of "exciting" requirements, whether domain, interface, or machine requirements. Another thing is to ensure that these many individually conceived requirements "harmonise": "Fit together", ie., do not create inconsistencies or conflicts when the "software–to–be" is the basis of computations. Proper formal requirements models allow systematic, formal search for such anomalies [30, 31, 29]. Other than mentioning this 'feature interaction' problem, we shall not cover the problem further. But a treatment of some aspects of requirements engineering would not be satisfying if it completely omitted any reference to the problem.

2.8 Discussion

We have attempted a near–exhaustive listing and partial survey of as complete a bouquet of requirements prescription issues as possible. We have done so in order to delineate the scope and span of formal techniques, as well as the relations, "backward", to domain descriptions, and, as we shall later see, "forward" to software design.

A major thesis of our treatment, maybe not so fully convincingly demonstrated here, but then perhaps more so in our lecture notes [7], is to demonstrate these relationships, to demonstrate that requirements, certainly domain requirements, can be formalised, and to provide sufficiently refined requirements prescription techniques — especially for domain requirements.

We have tried, in contrast to todays software engineering (including requirement engineering) text books, to provide some principles and techniques for structuring the requirements documents to be constructed by requirements engineers.

3 Software Design

Requirements prescriptions do not specify software designs. Where a requirements prescription is allowed to leave open may ways of implementing some entities (ie., data) and functions, a software design, initially an abstract one, in the form of an architecture design, makes the first important design decisions. Incrementally, in stages, from architecture, via program organisation based on identified components, to module design and code, these stages of software design concretises previously abstract entities and functions.

Where requirements selected parts of a domain for computerisation by only stating such requirements for which a computable representation can be found, software design, one–by–one selects these representations.

3.1 Architectures

By an architecture design we understand a software specification that implemenents the domain and, maybe, some of the interface requirements. The domain requirements of client_4, staff_4, and timtbl_5, are first transformed, and this is just a proposal, as a system of three parallel processes client_arch, staff_arch, and timtbl_arch. Where client_4 and staff_4, embedded within timtbl_5, we now "factor" them out of timtbl_5, and hence we must provide channels that allow client_arch and staff_arch to communicate with timtbl_arch. The communicated values are the denotations, cf. `aplets`, of query and update commands. Whereever client_arch and staff_arch had time tables as arguments they must now communicate the function denotations, that were before applied to time tables, to the timtbl_arch process.

```
scheme ARCH =
  extend ... with
    class
      channel
        ctt QU, ttc VAL, stt UP, tts RES
    value
      system_arch: TT → Unit, system_arch(tt) ≡
                            client_arch() ‖ staff_arch() ‖ timtbl_arch(tt)

      client_arch: Unit → out ctt  in ttc  Unit
      client_arch() ≡ let q:Query in ctt ! Mq(q) ; ttc ? ; client_arch() end

      staff_arch: Unit → out stt  in tts  Unit
      staff_arch() ≡ let u:Update in stt ! Mu(u) ; tts ? ; staff_arch() end

      timtbl_arch: TT → in ctt,stt  out ttc,tts  Unit
      timtbl_arch(tt) ≡
        (let q = ctt ? in ttc ! q(tt) end timtbl_arch(tt))
        []
        (let u = stt ? in let (tt′,r) = u(tt) in tts ! r ; timtbl_arch(tt′) end end)
    end
```

Notice how we have changed the non-deterministic behaviour from being internal ⌈⌉ for timtbl_5 to becoming external [] for timtbl_arch. One needs to argue some notion of correctness of this.

An interface requirements was not stated above, so we do it here, namely there shall be a number of separate client_arch_1 processes, each having its identity as a constant parameter. Figure 1[2] illustrates the idea.

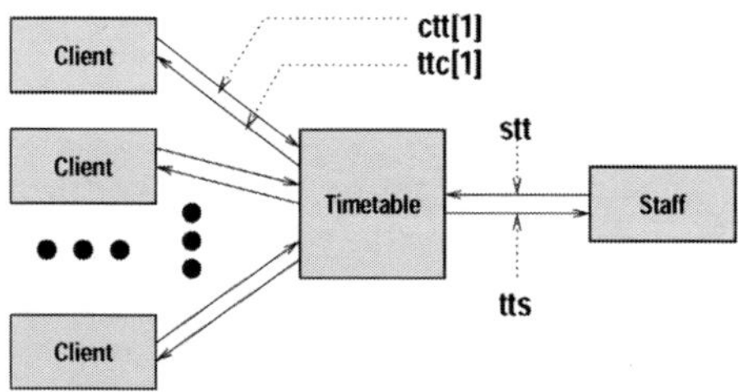

Architecture: A Time–table with Clients and St

Fig. 1.

[2] Figures 1–5 also illustrates the use of a diagrammatic language. It is very closely related to the CSP subset of RSL. Other than showing both **scheme** ARCH and Figure 1 we shall not "explain" this diagrammatic language — but it appears to be straightforward. We shall hence 'reason' over constructs (complete diagrams) of this diagrammatic language.

The system_arch_1 now consists of n client_arch_1 parallel processes in parallel with a basically unchanged staff_arch_1 process and a slightly modified timtbl_arch_1 process. The slightly modified timtbl_arch_1 process expresses willingness to input from any client_arch_1 process, in an external non–deterministic manner. Etcetera:

```
value
   n:Nat
type
   CIdx = {| 1..n |}
channel
   ctt[1..CIdx] QU, ttc[1..CIdx] VAL, stt UP, tts RES
value
   system_arch_1: TT → Unit
   system_arch_1(tt) ≡ || { client_arch_1(i) | i:CIdx } || staff_arch_1() || timtbl_arch_1(tt)

   client_arch_1: CIdx → out ctt  in ttc  Unit
   client_arch_1(i) ≡ let q:Query in ctt[i] ! Mq(q) ; ttc[i] ? ; client_arch_1(i) end

   staff_arch_1: Unit → out stt  in tts  Unit
   staff_arch_1() ≡ let u:Update in stt ! Mu(u) ; tts ? ; staff_arch_1() end

   timtbl_arch_1: TT → in { ctt[i],stt[i] i:CIdx }  out ttc,tts  Unit
   timtbl_arch_1(tt) ≡
      ⌷ { let q = ctt[i] ? in ttc[i] ! q(tt) end timtbl_(tt) | i:CIdx }
      ⌷ (let u = stt ? in let (tt′,r) = u(tt) in tts ! r ; timtbl_arch_1(tt′) end end)
```

3.2 Component Design

By a component design (as action) we understand a set of transformations, from a software architecture design, that implements the remaining interface requirements and major machine requirements, to the component design (as document). Whereas a software architecture design may have been expressed in terms of rather comprehensive processes, component design, as the name intimates, seeks to further decompose the architecture design into more manageable parts. Object modularisation (ie., module design) goes hand-in-hand with component design, but takes a more fine-grained approach. We are not yet ready, in our research, to relate these "posit & prove transformations" to the refinement calculus of for example Ralph Johan Back [21]. There are (at least) points: First there are too many issues predicating which refinements to choose. These issues represent the judicious prioritisation between a multitude of domain, interface and machine requirements: Which to consider and implement before others? Secondly the "refinement steps" illustrated next seem rather large. Hence for a proper refinement calculus to be proposed we need express the "large" steps, it seems, in terms of sequences of "smaller" steps. We are far from ready to embark on such an endeavour.

This is why we have used the phrase: *Posit & Prove Calculus* in the title of this communication.

One may say, colloquially speaking, that where component design decomposes a software design (and as guided by (remaining interface and by) machine requirements) into successively smaller parts, module design composes these parts from initially smallest modules. The former is, so-to-speak "top–down", where the latter seems more "bottom–up"[3].

At this stage we will just sketch the introduction of new processes that handle the machine requirements of accessability, availability and adaptability. But, as it turns out, it is convenient to first tackle an issue of many users versus just one interface.

Multiplexing: Instead of designing a time table subsystem that must cater to $n+1$ users we design one that caters to just two users. Hence we must provide a multiplexor, a component which provides for a more–or–less generic interface between, "to one side" n identical (or at least similar) processes, and, "to the other side" one process.

Figure 2 illustrates the idea.

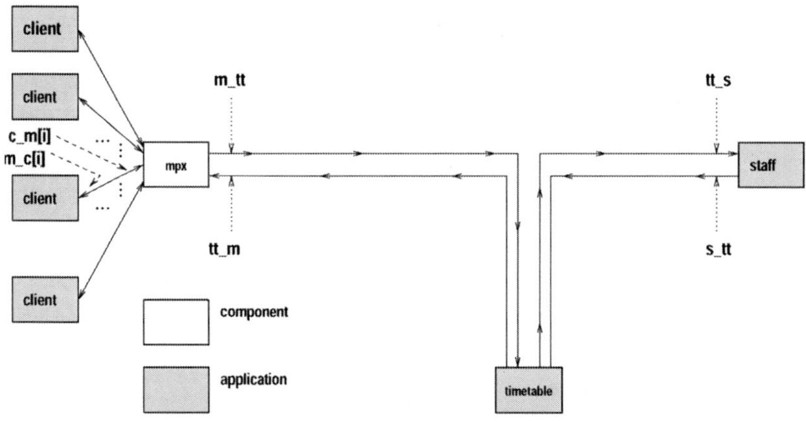

Program Organisation with Clients, Multiplexor, Staff, Timetable, and Channels

Fig. 2.

What we have done is to factor out the external non–deterministic choice amongst client process interactions, as documented in timtbl_4 by the distributed choice:

[3] But we normally refrain from these "figurations" as they depend on how one visualises matters: As a root of further roots, or as a tree of branches.

$\square$ { **let** q = ctt[i] ? **in** ... **end** | i:CIdx }

from that function into the mpx function. The external non–deterministic choice (remaining) among the one "bundled" client input and the staff will, see next, below, later be "moved" to an arbiter function.

We call such a component a multiplexor and leave its definition to the reader.

Accessability: To "divide & conquer" between requests for interaction with the time table process from either the ("bundled") clients (via the multiplexor) or the staff, we insert an arbiter component.

Figure 3 illustrates the idea.

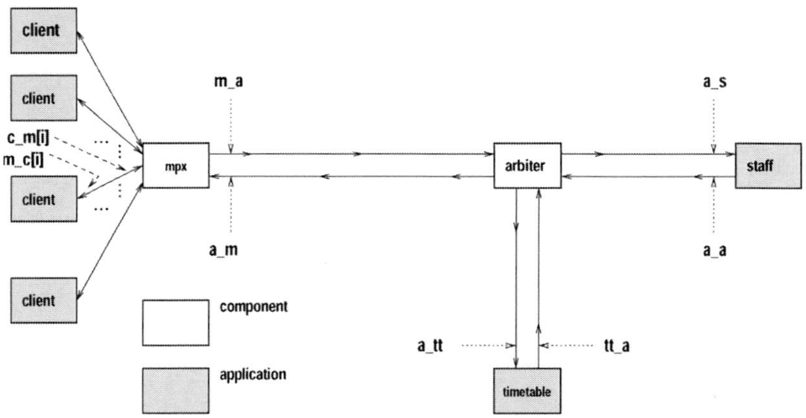

Program Organisation with Clients, Multiplexor, Arbiter, Staff, Timetable, and Channels

Fig. 3.

Its purpose is to create some illusion of fairness in handling non–determinism. If the arbiter ensures to "listen fairly" to the ("bundled") client and the staff "sides", for example for every f times it handles requests from the client side to then switch to handling one from the staff side, then perhaps some such fairness is achieved. The determination of f, or, for that matter, the arbiter algorithm, is subject to statistical knowledge about the traffic from either side and the service times for respective updates.

This issue of requiring 'fairness' also "spills" over to the multiplexor function.

Letting the arbiter also handle urgency of requests is natural. It would, in our view, be a further 'accessability' requirements.

We leave further specification to the reader.

Availability: The only component (ie., process) that may give rise to "loss of availability" is the time table process. Computing, for example the "at most n

change of flight" connections may take several orders of magnitude more time than to compute any other query or update. The idea is therefore to time–share the time table process, and, as a means of exploiting this time–sharing, to redesign (also) the multiplexor component and add a queue component.

Figure 4 illustrates the idea.

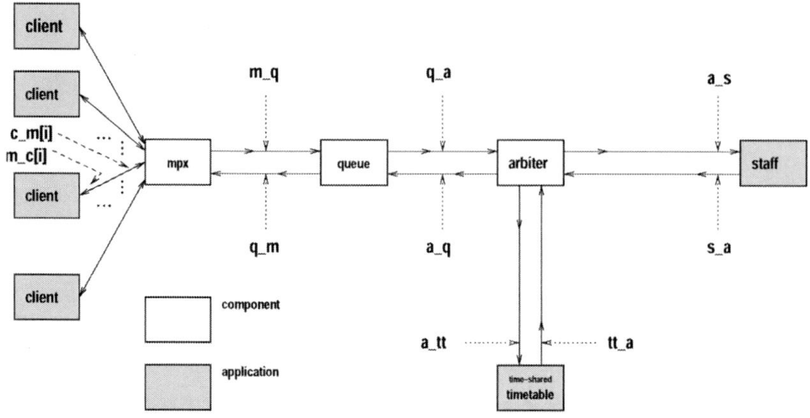

Program Organisation with Clients, Multiplexor, Queue, Arbiter, Staff, time–shared Timetable, and Channels

Fig. 4.

The multiplexor is now to accept successive requests for interaction from multiple clients (or even the same client). And the queueing component is to queue outstanding requests that are, at the same time sent to the time table process. It may respond to previously received requests, "out–of–order". The queueing component will track "back to which clients" request–responses shall be returned.

We leave further specification to the reader.

Adaptability: We have seen how the software design has evolved, on paper, in steps of component design development, into successively more components. Each of these, including those of the client, time table and staff processes may need be replaced. The client and staff components in response to new terminal (ie., PC) equipment, and the time table process in response, say to either new database management systems or new disks, or "both and all" !

If each of these components were developed with an intimate knowledge of (and hence dependency on) the special interfaces that these components may offer, then we may find that adaptability is being compromised. Hence we may decide to insert between neighbouring components so–called connectors. These are in fact motivated last, as in this "example sample development", but are suitably abstractly developed first. They "set standards" for exchange of information and control between components. That is, they define abstract, simple protocols. Once all components have been "inserted" one may refine the protocols to suit these compponents.

Figure 5 illustrates the idea.

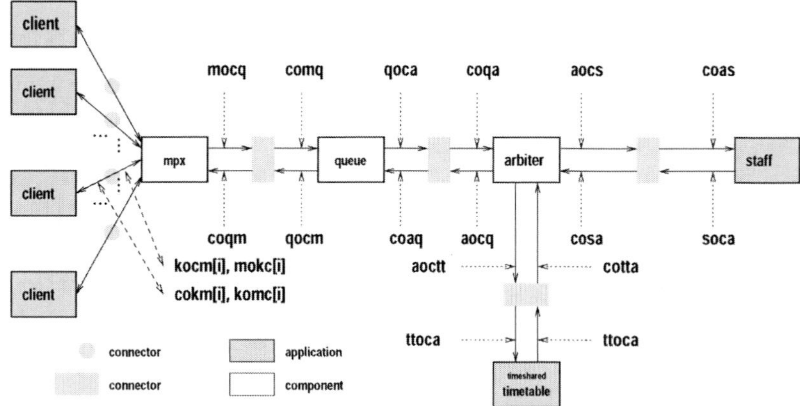

Program Organisation with Clients, Multiplexor, Queue, Arbiter, Staff, Timetable, Connectors and Channels

Fig. 5.

We leave further specification to the reader.

Architecture Vs. 'Componentry': We refer to work by David Garlan and his colleagues, work that relate very specifically to the above [3, 1, 13, 4, 22, 2, 12, 5]. What Garlan et al. call software architecture is not what we call software architecture. Ours is more abstract. Theirs is more at the level of interfacing components, that is of the connectors mentioned above under Adaptability. The CMU (ie., the Garlan et al.) work is much appreciated.

3.3 Towards "Posit & Prove Calculi" for Architecture and Component Structure Derivation

We have sketched a "posit & prove calculus" for deriving component structures. In each step of derivation the "operations" of the "component structure calculus" takes two "arguments". One "argument" is a specific machine (or interface) requirement. The other "argument" is a component structure (or, for the first step, the software architecture). The result of applying the "operation" is a new component structure.

We have still to develop: Identify, research and provide principles and more detailed techniques for when and how to deploy which machine (or interface) reqirements to which component structures. To wit: *"Should one apply the 'avail-*

ability' requirements before or after the 'accessability' requirements, etc. It is not yet clear whether the adaptability (and other maintenance "ility") requirements should be discharged, before, in step with, or after the discharge of each of the dependability "ilities". Etcetera.

We have not covered in this paper any "posit & prove calculus" aspects of deriving architectures from domain requirements.

4 Conclusion

4.1 Summary

We have completed a *"tour de force"* of example developments. Stepwise 'refinements' of domain descriptions, here for time tables, and phasewise transformation of domain descriptions into requirements prescriptions and the latter into stages of software designs: Architecture and component designs. It is soon time to conclude and to review our claims.

4.2 Validation and Verification

We have presented aspects of an almost "complete" chain of phases, stages and steps of development, from domains via requirements and software architecture to program organsation in terms of components and connectors. In all of this we have skirted the issues of validation and verification: Validating whether we are developing the right "product", and veryfying whether we develop that "product" right.

An issue that ought be mentioned, in passing, is that of some requirements, typically machine requirements, only being implementable in an approximate manner. One may, for example, have to check with runtime behaviour as to the approximation with which such machine requirements have been implemented [11].

Obviously more than 30 years of program correctness have not gone behind our back: With formalisations of many, if not most, phases, stages and steps it is now easier to state lemmas and theorems of properties and correctness. Properties of individual descriptions, prescriptions and specifications; correctness of one phase of development wrt. to the previous phase, respectively the same for stages and steps.

We have shown how to develop software "light". That is: Formally specifying phases, stages and steps, and, in a few, crucial cases, formulating lemmas and theorems (concerning "this and that"). We have found that developing software "light" seems to capture "most" development mistakes. In any case it is appropriate to end this, the 'triptych' section with the following:

Let $\mathcal{D}$, $\mathcal{R}$ and $\mathcal{S}$ stand for related $\mathcal{D}$omain descriptions, $\mathcal{R}$equirements prescriptions, repectively $\mathcal{S}$oftware specifications. Correctnes of the $\mathcal{S}$oftware with respect to its $\mathcal{R}$equirements can then be expressed as:

$$\mathcal{D}, \mathcal{S} \models \mathcal{R}$$

which, in words, imply: Proofs of correctness of $\mathcal{S}$ with respect to $\mathcal{R}$ typically require assumptions about the domain $\mathcal{D}$.

What could those assumptions be? Are they not already part of the requirements? To the latter the answer could be no, in which case it seems that we may have projected those assumptions "away"! And then these assumptions could be expressed, in the domain descriptions, in the form, for example, of constrained human or support technology behaviours, or of management behaviours, or they could be in the form of script languages in which to express rules & regulations, or they may be properties of the $\mathcal{D}$omain that can be proved in $\mathcal{D}$.

In [23] van Lamsweerde complements the above approximately as follows (our interpretation[4]):

Let $\mathcal{A}$ stand for a notion of 'Accuracy': *Non–functional goals requiring that the state of the input and output software objects accurately reflect the state of the corresponding monitored, respectively controlled objects they represent*, and let $\mathcal{G}$ stand for the set of goals:

$$\mathcal{A},\mathcal{S} \models \mathcal{R} \quad \text{with:} \quad \mathcal{A},\mathcal{S} \not\models \textbf{false} \qquad \text{and} \qquad \mathcal{D},\mathcal{R} \models \mathcal{G} \quad \text{with:} \quad \mathcal{D},\mathcal{R} \not\models \textbf{false}$$

We find this a worthwhile "twist", and expect more work done to fully understand and exploit the above.

4.3 Proper Identification of Components

"Varieties of requirements prescriptions lead to more stable identification of proper components": We hope that the development of components and connectors for the, albeit simple minded time table system of Section 3's subsection on 'Component and Object Design', "visualised" in Figures 2–5, can illustrate this claim: Each of the components — other than the client, time table and staff components, are components that relate primarily to machine (or, not shown, interface) requirements. Machine requirements are usually almost identical from application to application, and hence their components are "usually" reusable. But also the domain requirements components of clients, staff and time–shared time table, "cleaned" for all concerns of interface and machinerequirements, now appear in a form that is easier to parameterise and thus make reusable.

4.4 A Programme of Current Research

We briefly recall that there seems to be interesting research issues in better understanding and providing methodological support for the derivation of domain requirements and the derivation of component structures.

[4] As there are unexplained occurrence of $\mathcal{D}$ in van Lamsweerde formula: He additionally uses $\mathcal{A}s$ where we use $\mathcal{D}$

4.5 Acknowledgements

The author is tremendously grateful for a very careful review of a referee. I wish to state that many of the very reasonable concerns of the referee are indeed very valid concerns also of mine. Space, however, did not permit me, in a paper as "far sweeping" as this has become, to address each and all of these concerns.

4.6 A Caveat

This paper represents work in progress. It is based on presentations of *topics for discussion* at the IFIP Working Group 2.3. Such presentations are necessarily of "work in progress" — with the aim of the presentation being to solicit comments. As just said above, the anonymous referee has just done that. Thanks.

References

1. G. Abowd, R. Allen, and D. Garlan. Using style to understand descriptions of software architecture. *SIGSOFT Software Engineering Notes*, 18(5):9–20, December 1993.
2. G.D. Abowd, R. Allen, and D. Garlan. Formalizing style to understand descriptions of software architecture. *ACM Transactions on Software Engineering and Methodology*, 4(4):319–364, Oct 1995.
3. R. Allen and D. Garlan. A formal approach to software architectures. In *IFIP Transactions A (Computer Science and Technology); IFIP Wordl Congress; Madrid, Spain*, volume vol.A-12, pages 134–141, Amsterdam, Netherlands, 1992. IFIP, North Holland.
4. R. Allen and D. Garlan. Formalizing architectural connection. In *16th International Conference on Software Engineering (Cat. No.94CH3409-0); Sorrento, Italy*, pages 71–80, Los Alamitos, CA, USA, 1994. IEEE Comput. Soc. Press.
5. R. Allen and D. Garlan. A case study in architectural modeling: the AEGIS system. In *8th International Workshop on Software Specification and Design; Schloss Velen, Germany*, pages 6–15, Los Alamitos, CA, USA, 1996. IEEE Comput. Soc. Press.
6. Dines Bjørner. Domain Engineering: A "Radical Innovation" for Systems and Software Engineering ? In *Verification: Theory and Practice*, volume 2772 of *Lecture Notes in Computer Science*, page 54 pages, Heidelberg, October 7–11 2003. Springer–Verlag. The Zohar Manna International Conference, Taormina, Sicily 29 June – 4 July 2003.
7. Dines Bjørner. *The SE Book: Principles and Techniques of Software Engineering*, volume I: Abstraction & Modelling (750 pages), II: Descriptions and Domains (est.: 500 pages), III: Requirements, Software Design and Management (est. 450 pages). [Publisher currently (March 2003) being negotiated], I: Fall 2003, II: Spring 2004, III: Summer/Fall 2004 2003–2004.
8. A. Dardenne, S. Fikas, and Axel van Lamsweerde. Goal–Directed Concept Acquisition in Requirements Elicitation. In *Proc. IWSSD–6, 6th Intl. Workshop on Software Specification and Design*, pages 14–21, Como, Italy, 1991. IEEE Computer Society Press.
9. A. Dardenne, Axel van Lamsweerde, and S. Fikas. Goal–Directed Requirements Acquisition. *Science of Computer Programming*, 20:3–50, 1993.

10. R. Darimont and Axel van Lamsweerde. Formal Refinement Patterns for Goal–Driven Requirements Elaboration. In *Proc. FSE'4, Fourth ACM SIGSOFT Symp. on the Foundations of Software Enginering*, pages 179–190. ACM, October 1996.
11. M. Feather, S. Fikas, Axel van Lamsweerde, and C. Ponsard. Reconciling System Requirements and Runtime Behaviours. In *Proc. IWSSD'98, 9th Intl. Workshop on Software Specification and Design*, Isobe, Japan, April 1998. IEEE Computer Society Press.
12. D. Garlan. Formal approaches to software architecture. In *Studies of Software Design. ICSE '93 Workshop. Selected Papers*, pages 64–76, Berlin, Germany, 1996. Springer-Verlag.
13. D. Garlan and M. Shaw. *An introduction to software architecture*, pages 1–39. World Scientific, Singapore, 1993.
14. Joseph A. Goguen and M. Girotka, editors. *Requirements Engineering: Social and Technical Issues.* Academic Press, 1994.
15. Joseph A. Goguen and C. Linde. Techniques for Requirements Elicitation. In *Proc. RE'93, First IEEE Symposium on Requirements Engineering*, pages 152–164, San Diego, Calif., USA, 1993. IEEE Computer Society Press.
16. S. J. Greenspan, John Mylopoulos, and A. Borgida. A Requirements Modelling Language. *Information Systems*, 11(1):9–23, 1986. (About RML).
17. A. Hunter and B. Nuseibeh. Managing Inconsistent Specifications: Reasoning, Analysis and Action. *ACM Transactions on Software Engineering and Methodology*, 7(4):335–367, October 1998.
18. John Mylopoulos, L. Chung, and B. Nixon. Representing and Using Non–Functional Requirements: A Process–oriented Approach. *IEEE Trans. on Software Engineering*, 18(6):483–497, June 1992.
19. John Mylopoulos, L. Chung, and E. Yu. From Object–Oriented to Goal–Oriented Requirements Analysis. *CACM: Communications of the ACM*, 42(1):31–37, January 1999.
20. B. Nuseibeh, J. Kramer, and A. Finkelstein. A Framework for Expressing the Relationships between Multiple Views in Requirements Specifications. *IEEE Transactions on Software Engineering*, 20(10):760–773, October 1994.
21. Ralph-Johan Back and Joakim von Wright. *Refinement Calculus: A Systematic Introduction.* Graduate Texts in Computer Science. Springer-Verlag, Heidelberg, Germany, 1998.
22. C. Shekaran, D. Garlan, and et al. The role of software architecture in requirements engineering. In *First International Conference on Requirements Engineering (Cat. No.94TH0613-0); Colorado Springs, CO, USA*, pages 239–245, Los Alamitos, CA, USA, 1994. IEEE Comput. Soc. Press.
23. Axel van Lamsweerde. Requirements Engineering in the Year 00: A Research Perspective. In *Proceedings 22nd International Conference on Software Engineering*, ICSE'2000. IEEE Computer Society Press, 2000.
24. Axel van Lamsweerde, R. Darimont, and E. Letier. Managing Conflicts in Goal–Driven Requirements Engineering. *IEEE Transaction on Software Engineering*, 1998. Special Issue on Inconsistency Management in Software Development.
25. Axel van Lamsweerde and E. Letier. Integrating Obstacles in Goal–Driven Requirements Engineering. In *Proc. ICSE–98: 20th International Conference on Software Enginereering*, Kyoto, Japan, April 1998. IEEE Computer Society Press.
26. Axel van Lamsweerde and L. Willemet. Inferring Declarative Requirements Specification from Operational Scenarios. *IEEE Transaction on Software Engineering*, pages 1089–1114, 1998. Special Issue on Scenario Management.

27. Axel van Lamsweerde and L. Willemet. Handling Obstacles in Goal–Driven Requirements Engineering. *IEEE Transaction on Software Engineering*, 2000. Special Issue on Exception Handling.
28. E. Yu and John Mylopoulos. Understanding "why" in Software Process Modelling, Analysis and Design. In *Proc. 16th ICSE: Intl. Conf. on Software Engineering*, Sorrento, Italy, 1994. IEEE Press.
29. Pamela Zave. Classification of Research Efforts in Requirements Engineering. *ACM Computing Surveys*, 29(4):315–321, 1997.
30. Pamela Zave and Michael A. Jackson. Techniques for partial specification and specification of switching systems. In S. Prehn and W.J. Toetenel, editors, *VDM'91: Formal Software Development Methods*, volume 551 of *LNCS*, pages 511–525. Springer-Verlag, 1991.
31. Pamela Zave and Michael A. Jackson. Requirements for telecommunications services: an attack on complexity. In *Proceedings of the Third IEEE International Symposium on Requirements Engineering (Cat. No.97TB100086)*, pages 106–117. IEEE Comput. Soc. Press, 1997.

Distributed Concurrent Object-Oriented Software*

Manfred Broy

Institut für Informatik
Technische Universität München
D-80290 München, Germany
broy@in.tum.de

Abstract. In software engineering object-oriented development is today the most popular programming and design approach. However, in contrast to Dahl's original ideas object-orientation of today does not manage to address the needs of today's software construction in such a radical and fundamental way as needed in highly distributed interoperating software applications. In the following, we extend object-orientation to asynchrony and distribution for engineering large distributed software systems. We show how object-oriented techniques can be extended to a programming methodology and software engineering for concurrent distributed systems. This is strictly in the spirit of Ole-Johan Dahl.

1 Introduction

Object-orientation was fundamentally invented by Ole-Johan Dahl and Kristen Nygaard by their design of the programming language Simula 67 (see [Simula 67]). Before that, most programming languages were mainly influenced either by the commands of machine languages or by the logical foundations of computability such as λ-calculus. Only gradually programming languages were gaining step by step more abstract views of data and control structures. However, also these languages were mainly devoted to concepts of programming in the small and sequential, noninteractive programs. Typically, I/O, for instance, was considered a minor issue and therefore not part of the programming language definition for instance in ALGOL.

Simula 67 introduced radically new ideas by its concepts of co-routines and classes. Such an approach to programming and software development was badly needed to master the requirements of the development of large complex software systems, distributed over many computers connected by high-speed networks and thus operating concurrently and interacting asynchronously. These issues are addressed by the idea of distributed object-orientation as formulated for the first time in Simula 67.

Of course, in Simula 67 these ideas were realized by allowing objects to be co-routines, which was the best way at that time to imitate concurrent processes.

* Dedicated to Prof. Ole-Johan Dahl

O. Owe et al. (Eds.): From OO to FM (Dahl Festschrift), LNCS 2635, pp. 83–95, 2004.

Once you think of the objects as being independent of each other, concurrency among the actions performed by these objects is natural and almost inevitable. In today's world the obvious way would be to let (active) objects be concurrent processes, and one would obtain a distributed system by a set of objects running in parallel, interacting by remote method calls. Thus, the concepts of threads of Java (sharing the same object attributes) is not following the original OO ideas.

In the last three decades of software engineering object-orientation developed into the most popular programming and design approach. Object-orientation, it is claimed, offers better structuring features and more flexible concepts than conventional imperative, functional, or logical programming styles — especially for structuring programs as well as development and programming in the large.

Software development techniques and methods of today have to cope with a number of difficulties such as

- the growing complexity and size of software applications,
- interoperability demands,
- applications that are executed on large distributed networks,
- the long term perspective of legacy software systems being in operation over 30 years or more in a still quickly developing technology with rapidly changing requirements.

Therefore development in the large, management of change, and interoperability are key issues in software development and programming.

Unfortunately, object-orientation as mostly applied in practice today does not manage to address these needs of software construction of today in such a radical and fundamental way as intended by Ole-Johan Dahl. In many respects, object-orientation stays within the conventional approach to programming, mainly influenced by the sequential stand-alone machines of the early sixties.

One might object to those claims by saying that, for instance, Java as a recent object-orientated programming language is a modern programming language that addresses all the needs of today. However, being certainly an advantage over some of the programming languages available so far, Java is in many respects a rather conventional language. Moreover, the success of Java is not only due to its object-orientation. It is also due to its concept of portability and code mobility guaranteed by the idea of byte code, which is quite independent of object-orientation.

In the following we concentrate our discussion onto the following aspects of software development:

(1) interface abstraction and interaction
(2) concurrency and distribution

In particular, we discuss which interface abstractions are possible for object-oriented programs and how that relates to concurrency and distribution.

Why is the issue of distribution and concurrency so important? If we assume that a software is executed on a large network of computers where response times and transmission time is unpredictable a sequential execution model is not appropriate.

2 Object-Orientation in Practice Today — Its Characteristics

Let us begin our discussion by shortly rephrasing the main characteristics of object-orientation. Object-orientation is based on the following major concepts and principles:

- classes with attributes and methods as the major units for describing and structuring programs,
- access interfaces in terms of methods of objects and their attributes described by classes,
- creating objects as instances of classes,
- encapsulation of data and state represented by programming variables called attributes in classes and objects,
- persistence, meaning the durable storage of local attribute values within objects between method invocations,
- data abstraction and implementation hiding,
- identifying and addressing objects by object identifiers,
- inheritance and polymorphism.

One of the main claims of object-orientation is to provide the capabilities and potentials to support the following recognized design principles

- modularity of interfaces by state encapsulation,
- data abstraction,
- information hiding,
- dynamics and flexibility by object instantiation,
- reusability by inheritance and aggregation,
- well-specified interfaces.

Object-orientation is advocated both as a programming paradigm supported by a number of object-oriented programming languages and as a software development method supporting the entire spectrum of analysis, design, and implementation. In particular, in network applications such as the Internet or client/server systems object-orientation is claimed to be the better programming technique, superior to other programming styles.

In fact, object-oriented programming languages dominate these application areas. Java, for instance, provides the idea of portability and code mobility as a decisive feature in Internet applications.

In spite of the claims and the popularity of object-orientation in practice, there are severe shortcomings in object-orientation as it is used in practice today. These are in particular the limitations of object-oriented programming to:

- intrinsically sequential execution models following the paradigm of sequential control flow of procedural programs,
- code inheritance with a danger of violating the principle of information hiding and data abstraction,
- missing interface specification techniques for classes,
- missing concept of composition of classes into composite classes,
- instantiation of objects via references,
- missing concept of a component as a basis for software architectures.

Thus object-oriented programming languages of today miss some of the essential points of Simula 67. In fact, recent object-oriented programming languages offer a number of extensions to classical object-orientation to overcome some of these shortcomings. For instance, the syntactic interfaces of classes provide a useful concept for interface description. However, for most object-oriented languages abstract semantic interface description concepts do not exist. They only offer syntactic notions of interfaces. In fact, experiments and experiences with object-oriented frameworks show crucially the weakness of current practice of object-orientation in that respect.

The object-oriented paradigm as it is found in many object-oriented programming languages of today is inherently sequential. The reason lies in the interaction mechanism between objects, called method invocations, which are nothing but procedure calls. This way object-oriented programs have to be seen as operating on a large state space for which — according to encapsulation — only special scopes are introduced such that the access to attributes is only possible inside of the bodies of the respective classes. The effect of a method invocation including all the subinvocations of methods during the execution of the call has to be described as one state change on this global state space. This concept makes the execution model inherently sequential since all calls have to be seen as atomic actions.

The introduction of parallelism and concurrency brings in all the classical difficulties and complexities of shared memory parallelism such as the question which actions are indivisible, how to co-ordinate and synchronize and how to express waiting. The classical ways to introduce concurrency into state based systems do not lead to the high level abstract models of the real world as advocated and claimed by the basic philosophy of object-orientation.

However, most applications of today run in a highly concurrent distributed environment in networks of computers. Therefore, object-oriented programs have to interact and react to many concurrent activities. As a result, we want to model explicitly concurrent activities in object-oriented programs.

In the original work on Simula, it was clearly stated that an object would in general have its own activity, as well as data and procedure (methods). Objects with activity were referred to as "independent processes", and objects without activity were called passive. "Simula I" used the keyword activity (see [Simula 67]).

3 Concurrent Open Systems — Their Characteristics

Concurrent distributed systems show a number of characteristics that make them complex, and at the same time, flexible. These characteristics include the following notions:

- interaction
- distribution and structure
- concurrency

Nonconcurrent, noninteractive programs — sometimes called transformational programs — support powerful abstractions. They can be seen as functions, in functional programming between arbitrary types, in state-based programs as functions between states. In concurrent systems, interaction means that a system does not get all its input initially at the beginning of the computation and also that it does not produce all its output only at the end of a computation. Input is given step by step to the system, output is generated in response to portions of the input step by step. In fact, some of the input may depend on the output produced so far if a system runs in a feedback loop. Therefore to model the behavior of an interactive system we have to model it as a state transition system, or as a function or, relation on streams.

In the presence of concurrency, it is crucial to fix the granularity of a system because this determines for the state transition system at which intermediate state some interaction can take place such that input is accepted and output is produced. This is closely related to the issue of abstraction. In a noninteractive program we may abstract fully from the computation meaning the intermediate states generated in the course of the computation. In a concurrent, interactive program we have to represent all the intermediate states in which interaction can take place and this way may chance the course of the computation. Therefore the granularity of the state transition is essential. It determines which states are relevant for the interaction.

4 Object-Oriented Programming and Concurrency

In this section we argue about the question whether object-oriented programs differ from concurrent interactive programs or not. We argue that object-oriented programs show all the characteristics of interactive programs, but do not address concurrency properly. In that respect we conclude that although object-oriented programs do not support better abstractions than interactive concurrent programs they do not exploit all possibilities of concurrency, hierarchy, asynchronous communication, and composition.

We see this as severe shortcomings of today's practice object-oriented programming. In particular, we argue that according to these deficiencies object-orientation fails to address some of the requirements for a programming language and technique needed for writing large distributed software systems running on networks with long communication delays.

4.1 Classes as State Machine Descriptions

A class manifests the basic idea of a module in object-orientation. Classes are the fundamental building blocks in object-oriented programs. In some sense they are the only structuring means in object-orientation. They have to play the role of components although they are too fine grained for that.

For an interface specification we have to be able to describe the behavior of a component in an interface view. This means that we describe the observable behavior of a class. This is a description that identifies under what circumstances two different classes can be used in the same environment without any observable difference in their behavior. Such a notion is mandatory for a top down as well as for a bottom up specification and design approach.

For classes and objects, however, a simple description of their observable behavior is surprisingly complicated. The reason lies in the interaction mechanism between objects, called method invocations, which are, of course, nothing but procedure calls. Method invocations may change the state, given by values of the attributes of objects. They may also result in further invocations of methods and, therefore, change not only the state of the object addressed by the method invocation but, in addition, the state of other objects. This way method invocations in object-oriented programs have to be seen as operations on a large state space — the global program state. In contrast to the principle of state encapsulation, by object-orientation only special scopes are introduced such that the access to attributes is only possible inside of the bodies of the respective classes or name space. The effect of a method invocation including all the subinvocations of methods during the execution of the call has to be described as one state change on the global state space.

The specification of the observable behavior of classes and objects runs into all the difficulties of the description of distributed interactive systems — except issues of concurrency and action granularity (see below). In fact, object-orientation introduces by its concept of a class nearly everything needed and typical for concurrent interactive program execution, however, without being brave enough to carry out the final step into concurrency.

Ole-Johan Dahl's work on abstract specification of concurrent objects by means of histories, has to be mentioned as a possible solution towards "missing interface techniques for classes", and gives an abstract "interface view" as there is no other abstract state than that captured by the history. As the abstract state at any given time is reflected by a finite history, Ole-Johan Dahl was building up specification techniques around finite traces, and a central idea was to use right-append as a generator (in contrast to CSP) in order to describe new actions in terms of the history (thereby avoiding recursive definition of processes). For reasoning about calls that trigger other calls, Ole-Johan Dahl would separate initiation of a method call from its termination into two separate events. The semantics and rules for parallel composition in this setting has been described and pursued by several groups. Ole-Johan Dahl himself was mostly concerned with safety reasoning, using the concept of quiescence to deal with liveness, but others have done more general work towards liveness.

4.2 Interface Views onto Objects

Basically, there are two interface abstractions for object-oriented programs:

(1) *Closed view*: each method call is seen as one indivisible step defining a state transition for the object and all the objects changed by submethod calls.
(2) *Open view*: each method call consists of a sequence of steps, consisting of submethod calls and the state changes between the submethod calls.

In the presence of concurrency and distribution the closed view is not appropriate.

The early "Dahl School" on reasoning about OO systems builds on the idea of limiting direct access to attributes of an object from outside, either disallowing all remote variable access or allowing access to a some (seen as an abbreviation for implicit read and write operations). Keywords were also added to the Simula standard in order to control this. This means that one may give local invariants in a class and prove that a class invariant is established and maintained, by looking at the text of the class itself (and super-classes). When subclassing is restricted so that super-invariants are respected, reasoning about concurrent objects may be done without looking at the global state space: Hoare reasoning can be done locally in each class (implementation), and reasoning about a (sub)system of concurrent objects can be done by means of sets of possible traces (consisting of events reflecting the methods calls up to certain point in time). In particular, for concurrent objects there is no need for a reasoning about the global state.

4.3 Interaction Patterns

A typical property of most approaches to object-oriented programming is the use of methods (like procedures in conventional programming languages) with their method call and method return pattern of interaction. As long as there is no concurrency this pattern is sufficient, and at the same time simple and well-structured. Fig. 1 gives an idea of a simple method call hierarchy.

We get a slightly more complex call cascade if a call leads to a call of a method of the initially calling object.

In interactions by method calls, every call is eventually preceded by a return (we exclude for the moment the possibility of nontermination of method calls). In the presence of concurrency and distribution of the computing entities of networks with larger communication delays we immediately run into troubles. Since the computing entities may run concurrently and communication and calculation may take some time, a scheme as in Fig. 1 may no longer be acceptable. Keeping the idea of method calls we have to work differently. Fig. 3 shows method calls that mimic asynchronous communications.

But Fig. 3 is no longer a pattern of sequential method calls. In sequential method calls exactly one entity is active at a time and control is passed by the method calls and the return messages. Now several components are active concurrently. This leads to the question, what it means if an object, that is active

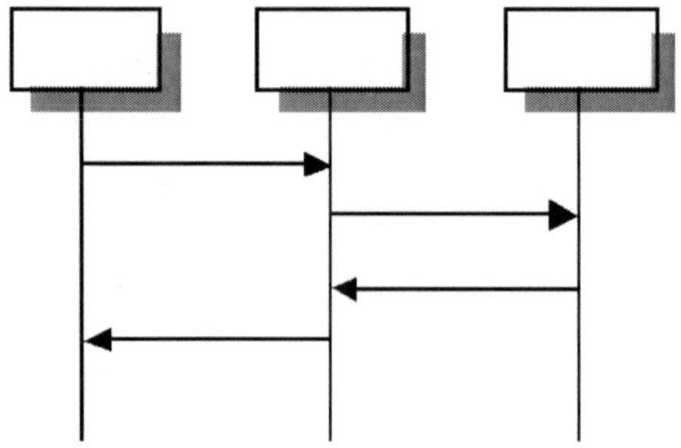

Fig. 1. Typical Method Call Cascade

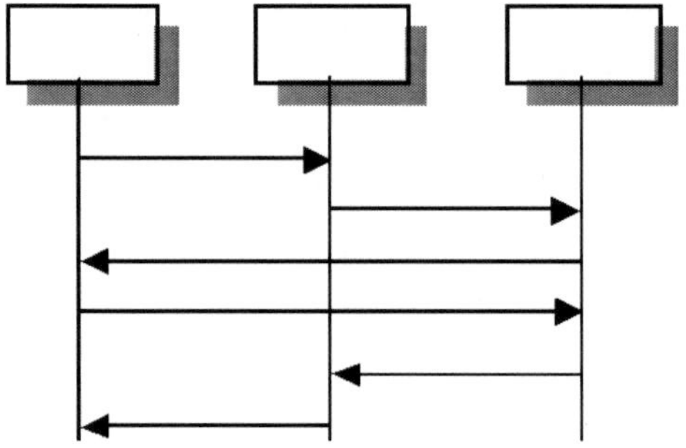

Fig. 2. Method call cascade with recursive subcalls

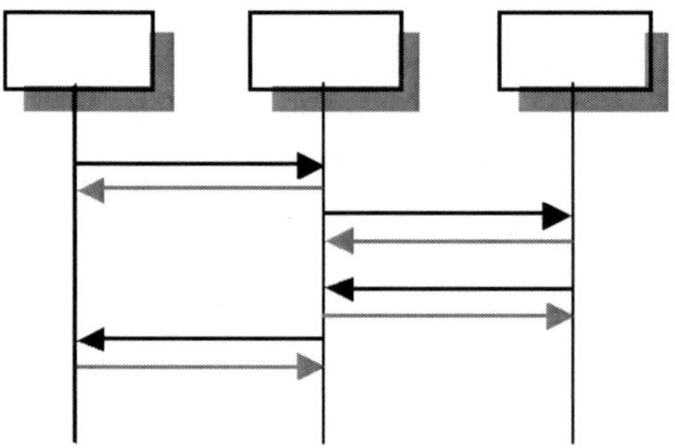

Fig. 3. Method call cascade to mimic asynchronous interaction

receives another method call. The sequential execution model for object-oriented systems is simple and clear. Each computing entity, and each object, is inactive, until a method call activates it. Then it calculates until it either returns from the method call or issues a method call itself, named a subcall. Then it stays inactive until it is called again or the submethod call returns.

In the presence of concurrency this simple idea is no longer sufficient, because a method call may arrive while an object is active. Also in Dahl's later work on specification of OO-systems, it is suggested that objects may be concurrent processes, interacting by method calls (with protected variables), see for instance the lift example [Dahl, Owe 91].

This leads to the question when and how an object accepts the method call. Basically, there are three possible answers:

(1) interrupt: the object immediately stops its current calculation and works on the incoming method calls;
(2) the method call is accepted as soon as the current activity is finished, for instance, if by the current activity a submethod call is issued;
(3) the method call is accepted only if the currently executed method call is completely finished.

We do not consider explicit concurrency within an object, i.e. the execution of two threads in an object simultaneously. Clearly (1) leads to an execution model where any concept of interface abstraction breaks down. Badly enough, solution (1) is not far from the concept of concurrent threads in Java where the interrupt can be explicitly controlled. Solution (3) is very coarse grain and forces to work with rather fine grain method calls. Solution (2) leads to several pending threads in objects and thus to a rather scattered execution model.

In concurrent systems we may also be interested in other patterns of interaction such as those given in Figs. 4 and 5.

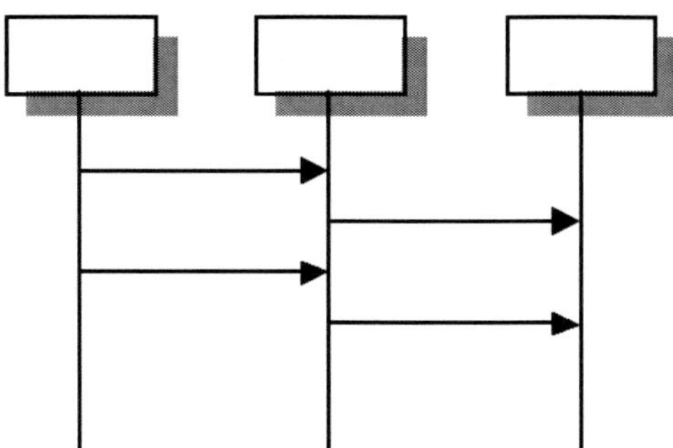

Fig. 4. Communication cascade for a pipeline

Figure 4 shows the fundamental interaction pattern of pipeline communication.

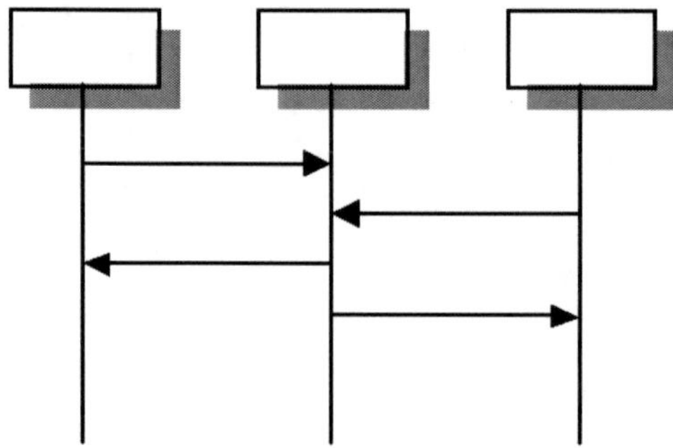

Fig. 5. Coordination by message exchange

There are two fundamental paradigms in programming: stacks and queues. Stacks are the fundamental idea of sequential programming while queues are the fundamental concept of distributed concurrent programming. Method calls are essentially based on the stack paradigm, which is not appropriate for distributed concurrent systems such as the Internet. There we need a concept based on the queue paradigm (see [Dahl, Owe 91]).

4.4 Software Architectures and Component Concept

The dominant concept in object-orientation is that of a class. From a methodological point of view the notion of a module or a component has to fulfill certain principles in the development of large software systems such as

- hierarchical composition/decomposition,
- interface specification,
- appropriate scaling up.

All these three requirements are not sufficiently well addressed and satisfied by the class concept in today's object-oriented programming languages.

Class Composition In object-orientation there is no explicit operator to compose several classes into another, composite class. There is no common concept of class composition. Note that the idea of multiple inheritance may look similar to class composition but it is, in fact, a completely different concept. Consequently there is no way in object-orientation to form larger subsystems structured in appropriate subunits. This is a serious flaw of object-orientation since a support for a hierarchical structuring of systems is badly needed for a programming language for large scale software systems.

In fact, it is rather surprising that the concept of class composition does not exist explicitly in object-orientation. It can and should be introduced into object-orientation without much overhead. The idea of an assembly of new classes by instantiations of old classes does not lead to a transparent structure.

Component Concept and Interfaces One of the severe drawbacks of object-orientation is a missing notion of component complementary to that of a class. Classes are certainly a too small, too fine grained concept. They rather are implementation units (such as modules) and therefore not appropriate for structuring large scale systems.

In fact, component notions are a prerequisite for software architectures. Components are larger grain units that should be hierarchically composable (again) from several components.

Software Architecture For the design of large software systems the notion of a software architecture is decisive. A software architecture is the structuring of a software system into components and their principles and forms of co-operation and interaction.

For small software systems, classes may be appropriate to form the structure of the software architecture. For large systems, however, in object-orientation we find hundreds or even thousands of classes. Then classes cannot be any longer the appropriate basis and level of granularity for a software architecture.

5 Concluding Remarks

Are we able to create an approach to software system design and to programming that does not show the weaknesses of object-orientation of today and nevertheless still manages to maintain most of its advantages? We think yes! There are approaches to the programming of distributed systems based on state machines (such as statecharts) that support asynchronous models of concurrent execution. An interesting approach in that direction is ROOM (see [Room 94]) that in a very consequent way introduces the required techniques.

A generalization of this model along the lines of Focus (see [Broy 98]) and the prototype CASE tool AutoFocus (see [AutoFocus 00]) shows many of the features described above. The introduction of the classical concepts of object-orientation into this model is an interesting exercise.

Ole-Johan Dahl in his original work was much closer to the idea of concurrent distributed systems as most of the so — called object — oriented programming languages of today.

6 Acknowledgement

I am grateful to remarks and hints by the referees on Ole-Johan Dahl's work on concurrency.

7 References

[AutoFocus 00] P. Braun, H. Lötzbeyer, B. Schätz, O. Slotosch: Consistent Integration of Formal Methods. In: Proc. 6th Intl. Conf on Tools and Algorithms for the Construction and Analysis of Systems (TACAS'00), 2000,

[Beeck 94] M. v. d. Beeck: A Comparison of Statecharts Variants. In: H. Langmaack, W.-P. de Roever, J. Vytopil (eds): Formal Techniques in Real Time and Fault-Tolerant Systems. Lecture Notes in Computer Science 863, Berlin: Springer 1994, 128-148

[Booch 91] G. Booch: Object Oriented Design with Applications. Benjamin Cummings, Redwood City, CA, 1991

[Broy 91a] M. Broy: Towards a Formal Foundation of the Specification and Description Language SDL. Formal Aspects of Computing 3, 21-57 (1991)

[Broy 92] M. Broy: Compositional Refinement of Interactive Systems. Journal of the ACM, Volume 44, No. 6 (Nov. 1997), 850-891. Also in: DIGITAL Systems Research Center, SRC 89, 1992.

[Broy 93] M. Broy: (Inter-)Action Refinement: The Easy Way. In: Broy, M. (ed.): Program Design Calculi. Springer NATO ASI Series, Series F: Computer and System Sciences, Vol. 118, pp. 121-158, Berlin, Heidelberg, New York: Springer 1993

[Broy 95b] M. Broy: Advanced Component Interface Specification. In: Takayasu Ito, Akinori Yonezawa (Eds.). Theory and Practice of Parallel Programming, International Workshop TPPP'94, Sendai, Japan, November 7-9, 1994, Proceedings, Lecture Notes in Computer Science 907, Berlin: Springer 1995

[Broy 98] M. Broy: Compositional Refinement of Interactive Systems Modeled by Relations. In: W.-P. de Roever, H. Langmaack, A. Pnueli (eds.): Compositionality: The Significant Difference. LNCS State of the Art Survey, Lecture Notes in Computer Science 1536, 1998, 130-149

[Dahl et al 72] O. Dahl, E.W. Dijkstra, C.A.R. Hoare (eds.): Structured Programming. Academic Press 1971

[Dahl, Owe 91] O.-J. Dahl, O. Owe: Formal development with ABEL. In: S. Prehn, W. J. Toetenel (eds.): VDM '91: formal software development methods: 4th International Symposium of VDM Europe. Noordwijkerhout, the Netherlands, October 21-25, 1991 proceedings. — Vol. 2, Tutorials. Lecture Notes in Computer Science 552, Berlin: Springer 1991, 320-362

[Dahl 92] O.-J. Dahl: Verifiable programming. Prentice Hall International Series in Computer Science. New York : Prentice Hall, 1992

[Grapes 90] GRAPES-Referenzmanual, DOMINO, Integrierte Verfahrenstechnik. Siemens AG, Bereich Daten- und Informationstechnik 1990

[Grosu 94] R. Grosu: A Formal Foundation for Concurrent Object-Oriented Programming. Dissertation, Fakultät für Informatik, Technische Universität München, December 94

[Harel 87] D. Harel: Statecharts: A Visual Formalism for Complex Systems. Science of Computer Programming 8, 1987, 231 - 274

[Jacobson 92] I. Jacobsen: Object-Oriented Software Engineering. Addison-Wesley, ACM Press 1992

[Milner et al. 92] R. Milner, J. Parrow, D. Walker: A calculus of mobile processes. Part i + ii, Information and Computation, 100:1 (1992) 1-40, 41-77

[Rumbaugh 91] J. Rumbaugh: Object-Oriented Modelling and Design. Prentice Hall, Englewood Cliffs: New Jersey 1991

[Philipps, Scholz 95] J. Philipps, P. Scholz: Compositional Specification of Embedded Systems with Statecharts. In: Theory and Practice of Software Development TAPSOFT'97, Lille, Lecture Notes in Computer Science 1214, Berlin: Springer 1995

[Room 94] B. Selic, G. Gullekson. P.T. Ward: Real-time Object Oriented Modeling. Wiley, New York 1994

[SDL 88] Specification and Description Language (SDL), Recommendation Z.100. Technical report, CCITT, 1988

[Simula 67] Dahl, O.-J., B. Myrhaug, K. Nygaard: Simula 67 - common base language. Technical Report N. S-22, Norsk Regnesentral (Norwegian Computing Center), Oslo.

[UML 97] G. Booch, J. Rumbaugh, I. Jacobson: The Unified Modeling Language for Object-Oriented Development, Version 1.0, RATIONAL Software Cooperation

[Wirsing 90] M. Wirsing: Algebraic Specification. Handbook of Theoretical Computer Science, Vol. B, Amsterdam: North Holland 1990, 675-788 14

Composing Hidden Information Modules over Inclusive Institutions

Joseph Goguen[1] and Grigore Roşu[2]

[1] Dept. Computer Science & Engineering, Univ. California, San Diego
goguen@cs.ucsd.edu
[2] Dept. Computer Science, Univ. Illinois, Urbana-Champaign
grosu@cs.uiuc.edu

Abstract. This paper studies the composition of modules that can hide information, over a very general class of logical systems called inclusive institutions. Two semantics are given for the composition of such modules using five familiar operations, and a property called conservativity is shown necessary and sufficient for these semantics to agree. The first semantics extracts the visible properties of the result of composing both the visible and hidden parts of modules, while the second uses only the visible properties of the components; the two semantics agree when the visible consequences of hidden information are enough to determine the result of the composition. A number of "laws of software composition" are proved relating the five composition operations. Inclusive institutions simplify many of the proofs. The approach has application to module composition technology, for both programs and specifications.

1 Introduction

Modularization reduces the complexity of large systems by breaking them into more comprehensible parts; this eases both initial construction and later modification, and it also facilitates reuse. Parameterized programming[3] significantly further enhances flexibility and reusability of modules, by providing *parameterized modules* along with *views*, also called *fitting morphisms*, which say how to fit the syntax of a formal parameter to an actual parameter in a convenient, flexible way, including defaults when there is only one reasonable choice; moreover, views can be parameterized, dependent types are supported through formal parameters that are parameterized by previously introduced formal parameters, and *module expressions* compose modules into systems [18,19]. We use essentially the same module composition operations as in the original Clear language [7], for aggregating, renaming, enriching, hiding, and instantiating parameterized modules. *Module expressions* are terms built from basic modules, parameterized modules, and views, using these five operations; we believe that making views first class citizens is key to realizing the full practical potential of modularization.

[3] As in [18,19], this term should be understood as applying to both specifications and programs, as well as to their combination.

O. Owe et al. (Eds.): From OO to FM (Dahl Festschrift), LNCS 2635, pp. 96–123, 2004.

The approach of this paper is by no means limited to specification languages, let alone to equational specification languages. In particular, the LILEANNA system has significantly extended the power and the efficiency of Ada generics by applying these ideas; LILEANNA module expressions are "executed" by combining the code in their modules, resulting in optimized, executable programs [42,26]. LILEANNA has been used in industry to build navigation system software for helicopters, and the original Clear and OBJ languages inspired aspects of parameterization in the module systems of Ada, ML, and C++.

There are many good reasons to hide information in modules. First, following Parnas [34], information hiding supports data abstraction, and more practically, allows replacing one module by another having the same semantics for its visible signature, but a different implementation, without having to worry that other modules might have used details of the implementation. Second, a classic result of Bergstra and Tucker [3] says that every computable algebra has a finite equational specification with some hidden operations, and examples show that the hidden operations are sometimes necessary (see [32] for a survey of this area). Third, [23] shows that every [finite] behavioral (also called observational, or hidden) algebraic specification [20,22,38,35] has an equivalent [finite] information hiding specification with the same models, but using ordinary satisfaction. However, the translation of finite behavioral specifications to hidden information modules in [23] does not explain context induction [28], and hence does not support behavioral proofs by induction. To overcome this, [36] gave an improved translation, that takes account of experiments and their recursive evaluation in a bottom-up fashion. This new translation justifies behavioral proofs by induction, even though neither induction nor equational reasoning are in general sound for behavioral equivalence. Some of the same ideas seem to have more recently appeared in [5], using a different notation.

Category theory and institutions are heavily used in this paper. Institutions (see Section 2.3) formalize the informal notion of logical system, with a balanced interplay of syntax and semantics, to support research that is independent of the underlying logic. An institution consists of: a category of signatures; a functor from signatures Σ to classes of Σ-sentences; a contravariant functor from signatures Σ to categories of Σ-models; and for every signature Σ, a relation of satisfaction $\models_\Sigma$ between Σ-sentences and Σ-models, such that $M' \models_{\Sigma'} \varphi(f)$ iff $\varphi(M') \models_\Sigma f$, for every signature morphism $\varphi\colon \Sigma \to \Sigma'$, every Σ'-model M', and every Σ-sentence f, where $\varphi(f)$ is the translation of f according to φ and $\varphi(M')$ is the reduct of M according to φ. Given a class A of Σ-sentences, let A^* denote the class of Σ-models that satisfy every sentence in A, and given a class V of Σ-models, let V^* denote the class of Σ-sentences that are satisfied by all models in V. Modularization has been one of the most important applications of institutions. Many logical systems have been shown to be institutions, and most recent algebraic specification languages have an institution-based semantics, e.g., CASL [9], CafeOBJ [14], OBJ3 [27], and BOBJ [25]. Other applications include translating between logics (see [24] for a survey), and database integration using meta-data expressed as theories in a suitable institution [1] (this work actually has further ambitions to meta-data management and integration for any kind of data [4]).

Defining and proving properties of module systems can be greatly simplified when the institution involved is *inclusive*, in the sense that its category of signatures satisfies certain natural conditions that axiomatize the notion of inclusion. (Our inclusive institutions are simpler than the original ones in [15] because we use the inclusive categories of [24]; see Section 2.2.) It appears that all institutions proposed for specification or programming are inclusive. Many properties of inclusive institutions are proved here, including a generalization of the Closure Lemma of classical institution theory.

Let $\mathcal{I}$ be a fixed inclusive institution. In this paper, we let the term *module* refer to a triple (Φ, Σ, A) where Φ is a subsignature of Σ, and A is a set of Σ-sentences, all from $\mathcal{I}$. Σ is called the *working signature*, and it includes both the public and the private operations of the module; Φ is called the *visible signature*, which defines the public interface; elements of A are called *axioms*. The *visible theorems* of $M = (\Phi, \Sigma, A)$, denoted $Vth(M)$, are the Φ-sentences in the "double star closure" A^{**} of A. A *model* of M is a Φ-model satisfying all its visible theorems. A *transparent module* has $\Phi = \Sigma$; these correspond to specifications without information hiding.

In the first semantics, the meaning of a module expression is the visible theory of the result of evaluating the module expression compositionally (i.e., recursively) over the five operations. For example, if $M = (\Phi, \Sigma, A)$ then $[\![M]\!]_1 = Vth(M)$, and given also $M' = (\Phi', \Sigma', A')$, then $[\![M + M']\!]_1 = Vth(\Phi \cup \Phi', \Sigma \cup \Sigma', A \cup A')$. This semantics is the same as that in [26], except that signature union comes from inclusive categories rather than the extended set theory used in [26]. In the second semantics, following [37], meaning is directly compositional over visible theories. As before, $[\![M]\!]_2 = Vth(M)$, but now $[\![M + M']\!]_2 = ([\![M]\!]_2 \cup [\![M']\!]_2)^{**}$, where this closure is relative to the signature $\Phi \cup \Phi'$. Meanings in this semantics for the other module composition operations are similar, and do not use the hidden parts of component modules. Semantics similar to these have been given in the tradition of [39], but are defined as classes of models rather than as theories.

The first semantics is more comprehensive because it uses more information; it is a non-trivial theorem that the two semantics agree when all modules involved are conservative, where a module (Φ, Σ, A) is *conservative* iff every Φ-model of its visible theorems can be extended to a Σ-model of A. Transparent modules are obviously conservative, but in general, testing for conservativity depends on the institution involved, and can be difficult. The modules that arise in practice for equational institutions are conservative. One approach for showing conservativity in equational institutions is to show that every Φ-algebra can be enriched with hidden carriers and operations, such that it satisfies the axioms. Since each semantics gives a theory, each has an associated class of models, and these two classes also agree under conservativity. Example 2 shows that conservativity is necessary as well as sufficient, even for the equational institution.

This paper also proves a number of identities that hold among the meanings of simple module expressions. These can be considered "basic laws of software engineering" (though they are mostly very simple); such laws are used in the

LILEANNA system [42,26] to simplify module expressions before handing them over to the backend of the Ada compiler for optimization, and result in more efficient code than composing the same system in raw Ada. Example laws are $E + E' \equiv E' + E$ and $E + (E' + E'') \equiv (E + E') + E''$, where $E \equiv E'$ indicates that $[\![E]\!]_1 = [\![E']\!]_1$ for module expressions E, E'. Of course, these are very simple examples, the most interesting identities involve instantiation of parameterized modules. We have found that inclusive institutions significantly simplify the proofs of such laws.

1.1 Related Work

We mainly discuss work that directly influenced this paper; readers wanting more background or historical information should consult references in the cited papers. The most influential works for us were [26] and [15]. Many results of the present paper appear in a slightly more concrete form in [26], which considered the same module system as this paper, using a version of institutions in which signatures are structured set/tuple hierarchies, so that inclusions are directly available and need not be axiomatized. This approach is less general than that of the present paper[4], but has the advantage of making the techniques for implementing the module system more explicit. On the other hand, proofs are less elegant, and more difficult to discover, and the present paper supplies proofs that are missing from [26].

Modularization over inclusive institutions is studied in [15], but its modules do not hide information, and its notion of inclusion system is less general then the present one. [2] axiomatizes operations on modules and proves certain properties, including a normalization theorem; unfortunately, first order logic is built into their formalism for sentences, which limits the application of their results. When the institution is first order logic, the results in this paper prove from more basic principles all of the axioms in [2] that concern our operations.

Generalizing prior work of Cengarle for first order logic [8], Borzyszkowski [6] gives a nice proof that under certain sufficient conditions (semantic forms of amalgamation and interpolation are the main ones) the two semantics agree; however, [6] does not treat parameterized modules, uses a different notation in which one semantics is formulated as a deductive system, and uses a different notion of institution that seems unnecessarily complex. Since the assumptions of the present paper are necessary and sufficient, it would be interesting to see how they relate to those of [6], despite the different notions of institution employed; the relation between interpolation and conservativity seems worthy of further investigation.

Inclusive institutions seem an attractive alternative to approaches like "institutions with symbols" [33], which assign sets of symbols to signatures, because inclusions automatically keep track of shared symbols in subsignatures, while allowing the usual operations on modules to be easily and naturally expressed; the approach of [33] was developed for the semantics of the European CASL

[4] Although it seems to include all the standard examples.

[9] specification language. Diaconescu [12] studies modules without information hiding for equational-like logics, using category-based equational logic (CBEL). We believe that under some mild conditions, CBEL is an inclusive institution, so that results in this paper would apply.

In contrast[5] to [40,39], it is our view that parameterized programs can be considered parameterized theories, by using an appropriate institution, having programs as sentences and executions as models (though it would of course be a substantial task to write out all the details of such an institution, e.g., for the C language). We also disagree with the view expressed forcefully in [40,39] that it is necessary to hybridize algebraic specification with type theory in order to address concerns that blend specification and programming. In particular, we disagree with their claim that colimits are not adequate for parameterized programs, which should instead be treated using dependent types. Indeed, LILEANNA, which is an implemented programming and specification system based on the same approach as this paper, shows that this claim is false [42,26]. LILEANNA module expressions tell the system how to combine the Ada intermediate compiled code for components, which is then passed to the compiler backend, resulting in efficient executable composed programs. The Specware system takes a somewhat different approach to generating code, but still uses colimits for composition [30]. The existence of institutions with programs as sentences explains why colimit constructions work for module composition at the code level, not just at the specification level. Some confusion perhaps arises because of the familiarity of institutions from mathematical logic, such as the lambda calculus and equational logic, which have been applied to certain classes of functional programs. Moreover, the relation between the Ada programs and the Anna specifications of LILEANNA is given by an institution of this more traditional kind.

Section 2 of this paper reviews notation and concepts from category theory, inclusive categories and institutions, while inclusive institutions are presented in Section 3, and Section 4 introduces modules. Section 5 is the heart of the paper, giving the five module operations with their semantics and the basic laws, while Section 6 gives some conclusions and future directions. We consider this paper a natural next step in the research on parameterized programming begun in [18,19] for the OBJ specification and term rewriting language [27], inspired by the Clear module system [7], and further developed in [26] and [15].

2 Preliminaries

Categories, inclusions and institutions are heavily used in this paper, and this section briefly introduces our notation and terminology for these concepts.

[5] This paragraph and some related footnotes were written reluctantly, at the request of a referee, and many details are omitted, because we feel that such discussions tend to distract from technical content.

2.1 Categories

The reader is assumed to be familiar with basics of category theory, including limits, colimits, functors, and adjoints [31,29]. $|\mathcal{C}|$ denotes the class of objects of a category $\mathcal{C}$, and $\mathcal{C}(A, B)$ denotes the set of morphisms in $\mathcal{C}$ from object A to object B. The composition of morphisms is written in diagrammatic order, that is, $f;g\colon A \to C$ is the composition of $f\colon A \to B$ with $g\colon B \to C$. Let **Cat** denote the (quasi-)category with locally small categories as objects and with functors as morphisms. A family of morphisms $\{e_i\colon A_i \to B \mid i \in I\}$ is **epimorphic** iff for any two morphisms $f, g\colon B \to C$, if $e_i; f = e_i; g$ for each $i \in I$ then $f = g$.

A functor $\mathcal{F}\colon \mathcal{C} \to \mathcal{D}$ is **full** (**faithful**) if its restrictions $\mathcal{F}\colon \mathcal{C}(A, B) \to \mathcal{D}(\mathcal{F}(A), \mathcal{F}(B))$ are surjective (injective) for all objects A, B in $\mathcal{C}$. $\mathcal{F}$ is **dense** provided that for each $D \in |\mathcal{D}|$ there is some $C \in |\mathcal{C}|$ such that $\mathcal{F}(C)$ is isomorphic to D. A **full subcategory** is a subcategory such that the inclusion functor is full. A category is **skeletal** iff isomorphic objects are identical. A **skeleton** of a category $\mathcal{C}$ is a maximal full skeletal subcategory of $\mathcal{C}$; it can be shown that any two skeletons of a category are isomorphic in **Cat**. A category $\mathcal{C}$ is **equivalent** to a category $\mathcal{D}$ iff C and $\mathcal{D}$ have isomorphic skeletons. It is known [31] that two categories $\mathcal{C}$ and $\mathcal{D}$ are equivalent iff there exists a functor $\mathcal{F}\colon \mathcal{C} \to \mathcal{D}$ which is full, faithful and dense.

Pullbacks in **Cat** have the following special property: if a pair of functors $\mathcal{F}_1\colon \mathcal{P} \to \mathcal{C}_1$ and $\mathcal{F}_2\colon \mathcal{P} \to \mathcal{C}_2$ is a pullback in **Cat** of $\mathcal{G}_1\colon \mathcal{C}_1 \to \mathcal{D}$ and $\mathcal{G}_2\colon \mathcal{C}_2 \to \mathcal{D}$, and if $C_1 \in |\mathcal{C}_1|$ and $C_2 \in |\mathcal{C}_2|$ are such that $\mathcal{G}_1(C_1) = \mathcal{G}_2(C_2)$, then there is a *unique* object P in $\mathcal{P}$ such that $\mathcal{F}_1(P) = C_1$ and $\mathcal{F}_2(P) = C_2$.

2.2 Inclusive Categories

Many categories have certain morphisms which are intuitively inclusions. The problem of characterizing such morphisms was raised in [21], first solved in [15] with the notion of inclusion system, and further developed and simplified in [10,11,37,24]. The simplest version occurs in [24]: An **inclusive category** $\mathcal{C}$ is a category having a broad subcategory[6] $\mathcal{I}$ which is a poclass (i.e., its objects are a class such that each $\mathcal{I}(A, B)$ has at most one element, and if both $\mathcal{I}(A, B)$ and $\mathcal{I}(B, A)$ are non-empty, then $A = B$) with finite products and coproducts, called **intersection** (denoted $\cap$) and **union** (denoted $\cup$ or possibly $+$), respectively, such that for every pair A, B of objects, $A \cup B$ is a pushout of $A \cap B$ in $\mathcal{C}$; morphisms in $\mathcal{I}$ are written $\hookrightarrow$ and called **inclusions**. In particular, $\mathcal{C}$ and $\mathcal{I}$ have an initial object, which we denote $\emptyset$, and $A_1, ..., A_n$ are **disjoint** iff $A_i \cap A_j = \emptyset$ for $i \neq j$. $\mathcal{C}$ is **distributive** iff $\mathcal{I}$ is distributive, in the sense that $A \cup (B \cap C) = (A \cup B) \cap (A \cup C)$ (which, as in lattice theory, is equivalent to $A \cap (B \cup C) = (A \cap B) \cup (A \cap C)$) in $\mathcal{I}$.

[6] In the sense that it has the same objects as $\mathcal{C}$.

Proposition 1. *In any inclusive category $\mathcal{C}$:*

1. *The family of inclusions $A_i \hookrightarrow \bigcup_{j=1}^n A_j$ for $i = 1, ..., n$ is epimorphic.*
2. *$\bigcup_{j=1}^n A_j$ is a colimit in $\mathcal{C}$ of the diagram given by the pairs of inclusions $A_i \cap A_j \hookrightarrow A_i$ and $A_i \cap A_j \hookrightarrow A_j$ for $i, j = 1, ..., n$.*

The proof is elementary and fun, but a bit tedious. We leave its proof as an exercise for the tenacious reader, emphasizing that distributivity of $\mathcal{C}$ is indeed not *necessary.*

We say that morphisms $h_i\colon\ A_i \to B_i$ in $\mathcal{C}$ for $i = 1, ..., n$ **have a union**, written $\bigcup_{j=1}^n h_j$, iff there is a morphism $h\colon\ \bigcup_{j=1}^n A_j \to \bigcup_{j=1}^n B_j$ such that $(A_i \hookrightarrow \bigcup_{j=1}^n A_j); h = h_i; (B_i \hookrightarrow \bigcup_{j=1}^n B_j)$ for $i = 1, ..., n$. Such a morphism h is unique if it exists, and $h_1, ..., h_n$ have a union whenever $A_1, ..., A_n$ are disjoint. $\mathcal{C}$ **has pushouts which preserve inclusions** iff for any pair of arrows $(A \hookrightarrow B, A \to A')$ there are pushouts of the form $(A' \hookrightarrow B', B \to B')$. A functor between two inclusive categories is **inclusive** (or **preserves inclusions**) iff it takes inclusions in the source category to inclusions in the target category.

2.3 Institutions

Institutions were introduced by Goguen and Burstall [21] to formalize the intuitive notion of logical system. An **institution** consists of a category **Sign** whose objects are called **signatures**, a functor **Sen**: **Sign** $\to$ **Set** giving for each signature a set whose elements are called **Σ-sentences**, a functor **Mod**: **Sign** $\to$ **Cat**^{op} giving for each signature Σ a category of **Σ-models**, and a signature-indexed relation called **satisfaction**, $\models\ = \{\models_\Sigma \mid \Sigma \in \mathbf{Sign}\}$, where $\models_\Sigma \subseteq |\mathbf{Mod}(\Sigma)| \times \mathbf{Sen}(\Sigma)$, such that for each signature morphism $h\colon\ \Sigma \to \Sigma'$, the **satisfaction condition**, $m' \models_{\Sigma'} \mathbf{Sen}(h)(a)$ iff $\mathbf{Mod}(h)(m') \models_\Sigma a$, holds for all $m' \in |\mathbf{Mod}(\Sigma')|$ and $a \in \mathbf{Sen}(\Sigma)$. We may write h for $\mathbf{Sen}(h)$ and $\_\lceil_h$ for $\mathbf{Mod}(h)$; $m\lceil_h$ is called the h-**reduct** of m. The satisfaction condition then takes the simpler form $m' \models_{\Sigma'} h(a)$ iff $m'\lceil_h \models_\Sigma a$. We may omit the subscript Σ when it can be inferred from context. Given a set A of Σ-sentences, let

$$A^* = \{m \in \mathbf{Mod}(\Sigma) \mid m \models_\Sigma a \text{ for all } a \in A\}\ ,$$

and given a class V of Σ-models, let

$$V^* = \{a \in \mathbf{Sen}(\Sigma) \mid m \models_\Sigma a \text{ for all } m \in V\}\ .$$

Then the **closure** of a set of Σ-sentences A is $A^\bullet = A^{**}$, and $\_^\bullet$ is a closure operator, i.e., it is extensive, monotonic and idempotent; the sentences in $A^\bullet$ are called the **theorems of** A.

A **specification** or **presentation** is a pair (Σ, A) where Σ is a signature and A is a set of Σ-sentences. A **specification morphism** from (Σ, A) to (Σ', A') is a signature morphism $h\colon\ \Sigma \to \Sigma'$ such that $h(A) \subseteq A'^\bullet$. Specifications and specification morphisms form a category denoted **Spec**. A **theory** (Σ, A) is a specification with $A = A^\bullet$; the full subcategory of theories in **Spec** is denoted **Th**. Given a specification (Σ, A), $\mathbf{Mod}(\Sigma, A)$ denotes the full subcategory of $\mathbf{Mod}(\Sigma)$ of models that satisfy A; given a morphism $h\colon\ (\Sigma, A) \to (\Sigma', A')$,

$\_\lceil_h$ takes models of A' to models of A. We will also write $A \models_\Sigma B$ when $\mathbf{Mod}(\Sigma, A) \subseteq \mathbf{Mod}(\Sigma, B)$. **Th** and **Spec** are equivalent categories, where the equivalence functor is just the inclusion $\mathcal{U}\colon \mathbf{Th} \to \mathbf{Spec}$. This functor has a left-adjoint-left-inverse $\mathcal{F} : \mathbf{Spec} \to \mathbf{Th}$, given by $\mathcal{F}(\Sigma, A) = (\Sigma, A^\bullet)$ on objects and the identity on morphisms; note that $\mathcal{F}$ is also right adjoint to $\mathcal{U}$, so that **Th** is a reflective and coreflective subcategory of **Spec**.

A theory morphism $h\colon (\Sigma, A) \to (\Sigma', A')$ is **conservative** iff for any (Σ, A)-model m there is a (Σ', A')-model m' such that $m'\lceil_h = m$, i.e., iff its retract map $\_\lceil_h\colon \mathbf{Mod}(\Sigma', A') \to \mathbf{Mod}(\Sigma, A)$ is surjective. A signature morphism $h\colon \Sigma \to \Sigma'$ is **conservative** iff it is conservative as a morphism of *void* theories, i.e., iff $h\colon (\Sigma, \emptyset^\bullet) \to (\Sigma', \emptyset'^\bullet)$ is conservative. An important result of [21] is that **Th** has whatever colimits **Sign** has; in particular, **Th** has pushouts whenever **Sign** does, and if $h_1 : (\Sigma, A) \to (\Sigma_1, A_1)$ and $h_2 : (\Sigma, A) \to (\Sigma_2, A_2)$ are theory morphisms, and if $(h'_1 : \Sigma_1 \to \Sigma',\ h'_2 : \Sigma_2 \to \Sigma')$ is a pushout of (h_1, h_2) in **Sign**, then $(h'_1 : (\Sigma_1, A_1) \to (\Sigma', A'),\ h'_2 : (\Sigma_2, A_2) \to (\Sigma', A'))$ is a pushout of h_1, h_2 in **Th**, where $A' = (h'_1(A_1) \cup h'_2(A_2))^\bullet$. Moreover,

Proposition 2. *Given $h\colon \Sigma \to \Sigma'$, $A, A' \subseteq \mathbf{Sen}(\Sigma)$, and $a \in \mathbf{Sen}(\Sigma)$, then:*

1. *Closure Lemma: $h(A^\bullet) \subseteq h(A)^\bullet$, i.e., $A \models_\Sigma a$ implies $h(A) \models_{\Sigma'} h(a)$.*
2. *If h is conservative, then $A \models_\Sigma a$ iff $h(A) \models_{\Sigma'} h(a)$.*
3. *$h(A^\bullet)^\bullet = h(A)^\bullet$.*
4. *$(A^\bullet \cup A')^\bullet = (A \cup A')^\bullet$.*

If any reader is disturbed by the size of the categories involved in the notion of institution, it may be reassuring that, for the purposes of this paper at least, little is lost by restricting categories of signatures to be small categories. Indeed, if signatures are finite constructions using symbols drawn from a fixed countable set, as is usual in computer science, then we could even assume that signature categories have only a countable number of objects. Similar restrictions could be given for the values of the sentence and model functors; although this entails weaker completeness properties, the practical applications to module composition only require *finite* colimits of theories.

3 Inclusive Institutions

The semantics of module systems over an institution is much simplified when signature inclusions are available, in the following sense:

Definition 1. *An institution is* **inclusive** *iff* **Sign** *is inclusive and has pushouts which preserve inclusions,* **Sen** *is inclusive, and* **Mod** *preserves pushouts which preserve inclusions, i.e., takes them to pullbacks in* **Cat**. *An inclusive institution is* **distributive** *iff its category of signatures is distributive.*

We now fix an inclusive institution and refer to it as the "given institution." Many natural properties can be expressed intuitively in inclusive institutions, for example, if A and A' are sets of Σ- and Σ'-sentences, respectively, then

$(A^\bullet \cup A'^\bullet)^\bullet = (A \cup A')^\bullet$, where the outermost closures are over $\Sigma \cup \Sigma'$-sentences; also, if $\Phi \hookrightarrow \Sigma$, $a \in \mathbf{Sen}(\Phi)$, and $A \subseteq \mathbf{Sen}(\Phi)$, then $A \models_\Phi a$ implies $A \models_\Sigma a$, with equivalence when $\Phi \hookrightarrow \Sigma$ is conservative. The category **Th** tends to have the same properties as **Sign**. In particular,

Proposition 3. *For any inclusive institution,* **Th** *is inclusive and has pushouts that preserve inclusions, where the inclusions* $\mathcal{I}_{\mathbf{Th}}$ *in* **Th** *are morphisms* $(\Sigma, A) \hookrightarrow (\Sigma', A')$ *where* $\Sigma \hookrightarrow \Sigma'$ *is an inclusion in* **Sign** *and* $A \subseteq A'$.

Proof: It is easy to check that $\mathcal{I}_{\mathbf{Th}}$ is a poclass with the same objects as **Th**. Define the union of theories (Σ, A), (Σ', A') by $(\Sigma, A) \cup (\Sigma', A') = (\Sigma \cup \Sigma', (A \cup A')^\bullet)$ where the closure is over $(\Sigma \cup \Sigma')$-sentences, and define their intersection by $(\Sigma, A) \cap (\Sigma', A') = (\Sigma \cap \Sigma', A \cap A')$. We now show correctness of these definitions. That union is a pushout of an intersection in $\mathcal{I}_{\mathbf{Th}}$ follows from the construction of pushouts in **Th**. Now consider an inclusion $(\Sigma, A) \hookrightarrow (\Sigma_1, A_1)$ in **Th** and a morphism $h\colon (\Sigma, A) \to (\Sigma_2, A_2)$ in **Th**. Let $(\Sigma_2 \hookrightarrow \Sigma', h_{\Sigma'}\colon \Sigma_1 \to \Sigma')$ be a pushout of $(\Sigma \hookrightarrow \Sigma_1, h\colon \Sigma \to \Sigma_2)$ in **Sign** which preserves the inclusion. Then $((\Sigma_2, A_2) \hookrightarrow (\Sigma', A'), h_{\Sigma'}\colon (\Sigma_1, A_1) \to (\Sigma', A'))$ is the desired pushout in **Th**, where $A' = (A_2 \cup h_{\Sigma'}(A_1))^\bullet$, again by the construction of pushouts in **Th**. □

Convention 1 We do not assume any particular way to calculate pushouts of signatures, nor do we require these pushouts to have any special properties, but for notational convenience, we assume *fixed* pushouts that preserve the inclusions; let $(\Phi' \hookrightarrow \Sigma_h,\ h_\Sigma\colon \Sigma \to \Sigma_h)$ denote this pushout for $(\Phi \hookrightarrow \Sigma,\ h\colon \Phi \to \Phi')$. We say that a choice of such pushouts is **closed under horizontal** and/or **vertical composition** iff for any $(\Phi \hookrightarrow \Sigma,\ h\colon \Phi \to \Phi')$, $\Sigma'_{(h_\Sigma)} = \Sigma'_h$ and $\Sigma \hookrightarrow \Sigma'$ and/or iff $(\Sigma_h)_g = \Sigma_{h;g}$ for any signature morphism g with source Φ'. Also, we may say **theory extension** for theory inclusion.

Open Problem It would be useful to have an algorithm for pushouts of the usual signatures, that is closed under horizontal and/or vertical composition, i.e., such that $\Sigma'_{(h_\Sigma)} = \Sigma'_h$ for any $(\Phi \hookrightarrow \Sigma,\ h\colon \Phi \to \Phi')$ and $\Sigma \hookrightarrow \Sigma'$, and such that $(\Sigma_h)_g = \Sigma_{h;g}$ for any signature morphism g with source Φ'.

Definition 2. *Given* $\imath\colon \Phi \hookrightarrow \Sigma$ *in* **Sign** *and* $A \subseteq \mathbf{Sen}(\Sigma)$, *let* $Th^\Sigma_\Phi(A)$ *denote* $\imath^{-1}(A^\bullet) \subseteq \mathbf{Sen}(\Phi)$, *called the* **$\Phi$-visible theorems of** A *(over* Σ*).*

$Th^\Sigma_\Phi(A)$ contains all the Φ-sentences that are consequences of A. When $\imath$ is an identity, then $Th^\Sigma_\Sigma(A) = A^\bullet$.

Example 1 Assume a logic where equational reasoning and induction are sound, and let *LIST* be a specification of lists containing at least the sorts *Elt* and *List*, a constant *nil* of sort *List*, and a constructor $cons\colon Elt \times List \to List$. Let Φ extend this signature by a reverse operation $rev\colon List \to List$, let Σ extend Φ by a private operation $aux\colon List \times List \to List$, and let A contain the equations

$(\forall L : List)\ rev(L) = aux(L, nil).$
$(\forall P : List)\ aux(nil, P) = P.$
$(\forall E : Elt; L, P : List)\ aux(cons(E, L), P) = aux(L, cons(E, P)).$

Then the following are two Φ-visible theorems of A over Σ:

$$rev(nil) = nil\ ,$$
$$(\forall L : List)\ rev(rev(L)) = L\ .$$

The proof of the second requires induction and two lemmas. □

The following properties are familiar for many particular logics, because they hold in any inclusive institution:

Proposition 4. *If* $\Psi \hookrightarrow \Phi \hookrightarrow \Sigma$, $A \subseteq A' \subseteq \mathbf{Sen}(\Sigma)$, *and* $B \subseteq \mathbf{Sen}(\Phi)$, *then:*

1. $B \subseteq Th^{\Sigma}_{\Phi}(B)$.
2. $Th^{\Phi}_{\Psi}(B) \subseteq Th^{\Sigma}_{\Psi}(B)$.
3. $Th^{\Phi}_{\Psi}(B) = Th^{\Sigma}_{\Psi}(B)$ *if* $\Phi \hookrightarrow \Sigma$ *is conservative.*
4. $Th^{\Sigma}_{\Psi}(A) \subseteq Th^{\Sigma}_{\Phi}(A)$.
5. $Th^{\Sigma}_{\Phi}(A) \subseteq Th^{\Sigma}_{\Phi}(A')$.
6. $Th^{\Sigma}_{\Psi}(A) \subseteq Th^{\Sigma}_{\Phi}(Th^{\Sigma}_{\Psi}(A))$.
7. $Th^{\Sigma}_{\Psi}(Th^{\Sigma}_{\Phi}(A)) \subseteq Th^{\Sigma}_{\Psi}(A)$.
8. $Th^{\Sigma}_{\Phi}(Th^{\Sigma}_{\Phi}(A)) = Th^{\Sigma}_{\Phi}(A)$.
9. $Th^{\Phi}_{\Phi}(Th^{\Sigma}_{\Phi}(A)) = Th^{\Sigma}_{\Phi}(A)$.
10. $Th^{\Phi}_{\Psi}(Th^{\Sigma}_{\Phi}(A)) = Th^{\Sigma}_{\Psi}(A)$.

Proof: Let $\imath' : \Psi \to \Phi$ and $\imath : \Phi \to \Sigma$ be the two inclusions.

1. If $b \in B$ then $B \models_{\Sigma} b$, i.e., $b \in Th^{\Sigma}_{\Phi}(B)$.
2. By 1. of Proposition 2.
3. This is exactly 2. in Proposition 2.
4. Since **Sen** is a morphism of inclusion systems, a is in $\mathbf{Sen}(\Phi)$ whenever a is in $\mathbf{Sen}(\Psi)$.
5. This is equivalent to $\imath^{-1}(A^{\bullet}) \subseteq \imath^{-1}(A'^{\bullet})$, which holds because $A^{\bullet} \subseteq A'^{\bullet}$.
6. This follows from 1. with $Th^{\Sigma}_{\Psi}(A)$ for B.
7. This is equivalent to $(\imath';\imath)^{-1}(\imath^{-1}(A^{\bullet})) \subseteq (\imath';\imath)^{-1}(A^{\bullet})$, which is true because $\imath^{-1}(A^{\bullet}) \subseteq A^{\bullet}$.
8. This follows from 6. and 7., with $\Psi = \Phi$.
9. By 1., $Th^{\Sigma}_{\Phi}(A) \subseteq Th^{\Phi}_{\Phi}(Th^{\Sigma}_{\Phi}(A))$. On the other hand, $Th^{\Phi}_{\Phi}(Th^{\Sigma}_{\Phi}(A)) \subseteq Th^{\Sigma}_{\Phi}(Th^{\Sigma}_{\Phi}(A))$ by 2., and also $Th^{\Phi}_{\Phi}(Th^{\Sigma}_{\Phi}(A)) \subseteq Th^{\Sigma}_{\Phi}(A)$ by 8.
10. This is equivalent to $\imath'^{-1}(\imath^{-1}(A^{\bullet})) = (\imath';\imath)^{-1}(A^{\bullet})$, which is true.

□

Lemma 1. <u>**Generalized Closure Lemma:**</u> *Given* $A \subseteq \mathbf{Sen}(\Sigma)$*, inclusions* $\imath\colon \Phi \hookrightarrow \Sigma$*,* $\imath'\colon \Phi' \hookrightarrow \Sigma'$*, and morphisms* $h\colon \Phi \to \Phi'$ *and* $g\colon \Sigma \to \Sigma'$ *such that*

$$\begin{array}{ccc} \Phi & \xrightarrow{\imath} & \Sigma \\ {\scriptstyle h}\downarrow & & \downarrow{\scriptstyle g} \\ \Phi' & \xrightarrow[\imath']{} & \Sigma' \end{array}$$

commutes, then $h(Th_{\Phi}^{\Sigma}(A)) \subseteq Th_{\Phi'}^{\Sigma'}(g(A))$*.*

Proof: Let a be a Φ-sentence in $Th_{\Phi}^{\Sigma}(A)$, so that $A \models_{\Sigma} a$. Then $g(A) \models_{\Sigma'} g(a)$ by the classic Closure Lemma (1. of Proposition 2). But $g(a) = h(a)$ because **Sen** preserves inclusions, and so $h(a)$ is in $Th_{\Phi'}^{\Sigma'}(g(A))$. □

The classic Closure Lemma is the special case of the above where $\imath, \imath'$ are identities, that is, where nothing is hidden.

4 Modules

Our modules, like those in [26], extend the usual algebraic specifications by allowing them to hide some information, which however may be used in defining their visible features.

Definition 3. *A* **module** *is a triple* (Φ, Σ, A)*, where* $\Phi \hookrightarrow \Sigma$ *are signatures and* A *is a set of* Σ*-sentences;* Φ *is called the* **visible signature***,* Σ *the* **working signature***,* $Th(M) = Th_{\Sigma}^{\Sigma}(A)$ *the* **working theorems***, and* $Vth(M) = Th_{\Phi}^{\Sigma}(A)$ *the* **visible theorems***. A* **morphism** $h\colon M \to M'$ *of modules is a morphism of their visible signatures such that* $h(Vth(M)) \subseteq Vth(M')$*.*

Modules together with module morphisms form a category **MSpec**. The functor $\mathcal{M}$ from **Th** to **MSpec** defined by $\mathcal{M}(\Sigma, A) = (\Sigma, \Sigma, A)$ and $\mathcal{M}(h) = h$, is full, faithful and dense, i.e., is an equivalence of categories. Further (by Theorem 1, page 91 of [31]), $\mathcal{M}$ is part of an adjoint equivalence, with left adjoint $\mathcal{T}\colon$ **MSpec** $\to$ **Th** defined by $\mathcal{T}(\Phi, \Sigma, A) = (\Phi, Th_{\Phi}^{\Sigma}(A))$ on objects, and the identity on morphisms; the unit of this adjunction is $1_{\Phi}\colon (\Phi, \Sigma, A) \to (\Phi, \Phi, Th_{\Phi}^{\Sigma}(A))$. We let $\mathcal{U}\colon$ **MSpec** $\to$ **MSpec** denote the functor $\mathcal{T};\mathcal{M}$, taking modules (Φ, Σ, A) to modules $(\Phi, \Phi, Th_{\Phi}^{\Sigma}(A))$. Notice that $\mathcal{T}$ is also a right adjoint of $\mathcal{M}$, so that **Th** is (modulo isomorphism) a reflective and coreflective subcategory of **MSpec**. Since the two categories are equivalent, every categorical property [29] of **Th** is also a property of **MSpec**. In particular, pushouts are preserved and reflected by $\mathcal{M}$ and $\mathcal{T}$, and **MSpec** is cocomplete whenever **Sign** is cocomplete, since **Th** is cocomplete (by [21]).

Definition 4. *A* Φ*-model* m **satisfies** $M = (\Phi, \Sigma, A)$ *iff* $m \models_{\Phi} Vth(M)$*; in this case, we write* $m \models M$*.*

If $h\colon M \to M'$ is a module morphism and $m' \models M'$, then $m'{\restriction}_h \models M$. Therefore in any inclusive institution, the functor **Mod** extends to **MSpec** by mapping a module M to the full subcategory $\mathbf{Mod}(M)$ of $\mathbf{Mod}(\Phi)$ with the Φ-models satisfying M as its objects.

It is common to call a theory extension $(\Sigma, A) \hookrightarrow (\Sigma, A')$ conservative when $A = A' \cap \mathbf{Sen}(\Sigma)$; we call this notion **syntactic conservativity** to distinguish it from the semantic version. Notice that for any module $M = (\Phi, \Sigma, A)$, the theory inclusion $(\Phi, \mathit{Vth}(M)) \hookrightarrow (\Sigma, \mathit{Th}(M))$ is syntactically conservative, because $\mathit{Vth}(M) = \mathit{Th}_{\Phi}^{\Sigma}(A) = \{a \in \mathbf{Sen}(\Phi) \mid A \models_{\Sigma} a\} = \{a \in \mathbf{Sen}(\Phi) \mid a \in \mathit{Th}(M)\} = \mathit{Th}(M) \cap \mathbf{Sen}(\Phi)$. As shown in [15], syntactic conservativity is a necessary but insufficient condition for semantic conservativity. So it is not surprising that we also need a stronger conservativity for modules:

Definition 5. *A module M is* **conservative** *if and only if the theory inclusion $(\Phi, \mathit{Vth}(M)) \hookrightarrow (\Sigma, \mathit{Th}(M))$ is conservative.*

Transparent modules, with $\Phi = \Sigma$, are always conservative. But there are simple non-conservative modules, even for unsorted equational logic, such as the following (after [15]):

Example 2 Let Φ contain a constant a and a unary operation $-$, let Σ additionally contain a constant c, and let A contain the equation $c = -c$. Then the visible theorems of this module form an empty theory, but there are Φ-models that cannot be extended to Σ-models satisfying A, such as $m = \{1, -1\}$ with $m_a = 1$, $m_-(1) = -1$ and $m_-(-1) = 1$. □

5 Module Composition Operations

We give two semantics and a definition, for five module composition operations from original Clear paper [7], over any inclusive institution. These are functions defined on module expressions, i.e., terms involving basic modules, parameterized modules, and the five operations. The definition follows [26], and is module valued, saying what must be implemented, e.g., in LILEANNA, is denoted $|E|$ where E is a module expression. The first semantics (also from [26]), denoted $[\![E]\!]_1$, takes the visible theorems of the combined module, while the second semantics (from [37]), denoted $[\![E]\!]_2$, combines the visible theorems of the component modules. Thus the first semantics uses the definitions of the module combination operations, including renamings to avoid name conflicts, while the second semantics directly combines their visible theorems. The first semantics is more comprehensive because it makes use of more information, and the two agree only under special conditions, when interactions among hidden information can safely be ignored. A major result is that conservativity is a necessary and sufficient condition for the two semantics to agree; this characterizes when it is safe to ignore interactions among hidden parts. All five module operations preserve conservativity under natural conditions. When proving theorems about composed systems, it is often easier to use hidden information than to use only its consequences; for example, the former may be finite while the latter is infinite. Therefore a theorem prover should have access to all of the hidden information, e.g., the combined module given by the definitions, or the module expression itself, which provides additional structuring information.

5.1 Aggregation

The aggregation of modules is essentially the componentwise union of their parts. However, this simple view is complicated by the need to handle symbols having the same name but defined in different modules, and symbols coming from shared submodules. A standard way to prevent such name clashes is to tag symbols with the name of the module where they are defined; symbols defined in shared submodules are then tagged just once. Some languages with overloaded operators have complex symbol resolution algorithms, while others take the simple union of all symbols, leaving the name collision problem to the user. The latter approach is actually quite appropriate for investigating the role of hidden symbols in the semantics of aggregation, and of module composition more generally. Moreover, if symbols are already tagged with their originating module when they are declared, with their untagged name available as a convenient abbreviation when it is unambiguous (as is done in implementations of the OBJ systems [27,25]), then this approach is actually equivalent to the standard one.

We will show that the two semantics for aggregation agree when the component modules are conservative and all the symbols that they share are visible, and we will give counterexamples showing that both of these requirements are necessary. We will also give some simple "laws of software composition" for aggregation, and prove some other basic properties of aggregation.

Definition 6. *Given modules* $M = (\Phi, \Sigma, A)$ *and* $M' = (\Phi', \Sigma', A')$*, their* **aggregation** *is defined to be* $(\Phi \cup \Phi', \Sigma \cup \Sigma', A \cup A')$*, or more formally,* $|M + M'| = (\Phi \cup \Phi', \Sigma \cup \Sigma', A \cup A')$*. Moreover, we let* $[\![M + M']\!]_1 = Vth(\Phi \cup \Phi', \Sigma \cup \Sigma', A \cup A')$*, and* $[\![M + M']\!]_2 = (Vth(M) \cup Vth(M'))^\bullet$*, where the closure is with respect to* $\Phi \cup \Phi'$*.*

This makes sense because $\Phi \cup \Phi' \hookrightarrow \Sigma \cup \Sigma'$ and $A \cup A'$ is a set of $(\Sigma \cup \Sigma')$-sentences, since **Sen** preserves inclusions. Because $M + M'$ is a formal expression, it is an abuse of notation to write $M + M' = (\Phi \cup \Phi', \Sigma \cup \Sigma', A \cup A')$, but it is often convenient, and we will use this convention for the other module combination operations, as well as for aggregation. In particular, we may write $E = M$ for the more precise $|E| = M$ where E is a module expression and M is a module. Note that $|M| = M$, and that[7] here and hereafter, $[\![M]\!]_1 = Vth(|M|)$. Since each of the three formal semantic definitions extends recursively over the module combination operations to all module expressions, it also makes sense to write $E = E'$ for $|E| = |E'|$ where E, E' are both module expressions, as is (implicitly) done in the following:

Fact 1 *Aggregation is commutative, associative and idempotent.*

[7] For some reason, the expression $Vth(E')$ where $E' = |E|$ is called the *normal form* of E in the tradition of [40,39,6].

A precise form of the first assertion is $|M + M'| = |M' + M|$. The proof of this fact uses that union has the three corresponding properties. It also follows that $[\![M + M']\!]_1 = [\![M' + M]\!]_1$ and that $[\![M + M']\!]_2 = [\![M' + M]\!]_2$. Hereafter, we will systematically employ the abuse of notation discussed above.

Proposition 5. *If $\imath$ and $\imath'$ denote the inclusions $\Phi \hookrightarrow \Phi \cup \Phi'$ and $\Phi' \hookrightarrow \Phi \cup \Phi'$, respectively, then $\imath\colon M \to M{+}M'$ and $\imath'\colon M' \to M{+}M'$ are module morphisms. Therefore $m \models M + M'$ implies $m{\restriction_\Phi} \models M$ and $m{\restriction_{\Phi'}} \models M'$ for any $(\Phi \cup \Phi')$-model m.*

Proof: This is immediate, noting that $M + M'$ denotes the module $|M + M'|$.
□

The following technically important result informally says that if all common symbols of two conservative modules are visible, then any model of both sets of visible theorems extends to a model of both sets of working theorems:

Theorem 1. *If modules $M = (\Phi, \Sigma, A)$ and $M' = (\Phi', \Sigma', A')$ are conservative and if $\Phi \cap \Phi' = \Sigma \cap \Sigma'$, then for any $(\Phi \cup \Phi')$-model m such that $m \models_{\Phi\cup\Phi'} Vth(M) \cup Vth(M')$ there is a $(\Sigma \cup \Sigma')$-model m' such that $m'{\restriction_{\Phi\cup\Phi'}}= m$ and $m' \models_{\Sigma\cup\Sigma'} Th(M) \cup Th(M')$.*

Proof: By the Satisfaction Condition, $m{\restriction_\Phi} \models_\Phi Th^{\Sigma}_{\Phi}(A)$ and $m{\restriction_{\Phi'}} \models_{\Phi'} Th^{\Sigma'}_{\Phi'}(A')$. Since (Φ, Σ, A) and (Φ', Σ', A') are conservative, there exist a Σ-model m_Σ of A and a Σ'-model $m_{\Sigma'}$ of A' such that $m_\Sigma{\restriction_\Phi}= m{\restriction_\Phi}$ and $m_{\Sigma'}{\restriction_{\Phi'}}= m{\restriction_{\Phi'}}$.

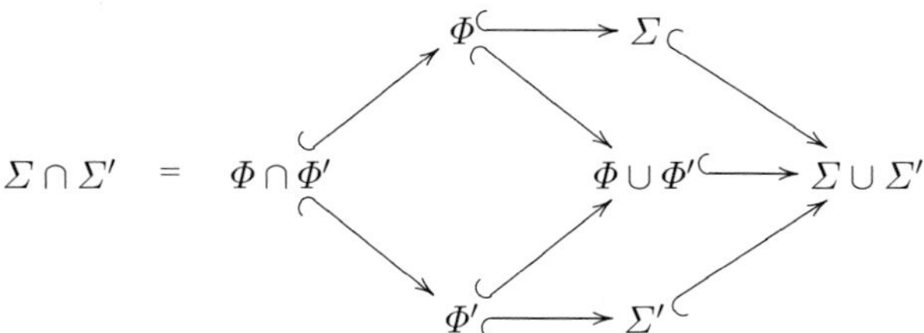

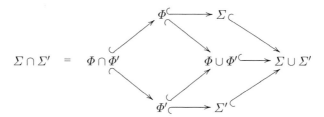

Then by the functoriality of reducts, $m_\Sigma{\restriction_{\Phi\cap\Phi'}}= (m_\Sigma{\restriction_\Phi}){\restriction_{\Phi\cap\Phi'}}= (m{\restriction_\Phi}){\restriction_{\Phi\cap\Phi'}}= m{\restriction_{\Phi\cap\Phi'}}= (m{\restriction_{\Phi'}}){\restriction_{\Phi\cap\Phi'}}= (m_{\Sigma'}{\restriction_{\Phi'}}){\restriction_{\Phi\cap\Phi'}}= m_{\Sigma'}{\restriction_{\Phi\cap\Phi'}}$. Since $\Sigma \cap \Sigma' = \Phi \cap \Phi'$, and **Mod** preserves intersection-union pushouts, and by the construction of pullbacks in **Cat**, there is a (unique) $(\Sigma \cup \Sigma')$-model m' such that $m'{\restriction_\Sigma}= m_\Sigma$ and $m'{\restriction_{\Sigma'}}= m_{\Sigma'}$; thus $m'{\restriction_\Sigma} \models_\Sigma A$ and $m'{\restriction_{\Sigma'}} \models_{\Sigma'} A'$. Therefore the Satisfaction Condition gives $m' \models_{\Sigma\cup\Sigma'} A \cup A'$. The reader may check that this essentially says that m' is a model of both $Th(M)$ and $Th(M')$, and that $(m'{\restriction_{\Phi\cup\Phi'}}){\restriction_\Phi}= m{\restriction_\Phi}$ and $(m'{\restriction_{\Phi\cup\Phi'}}){\restriction_{\Phi'}}= m{\restriction_{\Phi'}}$. Therefore $m'{\restriction_{\Phi\cup\Phi'}}$ satisfies the conditions that are uniquely satisfied by m (because the union of Φ and Φ' is a pushout of their intersection, because **Mod** preserves it, and because of the way pullbacks are built in **Cat**). Therefore $m'{\restriction_{\Phi\cup\Phi'}}= m$. □

Proposition 6. *If M and M' are modules as in Theorem 1, then*

1. $[\![M + M']\!]_1 = [\![M + M']\!]_2$.
2. $m \models M + M'$ *iff* $m\lceil_{\Phi} \models M$ *and* $m\lceil_{\Phi'} \models M'$ *for any* $(\Phi \cup \Phi')$*-model* m.
3. $M + M'$ *is conservative.*

Proof: 1. is equivalent to $Th^{\Sigma\cup\Sigma'}_{\Phi\cup\Phi'}(A \cup A') = Th^{\Phi\cup\Phi'}_{\Phi\cup\Phi'}(Th^{\Sigma}_{\Phi}(A) \cup Th^{\Sigma'}_{\Phi'}(A'))$. By Proposition 4, $Th^{\Sigma}_{\Phi}(A) \subseteq Th^{\Sigma\cup\Sigma'}_{\Phi\cup\Phi'}(A \cup B)$ and $Th^{\Sigma'}_{\Phi'}(B) \subseteq Th^{\Sigma\cup\Sigma'}_{\Phi\cup\Phi'}(A \cup B)$, so $Th^{\Phi\cup\Phi'}_{\Phi\cup\Phi'}(Th^{\Sigma}_{\Phi}(A) \cup Th^{\Sigma'}_{\Phi'}(B)) \subseteq Th^{\Sigma\cup\Sigma'}_{\Phi\cup\Phi'}(A \cup B)$. Conversely, consider a $(\Phi \cup \Phi')$-sentence a such that $A \cup A' \models_{\Sigma\cup\Sigma'} a$, and let m be a $(\Phi\cup\Phi')$-model for $Th^{\Sigma}_{\Phi}(A)$ and $Th^{\Sigma'}_{\Phi'}(A')$. By Theorem 1, there exists a $(\Sigma \cup \Sigma')$-model m' of $A \cup A'$ such that $m'\lceil_{\Phi\cup\Phi'} = m$. Then $m' \models_{\Sigma\cup\Sigma'} a$, and so by the Satisfaction Condition, $m'\lceil_{\Phi\cup\Phi'} \models_{\Phi\cup\Phi'} a$, that is, $m \models_{\Phi\cup\Phi'} a$. Consequently, a is in $Th^{\Phi\cup\Phi'}_{\Phi\cup\Phi'}(Th^{\Sigma}_{\Phi}(A) \cup Th^{\Sigma'}_{\Phi'}(A'))$. This shows that $Th^{\Sigma\cup\Sigma'}_{\Phi\cup\Phi'}(A \cup A') \subseteq Th^{\Phi\cup\Phi'}_{\Phi\cup\Phi'}(Th^{\Sigma}_{\Phi}(A) \cup Th^{\Sigma'}_{\Phi'}(A'))$.

2. follows from the equivalences:

$$\begin{array}{ll}
m \models M + M' & \text{iff} \\
m \models_{\Phi\cup\Phi'} Vth(M + M') & \text{iff (by 1.)} \\
m \models_{\Phi\cup\Phi'} (Vth(M) \cup Vth(M'))^{\bullet} & \text{iff} \\
m \models_{\Phi\cup\Phi'} Vth(M) \cup Vth(M') & \text{iff} \\
m \models_{\Phi\cup\Phi'} Vth(M) \text{ and } m \models_{\Phi\cup\Phi'} Vth(M') & \text{iff} \\
m\lceil_{\Phi} \models_{\Phi} Vth(M) \text{ and } m\lceil_{\Phi'} \models_{\Phi'} Vth(M') & \text{iff} \\
m\lceil_{\Phi} \models M \text{ and } m\lceil_{\Phi'} \models M' \,. &
\end{array}$$

Only the right to left implication is interesting, since the other direction needs neither conservativity nor that $\Phi \cap \Phi' = \Sigma \cap \Sigma'$.

For 3., take a $(\Phi \cup \Phi')$-model m of $Th^{\Sigma\cup\Sigma'}_{\Phi\cup\Phi'}(A \cup A')$. Then m is also a $(\Phi \cup \Phi')$-model of $Th^{\Sigma}_{\Phi}(A)$ and $Th^{\Sigma'}_{\Phi'}(A')$, and by Theorem 1 there is a $(\Sigma \cup \Sigma')$-model m' of $A \cup A'$ such that $m'\lceil_{\Phi\cup\Phi'} = m$. Therefore, m' is a $(\Sigma \cup \Sigma')$-model of $Th^{\Sigma\cup\Sigma'}_{\Sigma\cup\Sigma'}(A \cup A')$; this shows that $(\Phi, \Sigma, A) + (\Phi', \Sigma', A')$ is conservative. □

Despite its somewhat complex proof, this result looks so natural that one might be tempted to think its hypothesis too strong. But visibility of shared symbols really is needed, as shown by the following:

Example 3 Let M have a visible constant 0, a hidden constant c and the sentence $0 = c$, while M' has a constant 1, the same hidden c, and the sentence $1 = c$. Then $(Vth(M) \cup Vth(M'))^{\bullet}$ is empty while $Vth(M + M')$ contains $0 = 1$. This suggests that an implementation of aggregation should rename all shared private symbols even if they occurred as a consequence of enriching a shared module. □

Example 4 Conservativity of M and M' is also needed. Let Φ be the signature with constants $0, 1$ and a binary operation $+$, let Σ add to Φ a hidden constant c, let A have the equation $0 + c = 1 + c$, let $\Sigma' = \Phi' = \Phi$, and let A' have the equations $(\forall X)\ X + X = 0$ and $(\forall X, Y, Z)\ X + (Y + Z) = (X + Y) + Z$. Then the equation $0 = 1 + 0$ is in $Vth(M + M')$ but not in $(Vth(M) \cup Vth(M'))^\bullet$, and this occurs because M is not conservative. □

The two semantics naturally extend to an arbitrary number of modules: $[\![M_1 + \cdots + M_n]\!]_1 = Vth(M_1 + \cdots + M_n)$, and $[\![M_1 + \cdots + M_n]\!]_2 = (Vth(M_1) \cup ... \cup Vth(M_n))^\bullet$, where the closure is over $\Phi_1 \cup ... \cup \Phi_n$. We then have

Corollary 1. *If the given institution is distributive and if $M_j = (\Phi_j, \Sigma_j, A_j)$ for $j = 1, ..., n$ are conservative such that $\Sigma_i \cap \Sigma_j = \Phi_i \cap \Phi_j$ for $i, j = 1, ..., n$ with $M_i \neq M_j$, then:*

1. $[\![M_1 + \cdots + M_n]\!]_1 = [\![M_1 + \cdots + M_n]\!]_2$.
2. *$m \models M_1 + \cdots + M_n$ iff $m{\restriction}_{\Phi_j} \models M_j$ for $j = 1, ..., n$, where m is a $(\Phi_1 \cup ... \cup \Phi_n)$-model.*
3. *$M_1 + \cdots + M_n$ is conservative.*

5.2 Renaming

Renaming is straightforward for transparent algebraic specifications: given a specification (Σ, A) and a morphism $h \colon \Sigma \to \Sigma'$, the *renaming of* (Σ, A) *by* h, denoted $(\Sigma, A)\star h$, is obtained by renaming each Σ-sentence in A, i.e., $(\Sigma, A)\star h = (\Sigma', h(A))$. The situation is more complex for modules with hiding, because only the visible symbols are renamed, and because renamed symbols could clash with private names. These problems are handled abstractly by signature pushouts.

Definition 7. *Given $M = (\Phi, \Sigma, A)$ and $h \colon \Phi \to \Phi'$,* **the renaming of** M **by** *h, written $M \star h$, is the module $(\Phi', \Sigma_h, h_\Sigma(A))$ (see Convention 1). Moreover, $[\![M \star h]\!]_1 = Vth(\Phi', \Sigma_h, h_\Sigma(A))$, and $[\![M \star h]\!]_2 = h(Vth(M))^\bullet$, where the closure is over Φ'.*

The morphism h is first extended to the morphism h_Σ on the whole working signature, and then A is renamed by h_Σ. This is well defined because $\Phi' \hookrightarrow \Sigma_h$ and $h_\Sigma(A)$ is a set of Σ_h-sentences. Notice that $h \colon M \to M \star h$ is a module morphism by the Generalized Closure Lemma (Lemma 1), so $m \models M \star h$ implies $m{\restriction}_h \models M$ for any Φ_h-model m.

The next result says that, assuming conservativity, the two semantics coincide: the visible theorems of a renamed module are exactly those generated by the renamed visible theorems of the initial module, i.e., the models of the renamed module are *exactly* those whose reducts are models of the initial module; moreover, conservativity is preserved under renaming.

Proposition 7. *If $M = (\Phi, \Sigma, A)$ is a conservative module, then*

1. $[\![M \star h]\!]_1 = [\![M \star h]\!]_2$.
2. *$m \models M \star h$ iff $m{\restriction}_h \models M$ for any Φ'-model m.*
3. *$M \star h$ is conservative.*

Proof: For 1., we need $Th_{\Phi'}^{\Phi'}(h(Th_{\Phi}^{\Sigma}(A))) = Th_{\Phi'}^{\Sigma_h}(h_{\Sigma}(A))$. Lemma 1 implies $h(Th_{\Phi}^{\Sigma}(A))) \subseteq Th_{\Phi'}^{\Sigma_h}(h_{\Sigma}(A))$; applying $Th_{\Phi'}^{\Phi'}$ to this inclusion, Proposition 4 gives $Th_{\Phi'}^{\Phi'}(h(Th_{\Phi}^{\Sigma}(A))) \subseteq Th_{\Phi'}^{\Sigma_h}(h_{\Sigma}(A))$. Conversely, let $a \in \mathbf{Sen}(\Phi')$ such that $h_{\Sigma}(A) \models_{\Sigma_h} a$ and let m' be a Φ'-model such that $m' \models_{\Phi'} h(Th_{\Phi}^{\Sigma}(A))$. We need to show $m' \models_{\Phi'} a$. By the Satisfaction Condition, $m'\lceil_h \models_{\Phi} Th_{\Phi}^{\Sigma}(A)$. Since (Φ, Σ, A) is conservative, there is a Σ-model m such that $m\lceil_{\Phi} = m'\lceil_h$ and $m \models_{\Sigma} Th_{\Sigma}^{\Sigma}(A)$. By the construction of pullbacks in **Cat** (Section 2.1), and since **Mod** preserves intersection-union pushouts (Definition 1), there is a Σ_h-model, say m_h, such that $m_h\lceil_{h_\Sigma} = m$ and $m_h\lceil_{\Phi'} = m'$. Then $m_h\lceil_{h_\Sigma} \models_{\Sigma} A$ (because $m \models_{\Sigma} Th_{\Sigma}^{\Sigma}(A)$ and $A \subseteq Th_{\Sigma}^{\Sigma}(A)$), and so $m_h \models_{\Sigma_h} h_{\Sigma}(A)$. Further, $m_h \models_{\Sigma_h} a$ because $h_{\Sigma}(A) \models_{\Sigma_h} a$. Finally, if $\imath'$ is the inclusion $\Phi' \hookrightarrow \Sigma_h$ then $m_h \models_{\Sigma_h} \imath'(a)$, so $m_h\lceil_{\imath'} \models_{\Phi'} a$; therefore $m' \models_{\Phi'} a$.

2. follows since $m\lceil_h \models M$ iff $m\lceil_h \models_{\Phi} Vth(M)$ iff $m \models_{\Phi'} h(Vth(M))$ (Satisfaction Condition) iff $m \models_{\Phi'} h(Vth(M))^{\bullet}$ iff $m \models_{\Phi'} Vth(M \star h)$ (by 1.) iff $m \models M \star h$.

For 3., let m be a Φ'-model of $Th_{\Phi'}^{\Sigma_h}(h_{\Sigma}(A))$, that is, $m \models M \star h$. By 2., $m\lceil_h$ is a Φ-model of $Th_{\Phi}^{\Sigma}(A)$. Then by conservativity of (Φ, Σ, A), there is a Σ-model m_{Σ} of A such that $m_{\Sigma}\lceil_{\Phi} = m\lceil_h$. But the pair of morphisms h_{Σ} and $\Phi' \hookrightarrow \Sigma_h$ is a pushout of h and $\Phi \hookrightarrow \Sigma$; therefore, since **Mod** preserves these pushouts (see Definition 1), by the construction of pullbacks in **Cat**, there is a Σ_h-model m' such that $m'\lceil_{(h_\Sigma)} = m_{\Sigma}$ and $m'\lceil_{\Phi'} = m$. Then by the Satisfaction Condition, $m' \models_{\Sigma_h} h_{\Sigma}(A)$, that is m' is a Σ_h-model of $Th_{\Sigma_h}^{\Sigma_h}(h_{\Sigma}(A))$. Therefore, for a Φ'-model m of $Vth(M \star h)$ we have a Σ_h-model m' of $Th(M \star h)$ such that $m'\lceil_{\Phi'} = m$. This shows that $M \star h$ is conservative. □

The following shows that conservativity is necessary here:

Example 5 Consider the unsorted equational logic module $M = (\Phi, \Sigma, A)$ where Φ contains constants a, b and a binary operation f, Σ adds one more constant c, and A contains the equations $f(a, c) = a$ and $f(b, c) = f(a, a)$; suppose also that Φ' consists of only one constant d and that h takes both a and b to d. Then $h(Vth(M))^{\bullet}$ is an empty theory because $Vth(M)$ is empty, while $Vth(M \star h)$ contains the equation $f(d, d) = d$. Notice that M is not conservative. □

A desirable property of renamings is that they can be composed, in the sense that $(M \star h) \star g = M \star (h; g)$ for any appropriate h and g. This is straightforward for transparent specifications, but it can be hard to insure when hiding is allowed because of the variety of conventions for renaming hidden symbols to prevent name clashes with the visible symbols in the result (this is similar to the variety of choices for h_{Σ} discussed in Convention 1).

Proposition 8. *If pushouts of inclusions in* **Sign** *are chosen such that they can be composed vertically (in the sense of Convention 1), then* $(M \star h) \star g = M \star (h; g)$ *for any module* $M = (\Phi, \Sigma, A)$ *and any morphisms* $h\colon \Phi \to \Phi'$ *and* $g\colon \Phi' \to \Phi''$.

Proof: We calculate as follows:

$$\begin{aligned}((\Phi,\Sigma,A)\star h)\star g &= (\Phi',\Sigma_h,h_\Sigma(A))\star g && \text{by Definition 7}\\ &= \Phi'',(\Sigma_h)_g,g_{(\Sigma_h)}(h_\Sigma(A))) && \text{also by Definition 7}\\ &= (\Phi'',\Sigma_{h;g},(h;g)_\Sigma(A)) && \text{by hypothesis}\\ &= (\Phi,\Sigma,A)\star(h;g) && \text{again by Definition 7.}\end{aligned}$$

□

5.3 Enrichment

A common way to reuse software and specification is through enrichment, which adds functionality to an existing module. For example, LILEANNA [42] implements enrichment by adding a partial signature to the given signature and then adding code over the resulting signature. However, it is simpler to use extensions of total signatures.

Definition 8. *Given modules $M = (\Phi, \Sigma, A)$ and (Φ', Σ', A') with $\Phi \hookrightarrow \Phi'$ and $\Sigma \hookrightarrow \Sigma'$, the* **enrichment of** M **by** (Φ', Σ', A')*, written $M@(\Phi', \Sigma', A')$, is the module $(\Phi', \Sigma', A \cup A')$, and $[\![M@(\Phi', \Sigma', A')]\!]_1 = Vth(\Phi', \Sigma', A \cup A')$ and $[\![M@(\Phi', \Sigma', A')]\!]_2 = Vth(\Phi', \Phi' \cup \Sigma, A \cup Vth(\Phi' \cup \Sigma, \Sigma', A'))$.*

Both visible (Φ') and private (Σ') symbols can be added, as well as new sentences (in A') involving all these symbols. Note that if $\imath$ is the inclusion $\Phi \hookrightarrow \Phi'$ then $\imath\colon M \to M@(\Phi', \Sigma', A')$ is a morphism of modules, so $m \models M@(\Phi', \Sigma', A')$ implies $m\restriction_\Phi \models M$ for any Φ'-model m.

The first semantics is straightforward, but the second requires some explanation. The key is to take a *working-in-M* perspective, similar to the intuition for module enrichment in software engineering, and to consider how the newly added features affect the semantics of the current working environment, regarded as visible. Since new visible symbols are added to M, those symbols extend the working signature to $\Phi' \cup \Sigma$, and their effect on the working environment is the visible theorems of the module $(\Phi' \cup \Sigma, \Sigma', A')$. We first prove the following:

Lemma 2. *In the context of Definition 8, if $\Sigma \hookrightarrow \Psi \hookrightarrow \Sigma'$ is such that (Ψ, Σ', A') is conservative, then $Th_\Psi^{\Sigma'}(A \cup A') = Th_\Psi^{\Psi}(A \cup Th_\Psi^{\Sigma'}(A'))$.*

Proof: Since $A \subseteq Th_\Psi^{\Sigma}(A \cup A')$ and $Th_\Psi^{\Sigma}(A') \subseteq Th_\Psi^{\Sigma'}(A \cup A')$, it follows by Proposition 4 that $Th_\Psi^{\Psi}(A \cup Th_\Psi^{\Sigma'}(A')) \subseteq Th_\Psi^{\Sigma'}(A \cup A')$. Conversely, let a be a Ψ-sentence in $Th_\Psi^{\Sigma'}(A \cup A')$. In order to prove that a is in $Th_\Psi^{\Psi}(A \cup Th_\Psi^{\Sigma'}(A'))$, take a Ψ-model m of $A \cup Th_\Psi^{\Sigma'}(A')$. Since (Ψ, Σ', A') is conservative, there is a Σ'-model m' of A' such that $m'\restriction_\Psi = m$. But $m \models_\Psi A$, that is, $m'\restriction_\Psi \models_\Psi A$; then by the satisfaction condition we get $m' \models_{\Sigma'} A$. Therefore $m' \models_{\Sigma'} A \cup A'$, and so $m' \models_{\Sigma'} a$, because we supposed that $A \cup A' \models_{\Sigma'} a$. Consequently, the satisfaction condition implies $m'\restriction_\Psi \models_\Psi a$, i.e., $m \models_\Psi a$. Therefore, a is in $Th_\Psi^{\Psi}(A \cup Th_\Psi^{\Sigma'}(A'))$. □

Proposition 9. *In the context of Definition 8, if* $(\Phi' \cup \Sigma, \Sigma', A')$ *is conservative then*

1. $[\![M@(\Phi', \Sigma', A')]\!]_1 = [\![M@(\Phi', \Sigma', A')]\!]_2$,
2. $M@(\Phi', \Sigma', A')$ *is conservative if* $(\Phi', \Phi' \cup \Sigma, A \cup \mathit{Vth}(\Phi' \cup \Sigma, \Sigma', A'))$ *is conservative.*

Proof: Replacing Ψ by $\Phi' \cup \Sigma$ and then taking the Φ'-visible theorems of the two sides in the equality given by Lemma 2, we get $\mathit{Th}_{\Phi'}^{\Sigma'}(A \cup A') = \mathit{Th}_{\Phi'}^{\Phi' \cup \Sigma}(A \cup \mathit{Th}_{\Phi' \cup \Sigma}^{\Sigma'}(A'))$. Equation 1. now follows from the calculation

$$\begin{aligned} [\![M@(\Phi', \Sigma', A')]\!]_1 &= \mathit{Vth}(\Phi', \Sigma', A \cup A') \\ &= \mathit{Th}_{\Phi'}^{\Sigma'}(A \cup A') \\ &= \mathit{Th}_{\Phi'}^{\Phi' \cup \Sigma}(A \cup \mathit{Th}_{\Phi \cup \Sigma}^{\Sigma'}(A')) \\ &= \mathit{Vth}(\Phi', \Phi' \cup \Sigma, A \cup \mathit{Vth}(\Phi' \cup \Sigma, \Sigma', A')) \\ &= [\![M@(\Phi', \Sigma', A')]\!]_2 \ . \end{aligned}$$

For 2., let m be a Φ'-model of $\mathit{Vth}(M@(\Phi', \Sigma', A'))$. Then by Proposition 4, m is also a Φ'-model of $\mathit{Vth}(\Phi', \Phi' \cup \Sigma, A \cup \mathit{Vth}(\Phi' \cup \Sigma, \Sigma', A'))$ and so by conservativity, there is a $(\Phi' \cup \Sigma)$-model m'' of $A \cup \mathit{Vth}(\Phi' \cup \Sigma, \Sigma', A')$ such that $m''{\restriction_{\Phi'}} = m$. Now, since $(\Phi' \cup \Sigma, \Sigma', A')$ is conservative, there is a Σ'-model m' of A' such that $m'{\restriction_{\Phi' \cup \Sigma}} = m''$. By the Satisfaction Condition, $m' \models_{\Sigma'} A$, so that $m' \models_{\Sigma'} A \cup A'$ and, of course, $m'{\restriction_{\Phi'}} = m$. □

One can enrich an imported module with essentially anything, including inconsistent sentences. But an important special case is when no new visible symbols are added. This is useful when refining an incomplete module that declares an interface, or when one wants to further constrain an existing module in order to change its intended semantics (for example, adding the equation $10 = 0$ to the module that specifies integers to get integers modulo 10).

Corollary 2. *If* $M' = (\Sigma, \Sigma', A')$ *is a conservative module, then*

1. $\mathit{Vth}(M@(\Phi, \Sigma', A')) = \mathit{Vth}(\Phi, \Sigma, A \cup \mathit{Vth}(M'))$, *and*
2. $M@(\Phi, \Sigma', A')$ *is conservative if* $(\Phi, \Sigma, A \cup \mathit{Vth}(M'))$ *is conservative.*

Proof: This follows by Proposition 9, replacing Φ' by Φ. □

Technically, enriching is a special case of aggregation in our approach, because $M@(\Phi', \Sigma', A') = M + (\Phi', \Sigma', A')$. However, the results that were developed for aggregation assumed that the aggregated modules did not have common private symbols, which fails for enrichment, where all the private symbols of the enriched module are available.

5.4 Hiding

Hiding information is very natural in our approach; it just restricts visibility to a deeper subsignature.

Definition 9. *If $M = (\Phi, \Sigma, A)$ is a module and Ψ is a subsignature of Φ, then $\Psi \Box M$ is the module (Ψ, Σ, A); also $[\![\Psi \Box M]\!]_1 = Vth(\Psi, \Sigma, A)$, and $[\![\Psi \Box M]\!]_2 = (\Psi, \Phi, Vth(M))$. We call $\Box$ the* **information hiding operator**.

Fewer theorems remain visible after an information hiding operation. The term "export operator" is used for $\Box$ in [2], but we prefer the more explicit term, after [15]; this operation is essentially the same as the "derive" operation of Clear [7]. If $\imath \colon \Psi \hookrightarrow \Phi$, then $\imath \colon \Psi \Box M \to M$ is a module morphism, so $m \models M$ implies $m\restriction_{\Psi} \models \Psi \Box M$ for any Φ-model m. The following shows the relationship between the visible theorems of $\Psi \Box M$ and the visible theorems of M, that is, a relationship between the two semantics, and it also gives a sufficient condition under which hiding preserves conservativity.

Proposition 10. *If $M = (\Phi, \Sigma, A)$ is a module and $\Psi \hookrightarrow \Phi$ is a signature inclusion, then*

1. *$[\![\Psi \Box M]\!]_1 = [\![\Psi \Box M]\!]_2$ and*
2. *$\Psi \Box M$ is conservative if M and $(\Psi, \Phi, Vth(M))$ are conservative.*

Proof: 1. is equivalent to $Th^{\Sigma}_{\Psi}(A)) = Th^{\Phi}_{\Psi}(Th^{\Sigma}_{\Phi}(A))$, which is 10. of Proposition 4. For 2., let m be a Ψ-model of $Th^{\Sigma}_{\Psi}(A))$. Since $Th^{\Sigma}_{\Psi}(A)) = Th^{\Phi}_{\Psi}(Th^{\Sigma}_{\Phi}(A))$, by the conservativity of $(\Psi, \Phi, Th^{\Sigma}_{\Phi}(A))$, there is a Φ-model m' of $Th^{\Phi}_{\Phi}(Th^{\Sigma}_{\Phi}(A)) = Th^{\Sigma}_{\Phi}(A)$ such that $m'\restriction_{\Psi} = m$. Then by the conservativity of (Φ, Σ, A) there is a Σ-model m'' of $Th^{\Sigma}_{\Sigma}(A)$ with $m''\restriction_{\Phi} = m'$. Therefore $m''\restriction_{\Psi} = m$, and so (Φ, Σ, A) is conservative. $\Box$

Although conservativity is not needed to show equivalence of the two semantics for hiding, it is needed for equivalence of the semantics for the other operations. This is why we always give sufficient conditions for conservativity of resulting modules. Notice that conservativity of M does not guarantee conservativity of $\Psi \Box M$: for example, for M a transparent module (which is automatically conservative) and Ψ such that $\Psi \Box M$ is not conservative, as in Example 4.

Testing conservativity of a module (Ψ, Σ, A) can be difficult, and depends on the underlying logic. In many sorted equational logics, one can enrich a Ψ-algebra with new carriers for private sorts (in $\Sigma - \Psi$), and with new private operations, and then show that the new Σ-algebra satisfies A. Of course, the fewer private symbols, the easier this is. For this reason, we prefer to reduce showing the conservativity of a module with visible signature Ψ and working signature Σ, to the conservativity of other two modules: one with visible signature Ψ and working signature Φ, for $\Psi \hookrightarrow \Phi \hookrightarrow \Sigma$, and the other with visible signature Φ and working signature Σ, as in the above proposition.

5.5 Parameterization

One of the most effective supports for software reuse is parameterization. Many expositions only treat the one parameter case, saying that it generalizes to many parameters in an obvious way. Since one of our goals is conditions for the correctness of logic-independent algorithms to flatten complex module structures, and since shared features of parameters are important in this, we treat multiple parameterization explicitly, and prove that it is a colimit.

Definition 10. *A* **parameterized module** $M[\alpha_1 :: P_1, ..., \alpha_n :: P_n]$ *is a set of module morphisms* $\alpha_j; \imath_j : P_j \to M$*, where* $M = (\Phi, \Sigma, A)$ *and* $P_j = (\Phi'_j, \Sigma'_j, B_j)$ *for* $j = 1, ..., n$*, such that:*

1. $\alpha_j : \Phi'_j \to \Phi_j$ *are isomorphisms of signatures,*
2. $\imath_j : \Phi_j \hookrightarrow \Phi$ *are inclusions of signatures, and*
3. $\Phi_1, ..., \Phi_n$ *are disjoint.*

We say that M *is* **parameterized** *by* $\alpha_1, ..., \alpha_n$. $P_1, ..., P_n$ *are called the* **interfaces** *and* M *the* **body**. *Given a parameterized module* $M[\alpha_1 :: P_1, ..., \alpha_n :: P_n]$ *and morphisms* $h_j : P_j \to M_j$ *with* $M_j = (\Psi_j, \Omega_j, A_j)$ *for* $j = 1, ..., n$*, the* **instantiation of** M **by** $h_1, ..., h_n$*, written* $M[h_1, ..., h_n]$*, is the module*

$$(\Phi_h,\ \Sigma_{(h_\Phi)} \cup \bigcup_{j=1}^{n} \Omega_j,\ (h_\Phi)_\Sigma(A) \cup \bigcup_{j=1}^{n} A_j)\ ,$$

where $h = \bigcup_{j=1}^{n} \alpha_j^{-1}; h_j$ *(see Section 2.2 and Convention 1).*

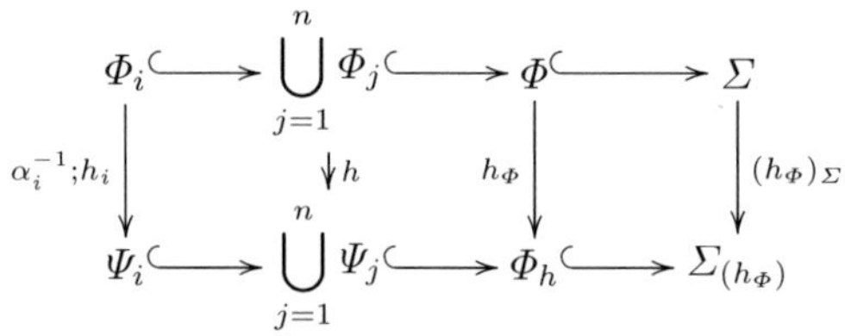

$$\begin{array}{ccccccc}
\Phi_i & \hookrightarrow & \bigcup_{j=1}^{n} \Phi_j & \hookrightarrow & \Phi & \hookrightarrow & \Sigma \\
\downarrow{\scriptstyle \alpha_i^{-1};h_i} & & \downarrow{\scriptstyle h} & & \downarrow{\scriptstyle h_\Phi} & & \downarrow{\scriptstyle (h_\Phi)_\Sigma} \\
\Psi_i & \hookrightarrow & \bigcup_{j=1}^{n} \Psi_j & \hookrightarrow & \Phi_h & \hookrightarrow & \Sigma_{(h_\Phi)}
\end{array}$$

This complex looking definition has a natural interpretation. First, it says that parameters have disjoint interface signatures in the parameterized module; this condition, called *non-shared parameterization* in CafeOBJ [14], avoids obvious name clashes, and is easily achieved in practice by tagging parameter signatures with their parameter names. Second, informally speaking, it says that the instantiation of a module is computed as follows:

1. Calculate $\alpha_i^{-1}; h_i$, which gives for each symbol in M belonging to a parameter P_i its actual instance symbol;
2. store all these mappings in a table h;
3. Calculate h's pushout h_Φ, which "knows" how to avoid name clashes between visible symbols defined in M and visible symbols that may accidentally occur in some of the actual parameters;
4. Calculate h_Φ's pushout $(h_\Phi)_\Sigma$, which solves further name conflicts with M's private symbols; and
5. Rename all sentences declared in M accordingly.

Notice that all these steps are purely textual and can be efficiently implemented.

Proposition 11. *In the context of Definition 10,*

1. $h_\Phi : M \to M[h_1, ..., h_n]$ *is a module morphism,*
2. $\bigcup_{j=1}^{n} \Psi_j \hookrightarrow \Phi_h : M_1 + \cdots + M_n \to M[h_1, ..., h_n]$ *is also a morphism, and*
3. $M[h_1, ..., h_n] = M \star h_\Phi + M_1 + \cdots + M_n$.

Proof: For 1., $h_\varphi : M \to M[h_1, ..., h_n]$ is a morphism because:

$$\begin{aligned} h_\Phi(Vth(M)) &= h_\Phi(Th^{\Sigma}_{\Phi}(A)) \\ &\subseteq Th^{\Sigma_{(h_\Phi)}}_{\Phi_h}((h_\Phi)_\Sigma(A)) & \text{(Lemma 1)} \\ &\subseteq Th^{\Sigma_{(h_\Phi)} \cup \bigcup_{j=1}^n \Omega_j}_{\Phi_h}((h_\Phi)_\Sigma(A) \cup \bigcup_{j=1}^n A_j) & \text{(Proposition 4)} \\ &= Vth(M[h_1, ..., h_n]) \ . \end{aligned}$$

2. is straightforward, because by Proposition 4,

$$Th^{\bigcup_{j=1}^n \Omega_j}_{\bigcup_{j=1}^n \Psi_j}(\bigcup_{j=1}^{n} A_j) \subseteq Th^{\Sigma_{(h_\Phi)} \cup \bigcup_{j=1}^n \Omega_j}_{\Phi_h}((h_\Phi)_\Sigma(A) \cup \bigcup_{j=1}^{n} A_j) \ .$$

3. follows from the equalities

$$\begin{aligned} & M \star h_\Phi + M_1 + \cdots + M_n \\ &= (\Phi, \Sigma, A) \star h_\Phi + (\Psi_1, \Omega_1, A_1) + \cdots + (\Psi_n, \Omega_n, A_n) \\ &= (\Phi_h, \Sigma_{(h_\Phi)}, (h_\Phi)_\Sigma(A)) + (\Psi_1, \Omega_1, A_1) + \cdots + (\Psi_n, \Omega_n, A_n) & \text{(Def. 7)} \\ &= (\Phi_h \cup \bigcup_{j=1}^n \Psi_j, \Sigma_{(h_\Phi)} \cup \bigcup_{j=1}^n \Omega_j, (h_\Phi)_\Sigma(A) \cup \bigcup_{j=1}^n A_j) & \text{(Def. 6)} \\ &= (\Phi_h, \Sigma_{(h_\Phi)} \cup \bigcup_{j=1}^n \Omega_j, (h_\Phi)_\Sigma(A) \cup \bigcup_{j=1}^n A_j) \\ &= M[h_1, ..., h_n] \ , & \text{(Def. 10)} \end{aligned}$$

using Proposition 4. □

This proposition suggests the following for the two semantics of instantiating a parameterized module:

Definition 11. *Using the same context and notation as in Definition 10, let* $[\![M[h_1, ..., h_n]]\!]_1 = Vth(\Phi_h, \Sigma_{(h_\Phi)} \cup \bigcup_{j=1}^n \Omega_j, (h_\Phi)_\Sigma(A) \cup \bigcup_{j=1}^n A_j)$ *and also let* $[\![M[h_1, ..., h_n]]\!]_2 = (h_\Phi(Vth(M)) \cup \bigcup_{j=1}^n Vth(M_j))^\bullet$*, where closure is over* Φ_h.

The following gives sufficient and necessary conditions under which the two semantics for the result module coincide, and shows that conservativity of the result module does not depend on conservativity of its original interface:

Proposition 12. *In the context of Definition 10, if the given institution is distributive and if*

1. $M, M_1, ..., M_n$ *are conservative,*
2. $\Sigma_{(h_\Phi)} \cap \Omega_j = \Psi_j$ *for* $j = 1, ..., n$*, and*
3. $\Omega_i \cap \Omega_j = \Psi_i \cap \Psi_j$ *for* $i, j = 1, ..., n$*, with* $M_i \neq M_j$*,*

then

1. $[\![M[h_1, ..., h_n]]\!]_1 = [\![M[h_1, ..., h_n]]\!]_2$,
2. $m \models M[h_1, ..., h_n]$ *iff* $m\restriction_{h_\Phi} \models M$ *and* $m\restriction_{\Phi_j} \models M_j$ *for any* Φ_h*-model* m*,*
3. $M[h_1, ..., h_n]$ *is conservative.*

Proof: By Propositions 11 and 7, $Vth(M \star h_\Phi) = h_\Phi(Vth(M))^\bullet$ and $M \star h_\Phi$ is conservative, where the closure is over Φ_h-sentences. Since $M[h_1, ..., h_n] = M \star h_\Phi + M_1 + \cdots + M_n$, iteratively applying Propositions 11 and 6 we get that $Vth(M[h_1, ..., h_n]) = (h_\Phi(Vth(M))^\bullet \cup \bigcup_{j=1}^n Vth(M_j))^\bullet$ and $M[h_1, ..., h_n]$ is conservative, where the closures are over Φ_h-sentences. □

The conservativity of $M, M_1, ..., M_n$ and the equalities $\Omega_i \cap \Omega_j = \Psi_i \cap \Psi_j$ are needed because of 3. in Proposition 11 and because of their necessity in Propositions 6 and 7. The condition $\Sigma_{(h_\Phi)} \cap \Omega_j = \Psi_j$ may look restrictive, but in practice it is not, since informally, it says that an implementation should either rename some private symbols in M in the instantiated module to avoid conflicts with private symbols in M_j, or else rename some symbols in M_j before the instantiation is done. This assumption is needed because Proposition 6 requires that the modules involved in a sum have pairwise disjoint private symbols; condition 2. concerns the pairs involving the module $M \star h_\Phi$, while condition 3. concerns the remaining pairs.

An important general property of parameterization is that the instantiated module is a colimit. This can be proved in a logic independent framework for modules which respect the above natural requirements:

Theorem 2. *In the context of Proposition 12, if S_{ij} are $(\Psi_i \cap \Psi_j)$-modules*[8] *such that $Vth(S_{ij}) \subseteq Vth(M_i) \cap Vth(M_j)$, then $M[h_1, ..., h_n]$ is a colimit of*

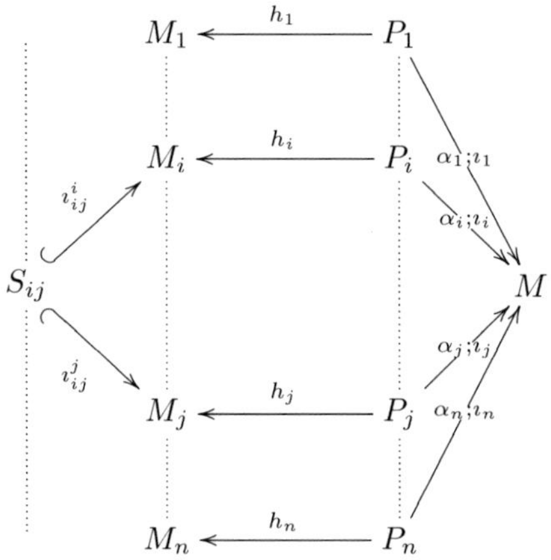

where $\imath^i_{ij}$ is the inclusion $\Psi_i \cap \Psi_j \hookrightarrow \Psi_i$, for $i, j = 1, ..., n$.

Proof: Notice that $\imath^i_{ij} \colon S_{ij} \to M_i$ are module morphisms, and that giving a cocone of the diagram above is equivalent to giving a module C, a morphism $f \colon M \to C$, and morphisms $g_j \colon M_j \to C$ such that

1. $h_i; g_i = \alpha_i; \imath_i; f$ for $i = 1, ..., n$, and
2. $\imath^i_{ij}; g_i = \imath^j_{ij}; g_j$ for $i, j = 1, ..., n$.

The diagram below may help the reader follow the rest of this proof.

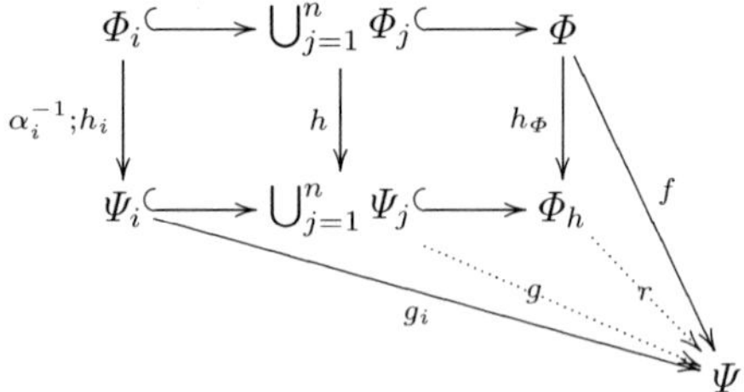

[8] Think of S_{ij} as the shared modules of M_i and M_j.

First we show that $h_\Phi\colon M \to M[h_1,...,h_n]$ with $\Psi_i \hookrightarrow \Phi_h\colon M_i \to M[h_1,...,h_n]$ for $i = 1,...,n$ is a cocone:

$$\begin{aligned}
h_i;(\Psi_i \hookrightarrow \Phi_h) &= (\alpha_i;\alpha_i^{-1});h_i;((\Psi_i \hookrightarrow \textstyle\bigcup_{j=1}^n \Psi_j);(\bigcup_{j=1}^n \Psi_j \hookrightarrow \Phi_h))\\
&= \alpha_i;((\alpha_i^{-1};h_i);(\Psi_i \hookrightarrow \textstyle\bigcup_{j=1}^n \Psi_j));(\bigcup_{j=1}^n \Psi_j \hookrightarrow \Phi_h)\\
&= \alpha_i;((\Phi_i \hookrightarrow \textstyle\bigcup_{j=1}^n \Phi_j);h);(\bigcup_{j=1}^n \Psi_j \hookrightarrow \Phi_h)\\
&= \alpha_i;(\Phi_i \hookrightarrow \textstyle\bigcup_{j=1}^n \Phi_j);(h;(\bigcup_{j=1}^n \Psi_j \hookrightarrow \Phi_h))\\
&= \alpha_i;(\Phi_i \hookrightarrow \textstyle\bigcup_{j=1}^n \Phi_j);((\bigcup_{j=1}^n \Phi_j \hookrightarrow \Phi);h_\Phi)\\
&= \alpha_i;((\Phi_i \hookrightarrow \textstyle\bigcup_{j=1}^n \Phi_j);(\bigcup_{j=1}^n \Phi_j \hookrightarrow \Phi));h_\Phi\\
&= \alpha_i;\imath_i;h_\Phi\ .
\end{aligned}$$

Also, it is straightforward that $\imath_{ij}^i;(\Psi_i \hookrightarrow \Phi_h) = \imath_{ij}^j;(\Psi_j \hookrightarrow \Phi_h)$, because there is only one inclusion $\Psi_i \cap \Psi_j \hookrightarrow \Phi_h$.

Now let $f\colon M \to C$ and $g_i\colon M_i \to C$ for $i = 1,...,n$ be another cocone, with $C = (\Psi,\Omega,B)$. Then Ψ with the signature morphisms $g_i\colon \Psi_i \to \Psi$ for $i = 1,...,n$ form a cocone in **Sign** for the diagram given by the pairs of inclusions

$$\Psi_i \hookleftarrow \Psi_i \cap \Psi_j \hookrightarrow \Psi_j$$

for $i,j = 1,...,n$, so by 2. of Proposition 1, there is a unique signature morphism, let us call it $g\colon \bigcup_{j=1}^n \Psi_j \to \Psi$, such that $(\Psi_i \hookrightarrow \bigcup_{j=1}^n \Psi_j);g = g_i$. Since

$$\begin{aligned}
(\Phi_i \hookrightarrow \textstyle\bigcup_{j=1}^n \Phi_j);((\bigcup_{j=1}^n \Phi_j \hookrightarrow \Phi);f) &= ((\Phi_i \hookrightarrow \textstyle\bigcup_{j=1}^n \Phi_j);(\bigcup_{j=1}^n \Phi_j \hookrightarrow \Phi));f\\
&= \imath_i;f\\
&= (\alpha_i^{-1};\alpha_i);\imath_i;f\\
&= \alpha_i^{-1};(\alpha_i;\imath_i;f)\\
&= \alpha_i^{-1};(h_i;g_i)\\
&= (\alpha_i^{-1};h_i);g_i\\
&= (\alpha_i^{-1};h_i);((\Psi_i \hookrightarrow \textstyle\bigcup_{j=1}^n \Psi_j);g)\\
&= ((\alpha_i^{-1};h_i);(\Psi_i \hookrightarrow \textstyle\bigcup_{j=1}^n \Psi_j));g\\
&= ((\Phi_i \hookrightarrow \textstyle\bigcup_{j=1}^n \Phi_j);h);g\\
&= (\Phi_i \hookrightarrow \textstyle\bigcup_{j=1}^n \Phi_j);(h;g)\ ,
\end{aligned}$$

by 1. of Proposition 1, we get $(\bigcup_{j=1}^n \Phi_j \hookrightarrow \Phi);f = h;g$. But the rightmost square in the diagram at the beginning of this proof is a pushout, so there is a unique $r\colon \Phi_h \to \Psi$ such that $h_\Phi;r = f$ and $(\bigcup_{j=1}^n \Psi_j \hookrightarrow \Phi_h);r = g$.

We claim that r is a module morphism, from $M[h_1,...,h_n]$ to C. Indeed,

$$\begin{aligned}
r(Vth(M[h_1,...,h_n])) &= r((h_\Phi(Vth(M)) \cup \textstyle\bigcup_{j=1}^n Vth(M_j))^\bullet)\\
&\subseteq r(h_\Phi(Vth(M)) \cup \textstyle\bigcup_{j=1}^n Vth(M_j))^\bullet\\
&= (r(h_\Phi(Vth(M))) \cup \textstyle\bigcup_{j=1}^n r(Vth(M_j)))^\bullet\\
&= (f(Vth(M)) \cup \textstyle\bigcup_{j=1}^n g_j(Vth(M_j)))^\bullet\\
&\subseteq Vth(C)^\bullet\\
&= Vth(C)\ .
\end{aligned}$$

The first line above follows by 1. of Proposition 12, and the second by the Closure Lemma. The uniqueness of $r\colon M[h_1,...,h_n] \to C$ follows from the uniqueness of $r\colon \Phi_h \to \Phi$ as a signature morphism. Let $r'\colon M[h_1,...,h_n] \to C$ be another morphism such that $h_\Phi; r' = f$ and $(\Psi_i \hookrightarrow \Phi_h); r' = g_i$ for $i = 1, ..., n$. Since the inclusions $\Psi_i \hookrightarrow \bigcup_{j=1}^n \Psi_j$ are an epimorphic family and

$$\begin{aligned}(\Psi_i \hookrightarrow \textstyle\bigcup_{j=1}^n \Psi_j);((\bigcup_{j=1}^n \Psi_j \hookrightarrow \Phi_h); r') &= ((\Psi_i \hookrightarrow \textstyle\bigcup_{j=1}^n \Psi_j);(\bigcup_{j=1}^n \Psi_j \hookrightarrow \Phi_h)); r' \\ &= (\Psi_i \hookrightarrow \Phi_h); r' \\ &= g_i \\ &= (\Psi_i \hookrightarrow \textstyle\bigcup_{j=1}^n \Psi_j); g\ ,\end{aligned}$$

by 1. of Proposition 1, $(\bigcup_{j=1}^n \Psi_j \hookrightarrow \Phi_h); r' = g$. By the uniqueness of $r\colon \Phi_h \to \Psi$ with $h_\Phi; r = f$ and $(\bigcup_{j=1}^n \Psi_j \hookrightarrow \Phi_h); r = g$, it follows that $r' = r$. □

Many practical modules have just one parameter, in which case sharing between actual parameters is not a problem, and a simpler result can be stated:

Corollary 3. *In the context of Proposition 12, if* $M[\alpha_1 :: P_1]$ *is a parameterized module and if* $h_1\colon P_1 \to M_1$ *is a module morphism, then the square*

$$\begin{array}{ccc} P_1 & \xrightarrow{\alpha_1;\imath_1} & M \\ {\scriptstyle h_1}\downarrow & & \downarrow{\scriptstyle h_\Phi} \\ M_1 & \xrightarrow[\imath]{} & M[h_1] \end{array}$$

is a pushout in **MSpec**, *where* $h = \alpha^{-1}; h_1$ *and* $\imath\colon \Psi_1 \hookrightarrow \Phi_h$.

Proof: By Theorem 2 with $S_{11} = M_1$. □

6 Conclusions and Future Research

This paper studies the composition of modules that can hide information, over inclusive institutions, a class which appears to include all logical systems of practical interest. Two different semantics for composed modules were defined, and it was shown that they agree if all the modules involved are conservative. In addition, a number of basic "laws of software composition" were proved; these assert that two different module compositions have the same semantics, for all instances of their variables that range over modules. An important conclusion is that inclusive institutions can greatly simplify the kind of proofs done in this paper. This setting also allows algorithms for flattening compositions to be presented as mainly based on signatures pushouts, which is a purely textual operation for concrete institutions. In addition, we have given a brief institutional explanation for why our approach applies to programs as well as to specifications.

In addition to the applications discussed in the introduction to powerful module systems for programming and specification languages, and its emerging applications to database and meta-data integration, the ideas of parameterized programming, as refined and extended in this paper, seem promising for many other areas involving knowledge representation, as was already suggested in the original paper on Clear [7]. Examples of such promising areas include the semantic web [16], ontologies for scientific research, cognitive linguistics [17], and business workflow models.

Some interesting directions for future theoretical research include the following: extend the results of this paper to a multi-institutional framework (e.g., see [13,41]) to accommodate multi-paradigm specification languages; prove further laws, such as distributivity (see [2,15]); and adapt the normalization theorem of [2] to our setting. It would also be interesting to develop an algorithm for pushouts of the usual signatures, that is closed under horizontal and/or vertical composition in the sense of Convention 1; an implementation (e.g., in Perl) of the composition operations using this algorithm could be useful for a wide range of applications.

Acknowledgements. The authors thank Virgil Emil Căzănescu for his ongoing collaboration on inclusion systems, and Răzvan Diaconescu for stimulating debates on institution-based modularization.

Dedication. This paper is dedicated to Ole-Johan Dahl, a gentleman of the old school, and a pioneer in language design, whose work always exhibited the good taste and elegance of its author. He will be sorely missed.

References

1. Suad Alagic and Philip Bernstein. A model theory for generic schema management. In Giorgio Ghelli and Gösta Grahne, editors, *Proceedings, Database Programming Languages 2001*, pages 228–246. Springer, 2002. Lecture Notes in Computer Science, volume 2397.
2. Jan Bergstra, Jan Heering, and Paul Klint. Module algebra. *Journal of the Association for Computing Machinery*, 37(2):335–372, 1990.
3. Jan Bergstra and John Tucker. Equational specifications, complete term rewriting systems, and computable and semicomputable algebras. *Journal of the Association for Computing Machinery*, 42(6):1194–1230, 1995.
4. Philip Bernstein. Applying model management to classical meta data problems. In *Proceedings, Conf. on Innovative Database Research*, pages 209–220, 2003.
5. Michel Bidoit and Rolf Hennicker. Constructor-based observational logic. Technical Report LSV–03–9, Laboratoire Spcification et Verification, CNRS de Cachan, March 2003.
6. Tomasz Borzyszkowski. Completeness of a logical system for structured specifications (wadr'97). In Francesco Parisi Presicce, editor, *Recent Trends in Algebraic Development Techniques*, pages 107–121. Springer, 1997. Notes in Theoretical Computer Science, volume 1376.
7. Rod Burstall and Joseph Goguen. Putting theories together to make specifications. In Raj Reddy, editor, *Proceedings, Fifth International Joint Conference on Artificial Intelligence*, pages 1045–1058. Department of Computer Science, Carnegie-Mellon University, 1977.
8. María Victoria Cengarle and Martin Wirsing. A calculus of higher order parameterization for algebraic specification. *Bulletin of the Interest Group in Pure and Applied Logics*, 3(4):615–641, 1995.
9. CoFI. CASL summary, 2002. `www.cofi.info`.
10. Virgil Emil Căzănescu and Grigore Roşu. Weak inclusion systems. *Mathematical Structures in Computer Science*, 7(2):195–206, 1997.

11. Virgil Emil Căzănescu and Grigore Roşu. Weak inclusion systems; part 2. *Journal of Universal Computer Science*, 6(1):5–21, 2000.
12. Răzvan Diaconescu. Category-based modularization for equational logic programming. *Acta Informatica*, 33(5):477–510, 1996.
13. Răzvan Diaconescu. Extra theory morphisms in institutions: logical semantics for multi-paradigm languages. *Applied Categorical Structures*, 6(4):427–453, 1998.
14. Răzvan Diaconescu and Kokichi Futatsugi. *CafeOBJ Report: The Language, Proof Techniques, and Methodologies for Object-Oriented Algebraic Specification.* World Scientific, 1998. AMAST Series in Computing, volume 6.
15. Răzvan Diaconescu, Joseph Goguen, and Petros Stefaneas. Logical support for modularization. In Gerard Huet and Gordon Plotkin, editors, *Logical Environments*, pages 83–130. Cambridge, 1993.
16. Tim Berners-Lee *et al.* Semantic web, 2003. `www.w3.org/sw/`.
17. Gilles Fauconnier and Mark Turner. *The Way We Think.* Basic, 2002.
18. Joseph Goguen. Parameterized programming. *Transactions on Software Engineering*, SE–10(5):528–543, September 1984.
19. Joseph Goguen. Principles of parameterized programming. In Ted Biggerstaff and Alan Perlis, editors, *Software Reusability, Volume I: Concepts and Models*, pages 159–225. Addison Wesley, 1989.
20. Joseph Goguen. Types as theories. In George Michael Reed, Andrew William Roscoe, and Ralph F. Wachter, editors, *Topology and Category Theory in Computer Science*, pages 357–390. Oxford, 1991. Proceedings of a Conference held at Oxford, June 1989.
21. Joseph Goguen and Rod Burstall. Institutions: Abstract model theory for specification and programming. *Journal of the Association for Computing Machinery*, 39(1):95–146, January 1992.
22. Joseph Goguen and Grant Malcolm. A hidden agenda. *Theoretical Computer Science*, 245(1):55–101, August 2000.
23. Joseph Goguen and Grigore Roşu. Hiding more of hidden algebra. In *Formal Methods 1999 (FM'99)*, volume 1709 of *Lecture Notes in Computer Sciences*, pages 1704–1719. Springer-Verlag, 1999.
24. Joseph Goguen and Grigore Roşu. Institution morphisms. *Formal Aspects of Computing*, 13:274–307, 2002.
25. Joseph Goguen, Grigore Roşu, and Kai Lin. Conditional circular coinductive rewriting. In *Recent Trends in Algebraic Development Techniques, 16th International Workshop, WADT'02.* Springer, Lecture Notes in Computer Science, to appear 2003. Selected papers from a workshop held in Frauenchiemsee, Germany, 24–27 October 2002.
26. Joseph Goguen and William Tracz. An implementation-oriented semantics for module composition. In Gary Leavens and Murali Sitaraman, editors, *Foundations of Component-based Systems*, pages 231–263. Cambridge, 2000.
27. Joseph Goguen, Timothy Winkler, José Meseguer, Kokichi Futatsugi, and Jean-Pierre Jouannaud. Introducing OBJ. In Joseph Goguen and Grant Malcolm, editors, *Software Engineering with OBJ: algebraic specification in action*, pages 3–167. Kluwer, 2000.
28. Rolf Hennicker. Context induction: a proof principle for behavioral abstractions. *Formal Aspects of Computing*, 3(4):326–345, 1991.
29. Horst Herrlich and George Strecker. *Category Theory.* Allyn and Bacon, 1973.
30. Kestrel Institute. SpecWare language manual, version 4.0, 2003. `www.specware.org/doc.html`.

31. Saunders Mac Lane. *Categories for the Working Mathematician.* Springer, 1971.
32. José Meseguer and Joseph Goguen. Initiality, induction and computability. In Maurice Nivat and John Reynolds, editors, *Algebraic Methods in Semantics*, pages 459–541. Cambridge, 1985.
33. Till Mossakowski. Specifications in an arbitrary institution with symbols. In *Proceedings, WADT'99*, volume 1827 of *Lecture Notes in Computer Science*, pages 252–270. Springer, 2000.
34. David Parnas. Information distribution aspects of design methodology. *Information Processing '72*, 71:339–344, 1972. Proceedings of 1972 IFIP Congress.
35. Grigore Roşu. *Hidden Logic.* PhD thesis, University of California at San Diego, 2000. `http://ase.arc.nasa.gov/grosu/phd-thesis.ps`.
36. Grigore Roşu. Inductive behavioral proofs by unhiding. In *Proceedings of Coalgebraic Methods in Computer Science (CMCS'03)*, volume 82 of *Electronic Notes in Theoretical Computer Science.* Elsevier Science, 2003.
37. Grigore Roşu. Abstract semantics for module composition. Technical Report CSE2000–0653, University of California at San Diego, May 2000.
38. Grigore Roşu and Joseph Goguen. Hidden congruent deduction. In Ricardo Caferra and Gernot Salzer, editors, *Automated Deduction in Classical and Non-Classical Logics*, volume 1761 of *Lecture Notes in Artificial Intelligence*, pages 252–267. Springer, 2000. Papers from First Order Theorem Proving '98 (FTP'98).
39. Donald Sannella, Stefan Sokolowski, and Andrzej Tarlecki. Toward formal development of programs from algebraic specifications: parameterisation revisited. *Acta Informatica*, 29:689–736, 1992.
40. Donald Sannella and Andrzej Tarlecki. Specifications in an arbitrary institution. *Information and Control*, 76:165–210, 1988.
41. Andrzej Tarlecki. Moving between logical systems. In Magne Haveraaen, Olaf Owe, and Ole-Johan Dahl, editors, *Recent Trends in Data Type Specification*, volume 1130 of *Lecture Notes in Computer Science*, pages 478–502. Springer, 1996.
42. William Tracz. LILEANNA: a parameterized programming language. In *Proceedings, Second International Workshop on Software Reuse*, pages 66–78, March 1993. Lucca, Italy.

Towards the Verifying Compiler

Tony Hoare

Microsoft Research Ltd.
Cambridge
UK

Abstract. A verifying compiler is one that proves mechanically that a program is correct before allowing it to be run. Correctness of a program is defined by placing assertions at strategic points in the program text, particularly at the interfaces between its components. From recent enquiries among software developers at Microsoft, I have discovered that assertions are already used widely in program development practice. Their main rôle is as test oracles, to detect programming errors as close as possible to their place of occurrence. Further progress in reliable software engineering is currently supported by programmer productivity tools. I conjecture that these will be developed to exploit assertions of various kinds in various ways at all stages in program development. Eventually assertions will be used more widely for their original purpose of establishing important aspects of the correctness of large programs. However, the construction of a fully verifying compiler remains as a long-term challenge for twenty-first century Computing Science.

1 Historical Introduction

An assertion in its most familiar form is a Boolean expression that is written as an executable statement at any point in the program text. It can in principle or in practice be evaluated by the computer, whenever control reaches that point in the program. If an assertion ever evaluates to false, the program is by definition incorrect. But if all assertions always evaluate to true, then at least no program defect has ever been detected. But best of all, if it can be proved that the assertion will always evaluate to true on every possible execution, then the program is certainly correct, at least insofar as correctness has been captured by the assertions embedded in it. The construction and validation of such proofs are the goal of the verifying compiler.

An understanding of the rôle of assertions in Checking a Large Routine [Turing] goes back to Alan Turing in 1949. The idea of a verifying compiler, which uses automatic theorem proving to guarantee the correctness of the assertions, goes back to Bob Floyd [Floyd]. And the idea of writing the assertions even before writing the program was propounded in 1968 by Edsger Dijkstra in an article on a Constructive Approach to the Problem of Program Correctness [Dijkstra]. Dijkstra's insight has been the inspiration of much of the research in formal methods of software engineering conducted in University Computing Departments over the last thirty years.

O. Owe et al. (Eds.): From OO to FM (Dahl Festschrift), LNCS 2635, pp. 124–136, 2004.

Ole-Johan Dahl has made many contributions to research on program correctness. He began by extending program correctness reasoning to semicoroutines [Dahl1], a disciplined structure for quasi-parallel programming which had been introduced in Simula. In [Dahl2] he discussed a question that still deserves an answer today: can program proving be made practical? In [Dahl3] and [Dahl4] he began to extend specification and verification technology to object-oriented programming. In [Dahl,Owe] and [Dahl5] he applied formal analytic techniques based on assertions to the design of new programming language features, particularly those that are relevant for reliable exploitation of concurrency. Correctness of concurrent object-oriented programs is of increasing concern in the present day. Finally, a complete treatment of verifiable programming is the topic of his major textbook [Dahl6].

([Dahl5] reports a presentation that Ole-Johan gave at a symposium to mark my retirement from Oxford University in 1999. During his presentation, all the lights in the building went out. He was able to complete his presentation in darkness, maintaining the rapt attention of his audience. None of the subsequent speakers were prepared to match this achievement, so the symposium adjourned until the electricians could restore power.)

Early attempts to implement a verifying compiler were frustrated by the inherent difficulties of mechanical theorem proving. These difficulties have inspired productive research in a number of directions, and with the aid of massive increases in computer power and capacity considerable progress has been made. I suggest that an intensification of cooperative research efforts will result in the emergence of a workable verifying compiler some time in the current century.

A second problem has been that meaningful assertions are notoriously difficult to write. Computers are most widely applied in areas such as commerce and in social interactions, where there is no generally accepted framework of scientific concepts to help in the formulation of specifications and the elucidation of assumptions and preconditions for the successful use of a software service. Much of the code in use today contains very few assertions. Few of the internal interfaces have any sort of formal specification. This means that there is no body of test material against which progress in program verification can be assessed. A third problem has been that the benefits of assertions have been insufficiently recognised to motivate their wider use by programmers. Many graduates of reputable Computing Science degrees never encounter assertions in their entire university education. Assertions are not adequately supported by current programming languages, and they are not widely exploited in current program development environments. But these negative factors are gradually being overcome. In sections 2 and 3, I will present evidence for the increasing rôle of assertions in todays programming practice.

But by far the greatest problem for program verification has always been lack of market demand. For many years, my friends in the software industry have told me that in all surveys of customer requirements the top two priorities have always been firstly an increase in features, and secondly an increase in performance. Reliability takes only the third place. But now it seems that widely available software already provides enough features to satisfy nearly all demands, and widely available hardware already satisfies most demands for performance and capacity. The main remaining obstacle to the full integration of computers into industry and commerce and into the life of society as a whole is a wide-spread and well-justified reluctance to trust the software. A recent email [Gates] by Bill Gates to Microsoft and all its subsidiaries has put trustworthy computing at the head of the policy agenda. This policy has already been put into force by devoting the efforts of the entire Microsoft Windows team during the whole month of February 2002 to a software security drive. Expensive it has been, but not as expensive as some recent viruses like Code Red, which have led to worldwide losses estimated at over a billion dollars. In the long run, it is satisfaction of market demand for software reliability, and reduction in the high cost of program testing, that will motivate adoption of a verifying compiler in normal program development practice.

2 Assertions in Program Testing

In my thirty years as an academic scientist, I pursued the traditional academic ideals of rigour and precision in scientific research. I sought to enlarge our understanding of the theory of programming to show that large-scale programs can be fully specified and proved to be correct with absolute mathematical certainty. I hoped that increased rigour in top-down program development would significantly reduce if not eliminate the burden of program testing and debugging. I would quote with approval the famous dictum of Dijkstra, that program testing can prove the existence of program bugs, but never their absence.

A very similar remark was made by the famous philosopher Karl Popper. His Philosophy of Science is based on the principle of falsification, namely that a scientific theory can never be verified by scientific experiment; it can only be falsified. I accept his view that a scientific advance starts with a theory that has some a priori grounds for credibility, for example, by deduction from the principle that a force has an effect that is inversely proportional to the square of the distance at which it acts. A new theory that applies such a principle to a new phenomenon is subjected to a battery of tests that have been specifically designed, not to support the theory, but rather to refute it. If the theory passes all the tests, it will be used with confidence to help in the formulation and test of further and more advanced theories, and in the design of experiments to refute them.

Extending this analogy to computer software, we can see clearly why program testing is in practice such a good assurance of the reliability of software. A competent programmer always has a prior understanding, perhaps quite intuitive, of the reasons why the program is going to work. If this hypothesis survives a rigorous testing regime, the software has proved itself worthy of delivery to a customer. If a few small changes are needed to correct minor anomalies in the program, they are quickly made — unfortunate perhaps, but that happens to scientific theories too. In Microsoft, every project has assigned to it a team of testers, recruited specially for their skill as experimental scientists; they constitute about a half of the entire program development staff on each project.

This account of the vital rôle of testing in the progress of science is reinforced by consideration of the rôle of test in engineering. In all its branches, rigorous product test is an essential prerequisite before shipping a new or improved product to the customer. For example, in the development of a new aero jet engine, an early working model is installed on an engineering test bench for exhaustive trials. This model engine will first be thoroughly instrumented by insertion of test probes at every accessible internal and external interface. An exhaustive test schedule is designed to exercise the engine at all the extremes of its intended operating range. By continuously checking tolerances at all the crucial internal interfaces, the engineer detects incipient errors immediately, and never needs to test the assembly as a whole to destruction. By continuously striving to improve the set points and tighten the tolerances at each interface, the quality of the whole product can be gradually raised. That is the essence of the six sigma quality improvement philosophy, which has been widely applied in manufacturing industry to increase profits at the same time as customer satisfaction.

In the engineering of software, assertions at the interfaces between modules of the program play the same rôle as test probes in engine design. This analogy with engineering instrumentation suggests that programmers should devote effort to increase in the number and strength of assertions in their code. This will make their system more likely to fail under test; but the reward is that it is subsequently much less likely to fail in the field.

In the three years since I retired from academic life, I have been working in the software industry. This has enabled me to balance the idealism that inspires academic research with the practical compromises that are essential to industrial engineering. In particular, I have radically changed my attitude towards program testing, which I now understand to be entirely complementary to scientific design and verification methods; testing makes an equally essential contribution to the development of reliable software on an industrial scale. It is no accident that program testing exploits the same kind of specifications by assertions that form the basis of program verification.

3 Assertions in Current Microsoft Development Practice

In this section I will describe some of the ways in which I have found that assertions are already exploited by program developers in Microsoft Corporation. I have grounds for believing that many other Companies find them just as useful. Their main use is not for program verification but as a test oracle during the debugging phase of development. The fact that they are useful for many purposes besides verification is encouraging, because it shows that programmers can already be persuaded to annotate their programs with reliable assertions. Indeed, because they are so thoroughly tested every time the program is changed, they are widely regarded as the only reliable form of program documentation.

The defining characteristic of an engineering test probe is that it is removed from the engine before manufacture and delivery to the customer. In computer programs, this effect is achieved by means of a conditionally defined macro. The macro is resolved at compile time in one of two ways, depending on a compile-time switch called `DEBUG`, set for a debugging run, and unset when compiling code that will be shipped to the retail customer. An assertion may be placed anywhere in the middle of executable code by means of this `ASSERT` macro, which is typically declared

```
#ifdef DEBUG
#define ASSERT(b,str)
  if (b)
  else report (str); assert (false)
#else #define ASSERT(b,str)
#endif
```

In addition to their rôle in product test, assertions are widely recommended as a form of program documentation. This is of vital concern to major software suppliers today, because their main development activity is the continuous evolution and improvement of old code to meet new market needs. Even quite trivial assertions, like the following, give added value when the code is modified for a subsequent release of the product.

```
if (a >= b) ... a++ ; ... ;
    ...
ASSERT(a != b, ?a has just been incremented to avoid equality') ;
x = c/(a - b)
```

One development manager in Microsoft recommends that for every bug corrected in test, an assertion should be added to the code which will fire if that bug ever occurs again. Ideally, there should be enough assertions in a program that nearly all bugs are caught by assertion failure, because that is much easier to diagnose than other forms of failure, for example, a crash. Some developers are willing to spend a whole day to design precautions that will avoid a week's work tracing an error that may be introduced later, when the code is modified by a less experienced programmer. Success in such documentation by assertions depends on long experience and careful judgment in predicting the most likely errors a year or more from now. Not everyone can spare the time to do this under pressure of tight delivery schedules. But it is likely that a liberal sprinkling of assertions in the code would increase the accumulated value of legacy, when the time comes to develop a new release of the software.

In the early testing of a prototype program, the developer wants to check out the main paths in the code before dealing with all the exceptional conditions that may occur in practice. In order to document such a development plan, some developers have introduced a variety of assertion which is called a simplifying assumption.

```
SIMPLIFYING_ASSUMPTION
(strlen(input) < MAX_PATH, 'not yet checking for overflow')
```

The assumption documents exactly the cases which the developer is not yet ready to treat, and it also serves as a reminder of what remains to do later. Violation of such assumptions in test will simply cause a test case to be ignored, and should not be treated as an error. Of course, in compiling retail code for delivery to the customer, the debug flag is not set; and then the macro will give rise to a compile-time error; it will not just be ignored like an ordinary assertion. This gives a guarantee against the risk incurred by more informal comments and messages about known bugs and work that is still TO DO; such comments have occasionally and embarrassingly found their way into code shipped by Microsoft.

All the best fault diagnoses are those given at compile time, since that is much cheaper than diagnosis of errors by test. In one product team in Microsoft, a special class of assertion has been implemented called a compile-time check, because its value, true or false, can be computed at compile time.

```
COMPILE_TIME_CHECK (sizeof(x)==sizeof(y),
          'addition is undefined for arrays of different sizes')
```

The compile time error message is generated by a macro that expands to an invalid declaration (negative array bound) in C when the condition evaluates to false; of course, each use of the compile time assertion must be restricted to use only values and functions computable by the compiler. (The compiler will complain if not.) The example above shows a test of conformity of the size of two array parameters for a method. Of course, as we make progress towards a verifying compiler, the aim will be to increase the proportion of assertions whose potential violation will be detected at compile time.

Assertions can help a compiler produce better code. For example, in a C-style case statement, a default clause that cannot be reached can be marked with an `UNREACHABLE` assertion, and a compiler (for example Visual C) avoids emission of unnecessary code for this case.

```
switch (condition)
case 0:  ...   ; break;
case 1:  ...   ; break;
default: UNREACHABLE('condition is really a boolean');
```

In future, perhaps assertions will give further help in optimisation, for example by asserting that pointers or references do not point to the same location. Of course, if such an assertion were false, the effect of the optimisation could be awful. But fortunately assertions which have been frequently tested are remarkably reliable; indeed, they are widely believed to be the only believable form of program documentation. When assertions are automatically proved by a verifying compiler, they will be even more believable.

A global program analysis tool called PREfix [Bush] is now widely used by Microsoft development teams. Like Lint [Johnson], its rôle is to detect program defects at the earliest possible stage, even before the program is compiled.

Typical defects are a NULL pointer reference, an array subscript out of bound, a variable not initialised. PREfix works by analysing all paths through each method body, and it gives a report for each path on which there may be a defect. The trouble is that most of the paths can never in fact be activated. The resulting false positive messages are called noise, and they still require considerable human effort to analyse and reject; and the rejection of noise is itself highly prone to error. It is rumoured that the recent Code Red virus gained access through a loophole that had been detected by PREfix and deliberately ignored.

Assertions can help the PREfix anomaly checker to avoid unnecessary noise. If something has only just three lines ago been inserted in a table, it is annoying to be told that it might not be there. A special `ASSUME` macro allows the programmer to tell PREfix relevant information about the program that cannot at present be automatically deduced.

```
pointer = find (something);
PREFIX_ASSUME ( pointer != NULL,
    'see the insertion three lines back');
pointer ->mumble = blat  ;
```

Assertions feature strongly in the code for Microsoft Office — around a quarter of a million of them. They are automatically given unique tags, so that they can be tracked in successive tests, builds and releases of the product, even though their line-number changes with the program code. Assertion violations are recorded in RAID, the standard data base of unresolved issues. When the same fault is detected by two different test cases, it is twice as easy to diagnose, and twice as valuable to correct. This kind of fault classification defines an important part of the team's programming process.

In Microsoft, over half the effort devoted to program development is attributed to test. For legacy code, there is an accumulation of regression tests that are run for many weeks before each new release. It is therefore very important to select tests that are exceptionally rigorous, so as to increase the chance of catching bugs before delivery. Obviously, tests that have in the past violated assertions are the most important to run again. Violation of a simplifying assumption is a particular reason for increasing the priority of a test, because it is likely to exercise a rare and difficult case.

The original purpose of assertions was to ensure that program defects are detected as early as possible in test, rather than after delivery. But the power of the customer's processor is constantly increasing, and the frequency of delivery of software upgrades is also increasing. It is therefore more and more cost-effective to leave a moderate proportion of the assertions in shipped code; when they fire they generate an exception, and the choice is offered to the customer of sending a bug report to Microsoft. The report includes a dump of the stack of the running program. About a million such reports arrive in Redmond every day for statistical assessment, and the more frequent ones are corrected in service packs. A controlled restart resulting from assertion failure is much better than a crash, which is otherwise a likely result of entry into a region of code that has never been encountered in test.

4 Assertions in Programming Languages

The examples of the previous section have all been implemented as macro definitions by various teams in Microsoft, and each of them is used only by the team which implemented them. In the code for Microsoft Windows, we have found over a thousand different assertion macro declarations. This constitutes a serious impediment to the deployment of a standard programming analysis tool to exploit assertions. The best way of solving this problem in the long term is to include an adequate range of assertions into the basic programming language. A standard notation is likely to be more widely accepted, more widely taught, and more widely used than a macro devised by an individual programmer or programming team. Furthermore, inclusion of assertions in the language would remind the language designer of the desirability of helping programmers in their most difficult task, namely that of establishing confidence in the correctness of their programs. As I suggested when I first started research on assertions [Hoare1], provision of support for sound reasoning about program correctness is a suitably objective and scientific criterion for judging the quality of a programming language design.

Significant progress towards this goal has been made by Bertrand Meyer in his design of the Eiffel programming language [Meyer]. Assertions are recommended as a sort of contract between the implementers and the users of a library of classes; each side undertakes certain obligations in return for corresponding guarantees from the other. The same ideas are incorporated in draft proposals for assertion conventions adapted for specifying Java programs. Two examples are the Java modelling language JML [Leavens et al.] and the Extended Static Checker ESC for Modula 3 and Java [Leino et al.]. ESC is already an educational prototype of a verifying compiler.

Assertions at interfaces presented by a library give exceptionally good value. Firstly, they are exploited at least twice, once by the implementer of the interface and possibly many times by all its users. Secondly, interfaces are usually more stable than code, so the assertions that define an interface are used repeatedly whenever library code or user code is enhanced for a later release. Interface assertions permit unit testing of each module separately from the programs that use it; and they give guidance in the design of rigorous test cases. Finally, they enable the analysis and proof of a large system to be split into smaller parts, designed and checked separately for each module. This is absolutely critical. Even with fully modular checking, the first application of PREfix to a twenty million line product took three weeks of machine time to complete the analysis; and even after a series of optimisations and compromises, it still takes three days. A faster analysis tool is now available for more frequent modular use.

Three useful kinds of assertions at interfaces are preconditions, postconditions and invariants. A *precondition* is defined as an assertion made at the beginning of a method body. It is the caller of the method rather than the implementer who is responsible for the validity of the precondition on entry; the implementer of the body of the method can just take it as an assumption. Recognition of this division of responsibility protects the virtuous writer of a precondition from having to inspect faults which have been caused by a careless caller of the method. In the design of test cases for unit test, each case must be generated or designed to satisfy the precondition, preferably at the edges of its range of validity.

A *post-condition* is an assertion which describes (at least partially) the purpose of a method call. The caller of a method is allowed to assume its validity. The obligation is on the writer of the method to ensure that the post-condition is always satisfied. Test cases for unit test must be generated or designed with the best possible chance of falsifying the postcondition. In fact, postconditions and other assertions should be so strong that they are almost certain to find any defect in the program. As with a scientific theory, it should be almost inconceivable that an incorrect program will escape detection by one of the tests.

In object oriented programs, preconditions and post-conditions document the contract between the implementer and the user of the methods of a class. The interface between successive calls of different methods of an object of the class is specified by means of an invariant. An *invariant* is defined as an assertion that is intended to be true of every object of a class at all times except while the code of the class is executing. It can be specified as a suitably named boolean method of the same class. An invariant does not usually feature as part of the external specification of a class; but rather describes the strategy of the implementation of the individual methods. For example, in a class that maintains a private list of objects, the invariant could state the implementer's intention that the list should always be circular. While the program is under test, the invariant can be retested after each method call, or even before as well.

Invariants are widely used today in software engineering practice, though not under the same name. For example, every time a PC is switched on, or a new application is launched, invariants are used to check the integrity of the current environment and of the stored data base. In the Microsoft Office project, invariants on the structure of the heap are used to help diagnose storage leaks. In the telephone industry, they have been used by a software auditing process, which runs concurrently with the switching software in an electronic exchange. Any call records that are found to violate the invariant are just re-initialised or deleted. It is rumoured that this technique once raised the reliability of a newly developed telephone switching system from undeliverable to irreproachable.

In Microsoft, I see a future rôle for invariants in post-mortem dump-cracking, to check whether a failure was caused perhaps by some incident long ago that corrupted data on the heap. This test has to be made on the customer machine, because the heap is too voluminous to communicate in totality to a central server. There is a prospect that the code to conduct the tests will be injected into the customer's software as the occasion demands.

In summary, the primary use of assertions today is for program instrumentation; they are inserted as probes in program testing, and they serve as a test oracle to give early warning of program defects, close to the place that they occur. They are also used for program documentation, to assist later developers to evolve the product to meet new market needs. In particular, they specify interfaces between major software components, such as libraries and application programs. Assertions are just beginning to be used by the C compiler in code optimisation. They are used to classify and track defects between customer sites, between test cases, and between code changes. Assertions are being introduced into program analysis tools like PREfix, to raise the precision of analysis and reduce the noise of false positives. Increasingly, assertions are shipped to the customer to make a program more rugged, by forestalling errors that might otherwise lead to a crash.

At present, Microsoft programmers find it profitable to formulate assertions that achieve each of these benefits separately. Even more profitable would be to obtain all these benefits together, by reusing the same assertion again and again for different purposes at different stages in the progress of a project. In this way, programmers will be encouraged to introduce assertions as early as possible into the development process. They can then play a guiding rôle in a top-down process of program design, as suggested in Dijkstra's original constructive approach to correctness.

5 The Future

I expect that assertions will bring even greater benefits in the future, when they are fully supported by a range of programmer productivity tools. They will help in deep diagnosis of post-mortem dumps. They will serve as a guide in test case generation and prioritisation. They will help to make code concurrency-safe, and to reduce security loop-holes. In dealing with concurrency and security, there is still plenty of scope for fundamental research in the theory of programming.

In conclusion, I would like to re-iterate the research goal which I put forward [Hoare1] when I first embarked on research into program correctness based on assertions. It was to enable future programming languages and features to be designed from the beginning to support reasoning about the correctness of programs. In this way, I hoped to establish an objective criterion for evaluating the quality of the language design. I believe that modern language designers, including the designers of Java and C#, are beginning to recognise this as a valuable goal, though they have not yet had the idea of using assertions to help them achieve it. As a result, these languages still include a number of fashionable features, and low-level constructions which are often motivated by the desire to contribute to efficiency. Unfortunately, these features can make it difficult or impossible to use local reasoning about the correctness of a component, in the assurance that correctness will be preserved when the components are assembled into a large system.

Fortunately, these problems are soluble even without a switch to a more disciplined programming language. Program analysis tools like PREfix show the way [Bush, Evans]. By conducting an analysis of the source code for the entire system, it is possible to identify the use of the more dangerous features of a programming language, which can be objectively identified as those which violate modularity and invalidate normal correctness reasoning. A notorious example is the introduction of aliasing by passing the same (or overlapping) parameter more than once by reference to the same procedure call. Such violations are flagged by a warning message. Of course, the warnings can be ignored. But in Microsoft, at least, there is a growing reluctance to ignore warning messages. It is a brave programmer who has the confidence to guarantee program correctness in the face of such a warning, when the penalty for incorrectness is the introduction of a virus that causes a billion dollars of damage. And when all programmers rewrite their code to eliminate all such warnings, they are effectively already using a much improved programming language, essentially a safe subset of the original legacy language.

A second promising development for users of legacy languages is the design pattern [Gamma et al.]. A design pattern is based on some coherent program structuring concept, whose purpose is carefully explained. It consists of a collection of code fragments that can be inserted into the users own program, together with a set of protocols and design disciplines to be observed in the rest of the program, to ensure the integrity of the program structure. It is likely that program analysis tools will evolve to police the observance of such disciplines. In effect, an advanced program analyser will come to resemble a compiler for an improved language, with new and potentially verifiable features included as design patterns, and known defects of existing languages removed. And these benefits are obtained effectively without any abrupt change of notation for writing the code.

These are the reasons for optimism that professional programmers in the software industry will be ready to accept and use a verifying compiler, when it becomes available. In industry, work towards the evolution of a verifying compiler will progress gradually by increasing the sophistication of program analysis tools. But there is a splendid opportunity for academic research to lead the way towards the longer term future. I have already mentioned the verifying compiler as one of the major challenges of Computing Science in the twenty first century. To meet the challenge we will need to draw on contributions from all the different technologies relevant to mechanised proof. Like the Human Genome project, or the launch of a new scientific satellite, or the design of a sub-atomic particle accelerator, progress on such a vast project will depend on a degree of collaboration among scientists that is so far unprecedented in Computer Science.

There is now a great mass of legacy software available as test material for evaluating progress towards software verification. Work can start by annotating and improving the quality of the interfaces to the base class libraries, which come with the major object oriented languages. The work will be meticulous, exhausting and like most of scientific research, it will include a large element of routine. It will require deep commitment, and wide collaboration, and certainly the occasional breakthrough. Fortunately, the goal of the project is closely aligned with the ideals of the open source movement, which seeks to improve quality by contributions from many workers in the field.

We will also need to recognise the complementary rôle of rigorous program testing; we must integrate verification with all the other productivity tools that are aimed at facilitating the program development process, including the maintenance and enhancement of legacy code. I expect that the use of full program verification will always be expensive; and the experienced software engineer will always have to use good engineering judgement in selecting a combination of verification and validation techniques to achieve confidence in correctness, reliability and serviceability of software. For safety critical software, the case for full verification is strongest. For operating system kernels and security protocols, it is already known that there is no viable alternative. For assurance of the structural integrity of a large software system, proof of avoidance of overflows and interference is extremely valuable. There will also be many cases where even a partial verification will permit a significant reduction in the volume and the cost of testing, which at present accounts for more than half the total cost of software development. Reduction in the high cost of testing and reduction in the interval to delivery of new releases will be major commercial incentives for the expansion of the rôle of verification; they will be just as persuasive as the pursuit of an ideal of absolute correctness, which has been the inspiration of scientific research in the area. In this respect, software engineering is no different from other branches of engineering, where well-judged compromises in the light of costs and timescales are just as important as an understanding of the relevant scientific principles, and skill in the application of the various tools. For further details about prospects for fulfilling the challenge of a Verifying Compiler, see [Hoare2].

The fact that formal software verification will not by itself solve all the problems of software reliability should not discourage the scientific community from taking up the challenge. Like other major scientific challenges, the appeal of the project must be actually increased by its inherent difficulty. But the primary motivation must be scientific: the pursuit of the old academic ideals of purity and integrity, and the enlargement of understanding by the discovery and exploitation of scientific truth.

6 Acknowledgements

My thanks to all my new colleagues in Microsoft Research and Development, who have told me about their current use of assertions in programming and testing. Their names include Rick Andrews, Chris Antos, Tom Ball, Pete Collins, Terry Crowley, Mike Daly, Robert Deline, John Douceur, Sean Edmison, Kirk Glerum, David Greenspoon, Yuri Gurevich, Martyn Lovell, Bertrand Meyer, Jon Pincus, Harry Robinson, Hannes Ruescher, Marc Shapiro, Kevin Schofield, Wolfram Schulte, David Schwartz, Amitabh Srivastava, David Stutz, James Tierney.

Acknowledgments also to all my colleagues in Oxford and many other Universities, who have explored with me the theory of programming and the practice of software engineering. In my present rôle as Senior Researcher in Microsoft Research, I have the extraordinary privilege of witnessing and maybe even slightly contributing to the convergence of academic and industrial research, and I have good hope of seeing results that contribute back to the development of the theory and also to the practice of programming.

7 References

[Bush et al] W.R. Bush, J.D. Pincus, and D.J. Sielaff: A static analyzer for finding dynamic programming errors, Software — Practice and Experience 2000 (30) 775–802.

[Dahl1] O.-J. Dahl: An approach to correctness proofs of semicoroutines, Mathematical Foundations of Computer Science, 3rd Symposium, Springer LNCS 28, (1975) 157–174.

[Dahl2] O.-J. Dahl: Can program proving be made practical? In Les fondements de la programmation, Institut de recherch dinformatique et dautomatique 57–114. (In English: ISBN 2726101844).

[Dahl3] O.-J. Dahl: Time sequences as a tool for describing program behaviour. In Abstract Software Specifications, Springer LNCS 86 (1979), 274–290.

[Dahl4] O.-J. Dahl: Object-orientation and formal techniques. In VDM 90, Formal methods in Software Development, Springer LNCS 428 (1992), 1–11.

[Dahl5] O.-J. Dahl: A note on monitor versions. In Millennial Perspectives in Computer Science, Palgrave (2000), 91–98.

[Dahl6] O.-J. Dahl: Verifiable programming, Prentice Hall (1992), 269 pages.

[Dahl,Owe] O.-J. Dahl and O. Owe: Formal development with ABEL. In Proceedings of Formal Software Development Methods, VDM 91, Springer LNCS 552 (1991), 320–362.

[Dijkstra] E.W. Dijkstra: A Constructive Approach to the problem of Program Correctness. In BIT 8 (1968) 174–186

[Evans, Larochelle] D. Evans and D. Larochelle: Improving Security Using Extensible Lightweight Static Analysis, IEEE Software, Jan/Feb 2002.

[Floyd] R.W. Floyd: Assigning meanings to programs, Proc. Amer. Soc. Symp. Appl. Math. 19, (1967) 19–31

[Gamma et al.] E. Gamma, R. Helm, R. Johnson and J. Vlissides: Design Patterns: Elements of Reusable Object-Oriented Software, Addison-Wesley, 1995.

[Gates] W.H. Gates: internal communication, Microsoft Corporation, 2002

[Hoare1] C.A.R. Hoare: An Axiomatic Basis for Computer Programming, Comm. ACM, 12(10) Oct 1969, 576–580, 583.

[Hoare2] C.A.R. Hoare: The Verifying Compiler: a Grand Challenge for Computer Research, JACM (50) 1, (2003) 63–69

[Johnson] S.C. Johnson: Lint, a C program Checker. In UNIX Programmers Manual, vol 2A, 292–303.

[Leavens et al.] G.T. Leavens, A.L. Baker and C. Ruby: Preliminary design of JML: a behavioural interface specification language for Java, Technical Report 98-060, Iowa State University, Department of Computer Science, August 2001.

[Leino et al.] K.R.M. Leino, G. Nelson and J.B. Saxe: ESC/Java users manual. Tech note 2002.002, Compaq SRC, Oct. 2000.

[McCarthy] J. McCarthy: Towards a mathematical theory of computation, Proc. IFIP Cong. 1962, North Holland, (1963)

[Meyer] B. Meyer: Object-Oriented Software Constrcution, 2nd edition, Prentice Hall, (1997)

[Turing] A.M. Turing: Checking a large routine, Report on a Conference on High Speed Automatic Calculating machines, Cambridge University Math. Lab. (1949) 67–69

Object-Oriented Specification and Open Distributed Systems

Einar Broch Johnsen[1,2] and Olaf Owe[2]

[1] BISS, FB3, University of Bremen, Germany
[2] Dept. of Informatics, University of Oslo, Norway
{einarj, olaf}@ifi.uio.no

Abstract. An object-oriented approach to program specification and verification was developed by Ole-Johan Dahl with the long-term ABEL project. Essential here was the idea of reasoning about an object in terms of its observable behavior, where the specification of an object's present behavior is given by means of its past interactions with the environment. In this paper, we review some of the ideas behind this approach and show how they can be fruitfully extended for reasoning about black-box components in open object-oriented distributed systems.

1 Introduction

Object-orientation was introduced by Ole-Johan Dahl and Kristen Nygaard with the programming language Simula [14, 15, 41, 13] in 1966. Since then, object-oriented programming (OOP) has become an increasingly widespread and popular programming paradigm, lately with Java. Also for system specification, many formalisms have adapted ideas from OOP to better organize specifications; for example, Actors [2], Maude [9], Object-Z [46], UML [7], and the π-calculus [38] all support some object-oriented concepts. The term *object-based* has emerged to describe formalisms that support objects, i.e., that incorporate notions of object identity and encapsulation in the language [40]. To be fully object-oriented, a formalism should also have an inheritance mechanism reminiscent of OOP. We will now explain what we mean by the central object-oriented concepts of object identity, encapsulation, and inheritance in the context of specification notations:

Identity. Objects have explicit identifiers. When communication occurs between named objects, an object knows which objects it addresses with a given communication. Object identifiers can be transmitted from one object to another during such communication. An object's awareness of other objects in its environment can thus increase over time.

Encapsulation and information hiding. An object encapsulates its internal variables (attributes), so these are not directly perceived from outside the object. This has some noteworthy consequences. *Internally*, we gain control of how the object's variables are manipulated. Variables can only be manipulated by operations (methods) that the object offers to its environment, so the state space of an object resembles an abstract data type. *Externally*, an object

O. Owe et al. (Eds.): From OO to FM (Dahl Festschrift), LNCS 2635, pp. 137–164, 2004.

appears as a black box that reacts in a (more or less) predictable manner to impulses from its environment. To use an object, knowledge of its implementation is not needed, only of the available methods. (Explicit hiding mechanisms were not present in the first version of Simula.)

Inheritance. A subclass inherits a superclass by adding attributes and modifying or extending its methods. Class inheritance, introduced in Simula, is a powerful structuring mechanism for developing large systems. However, to really be of value, inheritance should not only allow reuse of code, but also of the reasoning done for the superclass [48]. A similar notion of inheritance or reuse at the level of reasoning can be found in behavioral (or predicate) subtyping [35]. In principle, these two notions of inheritance are not directly related, but when class inheritance is restricted to behavioral subtyping, we get *substitutability*, by which we mean that an object of a class C can be replaced by an object of a subclass of C at the level of reasoning.[3]

Restricting class inheritance to ensure behavioral subtyping comes at the expense of free code reuse and may seem too limiting in the eyes of many programmers. Also, combining these notions lead to the so-called inheritance anomalies [37]. In contrast, in the ABEL project [10, 11, 16, 12], Dahl takes the approach that reasoning is done at the specification level, and code is shown to implement specifications, for instance by means of type simulation. Hence, in ABEL, a class can simulate a type. Requirement specification of a concurrent object is in terms of its *observable behavior* and may be implemented using (internal) state transitions. The observable behavior of an object up to some point in time is recorded in its communication history (or finite trace), which gives us an abstract view of the object's state, and present behavior can be specified as a function on the history. Traces are well-known from process algebra, for example CSP [25]. However, generator inductive specifications of the permissible traces as suggested by Dahl [10], where fix-points are not needed in the underlying semantics, are different from the process algebraic approach (as explained in Section 2.2). In contrast to approaches based on streams [33, 8], specifications can be expressed by finite traces since the history at any given time is finite.

In this paper, our focus is on formal reasoning and specification of open distributed systems (ODS). These systems are subject to change at runtime, so we consider concurrent objects, and more generally components, that exist in an evolving environment. For instance, new objects can be introduced into the system and old objects can be upgraded or replaced. Objects will often be supplied by third party manufacturers and we cannot generally expect to have knowledge of implementation details concerning objects in the environment. Instead, the behavior of an object can be locally determined by its interaction with other objects in the environment [2], i.e. by its observable behavior. Due to the complexity of ODS, it is often advocated that system descriptions be aspectwise, in so-called viewpoints [26]. In this paper, we address the issue of specifying ODS

[3] An early work on substitutability in the setting of class invariants, pre- and postconditions on methods, and related requirements on method redefinition and external attribute access, is the thesis of Wang [50], supervised by Dahl.

by viewpoints of observable object behavior, based on the tradition in object-oriented specification from ABEL.

The paper is structured as follows. In the next section, we give a brief overview of some important principles of object-oriented specification in ABEL and suggest extensions towards ODS. Section 3 considers openness within the object-oriented framework. Section 4 introduces object viewpoints and behavioral interfaces in an assumption guarantee specification style [32], inspired by these principles. Section 5 illustrates the use of this formalism by a specification of a software bus, i.e. an open communication infrastructure. Section 6 discusses composition of assumption guarantee specifications in this setting and Section 7 relates this work to other formalisms for specifying ODS and outlines future research issues before we conclude in Section 8.

2 Object-Oriented Specification

The Abstraction Building, Experimental Language (ABEL) is a long-term research project at the University of Oslo, centered around a student course in formal methods and the development of a theorem prover. ABEL is a wide spectrum language, expressing requirement specifications, constructive specifications (models), and classes. The most important sources of ideas for ABEL are *object-orientation*, especially the notions of class and subclass, which originated from the work on Simula; *generator induction*, from the work on Larch [23]; and *order-sorted algebras*, from the work on OBJ [22]. Program development in ABEL consists of three steps:

Applicative level. Specification in terms of observable behavior uses abstract data types, generator induction, and the local communication history. Subtypes are either syntactical (cf. examples) or predicative. ABEL supports partial functions with partial logic [42].

Imperative level. Class implementation is state-based, establishing invariants by means of Hoare logic [24, 12], with the history as a mythical variable.

Integration. The two levels are integrated by means of weak or strong simulation. A type can be simulated by a class.

We will now consider each of the three steps and develop a brief example.

2.1 The Applicative Level of ABEL

At an applicative level, specifications of concurrent objects are expressed by permissible observable behavior, i.e. by the time sequence of input and output to the program. This fits well with the object-oriented notion of encapsulation; only visible operations are considered at the applicative level and the realization of the object by means of internal data structures and implementation of operations is postponed to the imperative level. An execution can be represented by a sequence of communication events. In the case of non-terminating executions, the sequences are infinite. However, infinite sequences are not easy to reason about. In order to avoid infinite sequences, specifications are expressed in terms of the finite initial segments of the executions, which express the abstract states of the object. These sequences are commonly referred to as histories [10] or traces [25]. An *invariant* on the history defines a set of traces by the prefix-closure of the set of executions, so history invariants express safety properties in the sense of Alpern and Schneider [3].

Dahl remarks that specifications in a generator inductive style closely resemble programs in an applicative programming language [12]. The values of an abstract data type are completely defined by its set of generator functions (or constructors) in the sense that all inhabitants of the type can be generated by successive applications of the constructors. The definition $f(x_1, \ldots, x_n) == RHS$ is *terminating* and *generator inductive* (TGI) if the right hand side RHS of the equation uses the variables $x_1, \ldots, x_n$, the constructors, case constructs, f itself, and other TGI defined function symbols. In case of direct or indirect recursion, syntactic requirements guarantee termination. Specifications where all expressions are well-defined and only use TGI defined functions, can be evaluated in a convergent term rewrite system. Furthermore, for TGI defined functions, inductive arguments can be used in proofs; to each constructor corresponds one hypothesis in the proof rule. Such proofs can also to a large extent be mechanized by term rewrite systems.

Finite sequences. We present an abstract data type specification in the ABEL style for finite sequences parameterized over some type T. The type (schema) Seq[T] is defined as the union of two subtypes, Eseq, which is the type of the empty sequence over type T, and Seq1[T], which is the type of non-empty sequences over type T.

typeSeq[T] **by** Eseq, Seq1[T] ==
module
  func ε $: \to$ Eseq
  func $\hat{}\vdash\hat{}$: Seq[T] $\times\, T \to$ Seq1[T]
  genbas $\varepsilon, \hat{}\vdash\hat{}$
endmodule

where $\hat{}$ denotes argument positions of functions with mixfix notation. Here, the keyword **genbas** is used to indicate the functions used as a generator basis for the type, so the finite sequences are constructed from two generator functions; ε generates an empty sequence and $s \vdash x$ generates a non-empty sequence from a sequence s and en element x of type T. In ABEL, finite sequences are defined by means of right append (suffix) rather than left append (prefix).

Using TGI definitions, several functions can be constructively defined on the type of finite sequences Seq[T]. For instance, we can define left append $\hat{}\dashv\hat{} : T \times \text{Seq}[T] \to \text{Seq1}[T]$, concatenation $\hat{}\vdash\!\dashv\hat{} : \text{Seq}[T] \times \text{Seq}[T] \to \text{Seq}[T]$, and length $\sharp\hat{} : \text{Seq}[T] \to \text{Nat}$ by (case-free) equations:

$$
\begin{array}{lll}
x \dashv \varepsilon = \varepsilon \vdash x & s \vdash\!\dashv \varepsilon = s & \sharp\varepsilon = 0 \\
x \dashv (s \vdash y) = (x \dashv s) \vdash y & s \vdash\!\dashv (t \vdash x) = (s \vdash\!\dashv t) \vdash x & \sharp(s \vdash x) = \sharp s + 1
\end{array}
$$

In these function definitions, the free variables in each equation have an implicit universal quantifier, reminiscent of for instance ML, and each line corresponds to a possible generator case.

Many useful functions are only partially defined on Seq[T], but TGI defined and total on the subtype Seq1[T], which has only one generator ($\vdash$). For instance, we can define selector functions: right rest $rr(\hat{\ })$: Seq1[T] $\rightarrow$ Seq[T] and left term $lt(\hat{\ })$: Seq1[T] $\rightarrow T$ by

$$rr(\varepsilon \vdash x) = \varepsilon \qquad lt(\varepsilon \vdash x) = x$$
$$rr((s \vdash y) \vdash x = rr(s \vdash y) \vdash x \qquad lt((s \vdash y) \vdash x) = lt(s \vdash y)$$

The type of finite sequences and the functions we have defined above will now be used in an example specification.

Example 1: We illustrate the applicative level of the ABEL language by the specification of an unbounded buffer object. The buffer receives input by means of a *get* operation and transmits output by a *put* operation. The history of the buffer is a sequence of operation calls, conventionally denoted $\mathcal{H}$, and new method invocations are recorded in the history by suffixing. Hence, the history until present time is always available for reasoning, and present behavior of the buffer is specified in terms of preceding activity. If we represent by a type $Calls$ the *put* and *get* operations ranging over the values of a given type T, then $\mathcal{H}$: Seq[$Calls$]. Given a history sequence, we define a function *cnt* that computes the implicit content of the buffer, *cnt* : Seq[$Calls$] $\rightarrow$ Seq[T]. Thus, the history gives us an abstract view of the state. The invariant of the specification is defined as a predicate on the history, which is updated after every method call. It follows that the history invariant is implicitly both pre- and postcondition of every operation in the interface.

interface BufferSpec [$T : Type$]
begin
  opr put(**in** $x : T$)
  opr get(**out** $x : T$)
 inv $I(\mathcal{H})$
where
 $I(\varepsilon) = \varepsilon$
 $I(\mathcal{H} \vdash put(x)) = I(\mathcal{H})$
 $I(\mathcal{H} \vdash get(x)) = I(\mathcal{H}) \wedge$ **if** $cnt(\mathcal{H}) \neq \varepsilon$ **then** $x = lt(cnt(\mathcal{H}))$ **else false fi**

 $cnt(\varepsilon) = \varepsilon$
 $cnt(\mathcal{H} \vdash put(x)) = cnt(\mathcal{H}) \vdash x$
 $cnt(\mathcal{H} \vdash get(x)) = rr(cnt(\mathcal{H}))$
end

Both the invariant and the auxiliary function *cnt* are defined by terminating generator induction. An invocation $get(x)$ updates the mythical variable: $\mathcal{H} := \mathcal{H} \vdash get(x)$. As new values are added to the right of the content sequence (calculated by $cnt(\mathcal{H})$), the first value is retrieved by the left term function $lt(cnt(\mathcal{H}))$ and the remaining content by the right rest function $rr(cnt(\mathcal{H}))$. □

2.2 The Imperative Level of ABEL

For the implementation of specifications in program code, a state-based guarded command language is suggested. The invocation of an operation implemented by $G \longrightarrow S$, where G is a guard and S is a program statement, must wait until G holds and results in the execution of S. The communication history is available at the implementation level as a "mythical" variable [12], which is implicitly updated with a new event representing the invocation of an operation after evaluation of the operation body. For verifying operations, ABEL relies on Hoare-logic. Given a history invariant, verifying an operation call $op(x)$ consists of establishing the validity of the formula $\{G \wedge I(\mathcal{H})\}\ S\ \{I(\mathcal{H} \vdash op(x))\}$.

Example 2: In this example, we propose a program code for the unbounded buffer specified in Example 2.1. The content of the buffer is stored in an internal variable $cont$: Seq[T]. The program invariant is given by the relationship between the implicit content of the buffer, as extracted from the history, and the actual content which is stored in $cont$.

class BufferClass [T : $Type$]
  implements BufferSpec [T]
begin
  var $cont$: Seq[T]
    opr put(**in** $x : T$) $== cont := cont \vdash x$
    opr get(**out** $x : T$) $== cont \neq \varepsilon \longrightarrow [x := lt(cont); cont := rr(cont)]$
  inv $cont = cnt(\mathcal{H})$
end

□

The constructive nature of this form of applicative specifications is close to implementation, as illustrated by this program code for the specification of Example 2.1. In fact, this class implementation can be derived directly from the specification and the class invariant. (To obtain single transition systems, program statements can be restricted to multiple assignment operations although this is not done here.)

In ABEL, the history is constructed by sequence suffixing, using right append as the constructor in contrast to prefixing by means of left append. The history is always available for reasoning, as an abstract representation of the state, from which we can extract information. Consequently, the correct behavior of the specified object can be determined by a predicate. Choosing the prefix constructor instead would bring us to a recursive setting, similar to process algebras such as CSP. In this case, the history is not available for reasoning and information concerning the state must be passed along in process parameters that reveal parts of the internal structure of the program. An illustrative example here is the formalism CSP-OZ [20], which combines CSP with Object-Z. In this formalism, objects specified in Object-Z are represented as CSP processes by including all attributes as process parameters. ABEL specifications do not need to reveal the internal structure of the program, so they are in this sense more abstract than the corresponding process algebraic specifications. In particular, recursive definition of processes and the resulting fix-point semantics are avoided.

Type simulation. In order to show that program code implements the intended specification, ABEL uses type simulation techniques [12]. An abstract type simulates a concrete type by means of an abstraction function. There are many techniques for type simulation. In ABEL, focus has been on both strong simulation, where every function, and thereby every value, on the abstract type is simulated by a function on the concrete type, and on weak simulation, where concrete values at best approximate an abstract value, for instance giving room for capacity constraints at the concrete level. Type approximation corresponds to one possible method of data refinement. There is a rich literature on data refinement; for a recent overview, the reader may consult de Roever and Engelhardt [18]. Although less standard, ABEL's refinement by type approximation reflects a profound concern for the practical applicability of formal methods.

2.3 Explicit Object Identities

In this section, we show how the formalism presented above can be extended in order to capture object interaction in systems with many objects. When we consider concurrent objects that communicate in parallel systems, an object may talk to several other objects. In this setting it is therefore not satisfactory to model the object's behavior by its interaction with an implicit environment that consists of a *single entity*, as we did in the previous examples. Instead, we now consider the environment of an object as an unbounded set of other objects. When we specify an object in such a system, we will refer to this set as the object's (communication) environment. For object systems, the history records communication between objects in the form of remote method calls. Therefore, we introduce object identifiers in the events that are recorded in the communication traces, so that every communication event contains the identity of the transmitting object. This lets us express properties that should hold for a single calling object, a particular calling object, or for all calling objects by projections on the history. Also, we can specify how calls from different objects in the environment are interleaved. We illustrate specifications with implicit object identities in communication events by an example, following [17].

Example 3: Consider an object controlling write access to some shared data resource. All objects in its environment are allowed to perform write operations on the shared data, but only one object at a time; we want to specify that write access is sequential. Assume that every event has an implicit sender identifier. Now, we can project traces on an object identifier to express projection on the set of all events associated with that identifier (ranging over operations) or on the name of an operation to express projection on the set of events associated with that operation (ranging over object identifiers).

Let OW represent (the completion of) an *open_write* operation, W a *write* operation, and CW a *close_write* operation. Let the predicate t **prs** Reg express that a trace t is a prefix of a trace in the regular language Reg. The **prs** predicate will be used to express invariant properties on the history. As before, $\mathcal{H}$ denotes the history of communication events involving the current object. We denote by $\mathcal{E}$ the current environment of the object we are specifying.

interface SeqWrite $[T : Type]$
begin
    opr OW
    opr W
    opr CW
  inv $\mathcal{H}$ **prs** $[OW\ W^*\ CW]^* \wedge \forall o \in \mathcal{E} : (\mathcal{H}/o)$ **prs** $[OW\ W^*\ CW]^*$

  lemma $\forall \mathcal{H} : 0 \leq \sharp(\mathcal{H}/OW) - \sharp(\mathcal{H}/CW) \leq 1$
end

The regular expression ensures that *write* operations W are performed between an *open_write* operation OW and a *close_write* operation CW. We want the regular expression to hold for every object in the environment so we quantify over object identifiers. The predicate $\forall o \in \mathcal{E} : (\mathcal{H}/o)$ **prs** $[OW\ W^*\ CW]^*$ quantifies over objects in the environment. By projecting the history on events associated with every calling object, we consider the (pointwize) communication between the objects of the environment and the object of the interface. The predicate above therefore states that every object in the environment adheres to this behavior. The other conjunct $\mathcal{H}$ **prs** $[OW\ W^*\ CW]^*$ states that the full history of the object adheres to this behavior as well. This means that *write* operations only occur when $\sharp(\mathcal{H}/OW) - \sharp(\mathcal{H}/CW) = 1$, for every object in the environment, and the lemma follows. Therefore, at most one object in the environment can perform write operations with the given invariant. □

Observe that in this example, the specified object is *passive* because it only receives and never transmits calls. In order to specify objects that are *active* as well, we need to reason about events that are transmitted from the object (output) to different objects in the environment, so communication events need to be equipped with the object identities of both the sender and receiver.

3 Object-Orientation and Openness

In open systems software may be changed, interchanged, and updated. This makes program reasoning more difficult as old invariants can be violated by new software, and also static typing can be too restrictive. Although there are applications where this does not seem to be a problem, it is interesting to see how and to what extent strong typing and incremental, textual, and compositional reasoning can be combined with openness. Strong typing alone can ensure essential safety properties, such as providing limited access rights. We will here explore some possibilities for controlled openness within the object-oriented framework.

In order to solve the conflict between unrestricted reuse of code in subclasses, and behavioral subtyping and incremental reasoning control, we suggest to use behavioral interfaces as presented in the previous section to type object variables, and consider multiple inheritance at the interface level as well as at the class level. Interface inheritance is restricted to a form of behavioral subtyping [35], whereas class inheritance may be used freely. Inherited class (re)declarations are resolved by disjoint union. A class may implement several interfaces, provided that it satisfies the syntactic and semantic requirements stated in the interfaces. An object of class C supports an interface I if the class C implements I.

Reasoning control is ensured by substitutability at the level of interfaces: *an object supporting an interface I may be replaced by another object supporting I or a subinterface of I*. Subclassing is unrestricted with the consequence that interface implementation claims are not preserved by subclassing. If a class C implements an interface I, this property is not always guaranteed by a subclass of C, as a method redefinition may violate semantic requirements of I. Therefore, implementation claims (as well as class invariants) are not in general inherited.

Strong typing. We consider typing where two kinds of variables are declared; an object variable by an interface and an ordinary variable by a data type. Strong typing ensures that for each method invocation $o.m(inputs;\ outputs)$, where I is the declared interface of o, the actual object o (if not nil) will support I and the method m will be understood, with argument types "including" the types of the actual ones. Inclusion is defined as the pointwise extension of the subtype and subinterface relation, using co- and contravariance for in- and out-parameters, respectively. Explicit hiding of class attributes and methods is not needed, because typing of object variables is based on interfaces and only methods mentioned in the interface (or its super-interfaces) are visible.

Modifiability. An obvious way to provide some openness is to allow addition of new (sub)classes and new (sub)interfaces. In our setting, this mechanism in itself does not violate reasoning control, in the sense that old proven results still hold. Also, additional implementation claims may be stated and proved. However, old objects may not use new interfaces that require new methods.

A natural way to overcome this limitation is through a dynamic class construct, allowing a class to be *replaced* by a subclass. Thus a class C may be modified by adding attributes (with initialization) and methods, redefining methods, as well as extending the inheritance and implements lists. (In order to avoid circular inheritance graphs, C may not inherit from a subclass of C.) Unlike addition of a subclass of C, all existing objects of class C or a subclass become renewed in this case and support the new interfaces. Reasoning control is maintained when the dynamic class construct is restricted to behavioral subtyping, which can be ensured by verification conditions associated with the class modification [43]. Unrestricted use of the dynamic class construct, which may sometimes be needed, has the impact that objects of class C may violate behavior specified earlier, and constraints on compositions involving objects of class C must be reproved (or weakened).

Notice that as a special case of class modification, one may posteriorly add super-classes to an established class hierarchy. This would be an answer to a major criticism against object-oriented design [21], namely that the class hierarchy severely limits restructuring the system design.

The run-time implementation of dynamic class constructs is non-trivial [36], even typing and virtual binding need special considerations:

- The removal of a method or attribute from a class C violates strong typing, since such a method or attribute may be used in an old subclass of C and by strong typing the method or attribute must exist. This indicates that removal of methods or attributes should not be allowed.
- A modified class C may add an attribute or a method m and thereby an old subclass D inherits m. The subclass may also inherit m (with the same parameter types) from another superclass of D. An implication is that the virtual binding mechanism must give priority to the old m, otherwise objects of class D will behave unpredictably and reasoning control is clearly lost. This can be implemented by a table associated with each class at run-time, updated whenever a superclass is modified.
- The typing and well-formedness of a modification of a class C should not depend on any existing subclass of C. Consider the case where a new method m is added to a class C. This should be legal even if a subclass D already has a method m. The parameter types may well be the same, and this case predicts that we must accept unrestricted method redefinition in a subclass!
- Parameter types may be only slightly changed in class C (say, only for the out-parameters of a method m), in which case we must tolerate arbitrary overloading in a subclass. Invocations of m on objects of a subclass D must respect old behavior, otherwise these objects will behave unpredictably and reasoning control is lost. An implication is that the virtual binding mechanism must give priority to local methods (that include the actual parameter types) over inherited ones.

These implications give independent justification for declaring interfaces for object variables, while allowing unrestricted subclassing. In the next section, we consider specification and reasoning with behavioral interfaces more closely.

4 Viewpoints to ODS

In ODS, we can represent components by (collections of) objects that run in parallel and communicate asynchronously by means of remote method calls with input and output parameters. Often, such objects are supplied by third-party manufacturers unwilling to reveal the implementation details of their design. Therefore, reasoning about such systems must be done relying on abstract specifications of the system's components. We find specification in terms of observable behavior particularly attractive in this setting and imagine that components come equipped with behavioral interfaces that instruct us on how to use them. Furthermore, as a component may be used for multiple purposes, it can come equipped with multiple specifications. This section presents a formalism for reasoning about object viewpoints in the setting of ODS, extending the formalism of Section 2. Further details about this work can be found in [29, 28, 43].

4.1 Semantics

We now propose a formalization of viewpoint specifications for objects communicating asynchronously by means of remote method calls, restricting ourselves to safety aspects. Let *Objects* and *Mtd* be unbounded sets of object identifiers and method names, respectively, and let *Data* be a set of data values including *Objects*. Denote by $\text{List}[T]$ the lists over a type T (and by $[\,]$ the empty list).

Definition 1 (Communication events). *A communication event is a tuple* $\langle o_1, o_2, m, t, \mathit{inputs}, \mathit{outputs}\rangle$ *such that* $o_1, o_2 \in \mathit{Objects}$, $o_1 \neq o_2$, $m \in \mathit{Mtd}$, $t \in \{i, c\}$, $\mathit{inputs}, \mathit{outputs} \in \text{List}[\mathit{Data}]$, *and* $t = i \Rightarrow \mathit{outputs} = [\,]$.

Intuitively, we can think of these events as initiations and completions of calls to a method m provided by an object o_2 by another object o_1. Initiation events have no output. Communication is asynchronous as other events can be observed in between the initiation and completion of any given call. (We here assume strong typing, so the number and types of input and output parameters are correct by assumption in the events.)

Definition 2 (Alphabet). *An alphabet for a set of objects* $\mathcal{O}$ *is a set* S *of communication events such that* $\langle o_1, o_2, m, c, \mathit{ins}, \mathit{outs}\rangle \in S \Rightarrow \langle o_1, o_2, m, i, \mathit{ins}, [\,]\rangle \in S$ *and* $\langle o_1, o_2, \ldots\rangle \in S \Rightarrow (o_1 \in \mathcal{O} \wedge o_2 \notin \mathcal{O}) \vee (o_2 \in \mathcal{O} \wedge o_1 \notin \mathcal{O})$.

At the specification level, the alphabet of an object supporting an interface is statically given by the interface. Denote by h/S and $h \setminus S$ the restrictions of a sequence h to elements of the set S and to the complement of S, respectively.

Definition 3 (Trace set). *A trace set over an alphabet* α *is a prefix-closed set of sequences* $t \in \text{Seq}[\alpha]$ *such that, for every sequence* t *in the set and every completion event* $\langle o_1, o_2, m, c, \mathit{inputs}, \mathit{outputs}\rangle \in \alpha$,

$$\sharp(t/\langle o_1, o_2, m, i, \mathit{inputs}, [\,]\rangle) \geq \sharp(t/\langle o_1, o_2, m, c, \mathit{inputs}, \mathit{outputs}\rangle).$$

Definition 4 (Specification). *A specification* Γ *is a triple* $\langle \mathcal{O}, \alpha, \mathcal{T}\rangle$ *where (1)* $\mathcal{O}$ *is a set of object identities,* $\mathcal{O} \subseteq \mathit{Objects}$*, (2)* α *is an infinite alphabet for* $\mathcal{O}$*, and (3)* $\mathcal{T}$ *is a prefix-closed subset of* $\text{Seq}[\alpha]$.

We call $\mathcal{O}$ the object set of the specification Γ, α the alphabet of Γ, and $\mathcal{T}$ the trace set of Γ. In shorthand, these are denoted $\mathcal{O}(\Gamma)$, $\alpha(\Gamma)$, and $\mathcal{T}(\Gamma)$, respectively. For a specification Γ, we can derive a *communication environment* $\mathcal{E}(\Gamma)$ of objects communicating with the objects of Γ, from $\mathcal{O}(\Gamma)$ and $\alpha(\Gamma)$. In an ODS setting, we generally think of the communication environment as unbounded. If the object set of a specification Γ is a singleton $\{o\}$, we say that

Γ is an *interface specification* (of o). A *component specification* may comprise several objects.

In order to increase readability, we will henceforth represent an initiation event $\langle o_1, o_2, m, i, [i_1, \ldots, i_n], [\,]\rangle$ visually by $o_1 {\rightarrow} o_2.m(i_1, \ldots, i_n)$ and a completion event $\langle o_1, o_2, m, i, [i_1, \ldots, i_n], [v_1, \ldots, v_p]\rangle$ by $o_1 {\leftarrow} o_2.m(i_1, \ldots, i_n; v_1, \ldots, v_p)$.

Example 4: Consider the specification SeqWrite from Example 2.3, which we now reformulate as an interface specification of an object o. Let $\mathcal{E} = \{x \in \mathit{Objects} \,|\, x \neq o\}$ and let Data be a set of data values. The specification only considers one object, so $\mathcal{O}(\text{SeqWrite}) = \{o\}$. The write method W has an input parameter ranging over Data. The alphabet of SeqWrite is now

$$\begin{aligned}\alpha(\text{SeqWrite}) \triangleq \{&x{\rightarrow}o.OW(), x{\leftarrow}o.OW(), x{\rightarrow}o.CW(), x{\leftarrow}o.CW() \,|\, x \in \mathcal{E}\} \\ \cup\{&x{\rightarrow}o.W(d), x{\leftarrow}o.W(d) \,|\, x \in \mathcal{E} \wedge d \in \mathit{Data}\}.\end{aligned}$$

Controlled write access is obtained by restricting the possible traces of SeqWrite. For this purpose, we use patterns, i.e. regular expressions extended with a binding operator $\bullet$, and extend the **prs** predicate accordingly. Define a pattern Wcycle by

$$\begin{aligned}&[[x{\rightarrow}o.OW()\ x{\leftarrow}o.OW() \\ &\quad [[x{\rightarrow}o.W(d)\ x{\leftarrow}o.W(d)] \bullet d \in \mathit{Data}]^* \\ &\qquad x{\rightarrow}o.CW()\ x{\leftarrow}o.CW()] \bullet x \in \mathcal{E}].\end{aligned}$$

The trace set is now specified by a prefix of the pattern:

$$\mathcal{T}(\text{SeqWrite}) \triangleq \{h : \text{Seq}[\alpha(\text{SeqWrite})] \,|\, h \ \mathbf{prs}\ \mathit{Wcycle}^*\}.$$

Here, x is bound for each traversal of the loop and this binding operator on calling objects ensures sequential write access. A caller may perform multiple write operations once it has access. Note that a set defined by a predicate h **prs** R is always prefix-closed and that $\mathcal{T}(\text{SeqWrite})$ is a trace set. □

Refinement. Refinement describes a correct transformation step from specifications to programs, usually by making the specification more deterministic in the sense of model-inclusion. In our setting of partial specifications, a step towards realization of the specification may involve considering additional communication events, suggesting that refinement in our case must be after projection.

Definition 5 (Refinement). *A specification Γ' refines another specification Γ, denoted $\Gamma' \sqsubseteq \Gamma$, if (1) $\mathcal{O}(\Gamma) \subseteq \mathcal{O}(\Gamma')$, (2) $\alpha(\Gamma) \subseteq \alpha(\Gamma')$, and (3) $\forall t \in \mathcal{T}(\Gamma') : t/\alpha(\Gamma) \in \mathcal{T}(\Gamma)$.*

Using projection as suggested here, dynamic class extension (Section 3) is well-behaved with respect to refinement: the new extended class refines the old class. When considering liveness, the refinement relation must be extended to exclude additional deadlocks in a refinement step (cf. Section 7).

Composition. When two viewpoint specifications are composed, they synchronize on common events. However, as our focus is on the observable behavior of the specifications, internal communication between the objects of the composed specification is hidden.

Definition 6. *The internal events of a set S of objects are all communication events between objects of the set,* $\mathcal{I}(S) \triangleq \bigcup_{o_1,o_2 \in S}\{\langle o_1, o_2, \ldots\rangle, \langle o_2, o_1, \ldots\rangle\}$.

We will write $\mathcal{I}(\Gamma)$ instead of $\mathcal{I}(\mathcal{O}(\Gamma))$. As we consider component viewpoints here, events that are internal in one specification may be observable in another. We say that two specifications are *composable* if this is not the case [29, 28].

Definition 7 (Composition). *Let Γ and Δ be composable component specifications. Then $\Gamma || \Delta$ is the specification $\langle \mathcal{O}, \alpha, \mathcal{T}\rangle$ where (1) $\mathcal{O} \triangleq \mathcal{O}(\Gamma) \cup \mathcal{O}(\Delta)$, (2) $\alpha \triangleq \alpha(\Gamma) \cup \alpha(\Delta) - \mathcal{I}(\mathcal{O})$, and (3) $\mathcal{T} \triangleq \{h/\alpha \,|\, h/\alpha(\Gamma) \in \mathcal{T}(\Gamma) \wedge h/\alpha(\Delta) \in \mathcal{T}(\Delta)\}$.*

4.2 Behavioral Interfaces

Clearly, the specifications of Section 4.1 can be given a syntax à la ABEL. In this section, we consider such a treatment for interface specifications in a generic manner. These specifications are behavioral interfaces; they can be supported by different objects. An interface can be implemented by different classes and a class can implement different interfaces. An interface has the following syntax:

interface F [⟨type parameters⟩] (⟨context parameters⟩)
  inherits $F_1, F_2, \ldots, F_m$
begin
  with G
    opr $m_1(\ldots)$
      ⋮
    opr $m_n(\ldots)$
  asm ¡formula on local trace restricted to one calling object¿
  inv ¡formula on local trace¿
where ¡auxiliary function definitions¿
end

Interfaces can have both type and context parameters, the latter typically describes the minimal environment representing static links needed by objects that support the interface. An initiation and a completion event is associated with each method declaration (ranging over method parameters). In the interfaces, we use the keyword "*this*" to denote the object supporting the interface and "*caller*" to denote an object in the environment. We shall now briefly consider the remaining parts of the syntax, for technical details and discussion the reader is referred to [29, 43]. The use of interfaces for specification purposes is illustrated by way of examples in Section 5.

Assumption guarantee predicates. In ODS, the environment in which an object exists is subject to change and specifications are relative to an assumed behavior of the environment. Hence, we use the assumption guarantee specification style [32], but we adapt it to our setting of observable behavior. Assumptions are the responsibility of the objects of the environment; therefore, assumption predicates consider traces that end with *input* to the current interface and only communication with a single object in the environment. An assumption predicate $A(x, y, h)$ ranges over objects x in the environment, supporting objects y, and traces h. Let $\mathbf{in}(h, o)$ and $\mathbf{out}(h, o)$ denote functions that return the longest prefix of a trace h ending with an input or output event to an object o, respectively. If A is an assumption predicate, define $A^{in}(x, h) \triangleq \forall o \in \mathcal{E} : A(o, x, \mathbf{in}(h, x))$ and $A^{out}(x, h) \triangleq \forall o \in \mathcal{E} : A(o, x, \mathbf{out}(h, x))$. Invariants are the responsibility of the object supporting the interface; they are guaranteed when the assumption holds and consider traces that end with *output* from the current interface. If $I(x, h)$ is an invariant predicate ranging over supporting objects x and traces h, define $I^{out}(x, h) \triangleq I(x, \mathbf{out}(h, x)) \wedge A^{out}(x, h)$. The trace set $\mathcal{T}(\Gamma)$ of a specification Γ with assumption predicate A_Γ and invariant predicate I_Γ is the largest prefix-closed subset of $\{h \in \mathrm{Seq}[\alpha(\Gamma)] \mid A^{in}_\Gamma(this, h) \Rightarrow I^{out}_\Gamma(this, h)\}$.

Inheritance. Multiple inheritance is allowed for interfaces, but cyclic inheritance graphs are not allowed. If an interface F is declared with an inheritance clause, the alphabets of the super-interfaces are included in the alphabet of F and the traces of F must be in the trace sets of the super-interfaces when restricted to the relevant alphabets. In the subinterfaces, we can declare additional methods and behavioral constraints. An interface will always refine its super-interfaces.

Mutual dependency. Because objects are typed by interface, we can specify that only objects of a particular interface (a cointerface) may invoke the methods of the current interface, using the keyword **with**. Furthermore, the current interface knows the methods of the caller visible through the cointerface. This gives strong typing in an asynchronous setting. Semantically, a cointerface declaration changes the alphabet of the current interface as the communication environment is reduced whereas new methods of the caller are added.

5 Case Study: the Software Bus

In this section, we illustrate the use of interface specifications to capture viewpoints concerning the dynamic nature of a software bus, a communication platform to which processes may register in order to share data and resources. (This is a stripped version of an actual system used for monitoring nuclear power plants, more details on the software bus and its specification can be found in [31].) We consider a distributed architecture for the software bus, with a *portmapper* and a collection of *data servers*. The general lay-out of the software bus is shown in Figure 1. Processes may connect (and disconnect) to any data server. The task of the portmapper is to manage registration of processes, and communicate information about processes to other processes, via their data servers. Data

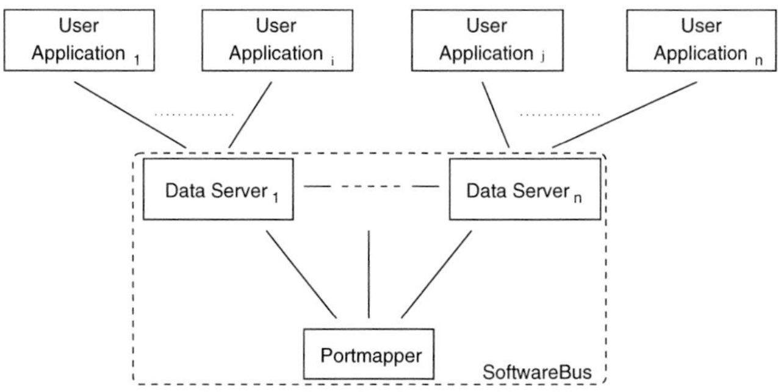

Fig. 1. Decomposition of **SoftwareBus**. Data servers have an interface **SB_Data** available to other data servers and an interface **SB_Connections** available to the portmapper. The portmapper offers an interface **SB_Portmapper** to data servers.

servers communicate with each other in order to share data processing tasks, on behalf of their processes. These tasks include the creation of variables, the assignment of values to variables, accessing the values of variables, and destroying variables. The software bus system is object-oriented: classes, functions, and variables are treated as software bus objects, i.e. as manipulatable data in the software bus system. An object in the system is identified either by reference or by a name and a reference to its parent. For specification purposes, we identify two types; **Name** for object names and **Ref** for object references. The latter will have subtypes, among them we find **ParentRef** for parent objects and **AppRef** for application processes. We shall now specify a data server interface **SB_Data** for manipulation of data, a data server interface **SB_Connections** for updating information on remote applications, and a portmapper interface **SB_Portmapper**.

5.1 Communication between Data Servers

The interface **SB_Data** considers methods for object manipulation between data servers in the **SoftwareBus**. For brevity, we will here only consider two such methods:

opr id (**in** name: **Name** , parent_ref: **ParentRef** ; **out** obj_ref: **Ref**)
opr del_obj (**in** obj_ref: **Ref**)

Intuitively, the method *id* obtains the reference to an object at a remote server and *del_obj* deletes an object at a remote server. It is assumed that a data server only attempts to delete an object to which it has obtained a reference (via *id*). If the object is already deleted by another remote server, the method call will not be completed (until the reference has been recreated). We here denote by

S_r the set of events that can be associated with a given reference r, $S_r = \{x \leftarrow y.id(\_,\_;r), x \rightarrow y.del\_obj(r), x \leftarrow y.del\_obj(r) \mid x, y \in Objects\}$, ignoring irrelevant parameters by underscore. The assumption can be formalized as follows:

$$\begin{aligned} A_d(x,y,h) = \forall r \in \mathbf{Ref} :& \\ & h/S_r \ \mathbf{prs}\ [[x \leftarrow y.id(\_,\_;r)]^+ \\ & \qquad x \rightarrow y.del\_obj(r)\ x \leftarrow y.del\_obj(r)]^* \end{aligned}$$

The invariant is concerned with output from the current object, in this case completion events to the methods *id* and *del_obj*. The assumption above states that a data server will wait for the completion of a call to the current data server before making new calls to this server. We check if there is a pending call to $del\_obj(r)$, using a predicate *pending*:

$$\begin{aligned} pending(mtd,x,y,h) = h/\{&x \rightarrow y.mtd(\ldots), x \leftarrow y.mtd(\ldots)\} \\ &\in [x \rightarrow y.mtd(\ldots), x \leftarrow y.mtd(\ldots)]^* x \rightarrow y.mtd(\ldots) \end{aligned}$$

As we ignore object creation in this example, we assume that an object exists once it has been assigned a reference in a call to *id*. Considering the entire history of a data server (seen through the **SB_Data** interface), we can identify traces after which we believe that a reference is to an existing object:

$$\begin{aligned} &\neg\, exists(r,\varepsilon) \\ &\neg\, exists(r, h \vdash x \leftarrow y.del\_obj(r)) \\ &\ \ exists(r, h \vdash x \leftarrow y.id(\_,\_;r)) \\ &\ \ exists(r, h \vdash \text{others}) = exists(r,h) \end{aligned}$$

In this definition, cases are in the considered order and '$h \vdash$ others' handles the remaining cases. The invariant $I_d(h,x)$ expresses that pending calls to $del\_obj(r)$ are only completed when the object with reference r is known to exist:

$$\begin{aligned} &I_d(x,\varepsilon) = \mathbf{true} \\ &I_d(x, h \vdash y \leftarrow x.del\_obj(r)) = pending(del\_obj, y, x, h) \wedge exists(r,h) \\ &I_d(x, h \vdash \text{others}) = true \end{aligned}$$

Remark how the case distinction with 'others' allows us to ignore irrelevant events in the above predicates. This way, the predicates can be given in a compact, readable format when only a few events of an alphabet need to be considered. Also, this predicate format facilitates reuse of the predicates in interfaces with extended alphabets, typically in subinterfaces.

We now define the interface **SB_Data** (types for method parameters are as given above).

```
interface SB_Data
begin
        opr id ( in name, parent_ref; out obj_ref )
        opr del_obj ( in obj_ref )
    asm A_d(caller, this, h)
    inv I_d(this, h)
end
```

This interface does not consider calls to other servers. The next step is to let **SB_Data** be inherited by a new interface **SB_DataAct**, which includes **SB_DataAct** as a cointerface and $\forall o \in \mathcal{E} : A_d(this, o, h)$ as invariant.

5.2 Communication with the Portmapper

In this section, we consider communication between the portmapper and the data servers. First, we specify an interface of the data server, which offers a method *going_down* to portmappers:

```
interface SB_Connections
begin
    with SB_Portmapper
        opr going_down( in ref: AppRef )
    asm true
    inv true
end
```

By declaring **SB_Connections** to be a cointerface of **SB_Portmapper**, the interface of the portmapper, the events associated with *going_down* are included in the alphabet of **SB_Portmapper** and we can specify the actual use of the method there. The method will be used to signal that applications in the environment are about to leave the **SoftwareBus**. When an application enters the software bus, its (current) data server will register it with the portmapper, and when it exits, likewise. Furthermore, a data server may contact the portmapper in order to know if (and where) an application is currently registered. The associated methods are

opr init (**in** name: **Name**)
opr exit (**in** name: **Name**)
opr conn_app (**in** appl_name: **Name** ; **out** appl_ref: **AppRef**)
opr disc_app (**in** appl_ref: **AppRef**)

Intuitively, *init* signals that an application enters the system, *exit* signals that an application leaves the system, *conn_app* establishes a logical connection to *appl_name*, and *disc_app* disconnects the logical connection to *appl_ref*. Obviously, logical connections should only be disconnected after having been established, which we formalize by the predicate

$$conns(x, y, h) = \forall r \in \mathbf{AppRef} : h/r \ \mathbf{prs}\ [x \leftarrow y.conn\_app(\_; r) \\ x \rightarrow y.disc\_app(r)\ x \leftarrow y.disc\_app(r)]^*$$

Furthermore, logical connections and disconnections from an application x may only occur when x is registered with the portmapper y.

$$is\_reg(x, y, h) = \\ h/x\ \mathbf{prs}\ x \rightarrow y.init(x)\ x \leftarrow y.init(x) \\ [x \rightarrow y.conn\_app(\_) \mid x \leftarrow y.conn\_app(\_; \_) \\ \mid x \rightarrow y.disc\_app(\_) \mid x \leftarrow y.disc\_app(\_)]^* \\ x \rightarrow y.exit(x)\ x \leftarrow y.exit(x)$$

The portmapper assumes that all data servers adhere to this behavior, so define its assumption by the formula

$$A_{pm}(x, y, h) = is\_reg(x, y, h) \wedge conns(x, y, h).$$

The invariant of **SB_Portmapper** considers when output from the portmapper should occur. For this purpose, we determine if an application is currently registered in the system by a predicate *up* on the history:

$$\begin{array}{l} \neg\, up(x, y, \varepsilon) \\ \;\; up(x, y, h \vdash z \leftarrow y.init(x)) \\ \;\; up(x, y, h \vdash \text{others}) = up(x, y, h) \end{array}$$

Similarly, we determine if an application a_1 has an established logical connection to another application a_2 via the portmapper p after history h by the predicate $conn\_up(a_1, a_2, p, h)$:

$$\begin{array}{l} \neg\, conn\_up(a_1, a_2, p, \varepsilon) \\ \;\; conn\_up(a_1, a_2, p, h \vdash a_1 \leftarrow p.conn\_app(a_2)) \\ \neg\, conn\_up(a_1, a_2, p, h \vdash a_1 \leftarrow p.disc\_app(a_2)) \\ \neg\, conn\_up(a_1, a_2, p, h \vdash p \leftarrow a_1.going\_down(a_2)) \\ \;\; conn\_up(a_1, a_2, p, h \vdash \text{others}) = conn\_up(a_1, a_2, p, h) \end{array}$$

We consider a logical connection closed (or broken) if a_1 gets a notification from the portmapper that $going\_down(a_2)$. (The events associated with this method come from the cointerface.) We use the abbreviation $notified(n, p, h)$ below for the the predicate $\forall a \in$ **AppRef** $: \neg\, conn\_up(a, n, p, h)$ and define the invariant of **SB_Portmapper** as follows:

$$\begin{array}{l} I_{pm}(p, \varepsilon) \\ I_{pm}(p, h \vdash a \leftarrow p.init(n)) = \\ \qquad \neg\, up(n, \_, h) \wedge pending(init(n), p, a, h) \wedge I_{pm}(p, h) \\ I_{pm}(p, h \vdash p \rightarrow a.going\_down(n)) = \\ \qquad conn\_up(a, n, p, h) \wedge pending(exit(n), p, \_, h) \wedge I_{pm}(p, h) \\ I_{pm}(p, h \vdash a \leftarrow p.exit(n)) = \\ \qquad up(n, \_, h) \wedge notified(n, p, h) \wedge pending(exit(n), p, a, h) \wedge I_{pm}(p, h) \\ I_{pm}(p, h \vdash a \leftarrow p.conn\_app(n, r)) = \\ \qquad \neg\, conn\_up(a, n, p, h) \wedge pending(conn\_app(n), p, a, h) \wedge I_{pm}(p, h) \\ I_{pm}(p, h \vdash a \leftarrow p.disc\_app(n)) = \\ \qquad conn\_up(a, n, p, h) \wedge pending(disc\_app(n), p, a, h) \wedge I_{pm}(p, h) \\ I_{pm}(p, h \vdash \text{others}) = I_{pm}(p, h) \end{array}$$

The invariant allows for asynchronous calls to the portmapper, as other events may occur between the initiation and completion of any given call. In particular, the invocation of *exit* explicitly results in calls *from* the portmapper. The **SB_Portmapper** interface is now specified (types for method parameters are as given above).

```
interface SB_Portmapper
begin
    with SB_Connections
        opr init( in n )
        opr exit( in n )
        opr conn_app( in n; out r )
        opr disc_app( in r )
    asm A_pm(caller, this, h)
    inv I_pm(this, h)
end
```

5.3 Internal Behavior of the Data Server

In this section, we consider how the two interfaces of the data servers can be combined in order to give a more complete specification of the data server in an interface **SB_DataServer**. In particular, we want to express that a data server can only make calls to another data server when it has an established logical connection to that data server. For convenience, we inherit auxiliary predicates as well as the semantics through interface inheritance.

This interface considers calls made by the current object, so we will strengthen the invariant of the data server (which we presently perceive as the conjunction of its two interface invariants, restricted to appropriate projections on traces). Define

$$
\begin{aligned}
&I_{ds}(x, \varepsilon)\\
&I_{ds}(x, h \vdash x{\rightarrow}y.id(\_)) = conn\_up(x, y, p, h) \wedge I_{ds}(x, h)\\
&I_{ds}(x, h \vdash x{\rightarrow}y.del\_obj(\_)) = conn\_up(x, y, p, h) \wedge I_{ds}(x, h)\\
&I_{ds}(x, h \vdash \text{others}) = I_{ds}(x, h)
\end{aligned}
$$

The interface **SB_DataServer** can now be specified by

```
interface SB_DataServer
    inherits SB_Connections, SB_Data
begin
    inv I_ds(this, h)
end
```

By definition, any data server with the **SB_DataServer** interface will also support the two super-interfaces **SB_Data** and **SB_Portmapper**. At the semantic level, super-interfaces are always refined by their subinterfaces.

6 Composing Assumption Guarantee Specifications

Just as multiple inheritance lets us combine interfaces that are supported by the same objects, we can *compose* specifications where this need not be the case. Definition 7 of Section 4.1 defined composition semantically. In this section we consider a composition rule for specifications made in the assumption guarantee style of interfaces, thus a specification Γ is on the form

$$\langle \mathcal{O}(\Gamma), \alpha(\Gamma), \{h \in \text{Seq}[\alpha(\Gamma)] | A^{in}_{\Gamma}(h) \Rightarrow I^{out}_{\Gamma}(h)\}\rangle,$$

where A_Γ and I_Γ are the assumption and invariant predicates associated with Γ. The supporting objects are here given by $\mathcal{O}(\Gamma)$, the functions $\mathbf{in}(h)$ and $\mathbf{out}(h)$ return the longest prefix of h that ends with input or output to any object in $\mathcal{O}(\Gamma)$, respectively. Let $\Gamma + \Delta$ denote the *syntactic* composition of two specifications Γ and Δ. We want to derive an assumption A and an invariant I that describe the traces of $\Gamma + \Delta$ from the predicates of Γ and Δ.

Composition should encapsulate internal communication, so the communication environment $\mathcal{E}(\Gamma + \Delta)$ excludes objects from the object sets $\mathcal{O}(\Gamma)$ and $\mathcal{O}(\Delta)$. Therefore, for the object set, communication environment, alphabet, and internal event set, we follow the semantics (Definition 7) and define $\mathcal{O}(\Gamma + \Delta) \triangleq \mathcal{O}(\Gamma||\Delta)$, $\mathcal{E}(\Gamma + \Delta) \triangleq \mathcal{E}(\Gamma||\Delta)$, $\alpha(\Gamma + \Delta) \triangleq \alpha(\Gamma||\Delta)$, and $\mathcal{I}(\Gamma + \Delta) \triangleq \mathcal{I}(\Gamma||\Delta)$. Let $h \in \mathrm{Seq}[\alpha(\Gamma + \Delta)]$. Now, define an assumption predicate for $\Gamma + \Delta$ by

$$\begin{aligned} A^{in}(h) &\triangleq A^{in}_\Gamma(h/\alpha(\Gamma)) \wedge A^{in}_\Delta(h/\alpha(\Delta)) \\ &= \forall o' \in \mathcal{E} : A_\Gamma(o, \mathbf{in}(h/o)) \wedge A_\Delta(o, \mathbf{in}(h/o)). \end{aligned}$$

Due to the quantification over objects in the environment, we have that $A_\Gamma(h) \Rightarrow A_\Gamma(h \setminus \mathcal{I}(\Gamma + \Delta))$. However, the assumption $A^{in}(h)$ above is not strong enough to guarantee either of the invariants I_Γ and I_Δ, because nothing has been assumed with regard to the internal communication between objects of the two specifications. This leads to the proof conditions (1) and (2) below.

In contrast to the assumption, the invariant does not quantify over the objects of the environment. Therefore, we cannot derive an invariant I directly from the invariants of Γ and Δ by removing internal communication; we need to consider the full alphabet. Let $h \in \mathrm{Seq}[\alpha(\Gamma) \cup \alpha(\Delta)]$. We first define the basic invariant I of the composition by

$$I^{\mathrm{basic}}(h) \triangleq I_\Gamma(\mathbf{out}(h/\alpha(\Gamma))) \wedge I_\Delta(\mathbf{out}(h/\alpha(\Delta))) \wedge A^{out}(h).$$

However, the basic invariant predicate takes internal events into account. It is well-known that hiding corresponds to the introduction of existential quantifiers [1]. For the invariant, we extend the alphabet of $\Gamma + \Delta$ with the hidden internal events, and hide the extension inside an existential quantifier. Without inherited specifications, the derived invariant is

$$I^{out}(h) \triangleq \exists h' \in \mathrm{Seq}[\alpha(\Gamma) \cup \alpha(\Delta)] : h = h' \setminus \mathcal{I}(\Gamma + \Delta) \wedge I^{\mathrm{basic}}(h').$$

Inheritance. We will assume that specifications can inherit other specifications like the interfaces of Section 4. Say that a specification Γ inherits another specification Σ. At the semantic level, inheritance is interpreted as refinement: for all traces $h \in \mathcal{T}(\Gamma)$, we have that $h/\alpha(\Sigma) \in \mathcal{T}(\Sigma)$. At the syntactic level, inheritance restricts the set of possible traces h defined by the assumption and invariant predicates by additional conjuncts of the form $A^{in}_\Sigma(h/\alpha(\Sigma)) \Rightarrow I_\Sigma(h/\alpha(\Sigma))$. However, in the composition $\Gamma + \Delta$, these additional conjuncts are only valid for the extended trace, so they must be placed *inside* the existential quantifier of the invariant. (Due to hiding, it is not the case that $\Gamma + \Delta$ directly inherits the super-interfaces of Γ and Δ.) Therefore, considering inheritance, we define the invariant of a composition as follows.

Definition 8. *For any specification S, we denote by A_S and I_S its assumption and invariant predicate, respectively. Consider two specifications Γ and Δ and denote by $\Sigma_1, \ldots, \Sigma_n$ the specifications inherited by either Γ or Δ. The invariant of the composition $\Gamma + \Delta$ is defined as*

$$I^{out}(h) \triangleq \exists h' \in \mathrm{Seq}[\alpha(\Gamma) \cup \alpha(\Delta)] : h = h' \setminus \mathcal{I}(\Gamma + \Delta) \land \\ (\forall i \in \{1, \ldots, n\} : A^{in}_{\Sigma_i}(h'/\alpha(\Sigma_i)) \Rightarrow I^{out}_{\Sigma_i}(h'/\alpha(\Sigma_i))) \land I^{\mathrm{basic}}(h'),$$

with the associated proof conditions

$$\forall h \in \mathrm{Seq}[\alpha(\Gamma)] : (A^{in}_{\Gamma}(h) \land I^{out}_{\Gamma}(h)) \Rightarrow A^{in}_{\Delta}(h/\mathcal{I}(\Gamma + \Delta)) \text{ and} \quad (1)$$
$$\forall h \in \mathrm{Seq}[\alpha(\Delta)] : (A^{in}_{\Delta}(h) \land I^{out}_{\Delta}(h)) \Rightarrow A^{in}_{\Gamma}(h/\mathcal{I}(\Gamma + \Delta)). \quad (2)$$

In order to maintain reasoning control for $\Gamma + \Delta$, output from Γ should not break the assumption of Δ and vice versa. The proof conditions (1) and (2) ensure that the internal communications of $\Gamma + \Delta$ respect the assumptions A_Γ and A_Δ of the two component specifications Γ and Δ. Circularity in compositional proofs is avoided because assumption predicates concern traces that end with input whereas invariants concern traces that end with output.

With the assumption and invariant predicates derived for $\Gamma + \Delta$, we define the trace set $\mathcal{T}(\Gamma + \Delta)$ as the largest prefix-closed subset of

$$\{h \in \mathrm{Seq}[\alpha(\Gamma + \Delta)] \mid A^{in}(h, o) \Rightarrow I^{out}(h)\}.$$

6.1 Soundness of the Composition Rule

In this section, the proof rule for composition is shown to be semantically *sound*, i.e. that any trace in the semantically defined composed specification is included in the trace set obtained through the proof rule: $\mathcal{T}(\Gamma || \Delta) \subseteq \mathcal{T}(\Gamma + \Delta)$. This corresponds to the notion of soundness for regular verification systems, see for instance Apt and Olderog [4]. Here, the soundness proof relies on the distinction between input and output events; when we consider communication between two objects, input to one is output from the other, so we can reason inductively about the communication traces between the two objects. The proof extends a proof made by Dahl and Owe [17] for a somewhat simpler formalism.

Proof. Let $\Gamma, \Delta, \Sigma_1, \ldots, \Sigma_n$ (where $n \geq 0$) be (component) specifications such that every Σ_i is inherited by either Γ or Δ. Assuming that the proof conditions (1) and (2) hold, we now show that $\mathcal{T}(\Gamma || \Delta) \subseteq \mathcal{T}(\Gamma + \Delta)$. Observe that, for any $h \in \mathcal{T}(\Gamma + \Delta)$, if one of $A^{in}_{\Gamma}(h/\alpha(\Gamma))$ and $A^{in}_{\Delta}(h/\alpha(\Delta))$ does not hold, neither does $A^{in}(h)$. Now, consider a trace $h \in \mathrm{Seq}[\alpha(\Gamma) \cup \alpha(\Delta)]$ such that $h \setminus \mathcal{I}(\Gamma + \Delta) \in \mathcal{T}(\Gamma + \Delta)$. By assumption, for any such trace h, we have that

$$A^{in}_{\Gamma}(h/\alpha(\Gamma)) \Rightarrow I^{out}_{\Gamma}(h/\alpha(\Gamma)), \text{ and} \quad (3)$$
$$A^{in}_{\Delta}(h/\alpha(\Delta)) \Rightarrow I^{out}_{\Delta}(h/\alpha(\Delta)). \quad (4)$$

We must show that if $A^{in}(h\backslash\mathcal{I}(\Gamma+\Delta))$ holds, then $I(h\backslash\mathcal{I}(\Gamma+\Delta))$ also holds. The proof is by induction over h, but we show a somewhat stronger result, namely

$$\begin{aligned}&\forall h : \mathrm{Seq}[\alpha(\Gamma) \cup \alpha(\Delta)] :\\ &\quad \forall i \in \{1,\ldots,n\} : A^{in}_{\Sigma_i}(h/\alpha(\Sigma_\mathrm{i})) \Rightarrow I^{out}_{\Sigma_i}(h/\alpha(\Sigma_\mathrm{i}))\\ &\qquad \wedge I^{out}_{\Gamma}(h/\alpha(\Gamma)) \wedge I^{out}_{\Delta}(h/\alpha(\Delta))\\ &\qquad\quad \wedge A_{\Gamma}(\mathbf{in}(h/\mathcal{I}(\Gamma+\Delta))) \wedge A_{\Delta}(\mathbf{in}(h/\mathcal{I}(\Gamma+\Delta))),\end{aligned} \tag{5}$$

from which the invariant follows. Two observations are in order at this point. First, due to quantification over the objects of the communication environment in assumptions, $A^{in}(h \setminus \mathcal{I}(\Gamma+\Delta))$ entails

$$A^{in}_{\Gamma}(h \setminus \mathcal{I}(\Gamma+\Delta)/\alpha(\Gamma)) \wedge A^{in}_{\Delta}(h \setminus \mathcal{I}(\Gamma+\Delta)/\alpha(\Delta)). \tag{6}$$

Second, inheritance graphs are acyclic, so we can inductively assume soundness for inherited specifications. Once we have established A^{in}_{Γ} and A^{in}_{Δ}, we get

$$A^{in}_{\Sigma_i}(h/\alpha(\Sigma_\mathrm{i})) \Rightarrow I^{out}_{\Sigma_i}(h/\alpha(\Sigma_\mathrm{i})) \text{ for } 0 < i \leq n. \tag{7}$$

We now proceed with the proof. As we are dealing with safety properties, the formula (5) holds for the empty trace ε. Next, consider the induction step. We assume that (5) holds for a trace h and show that it holds for $h \vdash m$, where $m \in \alpha(\Gamma) \cup \alpha(\Delta)$. Assume first that $m \in \alpha(\Gamma+\Delta)$, such that $A^{in}(h \vdash m)$. The induction hypothesis gives us

$$\begin{aligned}&A_{\Gamma}(\mathbf{in}(h \vdash m/\mathcal{I}(\Gamma+\Delta))) = A_{\Gamma}(\mathbf{in}(h/\mathcal{I}(\Gamma+\Delta))) \text{ and}\\ &A_{\Delta}(\mathbf{in}(h \vdash m/\mathcal{I}(\Gamma+\Delta))) = A_{\Delta}(\mathbf{in}(h/\mathcal{I}(\Gamma+\Delta))),\end{aligned}$$

so by observation (6), both $A^{in}_{\Gamma}(h \vdash m)$ and $A^{in}_{\Delta}(h \vdash m)$ hold. Then, by observations (3) and (4), the invariants

$$\begin{aligned}&I^{out}_{\Gamma}((h \vdash m)/\alpha(\Gamma)) \text{ and}\\ &I^{out}_{\Delta}((h \vdash m)/\alpha(\Delta))\end{aligned}$$

hold and by (1), (2), and (7), we can conclude that (5) holds for $h \vdash m$. Now, assume that $m \in \mathcal{I}(\Gamma+\Delta)$. We have four possibilities. If we consider two object identifiers o_1 and o_2 such that $o_1 \in \mathcal{O}(\Gamma)$ and $o_2 \in \mathcal{O}(\Delta)$, these possibilities are $o_1{\rightarrow}o_2.\mathrm{m}(\ldots)$, $o_1{\leftarrow}o_2.\mathrm{m}(\ldots)$, $o_2{\rightarrow}o_1.\mathrm{m}(\ldots)$, and $o_2{\leftarrow}o_1.\mathrm{m}(\ldots)$. In the first case, m is the initiation of a method m in o_2 by o_1. But then the event is an output event for Γ and hence, the assumption of Γ holds by the induction hypothesis:

$$\begin{aligned}A_{\Gamma}(\mathbf{in}((h \vdash m)/\mathcal{I}(\Gamma+\Delta))) &= A_{\Gamma}(\mathbf{in}(h/\mathcal{I}(\Gamma+\Delta) \vdash m))\\ &= A_{\Gamma}(\mathbf{in}(h/\mathcal{I}(\Gamma+\Delta))).\end{aligned}$$

Consequently, by observation (6), the assumption $A^{in}_{\Gamma}(h \vdash m)$ of specification Γ holds. Therefore, by assumption (3), the invariant $I^{out}_{\Gamma}(h \vdash m)$ of specification Γ holds. Now we know that both the assumption and invariant of Γ hold, so by proof condition (1), the assumption $A_{\Delta}(\mathbf{in}(h \vdash m/\mathcal{I}(\Gamma+\Delta)))$ holds. Then, by (6), we get the assumption of Δ and finally, by observation (4), the invariant $I_{\Delta}^{out}(h \vdash m)$ holds. As we have established the invariants of Γ and Δ, observation (7) lets us conclude.

In the next case, $m = o_1 \leftarrow o_2.\mathrm{m}(\ldots)$ is an output event from specification Δ. Here, we first consider the assumption A_Δ of Δ, which gives us:

$$A_\Delta(\mathbf{in}(h \vdash m/\mathcal{I}(\Gamma + \Delta))) = A_\Delta(\mathbf{in}(h/\mathcal{I}(\Gamma + \Delta))),$$

as m disappears by projection. The predicate holds by the induction hypothesis. By similar reasoning to the previous case, we can now establish the invariants of Γ and Δ, and (7) gives us the result. The two last cases are similar to these.

7 Discussion

The main objective of this paper has been to show how Dahl's notion of object-oriented specification can be extended for reasoning about open distributed systems, as object-orientation is a natural paradigm for ODS [26,17]. In this section, we draw some lines to related work and suggest some future extensions to the work we have presented in this paper.

Our approach is based on trace descriptions of (aspects of) the observable behavior of objects and components. Traces are well-known from the literature on processes, data flow networks, and modules [8,25,33,39,45]. These formalisms do not claim to be object-oriented and tend to be based on synchronous communication along channels, fix-point reasoning, and possibly infinite traces, in contrast to ABEL's approach. Object reference passing can be simulated using named channels instead of named objects, for example in the π-calculus [49], but using explicit object identifiers in the communication events allow a more natural representation. Explicit object identifiers may be found in languages such as Actors [2] and Maude [9]. Both these formalisms also allow asynchronous communication, exchange of object identities, and a large degree of modifiability. However, they are specialized towards system modeling rather than development and reasoning control, lacking for instance refinement notions that capture correctness for system development and modification.

We find specification in terms of observable behavior particularly attractive for reasoning about open distributed systems, where implementation detail need not be available for (client) objects in the environment. On the contrary, such detail can be intentionally hidden, being the intellectual property of some third-party manufacturer. In this respect, our approach is related to coalgebraic formulations of object-orientation such as [27], in which a class specification has assertions that equate sequences of observations on objects of the class. In general these assertions consider the entire history of the object and the conjunction of assertions thus resembles ABEL's history invariant. However, the coalgebraic approach does not seem to allow the kind of dynamic class extensions we have considered here, as the objects are semantically defined in terms of their statically given classes. Of course, state-based approaches may equally well supply a specification of an abstract state that does not directly reflect the implementation of a component. However, refinement becomes complicated when data structures change, in particular for aspects, described using different data structures, and dynamic extensions, captured in our formalism using projection on traces.

The idea of *separation of concerns* in specification seems to have originated with Parnas [44]. Partial specifications are perhaps best known for describing typical case-scenarios in specification notations such as Message Sequence Charts and UML. However, it is unclear how different cases relate to each other through composition and refinement in these notations. The use of interrelated viewpoints is recommended for ODS by the ITU [26] and work on combining viewpoints in this setting has been based on e.g. Object-Z [19, 6] and timed automata [5]. Two major differences between these approaches and ours are, first, that they are state-based whereas we prefer to model objects at an early stage by observations and, second, they are synchronous whereas we find asynchronous communication natural for distributed systems. Viewpoints as presented in this paper resemble aspects of aspect-oriented programming [34], describing aspects by their observable behavior as system services cross-cutting an object grid. Composition in our formalism corresponds to synchronization of aspects, which suggests a formalism for specification and reasoning about the development of aspect-oriented programs. Further investigation in this context is future work.

Specifications using observable behavior let us describe objects in an abstract way, describing properties by extracting information from the history. Furthermore, we can model object behavior in a constructive *graphical* way with trace patterns. From such graphical specifications, the step to implementation in a state-based guarded command language is straightforward. Much work has been done on developing useful graphical specification notations, for instance with Statecharts, Petri nets, and UML, and on their formalization. Interestingly, there is also work on graphical representations of formal notations, an example being Actor specification diagrams [47]. Our trace patterns try to visualize behavior and could perhaps be expressed graphically in a similar way.

Finally, the formalism as presented here only considers safety specifications. In the context of open asynchronously communicating systems, liveness properties are largely dependent on the environment, which we do not control. A weak form of liveness is to identify *deadlock deterministic* objects, i.e. objects where deadlock is not due to internal non-determinism. For deadlock deterministic objects, we can to some extent reason about liveness properties by means of prefix-closed trace sets, without having to resort to a stronger apparatus including infinite traces, temporal logic, etc. We propose an incremental approach by including exceptions in the reasoning formalism through refinement, and in particular timeouts. Thus, we can reason about liveness properties of our own objects even when the environment is unstable. Initial research in this direction has been done in the context of fault tolerance [30], but more work remains.

8 Conclusion

The term "object-oriented specification" was coined by O.-J. Dahl for a specification style where the internal implementation details of objects are encapsulated and behavior is expressed in terms of permissible observable communication. An object's observable communication history represents an abstract view of its state, readily available for reasoning about past and present behavior. Using a (mythical) history variable, the behavior of an object is determined by its communication history up to present time. The approach emphasizes mathematically easy-to-understand concepts such as generator inductive function definitions and finite sequences, avoiding fix-point semantics and infinite traces.

In this paper, we have shown how this approach can be extended in order to reason about open distributed systems. In particular, we consider objects running in parallel, communicating by means of asynchronous remote method calls by which object identifiers can be exchanged. In accordance with the ITU [26], the approach supports partial specification by viewpoints, representing object behavior in behavioral interfaces. Openness appears in the formalism by allowing new (sub)classes, new interfaces for old classes, and a restricted form of dynamic class extension, while maintaining reasoning control.

Acknowledgments

In developing the ideas for this paper, the authors have benefited from collaboration with the members of the ADAPT-FT project, and in particular with Ole-Johan Dahl and Isabelle Ryl.

References

1. M. Abadi and L. Lamport. Conjoining specifications. *ACM Transactions on Programming Languages and Systems*, 17(3):507–534, May 1995.
2. G. A. Agha, I. A. Mason, S. F. Smith, and C. L. Talcott. A foundation for actor computation. *Journal of Functional Programming*, 7(1):1–72, Jan. 1997.
3. B. Alpern and F. B. Schneider. Defining liveness. *Information Processing Letters*, 21(4):181–185, Oct. 1985.
4. K. R. Apt and E.-R. Olderog. *Verification of Sequential and Concurrent Systems.* Texts and Monographs in Computer Science. Springer-Verlag, Berlin, 1991.
5. L. Blair and G. Blair. Composition in multi-paradigm specification techniques. In R. Ciancarini, A. Fantechi, and R. Gorrieri, editors, *Proc. 3rd International Conference on Formal Methods for Open Object-Based Distributed Systems (FMOODS'99)*, pages 401–418. Kluwer Academic Publishers, Feb. 1999.
6. E. Boiten, J. Derrick, H. Bowman, and M. Steen. Constructive consistency checking for partial specification in Z. *Science of Computer Programming*, 35(1):29–75, Sept. 1999.
7. G. Booch, J. Rumbaugh, and I. Jacobson. *The Unified Modeling Language User Guide.* Addison-Wesley, Reading, Mass., 1999.
8. M. Broy and K. Stølen. *Specification and Development of Interactive Systems.* Monographs in Computer Science. Springer-Verlag, 2001.

9. M. Clavel, F. Durán, S. Eker, P. Lincoln, N. Martí-Oliet, J. Meseguer, and J. F. Quesada. Maude: Specification and programming in rewriting logic. *Theoretical Computer Science*, 285:187–243, Aug. 2002.
10. O.-J. Dahl. Can program proving be made practical? In M. Amirchahy and D. Néel, editors, *Les Fondements de la Programmation*, pages 57–114. Institut de Recherche d'Informatique et d'Automatique, Toulouse, France, Dec. 1977.
11. O.-J. Dahl. Object-oriented specification. In B. Shriver and P. Wegner, editors, *Research Directions in Object-Oriented Programming*, Series in Computer Systems, pages 561–576. The MIT Press, 1987.
12. O.-J. Dahl. *Verifiable Programming.* International Series in Computer Science. Prentice Hall, New York, N.Y., 1992.
13. O.-J. Dahl. The roots of object orientation: the Simula language. In M. Broy and E. Denert, editors, *Software Pioneers: Contributions to Software Engineering.* Springer-Verlag, June 2002.
14. O.-J. Dahl and K. Nygaard. SIMULA, an ALGOL-based simulation language. *Communications of the ACM*, 9(9):671–678, Sept. 1966.
15. O.-J. Dahl, B. Myhrhaug, and K. Nygaard. (Simula 67) Common Base Language. Technical Report S-2, Norsk Regnesentral (Norwegian Computing Center), Oslo, Norway, May 1968.
16. O.-J. Dahl and O. Owe. Formal development with ABEL. In S. Prehn and H. Toetenel, editors, *Formal Software Development Methods (VDM'91)*, volume 552 of *Lecture Notes in Computer Science*, pages 320–362. Springer-Verlag, Oct. 1991.
17. O.-J. Dahl and O. Owe. Formal methods and the RM-ODP. Research Report 261, Department of informatics, University of Oslo, Norway, May 1998.
18. W.-P. de Roever and K. Engelhardt. *Data Refinement: Model-Oriented Proof Methods and their Comparison*, volume 47 of *Cambridge Tracts in Theoretical Computer Science.* Cambridge University Press, New York, NY, 1998.
19. J. Derrick, H. Bowman, and M. Steen. Viewpoints and objects. In J. P. Bowen and M. G. Hinchey, editors, *The Z Formal Specification Notation, 9th International Conference of Z Users (ZUM'95)*, volume 967 of *Lecture Notes in Computer Science*, pages 449–468. Springer-Verlag, Sept. 1995.
20. C. Fischer. CSP-OZ: a combination of Object-Z and CSP. In H. Bowman and J. Derrick, editors, *Proc. 2nd IFIP Workshop on Formal Methods for Open Object-Based Distributed Systems (FMOODS)*, pages 423–438. Chapman and Hall, London, 1997.
21. C. Ghezzi and M. Jazayeri. *Programming Language Concepts.* John Wiley & Sons, 3rd edition, 1998.
22. J. Goguen and J. Tardo. An introduction to OBJ: A language for writing and testing formal algebraic program specifications. In N. Gehani and A. McGettrick, editors, *Software Specification Techniques.* Addison-Wesley, 1986.
23. J. V. Guttag, J. J. Horning, S. J. Garland, K. D. Jones, A. Modet, and J. M. Wing. *Larch: Languages and Tools for Formal Specification.* Texts and Monographs in Computer Science. Springer-Verlag, 1993.
24. C. A. R. Hoare. An Axiomatic Basis of Computer Programming. *Communications of the ACM*, 12:576–580, 1969.
25. C. A. R. Hoare. *Communicating Sequential Processes.* International Series in Computer Science. Prentice Hall, Englewood Cliffs, NJ., 1985.
26. International Telecommunication Union. Open Distributed Processing — Reference Model parts 1–4. Technical report, ISO/IEC, Geneva, July 1995.

27. B. Jacobs. Inheritance and cofree constructions. In P. Cointe, editor, *10th European Conference on Object-Oriented Programming (ECOOP'96)*, volume 1098 of *Lecture Notes in Computer Science*, pages 210–231. Springer-Verlag, July 1996.
28. E. B. Johnsen and O. Owe. Composition and refinement for partial object specifications. In *Proc. 16th International Parallel & Distributed Processing Symposium (IPDPS'02), Workshop on Formal Methods for Parallel Programming: Theory and Applications (FMPPTA'02)*. IEEE Computer Society Press, Apr. 2002.
29. E. B. Johnsen and O. Owe. A compositional formalism for object viewpoints. In B. Jacobs and A. Rensink, editors, *Proc. 5th International Conference on Formal Methods for Open Object-Based Distributed Systems (FMOODS'02)*, pages 45–60. Kluwer Academic Publishers, Mar. 2002.
30. E. B. Johnsen, O. Owe, E. Munthe-Kaas, and J. Vain. Incremental fault-tolerant design in an object-oriented setting. In *Proc. Asian Pacific Conference on Quality Software (APAQS'01)*, pages 223–230. IEEE Computer Society Press, Dec. 2001.
31. E. B. Johnsen, W. Zhang, O. Owe, and D. B. Aredo. Combining graphical and formal development of open distributed systems. In M. Butler, L. Petre, and K. Sere, editors, *Proc. Third International Conference on Integrated Formal Methods (IFM'02)*, volume 2335 of *Lecture Notes in Computer Science*, pages 319–338, Turku, Finland, May 2002. Springer-Verlag.
32. C. B. Jones. *Development Methods for Computer Programmes Including a Notion of Interference*. PhD thesis, Oxford University, UK, June l981.
33. G. Kahn. The semantics of a simple language for parallel programming. In J. L. Rosenfeld, editor, *Information Processing 74: Proc. IFIP Congress 74*, pages 471–475. IFIP, North-Holland Publishing Co., Aug. 1974.
34. G. Kiczales, J. Lamping, A. Menhdhekar, C. Maeda, C. Lopes, J.-M. Loingtier, and J. Irwin. Aspect-oriented programming. In M. Akşit and S. Matsuoka, editors, *Proc. 11th European Conference on Object-Oriented Programming (ECOOP'97)*, volume 1241 of *Lecture Notes in Computer Science*, pages 220–242. Springer-Verlag, June 1997.
35. B. H. Liskov and J. M. Wing. A behavioral notion of subtyping. *ACM Transactions on Programming Languages and Systems*, 16(6):1811–1841, Nov. 1994.
36. S. Malabarba, R. Pandey, J. Gragg, E. Barr, and J. F. Barnes. Runtime support for type-safe dynamic Java classes. In E. Bertino, editor, *14th European Conference on Object-Oriented Programming (ECOOP'00)*, volume 1850 of *Lecture Notes in Computer Science*, pages 337–361. Springer-Verlag, June 2000.
37. S. Matsuoka and A. Yonezawa. Analysis of inheritance anomaly in object-oriented concurrent programming languages. In G. Agha, P. Wegner, and A. Yonezawa, editors, *Research Directions in Concurrent Object-Oriented Programming*, pages 107–150. The MIT Press, Cambridge, Mass., 1993.
38. R. Milner. *Communicating and Mobile Systems: the π-Calculus*. Cambridge University Press, May 1999.
39. J. Misra and K. M. Chandy. Proofs of networks of processes. *IEEE Transactions on Software Engineering*, 7(4):417–426, July 1981.
40. O. Nierstrasz. A survey of object-oriented concepts. In W. Kim and F. Lochovsky, editors, *Object-Oriented Concepts, Databases and Applications*, pages 3–21. ACM Press and Addison-Wesley, Reading, Mass., 1989.
41. K. Nygaard and O.-J. Dahl. Simula 67. In R. W. Wexelblat, editor, *History of Programming Languages*. ACM Press, 1981.
42. O. Owe. Partial logics reconsidered: A conservative approach. *Formal Aspects of Computing*, 5:208–223, 1993.

43. O. Owe and I. Ryl. A notation for combining formal reasoning, object orientation and openness. Research Report 278, Department of informatics, University of Oslo, Norway, Nov. 1999.
44. D. L. Parnas. On the criteria to be used in decomposing systems into modules. *Communications of the ACM*, 15(12):1053–1058, Dec. 1972.
45. D. L. Parnas and Y. Wang. The trace assertion method of module interface specification. Technical Report 89-261, Department of Computing and Information Science, Queen's University at Kingston, Kingston, Ontario, Canada, Oct. 1989.
46. G. Smith. *The Object-Z Specification Language.* Advances in Formal Methods. Kluwer Academic Publishers, 2000.
47. S. F. Smith and C. Talcott. Modular reasoning for actor specification diagrams. In R. Ciancarini, A. Fantechi, and R. Gorrieri, editors, *Proc. 3rd International Conference on Formal Methods for Open Object-Based Distributed Systems (FMOODS'99)*, pages 401–418. Kluwer Academic Publishers, Feb. 1999.
48. N. Soundarajan and S. Fridella. Inheritance: From code reuse to reasoning reuse. In P. Devanbu and J. Poulin, editors, *Proc. Fifth International Conference on Software Reuse (ICSR5)*, pages 206–215. IEEE Computer Society Press, 1998.
49. D. Walker. Objects in the π-calculus. *Information and Computation*, 116(2):253–271, Feb. 1995.
50. A. Wang. Generalized types in high-level programming languages. Research Report in Informatics 1, Institute of Mathematics, University of Oslo, Jan. 1974. Cand. Real thesis.

SIMULA and Super-Object-Oriented Programming*

Eugene Kindler

Ostrava University,
Faculty of Sciences,
Dvorakova 7, CZ-70103 Ostrava,
Czech Republic
Kindler@ksi.mff.cuni.cz

Abstract. Although SIMULA was proposed in 1967 and in details described in 1968, it offers more than object-oriented programming. Together with object orientation, its process orientation and block orientation offers to model systems containing modeling elements. The development of this direction of application is described, concluding by the simulation of systems in that there are simulating computers that influence those systems. The development goes through the nested modeling to the reflective modeling. Nested modeling uses models of the systems that contain elements using other models, while reflective modeling is a special case of nesting modeling, in which the elements of the modeled system use models of the system in which they occur. Simulation modeling appears the most important factor in that domain.

1 Preface — Historical Introduction and Personal Reminiscence

The 60-ies of the 20th century were the second entire decade when Czechoslovakia was a part of the Soviet block, i.e. when its life was in a totalitarian way governed from Kremlin. The instructions came in the Russian language. Only a few people know that it was the only one of the cultural languages, which had no term for computer simulation. A certain Russian term, which was intended to mean computer simulation and which could be translated into English as imitation modeling, was introduced not sooner than in the late 70-ies and came into common use only in the late 80-ies. In the 60-ies the governing forces seating in Kremlin were still under influence of the Stalinist ideology of refusing computers and although they did no more use slogans like "Cybernetic — pseudoscience of the obscurians" they understood the computing technique as an only auxiliary tool of mathematics, i.e. a tool for final (numerical) solution of mathematical entities that arose after a conventional analysis performed by pre-computer mathematicians. An iterative communication between a human and

* In honor of Ole-Johan Dahl, a genial scientist, an excellent musician and a very good person

O. Owe et al. (Eds.): From OO to FM (Dahl Festschrift), LNCS 2635, pp. 165–182, 2004.

a computer, which admitted a human to view the computer behavior as that of an experiment, and the human governing the computer as a deep rational mans reaction to the behavior of the computer, was behind the horizons of the totalitarian leaders of the East European science. Moreover, for the leading case of that attempt, i.e. for computer simulation, the same leaders of science met another drawback, namely the above mentioned absence of the term that could be applied in the centralized instructing in the East European science. Even in case the Kremlin bureaucrats had wanted to instruct the leaders of science in the satellite countries about the importance of computer simulation they would not be able to tell that. The persons in Czechoslovakia who were delegated by Kremlin to lead the development of science were old men without any contacts with the contemporary state of the sciences, they obeyed the Kremlin directives and were allusive and mistrust against the term (computer) simulation, considering it with a suspicion that it could be something of ideological diversion, i.e. of the highly punished behavior in the totalitarian society. Computer simulation was far from being mentioned at the University courses and a small number of persons who had recognized its importance had to grow it almost illegally.

In 1966 I entered the Faculty of General Medicine of Charles University in Prague to build there a computer laboratory in a department oriented to biophysics and nuclear medicine. The specialists in medicine and biology, whom I met there, were at a high level of their profession and wanted to apply computers but they were perplexed by them, by algorithmization and by transforming their questions and problems into the physics of computing technique. But after a few weeks I watched them to have used a rather exact tool, namely compartmental systems, i.e. systems composed of well stirred volumes of matter, connected by idealized channels able to let non-zero volume through, contrary to the fact that their volume is zero [1], [2]. I prepared (and during the following months implemented) a programming language that enabled the non-computer-oriented specialists to describe compartmental systems: the description used terms familiar to the common terminology of the compartmental systems practice and a compiler processed it to a computer program that generated data similar to those that could be measured at a real compartmental system [3].

Charles University printed a booklet [4] on the mentioned software product and distributed it abroad. The coming political relaxation of the so called Prague Spring caused a short independence of the Czechoslovak science on the control from Kremlin and that situation enabled such international activities and the events that followed: the booklet came also to Ole-Johan Dahls hands, who prepared the famous IFIP Working Conference on Simulation Programming Languages (May 1967 in Oslo). The conference must be really understood as famous, because O.-J. Dahl and K. Nygaard presented there the principles of language SIMULA 67, i.e. the principles that were many years later recognized as leading principles of the development of programming and knowledge representation and called *object-oriented programming.* O.-J. Dahl invited me to come to the conference and to present there my software product. So I learned that I practiced simulation and that I designed and implemented a simulation language.

I returned from the conference with a joyful intention to throw out my software product and to use SIMULA 67: in my consideration it appeared as an ideal tool for solving not only high problems of programming, modeling, simulation and knowledge representation, but also everyday obstacles, rooting in the general phenomenon that making a program in a certain professional domain stimulated immediate demands for its author to make further programs belonging to the same domain or to a kindred one. My information about SIMULA principles were positively accepted by some Czechoslovak specialists and several years later SIMULA implementations appeared at certain main frame computers like CDC Cyber, IBM 370 and its East European copy called JSEP 1040. The mentioned specialists met at seminars organized under the Czechoslovak Cybernetic Society in its Working Group of SIMULA Users. I informed about SIMULA also during my lectures taken at Charles University in Prague and later at new Czech Universities established in Ostrava and in Pilsen.

2 First Directions in SIMULA Applications in Czechoslovakia

In the seventies, the Czechoslovak specialists applied SIMULA as a powerful simulation tool in some domains like steel metallurgy, machine production, agriculture, services, computer design, nuclear power plants, internal logistic of factories, medicine and ecology. In a smaller extent, SIMULA was also used outside simulation, like in musical science (analysis and synthesis of melodies and polyphonies, dodecaphonic music theory), in airplane production scheduling and in system optimization.

All those applications did not overpass the conventional view to general systems, that was interpreted by the habitual scheme of class nesting used by every SIMULA user: one class (called *main class*), representing a certain *world viewing* (or a problem oriented language fully defined in SIMULA, or a formal theory defined in SIMULA) contained other classes (let us call them *elementary classes*), representing the concepts applied in that world viewing (or in that problem oriented language or in that formal theory). A block prefixed by the main class represented a pattern of a model: when the computing process entered into such a block a new model arose and when the computing process left the block the model disappeared. If the main class introduced a simulated time axis the time flow arose and disappeared together with the model. A cycle containing such a block represented a simulation study, i.e. a sequence of simulation experiments so that each of them had its own time flow, which was not bound with those of the other experiments.

Already in that phase of SIMULA applications we realize that the block orientation of SIMULA allows *class nesting*: inside the main class (for example class `geometry` on page 168) other classes were nested (for example classes `point`, `line`, `circle` etc.).

```
class geometry;
begin class point(x,y); real x,y;... ;
      class circle(center, radius);
            ref(point)center; real radius; ... ;
      class line(...); ... ;
      ref(point)O; ref(line)x_axe,y_axe;
      O:-new point(0,0);
      x_axe:-new line(...); y_axe:-new line(...);
      ...
end of geometry;
```

We did not met anything similar later, when we studied other object-oriented programming languages (C++, SmallTalk, Eiffel etc.), which were presented to the world professional community. Main class seemed being nearer to the modeled world than "class libraries" or "class packages" that were offered by those languages and that were too distant from the real world and too fixed with the computers: one cannot forget that one of the principal advantages of the object-oriented programming was that the programmer was not forced to formulate what should happen in the computer and instead of it he was led to describe directly the thing to be modeled.

During our studying of SIMULA (and during university lectures on it) we have been meeting the fact that class nesting can be iterated. For example, a main class can contain classes that are also main classes and contain other classes. Or a main class can contain a process with its own statements (we call them "life rules"), and among these statements there is a block containing formulations of classes, or even a block prefixed by a main class.

Moreover, SIMULA introduced quasi-parallel systems that allowed switching the life rules of different objects. A new quasi-parallel system should rise when the computing process enters a block containing formulations of classes: the instances of these classes can enter the corresponding quasi-parallel system (as a more suitable, this rule replaced the original rule existing in the first definition of SIMULA, according to which a quasi-parallel system arose when the computing process entered a prefixed block). As the blocks can be nested the quasi-parallel systems can be also nested, i.e. an element of a quasi-parallel system can enter a phase (a subblock of its life rules) deepened by its own quasi-parallel system. We slowly penetrated to the meaning of the nesting of classes and of quasi-parallel systems, and namely to their importance.

3 Semantics of Nesting Main Classes and Quasi-Parallel Systems

Later it appeared to us why the mentioned penetrating was so difficult. The reason rooted in the fact that one could not support his consideration by means of a result or an analogy discovered in another exact science like mathematics, logic or even physics or chemistry. If we view a main class as a computer image of a formal theory (or a world viewing or a language), the nesting of the main classes has to be viewed as a formal theory the entities of that are able viewing to other ("their proper, private") formal theories (and — analogously — as a world viewing which admits that the viewed components of the world have their own world viewings, or as a language that allows its words to manipulate with their own "internal" languages).

Naturally, such attempt is not habitual and was not exactly studied by sciences. Nevertheless, in case of the interpretations by means of the formal theories and/or of the world viewings, certain analogies in the real world exist; we discovered some of them and then we included them into our work to implement computer models. This will be described in the next sections. The interpretation in case main class = language seems to fail any suitable application.

A more difficult interpretation expected us in case of nested quasi-parallel systems but the first steps in mental governing the class nesting enabled to understand also the nesting of the quasi-parallel systems.

4 First Steps in Nesting Modeling-Theory

The basic scheme of main class nesting in SIMULA can be outlined by means of the following block:

```
begin class main1;
      begin class concept1; ... ;
          class concept2; ... ;
            ... etc. other declarations;
          class internal_modeller;
          begin class main2;
            begin class conceptA; ... ;
                        class conceptB; ... ;
                        ... etc. other declarations;
                        possibly: statements of main2 ...
                  end of class main2;
                  possibly: statements of
                            internal_modeller;
            end of internal_modeller;
            possibly: statements of main1;
      end of main1; possibly: statements of the block
end of the block;
```

One can see that in the block a certain world viewing called `main1` is introduced so that it contains some concepts called `concept1, concept2, ...`, which are "habitual and conventional" for that world viewing, and a concept called `internal_modeller` that has his own world viewing called `main2` and using concepts called `conceptA, conceptB, ...` What happens in the "mind" of that modeler can be independent of what happens in the "world" composed of the instances of concepts belonging to `main1`, but can interact with them. Note that among the instances, those of the "habitual and conventional" concepts can occur and those of the `internal_modeller` as well. Let us present an example.

The block is a model of dining mathematicians. `concept1, concept2` etc. are dishes, plates, knives, forks, serving persons, tables, chairs etc., while the class `internal_modeller` is a concept of dining mathematician who cannot eat without thinking on geometry; in case he is eating together with other similar mathematicians he wishes to discuss with them about the professional questions he is having in his mind. The classes `conceptA`, `conceptB` etc. occurring in class `main2` are e.g. classes `point, line, circle` etc., occurring in class geometry mentioned in Section 2.

In place of dining mathematicians we can consider dining staff officers who do not thing on a static world of geometry but who imagine the battle that expects them: each of them has his own vision, he controls it by the rules of causality, probability and time flow and exchanges information on the imaginary battle with his staff colleagues. Note that two sorts of time occur in such a metaphor: the time during that the officers are eating and discussing, and the imagined time of the future battle. That natural metaphor leads us to attempt to quasi-parallel system nesting and to nesting of simulation models.

Although both the examples can seem rather strange, they led to modifications that could be applied in practice, even in industrial domain. The dining mathematicians should be replaced by working persons, because the persons can mutually interact not only during eating but during working, too, and they can govern not only things serving for eating but also components of the production and/or logistic systems in which they are working. The session of dining officers can be replaced by that of discussing experts who should decide of a certain — hopefully optimal — variant of a system that they have to design.

And — moreover — the thinking human can be replaced by a computer or by a human with his own computer that helps him to make decisions; namely a simulating computer can help a person to improve his imagining, which could be viewed as imperfect and poor "mental simulation". Such a transformation appears to be useful in case one should automate a system and tries to transfer the humans mental processes to those of computing automatons.

In the community of SIMULA users a habitude started in 1993: the object-oriented programming admitting the objects to have their "private" classes and thus enabling them to use these classes for to model "thinking", imagining, simulation and in general modeling was called *super-object-oriented programming* [5], [6].

5 Further Steps in Nesting Modeling — Pseudosimulation

The roots of the first real experiences with application of nesting modelling arose in use of a so called *pseudosimulation* or *fictitious simulation* [7]. The contents of those terms can be explained as follows:

Simulation programming tools were designed to make easier the implementation of simulation models: using these languages, a simulationist does not need to describe what should happen in the computer (i.e. an algorithm) but what happens (or should happen) in the simulated system. The automatic scheduling of events (and — for some simulation languages — of processes) at a common simulation time axis is one of the most impressive helping aspects of the discrete event simulation languages. Besides describing real systems or systems that are considered as possible real things in a future, one can use the simulation languages to describe systems that are evidently fictitious. Ole-Johan Dahl shown already in 1966 that such an affair can be used to make easier an implementation of certain algorithms [8]: instead to describe them in a traditional programming language one imagines a system that could produce the same data as the desired algorithm, and describes it in a simulation language. Dahl presented two examples, namely Eratosthenes sieve to compute prime numbers, and determining the shortest path in a graph. The last example was implemented as a simulation model of the following fictitious system.

Certain "pulses" leave the start node along all possible connections leading out from it. The rates of movement are the same. Any branching of the graph is in one of two following states: marked or free; at the beginning, every branching is free. When a pulse enters a free branching it marks it and then it multiplies (similarly as microorganisms and — in general — cells do) so that its "descendants" occupy all connections leading from the branching. When a pulse enters a marked branching it disappears. Each of the pulses carries information on its "ancestor" and on the connection along it moved. When a pulse enters the target point, it and its "genealogy" determine the shortest path. It is evident that a good discrete event simulation language makes easy not only scheduling the pulses marking of nodes and their multiplying, but also enables to formulate only one class of pulses with its life rules for a general concept of pulse. Naturally, something like the multiplying pulses is a fictitious affair.

The shortest path is often determined in the production and logistic systems, and nesting a subroutine for it is often necessary in simulation models of such systems. We mapped that subroutine to a simulation model of the system of pulses presented above. Its nesting in a simulation model of a real systems was described in SIMULA according to the following principles:

```
real_system_model: SIMULATION
begin class node; begin ref(head)environment; ... ;
      class connection(start_node, end_node); ... ;
      process class fixed_machine; ... ;
      process class conveyor;
      begin ref(node)present_place;
            procedure give_the_shortest_path_to(target);
            begin fictitious_system_model: SIMULATION
                  begin process class pulse
                         (start_place, father, way); ... ;
                        activate new pulse
                         (present_place, none,...);
                        ...
```

```
                    end of the fictitious system model;
              end of the shortest path routine;
              ... life rules of conveyor (sometimes calling
              the procedure give_the_shortest_path_to) ...
        end of class conveyor;
        ... forming the structure of real system model,
        activating conveyors, etc.
  end of the real system model;
```

In 1990, we started with using that principle in simulation of machinery production systems using induction carriages for its operation logistics [10], and then we proceed by a lot of other applications (see e.g. a detailed description of many SIMULA texts at pages 175–278 of [11]).

In the SIMULA text there are two occurrences of `SIMULATION` applied as prefixes at different block levels. This phenomenon is not in a contradiction to SIMULA principle forbidding subclassing across block levels, because each of the occurrences is considered as an identifier completely different from the other one. According our experience, every SIMULA compiler for PC compatible machines behaves in that manner.

6 Other Applications of Pseudosimulation

A description of application of pseudosimulation using other fictitious models than that of the pulses and applied for other reasons that the shortest paths computing, can be seen in [7]. In a greater part, they applied pseudosimulation nesting in a simulation model. But the nesting can be realized inversely, namely so that a simulation was nested in a model of a fictitious system that governed a simulation study (a sequence of simulation experiments controlled to lead to some target).

An excellent example was presented in [12] and [13]. It roots in the metaphor of the dining mathematicians presented in Section 4. Let us describe it.

The fictitious system is a session of several experts (may be from 5 to 10), each of them having a computer. The task of the session is to get a proposal of a (sub)optimal variant of a certain dynamic system.

At the beginning, each of the experts simulates the system from (simulated) time equal zero so that he respects his own opinion on the optimum variant. The experts simulate contemporarily and interrupt the simulation experiments when accessing a certain (simulated) time T.

Then they observe the results — often time integrals of some variables (e.g. of queue lengths, waiting times, income or expenditure) — and exchange information about that. One of the experts — let us call him W — recognizes his variant having led to the worst results; inspired by the variants of his colleagues, he processes the parameters of their variants to form a new variant for himself.

Then his colleagues continue their simulation experimenting from to $T + D$. SIMULA allows to model the experts so that they can simply proceed the simulation computing from (simulated) time T. Only W has to start the simulation of his new variant from the beginning, i.e. from time equal to zero, but he leads the simulation until the same time as his colleagues do, i.e. to $T + D$. Then the information exchange among the experts, leading to a new refusing of a variant and replacing it by that with — hopefully — better behavior takes place.

The experts simulate until time $T+2D$, and the cycle <simulation — communication — formulation of a new variant> is repeated until a certain (simulated) time $T + KD$ (where K uses to be from 100 to 500). In that state the experts come near to the optimum variant and in commercial applications the best variant being handled by them is sufficient. The theory says that such a way to the optimum realized during the simulation experimenting should take 50% of the computing time necessary for the conventional optimizing, which tests any variant by a simulation from zero until $T + KD$. Nevertheless commercial applications in steel metallurgy, machine production, neurophysiology, services and other branches demonstrated that the described method needs less computing time than about 15 percent of the time necessary for the conventional optimizing.

A natural question exists whether it would be necessary to apply conventional optimizing with simulation up to $T + KD$. There is a simple positive answer to such a question, which is supported by the following fact.

Simulation is applied for getting information on complex systems. For such systems it is difficult to determine the duration of the initial transitive phase during which the behavior of the system is exceptional and cannot be used for any decision concerning the optimum; the optimum design of a system should be designed according to its behavior in its *steady state*, which takes place after the initial phase. The information on the important behavior of the system (and therefore its optimizing, too) should be based at simulation experiments that map the system behavior during a certain duration T_S of its steady state. Nevertheless — because of the complexity of the simulated system — the duration of the initial phase is not known and one can formulate an extreme *optimistic* hypothesis T_{OPT} or an extreme *pessimistic* hypothesis T_{PES} about it, accepting that the true value T_X is somewhere between them. But it is just the method described above that enables to use the true duration for the optimizing: T is taken as $T_{OPT} + T_S$ and $T + KD$ as $T_{PES} + T_S$, which imply $D = \frac{T_{PES} - T_{OPT}}{K}$.

7 Reflective Simulation

When a system S is to be designed simulation is often used to give data that tell the designers about the behavior of various variants that they think on. Simulation models for that purpose can be called *external.* S can use simulation when it will operate: such a simulation can for instance test possible consequences of the decisions made during the operating of S. Let the simulation models used during the real existence of S and existing as its components be called *internal ones.* It is evident that both the internal models and the external ones concern the same thing and that it would be dummy to describe the external model in a language different from that applied for describing the internal ones.

The simulationists often say with humor that simulation is the worst way to get data about a system and that it should be replaced by a better way in case such a way exists (e.g. an analytical method, a direct experiment, a heuristic technique, or a search in a data base). They can say it, because they know that in case of complex systems there is no way to get data on them, excepting simulation. When the designers think about a system to contain a simulating computer, they have to accept that simulation is quite necessary, otherwise they would demonstrate their low professional level.

The consequence is that the external model should reflect not only "hard elements" of the designed system (machines, buildings, storages, ...) but also "soft elements", namely computers that exist contemporaneously with the hard elements and that sometimes simulate. To neglect the simulating computers in the external model would be a demonstration of one of two errors of the designers: if in such a state the external model gives good information the internal models can be rejected from the real system, too, and — oppositely — if the internal models are necessary to serve to the operation of the designed system, the external model without them would give false data about the studied system.

Therefore the external model of S has to contain the images of its simulating soft elements, i.e. the internal models should be nested in the external model. The phenomenon that it is not practiced roots in the fact that with use of common simulation tools (simulation languages, packages and object-oriented programming systems) it is too difficult to implement such an external model. Nevertheless SIMULA allows it; in principle the internal models can be nested in the external model similarly as outlined at the end of Section 5: `real_system_model` corresponds to the external model while `fictitious_system_model` represents the internal one.

There is a special property in the case presented in this Section: as it was mentioned, both the models concern the same thing and therefore what is formulated in `real_system_model` should be almost the same as what is declared in `fictitious_system_model`, which — of course — cease being a model of a fictitious system. In such a case we speak on reflective simulation, because the internal model should reflect what exists (or may exist) in the external one.

The practice of the reflective simulation carries some obstacles that were already overcome (see e.g. exhausting recommendations in manuals [14] and [15]). But there is a special aspect of the reflective simulation that has to be analyzed in some details. In concerns a programming error that can come just in case of reflective simulation and that is called *transplantation*. Let us describe that error and its possible consequences.

We already wrote that in case of the reflective simulation the language used for the description of the internal model should be almost the same as that used for the description of the external model. Suppose Q to be a name of a storage and R a name of an element that can enter Q. What can happen in the external model must be admitted for being mapped in the internal one and therefore the fact that R enters Q can occur in both the models. But what happens when one makes an error and writes in his model that R of the internal model enters Q of the external one?

Such an event has no analogy in the real world, because it means that something represented by means of electronic phenomena inside a computer existing in the real world enters into a storage that exists in the same real way as the computer. Nevertheless, one could say transplantation to be a certain analogy of the non-Euclidean geometries, about which 200 years ago one thought to be without sense and then their meaning and even their importance was discovered: although they seemed dummy they contain no internal contradiction. But it cannot be said about the transplantation [16]. If R enters Q it is handled as a component of the external model. It can have a neighbor P in Q, which belongs to the external model similarly as Q. But R can have a relation to another element M, which was introduced in an ordinary way before the transplantation; therefore M should belong to the internal model. Then, through the way M–R–neighbor of R, the computing process can handle P as if it would be an element of the internal model. An equivalent event can be accessed by the way M–R–storage of R: Q will be handled as a component of the internal model. Similar steps can be repeated, until both the external and internal models are hopelessly intermixed, and then the computing process fail into a collapse, emitting a message like "non-existing address". A reverse reconstruction of the steps from the message to the first erroneous step is impossible and therefore the place of the real programmer's error cannot be determined and repaired. Detailed experimenting leading to the collapses were presented in [16].

The ways of making the users safe against transplantation can be built in the run time phase or in the compiling one. The run time phase ways against transplantation do not limit the user's freedom but lead to an enormous prolongation of the run: every assignment must be tested whether it does not perform a transplantation. The security built in a compiler does not enlarge the run of the compiled program but implies restrictions of the language. Especially in case of SIMULA, we thought during 25 years it being secure against transplantation so strongly that it did not allow any communication between the external and internal models. Not sooner than in 1993 (therefore 26 years after the first proposal of the SIMULA principles and 25 years after the exact definition of its syntax and semantics) we discovered how to overcome the limitations (it is a splendid property of SIMULA that the tricky ways of the overcoming did not lead to any violation of its security!).

The SIMULA security roots in two syntactical restrictions: one of them asserts that a quasi-parallel system exists only contemporary with a subblock, while the second one states that the subblocks cannot get names (identifiers). As the simulation needs quasi-parallel systems, the internal and external models must be programmed as subblocks, but the consequence is that neither the external model nor the internal one cannot get names. Therefore one cannot express whether a name of an element (e.g. M, P, Q and R used in the example presented above) concerns the internal model or the external one, and the only "common rule of nesting blocks" is applicable: inside the block corresponding to the internal model such names point to its elements while the elements of the external model having the same names are not accessible there, and outside this block the names point to the elements of the external model while those of the internal one are inaccessible.

After the mentioned long period of 25 years, we discovered a trick, that will be demonstrated at the example of the name `Q`. Let us start from the example presented at the end of Section 5, and modify it slightly: let us introduce `external_model` in place of `real_system_model` and `internal_model` in place of `fictitious_system_model`, let us change the classes reflecting the simulated object (we are no oriented to the conveyor and its shortest path treatments more), and let us make a rather poetical (or dadaistic?) step by using name `world` for the class of computers that use the internal models. Let us introduce class `helping_force` and a name `assistant` for one of its instances; it reflects no real entity of the simulated system but will help to overcome the barriers given by SIMULA: when the `assistant` is demanded to give `Q_` it turns to what is called `Q` and presents it as `Q_`. As the assistant exists in the external model and out of the internal model, it handles `Q` belonging to the external model.

Now let us turn to class `world`. It contains a subblock internal_model. Outside this block, `world` contains function called `Q`, which is defined so that it delegates the assistant to give its `Q_`; the assistant gives `Q` of the external model and therefore — according to the rules of SIMULA — when this `world.Q` is met inside `world`, it points to `Q` of the external model. It holds also inside the internal model but if in that model an isolated text `Q` is met, the SIMULA rules determine that it is `Q` of the internal model. Therefore in the internal model one can distinguish between the both storages by using `Q` and `this world.Q`: `Q` points to `Q` of the internal model while this `world.Q` points to `Q` of the external one. Thus — for example — `Q.capacity:=this world.Q.capacity` expresses copying the value of attribute `capacity` of the storage `Q` existing in the external model, as the value of attribute capacity of the image of `Q` in the internal model. In SIMULA, `this world.Q` is to be read as "`Q` of this `world`", which illustrates the reason of the strange name given to the computer.

```
external_model: SIMULATION
begin class storage; ... ;
      ref(storage)Q;
      process class conveyor; ... ;
      class helping_force;
      begin ref(storage)procedure Q_; Q_:-Q;
      ...
      end of class helping_force;
      ref(helping_force)assistant;
      process class world;
      begin ref(storage)procedure Q; Q:-assistant.Q_;
            procedure simulate(...);
            begin internal_model: SIMULATION
                  begin class storage; ... ;
```

```
                        ref(storage)Q;
                        ...
                  end of the internal model;
            end of procedure simulate;
            ... life rules of class world ...
      end of class world;
      assistant:-new helping_force;
      ... forming the structure of real system model ...,
      activating its components ... ;
      activate new world;
      ...
end of the external model;
```

At the present time, a software system is implemented to translate a conventional simulation model written in SIMULA into an (external) model with computers that are able to observe the state of the system in that they occur, to generate a simulation model according it and to use it as internal model [17], [18]. Naturally, both the purpose of the internal model and the moments when it is to be applied depend on the users wishes and cannot be automatically generated. The software was made under the Barrande programme (bilateral cooperation between French and Czech universities, namely between the University of Ostrava and Blaise Pascal University in Clermont-Ferrand) and also supported by the institutional research scheme of the University of Ostrava.

8 An Example

During 1995–2000 the author of this paper was a member of an international consortium working under support of the European Commission at two Copernicus projects oriented to modernization of sea harbors by means of using modern information technologies [11], [19], [20]. Among the necessary tasks of the consortium work, an implementation of programming tools for simulation of container yards appeared. The tools had to be as general as possible, reflecting the wide spectrum of the container yards over the world.

The author of this paper oriented his work to that subject and used SIMULA to implement the mentioned tools: the subclassing, enabled by this language, appeared very suitable to realize the task (note that it was not only the subclassing of elementary classes like those of containers, transport tools etc. but also subclassing of main classes, i.e. in case of different "world viewings" to the container yards).

Using SIMULA there were no essential problems [21]. For computing the path of the ground-moving transport tools (further: GMTT, e.g. forklifts), the pseudosimulation of distributed pulses was applied similarly as it was presented in Section 5. Therefore the elaborated simulation models of the container yards contained nested simulation models of fictitious systems [22].

When a transport tool gets an instruction to move to a certain place a path is computed for its moving. In case of a GMTT the path must be composed of free places of the labyrinth among the stored containers, i.e. of places at which there is no container and no GMTT. The path is computed immediately when the instruction for moving is emitted and the computation is based on using the places that are free at the moment of the computing (the duration of the computing is neglected). But the computed path is then used during a certain non-zero time and during it the configuration of the free places can change: moving along the computed path, the GMTT can face to a barrier formed by a (temporarily) stored container or by another GMTT. Note that such barriers can arise only in case that more than one GMTT can contemporaneously operate in a container yard, but so it is just in many real situations.

A lot of control algorithms were proposed for what a GMTT should do when meeting a barrier. Hundreds of simulation experiments shown that any proposed algorithm led the system to deadlocks that stepwise cumulated in time until a complete collapse of moving in the whole yard. The solution was found in testing the computed path by simulation, in the following way.

Suppose at time t a GMTT F gets an instruction to move. We will say F to be *semiactive*. There may be other GMTTs that are already moving; their ways were already computed, tested and fixed at a time less than t and cannot be changed. Let us call them *active* GMTT. The other GMTT — in case they exist — are not moving, i.e. they have no path and a path can be assigned them later, at a time greater than t. A path P is computed for F and then a certain future of the container yard is simulated, supposing that P is accepted. The simulation experiment reflects also all moves of the active GMTT and is concluded by one of the following two events: the *happy end* is the event when F accesses the end of P, and the *bad end* is a conflict between F and a barrier. In case of the happy end the path P is accepted and F moves along it. In case of the bad end the place of the barrier is marked by a fictitious container and the process is repeated: a new path is computed for F and tested by simulation; because of the fictitious container, it will differ from P. So the process of two nested simulations — that of system of fictitious pulses and that of the future of the container yard — is repeated until a safe path is got. Many simulation experiments shown that in a realistic situation a safe path is always accessed [23], [24]; only in case the external simulation experiment is started so that more (e.g. four) GMTTs are cumulated around the first manipulated container, a deadlock comes immediately at the start, but no practiced worker of a container yard begins with such a bizarre decision step.

9 New Horizons

As we already mentioned, the simulation models of container yards, organized according to the described structure are external models containing two different internal ones so that one of them causes their use to be reflective simulation. Nowadays, the classification of the simulation models to those of real systems and those of fictitious systems seems to be clear and useful, and therefore a classification of the nested models seems to be almost clear; we wrote "almost", because beside the reflective simulation and the simulation using nested pseudosimulation, the third sort can be taken into account, characterized so that in a model of a real system S there is another model nested, simulating a system that is real but very different from S. Although the idea is natural and SIMULA allows applying it, its real application does not exist (it offers to be applied in concurrent engineering [25]).

But SIMULA opens other horizons, the substance of which is in mixing properties of real and fictitious systems. Although it may seem crazy, such systems can be simulated, their models can be nested into those of "uncrazy" systems and may be applied. An impressive example presented Novak (a student of Charles University in Prague) in his master thesis (the substance was published in English in [26]).

Computing a path of a GMTT, we try to get it as short as possible. The consequence of this intention is, that we automatically exclude the variants in which the GMTT should wait or even return. In Section 5 it was shown that the fictitious system of pulses produces only paths without waiting and without return, because when a pulse returns to a marked place it disappears. Nevertheless the idea to exclude the waiting and returns is not good in case the configuration of free places can change. In general, a GMTT can move near to a barrier, then it can wait there some time and then it can continue to move when the barrier disappears, and the time necessary for accessing the target can be smaller than that necessary for a moving along a rather long path without waiting. Moreover, even the following situation can exist without implying a deadlock:

There is a narrow way W between two walls formed by stored containers; the end places of W are Y and Z. Between them, but near to Y, there is a place A at W and beside it there is a place C in one of the walls, where occasionally no container is placed; C forms a certain alcove of W. At a place B between A and Z, there is a GMTT called G moving to the end Y, while near Y there is another GMTT called F. Its task is to move behind place Z. If the return and waiting is not accepted F should use another path than that through W; such a deviation could take much time. If a possibility to return and to wait exists F can move to A and then to C, there it can wait until G moves to a place between A and Y. Then F can return from C to A and to continue to Z.

Novak included an ability to generate such decisions so that he united both the internal models into a certain mix in which the images of real (active) GMTTs and fictitious pulses exist in a common simulated time and mutually interact: when the shortest path for a GMTT has to be determined the fictitious pulses are interpreted as all logically possible future moves of the semiactive GMTT and the moves are faced to meet with those moves and barriers that were already determined before and are caused by the active GMTT. If a pulse meets a barrier it does not disappear but it waits and when an image of an active GMTT moves along marked places it liquidates their marks so that the waiting pulses can continue to move through them.

10 Conclusion

Computer models penetrate more and more into the world in that we exist. The models reflect components of this world and — if using the terms *hard* and *soft*, introduced in Section 7 — we can classify the models into two different groups: the models of the hard components (production/logistic systems, living organisms, their organs and their communities, physical systems, buildings and their complexes etc.) and those of the soft components (e.g. data bases, computer networks and operation systems). The number of the models of the hard components is much grater because our world was originally composed of such components. Contemporarily with the computerization and informatization of the human society, the models will have to reflect penetrating of the computer models into the systems composed of hard components, i.e. have to map that the hard components are more and more bound by the soft ones, or — more precisely — by the models the soft components carry. The nesting of models will reflect the fact that the modeled hard components of the world develop to be less and less autonomous, influenced by soft ones.

This historical process leads to a certain task, namely to the necessity of studying the models of systems using models or — equivalently — to study theories concerning entities that carry theories. But — as we already wrote in Section 3 — the sciences give no support for it (the genial contribution given to mathematical logic and to our civilization by Kurt Gdel is too elementary than to be used as an effective aid). SIMULA surprises not only because it is a very effective stimulus for the mentioned task but also because of applications it offers. Already 35 years ago, the authors of SIMULA contributed not only by their ideas but also by their hard work that led the ideas until implementation functioning independently of the human thinking.

References

1. Rescigno, A., Segre, G.: La Cinetica dei Farmaci e dei Traccianti Radioattivi. Boringhieri, Torino (1961)
2. Sheppard, C. W.: Basic Principles of the Tracer Method — Introduction to Mathematical Tracer Kinetics. Wiley New York London (1962)
3. Kindler, E.: Simulation System COSMO, its Language and Compiler. Kybernetika 5 (1969) 201-211
4. Kindler, E.: COSMO (Compartmental system modelling) — Description of Programming System. Charles University, Prague (1967)
5. Kindler, E.: SIMULA Above and Beyond the Object-Oriented Programming. ASU Newsletter 21 (1993) No. 1, 41-44
6. Islo, H. E.: SOOP Corner. ASU Newsletter 22 (1994) No. 2, 22-26
7. Kindler, E.: Simulation of Systems Containing Simulating Elements. In: Snorek, M., Sujansky, M. Verbraeck, A. (eds.): Modelling and Simulation — ESM95, The Society for Computer Simulation International, San Diego, 1995, 609-613
8. Dahl, O.-J.: Discrete Event Simulation Languages. Norsk Regnesentral, Oslo (1966). Reprinted in [9]

9. Genuys, F. (ed.): Programming Languages. Academic Press, London New York (1968)
10. Kindler, E., Brejcha, M.: An Application of Main Class Nesting — Lee's Algorithm. SIMULA Newsletter 13 (1990) No.3, 24-26
11. Blumel, E. et al.: Managing and Controlling Growing Harbour Terminals. The Society for Computer Simulation International, San Diego Erlangen Ghent Budapest (1997)
12. Weinberger, J.: Extremization of Vector Criteria of Simulation Models by Means of Quasi-Parallel Handling. Computers and Artificial Intelligence 1 (1987) pp. 71-79
13. Weinberger, J.: Evolutionary Approach to Extremization of Vector Criteria of Simulation Models. Acta Universitatis Carolinae Medica 34 (1988) No. 3/4, 249-257
14. Kindler, E.: Chance for SIMULA. In: Islo, H. E. (ed.): Proceedings of the 25th Conference of the ASU — System Modelling Using Object-Oriented Simulation and Analysis. ASU, Kisten, Sweden (1999) 29-53. Reprinted as [15]
15. Kindler, E.: Chance for SIMULA. ASU Newsletter, 26 (2000) No. 1, 2-26
16. Kindler, E.: Transplantation — what Causes it in MS-DOS SIMULA? In: Breckling, B., Islo, H. E. (eds.): Object Oriented Modelling and Simulation of Environmental, Human and Technical Systems Ecology Center, Kiel (1998) 155-164
17. Kindler, E., Krivy, I., Tanguy, A.: Tentative de simulation rflective des systmes de production et logistiques. In: Dolgui A., Vernadat, F. (eds.): MOSIM'01, Actes de la troisime confrence francophone de MOdlisation et SIMulation "Conception, analyse et gestion des systmes industriels". Society for Computer Simulation International, San Diego Erlangen Ghent Delft (2001) Volume 1, 427-434
18. Kindler, E., Krivy, I., Tanguy, A.: Towards Automatic Generating of Reflective Simulation Models. In: Stefan, J. (ed.): Proceedings of 36th International Conference MOSIS '02 Modelling and Simulation of Systems, MARQ, Ostrava (2002) Vol. I, 13-19
19. Novitski, L., Bluemel, E., Merkuryev, Y., Tolujev, J., Ginters, E., Lorenz, P., Kindler, E., Slagter, D., Viktorova, E.: Simulation and Modelling in Managing and Controlling of Container Harbours. In: Kaylan, A. R., Lehmann, A. (eds.): Proceedings of the 1997 European Simulation Multiconference, Society for Computer Simulation International, San Diego (1997) 600-604
20. Bluemel, E., Novitsky, L. (eds.): Simulation and Information Systems Design: Applications in Latvian Ports. JUMI Ltd., Riga (2000)
21. Kindler, E.: Object-Oriented Simulation of Container Yards. In: Deussen, O., Lorenz, P. (eds.): Simulation und Animation '97. Society for Computer Simulation International, Erlangen Ghent Budapest San Diego (1997) 111-122
22. Kindler, E.: Nested Simulation Models Inside Simulation of Container Terminal. In: Bruzzone, A. G., Kerkhoffs E. J. K. (eds.): Simulation in Industry, 8th European Simulation Symposium (ESS 96). Society for Computer Simulation International, San Diego (1966) Vol. I, 653–657
23. Kindler, E.: Simulation Model of a Container Yard Containing a Simulating Computer. In: Bruzzone, A. G. (ed.): Harbour, Maritime & Industrial Logistics Modelling and Simulation HMS. The Society for Computer Simulation International, San Diego (1999) 3–8
24. Kindler, E.: Nesting Simulation of a Container Terminal Operating with its own Simulation Model. JORBEL (Journal of the Belgian Operation Research Society) Special Issue on Operation Research Models in a Harbour and Maritime Environment (2002) in print

25. Kindler, E.: SIMULA and Concurrent Engineering. ASU Newsletter, 21, (1993) No 3, 1-16
26. Novak, P.: Reflective Simulation with Simula and Java. In: Schulze, T., Hinz, V., Lorenz, P. (eds.): Simulation und Visualisation 2000. The Society for Computer Simulation International European Publishing House, Ghent (2000) 183-196

Efficient Coroutine Generation of Constrained Gray Sequences*

Donald E. Knuth[1] and Frank Ruskey[2]

[1] Computer Science Department
Stanford University
Stanford, CA 94305-9045 USA
http://www-cs-faculty.stanford.edu/~knuth/
[2] Department of Computer Science
University of Victoria
Victoria, B.C. V8W 3P6 Canada
http://www.cs.uvic.ca/~fruskey/
fruskey@cs.uvic.ca

Abstract. We study an interesting family of cooperating coroutines, which is able to generate all patterns of bits that satisfy certain fairly general ordering constraints, changing only one bit at a time. (More precisely, the directed graph of constraints is required to be cycle-free when it is regarded as an undirected graph.) If the coroutines are implemented carefully, they yield an algorithm that needs only a bounded amount of computation per bit change, thereby solving an open problem in the field of combinatorial pattern generation.

Much has been written about the transformation of procedures from recursive to iterative form, but little is known about the more general problem of transforming *coroutines* into equivalent programs that avoid unnecessary overhead. The present paper attempts to take a step in that direction by focusing on a reasonably simple yet nontrivial family of cooperating coroutines for which significant improvements in efficiency are possible when appropriate transformations are applied. The authors hope that this example will inspire other researchers to develop and explore the potentially rich field of coroutine transformation.

Coroutines, originally introduced by M. E. Conway [2], are analogous to subroutines, but they are symmetrical with respect to caller and callee: When coroutine A invokes coroutine B, the action of A is temporarily suspended and the action of B resumes where B had most recently left off. Coroutines arise naturally in producer/consumer situations or multipass processes, analogous to the "pipes" of UNIX, when each coroutine transforms an input stream to an output stream; a sequence of such processes can be controlled in such a way that their intermediate data files need not be written in memory. (See, for example, Section 1.4.2 of [9].)

The programming language SIMULA 67 [3] introduced support for coroutines in terms of fundamental operations named `call`, `detach`, and `resume`.

* dedicated to the memory of Ole-Johan Dahl

O. Owe et al. (Eds.): From OO to FM (Dahl Festschrift), LNCS 2635, pp. 183–208, 2004.

Arne Wang and Ole-Johan Dahl subsequently discovered [20] that an extremely simple computational model is able to accommodate these primitive operations. Dahl published several examples to demonstrate their usefulness in his chapter of the book *Structured Programming* [4]; then M. Clint [1] and O.-J. Dahl [6] began to develop theoretical tools for formal proofs of coroutine correctness.

Another significant early work appeared in R. W. Floyd's general top-down parsing algorithm for context-free languages [8], an algorithm that involved "imaginary men who are assumed to automatically appear when hired, disappear when fired, remember the names of their subordinates and superiors, and so on." Floyd's imaginary men were essentially carrying out coroutines, but their actions could not be described naturally in any programming languages that were available to Floyd when he wrote about the subject in 1964, so he presented the algorithm as a flow chart. Ole-Johan Dahl later gave an elegant implementation of Floyd's algorithm using the features of SIMULA 67, in §2.1.2 of [5].

The coroutine concept was refined further during the 1970s; see, for example, [19] and the references cited therein. But today's programming languages have replaced those ideas with more modern notions such as "threads" and "closures," which (while admirable in themselves) support coroutines only in a rather awkward and cumbersome manner. The simple principles of old-style coroutines, which Dahl called *quasi-parallel processes*, deserve to be resurrected again and given better treatment by the programming languages of tomorrow.

In this paper we will study examples for which a well-designed compiler could transform certain families of coroutines into optimized code, just as compilers can often transform recursive procedures into iterative routines that require less space and/or time.

The ideas presented below were motivated by applications to the exhaustive generation of combinatorial objects. For example, consider a coroutine that wants to look at all permutations of n elements; it can call repeatedly on a permutation-generation coroutine to produce the successive arrangements. The latter coroutine repeatedly forms a new permutation and calls on the former coroutine to inspect the result. The permutation coroutine has its own internal state — its own local variables and its current location in an ongoing computational process — so it does not consider itself to be a "subroutine" of the inspection coroutine. The permutation coroutine might also invoke other coroutines, which in turn are computational objects with their own internal states.

We shall consider the problem of generating all n-tuples $a_1a_2\ldots a_n$ of 0s and 1s with the property that $a_j \le a_k$ whenever $j \to k$ is an arc in a given directed graph. Thus $a_j = 1$ implies that a_k must also be 1; if $a_k = 0$, so is a_j. These n-tuples are supposed to form a "Gray path," in the sense that only one bit a_j should change at each step. For example, if $n = 3$ and if we require $a_1 \le a_3$ and $a_2 \le a_3$, five binary strings $a_1a_2a_3$ satisfy the inequalities, and one such Gray path is

$$000,\ 001,\ 011,\ 111,\ 101.$$

The general problem just stated does not always have a solution. For example, suppose the given digraph is

so that the inequalities are $a_1 \le a_2$ and $a_2 \le a_1$; then we are asking for a way to generate the tuples 00 and 11 by changing only one bit at a time, and this is clearly impossible. Even if we stipulate that the digraph of inequalities should contain no directed cycles, we might encounter an example like

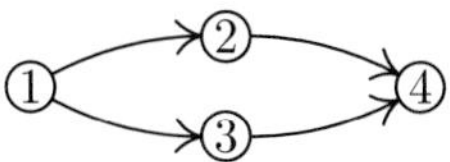

in which the Gray constraint cannot be achieved; here the corresponding 4-tuples

$$0000, 0001, 0011, 0101, 0111, 1111$$

include four of even weight and two of odd weight, but a Gray path must alternate between even and odd. Reasonably efficient methods for solving the problem without Grayness are known [17, 18], but we want to insist on single-bit changes.

We will prove constructively that Gray paths always do exist if we restrict consideration to directed graphs that are *totally acyclic*, in the sense that they contain no cycles even if the directions of the arcs are ignored. Every component of such a graph is a free tree in which a direction has been assigned to each branch between two vertices. Such digraphs are called *spiders*, because of their resemblance to arachnids:

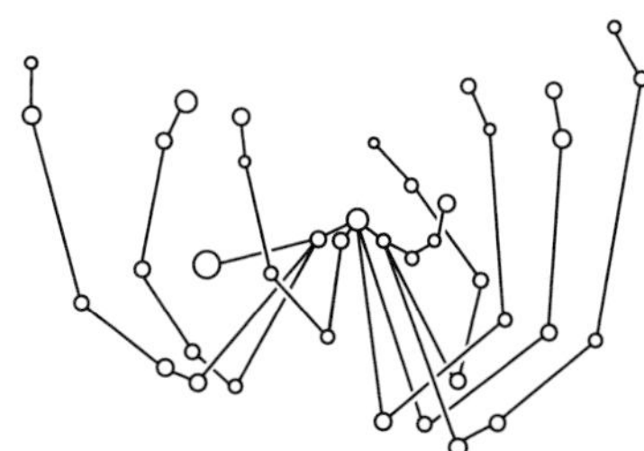

(In this diagram, as in others below, we assume that all arcs are directed upwards. More complicated graph-theoretical spiders have legs that change directions many more times than real spider legs do.) The general problem of finding all $a_1 \ldots a_n$ such that $a_j \le a_k$ when $j \to k$ in such a digraph is formally called the task of "generating the order ideals of an acyclic poset"; it also is called, informally, "spider squishing."

Sections 1–3 of this paper discuss simple examples of the problem in preparation for Section 4, which presents a constructive proof that suitable Gray paths always exist. The proof of Section 4 is implemented with coroutines in Section 5, and Section 6 discusses the nontrivial task of getting all the coroutines properly launched.

Section 7 describes a simple technique that is often able to improve the running time. A generalization of that technique leads in Section 8 to an efficient coroutine-free implementation. Additional optimizations, which can be used to construct an algorithm for the spider-squishing problem that is actually *loopless*, are discussed in Section 9. (A loopless algorithm needs only constant time to change each n-tuple to its successor.)

Section 10 concludes the paper and mentions several open problems connected to related work.

1 The Unrestricted Case

Let's begin by imagining an array of friendly trolls called T_1, T_2, ..., T_n. Each troll carries a lamp that is either off or on; he also can be either awake or asleep. Initially all the trolls are awake, and all their lamps are off.

Changes occur to the system when a troll is "poked," according to the following simple rules: If T_k is poked when he is awake, he changes the state of his lamp from off to on or vice versa; then he becomes tired and goes to sleep. Later, when the sleeping T_k is poked again, he wakes up and pokes his left neighbor T_{k-1}, without making any change to his own lamp. (The leftmost troll T_1 has no left neighbor, so he simply awakens when poked.)

At periodic intervals an external driving force D pokes the rightmost troll T_n, initiating a chain of events that culminates in one lamp changing its state. The process begins as follows, if we use the digits 0 and 1 to represent lamps that are respectively off or on, and if we underline the digit of a sleeping troll:

$\ldots 0000$ Initial state
$\ldots 000\underline{1}$ D pokes T_n
$\ldots 00\underline{1}1$ D pokes T_n, who wakes up and pokes T_{n-1}
$\ldots 00\underline{1}\underline{0}$ D pokes T_n
$\ldots 0\underline{1}10$ D pokes T_n, who pokes T_{n-1}, who pokes T_{n-2}
$\ldots 0\underline{1}1\underline{1}$ D pokes T_n
$\ldots 0\underline{1}\underline{0}1$ D pokes T_n, who pokes T_{n-1}

The sequence of underlined versus not-underlined digits acts essentially as a binary counter. And the sequence of digit patterns, in which exactly one bit changes at each step, is a *Gray binary* counter, which follows the well-known Gray binary code; it also corresponds to the process of replacing rings in the classic Chinese ring puzzle [12]. Therefore the array of trolls solves our problem of generating all n-tuples $a_1a_2\ldots a_n$, in the special case when the spider digraph has no arcs. (This troll-oriented way to generate Gray binary code was presented by the first author in a lecture at the University of Oslo in October, 1972 [10].)

During the first 2^n steps of the process just described, troll T_n is poked 2^n times, troll T_{n-1} is poked 2^{n-1} times, ..., and troll T_1 is poked twice. The last step is special because T_1 has no left neighbor; when he is poked the second time, all the trolls wake up, but no lamps change. The driver D would like to know about this exceptional case, so we will assume that T_n sends a message to D after being poked, saying '*true*' if one of the lamps has changed, otherwise saying '*false*'. Similarly, if $1 \le k < n$, T_k will send a message to T_{k+1} after being poked, saying '*true*' if and only if one of the first k lamps has just changed state.

These hypothetical trolls T_1, ..., T_n correspond to n almost-identical coroutines *poke*[1], ..., *poke*[n], whose actions can be expressed in an ad hoc Algol-like language as follows:

```
Boolean coroutine poke[k];
  while true do begin
    awake: a[k] := 1 - a[k];
       return true;
    asleep: if k > 1 then
                 return poke[k - 1]
              else
                 return false;
  end.
```

Coroutine *poke*[k] describes the action of T_k, implicitly retaining its own state of wakefulness: When *poke*[k] is next activated after having executed the statement '`return` *true*' it will resume its program at label 'asleep'; and it will resume at label 'awake' when it is next activated after '`return` *poke*[$k-1$]' or '`return` *false*'.

In this example and in all the coroutine programs below, the enclosing '`while` *true* `do begin` $\langle P \rangle$ `end`' merely says that program $\langle P \rangle$ should be repeated endlessly; all coroutines that we shall encounter in this paper are immortal. (This is fortunate, because Dahl [6] has observed that proofs of correctness tend to be much simpler in such cases.)

Our coroutines will also always be "ultra-lightweight" processes, in the sense that they need no internal stack. They need only remember their current positions within their respective programs, along with a few local variables in some cases, together with the global "lamp" variables $a[1], \ldots, a[n]$. We can implement them using a single stack, essentially as if we were implementing recursive procedures in the normal way, pushing the address of a return point within A onto the stack when coroutine A invokes coroutine B, and resuming A after B executes a `return`. (Wang and Dahl [20] used the term "semicoroutine" for this special case. We are, however, using `return` statements to return a value, instead of using global variables for communication and saying '`detach`' as Wang and Dahl did.) The only difference between our coroutine conventions and ordinary subroutine actions is that a newly invoked coroutine always begins at the point following its most recent `return`, regardless of who had previously invoked it. No coroutine will appear on the execution stack more than once at any time.

Thus, for example, the coroutines *poke*[1] and *poke*[2] behave as follows when $n = 2$:

00	Initial state
$0\underline{1}$	*poke*[2] = *true*
$\underline{1}1$	*poke*[2] = *poke*[1] = *true*
$\underline{1}\underline{0}$	*poke*[2] = *true*
10	*poke*[2] = *poke*[1] = *false*
$1\underline{1}$	*poke*[2] = *true*
$\underline{0}1$	*poke*[2] = *poke*[1] = *true*
$\underline{0}\underline{0}$	*poke*[2] = *true*
00	*poke*[2] = *poke*[1] = *false*

The same cycle will repeat indefinitely, because everything has returned to its initial state.

Notice that the repeating cycle in this example consists of two distinct parts. The first half cycle, before *false* is returned, generates all two-bit patterns in Gray binary order $(00, 01, 11, 10)$; the other half generates those patterns again, but in the *reverse* order $(10, 11, 01, 00)$. Such behavior will be characteristic of all the coroutines that we shall consider for the spider-squishing problem: Their task will be to run through all n-tuples $a_1 \ldots a_n$ such that $a_j \leq a_k$ for certain given pairs (j, k), always returning *true* until all permissible patterns have been generated; then they are supposed to run through those n-tuples again in reverse order, and to repeat the process ad infinitum.

Under these conventions, a driver program of the following form will cycle through the answers, printing a line of dashes between each complete listing:

```
⟨ Create all the coroutines ⟩;
⟨ Put each lamp and each coroutine into the proper initial state ⟩;
while true do begin
  for k := 1 step 1 until n do write(a[k]);
  write(newline);
  if not root then write("-----", newline);
end.
```

Here *root* denotes a coroutine that can potentially activate all the others; for example, *root* is *poke*[n] in the particular case that we've been considering. In practice, of course, the driver would normally carry out some interesting process on the bits $a_1 \ldots a_n$, instead of merely outputting them to a file.

The fact that coroutines *poke*[1], ..., *poke*[n] do indeed generate Gray binary code is easy to verify by induction on n. The case $n = 1$ is trivial, because the outputs will clearly be

```
0
1
----------
1
0
----------
```

and so on. On the other hand if $n > 1$, assume that the successive contents of $a_1 \ldots a_{n-1}$ are α_0, α_1, α_2, ... when we repeatedly invoke *poke*$[n-1]$, assuming that $\alpha_0 = 0 \ldots 0$ and that all coroutines are initially at the label 'awake'; assume further that *false* is returned just before α_m when m is a multiple of 2^{n-1}, otherwise the returned value is *true*. Then repeated invocations of *poke*$[n]$ will lead to the successive lamp patterns

$$\alpha_0 0,\ \alpha_0 1,\ \alpha_1 1,\ \alpha_1 0,\ \alpha_2 0,\ \alpha_2 1,\ \ldots,$$

and *false* will be returned after every sequence of 2^n outputs. These are precisely the patterns of n-bit Gray binary code, alternately in forward order and reverse order.

2 Chains

Now let's go to the opposite extreme and suppose that the digraph of constraints is an oriented path or chain,

$$1 \to 2 \to \cdots \to n.$$

In other words, we want now to generate all n-tuples $a_1 a_2 \ldots a_n$ such that

$$0 \le a_1 \le a_2 \le \cdots \le a_n \le 1,$$

proceeding alternately forward and backward in Gray order. Of course this problem is trivial, but we want to do it with coroutines so that we'll be able to tackle more difficult problems later.

Here are some coroutines that do the new job, if the driver program initiates action by invoking the root coroutine *bump*$[1]$:

```
Boolean coroutine bump[k];
  while true do begin
     awake0: if k < n then while bump[k+1] do return true;
        a[k] := 1; return true;
     asleep1: return false; comment a_k ... a_n = 1...1;
     awake1: a[k] := 0; return true;
     asleep0: if k < n then while bump[k+1] do return true;
        return false; comment a_k ... a_n = 0...0;
  end.
```

For example, the process plays out as follows when $n = 3$:

000	Initial state	123
$00\underline{1}$	*bump*$[1]$ = *bump*$[2]$ = *bump*$[3]$ = *true*	$12\underline{3}$
$0\underline{1}1$	*bump*$[1]$ = *bump*$[2]$ = *true*, *bump*$[3]$ = *false*	$1\underline{2}$
$\underline{1}11$	*bump*$[1]$ = *true*, *bump*$[2]$ = *false*	$\underline{1}$
111	*bump*$[1]$ = *false*	1
$\underline{0}11$	*bump*$[1]$ = *true*	$\underline{1}2$
$\underline{0}\underline{0}1$	*bump*$[1]$ = *bump*$[2]$ = *true*	$\underline{1}\underline{2}3$
$\underline{0}\underline{0}\underline{0}$	*bump*$[1]$ = *bump*$[2]$ = *bump*$[3]$ = *true*	$\underline{1}\underline{2}\underline{3}$
000	*bump*$[1]$ = *bump*$[2]$ = *bump*$[3]$ = *false*	123

Each troll's action now depends on whether his lamp is lit as well as on his state of wakefulness. A troll with an unlighted lamp always passes each bump to the right, without taking any notice unless a *false* reply comes back. In the latter case, he acts as if his lamp had been lit — namely, he either returns *false* (if just awakened), or he changes the lamp, returns *true*, and nods off. The Boolean value returned in each case is *true* if and only if a lamp has changed its state during the current invocation of *bump*[k].

(*Note:* The numbers '123', '12$\underline{3}$', ... at the right of this example correspond to an encoding that will be explained in Section 8 below. A similar column of somewhat inscrutable figures will be given with other examples we will see later, so that the principles of Section 8 will be easier to understand when we reach that part of the story. There is no need to decipher such notations until then; all will be revealed eventually.)

The dual situation, in which all inequalities are reversed so that we generate all $a_1a_2\ldots a_n$ with

$$1 \geq a_1 \geq a_2 \geq \cdots \geq a_n \geq 0,$$

can be implemented by interchanging the roles of 0 and 1 and starting the previous sequence in the midpoint of its period:

```
Boolean coroutine cobump[k];
  while true do begin
    awake0: a[k] := 1; return true;
    asleep1: if k < n then
                 while cobump[k + 1] do return true;
          return false;  comment a_k ... a_n = 1...1;
    awake1: if k < n then
                 while cobump[k + 1] do return true;
         a[k] := 0; return true;
    asleep0: return false;  comment a_k ... a_n = 0...0;
  end.
```

A mixed situation in which the constraints are

$$0 \leq a_n \leq a_{n-1} \leq \cdots \leq a_{m+1} \leq a_1 \leq a_2 \leq \cdots \leq a_m \leq 1$$

is also worthy of note. Again the underlying digraph is a chain, and the driver repeatedly bumps troll T_1; but when $1 < m < n$, the coroutines are a mixture of those we've just seen:

```
Boolean coroutine mbump[k];
  while true do begin
     awake0: if k < m then
                 while mbump[k + 1] do return true;
          a[k] := 1; return true;
     asleep1: if m < k ∧ k < n then
                 while mbump[k + 1] do return true;
```

```
      if k = 1 ∧ m < n then
         while mbump[m + 1] do return true;
      return false;
   awake1: if m < k ∧ k < n then
         while mbump[k + 1] do return true;
      if k = 1 ∧ m < n then
         while mbump[m + 1] do return true;
      a[k] := 0; return true;
   asleep0: if k < m then
         while mbump[k + 1] do return true;
      return false;
end.
```

The reader is encouraged to simulate the *mbump* coroutines by hand when, say, $m = 2$ and $n = 4$, in order to develop a better intuition about coroutine behavior. Notice that when $m \approx \frac{1}{2}n$, signals need to propagate only about half as far as they do when $m = 1$ or $m = n$.

Still another simple but significant variant arises when several separate chains are present. The digraph might, for example, be

in which case we want all 6-tuples of bits $a_1 \ldots a_6$ with $a_1 \le a_2$ and $a_4 \le a_5 \le a_6$. In general, suppose there is a set of endpoints $E = \{e_1, \ldots, e_m\}$ such that

$$1 = e_1 < \cdots < e_m \le n,$$

and we want

$$a_k \in \{0, 1\} \quad \text{for } 1 \le k \le n; \qquad a_{k-1} \le a_k \quad \text{for } k \notin E.$$

(The set E is $\{1, 3, 4\}$ in the example shown.) The following coroutines $ebump[k]$, for $1 \le k \le n$, generate all such n-tuples if the driver invokes $ebump[e_m]$:

```
Boolean coroutine ebump[k];
  while true do begin
  awake0: if k+1∉E∪{n+1} then while ebump[k+1] do return true;
     a[k] := 1; return true;
  asleep1: if k ∈ E \ {1} then return ebump[k′]
           else return false;
  awake1: a[k] := 0; return true;
  asleep0: if k+1∉E∪{n+1} then while ebump[k+1] do return true;
     if k ∈ E \ {1} then return ebump[k′]
     else return false;
end.
```

Here k' stands for e_{j-1} when $k = e_j$ and $j > 1$. These routines reduce to *poke* when $E = \{1, 2, \ldots, n\}$ and to *bump* when $E = \{1\}$. If $E = \{1, 3, 4\}$, they will generate all 24 bit patterns such that $a_1 \le a_2$ and $a_4 \le a_5 \le a_6$ in the order

$$\begin{gathered}
000000,\ 00000\underline{1},\ 0000\underline{1}1,\ 000\underline{1}11,\ 00\underline{1}111,\ 00\underline{1}\underline{0}11,\ 00\underline{1}\underline{0}\underline{0}1,\ 00\underline{1}\underline{0}\underline{0}\underline{0},\\
0\underline{1}1000,\ 0\underline{1}100\underline{1},\ 0\underline{1}10\underline{1}1,\ 0\underline{1}1\underline{1}11,\ 0\underline{1}\underline{0}111,\ 0\underline{1}\underline{0}\underline{0}11,\ 0\underline{1}\underline{0}\underline{0}\underline{0}1,\ 0\underline{1}\underline{0}\underline{0}\underline{0}\underline{0},\\
\underline{1}10000,\ \underline{1}1000\underline{1},\ \underline{1}100\underline{1}1,\ \underline{1}10\underline{1}11,\ \underline{1}1\underline{1}111,\ \underline{1}1\underline{1}\underline{0}11,\ \underline{1}1\underline{1}\underline{0}\underline{0}1,\ \underline{1}1\underline{1}\underline{0}\underline{0}\underline{0};
\end{gathered}$$

then the sequence will reverse itself:

$$\begin{gathered}
111000,\ 11100\underline{1},\ 1110\underline{1}1,\ 111\underline{1}11,\ 11\underline{0}111,\ 11\underline{0}\underline{0}11,\ 11\underline{0}\underline{0}\underline{0}1,\ 11\underline{0}\underline{0}\underline{0}\underline{0},\\
\underline{0}10000,\ \underline{0}1000\underline{1},\ \underline{0}100\underline{1}1,\ \underline{0}10\underline{1}11,\ \underline{0}1\underline{1}111,\ \underline{0}1\underline{1}\underline{0}11,\ \underline{0}1\underline{1}\underline{0}\underline{0}1,\ \underline{0}1\underline{1}\underline{0}\underline{0}\underline{0},\\
\underline{0}\underline{0}1000,\ \underline{0}\underline{0}100\underline{1},\ \underline{0}\underline{0}10\underline{1}1,\ \underline{0}\underline{0}1\underline{1}11,\ \underline{0}\underline{0}\underline{0}111,\ \underline{0}\underline{0}\underline{0}\underline{0}11,\ \underline{0}\underline{0}\underline{0}\underline{0}\underline{0}1,\ \underline{0}\underline{0}\underline{0}\underline{0}\underline{0}\underline{0}.
\end{gathered}$$

In our examples so far we have discussed several families of cooperating coroutines and claimed that they generate certain n-tuples, but we haven't proved anything rigorously. A formal theory of coroutine semantics is beyond the scope of this paper, but we should at least try to construct a semi-formal demonstration that *ebump* is correct.

The proof is by induction on $|E|$, the number of chains. If $|E| = 1$, *ebump*$[k]$ reduces to *bump*$[k]$, and we can argue by induction on n. The result is obvious when $n = 1$. If $n > 1$, suppose repeated calls on *bump*$[2]$ cause $a_2 \ldots a_n$ to run through the $(n-1)$-tuples α_0, α_1, α_2, $\ldots$, where *bump*$[2]$ is *false* when it produces $\alpha_t = \alpha_{t-1}$. Such a repetition will occur if and only if t is a multiple of n, because n is the number of distinct $(n-1)$-tuples with $a_2 \le \cdots \le a_n$. We know by induction that the sequence has reflective symmetry: $\alpha_j = \alpha_{2n-1-j}$ for $0 \le j < n$. Furthermore, $\alpha_{j+2n} = \alpha_j$ for all $j \ge 0$. To complete the proof we observe that repeated calls on *bump*$[1]$ will produce the n-tuples

$$\begin{aligned}
&0\alpha_0,\ 0\alpha_1,\ \ldots,\ 0\alpha_{n-1},\ \underline{1}\alpha_n,\\
&1\alpha_n,\ \underline{0}\alpha_n,\ \underline{0}\alpha_{n+1},\ \ldots,\ \underline{0}\alpha_{2n-1},\\
&0\alpha_{2n},\ 0\alpha_{2n+1},\ \ldots,\ 0\alpha_{3n-1},\ \underline{1}\alpha_{3n},
\end{aligned}$$

and so on, returning *false* every $(n+1)^{\text{st}}$ step as desired.

If $|E| > 1$, let $E = \{e_1, \ldots, e_m\}$, so that $e'_m = e_{m-1}$, and suppose that repeated calls on *ebump*$[e_{m-1}]$ produce the $(e_m - 1)$-tuples α_0, α_1, α_2, $\ldots$. Also suppose that calls on *ebump*$[e_m]$ would set the remaining bits $a_{e_m} \ldots a_n$ to the $(n+1-e_m)$-tuples β_0, β_1, β_2, $\ldots$, if E were empty instead of $\{e_1, \ldots, e_m\}$; this sequence β_0, β_1, β_2, $\ldots$ is like the output of *bump*. The α and β sequences are periodic, with respective periods of length $2M$ and $2N$ for some M and N; they also have reflective symmetry $\alpha_j = \alpha_{2M-1-j}$, $\beta_k = \beta_{2N-1-k}$. It follows that *ebump*$[e_m]$ is correct, because it produces the sequence

$$\begin{aligned}\gamma_0, \gamma_1, \gamma_2, \ldots = {} & \alpha_0\beta_0,\ \alpha_0\beta_1,\ \ldots,\ \alpha_0\beta_{N-1},\\ & \alpha_1\beta_N,\ \alpha_1\beta_{N+1},\ \ldots,\ \alpha_1\beta_{2N-1},\\ & \vdots\\ & \alpha_{M-1}\beta_{(M-1)N},\ \alpha_{M-1}\beta_{(M-1)N+1},\ \ldots,\ \alpha_{M-1}\beta_{MN-1},\\ & \alpha_M\beta_{MN},\ \alpha_M\beta_{MN+1},\ \ldots,\ \alpha_M\beta_{(M+1)N-1},\\ & \vdots\\ & \alpha_{2M-1}\beta_{(2M-1)N},\ \alpha_{2M-1}\beta_{(2M-1)N+1},\ \ldots,\ \alpha_{2M-1}\beta_{2MN-1},\ \ldots\end{aligned}$$

which has period length $2MN$ and satisfies

$$\gamma_{Nj+k} = \alpha_j\beta_{Nj+k} = \alpha_{2M-1-j}\beta_{2MN-1-Nj-k} = \gamma_{2MN-1-Nj-k}$$

for $0 \le j < M$ and $0 \le k < N$.

The patterns output by *ebump* are therefore easily seen to be essentially the same as the so-called *reflected Gray paths* for radices $e_2+1-e_1, \ldots, e_m+1-e_{m-1}$, $n+2-e_m$ (see [12]); the total number of outputs is

$$(e_2+1-e_1)\ldots(e_m+1-e_{m-1})(n+2-e_m).$$

3 Ups and Downs

Now let's consider a "fence" digraph

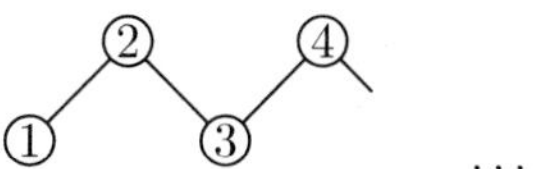

$\ldots,$

which leads to n-tuples that satisfy the up-down constraints

$$a_1 \le a_2 \ge a_3 \le a_4 \ge \cdots.$$

A reasonably simple set of coroutines can be shown to handle this case, rooted at *nudge*[1]:

```
Boolean coroutine nudge[k];
  while true do begin
    awake0: if k′ ≤ n then while nudge[k′] do return true;
       a[k] := 1; return true;
    asleep1: if k″ ≤ n then while nudge[k″] do return true;
       return false;
    awake1: if k″ ≤ n then while nudge[k″] do return true;
       a[k] := 0; return true;
    asleep0: if k′ ≤ n then while nudge[k′] do return true;
       return false;
  end.
```

Here $(k', k'') = (k+1, k+2)$ when k is odd, $(k+2, k+1)$ when k is even. But these coroutines do *not* work when they all begin at 'awake0' with $a_1 a_2 \ldots a_n = 00\ldots0$; they need to be initialized carefully. For example, when $n = 6$ it turns out that exactly eleven patterns of odd weight need to be generated, and exactly ten patterns of even weight, so a Gray path cannot begin or end with an even-weight pattern such as 000000 or 111111. One proper starting configuration is obtained if we set $a_1 \ldots a_n$ to the first n bits of the infinite string $000111000111\ldots$, and if we start coroutine *nudge*$[k]$ at 'awake0' if $a_k = 0$, at 'awake1' if $a_k = 1$. For example, the sequence of results when $n = 4$ is

0001	Initial configuration	124
$000\underline{0}$	*nudge*[1] = *nudge*[2] = *nudge*[4] = *true*	$12\underline{4}$
$0\underline{1}00$	*nudge*[1] = *nudge*[2] = *true*, *nudge*[4] = *false*	$1\underline{2}34$
$0\underline{1}0\underline{1}$	*nudge*[1] = *nudge*[2] = *nudge*[3] = *nudge*[4] = *true*	$1\underline{2}3\underline{4}$
$0\underline{1}\underline{1}1$	*nudge*[1] = *nudge*[2] = *nudge*[3] = *true*, *nudge*[4] = *false*	$1\underline{2}\underline{3}$
$\underline{1}111$	*nudge*[1] = *true*, *nudge*[2] = *nudge*[3] = *false*	$\underline{1}3$
$\underline{1}1\underline{0}1$	*nudge*[1] = *nudge*[3] = *true*	$\underline{1}\underline{3}4$
$\underline{1}1\underline{0}\underline{0}$	*nudge*[1] = *nudge*[3] = *nudge*[4] = *true*	$\underline{1}\underline{3}\underline{4}$
1100	*nudge*[1] = *nudge*[3] = *nudge*[4] = *false*	134
$110\underline{1}$	*nudge*[1] = *nudge*[3] = *nudge*[4] = *true*	$13\underline{4}$
$11\underline{1}1$	*nudge*[1] = *nudge*[3] = *true*, *nudge*[4] = *false*	$1\underline{3}$
$\underline{0}111$	*nudge*[1] = *true*, *nudge*[3] = *false*	$\underline{1}23$
$\underline{0}1\underline{0}1$	*nudge*[1] = *nudge*[2] = *nudge*[3] = *true*	$\underline{1}2\underline{3}4$
$\underline{0}1\underline{0}\underline{0}$	*nudge*[1] = *nudge*[2] = *nudge*[3] = *nudge*[4] = *true*	$\underline{1}2\underline{3}\underline{4}$
$\underline{0}\underline{0}00$	*nudge*[1] = *nudge*[2] = *true*, *nudge*[3] = *nudge*[4] = *false*	$\underline{1}\underline{2}4$
$\underline{0}\underline{0}0\underline{1}$	*nudge*[1] = *nudge*[2] = *nudge*[4] = *true*	$\underline{1}\underline{2}\underline{4}$
0001	*nudge*[1] = *nudge*[2] = *nudge*[4] = *false*	124

Again the cycle repeats with reflective symmetry; and again, some cryptic notations appear that will be explained in Section 8. The correctness of *nudge* will follow from results we shall prove later.

4 The General Case

We have seen that cleverly constructed coroutines are able to generate Gray paths for several rather different special cases of the spider-squishing problem; thus it is natural to hope that similar techniques will work in the general case when an arbitrary totally acyclic digraph is given. The spider

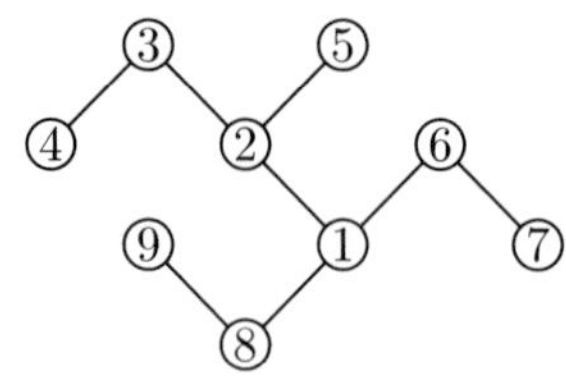

illustrates most of the complications that might face us, so we shall use it as a running example. In general we shall assume that the vertices have been numbered in *preorder*, as defined in [9, Section 2.3.2], when the digraph is considered to be a forest (ignoring the arc directions). This means that the smallest vertex in each component is the root of that component, and that all vertex numbers of a component are consecutive. Furthermore, the children of each node are immediately followed in the ordering by their descendants. The descendants of each node k form a subspider consisting of nodes k through scope(k), inclusive; we shall call this "spider k." For example, spider 2 consists of nodes $\{2,3,4,5\}$, and scope(2) $= 5$. Our sample spider has indeed been numbered in preorder, because it can be drawn as a properly numbered tree with directed branches:

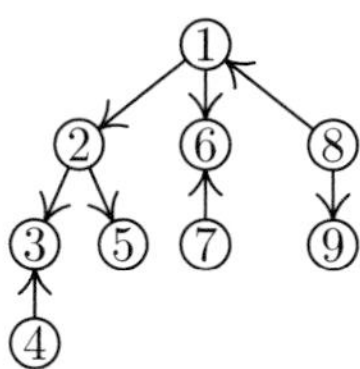

The same spider could also have been numbered in many other ways, because any vertex of the digraph could have been chosen to be the root, and because the resulting trees can be embedded several ways into the plane by permuting the children of each family.

Assume for the moment that the digraph is connected; thus it is a tree with root 1. A nonroot vertex x is called *positive* if the path from 1 to x ends with an arc directed towards x, *negative* if that path ends with an arc directed away from x. Thus the example spider has positive vertices $\{2,3,5,6,9\}$ and negative vertices $\{4,7,8\}$.

Let us write $x \to^* y$ if there is a directed path from x to y in the digraph. Removing all vertices x such that $x \to^* 1$ disconnects the graph into a number of pieces having positive roots; in our example, the removal of $\{1,8\}$ leaves three components rooted at $\{2,6,9\}$. We call these roots the *positive vertices near* 1, and we denote that set by U_1. Similarly, the *negative vertices near* 1 are obtained when we remove all vertices y such that $1 \to^* y$; the set of resulting roots, denoted by V_1, is $\{4,7,8\}$ in our example, because we remove $\{1,2,3,5,6\}$.

The relevant bit patterns $a_1 \ldots a_n$ for which $a_1 = 0$ are precisely those that we obtain if we set $a_j = 0$ whenever $j \to^* 1$ and if we supply bit patterns for each subspider rooted at a vertex of U_1. Similarly, the bit patterns for which $a_1 = 1$ are precisely those we obtain by setting $a_k = 1$ whenever $1 \to^* k$ and by supplying patterns for each subspider rooted at a vertex of V_1. Thus if n_k denotes the number of bit patterns for spider k, the total number of suitable patterns $a_1 \ldots a_n$ is $\prod_{u \in U_1} n_u + \prod_{v \in V_1} n_v$.

The sets U_k and V_k of positive and negative vertices near k are defined in the same way for each spider k.

Every positive child of k appears in U_k, and every negative child appears in V_k. These are called the *principal* elements of U_k and V_k. Every nonprincipal member of U_k is a member of U_v for some unique principal vertex v of V_k. Similarly, every nonprincipal member of V_k is a member of V_u for some unique principal vertex u of U_k. For example, the principal members of U_1 are 2 and 6; the other member, 9, belongs to U_8, where 8 is a principal member of V_1.

We will prove that the bit patterns $a_1 \ldots a_n$ can always be arranged in a Gray path such that bit a_1 begins at 0 and ends at 1, changing exactly once. By induction, such paths exist for the n_u patterns in each spider u for $u \in U_1$. And we can combine such paths into a single path that passes through all of the $\prod_{u \in U_1} n_u$ ways to combine those patterns, using a reflected Gray code analogous to the output of *ebump* in Section 3 above. Thus, if we set $a_k = 0$ for all k such that $k \to^* 1$, we get a Gray path P_1 for all suitable patterns with $a_1 = 0$. Similarly we can construct a Gray path Q_1 for the $\prod_{v \in V_1} n_v$ suitable patterns with $a_1 = 1$. Thus, all we need to do is prove that it is possible to construct P_1 and Q_1 in such a way that the last pattern in P_1 differs from the first pattern of Q_1 only in bit a_1. Then $G_1 = (P_1, Q_1)$ will be a suitable Gray path that solves our problem.

For example, consider the subspiders for $U_1 = \{2, 6, 9\}$ in the example spider. An inductive construction shows that they have respectively $(n_2, n_6, n_9) = (8, 3, 2)$ patterns, with corresponding Gray paths

$$\begin{aligned} G_2 &= 0000, 0001, 0101, 0100, 0110, 0111, 1111, 1101; \\ G_6 &= 00, 10, 11; \\ G_9 &= 0, 1. \end{aligned}$$

We obtain 48 patterns P_1 by setting $a_1 = a_8 = 0$ and using G_2 for $a_2a_3a_4a_5$, G_6 for a_6a_7, and G_9 for a_9, taking care to end with $a_2 = a_6 = 1$. Similarly, the subspiders for $V_1 = \{4, 7, 8\}$ have $(n_4, n_7, n_8) = (2, 2, 3)$ patterns, and paths

$$\begin{aligned} G_4 &= 0, 1; \\ G_7 &= 0, 1; \\ G_8 &= 00, 01, 11. \end{aligned}$$

We obtain 12 patterns Q_1 by setting $a_1 = a_2 = a_3 = a_5 = a_6 = 1$ and using G_4 for a_4, G_7 for a_7, and G_8 for a_8a_9, taking care to begin with $a_8 = 0$. Combining these observations, we see that P_1 should end with 011011100, and Q_1 should begin with 111011100.

In general, the last element of P_k and the first element of Q_k can be determined as follows: For all children j of k, set $a_j \ldots a_{\text{scope}(j)}$ to the last element of the previously computed Gray path G_j if j is positive, or to the first element of G_j if j is negative. Then set $a_k = 0$ in P_k, $a_k = 1$ in Q_k. It is easy to verify that these rules make $a_j = 0$ whenever $j \to^* k$, and $a_j = 1$ whenever $k \to^* j$, for all j such that $k < j \le \text{scope}(k)$. A reflected Gray code based on the paths G_u for $u \in U_k$ can be used to construct P_k ending at the transition values, having $a_k = 0$; and Q_k can be constructed from those starting values based on the paths G_v for $v \in V_k$, having $a_k = 1$. Thus we obtain a Gray path $G_k = (P_k, Q_k)$.

We have therefore constructed a Gray path for spider 1, proving that the spider-squishing problem has a solution when the underlying digraph is connected. To complete the construction for the general case, we can artificially ensure that the graph is connected by introducing a new vertex 0, with arcs from 0 to the roots of the components. Then P_0 will be the desired Gray path, if we suppress bit a_0 (which is zero throughout P_0).

5 Implementation via Coroutines

By constructing families of sets U_k and V_k and identifying principal vertices in those sets, we have shown the existence of a Gray path for any given spider-squishing problem. Now let's make the proof explicit by constructing a family of coroutines that will generate the successive patterns $a_1 \ldots a_n$ dynamically, as in the examples worked out in Sections 1–3 above.

First let's consider a basic substitution or "plug-in" operation that applies to coroutines of the type we are using. Consider the following coroutines X and Y:

```
Boolean coroutine X;
  while true do begin
    while A do return true;
    return false;
    while B do return false;
    if C then return true;
    end;

Boolean coroutine Y;
  while true do begin
    while X do return true;
    return Z;
    end.
```

Here X is a more-or-less random coroutine that invokes three coroutines A, B, C; coroutine Y has a special structure that invokes X and an arbitrary coroutine $Z \neq X, Y$. Clearly Y carries out essentially the same actions as the slightly faster coroutine XZ that we get from X by substituting Z wherever X returns *false*:

```
Boolean coroutine XZ;
  while true do begin
    while A do return true;
    return Z;
    while B do return Z;
    if C then return true;
    end.
```

This plug-in principle applies in the same way whenever all `return` statements of X are either '`return` *true*' or '`return` *false*'. And we could cast XZ into this same mold, if desired, by writing '**if** Z **then return** *true* **else return** *false*' in place of '**return** Z'.

In general we want to work with coroutines whose actions produce infinite sequences $\alpha_1, \alpha_2, \ldots$ of period length $2M$, where $(\alpha_M, \ldots, \alpha_{2M-1})$ is the reverse of $(\alpha_0, \ldots, \alpha_{M-1})$, and where the coroutine returns *false* after producing α_t if and only if t is a multiple of M. The proof at the end of Section 2 shows that a construction like coroutine Y above, namely

```
Boolean coroutine AtimesB;
  while true do begin
    while B do return true;
    return A;
    end
```

yields a coroutine that produces such sequences of period length $2MN$ from coroutines A and B of period lengths $2M$ and $2N$, when A and B affect disjoint bit positions of the output sequences.

The following somewhat analogous coroutine produces such sequences of period length $2(M+N)$:

```
Boolean coroutine AplusB;
  while true do begin
    while A do return true;
    a[1] := 1; return true;
    while B do return true;
    return false;
    while B do return true;
    a[1] := 0; return true;
    while A do return true;
    return false;
    end.
```

This construction assumes that A and B individually generate reflective periodic sequences α and β on bits $a_2 \ldots a_n$, and that $\alpha_M = \beta_0$. The first half of *AplusB* produces

$$0\alpha_0,\ \ldots,\ 0\alpha_{M-1},\ 1\beta_0,\ \ldots,\ 1\beta_{N-1},$$

and returns *false* after forming $1\beta_N$ (which equals $1\beta_{N-1}$). The second half produces the n-tuples

$$1\beta_N,\ \ldots,\ 1\beta_{2N-1},\ 0\alpha_M,\ \ldots,\ 0\alpha_{2M-1},$$

which are the first $M+N$ outputs in reverse; then it returns *false*, after forming $0\alpha_{2M}$ (which equals $0\alpha_0$).

The coroutines that we need to implement spider squishing can be built up from variants of the primitive constructions for product and sum just mentioned. Consider the following coroutines $gen[1], \ldots, gen[n]$, each of which receives an integer parameter l whenever being invoked:

```
Boolean coroutine gen[k](l); integer l;
  while true do begin
    awake0: if maxu[k]≠0 then while gen[maxu[k]](k) do return true;
      a[k] := 1; return true;
    asleep1: if maxv[k]≠0 then while gen[maxv[k]](k) do return true;
      if prev[k] > l then return gen[prev[k]](l) else return false;
    awake1: if maxv[k]≠0 then while gen[maxv[k]](k) do return true;
      a[k] := 0; return true;
    asleep0: if maxu[k]≠0 then while gen[maxu[k]](k) do return true;
      if prev[k] > l then return gen[prev[k]](l) else return false;
 end.
```

Here $maxu[k]$ denotes the largest element of $U_k \cup \{0\}$, and $prev[k]$ is a function that we shall define momentarily. This function, like the sets U_k and V_k, is statically determined from the given totally acyclic digraph.

The idea of '*prev*' is that all elements of U_l can be listed as u, $prev[u]$, $prev\big[prev[u]\big]$, …, until reaching an element $\leq l$, if we start with $u = maxu[l]$. Similarly, all elements of V_l can be listed as v, $prev[v]$, $prev\big[prev[v]\big]$, …, while those elements exceed l, starting with $v = maxv[l]$. The basic meaning of $gen[k]$ with parameter l is to run through all bit patterns for the spiders $u \leq k$ in U_l, if k is a positive vertex, or for the spiders $v \leq k$ in V_l, if vertex k is negative.

The example spider of Section 4 will help clarify the situation. The following table shows the sets U_k, V_k, and a suitable function $prev[k]$, together with some auxiliary functions by which $prev[k]$ can be determined in general:

k	scope(k)	U_k	V_k	$prev[k]$	ppro(k)	npro(k)
1	9	$\{2,6,9\}$	$\{4,7,8\}$	0	1	0
2	5	$\{3,5\}$	$\{4\}$	0	2	0
3	4	$\emptyset$	$\{4\}$	0	3	0
4	4	$\emptyset$	$\emptyset$	0	3	4
5	5	$\emptyset$	$\emptyset$	3	5	0
6	7	$\emptyset$	$\{7\}$	2	6	0
7	7	$\emptyset$	$\emptyset$	4	6	7
8	9	$\{9\}$	$\emptyset$	7	1	8
9	9	$\emptyset$	$\emptyset$	6	9	8

If u is a positive vertex, not a root, let v_1 be the parent of u. Then if v_1 is negative, let v_2 be the parent of v_1, and continue in this manner until reaching a positive vertex v_t, the nearest positive ancestor of v_1. We call v_t the *positive progenitor* of v_1, denoted ppro(v_1). The main point of this construction is that $u \in U_k$ if and only if k is one of the vertices $\{v_1, v_2, \ldots, v_t\}$. Consequently

$$U_k = U_l \cap \{k, k+1, \ldots, \text{scope}(k)\}$$

if l is the positive progenitor of k. Furthermore U_k and $U_{k'}$ are disjoint whenever k and k' are distinct positive vertices. Therefore we can define $prev[u]$ for all positive nonroots u as the largest element less than u in the set $U_k \cup \{0\}$, where $k = \text{ppro}(\text{parent}(u))$ is the positive progenitor of u's parent.

Every element also has a negative progenitor, if we regard the dummy vertex 0 as a negative vertex that is parent to all the roots of the digraph. Thus we define *prev* [v] for all negative v as the largest element less than v in the set $V_k \cup \{0\}$, where $k = \text{npro}(\text{parent}(v))$.

Notice that 9 is an element of both U_1 and U_8 in the example spider, so both *gen* [9](1) and *gen* [9](8) will be invoked at various times. The former will invoke *gen* [6](1), which will invoke *gen* [2](1); the latter, however, will merely flip bit a_9 on and off, because *prev* [9] does not exceed 8. There is only one coroutine *gen* [9]; its parameter l is reassigned each time *gen* [9] is invoked. (The two usages do not conflict, because *gen* [9](1) is invoked only when $a_1 = 0$, in which case $a_8 = 0$ and *gen* [8] cannot be active.) Similarly, *gen* [4] can be invoked with $l = 1, 2$, or 3; but in this case there is no difference in behavior because *prev* [4] $= 0$.

In order to see why *gen* [k] works, let's consider first what would happen if its parameter l were ∞, so that the test '*prev* [k] $> l$' would always be false. In such a case *gen* [k] is simply the *AplusB* construction applied to $A =$ *gen* [*maxu* [k]](k) and $B =$ *gen* [*maxv* [k]](k).

On the other hand when l is set to a number such that $k \in U_l$ or $k \in V_l$, the coroutine *gen* [k] is essentially the *AtimesB* construction, because it results when $Z =$ *gen* [*prev* [k]](l) is plugged in to the instance of *AplusB* that we've just discussed. The effect is to obtain the Cartesian product of the sequence generated with $l = \infty$ and the sequence generated by *gen* [*prev* [k]](l).

Thus we see that '`if` *maxu* [k] $\neq 0$ `then while` *gen* [*maxu* [k]](k) `do return` *true*' generates the sequence P_k described in Section 4, and '`if` *maxv* [k] $\neq 0$ `then while` *gen* [*maxv* [k]](k) `do return` *true*' generates Q_k. It follows that *gen* [k](∞) generates the Gray path G_k. And we get the overall solution to our problem, path P_0, by invoking the root coroutine *gen* [*maxu* [0]](0).

Well, there is one hitch: Every time the *AplusB* construction is used, we must be sure that coroutines A and B have been set up so that the last pattern of A equals the first pattern of B. We shall deal with that problem in Section 6.

In the unconstrained case, when the given digraph has no arcs whatsoever, we have $U_0 = \{1, \ldots, n\}$ and all other U's and V's are empty. Thus *prev* [k] $= k - 1$ for $1 \le k \le n$, and *gen* [k](0) reduces to the coroutine *poke* [k] of Section 1.

If the given digraph is the chain $1 \to 2 \to \cdots \to n$, the nonempty U's and V's are $U_k = \{k+1\}$ for $0 \le k < n$. Thus *prev* [k] $= 0$ for all k, and *gen* [k](l) reduces to the coroutine *bump* [k] of Section 2. Similar remarks apply to *cobump*, *mbump*, and *ebump*.

If the given digraph is the fence $1 \to 2 \leftarrow 3 \to 4 \leftarrow \cdots$, we have $U_k = \{k'\}$ and $V_k = \{k''\}$ for $1 \le k < n$, where $(k', k'') = (k+1, k+2)$ if k is odd, $(k+2, k+1)$ if k is even, except that $U_{n-1} = \emptyset$ if n is odd, $V_{n-1} = \emptyset$ if n is even. Also $U_0 = \{1\}$. Therefore *prev* [k] $= 0$ for all k, and *gen* [k](l) reduces to the coroutine *nudge* [k] of Section 3.

6 Launching

Ever since 1968, Section 1.4.2 of *The Art of Computer Programming* [9] has contained the following remark: "Initialization of coroutines tends to be a little tricky, although not really difficult." Perhaps that statement needs to be amended, from the standpoint of the coroutines considered here. We need to decide at which label each coroutine *gen*[k] should begin execution when it is first invoked: awake0, asleep1, awake1, or asleep0. And our discussion in Sections 3 and 4 shows that we also need to choose the initial setting of $a_1 \ldots a_n$ very carefully.

Let's consider the initialization of $a_1 \ldots a_n$ first. The reflected Gray path mechanism that we use to construct the paths P_k and Q_k, as explained in Section 4, complements some of the bits. If, for example, $U_k = \{u_1, u_2, \ldots, u_m\}$, where $u_1 < u_2 < \cdots < u_m$, path P_k will contain $n_{u_1} n_{u_2} \ldots n_{u_m}$ bit patterns, and the value of bit a_{u_i} at the end of P_k will equal the value it had at the beginning if and only if $n_{u_1} n_{u_2} \ldots n_{u_{i-1}}$ is even. The reason is that subpath G_{u_i} is traversed $n_{u_1} n_{u_2} \ldots n_{u_{i-1}}$ times, alternately forward and backward.

In general, let

$$\delta_{jk} = \prod_{\substack{u<j \\ u \in U_k}} n_u, \text{ if } j \in U_k; \qquad \delta_{jk} = \prod_{\substack{v<j \\ v \in V_k}} n_v, \text{ if } j \in V_k.$$

Let α_{jk} and ω_{jk} be the initial and final values of bit a_j in the Gray path G_k for spider k, and let τ_{jk} be the value of a_j at the transition point (the end of P_k and the beginning of Q_k). Then $\alpha_{kk} = 0$, $\omega_{kk} = 1$, and the construction in Section 4 defines the values of α_{ik}, τ_{ik}, and ω_{ik} for $k < i \leq \text{scope}(k)$ as follows: Suppose i belongs to spider j, where j is a child of k.

- If j is positive, so that j is a principal element of U_k, we have $\tau_{ik} = \omega_{ij}$, since P_k ends with $a_j = 1$. Also $\alpha_{ik} = \omega_{ij}$ if δ_{jk} is even, $\alpha_{ik} = \alpha_{ij}$ if δ_{jk} is odd. If $k \to^* i$ we have $\omega_{ik} = 1$; otherwise i belongs to spider j', where j' is a nonprincipal element of V_k. In the latter case $\omega_{ik} = \alpha_{ij'}$ if $\omega_{j'j} + \delta_{j'k}$ is even, otherwise $\omega_{ik} = \omega_{ij'}$. (This follows because $\omega_{j'j} = \tau_{j'k}$ and $\omega_{j'k} = (\tau_{j'k} + \delta_{j'k}) \bmod 2$.)
- If j is negative, so that j is a principal element of V_k, we have $\tau_{ik} = \alpha_{ij}$, since Q_k begins with $a_j = 0$. Also $\omega_{ik} = \alpha_{ij}$ if δ_{jk} is even, $\omega_{ik} = \omega_{ij}$ if δ_{jk} is odd. If $i \to^* k$ we have $\alpha_{ik} = 0$; otherwise i belongs to spider j', where j' is a nonprincipal element of U_k. In the latter case $\alpha_{ik} = \alpha_{ij'}$ if $\alpha_{j'j} + \delta_{j'k}$ is even, otherwise $a_{ik} = \omega_{ij'}$.

For example, when the digraph is the spider of Section 4, these formulas yield

k	n_k	Initial bits α_{jk}	Transition bits τ_{jk}	Final bits ω_{jk}
9	2	$a_9 = 0$	$*$	1
8	3	$a_8 a_9 = 00$	$*1$	11
7	2	$a_7 = 0$	$*$	1
6	3	$a_6 a_7 = 00$	$*0$	11
5	2	$a_5 = 0$	$*$	1
4	2	$a_4 = 0$	$*$	1
3	3	$a_3 a_4 = 00$	$*0$	11
2	8	$a_2 a_3 a_4 a_5 = 0000$	$*111$	1101
1	60	$a_1 a_2 \ldots a_9 = 000001100$	$*11011100$	111111100

Suppose j is a negative child of k. If n_u is odd for all elements u of U_k that are less than j, then $\delta_{ij} + \delta_{ik}$ is even for all $i \in U_j$, and it follows that $\alpha_{ik} = \tau_{ij}$ for $j < i \le \text{scope}(j)$. (If i is in spider j', where $j' \in U_j \subseteq U_k$, then α_{ik} is $\alpha_{ij'}$ or $\omega_{ij'}$ according as $\alpha_{j'j} + \delta_{j'k}$ is even or odd, and τ_{ij} is $\alpha_{ij'}$ or $\omega_{ij'}$ according as $\alpha_{j'j} + \delta_{j'j}$ is even or odd; and we have $\delta_{j'k} \equiv \delta_{j'j} \bmod 2$.) On the other hand, if n_u is even for some $u \in U_k$ with $u < j$, then δ_{ik} is even for all $i \in U_j$, and we have $\alpha_{ik} = \alpha_{ij}$ for $j < i \le \text{scope}(j)$. This observation makes it possible to compute the initial bits $a_1 \ldots a_n$ in $O(n)$ steps (see [13]).

The special nature of vertex 0 suggests that we define $\delta_{j0} = 1$ for $1 \le j \le n$, because we use path P_0 but not Q_0. This convention makes each component of the digraph essentially independent. (Otherwise, for example, the initial setting of $a_1 \ldots a_n$ would be $01\ldots1$ in the trivial "*poke*" case when the digraph has no arcs.)

Once we know the initial bits, we start *gen*$[k]$ at label awake0 if $a_k = 0$, at label awake1 if $a_k = 1$.

7 Optimization

The coroutines *gen*$[1]$, …, *gen*$[n]$ solve the general spider-squishing problem, but they might not run very fast. For example, the *bump* routine in Section 2 takes an average of about $n/2$ steps to decide which bit should be changed. We would much prefer to use only a bounded amount of time per bit change, on the average, and this goal turns out to be achievable if we optimize the coroutine implementation.

A brute-force implementation of the *gen* coroutines, using only standard features of Algol, can readily be written down based on an explicit stack and a switch declaration:

```
Boolean val; comment the current value being returned;
integer array stack[0 : 2 * n]; comment saved values of k and l;
integer k, l; comment the current coroutine and parameter;
integer s; comment the current stack height;
switch sw := p1, p2, p3, p4, p5, p6, p7, p8, p9, p10, p11;
integer array pos[0 : n]; comment coroutine positions;

⟨ Initialize everything ⟩;
p1: if maxu[k] ≠ 0 then begin
      invoke(maxu[k], k, 2);
      p2: if val then ret(1);
   end;
   a[k] := 1;  val := true;  ret(3);
p3: if maxv[k] ≠ 0 then begin
      invoke(maxv[k], k, 4);
      p4: if val then ret(3);
   end;
```

```
      if prev[k] > l then begin
         invoke(prev[k], l, 5);
         p5: ret(6);
      end
      else begin val := false;   ret(6); end;
   p6: if maxv[k] ≠ 0 then begin
         invoke(maxv[k], k, 7);
         p7: if val then ret(6);
      end;
      a[k] := 0;   val := true;   ret(8);
   p8: if maxu[k] ≠ 0 then begin
         invoke(maxu[k], k, 9);
         p9: if val then ret(8);
      end;
      if prev[k] > l then begin
         invoke(prev[k], l, 10);
         p10: ret(1);
      end
      else begin val := false; ret(1); end;
   p11: ⟨Actions of the driver program when k = 0⟩;
```

Here *invoke*(*newk*, *newl*, *j*) is an abbreviation for

```
pos[k] := j;   stack[s] := k;   stack[s + 1] := l;     s := s + 2;
k := newk;   l := newl;   go to sw[pos[k]]
```

and *ret*(*j*) is an abbreviation for

```
pos[k] := j;   s := s − 2;
l := stack[s + 1];   k := stack[s];   go to sw[pos[k]].
```

We can streamline the brute-force implementation in several straightforward ways. First we can use a well-known technique to simplify the "tail recursion" that occurs when *invoke* is immediately followed by *ret* (see [11, example 6a]): The statements '*invoke*(*prev*[*k*], *l*, 5); p5: *ret*(6)' can, for example, be replaced by

$$pos[k] := 6;\quad k := prev[k];\quad \texttt{go to}\ sw[pos[k]].$$

An analogous simplification is possible for the constructions of the form '`while` A `do return` *true*' that occur in *gen*[*k*]. For example, we could set things up so that coroutine A removes *two* pairs of items from the stack when it returns with *val* = *true*, if we first set *pos*[*k*] to the index of a label that follows the `while` statement. More generally, if coroutine A itself is also performing such a `while` statement, we could allow `return` statements to remove even more than two pairs of stack items at a time. Details are left to the reader.

8 The Active List

The *gen* coroutines of Section 5 perform $O(n)$ operations per bit change, as they pass signals back and forth, because each coroutine carries out at most two lines of its program. This upper bound on the running time cannot be substantially improved, in general. For example, the *bump* coroutines of Section 2 typically need to interrogate about $\frac{1}{2}n$ trolls per step; and it can be shown that the *nudge* coroutines of Section 3 typically involve action by about cn trolls per step, where $c = (5+\sqrt{5})/10 \approx 0.724$. (See [9, exercise 1.2.8–12].)

Using techniques like those of Section 7, however, the *gen* coroutines can always be transformed into a procedure that performs only $O(1)$ operations per bit change, amortized over all the changes. A formal derivation of such a transformation is beyond the scope of the present paper, but we will be able to envision it by considering an informal description of the algorithm that results.

The key idea is the concept of an *active list*, which encapsulates a given stage of the computation. The active list is a sequence of nodes that are either awake or asleep. If j is a positive child of k, node j is in the active list if and only if $k = 0$ or $a_k = 0$; if j is a negative child of k, it is in the active list if and only if $a_k = 1$.

Examples of the active list in special cases have appeared in the tables illustrating *bump* in Section 2 and *nudge* in Section 3. Readers who wish to review those examples will find that the numbers listed there do indeed satisfy these criteria. Furthermore, a node number has been underlined when that node is asleep; bit a_j has been underlined if and only if j is asleep and in the active list.

Initially $a_1 \ldots a_n$ is set to its starting pattern as defined in Section 6, and all elements of the corresponding active list are awake. To get to the next bit pattern, we perform the following actions:

1. Let k be the largest nonsleeping node on the active list, and wake up all nodes that are larger. (If all elements of the active list are asleep, they all wake up and no bit change is made; this case corresponds to $gen[maxu[0]](0)$ returning *false*.)
2. If $a_k = 0$, set a_k to 1, delete k's positive children from the active list, and insert k's negative children. Otherwise set a_k to 0, insert the positive children, and delete the negative ones. (Newly inserted nodes are awake.)
3. Put node k to sleep.

Again the reader will find that the *bump* and *nudge* examples adhere to this discipline.

If we maintain the active list in order of its nodes, the amortized cost of these three operations is $O(1)$, because we can charge the cost of inserting, deleting, and awakening node k to the time when bit a_k changes. Steps (1) and (2) might occasionally need to do a lot of work, but this argument proves that such difficult transitions must be rare.

Let's consider the spider of Section 4 one last time. The 60 bit patterns that satisfy its constraints are generated by starting with $a_1 \ldots a_9 = 000001100$, as we observed in Section 6, and the Gray path G_1 begins as follows according to the active list protocol:

$$\begin{array}{ll}
000001100 & 1235679 \\
00000110\underline{1} & 123567\underline{9} \\
000001\underline{0}01 & 12356\underline{7}9 \\
000001\underline{0}0\underline{0} & 12356\underline{7}\underline{9} \\
00000\underline{0}000 & 1235\underline{6}9 \\
00000\underline{0}00\underline{1} & 1235\underline{6}\underline{9} \\
0000\underline{1}0001 & 123\underline{5}69 \\
0000\underline{1}000\underline{0} & 123\underline{5}6\underline{9} \\
0000\underline{1}\underline{1}000 & 123\underline{5}\underline{6}79
\end{array}$$

(Notice how node 7 becomes temporarily inactive when a_6 becomes 0.) The most dramatic change will occur after the first $n_2 n_6 n_9 = 48$ patterns, when bit a_1 changes as we proceed from path P_1 to path Q_1:

$$\begin{array}{ll}
0\underline{1}1\underline{0}1\underline{1}\underline{1}0\underline{0} & 1\underline{2}\underline{4}\underline{6}\underline{7}\underline{9} \\
\underline{1}11011100 & \underline{1}4789
\end{array}$$

(The positive children 2 and 6 have been replaced by the negative child 8.) Finally, after all 60 patterns have been generated, the active list will be $\underline{1}\underline{4}\underline{7}\underline{8}\underline{9}$ and $a_1 \ldots a_9$ will be $\underline{1}11\underline{1}11\underline{1}\underline{0}\underline{0}$. All active nodes will be napping, but when we wake them up they will be ready to regenerate the 60 patterns in reverse order.

It should be clear from these examples, and from a careful examination of the *gen* coroutines, that steps (1), (2), and (3) faithfully implement those coroutines in an efficient iterative manner.

9 Additional Optimizations

The algorithm of Section 8 can often be streamlined further. For example, if j and j' are consecutive positive children of k and if V_j is empty, then j and j' will be adjacent in the active list whenever they are inserted or deleted. We can therefore insert or delete an entire family en masse, in the special case that all nodes are positive, if the active list is doubly linked. This important special case was first considered by Koda and Ruskey [14]; see also [12, Algorithm 7.2.1.1K].

Further tricks can in fact be employed to make the active list algorithm entirely *loopless*, in the sense that $O(1)$ operations are performed between successive bit changes in *all* cases — not only in an average, amortized sense. One idea, used by Koda and Ruskey in the special case just mentioned, is to use "focus pointers" to identify the largest nonsleeping node (see [7] and [12, Algorithm 7.2.1.1L]). Another idea, which appears to be necessary when both positive and negative nodes appear in a complex family, is to perform lazy updates to the active list, changing links only gradually but before they are actually needed. Such a loopless implementation, which moreover needs only $O(n)$ steps to initialize all the data structures, is described fully in [13]. It does not necessarily run faster than a more straightforward amortized $O(1)$ algorithm, from the standpoint of total time on a sequential computer; but it does prove that a strong performance guarantee is achievable, given any totally acyclic digraph.

10 Conclusions and Acknowledgements

We have seen that a systematic use of cooperating coroutines leads to a generalized Gray code for generating all bit patterns that satisfy the ordering constraints of any totally acyclic digraph. Furthermore those coroutines can be implemented efficiently, yielding an algorithm that is faster than previously known methods for that problem. Indeed, the algorithm is optimum, in the sense that its running time is linear in the number of outputs.

Further work is clearly suggested in the heretofore neglected area of coroutine transformation. For example, we have not discussed the implementation of coroutines such as

```
Boolean coroutine copoke[k];
  while true do begin
    if k < n then while copoke[k + 1] do return true;
    a[k] := 1 − a[k]; return true;
    if k < n then while copoke[k + 1] do return true;
    return false;
    end.
```

These coroutines, which are to be driven by repeatedly calling *copoke*[1], generate Gray binary code, so their effect is identical to repeated calls on the coroutine *poke*[n] in Section 2. But *copoke* is much less efficient, since *copoke*[1] always invokes *copoke*[2], ..., *copoke*[n] before returning a result. Although these *copoke* coroutines look superficially similar to *gen*, they are not actually a special case of that construction. A rather large family of coroutine optimizations seems to be waiting to be discovered and to be treated formally.

Another important open problem is to discover a method that generates the bit patterns corresponding to an *arbitrary* acyclic digraph, with an amortized cost of only $O(1)$ per pattern. The best currently known bound is $O(\log n)$, due to M. B. Squire [17]; see also [16, Section 4.11.2]. There is always a listing of the relevant bit patterns in which at most two bits change from one pattern to the next [15, Corollary 1].

The first author thanks Ole-Johan Dahl for fruitful collaboration at the University of Oslo during 1972–1973 and at Stanford University during 1977–1978; also for sharing profound insights into the science of programming and for countless hours of delightful four-hands piano music over a period of more than 30 years. The second author thanks Malcolm Smith and Gang (Kenny) Li for their help in devising early versions of algorithms for spider-squishing during 1991 and 1995, respectively. Both authors are grateful to Stein Krogdahl and to an anonymous referee, whose comments on a previous draft of this paper have led to substantial improvements.

References

[1] M. Clint, "Program proving: Coroutines," *Acta Informatica* **2** (1977), 50–63.

[2] Melvin E. Conway, "Design of a separable transition-diagram compiler," *Communications of the ACM* **6** (1963), 396–408.

[3] Ole-Johan Dahl, Bjørn Myhrhaug, and Kristen Nygaard, *SIMULA-67 Common Base Language*, Publication S-2 (Oslo: Norwegian Computing Center, 1968), 141 pages. Revised edition, Publication S-22 (1970), 145 pages. Third revised edition, Report number 725 (1982), 127 pages.

[4] Ole-Johan Dahl and C. A. R. Hoare, "Hierarchical program structures," in *Structured Programming* (Academic Press, 1972), 175–220.

[5] Ole-Johan Dahl, *Syntaks og Semantikk i Programmeringsspråk* (Lund: Studentlitteratur, 1972), 103 pages.

[6] Ole-Johan Dahl, "An approach to correctness proofs of semicoroutines," Research Report in Informatics, Number 13 (Blindern, Norway: University of Oslo, 1977), 20 pages.

[7] Gideon Ehrlich, "Loopless algorithms for generating permutations, combinations and other combinatorial configurations," *Journal of the Association for Computing Machinery* **20** (1973), 500–513.

[8] Robert W. Floyd, "The syntax of programming languages — A survey," *IEEE Transactions on Electronic Computers* **EC-13** (1964), 346–353.

[9] Donald E. Knuth, *Fundamental Algorithms*, Volume 1 of *The Art of Computer Programming* (Reading, Massachusetts: Addison–Wesley, 1968). Third edition, 1997.

[10] Donald E. Knuth, *Selected Topics in Computer Science, Part II*, Lecture Note Series, Number 2 (Blindern, Norway: University of Oslo, Institute of Mathematics, August 1973). See page 3 of the notes entitled "Generation of combinatorial patterns: Gray codes."

[11] Donald E. Knuth, "Structured programming with `go to` statements," *Computing Surveys* **6** (December 1974), 261–301. Reprinted with revisions as Chapter 2 of *Literate Programming* (Stanford, California: Center for the Study of Language and Information, 1992).

[12] Donald E. Knuth, "Generating all n-tuples," Section 7.2.1.1 of *The Art of Computer Programming*, Volume 4 (Addison–Wesley), in preparation. Preliminary excerpts of this material are available at `http://www-cs-faculty.stanford.edu/~knuth/news01.html`.

[13] Donald E. Knuth, SPIDERS, a program downloadable from the website `http://www-cs-faculty.stanford.edu/~knuth/programs.html`.

[14] Yasunori Koda and Frank Ruskey, "A Gray code for the ideals of a forest poset," *Journal of Algorithms* **15** (1993), 324–340.

[15] Gara Pruesse and Frank Ruskey, "Gray codes from antimatroids," *Order* **10** (1993), 239–252.

[16] Frank Ruskey, *Combinatorial Generation* [preliminary working draft]. Department of Computer Science, University of Victoria, Victoria B.C., Canada (1996).

[17] Matthew Blaze Squire, *Gray Codes and Efficient Generation of Combinatorial Structures*. Ph.D. dissertation, North Carolina State University (1995), x + 145 pages.

[18] George Steiner, "An algorithm to generate the ideals of a partial order," *Operations Research Letters* **5** (1986), 317–320.

[19] Leonard I. Vanek and Rudolf Marty, "Hierarchical coroutines: A method for improved program structure," *Proceedings of the 4th International Conference on Software Engineering* (Munich, 1979), 274–285.

[20] Arne Wang and Ole-Johan Dahl, "Coroutine sequencing in a block-structured environment," *BIT* **11** (1971), 425–449.

Consistency of Inheritance in Object-Oriented Languages and of Static, ALGOL-like Binding

Hans Langmaack

Institut für Informatik und Praktische Mathematik der
Christian-Albrechts-Universität zu Kiel
hl@informatik.uni-kiel.de

Abstract. ALGOL60 introduced the block level structure with its characteristic static binding and visibility scopes of identifiers, phenomena known before in predicate logics and λ-calculi outside programming. Misinterpretations and misimplementations of originally intended static scope semantics of ALGOL60 and Lisp have seduced language designers and practitioners to a notion of dynamic scope semantics which suppresses identifier renamings during program execution. Dynamic scoping has become popular above all in object-oriented programming, although the inventors of the latter and authors of Simula 67, O.-J. Dahl and K. Nygaard, explicitly based their ideas on ALGOL60 and static scoping. And there are follower languages which successfully combine object-orientation and static binding. The present article demonstrates that the implementation problems around the especially flexible and useful concept of many level or skew prefixing (inheritance) can well be solved, shown by LOGLAN'88, an extension of Simula 67.

1 Introduction: Origins of Static and Dynamic Identifier Binding

The higher programming language ALGOL60 introduced several remarkable software concepts. One is the *block concept*, essentially advocated by K. Samelson who was a member of the international ALGOL58- and ALGOL60-committees [PeS58, Nau60]. The block level structure and its characteristic storage allocation scheme are most important contributions of Samelson to programming science and technology [Sam55]. ALGOL58 [PeS58] and FORTRAN [Bac57] did not yet speak about binding and visibility scopes of identifiers, although these phenomena were known in predicate logics and λ-calculi since the 1930s [Her61].

ALGOL60's block concept has brought an essential syntactical and semantical clarification of the procedure concept. ALGOL60-procedures evolved from ALGOL58's notions procedure and do-statement. ALGOL-like, static binding of identifiers in ALGOL60's operational copy rule semantics was expressed by the requirement that procedure body and parameter replacements had to avoid binding violations (identifier clashes) by appropriate bound identifier renamings. The ALGOL60-report's formulations for language semantics, especially for semantics of procedures (function procedures and resultless procedures) would

O. Owe et al. (Eds.): From OO to FM (Dahl Festschrift), LNCS 2635, pp. 209–235, 2004.

have become much clearer to programmers and compiler constructors if the report had explicitly hinted at the α- and β-reductions in λ-calculi known already at that time. Such a hint would have helped to avoid many unfortunate developments of language definitions, of compilers and of run time systems, not only for ALGOL60, but also for many successor languages.

Samelson pointed out the idea of blocks and their characteristic data storage behaviour already in [Sam55]. He spoke about partial programs as open subprograms and library programs as closed subprograms. On the one hand he described how, during translation and evaluation of arithmetic formulas, intermediate results had to be stored in auxiliary storage cells where *last* stored results became available again *first*. The ground for that phenomenon was the left to right break down of formulas; the leftmost break down feasibilities were to be envisaged again and again; such proceeding is justified because evaluation of arithmetic formulas, also those known from school with their infix notations, bracket savings and priority rules, is *confluent*. The notation *number cellar* ("*Bauer-Samelsonscher Zahlkeller*") for pulsating of intermediate results appeared in the patent specification [BaS57] for the first time and afterwards in the article "Sequential Formula Translation" [SaB59]. On the other hand, also in 1955, Samelson described how run time pulsating of intermediate results extended to data storage cells for open and closed subprograms what was justified for confluence reasons as well. Subprograms had to cooperate with an indication of momentarily free storage entered in a fixed variable named *beginning free storage*.

With explicit references to [SaB59] E. W. Dijkstra described in "Recursive Programming" [Dij60] how the Bauer-Samelson-number cellar was to be extended towards a *run time stack* for blocks and procedures of ALGOL60. The variable *beginning free storage* was now named *stack pointer*, every procedure call generated a *procedure incarnation* for which an information unit with places for *procedure link, local parameters, local variables* and *intermediate results* was entered in the run time stack. In the procedure link Dijkstra established the *return address* of the procedure P called, the *dynamic pointer* pointing at the youngest preceding, not yet completed, incarnation (of that procedure Q wherein the call of P occured) and – what is crucial – the so called *static pointer* pointing at the *most recent*, not yet completed, incarnation of that first (i.e. smallest) procedure R lexicographically enclosing P. The static pointer is the instrument to access informations about *global procedure parameters* of P.

Unfortunately, Dijkstra's *most-recent-prescription* for static pointers does not fit ALGOL60's *copy rule semantics* and *static binding*: We can construct ALGOL60-programs which do not satisfy the so called *most-recent-property*, which means, there is a static pointer in a (corrected) run time system which does *not* point to the *most recent* incarnation of procedure R, but to one further down towards the stack bottom [GHL67]. There are astonishingly short programs with just two nested procedures, with procedure identifiers as formal and actual parameters and with formal procedure calls violating the most-recent-property as P. Kandzia demonstrated [Kan74]. Dijkstra's implementation causes unexpected changes of identifier meanings during execution, changes which the programmer is hardly able to pursue and understand so that she/he is surprised by curious final program results. If such changes of meaning are desired by language semantics definition then we speak of *dynamic binding* or *dynamic scope semantics.* Even the involved program example GPS (General Problem Solver) worked out in [RaR64] to demonstrate name parameter passing is not involved enough: GPS satisfies the most-recent-property.

Dijkstra's most-recent-prescription how to deal with static pointers has been used in implementations and in compiler building text books for ALGOL-like programming languages still in more recent years [WiM92]. This has led to discrepancies between originally intended language semantics and actual program executions. In order to avoid disappointments language Ada [Ich80] excluded procedures as arguments of procedure calls and language C [KeR78] disallowed any procedure nestings. Under these language restrictions static resp. dynamic scoping lead to equivalent program computations if the executed wellformed programs are *distinguished,* i.e. different defining identifier occurrences are denoted by different identifiers which, above that, must be different from standard ones (*Defining* occurrences are those places of identifiers in a program where their kinds, types etc. are introduced, all other identifiers occurrences are *applied* ones. An occurrence of a *free* identifier is an applied occurrence not bound to any defining occurrence. In a wellformed program every free identifier is to be standard).

There was a further influential publication which involuntarily brought dynamic binding to the attention of programmers. In "Lisp 1.5 Programmer's Manual" [McC65] J. McCarthy et al. published two Lisp-written interpreters in order to define an operational copy rule semantics of the functional language Lisp. McCarthy draw up Lisp as a user friendly setting of A. Church's (applied) λ-calculus with its static binding. But programming errors in the interpreters established a Lisp-semantics with dynamic binding such that even simple bound renamings showed different program results [Hoa90]. Langmaack found the programming errors in [McC65] during courses on compiler and run time system construction at the University of the Saarland 1970/71. He briefly repaired the Lisp-interpreters towards static binding and spoke of *natural* Lisp-semantics. Later the Lisp-community with CommonLisp [Ste84] has acknowledged the virtue of ALGOL-like, static binding.

The wording *"dynamic binding"* does not mean that this kind of binding offers clear advantages or higher potentials over *static binding.* At run time dynamic binding requires searching processes down the run time stack in order to load and store program variables resp. to load static pointers and display registers whereas static binding allows direct loadings. Dynamic binding leads to *regular procedure call trees* of programs and so to provable existence of *relatively complete Hoare proof calculi* [Old81] whereas static binding may generate *irregular* procedure call trees such that there are *no good* Hoare proof calculi for full ALGOL60 nor ALGOL68 [Wij^{+}69] nor Pascal [JeW75] [Cla79, LaO80]. In spite of these good news about dynamic binding program understanding and formulation of procedure pre- and postconditions is more difficult because for dynamic scope semantics there do not hold so mature substitution and bound renaming theorems as for static scope semantics.

2 Object-Orientation and Identifier Binding

Dynamic binding became popular above all in *object-oriented programming* although dynamic binding began from misinterpretations and misimplementations of originally intended language semantics and although O.-J. Dahl and K. Nygaard, the creators of the notions *object*, *class*, *inheritance* and of the language Simula67, explicitly based their ideas upon ALGOL60 with its block structure and static binding [DaN67, Dah01a]. Also follower languages like BETA [MMPN93] and LOGLAN'88 [KSW88] successfully combine object-orientation and static binding in a consistent manner. Comparatively old languages like ALGOL60 or Pascal allowed already that program parts, which were developed in parallel by separated software engineering groups, could be combined by procedure encapsulation without any problems. A dynamic binding regime would not so easily allow such software engineering practice because it is error prone or even impossible without full knowledge of local names in the other groups' program parts.

As mentioned before, Simula67 already had the inheritance idea incorporated, but demanded, for pragmatic reasons, *same level inheritance*, i.e. every inherited class must have the same module nesting level as the inheriting module. LOGLAN as well as BETA strived for *many level (skew) inheritance* so that programmers were not forced to write unnecessary class copies by hand and were enabled to install class libraries more flexibly. The serious problems how to define clear language semantics for many level inheritance under a static binding regime and how to establish efficient implementations were not yet foreseen in 1967 [Dah01b].

Goal of the present article is to show that these problems can well be solved. As a demonstration instrument we take LOGLAN'88, which extends Simula67 by prefixing at many levels, by inheriting in procedures, functions, processess, by concurrency, exceptions and signals and has been developed and implemented by the informatics research group around A. Kreczmar (†) and A. Salwicki at the University of Warsaw who are wellknown for their foundational work on algorithmic logic. LOGLAN's development began in the later 1970s and took its way via forerunners LOGLAN-77 and LOGLAN-82. We would like to give an informal description of the following more detailed sections 3 to 6 on how LOGLAN has solved the addressed problems:

For LOGLAN we may define an operational copy rule semantics – which is a variant of structural operational semantics – with static binding (scoping) as for other ALGOL-like languages. Not only procedure calls and object generations invoke copy rule applications, elimination of *inheritances* (*prefixings*) does so as well with which *modules* (*units*) like classes, blocks and procedures may be adhered with. This style of semantics definition is plainly at the high programming language level without any references to implementations nor processors [KKSL84].

The guiding idea for efficient implementation is that inheritance elimination may be imagined in a different semantics preserving way: Classes are transformed to procedures and inheriting modules are attached by new local procedures whose formal parameters are exactly those identifiers which can be reached via the inheritance (prefix) chain of the inheriting module. I.o.w.: Object orientation by classes and inheritances offers both a great structuring method and a pleasant shorthand (parameters saving) notation for ALGOL-programs.

Java's way how to define and treat semantics of inner classes and their many level prefixings by converting inner classes to toplevel ones is a different proceeding. The relations to static resp. dynamic scoping philosophies are to be clarified [Sun97, SaW02]. [SSB01] says explicitly that nested and inner classes are not treated.

Due to [Dij60] efficient block and procedure implementation for ALGOL can be done by the help of static pointer chains and *display registers*. All applied identifier occurrences which are bound to the same defining occurrence and, under static scoping, mean the same thing are coupled to the same register which is fixed by the module nesting level of the defining occurrence. Because of Simula67's same level inheritance regime ALGOL's display register allocation scheme is holding for Simula67 as well. The most pleasant and important implication is that no display register reloadings are necessary as long as a run time computation procedes from member to member of a whole prefix chain and does not leave that chain.

This ALGOL-Simula67-display register allocation scheme gets inadequate as soon as many level inheritance comes into scene. But the efficiency gaining Simula67-no-reloading property should urgently pertain for many level prefixing. There might be more display registers necessary than the maximal level of module nestings . So S. Krogdahl [Kro79] has proposed to optimize the BETA-codegenerator so that the minimal possible display register number is determined at translation time. [KKSL84] prove by systematic display register permutations that this minimal number is exactly the maximal module nesting level of the given program as we know from ALGOL60 or Simula67. A. Kreczmar and M. Warpechowski [KLKW85, KKLSW87] developed an elegant theory of L-algebras and their implementations for which LOGLAN-programs are models. Theory and implementation may be viewed as results of deliberations about what program language semantics with static scoping truly means.

3 Syntax and Static Semantics of MiniLOGLAN

In order to demonstrate proper specification of syntax, static semantics (context conditions) and dynamic semantics of programming languages with classes, inheritance (prefixing) and static scoping we present in appendix A a contextfree-like grammar for MiniLOGLAN which is a sublanguage of LOGLAN. So an implementation of the latter is also one of MiniLOGLAN. Its purpose is to abstract from less important details and to concentrate on the problem of meaning of identifiers in languages that have classes, objects, nesting of classes and inheritance without Simula 67's restrictions. So insights in MiniLOGLAN will show up ways which developments of other languages like Java can take.

Modules are blocks, procedures and classes. A module can be prefixed by at most one class; so we have inheritance or prefix chains. Procedures need not necessarily be prefixed. Their prefixing could be modeled by prefixing their bodies written as blocks if many level prefixing and static scoping with its bound identifier renamings are envisaged. A class initialization **new** ξ can be implemented by a simple prefixed block

$$\textbf{inh}\ \xi\ \textbf{block end}$$

with empty declaration and statement lists. The statement list Σ of a class body has to contain exactly one control statement **inner** with its *prologue* Σ_1 and *epilogue* Σ_2 :

$$\Sigma = \Sigma_1\ \textbf{inner}\ \Sigma_2 .$$

Should there be no explicit **inner** then **inner** is imagined to be the final statement of Σ with an empty epilogue Σ_2 .

There is a conceptual difference between a *substring* σ of a program π $(\pi = \alpha\ \sigma\ \omega)$ and of a *substring occurrence* ${}^i\sigma$ in π , a pair of σ and i with $i = |\alpha|+1$. The same substring σ may occur several times. That is especially true for identifiers. *Structured substring occurrences* are those which reduce to non-terminal symbols in the unambigously associated structure tree of π. Two structured substring occurrences are either disjoint or contained in each other.

Modules ${}^iM$ in π form a tree. They have *nesting levels* $\nu_{{}^iM} \geq 1$. The program itself is the largest module, a block module of level $\nu_{{}^1\pi} = 1$. Every module ${}^iM$ has an *associated binding range* ${}^rR$, the largest substring of ${}^iM$ which reaches from the keyword **block** resp. **class** resp. **proc** to the matching **end** and which, by definition, has the *same nesting level* $\nu_{{}^rR} = \nu_{{}^iM}$ as the module. Every structured substring ${}^j\sigma$ and especially every defining occurrence ${}^j\xi$ of an identifier inside the largest binding range (the associated binding range of π) has a so called *environment range* ${}^rR = env({}^j\sigma) = env({}^j\xi) = env(j)$ which is the smallest range which encloses ${}^j\sigma$ resp. ${}^j\xi$ resp. position j. If program π is named by ξ then the defining occurrence ${}^1\xi$ is defined to have *level* 0, the *level* of any other defining occurrence ${}^j\xi$ is that of $env({}^j\xi)$ which is ≥ 1. The *associated local identifier list locidl* $({}^rR)$ of a binding range is the ordered list of all defining identifier occurrences ${}^j\xi$ with $env({}^j\xi) = {}^rR$.

In a *wellformed program* π every identifier occurrence must be bound to at most one defining occurrence of that same identifier; all freely occurring identifiers must be standard with a predefined meaning; and all identifier applications have to be in type accordance with their associated definitions. So we have to establish a partially defined *binding function* $bdfct(i, \xi)$ which determines the associated defining occurrence ${}^j\xi$ of an identifier ξ if the searching process starts from position i (mostly ξ's applied position) :

$bdfct(i, \xi) :=$
if i is outside the largest binding range of π
then if π is a block named by ξ
then ${}^1\xi$
else undefined **fi**
else if ξ occurs in *locidl(env(i))*
then the rightmost entry ${}^j\xi$ in that local identifier list
else if $env(i) = {}^rR$ has an applied prefix class identifier occurrence ${}^l\eta$ with $l = r - 1$
then $bdfctpref\ (l\ ,\ \xi,\ {}^l\eta)$
else $bdfct\ (l\ ,\ \xi)$ **fi fi fi**

The auxiliary binding function $bdfctpref\ (i\ ,\ \xi,\ {}^l\eta)$ determines the associated defining occurrence ${}^j\xi$ of identifier ξ inside a so called prefix chain starting with class identifier occurrence ${}^l\eta$. i is the original starting point of the searching process for ξ, i is needed in case a defining occurrence of ξ cannot be found in the present prefix chain. Furtheron we see: Searching along a prefix chain has priority over searching through enclosing binding ranges. Be aware that prefix chains can be determined only in connection with the binding function *bdfct*, not in an independent manner.

$bdfctpref\ (i, \xi, {}^l\eta) :=$
if $bdfct\ (l, \eta)$ yields a defining class identifier occurrence ${}^k\eta$ with its class module ${}^{k-1}M$ and associated binding range ${}^rR$
then if ξ occurs in $locidl({}^rR)$
then the rightmost entry ${}^j\xi$ in this local identifier list
else if ${}^{k-1}M$ has an applied prefix class identifier occurrence ${}^{r-1}\zeta$
then $bdfctpref\ (i,\ \xi,\ {}^{r-1}\zeta)$
else $bdfct\ (i\ ,\ \xi)$ **fi fi**
else undefined **fi**

If ${}^l\eta$ is prefixing the module ${}^jM$ and ${}^i\eta = bdfct(l,\ \eta)$ is identifying class ${}^{j'}M'$ then this is called the *direct prefix module* $pref({}^jM)$. In a wellformed program all prefix chains, i.e. successive applications of function *pref*, must be acyclic. This additional demand for wellformedness cannot be concluded from existence of reasonable identifier binding.

If $bdfct(i, \xi) = {}^j\xi$ with $j \neq 1$ then there is the smallest module ${}^kM$ enclosing position i resp. occurrence ${}^i\xi$ such that ${}^j\xi$ is occuring in the local identifier list of a module ${}^{k'}M' = pref^n({}^kM), n \geq 0$ .We call ${}^{k'}M'$ the *declaring module* and ${}^kM$ the *vertex module* of ${}^i\xi$.

Wellformed MiniLOGLAN-programs π open up an important algebraic view, it will later help to create display register allocation for efficient static scope implementation. Let $\mathcal{M}$ be the set of all module occurrences ${}^jM$ in π. We have a partial nesting function $encl : \mathcal{M} \rightarrow \mathcal{M}$ which makes $\mathcal{M}$ a finite tree and a partial prefixing function $pref : \mathcal{M} \rightarrow \mathcal{M}$ which makes $\mathcal{M}$ a finite forest of finite trees. The definition is due to Kreczmar and Warpechowski [KLKW85, KKLSW87] :

Definition 3.1: An *L-algebra* is an algebra $L = < \mathcal{M}, encl, pref, \pi >$ where $\mathcal{M}$ is a non-empty finite set, *encl* and *pref* are partial functions defined on $\mathcal{M}$ into $\mathcal{M}$, π is an element of $\mathcal{M}$, and the following axioms are satisfied:
(A1) $encl(\pi)$ is undefined, and for every $a \in \mathcal{M}$ is $encl^*(a) = \pi$
(i.e. π is the root of the *encl*-tree $\mathcal{M}$);
(A2) for every $a \in \mathcal{M}$ $pref^+(a)$ is undefined (i.e. prefixing is acyclic);
(A3) for every $a \in \mathcal{M}$ if $pref(a)$ is defined then $encl\ pref\ (a)$ is defined and $pref^*\ encl^+\ (a) = encl\ pref\ (a)$ holds (i.e. if a diagram

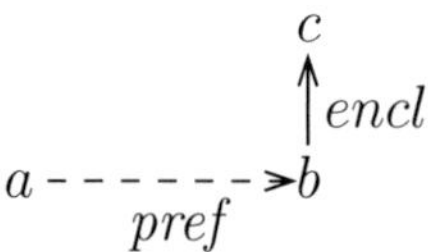

holds then it can be complemented

e.g. by vertex module d of identifier ${}^i\xi$ which prefixes module a ; c is the declaring module of ${}^i\xi$; vertex module d is the smallest module fulfilling the above diagram).

Theorem 3.2: $L = < \mathcal{M}, encl, pref, \pi >$ is an L-algebra.

In appendix B we present a wellformed program π_1 which shows many level prefixing. The L-algebra looks as follows

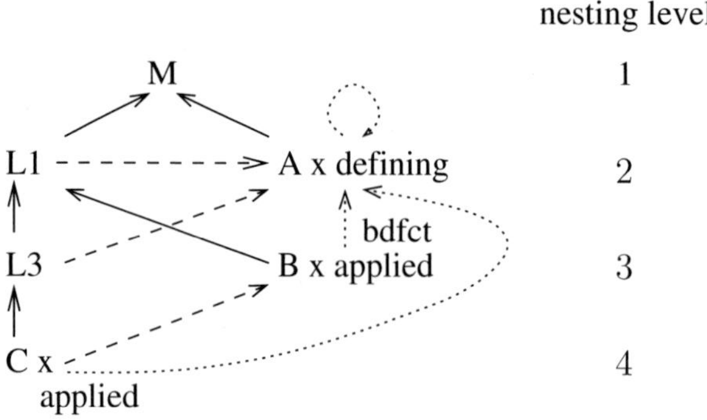

π_1 is not distinguished because there are two defining occurrences of x in the *main parts* (i.e. inside the binding ranges, but outside inner ones) of M and of A and two defining occurrences of y in the main parts of L1 and of L3.

A most important notion in L-algebras is that of the uniquely determined *complement module* $d = comp(a,\ b,\ c)$ for a triple of modules with $b = pref^*(a)$ and $c = encl^*(b)$ such that diagram

$$\begin{array}{ccc} d & \overset{*}{\dashrightarrow} & c \\ {\scriptstyle *}\uparrow & & \uparrow{\scriptstyle *} \\ a & \overset{*}{\dashrightarrow} & b \end{array}$$

holds. The existence of d is resulting from a *unique normal form* theorem basing on axiom (A3). In case $c = b$ then $d = a$, in case $a = b$ then $d = c$, in case $b = pref(a)$ and $c = encl(a)$ then $d = comp(a,\ b,\ c)$ is the smallest module satisfying diagram

$$\begin{array}{ccc} d & \overset{*}{\dashrightarrow} & c \\ {\scriptstyle +}\uparrow & & \uparrow{\scriptstyle +} \\ a & \overset{+}{\dashrightarrow} & b \end{array}$$

But be aware that this smallest module property does not hold for complement modules in general for $b = pref^+(a)$ and $c = encl^+(b)$, see a counterexample in appendix H of [KKSL84]. For implementation of static scoping with many level prefixing the following composition theorem is important:

Theorem 3.3: Complement module diagrams can be composed horizontally and vertically.

Be aware again: This theorem would not hold if we would have based the definition of complement modules on the above mentioned smallest module property.

4 Semantics of MiniLOGLAN

The (dynamic) semantics of programs with prefixing is based on the idea of prefix elimination which makes prefix chains shorter. We call this process *original prefix elimination* because in Section 5 we shall discuss a different elimination method.

Let π be a wellformed program. Let in π a class declaration

(1) **unit** η : **inh** ξ **class** Δ Σ **end** η

or a block

(2) $\quad \eta$: **inh** ξ **class** $\Delta\ \Sigma$ **end** η

be given, prefixed by ξ which identifies a class

(3) **unit** ξ : **inh** ξ' **class** $\Delta'\ \Sigma_1'$ **inner** Σ_2' **end** ξ

We have assumed that this class is again prefixed by ξ' what is not necessarily the case.

Prefix elimination replaces class (1) or block (2) by a class (1') or block (2') in the following way:

(1') **unit** η : **inh** ξ' **class** $\Delta'\ \Sigma_1'$ **gbegin** $\Delta\ \Sigma$ **end** Σ_2' **end** η

or

(2') $\quad \eta$: **inh** ξ' **block** $\Delta'\ \Sigma_1'$ **gbegin** $\Delta\ \Sigma$ **end** Σ_2' **end** η

If **inh** ξ' is not existent in (3) then **inh** ξ' is not existent in (1') nor (2'). Elimination of prefixes of procedures is done in an analogous way. We see especially that replaced modules remain modules of the same kind, namely classes, blocks or procedures.

Lemma 4.1: Original prefix elimination yields a new wellformed program π'

$$\pi \mid \overline{\text{orig pref elim}} \, \pi'$$

if π is distinguished. Otherwise π' does not necessarily result to be wellformed, not even *closed*, i.e. π' shows up free non-standard identifiers. If bound renamings are allowed and identifier clashes are avoided, e.g. by systematic renaming of programs in distinguished ones, then successive prefix elimination preserves wellformedness and is confluent.

If successive original prefix elimination under identifier clash avoidance, i.e. under static scoping regime, is applied to every prefixed module then (perhaps after infinitely many steps) the process ends up with an essentially uniquely determined (perhaps infinite) program π'' which has only redundant prefixing and redundant classes. It is actually sufficing to apply prefix elimination to every outermost prefixed module, i.e. outside any other prefixed module (and consequently outside class ξ itself if ξ is prefixed).

In appendix C we present a wellformed program π_2 with a structure of class and block modules

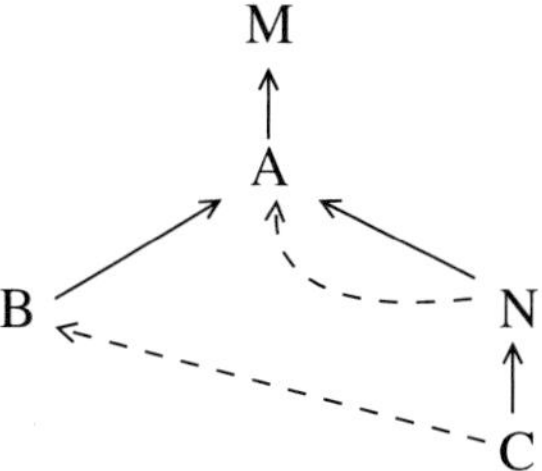

which has so called *recursive prefixing* without recursive procedures declared in π_2. Recursive prefixing is impossible in Simula67-like programs with their same level prefixing.

If we erase all classes in π'' (because they have got redundant) we have a wellformed ALGOL-program. It has a well defined operational resp. denotational semantics. This is defined to be the *(dynamic) semantics* of the given MiniLOGLAN-program π. Semantics definition is not hindered by infinity of π''.

In case we do dynamic scoping, i.e. disallow bound renamings of identifiers, and start from wellformed programs π (which are not distinguished in general) then we cannot preserve wellformedness nor achieve confluence. In order to preserve at least *closedness* of resulting programs π', every prefixing class ξ to be eliminated must have no prefix itself. Further on, in order to enforce confluence, prefix elimination must be applied to outermost prefixed modules only. These demands indicate , so to speak, that dynamic scoping leads to less robust semantics than static scoping does. And both semantics are differing as our program example π_1 in appendix B demonstrates:

Complete elimination of all prefixing in π_1 and of all classes A, B and C yields a program π_1'' in appendix D. Static scoping requires some renamings: Of x in class M to $\overline{x}$, of y in block L3 to $\overline{y}$, and of x, newly introduced in block L3 by prefix B elimination, to x'. Static scope semantics output of π_1'' and so by definition of π_1 is

$$2.0, 2.0, 3.0.$$

For dynamic scoping simply forget renamings in π_1''. Dynamic scope semantics output of ${\pi_1}''^{dyn}$ and so by definition of π_1 is

$$2.0, 4.0, 4.0.$$

Even if you turn π_1 to a distinguished program ${\pi_1}^{dist}$ (i.e. x in M to $\overline{x}$ and y in L3 to $\overline{y}$) and do prefix elimination under dynamic scoping you do not arrive at the static (nor the dynamic) scope semantics, but to the output

$$2.0, 2.0, 2.0,$$

see quasi static scope semantics in Section 6.1.

5 Prefix Elimination by Transforming to Procedures

As indicated already: If we deal within MiniLOGLAN only with Simula67-like programs π with their same level prefixing and static scoping regime then successive original prefix elimination needs only finitely many steps to reach a program π'' where all prefixings, class initializations and class declarations are redundant. So the resulting programs π'' may be called truly ALGOL-like.

Finitely many steps are not sufficing in general MiniLOGLAN. But in any case, a "final" π'' may be considered to be an ALGOL-like program, be it finite or infinite, it is established with a welldefined semantics.

But there is a different (new) prefix elimination process by transforming classes and prefixed blocks to procedures. This process is always finite. Let π be a distinguished wellformed program. We are allowed to assume there are no class initializations nor prefixed procedures in π.

Let a non-prefixed class declaration

$$\textbf{unit } \eta : \textbf{class } \ \Delta\ \Sigma_1 \textbf{ inner } \Sigma_2 \textbf{ end } \eta$$

in π be given which defines a module ${}^jM$ in π . Let

$${}^{i_1}\xi_1 \ldots {}^{i_n}\xi_n$$

be the local identifier list *locidl*(${}^jM$). **inner** indicates the only **inner**-statement in the main part of class η . Then the module above is transformed to

unit η : **proc** (η_f)
  Δ
  Σ_1 **call** $\eta_f(\xi_1 \cdots \xi_n)$ Σ_2
end η

where η_f is a new formal procedure identifier with an appropriate specification which we have deleted. It is induced by the declarations of $\xi_1 \ldots \xi_n$ in π in a well known way.

Now we consider a prefixed class declaration

$$\textbf{unit } \eta : \textbf{inh } \xi \textbf{ class } \ \Delta\ \Sigma_1 \textbf{ inner } \Sigma_2 \textbf{ end } \eta$$

in π which defines a module ${}^jM$ in π with its finite prefix chain

$$pref^{l-1}({}^jM) \leftarrow - - \cdots \leftarrow - - pref^0({}^jM)\ , l > 1,$$

and its local identifier lists

$${}^{j_1}\xi_1 \ldots {}^{j_n}\xi_n = locidl(pref^0({}^jM)),$$

$${}^{i_1}\zeta_1 \ldots {}^{i_m}\zeta_m = locidl(pref^{l-1}({}^jM)) \cdots locidl(pref^1({}^jM)).$$

Then the above module is transformed to

unit η : **proc** (η_f)
    unit η_g : **proc** $(\zeta_1 \cdots \zeta_m)$
      Δ

Σ_1 **call** $\eta_f(\zeta_1 \cdots \zeta_m\ \xi_1 \cdots \xi_n)\ \Sigma_2$
end η_g
call $\xi\ (\eta_g)$
end η

where η_f and η_g are new procedure identifiers with appropriate specifications which we have deleted. The specifications of η_f and η_g and $\zeta_1 \cdots \zeta_m$ in the resulting program are induced by the declarations of $\zeta_1 \cdots \zeta_m$ and $\xi_1 \cdots \xi_n$ in π.

A prefixed block is treated similarly: Let

$$\eta : \textbf{inh}\ \xi\ \textbf{block}\ \Delta\ \Sigma\ \textbf{end}\ \eta$$

be such a block in π which defines a module ${}^jM$ in π. This block is transformed to

η : **block**
unit η_g : **proc** $(\zeta_1 \cdots \zeta_m)$
Δ
Σ
end η_g
call $\xi\ (\eta_g)$
end η .

The symbols have the same meanings as before.

Now we should like to sketch a proof why the given MiniLOGLAN-program π and its transformed ALGOL-like program $\tilde{\pi}$ are semantically equivalent. Let us look at a non-prefixed class

(1) **unit** ξ : **class** $\Delta'\ \Sigma'_1$ **inner** Σ'_2 **end** ξ

which is prefix of a block

(2) η : **inh** ξ **block** $\Delta\ \Sigma$ **end** η

in π or in any program at any stage of the successive original prefix elimination process. We may assume that program to be distinguished. Let

$${}^{i_1}\zeta_1 \ldots {}^{i_n}\zeta_n$$

be the local identifier list of class ξ. The translated class and block look as follows

$(\tilde{1})$ **unit** ξ : **proc** (ξ_f)
Δ'
Σ'_1 **call** $\xi_f(\zeta_1 \ldots \zeta_n)\ \Sigma'_2$
end ξ

$(\tilde{2})$ η : **block**
unit η_g : **proc** $(\zeta_1 \ldots \zeta_n)$
Δ
Σ
end η_g
call $\xi(\eta_g)$
end η .

Now we compare original prefix elimination in (1), (2) and copy rule applications in $(\tilde{1})$, $(\tilde{2})$. Prefix elimination gives

η : **block**
Δ'
Σ'_1
gblock
Δ

Σ
end
Σ'_2
end η

and copy rule applications give,

first step:
η : **block**
  unit η_g : **proc** $(\zeta_1 \ldots \zeta_n)$
    Δ
    Σ
  end η_g
  gbegin
    Δ'
    Σ'_1 **call** $\eta_g(\zeta_1, \ldots, \zeta_n)$ Σ'_2
  end
end η ,

second step:
η : **block**
  unit η_g : **proc** $(\zeta_1 \ldots \zeta_n)$
    Δ
    Σ
  end η_g
  gbegin
    Δ'
    Σ'_1
    gbegin
      Δ
      Σ
    end
    Σ'_2
  end
end η .

We see: Prefix elimination and associated procedure call **call** $\xi(\eta_g)$ lead to equivalent program expansions since procedure η_g has become redundant. The other three cases

a block η prefixed by a prefixed class ξ,
a class η prefixed by a non-prefixed class ξ,
a class η prefixed by a prefixed class ξ

lead to analogous results.

Theorem 5.1: A given wellformed MiniLOGLAN-program π and its effectively transformed ALGOL-like program where all classes and prefixings have been eliminated and replaced by procedure declarations and calls are semantically equivalent.

Let us draw some conclusions from Section 5: By object-orientation via classes and inheritances Dahl and Nygaard have created a great program structuring method. This structuring can be achieved also by a systematic exploitation of ALGOL-procedure parameter transmission. But object-orientation offers a very pleasant shorthand notation for ALGOL-programs which comes along with drastic parameter savings.

Since many level prefixing is no hindrance the new prefix elimination technique in Section 5 is suggesting a program implementation method by use of display registers which is as efficient as for Simula67 or ALGOL60. It turns out that appropriate display register permutations can be determined at compile time what does not diminish run time efficiency. Section 6 shows the essential ideas.

Remark concerning Java: Both methods in sections 4 and 5 eliminate prefixing and so reduce semantics definition to programs without inheritances, but with nestings. Java's method removes class nestings and reduces semantics definition to flat programs with toplevel inheritances only. The connections between the methods are to be clarified [SaW02].

6 Implementation of MiniLOGLAN

6.1 Problem Review

Design of an efficient implementation for LOGLAN with many level prefixing and pure static scope semantics is a problem more severe than for ALGOL60 or Simula67. The idea to start with is Dijkstra's [Dij60], namely to enter *activation records* or *incarnations* in a *run time stack* when modules are activated and to use compile time determinable *display (index) registers* and *offsets (relative addresses)* for fast access to contents of variable and parameter places. As for Simula67, incarnations of modules in one prefix chain shall be grouped as one so called *object instance* or *object* in one activation record and no display register reloadings shall be needed as long as a computation is running through main parts of modules in a prefix chain. As an illustration look at the run time stack content (pure static scoping) of program π_1 in appendix E (with its environmental and prefix structure in Section 3) just before class C is terminating.

In Simula67 as in ALGOL60 or Pascal it is correct to associate every module M of level ν_M straight forwardly with a list of display registers numbered from 1 to ν_M, to associate every applied occurrence ${}^i\xi$ of a variable with a display register numbered $\nu_{bdfct({}^i\xi)}$ and, at run time, to load register ν_M to register 1 with pointers by going down the static pointers chain of the activated module M.

But this proceeding does no longer work out for many level prefixing. Krogdahl [Kro79] discusses this problem; he recommends to look for compile time optimization procedures to minimize display register loadings and reloadings at run time.

The first implementation of LOGLAN-77/82 used a 1-1-association of modules and display registers in order to avoid reloadings as long as a computation is residing in a prefix chain of a module. A total of 6 registers were needed for π_1 . But that implementation did not fit static scoping, output of π_1 showed

$$2.0, 2.0, 2.0 \quad \text{instead of the expected} \quad 2.0, 2.0, 3.0 \quad .$$

That phenomenon was observed 1983. So the implemented semantics was called *quasi static scope*.

The articles [KKSL84, KLKW85, KKLSW87] and Krause's dissertation [Kra86] prove that appropriate compile time determined display register permutations get along with a number ν_{max} of display registers which is the maximum module nesting level in a program. This works successfully for pure static scoping and many level prefixing, no reloadings inside prefix chains take place. Since ALGOL60- or Simula67-like programs already require this number ν_{max} we may state: The compile time determined display register permutations are a solution of Krogdahl's optimization problem. The fact that MiniLOGLAN is only a restricted LOGLAN and does not yet allow object reference storing nor remote (indirect) identifier access nor virtual procedures is no point against display register permutation. The missing language constructs can be added without problems, they do not overthrow the implementation idea.

Our program examples π_1 and π_2 in appendices B and C show the following permuted display register lists associated to modules.

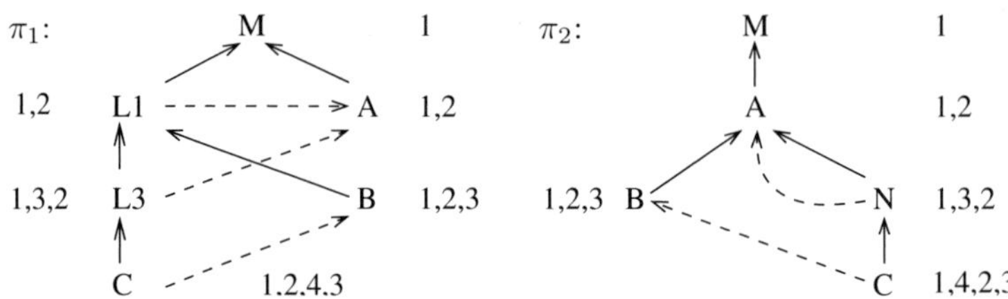

We see very clearly that many level prefixing induces non-trivial permutations.

Display register permutations for efficient implementation of MiniLOGLAN-programs (and LOGLAN-programs in general) are a result of viewing programs as L-algebras.

Static scoping is enabling that not only the set of modules in a wellformed program π may be seen as an L-algebra $\mathcal{M}$. This holds also for sets of the module instances in expanded programs $\bar{\pi}$ generated by successive prefix eliminations, class instantiations and copy rule applications. $\bar{\pi}$'s L-algebra $\overline{\mathcal{M}}$ is a so called *implementation* of π's L-algebra $\mathcal{M}$ with a characteristic *embedding homomorphism* h from $\overline{\mathcal{M}}$ into $\mathcal{M}$: The *pref*-trees in $\overline{\mathcal{M}}$ are linear paths *(object instances)*. If $M = h(\overline{M})$, then any path of *pref-* and *encl*-applications starting from M can be lifted to an analogous path starting from $\overline{M}$ (the other way round is clear by the notion homomorphism). Similarly for complement diagrams: If $M = h(\overline{M}),\ M' = h(\overline{M}'),\ M'' = h(\overline{M}''),\ \overline{M}' = pref^*(\overline{M}), \overline{M}'' = encl^*(\overline{M}')$ then $comp(M, M', M'') = h(comp(\overline{M}, \overline{M}', \overline{M}''))$.

We define display register association and present a correctness proof basing on L-algebras and their implementations.

6.2 Association of Lists of Display Registers to Modules and Its Correctness

At compile time every module M of level $\nu_M \geq 1$ of program π shall be associated with ν_M display registers numbered

$$d_M(1), \ldots, d_M(\nu_M)$$

with $1 \leq d_M(\mu) \leq \nu_M$ for $\mu = 1, \dots, \nu_M$. So d_M is a permutation of the numbers $1, \dots, \nu_M$. Main purpose of M's display registers is to have fast access to a local or global variable or parameter ${}^i\xi$ of M with its defining occurrence ${}^j\xi$ in its declaring module ${}^{k'}M'$ which is in the prefix chain of the vertex module ${}^kM$ of ${}^i\xi$.

But our wishes go further. Display register association shall be so intelligent that no display register reloadings are necessary as long as a computation is running in the main parts of M's prefix chain

$$M = pref^0(M) - - \rightarrow pref^1(M) - - \rightarrow \cdots - - \rightarrow pref^{l_M - 1}(M)$$

where $pref^{l_M}(M)$ is undefined and $l_M \geq 1$ is the length of M's prefix chain. This requires a uniformity condition to be fulfilled which bases on the notion of a complement modules chain.

Module M has its *enclosing modules chain*

$$M = M_{\nu_M} = encl^0(M) \rightarrow M_{\nu_M - 1} = encl^1(M) \rightarrow \dots$$
$$\rightarrow M_1 = encl^{\nu_M - 1}(M) = \pi$$

Let $M' = pref^l(M), 0 \leq l \leq l_M - 1$, be any module in the prefix chain of module M and let

$$M' = M'_{\nu_{M'}} \rightarrow M'_{\nu_{M'}-1} \rightarrow \dots \rightarrow M'_1 = \pi$$

be M' 's enclosing modules. This chain has a *complement modules chain*

$$M = M_{\lambda(\nu_{M'})} \stackrel{+}{\rightarrow} M_{\lambda(\nu_{M'}-1)} \stackrel{+}{\rightarrow} \cdots \stackrel{+}{\rightarrow} M_{\lambda(1)} = \pi$$

of length $\nu_{M'}$ inside M's enclosing modules chain such that

$$\nu_M = \lambda(\nu_{M'}) \leq \lambda(\nu_{M'} - 1) \leq \dots \leq \lambda(1) = 1\,.$$

$\lambda(\mu')$ is the level $\nu_{M_{\lambda(\mu')}}$ of the complement module $M_{\lambda(\mu')}$ of $M, M', M'_{\mu'}$ for $1 \leq \mu' \leq \nu_{M'}$. The decisive uniformity condition to be fulfilled is:

Condition 6.2.1:
$d_M(\lambda(\mu')) = d_{M'}(\mu')$ resp. $\lambda(\mu') = d_M^{-1} \circ d_{M'}(\mu')$
for all μ' with $1 \leq \mu' \leq \nu_{M'}$.

Is such an association d_M of lists of display register numbers to modules M possible? Yes. We define d_M by induction over the lexicographical ordering of couples (ν_M, l_M) of levels ν_M and prefix chain lengths l_M .

Induction beginning $(\nu_M, l_M) = (1, 1)$:
$d_M(1) := 1$
is the only choice possible.
Induction step $(\nu_M, l_M) \neq (1, 1)$, first case $l_M = 1$: Then $\nu_M > 1$ and there is an M' with

$$M \to M' \ ,$$

$\nu_{M'} = \nu_M - 1$, and $(\nu_{M'}, l_{M'})$ precedes $(\nu_{M'}, l_M)$ lexicographically. So $d_{M'}$ may be assumed to be defined.

$$d_M(\mu) := \begin{cases} d_{M'}(\mu) \text{ for } \mu = 1, \ldots, \nu_{M'} \\ \nu_M \qquad \text{for } \mu = \nu_M \quad . \end{cases}$$

Second case $l_M > 1$: Then there is an M' with

$$M \dashrightarrow M' \ ,$$

$\nu_{M'} \leq \nu_M$, $l_{M'} = l_M - 1$, and $(\nu_{M'}, l_{M'})$ precedes (ν_M, l_M) lexicographically. So $d_{M'}$ may be assumed to be defined.

$$d_M(\mu) := \begin{cases} d_{M'}(\mu') \text{ if } M_\mu \text{ and } M'_{\mu'} \text{ are in the enclosing modules chains} \\ \qquad \text{of } M \text{ and } M' \text{ and } M_\mu = comp(M, M', M'_{\mu'}), \mu = \lambda(\mu') \\ \\ \nu_{M'} + \delta \text{ if } M_\mu \text{ is in the enclosing modules chain of } M, \text{but} \\ \qquad \text{outside the complement modules chain of } M', \text{and} \\ \qquad M_\mu \text{ is the } \delta\text{-largest module of that kind,} \\ \qquad 1 \leq \delta \leq \nu_M - \nu_{M'} \end{cases}$$

In case we have same level prefixing as in Simula67 then case $d_M(\mu) = \nu_{M'} + \delta$ never applies and all d_M are identical mappings. Due to definition of the notion complement module and due to composition theorem 3.3 the following holds:

Lemma 6.2.2 : Our defined display register permutations d_M satisfy the uniformity condition 6.2.1.

For a correctness proof of our definition of d_M we have to explain beforehand what is to be proved: In practice the contents of display registers $Dr[d_M(\mu)]$ are linkage addresses of object instances (prefix chains of module incarnations). Since we would like to base our proof on L-algebra implementation

$$h : \overline{\mathcal{M}} \longrightarrow \mathcal{M}$$

we take object instances themselves, i.e. maximal prefix paths in $\overline{\mathcal{M}}$, as contents of display registers. Every module instance $\overline{M} \in \overline{\mathcal{M}}$ is an element of exactly one maximal prefix path, these paths define a partition of $\overline{\mathcal{M}}$ and an equivalence relation $\approx$ in $\overline{\mathcal{M}}$.

Let module $M \in \mathcal{M}$ be activated at runtime by instance $\overline{M} \in \overline{\mathcal{M}}$ with $h(\overline{M}) = M$. So the runtime system loads display register $Dr[d_M(\nu_M)]$ with $\overline{M}$'s maximal prefix chain

$$\overline{M} = pref^0(\overline{M}) \dashrightarrow \ldots \dashrightarrow pref^{l_{\overline{M}}-1}(\overline{M}) \ , \ l_{\overline{M}} = l_M \ ,$$

which is the equivalence class $[\overline{M}]_\approx$ of $\overline{M}$. Every display register $Dr[d_M(\mu)]$, $1 \leq \mu < \nu_M$, is loaded with $[\overline{M}_\mu]_\approx$ where $\overline{M}_\mu$ is that instance of level μ in the enclosing chain

$$\overline{M} = \overline{M}_{\nu_{\overline{M}}} \to \overline{M}_{\nu_{\overline{M}}-1} \to \ldots \to \overline{M}_\mu \to \ldots \to \overline{M}_1 = \bar{\pi} \ , \nu_{\overline{M}} = \nu_M .$$

This same loading is done when at run time after an interruption the computation is returning to or is resumed by object instance $[\overline{M}]_{\approx}$.

Now let M' be in the prefix chain of M , i.e. $M \overset{*}{--\rightarrow} M'$ and correspondingly $\overline{M} \overset{\star}{--\rightarrow} \overline{M}'$ with $h(\overline{M}') = M'$. Let ${}^{i}\xi'$ be a local or global variable or parameter occurrence in the main part of M' with its defining occurrence ${}^{j}\xi'$ in its declaring module ${}^{k'}M''$ which is in the prefix chain of the vertex module ${}^{k}M'$ of ${}^{i}\xi'$. To have a fast access to the storage place of ${}^{i}\xi'$ resp. ${}^{j}\xi'$ we couple (in fact, the compiler generated target code couples) the applied occurrence ${}^{i}\xi'$ with display register $Dr[d_{M'}(\mu')]$ where μ' is the level of the vertex module ${}^{k}M' = M'_{\mu'}$ in M''s enclosing chain

$$M' = M'_{\nu_{M'}} \rightarrow \ldots \rightarrow M'_{\mu'} \rightarrow \ldots \rightarrow M'_1 = \pi \ , \ \nu_{M'} \leq \nu_M .$$

Our claim is: As long as computation is running in object instance $[\overline{M}]_{\approx}$ display register $Dr[d_{M'}(\mu')]$ is already correctly loaded at object activation resp. resumption time. Bare transitions between module instances inside $[\overline{M}]_{\approx}$ need no reloading. This means more precisely: Consider the enclosing chain

$$\overline{M}' = \overline{M}'_{\nu_{\overline{M}'}} \rightarrow \ldots \rightarrow \overline{M}'_{\mu'} \rightarrow \ldots \rightarrow \overline{M}'_1 = \bar{\pi} \ , \ \nu_{\overline{M}'} = \nu_{M'},$$

for $\overline{M}'$. M' 's display registers are said to be *correctly loaded* if

$$\overline{M}'_{\nu_{\overline{M}'}} \in Dr[d_{M'}(\nu_{\overline{M}'})], ..., \overline{M}'_{\mu'} \in Dr[d_{M'}(\mu')], ..., \overline{M}'_1 \in Dr[d_{M'}(1)] \ .$$

We have a diagram

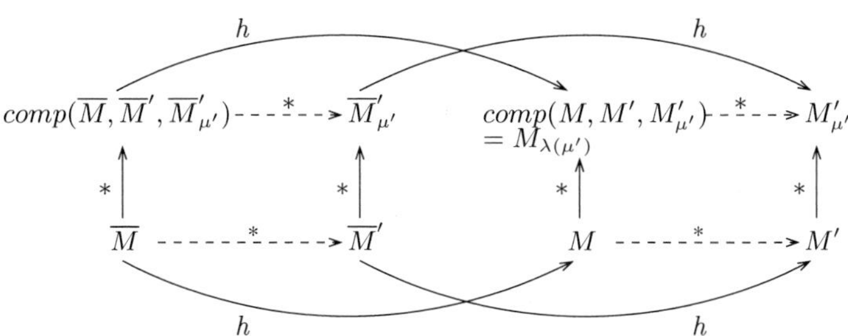

So $comp(\overline{M}, \overline{M}', \overline{M}'_{\mu'})$ is $\overline{M}_{\lambda(\mu')}$ which is $\in Dr[d_M(\lambda(\mu'))]$ by explicit loading and $\in Dr[d_{M'}(\mu')]$ due to uniformity guaranteed by lemma 6.2.2. So $\overline{M}'_{\mu'} \in Dr[d_{M'}(\mu')]$ because display registers of M are loaded with maximal prefix chains in $\mathcal{M}$ and $\overline{M}'_{\mu'}$ with $h(\overline{M}'_{\mu'}) = M'_{\mu'} = {}^{k}M'$ is a prefix of $\overline{M}_{\lambda(\mu')}$. We see: M''s display registers are correctly loaded in the sense above.

Why does this guarantee the right access to ${}^{i}\xi'$'s storage place? Remember that the declaring module ${}^{k'}M''$ is in the prefix chain of vertex module ${}^{k}M' = M'_{\mu'}$. So the defining occurrence ${}^{j}\xi'$ has a storage place in a corresponding instance $\overline{M}''$ with $h(\overline{M}'') = {}^{k'}M''$ which is in the prefix chain of $\overline{M}'_{\mu'}$. So

$\overline{M}'' \epsilon \; Dr[d_{M'}(\mu')]$, and this demonstrates the coupling of applied occurrence ${}^{i}\xi'$ with display register $Dr[d_{M'}(\mu')]$ is correct. This proves the correctness theorem:

Theorem 6.2.3: The display register associations d_M are correct. A module needs only ν_M registers. The associations are efficient in the sense that no reloadings are needed as long as a computation does not leave a prefix chain.

Important remark: It is well possible that different applied occurrences of the same variable in one prefix chain must be coupled to different display registers. So it is with x in class B and x in class C of program π_1 which are coupled with display register 2 resp. 4. See appendix D and E.

7 Conclusion

We would like this partly historical essay to be viewed as our high appreciation of O.-J. Dahl's and K. Nygaard's software engineering research on object orientation and its persistent combination with static binding which ALGOL60 has introduced in programming theory and practice and which has been known earlier in predicate logic and λ-calculus. Influential publications have unvoluntarily brought dynamic binding to the attention of programming practice. Dynamic binding became especially popular in object oriented programming although the inventors had a different view.

The Warsaw algorithmic logic and programming research group around A. Kreczmar and A.Salwicki has worked on object orientation in quite the same sense as the inventors. The Warsaw group defined and implemented several Simula 67-extensions, named LOGLAN77/82/88. One new language feature which Simula 67 excluded was many level (skew) prefixing. It was interesting to find out that the first many level prefixing implementation had deficiencies w.r.t. static binding. It proved to be a challenge to find a good efficient solution and a convincing justification. The problems that have come up were not foreseen in 1967 [Dah01b].

Our view of many level prefixed programs as classical ALGOL-programs with appropriate nested procedures and parameter transmissions have guided us to implement many level prefixing with the same display registers quantity and run time efficiency as same level prefixing, e.g. Simula 67. A right notion of complement module has given us the idea of display register permutation.

In order to prove the idea correct we view both original programs and their expansions and run time stack contents more abstractly as L-algebras. Expansions and stack contents, so called implementing L-algebras, are homomorphically embedded in the original programs. This L-algebraic view, enabled by static scoping, is sufficiently abstract such that typical object oriented language constructs like remote (indirect) addressing, object reference storing or virtual procedures are in concordance with the display register permutation idea.

I would like to thank my colleagues Grazyna Mirkowska, E. Börger, O.-J. Dahl, W. Goerigk, C.A.R. Hoare and A. Salwicki very heartily for many discussions around object orientation and static binding. Thanks also to an anonymous reviewer for his good suggestions. My conversations with O.-J. Dahl around the sd&m software pioneers conference at Bonn [Dah01a] have especially encouraged me to lecture anew on consistency of object inheritance and static binding [Lan01]. I am grateful to the editors who have invited me to contribute to the Festschrift in honour of our dear respected colleagues Ole-Johan Dahl and Kristen Nygaard. I thank Annemarie Langmaack and Moritz Zahorsky for typesetting the manuscript. Ole-Johan was a wonderful pianist; he together with Annemarie as a violinist enjoyed the participants of many informatics conferences since 1972.

References

[Bac57] J.W.Backus et al.. The FORTRAN Automatic Coding System. Proc. Western Joint Computing Conf. 11, 188-198, 1957

[BaS57] F.L.Bauer, K.Samelson. Verfahren zu automatischen Verarbeitung von kodierten Daten und Rechenmaschinen zur Ausübung des Verfahrens. Patentanmeldung Deutsches Patentamt, 1957

[Cla79] E.M. Clarke. Programming language constructs for which it is impossible to obtain good Hoare axiom systems. JACM 26:1, 129-147, 1979

[Dah01a] O.-J.Dahl. The Roots of Object Orientation: The Simula Language. In: M.Broy, E.Denert (Eds.). Software Pioneers, Contributions to Software Engineering. sd & m Conf. on Software Pioneers, Bonn 2001, Springer-Verlag, Berlin, Heidelberg, New York, 79-90, 2002

[Dah01b] O.-J.Dahl. Personal correspondence. Asker 2001

[DaN67] O.-J.Dahl, K.Nygaard. Class and Subclass Declarations. In: J.N.Buxton (ed.). Simulation Programming Languages. Proc. IFIP Work. Conf. Oslo 1967, North Holland, Amsterdam, 158-174, 1968

[Dij60] E.W.Dijkstra. Recursive Programming. Num. Math. 2, 312-318, 1960

[GHL67] A.A.Grau, U.Hill, H.Langmaack. Translation of ALGOL60. Handbook for Automatic Computation Ib, chief ed. K.Samelson. Springer-Verlag, Berlin, Heidelberg, New York 1967

[Her61] H.Hermes. Aufzählbarkeit, Entscheidbarkeit, Berechenbarkeit. Springer-Verlag, Berlin, Göttingen, Heidelberg 1961

[Hoa90] C.A.R.Hoare. Personal communications. EU-ESPRIT-BRA-Projekt "Provably Correct Systems - ProCoS", Oxford 1990, Cambridge 2001

[Ich80] J.D.Ichbiah. Ada Reference Manual. LNCS 106, Springer-Verlag, Berlin, Heidelberg, New York 1980

[JeW75] K.Jensen, N.Wirth. PASCAL-User Manual and Report, 2nd ed.. Springer Verlag, New York, Heidelberg, Berlin 1975

[Kan74] P.Kandzia. On the most-recent-property of ALGOL-like preograms. In: J.Loeckx (ed.). Automata, Languages and Programming. 2nd Coll. Univ. Saarbrücken 1974, LNCS14, Springer Verlag, Berlin, Heidelberg, New York, 97-111, 1974

[KeR78] B.W.Kernighan, D.M.Ritchie. The C Programming Language. Prentice Hall, Englewood Cliffs N.Y. 1978

[KKLSW87] M. Krause, A. Kreczmar, H. Langmaack, A. Salwicki, M. Warpechowski. Concatenation of Program Modules. Bericht 8701, Inst. f. Informatik u. Prakt. Math. Univ. Kiel, 1987

[KKSL84] A.Kreczmar, M.Krause, A.Salwicki, H.Langmaack. Specification and Implementation Problems of Programming Languages Proper for Hierarchical Data Types. Bericht 8410, Inst.Informatik Prakt. Math. CAU Kiel, 1984

[KLKW85] M.Krause, H.Langmaack, A.Kreczmar, M.Warpechowski. Concatenation of Program Modules, an Algebraic Approach to Semantic and Implementation Problems. In: A.Skowron (ed.). Computation Theory. Proc. 5th Symp. Zaborow 1984, LNCS 208, Springer Verlag, Berlin, Heidelberg, New York, 134-156, 1985

[Kra86] M. Krause. Die Korrektheit einer Implementation der Modulpräfidierung mit reiner Static-scope-Semantik, Bericht 8616, Inst. f. Informatik u. Prakt. Math. Univ. Kiel, 1986

[Kro79] S.Krogdahl. On the Implementation of BETA. Norwegian Comp. Centre, 1979

[KSW88] A.Kreczmar, A.Salwicki, M.Warpechowski. LOGLAN'88-Report on the Programming Language. LNCS 414, Springer-Verlag, Berlin, Heidelberg, New York 1990

[Lan01] H. Langmaack. Konsistenz von Vererbung in objektorientierten Sprachen und von statischer, ALGOL-artiger Bindung. In: K. Indermark, Thomas Noll (Hrsg.). Kolloquium Programmiersprachen und Grundlagen der Programmierung, Rurberg 2001. Aachener Informatik Berichte AIB-2001-11, RWTH Aachen, 47-52, 2001

[LaO80] H. Langmaack, E.-R. Olderog. Present day Hoare-like systems for programming languages with procedures: Power, limits, and most likely extensions. In: J.W. de Bakker, J. van Leeuwen. Proc. 7th Conf. Automata, Languages and Programming 1980, LNCS 25, Springer Verlag, Berlin, Heidelberg, New York, 363-373, 1980

[McC65] J.McCarthy et al.. Lisp 1.5 Programmer's Manual. The M.I.T. Press, Cambridge Mas. 1965

[MMPN93] O.L.Madsen, B.Møller-Pedersen, K.Nygaard. Object Oriented Programming in the BETA Programming Language. Addison Wesley / ACM Press, 1993

[Nau60] P.Naur (ed.) et al.. Report on the Algorithmic Language ALGOL60. Num. Math. 2, 106-136, 1960

[Old81] E.-R.Olderog. Sound and complete Hoare-like calculi based on copy rules. Acta Informatica, 16, 161-197, 1981

[PeS58] ACM Committee on Programming Languages and GAMM Committee on Programming, ed. by A.J.Perlis, K.Samelson. Report on the Algorithmic Language ALGOL. Num. Math. 1, 41-60, 1959

[RaR64] B.Randell, L.J.Russell. ALGOL60 Implementation. Academic Press, London, New York 1964

[SaB59] K.Samelson, F.L.Bauer. Sequentielle Formelübersetzung. Elektr. Rechenanl. 1, 4, 176-182, 1959

[Sam55] K.Samelson. Probleme der Programmierungstechnik. Intern. Koll. über Probleme der Rechentechnik, Dresden 1955, VEB Deutscher Verlag der Wissenschaften, Berlin, 61-68, 1957

[SaW02] A.Salwicki, M.Warpechowski. Combining Inheritance and Nesting Together: Advantages and Problems. Workshop Concurrency Specification and Programming CS&P '2002, 12 pp, Berlin 2002

[SSB01] R.F.Stärk, J.Schmid, E.Börger. Java and the Java Virtual Machine – Definition, Verification, Validation. Springer-Verlag, Berlin, Heidelberg, NewYork, 2001

[Ste84] G.L.Steele jr.. CommonLisp: The Language. Digital Press, 1984

[Sun97] Sun Microsystems. Inner Classes Specification. `http://java.sun.com/products/jdk/1.1/guide/innerclasses/`, 1997

[Wij+69] A.van Wijngaarden (ed.), B.J. Mailloux, J.E.L. Peck, C.H.A. Koster. Report on the Algorithmic Language ALGOL68. Num. Math. 14, 79-218, 1969

[WiM92] R.Wilhelm, D.Maurer. Übersetzerbau – Theorie, Konstruktion, Generierung. Springer-Verlag, Berlin, Heidelberg, NewYork, 1992

Appendix A : A contextfree-like grammar for MiniLOGLAN

The grammar is an adapted extraction from [KSW88]. *"Contextfree-like"*, as opposed to "contextfree", means that the productions are contextfree, but there may be infinitely many productions, terminal and non-terminal symbols. Terminal symbols or lexical entities are identifiers, literals, keywords and delimiters. Non-terminal symbols are written in angle brackets < > . Axiom is <program>. The production system is not complete. The reader is urged to add missing productions appropriately.

```
< program >          ::= < block >
< block >            ::= [< block idf. >:][inh < class idf. >]block < body >
                            [< block idf. >]
< body >             ::= < decl. >*< stm. >* end
< decl. >            ::= < var. decl. >
                       | < class decl. >
                       | < proc. decl. >
< var. decl. >       ::= var < var. spec. >
< class decl. >      ::= unit < class idf. >: [inh < class idf. >]class < body >
                            [< class idf. >]
< proc. decl. >      ::= unit < proc. idf. >: [inh < class idf. >]proc
                            (< form. par. spec. >*) < body > [< proc. idf. >]
< var. spec. >       ::= < var. idf. >:< var. type def. >
< var. type def. >   ::= < prim. type idf. >
                       | < class idf. >
< form. par. spec. > ::= < form. par. idf. >:< par. transm. mode >
                            {< type name > | < type >}
< type name >        ::= < prim. type idf. >
                       | < class idf. >
                       | < proc. idf. >
< stm. >             ::= < empty stm. >
                       | < assignm. stm. >
                       | call < proc. idf. > (< act. par. >*)
                       | new < class idf. >
                       | inner
                       | < block >
                       | < compound stm. >    like loop, conditional,
                                                    case statement
< act. par. >        ::= < var. idf. >
                       | < proc. idf. >
                       | < class idf. >
                       | < form. par. idf. >
```

Defining identifier occurrences are indicated by immediately following colons : , all other identifier occurrences are *applied* ones. Conditions for well-formedness (correct static semantics) of programs are formulated in Section 3. In order to handle prefix elimination and program semantics by copy rule applications and program expansions it is advisable to have an extra production

```
< stm.>          ::= gbegin <body>
```

which introduces so called *generated statements* or *instances* of modules. For later treatment of indirect (remote) identifier access productions like

```
<var. type def.> ::= <class idf.> . <var. type def.>
<type name>      ::= <class idf.> . <type name>
<var. name>      ::= <var idf.>
                   | <class idf.> . <var idf.>
```

ought to be added. For object generation (class instantiation) and storing object references a special assignment statement is needed

```
<assignm. stm.>  ::= <var. name> := new<class idf.>.
```

Appendix B:

Program example π_1

```
M: block
    var x: real;
    unit A: class
        var x: real;
        x:=3;
        inner
    end A;
    L1: inh A block
        var y: real;
        unit B: class
            x:=y; print(x);
            inner
        end B;
        y:=2;
        L2: new B;
        L3: inh A block
            var y: real;
            unit C: inh B class
                y:=x; print(y);
                inner
            end C;
            y:=4;
            L4: new C
        end L3
    end L1
end M
```

L2 and L4 are redundant statement labels.

Appendix C:

Program example π_2 with recursive prefixing. The original prefix elimination process is infinite.

```
M: block
    var y: real;
    unit A: class
        var x: real;
        unit B: class
            x:=y;
            inner
        end B;
        L1: new B;
        inner;
        unit N : inh A block
            var ȳ: real;
            unit C : inh B class
                ȳ:=x;
                inner
            end C;
            L2: new C;
        end N
    end A;
    L3: new A
end M
```

L1, L2, L3 are redundant statement labels.

Appendix D: Elimination of all prefixes in program π_1 yields π_1'' :

```
M: block
    var x̄: real;
                              (* class A deleted *)
    L1: block
        var x: real;
        x := 3;
        gbegin
        var y: real;
                              (* class B deleted *)
        y := 2;
        L2: block
            x := y; print(x);    (* see comment 1 *)
            gbegin
            end
        end L2;
        L3: block
            var x′: real;
            x′ := 3;
            gbegin
            var ȳ: real;
                              (* class C deleted *)
            ȳ := 4 ;
            L4: block
                x := y ; print(x);    (* see comments 2 and 3 *)
                gbegin
                ȳ := x′ ; print(ȳ);
                gbegin
                end
                end
            end L4
            end
        end L3
        end
    end L1
end M
```

Comment 1: The first output is 2.0, no matter whether static scoping, dynamic scoping or quasi static scoping (i.e. dynamic scoping starting from a distinguished program, renaming of x in M to $\overline{x}$, of y in L3 to $\overline{y}$), is done.

Comment 2: y is the first variable access where static scoping violates dynamic scoping because y does not access the most recent defining occurrence $\overline{y}$. The second output is 2.0 whereas dynamic scoping would yield 4.0. Quasi static scoping would still behave as static scoping and so yield the same second output 2.0 .

Comment 3: x is the first variable access where static scoping violates quasi static scoping because x does not access the most recent defining occurrence x' . The third output is 3.0 whereas quasi static scoping would yield again 2.0. Here static scoping deviates from Dijkstra's most-recent-behaviour in the same way as in the short ALGOL60-program examples of [GHL67] and [Kan74]. When class C, prefixed by B, is initialized then B does not store value 2.0 in that place reserved for B's global variable x within the most recent incarnation of class A, but within the older one. Observe that this deviation from most-recent-behaviour is generated by block enterings, class initializations and many level prefixing without any help of nested procedures with formal procedure identifiers as parameters.

Appendix E : Runtime stack of program π_1 just before class initalization **new** C terminates.

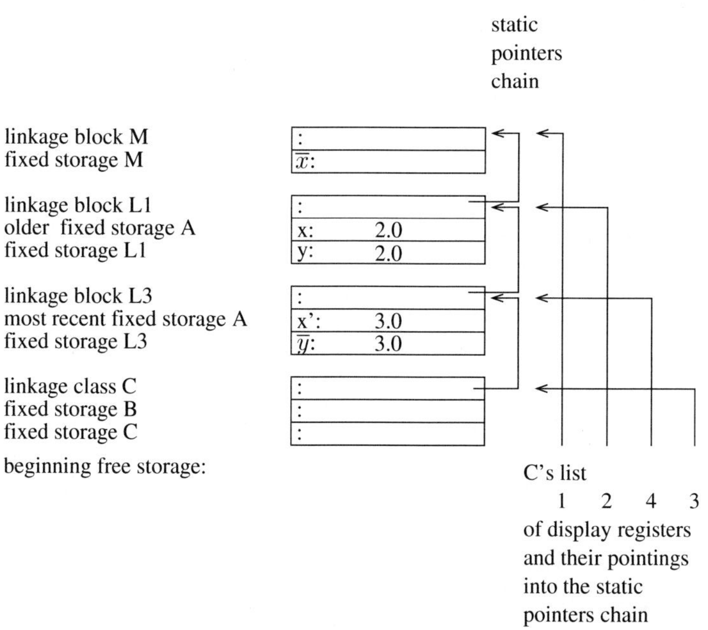

Both the block and class instances in the expanded program π_1'' and the incarnations in the run time stack above are L-algebras. Specific homomorphisms h from them into π_1's L-algebra make the L-algebras so called *implementations* of π_1's L-algebra. The static pointers of the object instances in the run time stack allow to determine the enclosing function *encl* of all incarnations implicitly. Observe: The applied occurrences of one and the same global variable x in class B and class C (the prefix chain of C) are coupled with different display registers 2 and 4.

The Power of Abstraction, Reuse, and Simplicity: An Object-Oriented Library for Event-Driven Design

Bertrand Meyer

ETH Zürich, Chair of Software Engineering
http://se.inf.ethz.ch
(also Eiffel Software, Santa Barbara, and Monash University)

Abstract. A new library for event-driven design, defining a general and extendible scheme yet easy to learn and use on both the publisher and subscriber sides, provides an opportunity to analyze such other approaches as the "Observer Pattern", the event-delegate mechanism of .NET and its "Web Forms", then to draw some general software engineering lessons.

1 Overview

Event-driven software design avoids any direct connection, in a system's architecture, between the unit in charge of executing an operation and those in charge of deciding when to execute it.

Event-driven techniques have gained growing usage because of their flexibility. They are particularly common for Graphical User Interface applications, where the operations come from an application layer and the decision to execute them comes from a GUI layer in response to events caused by human users. An event-driven scheme can shield the design of the application layer from concerns related to the user interface. Many application areas other than GUI design have used these ideas.

Closely related techniques have been proposed under such names as *Publish-Subscribe* and *Observer Pattern.*

This article describes the Event Library, a reusable component solution of broad applicability, covering all these variants. Intended to be easy to learn, the library consists in its basic form of one class with two features, one for the production of events and one for their consumption.

The discussion will compare this solution to the Observer Pattern and mechanisms recently introduced by .NET. It will expand on this analysis to examine more general issues of software engineering, including the role of abstraction, the transition from design patterns to reusable components, the concern for simplicity, and the contribution of object technology.

Section 2 quickly presents the essentials of the Event Library. Section 3 explains event-driven design and what makes it attractive. Sections 4, 5 and 6 analyze other solutions: the Observer Pattern, the .NET event handling mechanism, the Web Forms library of ASP.NET. Section 7 gives the remaining details of the Event Library. Section 8 examines the software engineering issues that led to this work and draws general conclusions.

O. Owe et al. (Eds.): From OO to FM (Dahl Festschrift), LNCS 2635, pp. 236-271, 2004.

2 Event Library Essentials

The Event Library consists at its core of one class, *EVENT_TYPE* with a feature *publish* for publishers and a feature *subscribe* for subscribers. The library is written in Eiffel; so are the usage examples in this section.

First the subscriber side. Assume you want to ensure that any future mouse click will cause execution of a certain procedure of your application

```
your_procedure (a, b: INTEGER)
```

passing to it the mouse coordinates as values for *a* and *b*. To obtain this effect, simply *subscribe* the desired procedure to the event type *mouse_click*:

```
mouse_click.subscribe (agent your_procedure)                     /1/
```

The argument to *subscribe* is an "agent" expression; an agent in Eiffel is an object representing a routine, here *your_procedure*.

In most cases this is all one needs to know on the subscriber side, for example to produce a graphical application using a GUI library. An advantage of the scheme is that it lets you start from an existing system and add an event-driven scheme such as a GUI without writing any connecting code. You'll just reuse the existing routines directly, linking them to event types through agent expressions as above. This extends to routines with extra arguments: assuming

```
other_procedure (text: STRING; a, b: INTEGER; date: DATE)
```

you can still subscribe the procedure without any "glue code" through

```
mouse_click.subscribe (agent other_procedure ("TEXT", ?, ?, Today)    /2/
```

where the question marks indicate the values to be filled in by the event. (The agent in form /1/ can be written more explicitly as **agent** *your_procedure* (**?**, **?**).)

So much for subscribers. The basic scheme for publishers is also straightforward. To trigger a mouse click event, all the GUI library will do is

```
mouse_click.publish ([x_position, y_position])                    /3/
```

It is also the publisher's responsibility to declare *mouse_click* and create the corresponding object. It can take care of both through

```
mouse_click: EVENT_TYPE [TUPLE [INTEGER, INTEGER]] is
    once
        create Result
    end                                                           /4/
```

Class *EVENT_TYPE* is generic; the parameter *TUPLE [INTEGER, INTEGER]* indicates that a mouse click produces event data consisting of two integers, representing the mouse coordinates, collected into a two-element "tuple".

Since *mouse_click* just represents an ordinary object — an instance of class *EVENT_TYPE* — the instruction that creates it could appear anywhere. One possibility, as shown, is to put it in a "once function" defining *mouse_click*. A once function is executed the first time it's called, whenever that is, the same result being returned by every subsequent call. This language mechanism addresses the issue of providing initialization operations without breaking the decentralized architecture of well-designed O-O systems. Here it creates the mouse click object when first needed, and retains it for the rest of the execution.

The scheme as described covers global events: the subscriber call /1/ subscribes *your_procedure* to any mouse click anywhere. Instead we may want to let subscribers select events in a given graphical element such as a button. We simply turn *mouse_click* into a feature of class *BUTTON*, so that subscriber calls will be

```
your_button.mouse_click.subscribe (agent your_procedure)          /5/
```

perhaps clearer as *your_button_click*.*subscribe* (**agent** *your_procedure*), retaining the original form /1/ with *your_button_click* set to *your_button*.*mouse_click*.

What we have just seen defines, for the majority of applications, the user's manual of the Event Library:

- On the publisher side, declare and create the event type object; trigger a corresponding event, when desired, by calling *publish*.
- On the subscriber side, call *subscribe* with an agent for the desired routine.

Only one class is involved, *EVENT_TYPE*; there is no need to define specific classes for each event type (mouse click, mouse movement etc.) as, for example, in the .NET model studied below — although you can do so if you wish by introducing descendants of *EVENT_TYPE* that specialize the event data. There is also no need for the publishers or the subscribers to inherit from any particular classes, such as the abstract classes *SUBJECT* and *OBSERVER* of the Observer Pattern, also studied below.

Section 7 will describe some of the more specialized features of the library. As is often the case when the basic design of a library uses a small number of abstractions tailored to the problem, it is possible to add special-purpose facilities without disturbing users who need only the basics.

To understand the rationale behind this design, we will now step back to examine the general issues of event-driven computation, and some previously proposed solutions.

3 Event-Driven Design

Event-driven design offers interesting architectural solutions when execution must respond to events whose order is hard to predict in the program text.

Putting the User in Control

GUI and WUI (Web User Interfaces) provide the most immediately visible illustration of why an event-driven scheme may be useful.

Consider this piece of WUI built with ASP.NET (the Web library for .NET):

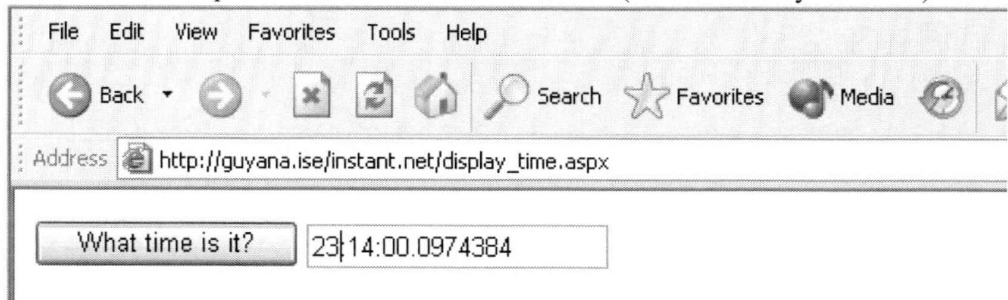

Figure 1: A Web User Interface under ASP.NET

The interface that we show to our user includes a text field and a button. There might be many more such "*controls*" (the Windows term for graphical elements, called "widgets" in the X Window system). We expect that the user will perform some input action, and we want to process it appropriately in our program. The action might be typing characters into the text field, clicking the button, or any other, such as menu selection, using controls not shown above.

But which of these will happen first? Indeed, will any happen at all?

We don't know.

In the early days, the problem didn't exist. Programs would just read user input, using for example a loop to consume successive lines, as in

```
from
    read_line
    count := 0
until
    last_line.is_empty
loop
    count := count + 1
        -- Store last_line at position count in Result:
    Result.put (last_line, count)
    read_line
end
```

This was good enough when we had a single sequential input medium and the program was in charge of deciding when, where and how to enjoin the user to enter some input, for example on a teletype console.

With current input techniques, a user sitting at a graphics workstation is free at any time to go to the text field, the button or any other control. He, not the program, is in control.

To support such modes of interaction, event-driven programming replaces a *control structure* by a *data structure*. A control structure means that the program decides when to execute things. Instead we want to let the user decide what to do next. We'll call these user decisions *events*. The system will use a data structure — let's call it the **event-action table** — to record in advance the actions that it has to execute when events of specific types occur. After that it relies on the event handling machinery to watch for events of recognized types and, when detecting one of them, trigger the corresponding action as found in the event-action table.

A role remains for control structures: each operation, while it executes, defines the scheduling of its own operations, using a control structure that can be arbitrarily complex. But when the operation terminates the event-driven scheme takes over again.

Overall, it's a major change. The program has relinquished direct control of global execution scheduling to a generic table-driven mechanism. For best results that mechanism should be a library, for example a GUI or WUI library, or — more generic yet — the Event Library, not tied to any specific application area.

This yields a clear division of tasks between such a general-purpose library and any particular application. The application is in charge of recording event-action associations; when the true show begins, the library is in charge of catching and processing events.

Application authors have their say, since what gets executed in the end are the actions — taken from the program — that they have planted in the table. But they do not directly control the scheduling of steps.

The library owns the event-action table, so that application programmers should not need to know anything about its implementation. With the Event Library they simply record event-action associations, through calls to *subscribe*; the library takes care of maintaining these associations in the appropriate data structure. We'll see that in some other frameworks, such as .NET, programmers work at a lower level of abstraction, closer to the internal representation of the event-action table.

Publishers and Subscribers

The overall scheme of programming in an event-driven style is this:

1 • Some part of the system is able to trigger events. We call it a **publisher**.

2 • Some part of the system wants to react to these events. We call it a **subscriber**. ("Observer" would also do, as in the "Observer Pattern", where the publisher is called a "subject".)

3 • The subscriber specifies actions that it wants to execute in connection with events of specified types. We'll say that the subscriber **registers** an action for an event type. The effect of registration is to record an association between an event type and a subscriber into the event-action table. Registrations usually happen during initialization, but subscribers can continue to register, or de-register, at any time of the execution; that's one of the advantages of using a table-driven scheme, since the table can be modified at any time.

4 • At any time during execution proper, after initialization, the publisher can trigger an event. This will cause execution of the routines that any registered subscribers have associated with the event's type.

For this discussion we must be careful about distinguishing between *events* and *event types*. The notion of mouse click is an event type; a user clicking his mouse will cause an event. Although the data structure is called the *event*-action table for brevity, its definition clearly specified that it records information about event types. Publishers, on the other hand, trigger events, each of a certain type.

Healthy skepticism should lead us to ask why we need all this. Instead of an indirect relationship through an event-action table, couldn't we just skip step 3 and let, in step 4, the subscriber call the publisher, or conversely?

A subscriber can indeed call its publishers directly through a generalization of the earlier sequential reading scheme: it will listen to events of several possible types rather than just one, pick up the first one that happens, select the appropriate action, and repeat. This has, however, two limitations. One is that you need to put the subscriber in charge of the application's control structure; that is not always appropriate. Another, more serious, is that it is not easy with this scheme to ensure that events raised by a publisher trigger actions in several subscribers.

Alternatively, the publisher could call the subscriber's routine directly

```
my_subscriber.routine (my_arguments)
```

using the standard object-oriented call mechanism. This works as long as the whole scheme is static: the publishers know their subscribers, and this information is defined once and for all so that publishers' code can include calls such as the above for each subscriber to each event type.

The limitations of both solutions indicate where event-driven programming becomes interesting. We may picture the general situation as one of those quantum physics experiments that bombard, with electrons or other projectiles, some screen with a little hole:

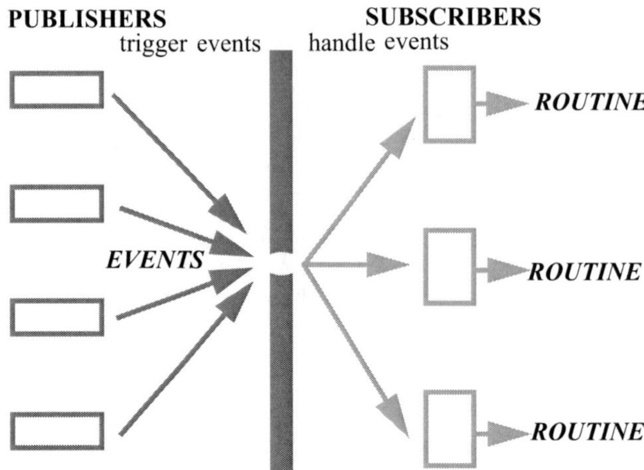

Figure 2: Triggering and handling events

The event-driven scheme decouples the subscribers from the publishers and may be attractive if one or more of the following conditions hold:

- *Publishers can't be required to know who the subscribers are*: they trigger events, but do not know who is going to process those events. This is typically the case if the publisher is a GUI or WUI library: the routines of the library know how to detect a user event such as a mouse click, but they should not have to know about any particular application that reacts to these events, or how it reacts. To an application, a button click may signal a request to start a compilation, run the payroll, or shut down the factory. To the GUI library, a click is just a click.

- *Subscribers may register and deregister while the application is running*: this generalizes the previous case by making the set of subscribers not only unknown to publishers but also variable during execution.

- *Any event triggered by one publisher may be consumed by several subscribers*. For example the event is the change of a certain value, say a temperature in a factory control system; then the change must be reflected in many different places that "observe" it, for example an alphanumeric display, a graphical display, and a database that records all historical values. Without an event mechanism the publisher would have to call routines in every one of these subscribers, causing too much coupling between different parts of the system. This would mean, in fact, that the publisher must know about all its subscribers, so this case also implies the first one.

- *The subscribers shouldn't need to know about the publishers*: this is less commonly required, but leads to the same conclusions.

In all such cases the event-driven style allows you to build a more flexible architecture by keeping publishers and subscribers at bay.

There is a downside: if you are trying to follow the exact sequence of run-time operations — for example when debugging an application — you may find the task harder, precisely because of the indirection. A plain call *x.f* (...) tells you exactly what happens: after the preceding instruction, control transfers to *f*, until *f*'s execution terminates, and then comes back to the instruction following the call. With an instruction that triggers an event, all you know is that some subscribers may have registered some routines to handle events of that kind, and if so they will execute these routines. But you don't immediately know who they are; indeed they may vary from execution to execution. So it is more delicate to track what's going on. One should weigh this objection — which some authors have proposed to address by replacing event-driven design with techniques inspired by parallel programming [18] — before deciding to embark on an event-driven architecture.

Controls

In cases such as GUI and WUI programming, the event-action table will generally contain not mere pairs — actions coupled with event types — but **triples**: we don't just specify "for events of this type, execute that action", but "for events of this type occurring in this *control*, execute that action", as in:

- "*If the user clicks the EXIT button, exit the application*".
- "*If the mouse enters this window, change the border color to red*".
- "*If this sensor reports a temperature above 40° C, ring the alarm*".

In the first case the control is a button and the event type is "mouse click"; in the second, they are a window and "mouse enter"; in the third, a temperature sensor and a measurement report.

A "control" is usually just a user interface element. As the last example indicates, the concept also applies outside of the UI world.

A common library interface to let subscribers deposit triples into the event-action table (we'll continue to call it that way) uses calls of the conceptual form

```
record_association (some_control, some_event_type, some_action)        /6/
```

and leaves the rest to the underlying GUI or WUI machinery. That's the essence of event-driven programming as supported by many modern graphics toolkits, from Smalltalk to EiffelVision to the Windows graphical API and the Web Forms of .NET. The most common variant is actually

```
add_association (some_control, some_event_type, some_action)
```

which adds *some_action* to the actions associated with *some_event_type* and *some_control*, so that you can specify executing *several* actions for a given event-control pair. We'll retain the first form /6/ since it corresponds to the most frequent need; it includes the second one as a special case if we assume a provision for composite actions.

The Event Library seemed at first not to support controls since the basic mechanism *mouse_click.subscribe* (...) /1/ did not make them explicit; but we saw that it's just a matter of making an event type belong to a control object, then use *your_button.mouse_click.subscribe* (...) /5/, which directly provides the general scheme /6/.

Actions as Objects

In a classical O-O language, we have a problem. Even though we don't need to manipulate the event-action table directly, we know it will exist somewhere, managed by a graphical library, and that it's a data structure — a structure made of objects, or (more realistically) references to objects. In each entry we expect to find a triple containing references to:

- One control.
- One event type.
- One action — or, as a result of the last observation, one list of actions.

Are these things objects? Controls, definitely. Any graphical O-O library provides classes such as *WINDOW* and *BUTTON* whose instances are objects representing controls — windows, buttons and so on. Event types too can be defined as objects in an O-O language; we saw how the Event Library does it. But what about actions?

Actions are given by our program's code. In an O-O program, the natural unit for an action is a routine of a class. But a routine is not an object.

This won't be too much of a concern for a C++ programmer, who may just use a *function pointer*: an integer denoting the address where a routine's code is stored, providing a way to execute the routine. But that's not type-safe, since one can do too many other things with the pointer. As a consequence, O-O languages intent on providing the benefits of static typing do not provide function pointers.

The notion of *agent* used in the Event Library is an object-oriented mechanism that addresses the issue within the constraints of type checking. An Eiffel agent is an object that represents a routine ready to be called.

> Some of its operands (target and arguments) can be fixed, or *closed*, at the time the agent is defined; the others, called *open* operands and expressed — when needed — as question marks **?** in earlier examples, must be provided at the time of each call. In **agent** *some_routine* all arguments are open; in **agent** *some_routine* (*1*, **?**, **?**, "*SOME TEXT*") the first and last arguments are closed, the others open. You can also make the *target* open, as in **agent** {*TARGET_TYPE*}**.***some_routine* (*1*, **?**, **?**, "*SOME TEXT*").

Some languages provide comparable mechanisms under the name "block" or "closure". The "delegates" of .NET and C# are a limited form of agent where arguments are always open and the target is always closed.

Java doesn't have such notion, meaning that to represent an action as object you have to create a little class that includes the corresponding routine. The availability of "nested classes" limits the amount of code that must be written for such classes, but the solution lacks extendibility and scalability.

Avoiding Glue

When building an event-driven application, you will need at some stage to connect the subscribers with the publishers. One of the guiding concerns — reflected in the design of the Event Library — must be to keep such connections as light as possible.

This goal is particularly relevant to the common case of restructuring an existing application to give it an event-driven architecture. The application may provide many functions, perhaps developed over a long period and embodying a sophisticated "business model" for a certain domain. The purpose of going event-driven might be to make these functions available through a graphical or Web interface, taking advantage of an event-driven GUI or WUI library. In this case both the business model and the library predate the new architecture.

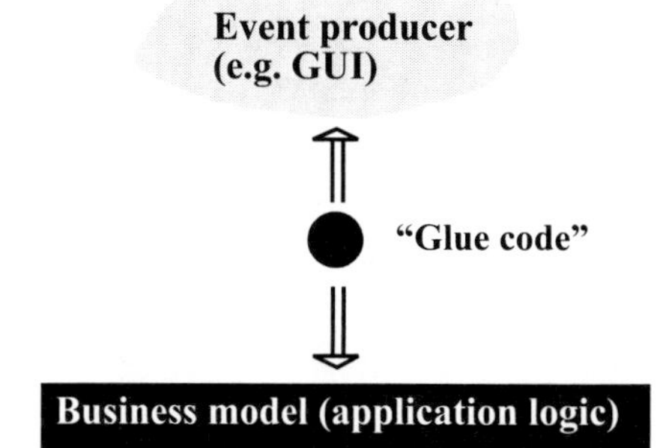

Figure 3: Connecting publishers and subscribers

Common names for the three parts appearing on the figure follow from the Smalltalk "MVC" scheme that inspired many event-driven GUI designs: *Model* for the existing application logic, *View* for the user interface, and *Controller* for the connection between the two.

With such terminology the above goal is easily stated: we seek to get rid of the Controller part, or reduce it to the conceptually inevitable minimum.

The Event Library offers two complementary styles to achieve this. In the first style, we let the application consume events by becoming a subscriber through calls of the form seen earlier

```
some_event_type.subscribe (agent some_routine)                    /7/
```

explicitly making the consumer application event-driven.

In many cases this is appropriate. But what if you want to reuse *both* the event producer and the event consumer (the application) exactly as they are? The Event Library and the agent mechanism allow this too. You'll leave both the producer and the consuming application alone, connecting application routines to producer events through a simple intermediary. Just add an explicit target to the agent expression: instead of **agent** *some_routine* as used above, which denotes the routine ready to be applied to the current object, you may select any other object as target of the future call:

```
some_event_type.subscribe (agent other_object.some_routine)       /8/
```

By using either form, you can select the style that you prefer:

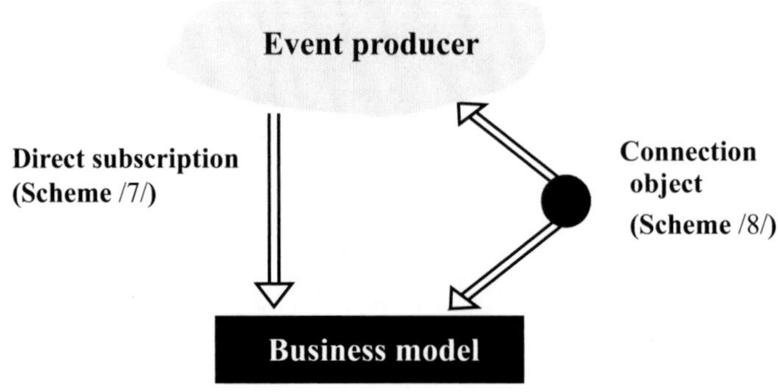

Figure 4: Two connection styles

Either may be appropriate depending on the context:

- Scheme /7/ adds event-driven scheduling to an existing application by plugging in routines of that application directly.
- Scheme /8/ lets you reuse both pre-existing event producers (publishers) and pre-existing event consumers (subscribers), unchanged. By definition, you'll need some glue code then. Scheme /8/ reduces it to the minimum possible: calls to *subscribe* using agents with explicit targets. One of the benefits of this style is that it lets you provide *several* interfaces to a given application, even within a single program.

To reduce the need for glue code even further, you may take advantage of the agent mechanism's support for combining *closed* and *open* arguments. Assume that an existing meteorological application includes a routine

```
show_rainfall (x, y: INTEGER; start, end : DATE): REAL
    -- Display amount of rain recorded between start and end at coords x, y.
```

You build a graphical interface that shows a map with many cities, and want to ensure that once a user has chosen a starting and ending dates *Initial* and *Final* moving the mouse across the map will at each step display the rainfall at the corresponding map position. This means that when calling the procedure *show_rainfall* for each *mouse_move* event we should treat its first two arguments differently from the other two:

- The application sets *start* and *end* from *Initial* and *Final*.
- The GUI library mechanism will fill in a fresh *x* and *y* — event data — each time it triggers the event.

To achieve this effect, simply subscribe an agent that uses open arguments for the first set and closed arguments for the second set, as in /2/:

```
mouse_move.subscribe (agent show_rainfall (?, ?, Initial, Final )        /9/
```

(This could also use an explicit target as in /8/; the target could be closed or itself open.) The generality of this mechanism lets you tweak an existing routine to fit a new context: the subscriber freezes certain operands at subscription time, and leaves the others for the publisher to provide, as event data, at the time of event publication.

The benefit here is that the agent lets us reuse an existing four-argument routine, *show_rainfall*, at a place were we need a routine with only two arguments.

With other mechanisms such as the ones studied later in this chapter we would have to use two variables and write an explicit wrapper routine:

```
Initial, Final: DATE
        -- Start and end of rainfall data collection period

show_rainfall_at_initial_and_final (x, y: INTEGER) is                /10/
        -- Display amount of rain recorded at x, y between Initial and Final.
    do
        show_rainfall (Initial, Final, x, y)
    end
```

For a few routines and event types this approach is acceptable. When scaled up to real applications, it generates noise code that pollutes the architecture, making the program harder to understand, maintain and extend.

Agents and the Event Library help avoid these pitfalls and build stable solutions on both the publisher and subscriber sides, with minimum connection code between the two.

4 The Observer Pattern

To provide more perspective on event-driven architectures and the design of the Event Library, this section and the next two examine other approaches.

First, the "Observer Pattern". As presented in the book *Design Patterns* [6], it was one of the first descriptions of a general event-driven scheme.

The following figure illustrates the general structure of that solution. For ease of comparison with the rest of this article the names Observer and Subject used in the original have been changed to *SUBSCRIBER* and *PUBLISHER*. *APPCLASS* and *LIBCLASS* denote typical examples of effective (concrete) classes, one describing a typical subscriber and the other a typical publisher.

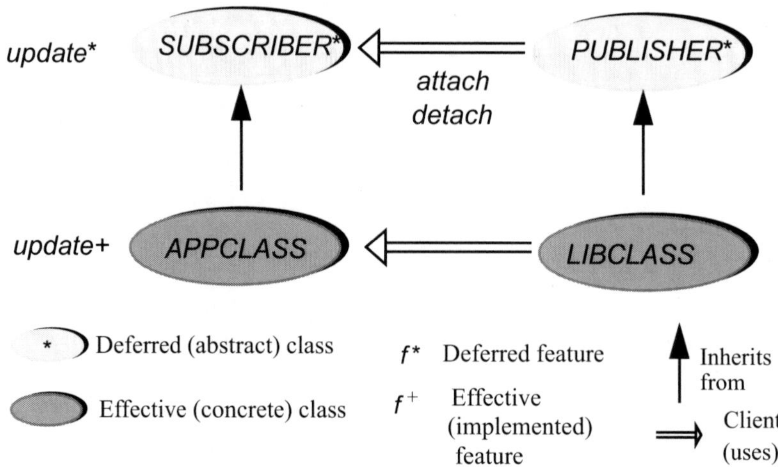

Figure 5: Observer Pattern architecture

Surprisingly, in the basic design it's the publishers that know about their observers, as shown by the direction of the client links on the figure: a publisher gets a new observer through the procedure *attach* and can remove it through *detach*. There is no equivalent to *register* on the subscriber side; in the primary example illustrating the pattern [6] — a clock that publishes ticks and two subscribers, both of them clock displays, one analog and the other digital — the subscriber objects get created with respect to a publisher, through a constructor (creation procedure) of the form

```
make (p: PUBLISHER) is
        -- Initialize this object as a subscriber to subject.
    do
        p.attach (Current)
    end
```

(where ***Current*** is the current object (also called *self*, *this*, *Me* in various O-O languages), so that the digital clock display gets created as

```
create digital_display.make (clock)
```

(in C++/Java/C# style: digitalDisplay = new DigitalDisplay (clock)).

An immediately visible limitation of the pattern is that it lacks a general solution for the publisher to pass information to the subscriber. That doesn't matter if all that characterizes an event is that it occurs. But many events will also need, as we have seen, to transmit *event data*, such as the mouse position for a mouse click. The Patterns book notes this issue (([6], page 298) and mentions two models for passing information, "push" and "pull", each implying even more coupling between the publisher and the subscriber. Each requires extra coding on both sides, taking into account the specific type of information being passed.

No reusable solution seems possible here — short of an explosion of the number of classes, as will be seen in the .NET model's approach in the next section — without both *genericity* and a *tuple type* mechanism as used by the Event Library. The Event Library represents event data through the generic parameter to *EVENT_TYPE*: when you introduce a new event type that generates, say, three pieces of information of types *A*, *B* and *C*, you will declare it of type *EVENT_TYPE* [*TUPLE* [*A*, *B*, *C*]]. Then the routine that you subscribe must take arguments of types *A*, *B*, *C*. This takes care of the connection, but is not possible in the C++/Java framework, used in most published discussions of patterns with the exception of the work of Jézéquel, Train and Mingins [8].

The Observer Pattern design raises two other immediate objections:

- The creation procedure — *make* or the corresponding C++ constructor — must be written anew for each subscriber class, leading to useless repetition of code, the reverse of object technology principles.

- It's too restrictive to force subscribers to register themselves with publishers at creation time, not only because subscriber classes may already exist and have other creation requirements, but also because the subscribers should be able to subscribe later.

We can alleviate both criticisms, at least in part, by adding to the class *SUBSCRIBER* a procedure *subscribe* which, on the subscriber side, mirrors what *attach* provides on the publisher side, and uses *attach* in its implementation:

```
subscribe (p: PUBLISHER) is
        -- Attach current subscriber to p.
    do
        p.attach (Current)
    end
```

This extension explicitly makes subscribers clients of their publishers. But other problems remain.

One is that a publisher sends notification of an event by calling a procedure *update* in each subscriber. The procedure is declared as deferred (abstract) in class *SUBSCRIBER* and effected (implemented) in each specific observer class such as *APPCLASS* to describe the subscriber's specific reaction to the event. Each publisher keeps a list of its subscribers, updated by *attach* and *detach*; when it triggers an event, it traverses this list and calls *update* on each element in turn, relying on dynamic binding to ensure that each subscriber uses its own version. But this means that altogether a subscriber may register only one action! As a consequence, it may subscribe to only one type of event, except for the trivial case of handling several event types in the same way. This is severely restrictive. An application component should be able to register various operations to various publishers. The Event Library places no limit, for a subscriber, on the number of calls of the form *some_control*.*some_event_type*.*subscribe* (**agent** *some_routine*).

The discussion in the Patterns book acknowledges the issue and proposes a solution ([6], page 297): add one argument to *update* to represent the publisher, which will pass ***Current*** when calling *update* to let the subscriber discriminate between publishers. But this is not satisfactory. Since there is still just one *update* procedure in each subscriber, that procedure will have to know about all relevant publishers and discriminate between them — a step back to the kind of know-them-all, consider-each-case-in-turn decision schemes from which object technology tries to free software architectures. Worse, this means a new form for procedure *update*, with one extra argument, invalidating the preceding class design for *PUBLISHER* and implying that we can't have a single reusable class for this concept. Reusability concerns yield to general guidelines that have to be programmed again, in subtly different ways, for each new application.

More generally the need for the subscribers to know the publishers is detrimental to the flexibility of the architecture. The direction of this knowledge relation is not completely obvious, since the last figure, drawn before we added *subscribe* to the pattern, only showed (like the corresponding UML diagram in the original Observer Pattern presentation) a client link from the publisher to the subscriber. That link indicates that each publisher *object* keeps a list of its subscribers. It has no harmful effect on the architecture since the text of publisher *classes* will, properly, not list subscribers.

Subscriber classes, however, do mention the publisher explicitly. In the pattern's original version, that's because the constructor of a subscriber uses the publisher as argument; our addition of *subscribe* as an explicit procedure made this requirement clearer. It causes undesirable coupling between subscribers and publishers. Subscribers shouldn't need to know which part of an application or library triggers certain events.

Yet another consequence is that the Observer Pattern's design doesn't cover the case of a single event type that any number of publishers may trigger. You subscribe to *one* event type from *one* publisher, which the subscriber's text must name explicitly.

It is also not clear with the Observer Pattern how we could — as discussed under "Avoiding glue" in section 3 — connect without glue code an existing business model and an existing event-driven interface library.

The Event Library overcomes all these limitations: publishers publish events of a certain event type; subscribers subscribe to such event types, not to specific publishers. The two sides are decoupled. All the specific schemes discussed in the Observer Pattern presentation are still possible as special cases. For all this extra generality, the interface is considerably simpler; it involves no abstract class and no inheritance relationship; it places no particular requirement on either subscriber or publisher classes, which can be arbitrary application or library elements. All a class must do to become a publisher or subscriber is to create objects of the appropriate type and call the desired features on them. In addition the solution is based on a reusable class, not on a design pattern, meaning that it does not require programmers to code a certain scheme from a textbook and change some aspects (such as the arguments to *update*) for each new application; instead they just rely on ready-to-use components.

It is legitimate to ask what caused the design of the Observer Pattern to miss the solution described here in favor of one that appears to be harder to learn, harder to use, less powerful, less reusable, and less general. Some of the reasons seem clear:

- Although solutions had been published before, the Design Patterns book was one of the first times the problem was approached in its generality, so it's not surprising that it didn't produce the last word. The simplest solution doesn't always come first, and it is easier to improve an original idea than to come up with it in the first place. This observation is also an opportunity to note that this article's technical criticism of the Observer Pattern and other existing designs only make sense when accompanied by the obvious acknowledgment of the pioneering insights of the patterns work and other more recent developments.

- The simpler and more advanced solution is only possible, as we have already noted in the case of event data representation, because of advanced language features: genericity, tuples, agents. The work on design patterns has been constrained by its close connection with C++ and then Java, both of which lack some of these features while sometimes adding their own obstacles. Take this comment in the presentation of the Observer Pattern: "*Deleting a* [publisher object] *should not produce dangling references in its* [subscribers]" ([6], page 297), followed by suggestions on how to avoid this pitfall. This reflects a problem of C++ (lack of standard garbage collection support) and has an adverse effect on the pattern.

- The Patterns work endeavors to teach programmers useful schemes. This is far from the goal of object technology, the Eiffel method in particular, which seeks to build reusable components so that programmers do *not* have to repeat a pattern that has been identified as useful.

We may also see another reason as possibly even more fundamental. The Observer Pattern design *uses the wrong abstractions* and in the process misses the right abstraction. Talk of right and wrong may sound arrogant, but seems justified here in light of the results. The abstractions "Subscriber" and "Publisher" (Subject and Observer in the original), although attractive at first, turn out to be too low-level, and force application designers to make relevant classes inherit from either *SUBSCRIBER* or *PUBLISHER*, hampering the reuse of existing software elements in new subscribing or publishing roles. Choosing instead *Event type* as the key abstraction — the only one introduced so far for the Event Library — leads to a completely different design.

With all the attraction of new development tools, concepts and buzzwords, it is easy to forget that the key to good software, at least in an object-oriented style (but is there really any other path?), is a task that requires insight and sweat: the discovery of good abstractions. The best hope for dramatically decreasing the difficulty and cost of software development is to capture enough of these abstractions in reusable components. Design patterns are a useful and sometimes required first step of this effort, but are not sufficient since they still require each developer to learn the patterns and reimplement them. Once we have spotted a promising pattern, we shouldn't stop, but continue to refine the pattern until we are able to turn it into a library ready for off-the-shelf reuse.

5 The .NET Event-Delegate Model

Probably inspired by the Observer Pattern but very different in its details, an interesting recent development for the spread of event-driven design is the Microsoft .NET object model, which natively supports two concepts directly related to event-driven design: *delegates*, a way to encapsulate routines into objects, and *event* types. The presence of these mechanisms is one of the principal differences between the .NET model and its most direct predecessor, the Java language; delegates, introduced in Microsoft's Visual J++ product, were at the center of Sun's criticism of that product [19].

We will examine how events and delegates address the needs of event-driven design.

The technology under discussion is not a programming language but the ".NET object model" providing a common substrate for many different languages. (Another article [14] discusses how the common object model and the programming languages manage to support different languages with their own diverse object models.)

The .NET delegate-event model is quite complex, as we found out in surveying it for a book on .NET [15]. The present description is partial; for a complete picture see the book.

C# and Visual Basic .NET, the two main languages directly provided by Microsoft to program .NET, have different syntax generally covering similar semantics — the semantics of the .NET object model. Event-delegate programming is one of the areas where the two languages show some significant differences; we'll stay closer to the C# variant.

The Basis for Delegates

The .NET documentation presents delegates as a type-safe alternative to function pointers. More generally, a delegate is an object defined from a routine; the principal operation applicable to such an object is one that calls the routine, with arguments provided for the occasion. That operation — corresponding to the feature *call* applicable to Eiffel agents — is called DynamicInvoke in the basic .NET object model.

The notion is easy to express in terms of the more general agent concept introduced earlier. Assuming, in a class *C*, a routine of the form

```
r (a1: A; b1: B)
```

with some argument signature, chosen here — just as an example — to include two argument types *A* and *B*, .NET delegates correspond to agents of the form

```
agent r                                                    /11/
```

or

```
agent x.r                                                  /12/
```

for *x* of type *C*. In either case, the delegate denotes a **wrapper object** for *r*: an object representing *r* ready to be called with the appropriate arguments. You would write such a call (still in Eiffel syntax for the moment) as

```
your_delegate.call ([some_A_value, some_B_value])                    /13/
```

where *your_delegate* is either of the above agents. /13/ has exactly the same effect as a direct call to *r*:

```
r (some_A_value, some_B_value)                                        /14/
x.r (some_A_value, some_B_value)                                      /15/
```

and hence is not interesting if it's next to the definition of *your_delegate*. The interest comes if the unit that defines *your_delegate* passes it to other modules, which will then execute /13/ when *they* feel it's appropriate, without knowing the particular routine *r* that the delegate represents.

The uncoupling will often go further, in line with the earlier discussion: the defining unit inserts *your_delegate* into an event-action table; the executing unit retrieves it from there, usually not knowing who deposited it, and executes *call* — DynamicInvoke in .NET — on it.

So far things are very simple. A delegate is like a restricted form of agent with all arguments open. There is no way to specify some arguments as "closed" by setting them at agent definition time, and leave some others open for filling in at agent call time, as in our earlier example *mouse_move*.*subscribe* (**agent** *show_rainfall* (**?**, **?**, *Initial*, *Final*) /9/. To achieve that effect you would have to write a special wrapper routine that includes the open arguments only and fills in the closed arguments to call the original, in the style of *show_rainfall_at_initial_and_final* /10/.

The only difference between the delegate form without an explicit target, /11/, and the form with *x* as a target, /12/, is that the first is only valid in the class *C* that defines *r* and will use the current object as target of future calls, whereas the second, valid anywhere, uses *x* as target. The direct call equivalent is /14/ in the first case and /15/ in the second. There is no way with delegates to keep the target open, as in the Eiffel notation **agent** {*TARGET_TYPE*}.*r*; to achieve such an effect you have again to write a special wrapper routine, this time with an extra argument representing the target.

In the examples so far the underlying routine *r* was a procedure, but the same mechanisms apply to a delegate built from a function. Then calling the delegate will return a result, as would a direct call to *r*.

So the basic idea is easy to explain: a delegate is an object representing a routine ready to be called on a target set at the time of the delegate's definition and arguments set at the time of the call.

The practical setup is more complicated. A delegate in .NET is an instance of a class that must be a descendant of a library class, Delegate, or its heir MulticastDelegate, which introduces the feature DynamicInvoke. We won't go into the details — see [15] — because these classes and features are not for direct use. They have a special status in the .NET runtime; programmers may not write classes that inherit from Delegate. It's a kind of magic class reserved for use by compiler writers so that they can provide the corresponding mechanisms as language constructs. In Eiffel, the agent mechanism (not .NET-specific) readily plays that role. C# with the keyword **delegate** and Visual Basic .NET with **Delegate** provide constructs closely mapped to the semantics of the underlying .NET classes.

Here is how it works in C#. You can't directly define the equivalent of **agent** *r* but must first define the corresponding **delegate type**:

```
public void delegate AB_delegate (A x, B y);                    /16/
```

In spite of what the keyword **delegate** suggests, the declaration introduces a delegate type, not a delegate.

The .NET documentation cheerfully mixes the two throughout, stating in places [16] that a delegate "*is a data structure that refers to a static method or to a class instance and an instance method of that class*", which defines a delegate as an object, and in others [17] that "*Delegates are a reference type that refers to a* Shared *method of a type or to an instance method of an object*" which, even understood as "*A* delegate *is...*", says that a delegate is a type. We'll stick to the simpler definition, that a delegate wraps a routine, and talk of **delegate type** for the second notion.

A delegate type declaration resembles a routine definition — listing a return type, here **void**, and argument types — with the extra keyword **delegate**.

Armed with this definition you can, from a routine *r* of a matching signature, define an actual delegate that wraps *r*:

```
AB_delegate r_delegate = new AB_delegate (r);                   /17/
```

The argument we pass to the constructor is the name of a routine, *r*. This particular instruction is type-wise valid since the signatures declared for the delegate and the routine match. Otherwise it would be rejected. A delegate constructor as used here is the only context in which C#, and more generally the .NET model, allow the use of a routine as argument to a call.

Instead of **new** AB_delegate (r) you can choose a specific call target *x* by writing **new** AB_delegate (x.r); or, if *r* is a static routine of class C, you can use **new** AB_delegate (C.r). (A static routine in C++ and successors is an operation that doesn't take a target.)

All we have achieved so far is the equivalent of defining the agent expression **agent** *r* or **agent** *x.r*. Because of typing constraints this requires defining a specific delegate type and explicitly creating the corresponding objects. The noise is due to the desire to maintain type safety in a framework that doesn't support genericity: you must define a delegate type for every single routine signature used in event handling.

Equipped with a delegate, you'll want to call the associated routine (see /13/). This is achieved, in C#, through an instruction that has the same syntactic form as a routine call:

```
AB_delegate (some_A_value, some_B_value);                    /18/
```

Visual Basic .NET offers corresponding facilities. To define a delegate type as in /16/ you will write:

```
Delegate Sub AB_delegate (x As A, y As B);
```

To create a delegate of that type and associate it with a routine as in /17/:

```
Dim r_delegate As New AB_delegate (AddressOf r);
```

The operator **AddressOf** is required since — unlike in C# — you can't directly use the routine name as argument.

Events

Along with delegates, .NET offers a notion of event. Unlike the Event Library's approach, the model doesn't use ordinary objects for that purpose, but a special built-in concept of "event". It's a primitive of the object model, supported by language keywords: **event** in C#, **Event** in Visual Basic .NET, which you may use to declare special features (members) in a class.

What such a declaration introduces is actually not an event but an event type. Here too the .NET documentation doesn't try very hard to distinguish between types and instances, but for this discussion we have to be careful. When a .NET class Button in a GUI or WUI library declares a feature Click as **event** or **Event** it's because the feature represents the event type "mouse click", not a case of a user clicking a particular button.

In the basic event handling scheme, the declaration of any *event* type specifies an associated *delegate* type. That's how .NET enforces type checking for event handling. It all comes together in a type-safe way:

1 • A delegate represents a routine.

2 • That routine has a certain signature (number and types of arguments, and result if a function).

3 • That signature determines a **delegate type**.

4 • To define an **event type**, you associate it with such a delegate type.

5 • Given the event type, any software element may *trigger* a corresponding event, passing to it a set of "event arguments" which must match the signature of the delegate. This matching is statically checkable; compilers for statically typed languages, and otherwise the type verifier of the .NET runtime, will reject the code if there is a discrepancy.

For step 4, Visual Basic .NET lets you specify a routine signature without explicitly introducing a delegate type as you must do in C#. Internally the VB.NET compiler will generate a delegate type anyway. We'll restrict ourselves to the C# style, also possible in VB.NET. You can declare an event type as

```
public event AB_delegate Your_event_type ;                              /19/
```

where the last item is what's being declared; the delegate type that precedes, here AB_delegate, is an extra qualifier like **public** and **event**.

What this defines is a new event type such that triggering an event of type Your_event_type will produce event data of a type compatible with the signature of AB_delegate; in this example, the event will produce a value of type A and a value of type B. As another example you might declare

```
public event Two_coordinate_delegate Click ;
```

to declare an event type Click whose triggering will produce two integers corresponding to the mouse coordinates. This assumes (compare /16/):

```
public void delegate Two_coordinate_delegate (int x, int y);            /20/
```

Note again that a particular mouse click is an event, but Click itself denotes the general notion of a user clicking the mouse.

Such event type definitions are the counterpart of the declarations of instances of *EVENT_TYPE* in the Event Library. Here, however, we have to introduce a new type declaration, referring to a delegate type, in each case. The reason is clear: the .NET model has neither tuples nor genericity. In the Event Library we could declare for example

```
mouse_click: EVENT_TYPE [TUPLE [INTEGER, INTEGER]]
```

always using the same generic base class, *EVENT_TYPE*, and varying the generic parameter as needed. The equivalent of Your_event_type /19/ would use *EVENT_TYPE* [*TUPLE* [*A*, *B*]]. In .NET, we have to introduce a new delegate type each time, and refer to it in declaring the event type.

Connecting Delegates to Event Types

We can now declare a delegate type corresponding to a certain routine signature; declare and create a delegate of that type, associated with a particular routine of matching signature; and define an event type that will generate event data also matching the delegate's type, so that the data can be processed by the routine. We need a facility enabling a subscriber to connect a certain delegate with a certain event type for a certain control.

We know the general idea: record a triple — control, event type, delegate — into an event-action table. In the .NET model and especially C#, however, the mechanism is expressed at a lower level. You will write

```
some_target.Some_event_type += some_delegate;
```

for example

```
your_button.Click += Two_coordinate_delegate;
```

where the highlighted **+=** operator means "append to the end of a list". This appends the delegate to the list associated with the target and the event type. Such a list automatically exists whenever some_target is of a type that, among its features, has an event type Some_event_type. Then if a publisher triggers an event, the underlying .NET mechanisms will traverse all the lists associated with the event's type, and execute their delegates in sequence.

Collectively, the set of all such lists constitutes the equivalent of the event-action table. The subscriber, however, will have to know about the individual lists and manage them individually. The only operations permitted are += and its inverse –= which removes a delegate.

The introductory discussion of event-driven design pointed out that in the general case each association we record is not just a pair (event type, action) but a triple, involving a control. The .NET model's basic association mechanism this_control.this_event_type **+=** this_action directly enforces this style. But then it doesn't cover the simpler case of subscribing to events that may occur anywhere, independent of any control. The Event Library gave us that flexibility: since an event type is just an object, you may create it at the level of the application /1/, or local to a particular control object such as a button /5/. You can achieve the former effect in .NET too, but this will require defining and creating a pseudo-control object and attach the event type to it, another source of extra code.

Raising Events

We haven't yet seen the publisher side. To raise an event of a type such as Your_event_type or Click you will, in C#, use the event type name as if it were a procedure name, passing the event data as arguments. Unfortunately, it is not enough to write Click (x_coordinate, y_coordinate) or, in the other example, Your_event_type (some_A_value, some_B_value). The proper idiom is

```
if (Click != null)
    {Click (this, x_mouse_coordinate, y_mouse_coordinate);}        /21/
```

The check for **null** is compulsory but can only be justified in reference to implementation internals. The name of the event type, here Click, denotes an internal list of delegates, to which you don't have access. (You can apply += and –=, but not to the whole list, only to the list for one control, such as your_button.Click.) If it's null because no delegate has been registered, trying to raise the event would cause an incorrect attempt to access a non-existent data structure.

It is incomprehensible that the mechanism puts the responsibility for this check to the publisher, for every triggering of any event. In the design of an API, one should avoid requiring client programmers to include an operation that's tedious to code and easy to forget, raising the risk that applications will experience intermittent failures. Probably because of that risk, the documentation for .NET recommends never writing the above code /21/ to raise an event directly, but encapsulating it instead in a routine

```
protected void OnClick (int x, int y)
   {if (Click != null)
        Click (this, x, y);
   }
```

then calling that routine to publish the event. The documentation actually says that you "*must*" use this style, including naming the routine On*EventType*, although in reality it's only a style recommendation. The strength of the advice indicates, however, the risks of not doing things right.

In comparing the .NET approach with the Event Library, we should also note that .NET's triggering of events requires some underlying magic. In the Event Library, the consequence of *mouse_click*.*publish* (*x*, *y*) is to execute the procedure *publish* of class *EVENT_TYPE*. That procedure looks up the event-action table to find all agents that have been associated with the *mouse_click* event type, an ordinary object. The table implementation is a plain *HASH_TABLE* from the standard EiffelBase library. You can see the whole implementation (only if you want to, of course) by looking up the source code of *EVENT_TYPE*. If you are not happy with the implementation you can write a descendant of *EVENT_TYPE* that will use different data structures and algorithms. In .NET, however, you have to accept that the instruction to register an event type, such as your_button.Click += your_delegate, somehow updates not only the list Click attached to your_button but also the mysterious global list Click which you can't manipulate directly, and in fact shouldn't have to know about except that you must test it against **null** anyway. So you have to trust the .NET runtime to perform some of the essential operations for you. Of course the runtime probably *deserves* to be trusted on that count, but there is really no reason for such mysteries. Implementing the action-event table is plain application-level programming that doesn't involve any system-level secrets and should have been done in a library, not in the built-in mechanisms of the virtual machine.

Event Argument Classes

If you have been monitoring the amount of extra code that various rules successively add to the basic ideas, you have one more step to go. For simplicity, our example event types, Click and Your_event_type, have relied on delegate types by specifying signatures directly: two integer arguments for Click /20/, arguments of types A and B in the other case /16/.

The recommended style is different. (Here too, the documentation suggests that this style is required, whereas it's in fact just a possible methodological convention.) It requires any delegate type used with events — meaning, really, any delegate type — to have exactly two arguments, the first one an Object representing the target and the second a descendant of the library class System.EventArgs. In our examples, you would declare

```
                                    // Compare with /16/:
public void delegate AB_delegate (Object sender, ABEventArgs e)

                                    // Compare with /20/:
public void delegate Two_coordinate_delegate (Object sender,
                                        TwoCoordinateEventArgs e)
```

with special classes ABEventArgs, describing pairs of elements of types A and B, and TwoCoordinateEventArgs describing pairs of integer elements representing mouse coordinates. For an event that doesn't generate event data, you would use the most general class System.EventArgs.

The reason for this rule seems to be a desire to institute a fixed style for all event handling, where events take exactly two arguments, the details of the event data being encapsulated into a specific class.

The consequence, however, is an explosion of small classes with no interesting features other than their fields, such as mouse coordinates *x* and *y*. In ordinary object-oriented methodology, the proliferation of such classes — really record types in O-O clothing — is often a sign of trouble with the design. It is ironic that mechanisms such as delegates succeed in countering a similar proliferation, arising from the presence of many "command classes", used for example in the Undo-Redo pattern [10]. Reintroducing numerous System.EventArgs classes, one per applicable signature, is a step backwards.

The resulting style is particularly heavy in the case of events with *no* data: instead of omitting arguments altogether, you must still pass **this** (the current object) as Sender, and a useless object of type System.EventArgs — an event data object containing no event data. Such overkill is hard to justify.

In the absence of compelling arguments for the System.EventArgs style, it would seem appropriate to advise .NET event programmers to disregard the official methodological rule. The style, however, is used heavily in the event-driven libraries of .NET, especially Windows Forms for GUI design and Web Forms for WUI design, so it's probably there to stay.

An Assessment of the .NET Form of Event-Driven Design

The event-delegate mechanism of .NET clearly permits an event-driven style of design. It lies at the basis of Windows Forms and Web Forms, both important and attractive libraries in the .NET framework. We must keep this in mind when assessing the details; in particular, none of the limitations and complications encountered justifies returning to a Java approach where the absence of a mechanism to wrap routines in objects causes even more heaviness.

The amount of noise code is, however, regrettable. Let's recapitulate it by restarting from the Event Library model, which seems to yield the necessary functionality with the conceptually minimal notational baggage. On the publisher side we must, returning to the mouse click example:

E1 •Declare an event type *click*: *EVENT_TYPE* [*TUPLE* [*INTEGER*, *INTEGER*]] typically as a once function that creates the object.

E2 •For every occurrence of the event, publish it: *click.publish* (*x*, *y*).

On the subscriber side, to subscribe a routine *r*, we execute, once:

E3 •*your_button.click.subscribe* (**agent** *r*)

Here is the equivalent in .NET, again using C#. Some element of the system (it can be the publisher or the subscriber) must:

D1 •Introduce a new descendant ClickArgs of EventArgs repeating the types of arguments of *r*. This adds a class to the system.

D2 •Declare a delegate type ClickDelegate based on that class. This adds a type.

Then the publisher must:

D3 •Declare a new event type ClickEvent based on the type ClickDelegate. This adds a type.

D4 •Introduce a procedure OnClick able to trigger a Click event, but protecting it against the **null** case. The scheme for this is always the same, but must be repeated for every event type.

D5 •For every occurrence of the event, create an instance of the ClickArgs class, passing x and y to its constructor. This adds a run-time object.

D6 •Also for every occurrence of the event, call Click with the newly created object as argument.

The subscriber must, to subscribe a routine *r*:

D7 •Declare a delegate rDelegate of type ClickDelegate.

D8 •Instantiate that delegate with *r* as argument to the constructor (this step can, in C#, be included with the previous step as a single declaration-initialization, see /17/).

D9 •Add it to the delegate list for the event type, through an instruction of the form your_button.Click += rDelegate.

In the case of an event type that is not specific to a control, it is also necessary, as we have seen, to add a class describing an artificial control. (With the Event Library you just *remove* the control, *your_button*, from E3.)

To all this encumbrance one must add the consequences of the delegate mechanism's lack of support for closed arguments and open targets, as permitted by agents. These limitations mean that it is less frequently possible, starting from an existing application, to reuse one of its routines directly ("without glue") and plug it into an event-driven scheme, for example a GUI or WUI. If the argument signature is just a little different, you will need to write new wrapper routines simply to rearrange the arguments. More glue code.

The combination of these observations explains why examples of typical event-driven code that would use a few lines with the Event Library can extend across many pages in .NET and C# books.

This does not refute the observation that .NET essentially provides the needed support for event-driven design. The final assessment, however, is that the practical use of these mechanisms is more complicated and confusing than it should be.

6 Events for Web Interfaces in ASP.NET

As a complement to the preceding discussion of .NET delegates and events it is interesting to note that the .NET framework does offer a simple and easy-to-learn mechanism for building event-driven applications. It's not part of the basic Common Language Runtime capabilities, but rather belongs to the application side, in the Web Forms mechanism of ASP.NET. Internally, it relies on the more complex facilities that we have just reviewed, but it provides a simpler set of user facilities. The "users" here are not necessarily programmers but possibly Web designers who will, from Web pages, provide connections to an underlying application. So the scope is far more limited — ASP.NET is a web development platform, not a general programming model — but still interesting for this discussion.

ASP.NET is a set of server-side tools to build "smart" Web pages, which provide not only presentation (graphics, HTML) but also a direct connection to computational facilities implemented on the Web server. Because ASP.NET is closely integrated with the rest of the .NET framework, these facilities can involve any software implemented on .NET, from database operations to arbitrarily complex programs written in any .NET-supported language such as C#, Visual Basic or Eiffel.

An event-driven model presents itself naturally to execute such server operations in response to choices — button click, menu entry selection… — executed by a visitor to the Web page. The screen shown at the beginning of this article was indeed extracted from an ASP.NET application:

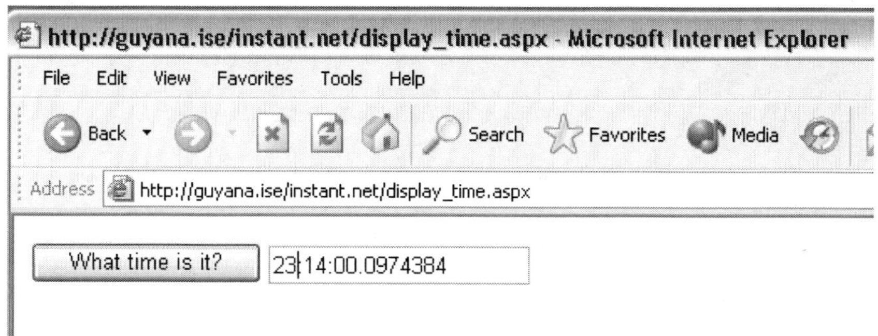

Figure 6: A Web User Interface under ASP.NET

If the visitor clicks What time is it?, the current time of day appears in the adjacent text field.

The code to achieve this is, even using C#, about as simple as might be hoped. The whole text reads:

```
<html>
   <body>
      <form runat="server">
                              <asp:Button OnClick = "display_time"
         Text = "What time is it?" runat = server/>

         <asp:TextBox id = "Output" runat=server/>

      </form>
   </body>

   <script language="C#" runat=server>
      private void display_time (Object sender, EventArgs e)
         {Output.Text= DateTime.Now.TimeOfDay.ToString();}
   </script>
</html>
```

The first part, the <body>, describes the layout of the page and the second part, <script>, provides the associated program elements, here in C#.

The <body> describes two ASP.NET controls: a button, and a text box called **Output**. ASP.NET requires making them part of a <form> to be runat the server side. The first highlighted directive sets the OnClick attribute of the button to **display_time**, the name of a procedure that appears in the <script> part. That's enough to establish the connection: when a Click event occurs, the procedure **display_time** will be executed.

The <script> part is C# code consisting of a single procedure, **display_time**, which computes the current time and uses it to set the Text property of the **Output** box.

This does what we want: a Click event occurring in the button causes execution of **display_time**, which displays the current time in the **Output** box.

The time computation uses class DateTime, where feature Now gives the current date and time, of type Date; feature TimeOfDay, in Date, extracts the current time; and ToString produces a string representation of that time, so that we can assign it to the Text feature of the TextBox.

Such simplicity is possible because ASP.NET takes care of the details. Since ASP.NET knows about the Click event type, controls such as asp:Button include an OnClick property, which you can set to refer to a particular procedure, here **display_time**. As a result, we don't see any explicit delegate in the above code; .NET finds the name of the procedure **display_time**, and takes care of generating the corresponding delegates.

The only hint that this involves delegates is in the signature of **display_time**, which involves two arguments: sender, of type object, and e, of type EventArgs. In the recommended style, as we have seen, they are the arguments representing event data, which delegate methods are expected to handle. Someone who just learns ASP.NET without getting the big picture will be told that (object sender, EventArgs e) is a magic formula to be recited at the right time so that things will work.

Clearly, the .NET machinery translates all this into the standard event-delegate mechanism discussed in the previous section. But it is interesting to note that, when the target audience is presumed less technical — Web designers rather than hard-core programmers — .NET can offer a simple and clear API.

The Event Library provides similar simplicity in a more general programming model.

7 Event Library Complements

The essential properties of the Event Library were given at the beginning of this discussion (section 2). Here are a few complementary aspects, to indicate perspectives for more specialized uses.

The library is available for free download, in source form, from se.inf.ethz.ch. Another reference [2] provides more details.

Basic Features

First let's examine some uses of the class and of the two features already introduced. The class is declared as

```
EVENT_TYPE [EVENT_DATA -> TUPLE]
```

meaning that the generic parameter represents an arbitrary tuple type. The two basic features, as we have seen, are *publish* and *subscribe*.

To introduce an event type you simply declare an entity, say *your_event_type*, with the type *EVENT_TYPE* [*TUPLE* [*A*, *B*, ...]] for some types *A*, *B*, ..., indicating that each occurrence will produce event data containing a value of type *A*, a value of type *B* and so on. If there is no event data use an empty tuple type as parameter: *EVENT_TYPE* [*TUPLE* []].

your_event_type will denote an ordinary object — an instance of *EVENT_TYPE* — and you may declare it using any of the generally available techniques. One possibility, as we have seen, is to make it a "once function" so that it will denote a single run-time object, created the first time any part of the software requests it. You may also attach it to every instance of a certain class representing a control, for example as a "once per object" function. Many other variants are possible.

The two basic procedures have the signatures

```
subscribe (action: PROCEDURE [ANY, EVENT_DATA])

publish (args: EVENT_DATA)
```

The type *PROCEDURE* [*G*, *H*], from the Kernel Library, describes agents built from any procedure declared in a descendant class of *G* and taking arguments conforming — when grouped into a tuple — to *H*, a tuple type. Here this means that for *EVENT_TYPE* [*TUPLE* [*A*, *B*, ...]] you may *subscribe* any procedure, from any class, that takes arguments of types *A*, *B*, ... (For details of agents see [4] or [11].)

The procedure *publish* takes an argument of type *TUPLE* [*A*, *B*, ...] — a sequence of values such as [*some_a_value*, *some_b_value*] denoting a tuple — enabling a publisher to trigger an event with appropriate event data through

```
your_event_type.publish ([some_a_value, some_b_value])
```

as in the earlier example /3/.

Introducing Specific Event Types

If for a certain event type you know the exact event data constituents, you can avoid using tuples by defining a specific heir of *EVENT_TYPE*. You might use this technique to cover a category of mouse events including left click, mouse click, right click, control-right-click, mouse movement etc. which all produce event data of a type *MOUSE_POSITION* represented by an existing class such as

```
class
    MOUSE_POSITION
feature -- Access
    x: INTEGER
        -- Horizontal position

    y: INTEGER
        -- Vertical position

    ... Other features (procedures in particular) ...
 end
```

Publishers of mouse events might have access to an object *current_position* of type *MOUSE_POSITION* representing the current mouse coordinates. By default they would trigger an event through calls such as

```
control_right_click.publish ([current_position.x, current_position.y])        /22/
```

But it may be more convenient to let them use the object *current_position* directly. If you define

```
class
    MOUSE_EVENT_TYPE
inherit
    EVENT_TYPE [TUPLE [INTEGER, INTEGER])
feature -- Basic operations
    publish_position (p: MOUSE_POSITION) is
            -- Trigger event with coordinates of p.
        do
            publish ([p.x, p.y])
        end
end
```

you can use this class rather than *EVENT_TYPE* to declare the relevant event types such as *control_right_click*, *left_click*, *mouse_movement* and so on, then publish mouse events, instead of /22/, through

```
control_right_click.publish_position (current_position)
```

or even, if you give class *MOUSE_EVENT_TYPE* access to *current_position*, enabling it to include a procedure *publish_current_position* with no argument, through just

```
control_right_click.publish_current_position
```

Classes such as *MOUSE_EVENT_TYPE* correspond, in the .NET model, to specific descendants of System.EventArgs. The difference is that you are not required to define such classes; you'll introduce one only if you identify an important category of event types with a specific form of event data, globally captured by an existing class, and — as a convenience — want to publish the event data as a single object rather than as a tuple. In all other cases you'll just use *EVENT_TYPE* directly, with tuples. So you avoid the proliferation of useless little classes, observing instead the object technology principle that enjoins to add a class to a system only if it represents a significant new abstraction.

Subscriber Precedence

If several agents are subscribed to an event type, the associated routines will by default be executed, when events occur, in the order of their subscription. To change this policy you may directly access the list of subscribers and change the order of its elements. To facilitate this, class *EVENT_TYPE* is a descendant of *LIST [ROUTINE [ANY, TUPLE[]]*, so that all the operations of the EiffelBase class *LIST* are applicable.

Although such uses of inheritance are appropriate — see the detailed discussion in [10] — they run contrary to some commonly held views on O-O design methodology. It would be possible to make *EVENT_TYPE* a client rather than heir of *LIST* by including a feature *subscribers* of type *LIST [ROUTINE [ANY, TUPLE[]]*; although making the class less easy to use, this change would not affect the rest of this discussion.

The principal factor in this decision to provide access to the list of subscribers was successful user experience with the EiffelVision 2 multi-platform GUI library [5], which follows the same convention. Reusing the EiffelBase list structures gives clients a whole wealth of list operations; the default *subscribe* is an *extend*, the operation that adds an element at the end of a list, but you can also use all the traversal operations, *replace* to replace a particular element, *put_front* to add an element at the beginning, the list deletion operations and others. This differs from .NET approach:

- In .NET, you *have* to consider an event type as a list. Here you can just use *subscribe* without bothering or knowing about lists. Only for advanced uses that need fine control over the subscriber list will you start manipulating it directly.
- In .NET, as noted, the list is always local to a control. Here it's just a standard list object and may appear anywhere in the software structure, at the level of the application or local to another object.
- The delegate lists associated with .NET events are very special structures, with only two applicable operations, += and –=. Here, they are general lists, to which you can apply all the EiffelBase list features.

Ignoring Some Publishers

Subscribers can be selective about an event's originating publisher. By default an event will cause the execution of subscribed routines regardless of the publisher. Call *ignore_publisher* (*p*: *ANY*) to exclude from consideration any event triggered by *p*. To ignore events except if they come from specific publishers, use *consider_only* (*p*: *ARRAY* [*ANY*]). To include a specific publisher explicitly, use *consider_publisher* (*p*: *ANY*). To cancel all subscriptions, use *ignore_all_publishers*; to reset to the default policy, use *consider_all_publishers*. These procedures are cumulative: a call to any of them complements or overrides the policy set by previous calls. To find out the resulting status you may use *ignored_publishers* and *considered_publishers*, both queries returning an *ARRAY* [*ANY*], the later meaningful only if the boolean query *specific_publishers_only* returns True.

To ignore all events temporarily and start considering them again, use *suspend_subscription* and *restore_subscription*. Unlike the *ignore* and *consider* variants these do not make any permanent change to the set of considered publishers.

This last set of facilities lends itself to criticism of pointless "featurism". As noted, however, such extra functionality does not harm simple uses of the library. It may have to be adapted or removed in the future.

8 Software Engineering Lessons

The first goal of this presentation has been immediate and pragmatic: to present the Event Library as a general tool for building event-driven software solutions. We may also draw some more general observations.

Limitations

The Event Library — like the other approaches surveyed — has so far been typically used for sequential or quasi-sequential applications, such as GUI development. Although its default ordering semantics is clear (procedures subscribed to the same event type will be executed, when an event occurs, in the order in which they have been subscribed), a generalization to full parallel computation would require precise rules on synchronization in the case of concurrent events.

In addition, the presentation of the mechanisms has not included any discussion of correctness; such a discussion should be based on the contracts associated with the routines that we encapsulate in agents.

Concurrency and correctness issues are clear candidates for further extensions of this work.

The Virtue of Simplicity

The word "simple" has occurred more than a few times in this presentation. Although claiming that something is simple doesn't make it so, we hope that the reader will have noticed the small number of concepts involved in using the Event Library.

This concern for simplicity applies not only to the library but also to the underlying language design, which attempts to maximize the "signal-to-noise ratio" both by providing powerful constructs, such as agents, and minimizing the noise by avoiding the provision of two solutions wherever one will do.

Although it may be tempting to dismiss the search for simplicity as a purely esthetic concern, the results seem clear when we compare the effort it takes for an ordinary user — an application builder who wants to use an event-driven library — to implement the Observer Pattern or use the .NET mechanisms (as discussed in the "assessment" at the end of section 5) rather than relying on the Event Library.

The Search for Abstractions

The key to the Event Library's simplicity is in the choice of its basic abstraction. Previous solutions used different ones:

- The Observer Pattern relies on abstractions "Subject" and "Observer" which, however intuitive, are not particularly useful since they have no relevant features.

- The .NET model produces complicated programs because it insists on defining a new delegate type — a new abstraction — for every routine signature to be used in handling events, and a new event type — again a new abstraction, with its own name — for every kind of event that a system may have to process. In the example discussed, it requires a new delegate type for procedures that take two integer arguments (where the Event Library simply uses an Eiffel agent expression, relying on genericity to ensure typing) and a new class to describe the mouse click event type. This leads to name and code explosion.

Both cases seem to result from what has been called "taxomania" [10]: overuse of inheritance and introduction of useless classes.

The Event Library identifies, as its key abstraction, the single notion of event type, characterized — as any proper abstraction in the abstract-data-type view at the basis of object technology — by relevant features: a subscriber can *subscribe* to be notified of events of a given type, and a publisher can *publish* an event of a given type. This choice of abstraction makes all the difference.

Lines of Research

This discussion has emphasized a certain path to software construction where the main task is to search for the right abstractions.

Such emphasis may seem remote from the concepts that seem currently to dominate discussions of design methodology, from UML and Aspect-Oriented Programming to Extreme Programming and Agile Methods. Indeed there is nothing new in the idea of identifying the problem's abstractions. But in light of the tendency to take object technology for granted [12], it is useful to note that resolving design problems may follow not just from new techniques but from the creative application of known principles. Good O-O design requires going back repeatedly to the basic question: "What *are* the main data abstractions behind this problem?".

From Patterns to Components

One of the design concepts that has amply proved its usefulness is the idea of design patterns. The patterns work has been instrumental in helping to identify and classify important algorithmic and architectural schemes.

When assessed against *reuse* goals, however, design patterns seem to go the other way, possibly contradicting some of the ideas that have made object technology attractive. Patterns are techniques that developers must learn and implement, like repertoires of traditional algorithms and data structures that one learns as a student and applies as a programmer. Coming after object and component technology, patterns seem to imply a return to recipes which, however elegant, must be applied afresh by every developer in every project.

This view that reusing packaged components is preferable to repeatedly handcrafting specific solutions leads to what we may call the *Pattern Elimination Conjecture*: that in the long term any useful pattern should be discarded as a pattern, and replaced by reusable components with a clear, simple, directly usable interface. Here the originators of the pattern idea would respond that typical patterns are too sophisticated to be encapsulated into components; but then the conjecture would assert that this difficulty of going from patterns to components is due to two factors:

- The limitations of the programming languages that served to describe the original patterns. (The "Prototype" pattern, for example, disappears as a pattern in Eiffel to become a direct application of the Kernel Library's built-in cloning mechanism.)
- Possibly insufficient effort or insight in previous attempts to turn patterns into components.

The Pattern Elimination Conjecture implies no criticism of the pattern idea; to the contrary, its recognizes the essential contribution of patterns to identifying the right components, part of what the reuse literature calls "domain analysis". It states that the natural goal for a pattern, once identified, is to cease being a pattern and become packaged as a component. As noted in [10], it's a natural ambition for object technology to make any statement of the form "*X* considered harmful" self-fulfilling — as soon as *X*, whatever it is, has been proved *useful* — by the simple observation that if it's useful it should be componentized.

This article's analysis of the Observer pattern and its introduction of the Event Library confirm the Pattern Elimination Conjecture in one case, since it's easier to use the library than to learn the architecture of the Observer pattern and apply it to a new program. This is of course just one example. Work by Karine Arnout and the author (see [1]) is currently exploring whether this partial result can be generalized to other important design patterns as described in the literature.

Types and Instances

It has been noted [10] [13] that publications on object technology too often use the terms "class" and "object" for one another. The prevalence of this confusion is surprising, as there is nothing difficult here: a class is a model, an object is an instance of such a model; classes exist in the software text, objects existing in memory at execution time. Yet one continues to come across design documents that state proudly that a program will include "an Employee object".

Some would argue that insisting on the distinction is just being fussy, and that readers understand what is meant in each case. Without having an absolute way to know, we may recall the lack of any attempt, in the .NET documentation, to distinguish between event types and events, or between delegate types and delegates, and conjecture that a more careful approach might have led to a different choice of basic abstraction and to a mechanism easier to understand and use.

Programming Language Constructs

Our final observation addresses the role of programming languages. The solution applied by the Event Library is made possible by the combination of a number of language features beyond the basic object-oriented concepts:

- Genericity (the key to avoiding a proliferation of little event and delegate classes), which a satisfactory object model should include in addition to inheritance [9].
- Tuple types (also important for this purpose, thanks to their support for variable-length sequences).
- *Constrained* genericity (used in the notation *EVENT_DATA –> TUPLE* in the declaration of *EVENT_TYPE*) to ensure that certain generic arguments can only represent tuples).
- Agents (and their typing properties).
- The possibility of using open as well as closed arguments in an agent, and of keeping the target open if desired (the key to avoiding a proliferation of glue code).
- Once functions (taking care of the problems of object initialization and sharing without breaking the decentralization of object-oriented architectures).
- Multiple inheritance (essential in particular to the structure of the underlying EiffelBase library).
- Covariance (for the needed type flexibility, in spite of the associated type checking issues).

With the growing acceptance of object-oriented ideas as a basis for new languages, there may be a tendency to assume that all O-O models are essentially equivalent. They are not. The features listed, many of them not supported by most O-O languages, make the difference in the ease of use, extendibility and reusability of the solutions encountered in this discussion.

Scope

Event-driven design is attractive in a number of situations illustrated by the examples of this article. It would be useful to conclude with a precise analysis of how it relates to other design styles, and how wide a range of applications it encompasses. We can, however, offer no firm answer on either count.

The most natural comparison is with concurrent computation mechanisms. Event-driven design indeed assumes some concurrency between the publishers and the subscribers, but that concurrency remains implicit in the model. Analogies that come to mind are with CSP [7], with its input and output events, and with the Linda approach to concurrent computation [3] whose general scheme involves clients depositing computational requests into a general "tuple space" which suppliers then retrieve and process based on pattern matching. We have not, however, explored such analogies further. Some work, already noted [18], is intended to *replace* event-driven design by concurrent computation mechanisms.

We are also not able to provide a clear assessment of the scope of the design style presented in this discussion. It undoubtedly works well in its usual areas of application, mainly GUI and now WUI building. How general is the idea, illustrated in figure 3, of publishers throwing events like bottled messages into the ocean, with the hope that some subscriber will pick them up? It may be a powerful paradigm that can affect the structure of many systems, not just their relation to their user interfaces; or maybe not.

On one issue, language-related, we now have unambiguous evidence: the usefulness of equipping an object-oriented language with a way to encapsulate routines into objects, such as Eiffel's agents or the delegate facility of .NET. The introduction of agents initially raised concern that they might in certain cases compete with the more traditional O-O constructs. Extensive experience with the mechanism has dispelled this concern; agents have a precise place in the object-oriented scheme, and in practice there is no ambiguity as to where they should be used and where not. The library-based scheme of event-driven computation described in this article is a clear example of when agents can provide an indispensable service.

Acknowledgments

This article rests on the work of the people who designed the agent mechanism: Paul Dubois, Mark Howard, Emmanuel Stapf and Michael Schweitzer. It also benefits from the design of the EiffelVision 2 library and its use of agents and event-driven mechanisms, due among others to Sam O'Connor, Emmanuel Stapf, Julian Rogers and Ian King. It takes advantage of comments from Karine Arnout and Volkan Arslan. It is indebted to the other designs discussed, especially Smalltalk's MVC, the Observer Pattern, the .NET event model, and its realization in C# and VB.NET. Without implying endorsement of the ideas expressed I gratefully acknowledge the comments received on earlier versions of this work from Éric Bezault, Jean-Marc Jézéquel, Piotr Nienaltowski, Claude Petitpierre and a referee who, when my request was granted to lift anonymity in light of the value of his criticism, turned out to be Tony Hoare.

References

[1] Karine Arnout, *Contracts and Tests*, research plan at se.inf.ethz.ch/people/arnout/ phd_research_plan.pdf, consulted June 2003.

[2] Volkan Arslan, Piotr Nienaltowski and Karine Arnout. *Event library: an object-oriented library for event-driven design*, to appear in JMLC 2003, Proceedings of Joint Modular Languages Conference, Klagenfurt (Austria), August 2003, ed. Laszlo Böszörmenyi, Springer-Verlag, 2003.

[3] Nicholas Carriero and David Gelernter: *How to Write Parallel Programs*, MIT Press, 1990. More recent (2000) Linda tutorial at lindaspaces.com/downloads/ lindamanual.pdf, consulted June 2003.

[4] Paul Dubois, Mark Howard, Bertrand Meyer, Michael Schweitzer and Emmanuel Stapf: *From Calls to Agents*, in *Journal of Object-Oriented Programming*, vol. 6, no. 12, September 1999.

[5] Eiffel Software: *Online EiffelVision2 documentation* at docs.eiffel.com/libraries/ vision2/, consulted June 2003.

[6] Erich GammaRichard Helm, Ralph Johnson and John Vlissides: *Design Patterns: Elements of Reusable Object-Oriented Software*, Addison-Wesley, 1995.

[7] C.A.R. Hoare: *Communicating Sequential Processes*, Prentice Hall, 1985.

[8] Jean-Marc Jézéquel, Michel Train and Christine Mingins: *Design Patterns and Contracts*, Addison-Wesley, 1999.

[9] Bertrand Meyer: *Genericity versus Inheritance*, in Norman K. Meyrowitz (Ed.): Conference on Object-Oriented Programming Systems, Languages, and Applications (OOPSLA'86), Portland, Oregon, Proceedings. SIGPLAN Notices 21(11), November 1986, pages 391-405. Updated version in appendix B of [10].

[10] Bertrand Meyer: *Object-Oriented Software Construction, 2nd edition*, Prentice Hall, 1997.

[11] Bertrand Meyer, Agent chapter in *Eiffel*: *The Language, 3rd edition*, in preparation, chapter text online at www.inf.ethz.ch/personal/meyer/publications/, consulted June 2003.

[12] Bertrand Meyer: *A Really Good Idea* (final installment of Object Technology column), IEEE *Computer*, vol. 32, no. 12, December 1999, pages 144-147. Also online at www.inf.ethz.ch/personal/meyer/publications/, consulted June 2003.

[13] Bertrand Meyer: *Assessing a C++ Text* (review of *Programming C#* by Jesse Liberty), IEEE *Computer*, vol. 35, no. 4, April 2002, pages 86-88. Also online at www.inf.ethz.ch/personal/meyer/publications/, consulted June 2003.

[14] Bertrand Meyer: *Multi-Language Programming; How .NET Does It*, published in three parts in *Software Development* Magazine, "Beyond Objects" column, May-July 2002. Also online at www.inf.ethz.ch/personal/meyer/publications/, consulted June 2003.

[15] Bertrand Meyer, Raphaël Simon, Emmanuel Stapf: *Instant .NET*, Prentice Hall, 2004, in preparation.

[16] *.NET Framework Class Library*: *Delegate Class*, part of Microsoft .NET documentation included with the .NET framework, also online at msdn.microsoft.com/library/default.asp?url=/library/en-us/cpref/html/frlrfSystemDelegateClassTopic.asp, consulted June 2003.

[17] *Visual Basic Language Reference*: *Delegate Statement*, part of Microsoft .NET documentation included with the .NET framework, also online at msdn.microsoft.com/library/default.asp?url=/library/en-us/vblr7/html/vastmDelegate.asp, consulted June 2003.

[18] Claude Petitpierre, *A Design Pattern for Interactive Applications*, École Polytechnique Fédérale de Lausanne, 2002.

[19] Sun Microsystems: *About Microsoft's "Delegates"*, 1997 white paper online at java.sun.com/docs/white/delegates.html, consulted June 2003.

Iterative Synthesis of Control Guards Ensuring Invariance and Inevitability in Discrete-Decision Games

Michel Sintzoff

Department of Computing Science and Engineering
Université catholique de Louvain
Place Sainte-Barbe 2, B-1348 Louvain-la-Neuve, Belgium
ms@info.ucl.ac.be

Abstract. Reactive and hybrid systems are modeled by games where players make strategic decisions in a temporally discrete manner. The dynamics of players use dense or discrete time. In order to guarantee invariance and inevitability properties, the proponent moves are restricted by "winning guards". The winning strategy determined by these guards does not exclude any initial state from which a winning strategy exists. Sets of such initial states constitute winning regions and are defined by fixed points. The iterates which yield winning regions are structured as unions of iterates which yield winning guards.

1 Introduction

The theory of games deals with interaction between dynamics. This is why it helps in understanding control systems, hybrid ones and reactive ones. For example, a control system can be presented as a noncooperative game where the controlling and controlled components are respectively the proponent and the opponent [Isa65]. There are various kinds of games [BaO98, Tho95]: plays may have a finite or infinite duration; time may be discrete or dense; players may cooperate or not; their strategic decisions may be taken continuously or discretely; each one may involve a finite or infinite set of choices; moves may be carried out in sequence or in parallel; they may be atomic, in one step, or durative, in any number of steps; goals may be qualitative or quantitative; informations on states may be perfect or imperfect; winning strategies may use additional memory or not.

A (strategic) decision is the selection of a move according to the strategy of a player. In "discrete-decision games", these decisions are separated by non-infinitesimal time-intervals. Hybrid systems can be modeled by discrete-decision games where the control moves by the proponent are atomic transitions [TLS00]. In general, the temporal discreteness of decisions is compatible with dense-time dynamics for proponents as well as for opponents; thus, the granularity of dynamics can be adapted and the roles of players can be exchanged. For the limited

O. Owe et al. (Eds.): From OO to FM (Dahl Festschrift), LNCS 2635, pp. 272–301, 2004.

problems tackled in this paper, it suffices to consider discrete-decisions games restricted as follows: the goals are qualitative; the information on states is perfect; the choice sets are finite; the winning strategies do not use additional memory.

Games are characterized by the dynamics of players, their roles and the winning conditions. Dynamics are expressed here by "processes", i.e. sets of trajectories. Roles determine cooperation or non-cooperation of players and are expressed by "pre-maps" associated with disjunctive or conjunctive decision modes. Pre-maps generalize predicate transformers [Dij76] and yield "preconditions", viz. sets of adequate initial states for given decision modes, processes and winning conditions. Winning conditions express goals for players and are represented by distinctive processes called "specifications". The binding of roles of players to their dynamics, viz. of pre-maps to processes, results in alternating, interacting processes called "coprocesses". A game thus consists of a coprocess and a specification. These components correspond to a graph-based arena and a winning set in the case of a discrete-time finite-state game [GTW02 (§ 2)].

The goal of the present work is the iterative synthesis of winning strategies for discrete-decision games. Iterative methods provide a structured framework for the systematic development of effective algorithms and they scale up well from finite domains to infinite ones. They can be used here thanks to the discreteness of decisions and the finiteness of choice sets. Game analysis follows iterative methods as a rule, especially for the generation of winning regions. Classical methods of game synthesis are based on the extraction of strategy functions from winning regions and are partially iterative [BaO98, Tho95].

In order to elaborate iterative synthesis techniques, we represent winning strategies by "winning guards" which restrict the domains of proponent moves. These guards ensure that all permitted plays satisfy the winning conditions; they do not need additional memory; their union includes each state in the winning region of the proponent. Thus, they determine a complete, finite-memory, winning strategy for the latter. We tackle the two primitive properties of dynamics, namely invariance and inevitability; they constitute the first level in the Borel hierarchy [Tho95]. The winning guards are synthesized iteratively on the basis of fixed-point definitions of winning regions: the iterates which generate winning regions are structured as unions of iterates which generate winning guards. This approach follows a method developed for the synthesis of correct guards in action systems, which amount to cooperative games with atomic moves defined by predicate transformers [vLS79].

The paper is organized as follows. Processes, specifications and preconditions are defined in Section 2. Coprocesses, their preconditions and discrete-decision games are presented in Section 3. Iterative synthesis techniques for winning strategies are developed in Section 4. Section 5 discusses related, current and further work, and concludes with some reflections.

The mathematical basis of the paper consists of a few results about lattices. Some developments are merely outlined. General formulations of definitions and properties may be replaced by typical instances. Proofs which are similar to previous ones may be summarized. The references indicate original, representative or recent works.

Notational conventions The set of functions from A to B is denoted by $A \to B$. A function application $f(u)$ may be written $f.u$ or fu when no ambiguity arises. Given a binary relation r, its converse $\{(x,y) \mid (y,x) \in r\}$ is denoted by $r^{\smile}$. The set of subsets of a set V is denoted by 2^V. A Cartesian product $V \times V$ may be denoted by V^2. An interval $\{c \mid a \leq c \leq b\}$ is denoted by $(a : b)$. The set of integers is denoted by $I\!N$, and $I\!R^+$ is the set of nonnegative real numbers. The symbol ∞ stands for $*$ or ω. For a set B and a predicate E, we abbreviate $(B \neq \emptyset) \wedge (\forall x \in B : E)$ by $\forall_+ x \in B : E$.

We write $\mu X : [f.X]$ for the least fixed-point of a monotone function f in a complete lattice, and $\nu X : [f.X]$ for the greatest one. The abbreviation $A =_\mu f.A$ stands for the equation $A = \mu X : [f.X]$, and similarly for $=_\nu$. Given the classical Knaster-Tarski Theorem, these fixed points are computable by transfinite iterations [Cou78, DN00, GTW02 (§ 20)]. In a finite lattice, finite iterations suffice. If f is continuous, e.g. $f.\cup_{i \in I} x_i = \cup_{i \in I} f.x_i$ for any increasing chain $(x_i)_{i \in I\!N}$, then it suffices to use infinite iterations on the form $X^{(0)} = a, \quad X^{(n+1)} = f.X^{(n)}$. For simplicity, iterative computations of fixed points are presented in terms of infinite iterations; versions using transfinite iterations can be obtained by systematic adaptations.

2 Processes, Specifications, and Their Preconditions

We present a compositional framework for processes a.k.a. behaviours, viz. sets of trajectories [Si96]. It allows for dense and discrete time and for temporal variants of classical operations of program composition.

Specifications are distinguished processes. They may represent winning conditions.

Pre-maps express selection modes. They yield preconditions which characterize the begin-points of trajectories matching a given specification and selected according to a given mode. These preconditions are analogous to starting basins for dynamics, to preconditions for programs and to winning regions for games.

2.1 Basic Processes and Operations

Let V be a non-empty set of *points*, viz. values or states. Let T be a set of *times*, with a total order, a minimum element 0, a commutative and associative addition with 0 as identity, and possibly an infinite element ω_T. We may write ω for ω_T if no ambiguity arises, and we may use an identifier T_ω for a time set containing an infinite element. Examples of time sets are $\{0,1\}$, $I\!N_\omega$, $I\!R^+$, or $I\!N_\omega \times I\!R^+_\omega$ with vector addition, lexicographic ordering and the infinite element $(\omega_{I\!N}, \omega_{I\!R^+})$. An element of a Cartesian product T is finite iff all its components are finite.

A *trajectory* b is a pair (d, g) where $Dur.b = d \in T$ is the *duration* and $g \in (0 : d) \to V$ is the *graph*; its *begin-* and *end-point* are respectively $Beg.b = g.0$ and $End.b = g.d$. A *process* B is a set of trajectories, and a *B-trajectory* is an element of B. The *duration of a process* B is *finite* iff the duration of each B-trajectory is finite.

Given $d \in T, P \subset V$, the process $[d]P$ is the set of trajectories with duration d and *range* P: $[d]P = \{(d, g) \mid g \in (0 : d) \to P\}$. We may write $[d]_T P$ to recall the time set T of interest. The *universal process over* P is $[\,]P = \bigcup_{d \in T}[d]P$, where T may include ω. The process $[*]P$ is $[\,]P \backslash [\omega]P$. The *universal process* is $[\,]V$. The *identity process* Id_P *over* P is $[0]P$. The *identity process* Id is Id_V.

The following set-operations can be used for processes: *union* $\cup$, *intersection* $\cap$, *finite union* $\bigcup_{i \in I}$, *finite intersection* $\bigcap_{i \in I}$ for a finite set I, and *complementation* $\backslash$. We write $-B$ for $([\,]V)\backslash B$ if $B \subset [\,]V$, and $-P$ for $V \backslash P$ if $P \subset V$.

A *cone* is a process where all trajectories begin with the same point. For $B \in [\,]V, x \in V$, the process $B(x)$ is the cone $\{b \mid b \in B \wedge (Beg.b = x)\}$. A process B is *deterministic* iff, for each $x \in V$, the cone $B(x)$ contains at most one trajectory.

Let be $c, d \in T, c \leq d$. The *prefix* $b(0 : c)$ of a trajectory $b = (d, g)$ is the trajectory (c, h) such that $\forall t \in (0 : c) : h.t = g.t$. For $B \subset [d]V$, $B(0 : c)$ is $\{b(0 : c) \mid b \in B\}$.

For a relation $r \subset V^2$, an *r-based process* R is $\{(1, g) \mid (g.0, g.1) \in r\} \subset [1]_{I\!N} V$. It is called a *relational process*. Similarly if $R = \{(1, g) \mid (g.(0, 0), g.(1, 0)) \in r\} \subset [(1, 0)]_{I\!N \times I\!R^+} V$.

Assume a dense-time process $B \subset [d]_{I\!R^+} V$ where $d \in I\!N, d \geq 1$. Then the *discrete-time sampling* of B is the discrete-time process $B_{I\!N} \subset [d]_{I\!N} V$ defined by

$$B_{I\!N} = \{(d, h) \mid \exists g : [\ (d, g) \in B \wedge \forall i \in (0 : d) \cap I\!N : h(i) = g(i)\ ]\ \}.$$

Similarly for time sets such as $I\!R^+_\omega$, $I\!N \times I\!R^+$ or $I\!N_\omega \times I\!R^+_\omega$.

Notes

1. Relational processes allow to integrate the relation-based view of dynamics, as used for automata and programs, into the process-based one. The Cartesian product $P \times P$ is isomorphic to the process $[1]_{\{0,1\}}P$ containing all the two-points trajectories with range $P \subset V$. The set P is isomorphic to the identity process Id_P over P.
2. The most abstract time-set is the singleton $\{0\}$. The abstract, binary time-set $\{0, 1\}$ consists of begin- and end-times only and may be used for atomic moves. Time sets such as $I\!N$ and $I\!R^+_\omega$ refine $\{0, 1\}$ and may be used for durative dynamics. The time set $I\!N_\omega \times I\!R^+_\omega$ is super-dense.
3. The infinite time ω can be excluded by using $[*]P$ or $T \backslash \{\omega\}$. When presenting a list of time sets which may include it, we often just give a few typical cases.

2.2 Temporal Composition of Processes

Basic operations for process composition are given in § 2.1. Processes may also be composed by means of temporal forms of sequential, concurrent and iterative composition.

2.2.1 Temporal Composition Operations

(a) Sequential composition The *sequential composition* of two processes $B_1 \subset [*]V$ and $B_2 \subset [\,]V$ is

$$B_1; B_2 = \{\, b_1; b_2 \mid b_1 \in B_1 \wedge b_2 \in B_2 \wedge (End.b_1 = Beg.b_2)\},$$
$$\text{where } (d_1, g_1); (d_2, g_2) \text{ is } (d_1 + d_2, g)$$
$$\text{such that } g(0 : d_1) = g_1(0 : d_1) \text{ and } \forall t \in (0 : d_2) : g.(d_1 + t) = g_2.t.$$

The sequential composition of processes is *fusion based*: in the trajectory $(b_1; b_2)$, b_1 and b_2 share the point $End.b_1 = Beg.b_2$. This is also the case for sequential composition of relations and programs.

Given a process $B \subset [*]V$, the *repetition* B^n is defined as follows, where $n, m \in I\!N$, $m < n$:

$$B^0 = Id, \qquad B^{m+1} = B^m; B.$$

The *pre-restriction* of a process $B \subset [\,]V$ by a *guard* $P \subset V$ is

$$P \rightharpoonup B \;=\; Id_P; B.$$

Thus, $P \rightharpoonup B \;= \{b \mid Beg.b \in P \wedge b \in B\}$, the cone $B(x)$ equals $\{x\} \rightharpoonup B$, and $B = V \rightharpoonup B$. By convention, $\bigcup_{i \in I} P_i \rightharpoonup B_i = \bigcup_{i \in I}(P_i \rightharpoonup B_i)$.

(b) Concurrent composition Let $V_1, V_2, V_1 \times V_2 \subset V$. The *local concurrent composition* of $B_1 \subset [\,]V_1, B'_2 \subset [\,]V_2$ is

$$B_1 \otimes B'_2 = \{\, b_1 \otimes b'_2 \mid b_1 \in B_1 \wedge b'_2 \in B'_2 \wedge (Dur.b_1 = Dur.b'_2)\},$$
$$\text{where } (d, g_1) \otimes (d, g'_2) \text{ is } (d, g) \text{ such that } \forall t \in (0 : d) : g.t = (g_1.t, g'_2.t).$$

The process $B_1 \otimes B'_2 \subset [\,](V_1 \times V_2)$ is a Cartesian, isochronous composition of the local processes B_1, B'_2, called *local branches*. This composition is not commutative. The operator $\otimes$ has priority over $\rightharpoonup, \in$ and $\subset$.

Let us now assume, for $i \in I, j \in J :\; G_i, G'_j \subset V_1 \times V_2,\; B_i \subset [\,]V_1,\; B'_j \subset [\,]V_2,\; B = \bigcup_{i \in I} G_i \rightharpoonup B_i \otimes [\,]V_2,$ and $B' = \bigcup_{j \in J} G'_j \rightharpoonup [\,]V_1 \otimes B'_j$. Then, the *(global) concurrent composition* of $B, B' \subset [\,](V_1 \times V_2)$ is

$$B \| B' \;=\; \bigcup_{i \in I, j \in J} G_i \cap G'_j \rightharpoonup B_i \otimes B'_j.$$

It is not commutative by definition of B, B'. In the *(left) branch* B, local processes $B_i \subset [\,]V_1$ are concurrent with universal local ones $[\,]V_2$ and are restricted by global guards G_i. Note $(B_i \otimes [\,]V_2) \cap ([\,]V_1 \otimes B'_j) = B_i \otimes B'_j$. Branches are processes and can be composed, for instance sequentially. The branch B may be written $\bigcup_{i \in I} G_i \rightharpoonup B_i$, and similarly for the *(right) branch* B'.

We have $B_1 \otimes B'_2 \;=\; V_1 \times V_2 \rightharpoonup B_1 \otimes B'_2 \;=\; (V_1 \times V_2 \rightharpoonup B_1 \parallel V_1 \times V_2 \rightharpoonup B'_2)$. Local concurrency is introduced for presentation purposes.

(c) Iterative composition Let $B \subset [*]V$. The *finite* and *infinite iteration* of the process B are respectively

$$B^* \;=\; \mu X : [Id \cup (X; B)] \quad \text{and} \quad B^\omega \;=\; \nu Y : [B; Y],$$

defined in the complete lattice $2^{[\,]V}$ of processes. The fixed point B^* is the limit of the iteration $X^{(0)} = \emptyset$, $X^{(n+1)} = Id \cup (X^{(n)}; B)$. The map $X \mapsto Id \cup (X; B)$ is continuous, hence monotone, because $((\bigcup_{i \in I\!N} B_i); B) \;=\; \bigcup_{i \in I\!N}(B_i; B)$. As a consequence, $B^* = \bigcup_{n \in I\!N} B^n$.

Similarly, B^ω is the limit of $Y^{(0)} \;=\; [\,]V$, $Y^{(n+1)} \;=\; (B; Y^{(n)})$. We have $Y^{(n+1)} \;=\; B^{n+1}; [\,]V \;=\; B^n; (B; [\,]V) \subset B^n; [\,]V \;=\; Y^{(n)}$.

Notes

1. To sum up, processes $B \subset [\,]_T V$ are mainly generated by the following rules:
   $B ::= B_a \mid [d]P \mid [*]P \mid [\,]P \mid$
   $B \cup B \mid B \cap B \mid \bigcup_{i \in I} B_i \mid \bigcap_{i \in I} B_i \mid -B \mid$
   $B; B \mid B \| B \mid B^{\varpi}$
   where $B_a \subset [\,]_T V$, $d \in T$, $P \subset V$, I is a finite set, the B_i's generate processes and $\varpi \in \mathbb{N} \cup \{*, \omega\}$. Primary processes B_a are constructed for example by automata, programs, or differential equations or inclusions. Accordingly, the composition operations on processes can be expressed by corresponding ones on transition systems or differential ones.
2. Discrete-time processes resemble temporal programs in a discrete-time, interval-based temporal logic with sequential and iterative composition [Mos98]. They are related to processes in the semantics of communicating concurrent programs [Hoa85]. Communications are represented here by concurrent readings in global states, viz. by global guards.
3. For all $P \subset V$ and $d_1, d_2 \in T$, the process $H = [d_1 + d_2]P$ verifies the closure property $H = H(0 : d_1); H(0 : d_2)$. Thus, the H-trajectories have no memory: any suffix of any trajectory is the prefix of another one. So to speak, H is full. This is akin to the semi-group axiom $f^{d_1+d_2} = f^{d_2} \circ f^{d_1}$ for flows generated by differential equations [BaC97]. In general, processes contain trajectories with memory. For instance, if $B \subset [2]V$ contains a single trajectory, then B does not necessarily include $B(0 : 1); B(0 : 1)$.
4. Classical relational approaches use a binary time-set and abstract from the intermediate points appearing in compositions [Abr96, BaW98].

2.2.2 Non-Zeno Assumption In this paper, we assume the following:

> The time set contains a finite number of distinguished elements different from 0 and called *non-Zeno times*. The duration of each considered trajectory is bounded below by a non-Zeno time.

This is a sufficient condition for excluding Zeno trajectories [DN00, Lyg03].

Notes Let $B^{\to\omega}$ be $\lim_{n\to\omega} B^n$ in an ultrametric structure [Ros 98].

1. Given the Non-Zeno assumption, each limit $B^{\to\omega}$ is the fixed point of a contracting map, using a prefix-based ultrametric distance d_u. Hence $B^{\to\omega} = B^{\to\omega}; [\,]V = B^{\omega}$. For example, $d_u(\,([1]V)^{\to\omega},\ (([1]V)^{\to\omega}; [\,]V)\,) = 0$, hence $([1]V)^{\to\omega} = ([1]V)^{\to\omega}; [\,]V = ([1]V)^{\omega}$.
2. Consider processes $R_0 \subset [(1,0)]_T V$ and $B_1 \subset \bigcup_{d \in \mathbb{R}^+} [(0,d)]_T V$, where $T = \mathbb{N}_\omega \times \mathbb{R}^+_\omega$. These processes may respectively model atomic control-transitions and durative plant-dynamics in hybrid systems [Lyg03]. To guarantee the Non-Zeno assumption, the non-Zeno times $(1,0)$ and $(0, 2^{-100})$ may for instance be used.
   In this case, the duration of each trajectory in the limit $(R_0; B_1)^{\to\omega}$ is the infinite time $(\omega_{\mathbb{N}}, \omega_{\mathbb{R}^+})$. Hence, the duration of each trajectory in $(R_0; B_1)^* \cup (R_0; B_1)^{\omega}$ is either finite or infinite: heterogeneous durations such as $(\omega_{\mathbb{N}}, 5.03)$ are excluded.

2.2.3 Properties

(a) Sequential composition of processes is monotone and associative.

(b) Concurrent and iterative compositions of processes are monotone.

(c) For $P, Q \subset V$ and $B \subset [\,]V$, $P \rightharpoonup (Q \rightharpoonup B) = (P \cap Q) \rightharpoonup B$.

(d) For V_1, V_2, $V_1 \times V_2 \subset V$, $[\,]V_1 \otimes [\,]V_2 = [\,](V_1 \times V_2)$.

(e) Assume $B_1 \subset [c]V$, $B_2 \subset [\,]V$ are left branches, and $B_1' \subset [c]V$, $B_2' \subset [\,]V$ are right branches, for $c \in T \backslash \{\omega\}$. Then

$$(B_1; B_2) \| (B_1'; B_2') = (B_1 \| B_1'); (B_2 \| B_2'),$$

$$(B_1{}^{\varpi} \| B_1'{}^{\varpi}) = (B_1 \| B_1')^{\varpi}, \qquad \text{where } \varpi \in I\!N \cup \{*, \omega\}.$$

(f) Assume $r_1 \subset V_1^2$, $r_2 \subset V_2^2$, $r = \{\ ((x_1, x_2), (y_1, y_2)) \mid (x_1, y_1) \in r_1 \wedge (x_2, y_2) \in r_2\} \subset (V_1 \times V_2)^2$. Let R_1, R_2, R be the r_1-, r_2-, r-based process, respectively. Then

$$R_1 \otimes R_2 = R.$$

2.3 Specifications

Specifications are distinguished processes which express desired dynamical patterns. They result from a restricted family of composition operations which abstract from time. In this paper, we focus on an operation serving to display sequential patterns of process ranges and called "chop" [Mos98]. Specifications are usually identified by W, to remind of *w*inning processes.

2.3.1 Definitions The *chop* of two sets $P, Q \subset V$ is the specification $P^\frown Q = [*]P; [\,]Q$. The chop of two specifications $W, W' \subset [\,]V$ is the specification $W^\frown W' = (W \cap [*]V); W'$.

The other composition operations for specifications are union, opposite, repetition and iteration; for $\varpi \in I\!N \cup \{*, \omega\}$, the definition of W^ϖ is $(W \cap [*]V)^\varpi$. *Specifications* $W \subset [\,]V$ are thus generated as follows:

$$W ::= P^\frown Q \mid W^\frown W \mid W \cup W \mid -W \mid W^\varpi \qquad (P, Q \subset V).$$

Notations Given a trajectory $b = (d, g)$, times $t, t' \in T$ such that $t \leq t' \leq d$, and $P, Q \subset V$,

$$b(t:t') \in P^\frown P \text{ iff } \forall s \in (t:t') : g.s \in P,$$
$$b(t:t') \in P^\frown Q \text{ iff } \exists s \in (t:t') \backslash \{\omega\} : b(t:s) \in P^\frown P \wedge b(s:t') \in Q^\frown Q.$$

2.3.2 Properties Assume $P, Q \subset V$.

(a) $P \cap Q = \emptyset \Rightarrow P^\frown Q = \emptyset$.

(b) Given $b_1, b_2 \in [\,]V$ and $End.b_1 = Beg.b_2$,

$$\begin{aligned} & b_1; b_2 \in P^\frown Q \\ \equiv\ & (b_1 \in P^\frown Q \wedge b_2 \in Q^\frown Q) \vee (b_1 \in P^\frown P \wedge b_2 \in P^\frown Q) \text{ in general,} \\ \equiv\ & b_1 \in P^\frown P \wedge b_2 \in P^\frown Q \quad \text{if } Q \subset P. \end{aligned}$$

For $b = (1, g) \in [1]_{I\!N} V$, we simply have

$$b \in P^\frown Q \ \equiv\ (g.0, g.1) \in (P \cap Q) \times Q \ \cup\ P \times (P \cap Q).$$

(c) Let $r \subset P \times Q$. Assume $R \subset [1]_{I\!N} V$ is r-based (§ 2.1). Then:

$R \subset P^\frown(P \cup Q)^\frown Q$ in general;

$R \subset P^\frown Q$ if $P \subset Q \vee Q \subset P$; $\quad R \subset P^\frown P$ if $P = Q$.

Proof: Let $T = I\!N$. For each $b = (1, g) \in R$, we have

$b \in R \subset [1]V$ by assumption on R. Hence

$b \in [1](P \cup Q)$ since $r \in P \times Q \subset (P \cup Q) \times (P \cup Q)$. Hence

$b \in Id_P; [1](P \cup Q); Id_Q$ since $g.0 \in P,\ g.1 \in Q$. Hence

$b \in P^\frown(P \cup Q)^\frown Q$ by § 2.3.1. Hence

$R \subset P^\frown(P \cup Q)^\frown Q$ given $b \in R$.

(d) Chop is associative and monotone.

2.3.3 Discrete Observability Assume $P, Q \subset V, d \in I\!N, d \geq 1$. Then, the chop $P^\frown Q$ is *discretely observable in a trajectory* $b = (d, g) \in [\,]_{I\!R^+} V$ iff the following holds, for $A = P$ or $A = Q$ and for all $n \in I\!N \cap (0 : d-1)$:

$$(g(n), g(n+1)) \in A \times A \Rightarrow b(n : n+1) \in A^\frown A,$$
$$(g(n), g(n+1)) \in P \times Q \Rightarrow b(n : n+1) \in P^\frown Q.$$

The chop $P^\frown Q$ is *discretely observable in a process* $B \subset [\,]_{I\!R^+} V$ iff it is discretely observable in each B-trajectory. Similarly for time sets such as $I\!R^+_\omega$ and $I\!N \times I\!R^+$.

2.3.4 Remarks

Chop and temporal logic The following equalities illustrate the use of chop in temporal specifications [Mos98], and thus in the present ones: $\Box P = P^\frown P$, $\Diamond P = V^\frown P^\frown V$, $P\mathcal{U}Q = P^\frown(P \cup Q)^\frown Q^\frown V$. The characteristic predicate of a set P is also denoted by P. Unlike chop, the until-operator $\mathcal{U}$ is not fusion-based; hence, P and Q can be disjoint. This explains the presence of $P \cup Q$ on the right-hand side (§ 2.3.2.c). The last occurrence of V is needed in case $P\mathcal{U}Q$ is followed by $\neg Q$. The discrete-time next-operator $\bigcirc P$ is not expressible using chops, which permit dense time.

Processes and specifications A process B satisfies a specification W iff $B \subset W$, viz. B conforms to the pattern defined by W. For example, $B \subset P^\frown P$ and $B' \subset Q^\frown Q$ entail $B; B' \subset P^\frown Q$. The choice of composition operations for specifications could be adapted without changing the main results; a relevant criterion could be the decidability of $B \subset W$.

2.4 Pre-maps and Preconditions for Processes

A *pre-map* ξ is a pre-image operator; it maps processes to functions from specifications to subsets of V called *preconditions*: $\xi \in 2^{[\,]V} \to (2^{[\,]V} \to 2^V)$. The precondition $\xi B.W$ is the set M such that W contains the B-trajectories which begin with points in M and which are selected according to the decision mode associated with ξ. We say precondition for a set by abuse of language.

As classical, we consider three decision modes for trajectory selection [BaW98, DN00]: the disjunctive mode expressing existence, the conjunctive one expressing universality or inexistence, and the combined one expressing universality and existence. They are respectively associated with the three pre-maps $\mathbf{E}, \mathbf{A}$ and $\mathbf{Æ}$, which are defined below and may be read *pre-exists*, *pre-all* and *pre-all-exists*.

The pre-map of a sequential composition of processes equals a nested composition of pre-maps of these processes. This allows to decompose a given chop into smaller ones.

Notations

Logical quantifiers: $L_{\mathbf{E}} = \exists,\ L_{\mathbf{A}} = \forall,\ L_{\mathbf{Æ}} = \forall_+$ (§ 1).

Dualities: $\mathbf{E}^{\sim} = \mathbf{A},\ \mathbf{A}^{\sim} = \mathbf{E}$.

Meta-variables: $\xi, \xi_i \in \{\mathbf{E}, \mathbf{A}, \mathbf{Æ}\},\quad \zeta, \zeta_i \in \{\mathbf{E}, \mathbf{Æ}\},\quad \eta, \eta_i \in \{\mathbf{E}, \mathbf{A}\}$, where $i \in I\!N$. Thus we use ζ for a pre-map expressing at least existence, and η for one of the dual pre-maps.

2.4.1 Definitions Given a process B and a specification W,

$$\begin{aligned}
\mathbf{E}B.W &= \{x \mid \exists b \in B(x) : b \in W\} = \{x \mid B(x) \cap W \neq \emptyset\},\\
\mathbf{A}B.W &= \{x \mid \forall b \in B(x) : b \in W\} = \{x \mid B(x) \subset W\},\\
\mathbf{Æ}B.W &= \{x \mid \forall_+ b \in B(x) : b \in W\} = (\mathbf{A}B.W) \cap (\mathbf{E}B.W).
\end{aligned}$$

In short, $\xi B.W = \{x \mid L_\xi b \in B(x) : b \in W\}$.

The cone $B(x)$ is defined in § 2.1. The pre-map $\mathbf{A}$ allows blocking, viz. inexistence of trajectories, but $\mathbf{E}$ and $\mathbf{Æ}$ forbid it: for instance, we have $\mathbf{A}\emptyset.W = V$ whereas $\mathbf{E}\,\emptyset.W = \emptyset$ and $\mathbf{Æ}\,\emptyset.W = V \cap \emptyset = \emptyset$. Both $\mathbf{A}$ and $\mathbf{Æ}$ can be defined from $\mathbf{E}$ since $\mathbf{A}B.W = -\mathbf{E}B. - W$.

Note There is an alternative way to define preconditions, in terms of sets of cones associated with a process B. Each set represents the selection mode defined by a pre-map; each selected cone is a subset of B:

$\mathbf{E}B = \{\{b\} \mid b \in B\}$,

$\mathbf{A}B = \{B\}$,

$\mathbf{Æ}B = \{B \mid B \neq \emptyset\}$.

Here, $\xi \in 2^{[\,]V} \to 2^{2^{[\,]V}}$ maps processes to sets of cones and $\xi B \in 2^{2^{[\,]V}}$ is a set of cones for any $B \in 2^{[\,]V}$.

The precondition of ξB wrt. a specification W is then obtained as follows, where $Pre \in 2^{2^{[\,]V}} \to (2^{[\,]V} \to 2^V)$ is a generic pre-map:

$Pre.\xi B.W = \{x \mid \exists B_0 \in \xi(B(x)) : B_0 \subset W\}$.

2.4.2 Remarks

Predicate transformers The pre-map $\text{\AE}$ is a temporal generalization of the predicate-transformer *wp* [Dij76]. For a given program, *wp* transforms a post-condition into a precondition, viz. a set of points into a set of points. For a given process, $\text{\AE}$ transforms a specification into a precondition, viz. a process into a set of points. Both *wp* and $\text{\AE}$ express universality and existence.

Path quantifiers The pre-maps $\mathbf{E}$ and $\mathbf{A}$ are analogous to the path quantifiers in branching-time temporal logics [CGP99, DN00]. The pre-map $\text{\AE}$ corresponds to no specific path-quantifier.

Operational interpretation From any x in the precondition $\mathbf{E}B.W$, there exists some $B(x)$-trajectory which belongs to W. To find one often requires a systematic search among the $B(x)$-trajectories. On the other hand, from any x in $\text{\AE}B.W$, each $B(x)$-trajectory belongs to W and at least one exists. Exhaustive exploration is then not needed. It is thus worthwhile to replace the process B by $B' \subset B$ such that the precondition $\text{\AE}B'.W$ is as large as possible.

2.4.3 Properties Assume $P, Q \subset V, \;\; B, B' \subset [\,]V$, and specifications W, W'.

(a) Begin set: $\zeta B.P^\frown Q \subset P$.

(b) Duality: $-\mathbf{E}B.W = \;\mathbf{A}B. - W$.

(c) Monotonicity: $\zeta B.W \subset \zeta B.(W \cup W')$.

(d) *Chop decomposition for processes*: given $B \subset [*]V$,

$$\begin{aligned}&\mathbf{E}(B;B').P^\frown Q\\ &= \mathbf{E}B.P^\frown Q^\frown(\mathbf{E}B'.Q^\frown Q) \cup \mathbf{E}B.P^\frown(\mathbf{E}B'.P^\frown Q) \quad \text{in general,}\\ &= \mathbf{E}B.P^\frown(\mathbf{E}B'.P^\frown Q) \quad \text{if } Q \subset P.\end{aligned}$$

Proof: by §§ 2.2.1.a, 2.3.2.b and the equality $(P^\frown P)^\frown Q = P^\frown Q$.
Similarly for $\text{\AE}$ instead of $\mathbf{E}$:

$$\text{\AE}(B;B').P^\frown Q = \text{\AE}B.P^\frown(\text{\AE}B'.P^\frown Q) \qquad \text{if } Q \subset P.$$

(e) For a deterministic process B (§ 2.1), $\mathbf{E}B.W = \mathbf{A}B.W = \text{\AE}B.W$. Moreover, $\mathbf{E}\mathit{Id}.P^\frown P = \mathbf{A}\mathit{Id}.P^\frown P = \text{\AE}\mathit{Id}.P^\frown P = P$.

(f) Case of pre-restrictions: by § 2.4.1, given $P_i \subset V, \; B_i \subset [\,]V$ for $i \in I$,

$$\mathbf{E}\textstyle\bigcup_{i\in I}(P_i \rightharpoonup B_i).W = \bigcup_{i\in I} P_i \cap (\mathbf{E}B_i.W)$$

$$\mathbf{A}\textstyle\bigcup_{i\in I}(P_i \rightharpoonup B_i).W = \bigcap_{i\in I}(-P_i \cup \mathbf{A}B_i.W).$$

In particular, $\mathbf{A}\bigcup_{i\in I} B_i.W = \bigcap_{i\in I} \mathbf{A}B_i.W$.

Note Chop decomposition (d) allows to decompose a proof into sub-proofs. It is thus similar to compositional proof rules in interval temporal logic [Mos98, Eqn (1)]. In general, it does not hold for the pre-map $\mathbf{A}$ which permits blocking; for instance, $\mathbf{A}(B;\emptyset).P^\frown Q = \mathbf{A}\emptyset.P^\frown Q = V$ whereas $\mathbf{A}B.P^\frown(\mathbf{A}\emptyset.P^\frown Q) = \mathbf{A}B.P^\frown V$.

2.4.4 Three Classical Properties of Dynamics Fundamental properties of dynamics can be expressed in terms of preconditions.

Let $P \subset V$. A trajectory b *stays in* P iff $b \in P^\frown P$. It *reaches* P iff $b \in V^\frown P$.

(a) Invariance without Termination, a.k.a. Safety For each x in the precondition $\text{Æ}B^\omega.P^\frown P$, each B^ω-trajectory beginning with x stays in P and does not terminate, and at least one such trajectory exists. Given the Non-Zeno assumption (§ 2.2.2), non termination implies infinite duration.

Similarly, for each x in $\mathbf{E}B^\omega.P^\frown P$, there exists at least one B^ω-trajectory which stays in P and never terminates. This precondition is akin to a viability domain [Aub91].

(b) Inevitability with Invariance, a.k.a. Safe Reachability Assume $Q \subset P$. For each x in the precondition $\text{Æ}B^*.P^\frown Q$, all trajectories in the non-empty cone $B^*(x)$ stay in P and reach Q.

The precondition $\text{Æ}B^\omega.P^\frown Q = \text{Æ}B^*.P^\frown(\text{Æ}B^\omega.Q^\frown Q)$ contains the points x such that all trajectories in the non-empty cone $B^\omega(x)$ stay in P for a finite duration and afterwards stay in Q for an infinite duration. This is a persistence property and can be expressed in terms of (a), (b) and chop decomposition.

(c) Liveness, a.k.a. Recurrence The precondition $\text{Æ}B^\omega.(V^\frown P)^\omega$ contains the points x such that all trajectories in the non-empty cone $B^\omega(x)$ do, from each time value, reach P.

Thus, the B^ω-trajectories beginning in this precondition verify the temporal-logic formula $\Box\Diamond P$.

2.5 Computation of Preconditions for Processes

We present a procedure for computing preconditions $\zeta B.W$. This procedure is not always effective because it does not treat all dense-time processes, and because limits of infinite or transfinite iterations may be needed. The procedure is effective at least in the case of discrete T and finite V.

The computation of $\zeta B.W$ follows the structure of B. The specification W is restricted to $P^\frown Q$ where $P, Q \subset V$. We first detail the computation of $\mathbf{E}B.P^\frown Q$. The computation of $\text{Æ}B.P^\frown Q$ is similar and summarized in a last case.

2.5.1 Case of Relational Processes If $r \subset V^2$ and R is the r-based process, then $\mathbf{E}R.P^\frown Q$ results from elementary relational computations:

$$\begin{aligned}
&\mathbf{E}R.P^\frown Q \\
&= (P \cap Q) \cap r^\smile(Q) \cup P \cap r^\smile(P \cap Q) \quad \text{in general, or} \\
&= P \cap r^\smile(P \cap Q) \quad \text{if } r \subset (-Q) \times V, \\
&= P \cap r^\smile(Q) \quad \text{if } P \subset Q \vee Q \subset P, \\
&= P \cap r^\smile(P) \quad \text{if } P = Q.
\end{aligned}$$

Proof: Let $T = I\!N$. For each $b = (1, g) \in R$:

$$\begin{aligned}&(1, g) \in P^\frown Q\\ &\equiv g.0 \in P \wedge \{g.0, g.1\} \subset Q \vee \{g.0, g.1\} \subset P \wedge g.1 \in Q \quad \text{by § 2.3.2.b},\\ &\equiv g.0 \in P \cap Q \wedge g.1 \in Q \ \vee \ g.0 \in P \wedge g.1 \in P \cap Q.\end{aligned}$$

Hence,

$$\begin{aligned}&\mathbf{E}R.P^\frown Q\\ &= \{x_0 \mid \exists (x_0, x_1) \in r : x_0 \in P \cap Q \wedge x_1 \in Q \ \vee \ x_0 \in P \wedge x_1 \in P \cap Q\}\\ &\qquad \text{by § 2.4.1},\\ &= (P \cap Q) \cap r^\smile(Q) \ \cup \ P \cap r^\smile(P \cap Q).\end{aligned}$$

2.5.2 Case of Sequential and Repeated Processes We repeatedly decompose chops (§ 2.4.3.d).

2.5.3 Case of Concurrent Processes They are reduced to relational, sequential or iterative processes, by distributivity and relational simplification (§ 2.2.3.e,f).

2.5.4 Case of Iterative Processes Fixed points are defined and computed as follows. We assume $Q \subset P \subset V$, $B \subset [*]V$.

(a) Preconditions for finitely iterated processes

$$\mathbf{E}B^*.P^\frown Q \ = \ \mu Y : [Q \cup \mathbf{E}B.P^\frown Y]$$

This least fixed-point is defined in the complete lattice 2^V of subsets of V, and it is computed by the iteration

$$Y^{(0)} = \emptyset, \quad Y^{(n+1)} = Q \cup \mathbf{E}B.P^\frown Y^{(n)}.$$

The function $Y \mapsto Q \cup \mathbf{E}B.P^\frown Y$ transforms a set of points into a set of points since the precondition $\mathbf{E}B.P^\frown Y$ is a set of points. Monotonicity follows from §§ 2.3.2.d, 2.4.3.c. Hence

$$Y^{(n+1)} = Y^{(n)} \cup X^{(n)}, \qquad \text{where } X^{(0)} = Q, \ X^{(n+1)} = \mathbf{E}B.P^\frown X^{(n)}.$$

The property $X^{(n)} = \mathbf{E}B^n.P^\frown Q$ is verified by induction as follows, for $n \geq 0$.

Basis: $X^{(0)} = \mathbf{E}\mathit{Id}.P^\frown Q = P \cap Q = Q$ by defns §§ 2.1, 2.4.1.

Induction step: assume $X^{(n)} = \mathbf{E}B^n.P^\frown Q$; then,

$$\begin{aligned}&X^{(n+1)}\\ &= \mathbf{E}B.P^\frown(\mathbf{E}B^n.P^\frown Q)\\ &\qquad \text{by the defn of } X^{(n+1)} \text{ and the induction hypothesis},\\ &= \mathbf{E}(B; B^n).P^\frown Q \quad \text{by chop decomposition (§ 2.4.3.d)},\\ &= \mathbf{E}B^{n+1}.P^\frown Q \quad \text{by defn of repetition (§ 2.2.1.a)}.\end{aligned}$$

(b) Preconditions for infinitely iterated processes

$$\mathbf{E}B^{\omega}.P^\frown P \;=\; \nu Z : [\mathbf{E}B.P^\frown Z].$$

This greatest fixed-point is defined in the complete lattice 2^P, and is computed by the iteration

$$Z^{(0)} = P, \quad Z^{(n+1)} = \mathbf{E}B.P^\frown Z^{(n)}.$$

Given § 2.4.3.a,c,d, $Z^{(n+1)} = \mathbf{E}B^n.P^\frown(\mathbf{E}B.P^\frown P) \subset Z^{(n)}$.

The property $Z^{(n)} = \mathbf{E}B^n.P^\frown P$ is proven by induction, as in (a).

Notes

1. For a repetition B^n, we clearly have $\mathbf{E}B^n.P^\frown Q = X^{(n)}$: this is the inductive property verified in (a).
2. The simplifying assumption $Q \subset P$ is not essential (§ 2.4.3.d).
3. The term $P^\frown Y$ is similar to the constructs using $\mathcal{U}_q$ and *Reach* in [Asa00, TLS00]; cf. § 2.3.4.
4. The fixed point $\nu Z : [\mathbf{E}B.P^\frown Z]$ in 2^P equals $\nu Z : [\mathbf{E}B.P^\frown(Z \cap P)]$ in 2^V. We use the first expression for simplicity.

2.5.5 Case of Dense-Time Processes Assume $P^\frown Q$ is discretely observable (§ 2.3.3) in a dense-time process B, and $B_{I\!N}$ is the discrete-time sampling (§ 2.1) of B. Then $\zeta B.P^\frown Q = \zeta B_{I\!N}.P^\frown Q$ which is computable by § 2.5.1-4.

The duration of the discrete steps depends on the regularity of the B-trajectories. By a suitable time re-scaling, any time quantum in B can match the time unit in $B_{I\!N}$.

2.5.6 Case of Æ-preconditions The computation of $ÆB.P^\frown Q$ is defined by a systematic adaptation of §§ 2.5.1-5, using chop decomposition (§ 2.4.3.d). In particular,

$$ÆB^*.P^\frown Q \;=\; \mu Y : [Q \cup ÆB.P^\frown Y],$$

computed in 2^V by

$$Y^{(0)} = Q,$$
$$Y^{(n+1)} = Y^{(n)} \cup X^{(n)}, \qquad \text{where } X^{(0)} = Q,\; X^{(n+1)} = ÆB.P^\frown X^{(n)}.$$

The property $X^{(n)} = ÆB^n.P^\frown Q$, for $n \geq 0$, is verified as in § 2.5.4.a.

3 Coprocesses and Their Preconditions

Introduction In order to express different interaction patterns, e.g. cooperation vs competition, we introduce "coprocesses" composed of applications of pre-maps to processes. That term hints at the interaction between processes bound to alternative decision-modes. The coprocesses $\mathbf{E}B_0$ and $\mathbf{A}B_1$ can be respectively seen as the proponent and the opponent in a finite, sequential, noncooperative game with two players. The max-min dynamics of this game can be defined by the iterative coprocess $(\mathbf{E}B_0; \mathbf{A}B_1)^*$. The specification could be $(-Win_1)^\frown Win_0$, where Win_0 and Win_1 are the winning sets of states for the proponent and the opponent, respectively.

Game dynamics can thus be described by coprocesses using $\mathbf{A}$ and $\mathbf{E}$; similarly, game trees can be generated by and/or-programs [Har80]. Coprocesses may also model reactive or hybrid systems, contracts [BaW98] or alternating transition systems [Hen00]. The interplay between the pre-maps $\mathbf{E}$ and $\mathbf{A}$ is characterized by that between $\exists$ and $\forall$ (§ 2.4.1). So, the interaction pattern in a coprocess is determined by the structure of pre-map alternations in it.

Coprocesses and their preconditions are defined in the following Sections. These preconditions can also be understood in terms of associated cones we introduce informally. Given a coprocess S, an *S-cone* is a cone generated as follows: the components of its trajectories belong to component processes of S and are collected according to the corresponding pre-maps (§ 2.4.1-Note). As an example, let S be $(\mathbf{E}B_1; \mathbf{Æ}B_2)$; then there exists one distinct S-cone $(\{b_1\}; B_2)$ for each trajectory $b_1 \in B_1$ such that $B_2(End.b_1) \neq \emptyset$. The set of S-cones is equivalent to the game-tree for S. The *precondition* $S.W$ is the set of points each of which begins at least one S-cone contained in W: from each such point, a winning strategy exists.

Given a coprocess S, an *S-trajectory* is an element of an S-cone, i.e. a B_S-trajectory where the process B_S is obtained by removing the pre-maps from S. The *duration* of S is *finite* iff the duration of each S-trajectory is finite.

Specifications and coprocesses respectively correspond to temporal formulae and their models [CGP99]; pre-maps are similar to path quantifiers (§ 2.4.2). We do not use path quantifiers in specifications given the limited problems considered in this paper. We use pre-maps in coprocesses in order to express different roles for players in games.

3.1 Structure of Coprocesses

A *basic coprocess* ξB is the application of a pre-map ξ to a process B; it transforms a specification into a precondition, viz. $\xi B \in 2^{[\,]V} \to 2^V$. A *concurrent coprocess* is a concurrent composition of basic or concurrent coprocesses. A *sequential coprocess* is a sequential composition of basic, concurrent or sequential coprocesses. An *iterative coprocess* is an iterative composition of basic, concurrent or sequential coprocesses. A *coprocess* $S \in 2^{[\,]V} \to 2^V$ is a basic, concurrent, sequential or iterative coprocess.

This stratified structure is restrictive: for instance, concurrent composition of sequential coprocesses is excluded. The resulting coprocesses are more tractable, and yet not trivial.

The preconditions for basic and composed coprocesses are respectively defined in § 2.4.1 and in the Sections below. Symbols for coprocess compositions are the same as for process compositions.

3.2 Sequential Composition of Basic Coprocesses

We define preconditions for sequential compositions of basic coprocesses only, in order to begin with a simple presentation of typical definitions and properties.

We assume B, B', B_i are processes ($i \in \mathbb{N}$), W, W' are specifications, and $P, Q \subset V$.

3.2.1 Definition We first give a simple case, where $B_1 \subset [*]V$, and then the m-ary one :

$$(\mathbf{E}B_1; \mathbf{Æ}B_2).W = \{x \mid \exists b_1 \in B_1(x) : \forall_+ b_2 \in B_2(End.b_1) : (b_1; b_2) \in W\},$$

$$\begin{aligned}&(\xi_1 B_1; \cdots; \xi_i B_i; \cdots; \xi_m B_m).W \\ &= \{x \mid L_{\xi_1} b_1 \in B_1(x) : \cdots : L_{\xi_i} b_i \in B_i(End.b_{i-1}) : \\ &\qquad \cdots : L_{\xi_m} b_m \in B_m(End.b_{m-1}) : (b_1; \cdots; b_i; \cdots; b_m) \in W\}.\end{aligned}$$

Note This precondition may be defined in terms of sets of cones; see the introduction above and the note in § 2.4.1. Assume $S = (\mathbf{E}B_1; \mathbf{Æ}B_2)$. Let $S(x) \in 2^{2^{[\,]V}}$ be the set of S-cones beginning with $x \in V$:
$S(x) = \{\{b_1\}; B_2 \mid b_1 \in B_1(x) \wedge (B_2(End.b_1) \neq \emptyset)\}$.
Then the precondition of S wrt. a specification W is
$Pre.S.W = \{x \mid \exists B \in S(x) : B \subset W\}$.

3.2.2 Properties We assume $B_1 \subset [*]V, B_2 \subset [\,]V$.

(a) Duality: $-(\eta_1 B_1; \eta_2 B_2).W = (\eta_1^{\sim} B_1; \eta_2^{\sim} B_2). - W$.
(b) Monotonicity: $(\zeta_1 B_1; \zeta_2 B_2).W \subset (\zeta_1 B_1; \zeta_2 B_2).(W \cup W')$,
(c) *Chop decomposition for basic coprocesses*:

$$\begin{aligned}&(\mathbf{E}B_1; \mathbf{Æ}B_2).P^\frown Q \\ &= \mathbf{E}B_1.P^\frown Q^\frown(\mathbf{Æ}B_2.Q^\frown Q) \cup \mathbf{E}B_1.P^\frown(\mathbf{Æ}B_2.P^\frown Q) \quad \text{in general,} \\ &= \mathbf{E}B_1.P^\frown(\mathbf{Æ}B_2.P^\frown Q) \qquad \text{if } Q \subset P.\end{aligned}$$

Proof: by § 2.3.2.b, as for § 2.4.3.d.
Similarly,

$$(\zeta_1 B_1; \zeta_2 B_2).P^\frown Q = \zeta_1 B_1.P^\frown(\zeta_2 B_2.P^\frown Q) \quad \text{if } Q \subset P.$$

(d) Case of pre-restrictions: assume $Q \subset P \subset V,\ B \subset [\,]V,\ P_i \subset V,\ B_i \subset [*]V$, for $i \in I$. By § 3.2.1, as in § 2.4.3.f,

$$\begin{aligned}(\mathbf{E}\textstyle\bigcup_{i\in I}(P_i \rightharpoonup B_i); \zeta B).P^\frown Q &= \textstyle\bigcup_{i\in I} P_i \cap (\mathbf{E}B_i; \zeta B).P^\frown Q, \\ (\mathbf{A}\textstyle\bigcup_{i\in I}(P_i \rightharpoonup B_i); \zeta B).P^\frown Q &= \textstyle\bigcap_{i\in I}(-P_i \cup (\mathbf{A}B_i; \zeta B).P^\frown Q).\end{aligned}$$

Hence $(\mathbf{Æ}\bigcup_{i\in I}(P_i \rightharpoonup B_i); \zeta B).P^\frown Q$ equals the conjunction of these two preconditions, since $(\forall_+ b \in B : E) \equiv (\exists b \in B : E) \wedge (\forall b \in B : E)$.

3.3 Concurrent Composition of Basic Coprocesses

We need to express a logical ordering between quantifiers, viz. between the premaps of branches, without introducing additional constraints on the dynamics.

Assume $B_1 \subset [\,]V_1,\ B_2 \subset [\,]V_2$ are processes, and $W, W' \subset [\,](V_1 \times V_2)$ are specifications.

3.3.1 Definition In the case of a local concurrent composition, we have

$$(\xi_1 B_1 \otimes \xi_2 B_2).W$$
$$= \{(x_1, x_2) \mid L_{\xi_1} b_1 \in B_1(x_1) : L_{\xi_2} b_2 \in B_2(x_2) : b_1 \otimes b_2 \in W\}.$$

E.g., $(\mathbf{E}B_1 \otimes \mathbf{A}B_2).W = \{(x_1, x_2) \mid \exists b_1 \in B_1(x_1) : \forall b_2 \in B_2(x_2) : b_1 \otimes b_2 \in W\}$.

In the case of a global concurrent composition, where $G_i, G_j \subset V_1 \times V_2,\ B_i \subset [\,]V_1,\ B'_j \subset [\,]V_2$, we have for instance

$$(\mathbf{E} \textstyle\bigcup_{i \in I} G_i \rightharpoonup B_i \parallel \text{Æ} \bigcup_{j \in J} G'_j \rightharpoonup B'_j).W$$
$$\begin{aligned} = \{(x_1, x_2) \mid \exists i \in I : [\,(x_1, x_2) \in G_i \wedge \exists b \in B_i(x_1) :& \\ [\,\forall j \in J : (\ (x_1, x_2) \in G'_j \Rightarrow \forall_+ b' \in B'_j(x_2) : b \otimes b' \in W)& \\ \wedge \exists j \in J : (\ (x_1, x_2) \in G'_j \wedge \forall_+ b' \in B'_j(x_2) : b \otimes b' \in W)]]\}.& \end{aligned}$$

3.3.2 Properties Assume B_1, B_2 are concurrent branches.

(a) Duality: $-(\eta_1 B_1 \| \eta_2 B_2).W = (\eta_1^{\sim} B_1 \| \eta_2^{\sim} B_2). - W$.

(b) Monotonicity: $(\zeta_1 B_1 \| \zeta_2 B_2).W \subset (\zeta_1 B_1 \| \zeta_2 B_2).(W \cup W')$.

3.4 Sequential Composition with Concurrent Coprocesses

Let be processes $B_1 \subset [*]V_1,\ B_2 \subset [*]V_2,\ B_3 \subset [*]V_3,\ B \subset [\,](V_1 \times V_2)$, and specifications $W, W' \subset [\,](V_1 \times V_2),\ W'' \subset [\,]((V_1 \times V_2) \times V_3)$.

3.4.1 Definition We give a typical case:

$$((\xi_1 B_1 \otimes \xi_2 B_2); \xi B).W = \{(x_1, x_2) \mid L_{\xi_1} b_1 \in B_1(x_1) : L_{\xi_2} b_2 \in B_2(x_2) :$$
$$L_\xi b \in B(End.(b_1 \otimes b_2)) : ((b_1 \otimes b_2); b) \in W\}.$$

Cases with global concurrency are obtained by systematic adaptations (§ 3.3.1). The general definition of preconditions for sequential coprocesses is obtained by combining the definitions given here and in § 3.2.1. The case of m-ary concurrent coprocesses is similar: e.g.,

$$((\xi_1 B_1 \otimes \xi_2 B_2) \otimes \xi_3 B_3).W''$$
$$= \{((x_1, x_2), x_3) \mid L_{\xi_1} b_1 \in B_1(x_1) : L_{\xi_2} b_2 \in B_2(x_2) :$$
$$L_{\xi_3} b_3 \in B_3(x_3) : (b_1 \otimes b_2) \otimes b_3 \in W''\}.$$

Given a basic, concurrent or sequential coprocess S, the *repetition* S^n is defined as follows, for $n, m \in I\!N$ and $m < n$:

$$S^0 = \text{Æ}\ Id, \qquad S^{m+1} = S^m; S.$$

3.4.2 Properties

(a) Duality: $-((\eta_1 B_1 \| \eta_2 B_2); \eta B).W = ((\eta_1^{\sim} B_1 \| \eta_2^{\sim} B_2); \eta^{\sim} B). - W$.

(b) Monotonicity: $((\zeta_1 B_1 \| \zeta_2 B_2); \zeta B).W \subset ((\zeta_1 B_1 \| \zeta_2 B_2); \zeta B).(W \cup W')$.

(c) *Chop decomposition for coprocesses*: assume $Q \subset P \subset V$, S is a basic, concurrent or sequential coprocess, S' is a basic or concurrent one, and both have a finite duration and only use the non-blocking pre-maps **E** or **Æ**; then

$$(S; S').P^{\frown}Q = S.P^{\frown}(S'.P^{\frown}Q).$$

This property generalizes § 3.2.2.c. Here is the proof for a typical case:

$$\begin{aligned} &((\zeta_1 B_1 \otimes \zeta_2 B_2); \zeta B).P^{\frown}Q \\ &= \{(x_1, x_2) \mid L_{\zeta_1} b_1 \in B_1(x_1) : L_{\zeta_2} b_2 \in B_2(x_2) : \\ &\qquad L_\zeta b \in B(End.(b_1 \otimes b_2)) : ((b_1 \otimes b_2); b) \in P^{\frown}Q\} \text{ by defn § 3.4.1,} \\ &= \{(x_1, x_2) \mid L_{\zeta_1} b_1 \in B_1(x_1) : L_{\zeta_2} b_2 \in B_2(x_2) : \\ &\qquad (b_1 \otimes b_2) \in P^{\frown}(\zeta B.P^{\frown}Q)\} \text{ by § 2.3.2.b,} \\ &= (\zeta_1 B_1 \otimes \zeta_2 B_2).P^{\frown}(\zeta B.P^{\frown}Q) \quad \text{by defn § 3.3.1.} \end{aligned}$$

3.5 Iterative Composition of Coprocesses

3.5.1 Assumptions The fixed-point definitions of preconditions for iterative processes (§ 2.5.4) depend on chop decomposition for processes (§ 2.4.3.d). The same holds for iterative coprocesses wrt. § 3.4.2.c. A coprocess S to be iterated must thus verify the following conditions:

(i) S is a basic, concurrent or sequential coprocess with pre-maps **E** or **Æ** only,
(ii) the duration S is finite.

The Non-Zeno assumption (§ 2.2.2) also concerns coprocesses: for each considered coprocess S, the duration of each S-trajectory is bounded below by a non-Zeno time.

The least and greatest fixed-points below generalize those defining preconditions for iterative processes. The structure of these fixed-point definitions match that of iterative coprocesses.

3.5.2 Preconditions for Finitely Iterated Coprocesses

$$S^*.P^{\frown}Q \;=\; \mu Y : [Q \cup S.P^{\frown}Y].$$

This fixed point is defined in the complete lattice 2^V and is computed by

$$Y^{(0)} = \emptyset, \quad Y^{(n+1)} = Q \cup S.P^{\frown}Y^{(n)}.$$

Thanks to monotonicity (§§ 2.3.2.d, 3.2.2.b),

$$Y^{(n+1)} = Y^{(n)} \cup X^{(n)}, \quad \text{where } X^{(0)} = Q, \quad X^{(n+1)} = S.P^{\frown}X^{(n)}.$$

The property $X^{(n)} = S^n.P^{\frown}Q$ is proven as in § 2.5.4, using §§ 3.4.2.c, 3.5.1.

3.5.3 Preconditions for Infinitely Iterated Coprocesses

$$S^{\omega}.P^{\frown}P \;=\; \nu Z : [S.P^{\frown}Z].$$

This fixed point is defined in the complete lattice 2^P and is computed by

$$Z^{(0)} = P, \quad Z^{(n+1)} = S.P^{\frown}Z^{(n)}.$$

The property $Z^{(n)} = S^n.P^{\frown}P$ is proven as in § 2.5.4, using §§ 3.4.2.c, 3.5.1.

Given §§ 3.2.1, 3.4.1, the set $Z^{(\omega_{I\!N})}$ is thus characterized by an $\omega_{I\!N}$-length $\forall/\exists$ formula.

3.6 Computation of Preconditions for Coprocesses

The procedure for computing preconditions for coprocesses follows the stratified structure of coprocesses. It is not always effective (§ 2.5). We only tackle specifications on the form $P^{\frown}Q$ for $Q \subset P \subset V$. If $Q \subset P$ does not hold, the general cases in §§ 2.3.2.b,c, 3.4.2.c should be used.

Case of basic coprocesses See § 2.5.

Case of concurrent coprocesses See § 3.3.1. As an example, we detail the case of local relational branches. Assume, for $i = 1, 2 : r_i \subset V_i \times V_i$, R_i is r_i-based, and $Q \subset P \subset V_1 \times V_2$. Then, by §§ 2.2.3.f, 2.3.2.b,

$$(\zeta_1 R_1 \otimes \zeta_2 R_2).P^{\frown}Q$$
$$= \{(x_1, x_2) \mid L_{\zeta_1}(x_1, y_1) \in r_1 : L_{\zeta_2}(x_2, y_2) \in r_2 : ((x_1, x_2), (y_1, y_2)) \in P \times Q\}$$

which is a relational computation.

To reduce the duration of concurrent coprocesses, one may reduce that of concurrent processes by using distributivity properties (§ 2.2.3.e).

Case of sequential and repeated coprocesses Their preconditions are decomposed into preconditions for basic or concurrent coprocesses, by repeatedly decomposing chops (§§ 3.2.2.d, 3.4.2.c).

Case of iterative coprocesses The fixed points in § 3.5 are computed by iterations. Each iterate is computed using the previous cases since S is a basic, concurrent or sequential coprocess.

3.7 Discrete-Decision Games and Winning Regions

Games are pairs of coprocesses and specifications. Winning regions are their preconditions. The definitions are detailed hereafter.

A *(noncooperative, iterative) game coprocess* is a coprocess S^{∞} where the *proponent* is a distinguished coprocess occurring in S and using the pre-map **E** or **Æ**; the *opponent* is the remainder of S. A *game* is a pair (S^{∞}, W) consisting of a game coprocess S^{∞} and a specification W. The *winning region* of a game (S^{∞}, W) is the precondition $S^{\infty}.W$. Moves and plays are S- and S^{∞}-trajectories, respectively. The game is finite, resp. infinite, if the duration of the plays is finite, resp. infinite.

Strategic decisions are made by players when their moves are selected, viz. when their pre-maps are elaborated. Given the stratification of coprocesses (§ 3.1), any two decisions generated by a coprocess S are generated either by a concurrent composition of coprocesses in S or by a sequential or iterative one; they are then said to be concurrent or sequential, respectively. A coprocess S is a *discrete-decision coprocess* iff any two sequential decisions generated by S are separated by a time interval bounded below by a non-Zeno time.

A *discrete-decision game* is a game (S^∞, W) where S^∞ is a discrete-decision game-coprocess verifying two additional assumptions. Firstly, the proponent coprocess ζB occurs at the left-most position in S, like a dominating existential quantifier: we seek a winning strategy for the proponent. Secondly, the choice set of the proponent is finite, namely B is a finite union $\bigcup_{i\in I} B_i$ or $\bigcup_{i\in I} G_i \rightharpoonup B_i$ (§ 2.2.1.b) where each B_i is deterministic. We could thus use the more complete expression "discrete-decision, finite-choice, dynamical game", where "dynamical" refers to dense- or discrete-time dynamics.

The Non-Zeno assumption entails each coprocess is a discrete-decision one. Let us check this. For any two sequential decisions in any coprocess S, the first one is generated by a basic coprocess S_0 in S. Hence their occurrence times are separated by at least the duration of an S_0-trajectory, which is bounded below by a non-Zeno time (§ 3.5.1). Hence S is a discrete-decision coprocess.

3.8 Related Work on Discrete-Decision Coprocesses

We briefly discuss related work on discrete-decision coprocesses such as reactive and hybrid systems. The time set is $I\!N_\omega \times I\!R^+_\omega$ (§ 2.2.2); the time set $I\!N_\omega$ may be represented by $I\!N_\omega \times \{0\}$. We use relational processes $R, R', R_i \subset [(1,0)]V$ and durative ones $B, B_i \subset \bigcup_{d\in I\!R^+} [(0,d)]V$, for $i = 1,2$. In discussions such as the present one, we do not consider the difference between $\mathbf{A}$ and $\mathbf{Æ}$ (§ 2.4.1).

Coprocesses $(\mathbf{E}R; \mathbf{A}R')^\omega$ on a finite state-space, e.g. in the case of Büchi automata, are treated in [BüL69, TB70, RW89]. Simple cooperative coprocesses $(\mathbf{E}R)^\omega$ on infinite state-spaces are considered in [vLS79]. Noncooperative coprocesses $(\mathbf{E}R; \mathbf{A}R')^\omega$ on infinite state-spaces are studied in [MP95, BaW98]. The local concurrent case $S^\omega = (\mathbf{E}R_1 \| \mathbf{A}R_2)^\omega$ is investigated in [AMP95, Hen 00]; the precondition $S.V^\frown Q$ is analogous to the set $\Psi_S^{CPre_1}(Q)$ in [Hen00].

Coprocesses $(\mathbf{E}R; \mathbf{A}B)^\omega$ model the hybrid systems considered in [AMP95, Asa00]. Richer coprocesses such as $((\mathbf{E}R_1 \| \mathbf{A}R_2); \mathbf{A}(B_1 \| B_2))^\omega$ model two concurrent hybrid systems, with control transitions in R_1, R_2 and plant trajectories in B_1, B_2, respectively [TLS00]. Variant or dual forms of the until-operator are introduced in [Asa00, TLS00] to take the durative B-trajectories into account (§ 2.5.4-Note.3).

Quasi-discrete games and games with K-strategies [Isa65] are discrete-decision games; they serve to approximate continuous-decision ones.

4 Iterative Synthesis of Winning Strategies

4.1 Preliminaries

4.1.1 Winning Transforms of Discrete-Decision Games Consider a discrete-decision game (S^∞, W) where the proponent is $\mathbf{E}B$ (§ 3.7). The winning plays for the proponent result from the search-based selection-mode $\mathbf{E}$. This mode is to be strengthened into the search-free one $\mathbf{Æ}$ (§ 2.4.2).

As a consequence, we aim at restricting the proponent process $B = \bigcup_{i \in I} B_i$ by the addition of guards $C_i \subset V$ which exclude B-moves steering plays outside of W. Let B_c be the union of pre-restrictions of the B_i's, i.e. $B_c = \bigcup_{i \in I} C_i \rightharpoonup B_i$. If the C_i's only permit B-moves which steer plays inside the winning process W, they are *winning guards*. In this case, the proponent $\mathbf{E}B$ can be replaced in S by $\mathbf{Æ}B_c$. A *winning transform* of the discrete-decision game (S^∞, W) is (S_c^∞, W) where S_c is the result of such a replacement. The winning transform represents a finite-memory strategy since the winning guards do not need additional memory. This winning strategy must be complete in the sense that $S^\infty.W = S_c^\infty.W$: the reduction of B to B_c may not reduce the winning region.

The goal is to construct such winning guards iteratively, given a discrete-decision game (S^∞, W) and a proponent $\mathbf{E} \bigcup_{i \in I} B_i$, or $\mathbf{E} \bigcup_{i \in I} G_i \rightharpoonup B_i$ in a concurrent coprocess.

4.1.2 Synthesis Problems We consider two basic properties of dynamics (§ 2.4.4.a,b). Let $P, Q \subset V$.

(I) Invariance without Termination Given a discrete-decision game $(S^\omega, P^\frown P)$, to find a winning transform $(S_c^\omega, P^\frown P)$ with the same winning region.

(II) Inevitability with Invariance Given a discrete-decision game $(S^*, P^\frown Q)$, to find a winning transform $(S_c^*, P^\frown Q)$ with the same winning region.

4.1.3 Solution Method We extend to coprocesses the method used for action systems [vLS79]. In the latter work, an action system amounts to an iteration $(\mathbf{E}R)^\infty$ of a basic, cooperative, relational coprocess on a finite or infinite state-space. The idea is simple: the iterates $C^{(n)}$ which yield a winning region C are structured as unions of iterates $C_i^{(n)}$ which yield winning guards C_i. The iteration function for $C^{(n)}$ is then refined into iteration functions for $C_i^{(n)}$.

We reuse the fixed-point definitions of winning regions (§§ 3.5, 3.7). Thus, the chop decomposition (§ 3.4.2.c) is as useful for iterative synthesis as for iterative analysis (§ 3.6). Following §§ 2 and 3, the synthesis methods below are defined for dense and discrete time. However, as in §§ 2.5, 3.6, the iterative techniques we propose are discrete or use discretization. Again, these techniques in general require induction, and thus give rise to procedures which are not always effective.

4.1.4 Assumptions In the considered synthesis problems, we assume the following:

(a) $S = (\mathbf{E}B; \mathbf{A}B')$ where $B = \bigcup_{i \in I} B_i$, , or $S = ((\mathbf{E}B \| \mathbf{A}B'); \mathbf{A}B'')$ where B is a left branch $\bigcup_{i \in I} G_i \rightharpoonup B_i$. The proponent is $\mathbf{E}B$.
(b) Each process B_i is deterministic. Hence $\mathbf{E}B_i = \text{Æ}B_i = \mathbf{A}B_i$ (§ 2.4.3.e).
(c) The opponent coprocess does not block, viz. $\mathbf{A}B = \text{Æ}B$ (§ 2.4.1). The assumption (a) may thus be replaced by $S = (\mathbf{E}B; \text{Æ}B')$ or $S = ((\mathbf{E}B \| \text{Æ}B'); \text{Æ}B'')$.
(d) S has a finite duration.
(e) $Q \subset P \subset V$.

Notes

1. The coprocesses $\mathbf{E}B$ and $(\mathbf{E}B \| \mathbf{A}B')$ are respectively equal to $(\mathbf{E}B; \mathbf{A}\mathit{Id})$ and $((\mathbf{E}B \| \mathbf{A}B'); \mathbf{A}\mathit{Id})$, which are instances of (a).
2. By assumption (b), the non-determinism of B is entirely expressed by the finite union $\bigcup_{i \in I} B_i$ (§ 2.1). The choice set in $\mathbf{E}B$ is thus finite. We do not use the more general assumption $B = \bigcup_{i \in I} \text{Æ}B_i$ because the composition of coprocesses is restricted (§ 3.1).
3. Assumption (c) can be ensured by taking $B \subset [d]V$ where d is sufficiently small so that blocking B-trajectories are excluded in the time interval $(0 : d)$.
4. Condition (i) in § 3.5.1 results from (c). Condition (ii) is (d).
5. The simplifying assumption (e) is not essential (§ 2.4.3.d).

4.2 Invariance without Termination

A point is loosing if it begins a play which leaves the set P or terminates. Loosing points are iteratively removed from the initially given domains of proponent moves. The set of remaining, winning points is a greatest fixed-point, as classical for invariance during infinite time.

4.2.1 Sequential Proponent Let $S = (\mathbf{E}B; \text{Æ}B')$; cf. § 4.1.4.c.

Problem To derive winning guards $C_i \subset V$ such that

$$S^\omega.P^\frown P = S_c^\omega.P^\frown P, \quad \text{where } S_c = (\text{Æ}B_c; \text{Æ}B') \text{ and } B_c = \bigcup_{i \in I} C_i \rightharpoonup B_i.$$

Solution Let C be the winning region $S^\omega.P^\frown P$ (§ 3.5.3):

$$C =_\nu S.P^\frown C.$$

The winning region C and the winning guards C_i are computed in the complete lattice 2^P by the following iterations, where $S_i = (\mathbf{E}B_i; \text{Æ}B')$, $i \in I$ and $n \in I\!N$:

$$C^{(n)} = \bigcup_{i \in I} C_i^{(n)},$$

$$C_i^{(0)} = P, \quad C_i^{(n+1)} = S_i.P^\frown C^{(n)}.$$

Proof The iterates $C_i^{(n)}$ and $C^{(n)}$ have limits, by monotonicity: $C_i^{(n+1)} \subset C_i^{(n)}$ and $C^{(n+1)} \subset C^{(n)}$. The limit of $C^{(n)}$ is the fixed point C because

$$C^{(0)} = P, \quad C^{(n+1)} = \bigcup_{i \in I} S_i.P^\frown C^{(n)} = S.P^\frown C^{(n)}.$$

Since $B_c \subset B$, we have $S_c^\omega.P^\frown P \subset S^\omega.P^\frown P$. Given $C = S^\omega.P^\frown P$, the requirement $S_c^\omega.P^\frown P = S^\omega.P^\frown P$ is thus implied by $C \subset S_c^\omega.P^\frown P$.

To prove the latter inclusion, let us verify that each S^∞-trajectory beginning in $C = \bigcup_{i \in I} C_i$ belongs to $P^\frown P$ and does not terminate. For each i, given § 4.1.4.b and the definition of $C_i^{(n)}$, we have $C_i \subset (\text{Æ}B_i; \text{Æ}B').P^\frown C$. Thus, each point in C_i begins $(B_i; B')$-trajectories which all stay in P and reach some $C_j \subset C$ again. Hence P is invariant and termination is excluded. Hence $C = \bigcup_{i \in I} C_i \subset S_c^\omega.P^\frown P$.

4.2.2. Concurrent Proponent Assume $S = ((\mathbf{E}B \| \text{Æ}B'); \text{Æ}B'') \subset [*](V_1 \times V_2)$, where $B = \bigcup_{i \in I} G_i \rightharpoonup B_i$ is a left branch, and $G_i \subset V_1 \times V_2$, $B_i \subset [*]V_1$, for $i \in I$.

Problem To derive winning global guards $C_i \subset V_1 \times V_2$ such that

$$S^\omega.P^\frown P = S_c^\omega.P^\frown P,$$
$$\text{where } S_c = ((\text{Æ}B_c \| \text{Æ}B'); \text{Æ}B'') \text{ and } B_c = \bigcup_{i \in I} (C_i \cap G_i) \rightharpoonup B_i.$$

Solution As in § 4.2.1, for $S_i = ((\mathbf{E}(G_i \rightharpoonup B_i) \| \text{Æ}B'); \text{Æ}B'')$.

Proof Similar to the proof in § 4.2.1. In particular:

We have $C_i \subset G_i \cap ((\text{Æ}B_i \| \text{Æ}B'); \text{Æ}B'').P^\frown C$. Thus, each point in C_i begins $((B_i \| B'); B'')$-trajectories all of which stay in P and reach C again. Hence P is invariant and termination is excluded.

4.3 Inevitability with Invariance

A point is winning if it begins plays all of which stay in P and inevitably reach Q. Winning points are iteratively added to the initially empty domains of proponent moves. The set of winning points is a least fixed-point, as classical for inevitability.

4.3.1. Sequential Proponent Let $S = (\mathbf{E}R; \text{Æ}B)$.

Problem To derive winning guards $C_i \subset V$ such that

$$S^*.P^\frown Q = S_c^*.P^\frown Q, \quad \text{where } S_c = (\text{Æ}B_c; \text{Æ}B') \text{ and } B_c = \bigcup_{i \in I} C_i \rightharpoonup B_i.$$

Solution Let C be such that $Q \cup C$ is the winning region $S^*.P^\frown Q$ (§ 3.5.2):

$$C =_\mu S.P^\frown Q \cup S.P^\frown C.$$

The set C and the winning guards C_i are computed in the complete lattice 2^V by the following iterations, where $S_i = (\mathbf{E}B_i; \text{Æ}B')$, $i \in I$ and $n \geq 1$:

$$C^{(n)} = \bigcup_{i \in I} C_i^{(n)},$$
$$C_i^{(1)} = S_i.P^\frown Q, \qquad C_i^{(n+1)} = C_i^{(n)} \cup (S_i.P^\frown C^{(n)}) \backslash C^{(n)}.$$

Proof Thanks to § 4.1.4.b, we have $S_i = (ÆB_i; ÆB')$. W.l.o.g., we assume B_i is not applicable in Q, viz. $B_i = (-Q \rightharpoonup B_i)$.

The iterates $C_i^{(n)}$ and $C^{(n)}$ have limits, by monotonicity (§ 3.5.2). The limit of $C^{(n)}$ is the fixed point C because

$$C^{(0)} = \bigcup_{i\in I} S_i.P^\frown Q = S.P^\frown Q,$$

$$C^{(n+1)} = (\bigcup_{i\in I} C_i^{(n)}) \cup \bigcup_{i\in I}(S_i.P^\frown C^{(n)})\backslash C^{(n)} = C^{(n)} \cup \bigcup_{i\in I} S_i.P^\frown C^{(n)}.$$

Since $B_c \subset B$, we have $S_c^*.P^\frown Q \subset S^*.P^\frown Q$. Given $Q \cup C = S^*.P^\frown Q$, the requirement $S_c^*.P^\frown Q = S^*.P^\frown Q$ is thus implied by $Q \cup C \subset S_c^*.P^\frown Q$.

To prove the latter inclusion, let us verify that each S^∞-trajectory beginning in C belongs to $P^\frown Q$. Assume, for $i \in I$ and $n \geq 1$,

$$D^{(n)} = \bigcup_{i\in I} D_i^{(n)},$$

$$D_i^{(1)} = C_i^{(1)}, \qquad D_i^{(n+1)} = C_i^{(n+1)}\backslash C^{(n)} = (S_i.P^\frown C^{(n)})\backslash C^{(n)}.$$

Thus, $C_i^{(n+1)} = C_i^{(n)} \cup D_i^{(n+1)}$ and $C = \bigcup_{n\geq 1} D^{(n)}$. The difference sets $D^{(n)}$ stratify C : for each $x \in C$, there is a unique n such that $x \in D^{(n)}$, because $D^{(n)} \cap D^{(m)} = \emptyset$ if $n \neq m$.

For all $n \geq 1$, each S^∞-trajectory beginning in $D^{(n)}$ is an S_c^n-trajectory which has a finite duration, stays in P and ends in Q. This property is verified by induction as follows.

Basis: Let be any $x \in D^{(1)} = \bigcup_{i\in I} C_i^{(1)} = \bigcup_{i\in I} S_i.P^\frown Q$. Hence each S^∞-trajectory b beginning with x begins in $C_j^{(1)}$ and is an S_j-trajectory, for some $j \in I$; it is then an S_c^1-trajectory by definition of B_c. Since $C_j^{(1)} = S_j.P^\frown Q$, the S_c^1-trajectory b has a finite duration, stays in P and ends in Q. No S_k-trajectory continues b since $B_k = (-Q \rightharpoonup B_k)$.

Induction step: Assume the thesis holds for n. Then:
Let be any $x \in D^{(n+1)} = \bigcup_{i\in I} D_i^{(n+1)} \subset \bigcup_{i\in I} S_i.P^\frown C^{(n)}$. Hence each S^∞-trajectory beginning with x has a prefix b_1 which is an S_j-trajectory for some $j \in I$. Each such b_1 begins in $D_j^{(n+1)} \subset C_j$ and is thus an S_c^1-trajectory. It has a finite duration, stays in P and ends with $y \in C^{(n)}$. Hence $y \in D^{(n)}$, since $x \notin C^{(n)}$.
Given the induction hypothesis, each S^∞-trajectory beginning with $y \in D^{(n)}$ is an S_c^n-trajectory b_n which has a finite duration, stays in P and ends in Q. By sequential composition of the S_c^1-trajectory b_1 and the S_c^n-trajectory b_n, each S^∞-trajectory beginning with $x \in D^{(n+1)}$ is an S_c^{n+1}-trajectory $(b_1; b_n)$ which has a finite duration, stays in P and ends in Q.

Thus, for each $n \geq 1$ and each $x \in D^{(n)}$, $x \in S_c^*.P^\frown Q$. Hence $Q \cup C = Q \cup \bigcup_{n\geq 1} D^{(n)} \subset S_c^*.P^\frown Q$.

4.3.2. Concurrent Proponent We merely summarize the results; the details and proofs integrate §§ 4.2.2, 4.3.1.

Problem As in § 4.2.2, using the requirement $S^*.P^\frown Q = S_c^*.P^\frown Q$.

Solution As in § 4.3.1, for $S_i = (\mathbf{E}(G_i \rightharpoonup B_i) \| \text{Æ}B'); \text{Æ}B'')$.

4.3.3 Remarks

Construction of a well-ordering The difference sets $D^{(n)}$ are well ordered by their rank n, and the latter is decremented by each S_c-trajectory. This ranking is related to value functions [BaO98, TLS00] and to minimum time-to-reach functions [BCT02]. Value functions are defined by difference equations in the discrete-time case and by differential equations in the dense-time case.

Consider classical synthesis methods for discrete-time games: iterations generate a winning region, an explicit well-ordering is found for the latter, and a strategy function is then elaborated [GTW02 (§ 2.5.1), Tho95]. Here, iterations directly generate winning guards while the well-ordering appears only in the proof. Strategy functions are not used since strategies are represented by process guards; this representation depends on the finiteness of choice sets (§ 3.7).

Simplification and deduction of winning guards If the considered game always begins in the winning region C, then each winning guard C_i can be simplified into C_i' such that $C_i' \cap C = C_i$.

In Problem (I), the C_i's can be deduced from the winning region C by means of $C_i = S_i.P^\frown C$. Here, the winning guards and the winning region are generated in a common iteration (§ 4.2). This illustrates the approach can be used uniformly for different properties of dynamics.

Synthesis vs. analysis The coprocess S may happen to be correct, in the sense that the proponent $\mathbf{E}B$ may be replaced by ÆB, viz. $B_c = B$. To verify S amounts thus to synthesize winning guards C_i such that $(C_i \rightharpoonup B_i) = B_i$; no restriction on $B = \bigcup_{i \in I} B_i$ is needed. This iterative verification is comparable to a model-checking procedure in the case it finds no errors [CGP99].

The present approach is also related to a method developed in the context of model checking [Cha00]. The latter considers temporal-logic queries about finite-state, discrete-time systems, and presents a procedure for computing the answers. This may be used for specification improvement and system inspection.

Non-deterministic strategies The proposed techniques generate winning guards which may well have non-empty intersections. It is thus possible to obtain non-deterministic winning strategies.

Alternative complete strategies The iteration scheme in § 4.3.1 is synchronous: it increments the rank n of each iterate $C_i^{(n)}$ at each iteration step. This iteration scheme may well become asynchronous, provided it remains fair: some iterates may progress more slowly than other ones, but none is left out forever [Cou78, Ber00 (Vol. II, § 1.3.2)].

The winning guards generated by asynchronous iterations determine alternative winning strategies where moves may receive other priorities. These alternative strategies are complete because fair asynchronous iterations preserve the equality $C = \bigcup_{i \in I} C_i$. Complete, alternative strategies determine different coprocesses S_c.

Liveness The liveness problem (§ 2.4.4.c) could be tackled by using nested fixed-points since $S^\omega.(V^\frown Q)^\omega = \nu X : [S^*.V^\frown Q^\frown X]$; this is classical for finite-state games [BüL69, Tho95]. Winning guards which ensure liveness would then be synthesized by nested iterations.

Continuous-decision games If the strategic decisions in a game are continuous, then the time set is dense. In continuous-decision coprocesses, the closest sequential decisions are separated by an infinitesimal time-interval. Accordingly, iterative techniques (§§ 3, 4) should be replaced by differential ones [BaO98, Vin00].

Discretizations Dense-time processes can be tackled by discrete-time sampling (§ 2.5.5), and time-to-reach functions for dense time can be computed through numerical discretization [BCT02]. Such discretizations may be organized in two levels:

(i) The abstraction (or approximation) of dense-time processes by discrete-time ones results in small-step iterations (§ 2.5).
(ii) The abstraction of continuous-decision coprocesses by discrete-decision ones results in big-step iterations (§ 3.6).

Discrete-time dynamics (*i*) induce discrete-decision interactions (*ii*), but not conversely: discrete-decision interactions in coprocesses may involve dense-time dynamics in processes.

5 Discussions and Conclusions

We briefly review related work on synthesis, summarize the present contributions, discuss further work and conclude with a few observations.

5.1 Related Work on Synthesis of Strategies

For related work on discrete-decision coprocesses, see § 3.8. The two synthesis problems discussed here are defined in § 4.1.2. Simple discrete-decision coprocesses are considered in § 4.1.4-Note.1. We use R, R' for relational processes and B, B' for general ones. The proponent is $\mathbf{E}R$.

Problem (I): Invariance without termination The classical solution for finite-state games is semi-iterative [BüL69, TB70, RW89]: relational coprocesses $(\mathbf{E}R; \mathbf{A}R')^\omega$ are considered; winning regions are synthesized iteratively; winning-strategy functions are then extracted from these. Problem (I) is solved iteratively for the cooperative coprocesses $(\mathbf{E}R)^\omega$ [vLS79]. In [AMP95, MPS95, Tho95, BaW98, Hen00], it is solved by a semi-iterative method for systems on the form $(\mathbf{E}R; \mathbf{A}R')^\omega$ or $(\mathbf{E}R \| \mathbf{A}R')^\omega$. A similar approach is used in [AMP95, Asa00, TLS00] for hybrid systems like $(\mathbf{E}R; \mathbf{A}B)^\omega$ or $((\mathbf{E}R \| \mathbf{A}R'); \mathbf{A}B)^\omega$.

For Problem (I), there is not much difference between iterative techniques and semi-iterative ones: the winning guards can be deduced from the winning region (§ 4.3.3) [Asa00]. More significant problems, e.g. liveness, have been solved by semi-iterative methods [Tho95]; they are not treated in this paper.

Problem (II): Inevitability with invariance Usually, the winning region of a finite-state game $((\mathbf{E}R; \mathbf{A}R')^*, P^\frown Q)$ is generated iteratively, but not the winning strategy: each state is given a rank during the computation of the iterates, and the strategy function decreases this rank [BüL69, TB70, MPS95, Tho95, BaW98]; see also § 4.3.3. An iterative method is available for the cooperative coprocesses $(\mathbf{E}R)^*$ [vLS79]. In [BKS98], the problem is solved by a systematic elimination of cycles in trajectories. In [HLM01], control guards are derived iteratively in an approach related to § 4.3. The algorithms elaborated in the latter two papers are respectively based on a graph model of discrete-event systems and on an automata model of hybrid systems.

Regarding Problem (II), iterative techniques compare as follows with semi-iterative ones. The winning guards generated by iterations directly determine a winning strategy, whereas the explicit elaboration of a well-ordering and of an associated strategy-function is less immediate, especially in the case of infinite state-spaces. On the other hand, the proposed iterative techniques yield strategies which are equivalent to those obtained by semi-iterative methods, at least in the case of finite-state, discrete-time games and synchronous iterations (§ 4.3.3).

Computations for dense-time dynamics Qualitative problems can be reduced to quantitative ones by using a binary set of quantities. Let us then look at optimization problems.

Dense-time optimization problems can often be expressed by Hamilton-Jacobi(-Bellman) differential equations based on a dense-time form of Bellman's principle of dynamic programming. These equations may be solved following Bellman's principle, as precised in viscosity solutions, or Pontryagin's principle of optimality [BaC97, Ber00, Vin00, AgS02]. It could prove fruitful to use such methods for computing preconditions for dense-time processes, in particular when discontinuities render sampling inadequate.

Similar observations apply to continuous-decision games. The max-min versions of the optimization problems yield the Hamilton-Jacobi(-Bellman)-Isaacs equations [Isa65, Lew94, BaC97, BaO98]. These can be solved by max-min variants of dense-time optimization methods. The iterative techniques used here present a similar structure (§ 4.3.3). In the case of continuous-decision games, the differential equations assume properties such as lower semicontinuity; in the case of discrete-decision games, the iterations assume monotonicity properties.

5.2 Contributions

In the proposed framework, coprocesses integrate atomic moves with durative ones, discrete-time dynamics with dense-time ones, and dynamics with their selection modes. As to constructive design, iterative techniques serve to synthesize guards which ensure basic dynamical properties. These techniques are based on fixed points as also used in game analysis. Complete, finite-memory winning-strategies can thus be generated iteratively for discrete-decision games with finite choice-sets and dense- or discrete-time dynamics.

The present results combine known ones, are not very original, treat limited problems so far, but may help to understand related approaches (§ 5.1). Note that a paper on the synthesis of correct guards for cooperative action-systems [vLS79] overlooks relevant previous work on the synthesis of winning strategies for noncooperative games [BüL69, TB70].

5.3 Further Work

Case studies A few examples were investigated while elaborating the framework and the synthesis techniques; they served both as guidelines and as test beds. Substantial case-studies should be developed too. They would foster a better grasp of the various approaches and improvements to methods of solution.

Framework It could prove fruitful to define coprocesses and specifications on the basis of temporal μ-calculi and ω-regular algebras [DN00, GTW02]. More properties of coprocesses should be established. Preconditions for processes and coprocesses could be defined in terms of sets of cones for coprocesses; such sets should then be given a general definition, after the example in § 3.2.1. The computation of preconditions $S.W$ should follow on an equal footing the structure of the coprocess S and that of the specification W. The relationships between discrete- and continuous-decision games should be analyzed thoroughly.

Unification We use one model, viz. that of discrete-decision coprocesses, two properties, viz. safety and reachability, and two forms of coprocesses to be iterated, viz. the sequential and concurrent ones. This yields two fixed-point equations and four solution techniques (§ 4), which have much in common. We may think of an integrated compositional method for a wider class of discrete-decision games. Other challenges exist: for instance, the use of stochastic processes; the unification and elaboration of analytical and computational methods for solving dense- and discrete-time problems efficiently; the synthesis of optimal strategies for quantitative games.

Time refinement The synthesis of winning moves is no less important than that of winning guards. The problem could be attacked by stepwise refinement as follows. Firstly, an abstract game is designed using a simple time-set. Secondly, a winning transform is synthesized. Thirdly, the winning transform is refined into a concrete game using a more detailed time-set. Process-based versions of refinement calculi should then be used [Lam94].

5.4 Conclusions

Discrete-decision games are characterized by the discreteness of strategic decisions made by players. The difference between discrete- and dense-time dynamics for players is secondary. In processes, time domains should thus be definable together with data domains.

Iterative approaches prove helpful: fixed-point definitions exhibit essential patterns and iterations provide a clear basis for effective procedures. Iterative schemes abstract differential ones; they should thus be investigated together.

Distinct frameworks are characterized by dense or discrete domains and by infinite or finite ones. Discrete-decision, finite-choice, dynamical games form just one class among many. This space should be explored systematically.

It is good to verify systems. It is better to verify systems or else to exhibit errors, as in model checking. It is still better to verify systems or else to remove errors, as in correctness-improving transformations. This is especially true if the thinking effort and computing cost appear comparable for these three modes of reasoning in system design.

Abstraction allows to analyze detailed, concrete systems in terms of simpler, qualitative ones [Bro03, CoC00, Hen00]. However, abstraction amounts to reverse refinement, the discovery of good abstractions appears as difficult as that of good refinements, and the techniques often prove related. It seems thus reasonable to consider synthesis and stepwise refinement on a par with analysis and stepwise abstraction.

The classical theory of interaction in systems is game theory. It is well-advised to take advantage of results in this field when developing models for cooperation and interaction. An example is the game-based approach for security problems. Clearly, the same holds wrt. control and optimization theory.

Dynamics of various kinds take part in the interactions between computing systems and their environments. Computing science should thus cooperate with mathematical analysis as actively as with algebra and logic. This would help to establish a scientific basis which can be shared by software engineering and classical engineering.

Acknowledgments

We gratefully acknowledge helpful comments by members of IFIP Working Group 2.3 on Programming Methodology, Jean-Raymond Abrial, a referee and Christophe Depasse.

References

[Abr96] Abrial, J.-R., *The B-Book*, Camdridge Univ. Press, Cambridge, 1996.

[AgS02] Agrachev, A.A., and Yu.L. Sachkov, *Control Theory from the Geometric Viewpoint*, Lecture Notes, Intern. School Advanced Studies, Trieste, 2002.

[AMP95] Asarin, E., O. Maler and A. Pnueli, Symbolic controller synthesis for discrete and timed systems, in: *Proc. 2nd Workshop Hybrid Systems*, LNCS 999, pp.1-20, Springer, Berlin, 1995.

[Asa00] Asarin, E., O. Bournez, T. Dang, O. Maler and A. Pnueli, Effective synthesis of switching controllers for linear systems, *Proc. IEEE 88*(7):1011-1025, 2000.

[Aub91] Aubin, J.-P., *Viability Theory*, Birkhaüser, Boston, 1991.

[BaC97] Bardi, M., and I. Capuzzo-Dolcetta, *Optimal Control and Viscosity Solutions of Hamilton-Jacobi-Bellman Equations*, Birkhaüser, Boston, 1997.

[BaO98] Başar, T., and G.J. Olsder, *Dynamic Noncooperative Game Theory*, Soc. Industr. and Appl. Math., Philadelphia, 1998.

[BaW98] Back, R.-J., and J. von Wright, *Refinement Calculus: A Systematic Introduction*, Springer, Berlin, 1998.

[BCT02] Bayen, A.M., E. Crück and C.J. Tomlin, Guaranteed overapproximations of unsafe sets for continuous and hybrid systems: solving the Hamilton-Jacobi equation using viability techniques, in: *Proc. 5th Workshop Hybrid Systems*, LNCS 2289, pp. 90-104, Springer, Berlin, 2002.

[Ber00] Berstekas, D.P., *Dynamic Programming and Optimal Control,* Athena Scientific, Belmont, Mass., 2nd ed., Vol.I, 2000, and Vol. II, 2001.

[BKS98] Barbeau, M., F. Kabanza, and R. St-Denis, A method for the synthesis of controllers to handle safety, liveness, and real-time constraints, *IEEE Trans. Automatic Control 43*(11): 1543-1559, 1998.

[Bro03] Broy, M., Abstractions from time, in: A. McIver and C. Morgan (eds.), *Programming Methodology,* pp. 95-107, Springer, Berlin, 2003.

[BüL69] Büchi, J.R., and L.H. Landweber, Solving sequential conditions for finite-state operators, *Trans. AMS 138*:259-311, 1969.

[CGP99] Clarke, E.M., O. Grumberg and D.A. Peled, *Model Checking,* MIT Press, Cambridge, 1999.

[Cha00] Chan, W., Temporal-logic queries, in: *Proc. 12th Conf. Computer-Aided Verification* , LNCS 1855, pp.450-463, Springer, Berlin, 2000.

[CoC00] Cousot, P., and R. Cousot, Temporal abstract interpretation, in: *Proc. 25th Symp. Principles Programming Lang.,* pp.12-25, ACM, New-York, 2000.

[Cou78] Cousot, P., *Méthodes Itératives de Construction et d'Approximation de Points Fixes d'Opérateurs Monotones sur un Treillis, Analyse Sémantique des Programmes,* Thèse de Doctorat Sci. Math., Univ. Sci. et Médicale de Grenoble, 1978.

[Dij76] Dijkstra, E.W., *A Discipline of Programming*, Prentice Hall, Englewood Cliffs, 1976.

[DN00] Davoren, J.M., and A. Nerode, Logics for hybrid systems, *Proc. IEEE 88*(7):985-1010, 2000.

[GTW02] Grädel, E., W. Thomas, and Th. Wilke (eds), *Automata, Logics, and Infinite Games,* LNCS 2500, Springer, Berlin, 2002.

[Har80] Harel, D., And/or programs: a new approach to structured programming, *ACM TOPLAS 2*(1):1-17, 1980.

[Hen00] Henzinger, Th.A., R. Majumdar, F. Mang and J.-F. Raskin, Abstract interpretation of game properties, in: *Proc. 7th Static Analysis Symp.*, LNCS 1824, pp.220-239, Springer, Berlin, 2000.

[HLM01] Heymann, M., F. Lin, and G. Meyer, Control of rate-bounded hybrid systems with liveness constraints, in: F. Colonius et al. (eds), *Advances in Mathematical Systems Theory,* pp.151-168, Birkhaüser, Boston, 2001.

[Hoa85] Hoare, C.A.R., *Communicating Sequential Processes*, Prentice Hall, Englewood Cliffs, 1985.

[Isa65] Isaacs, R., *Differential Games,* Wiley, New-York, 1965. Republished: Dover, New-York, 1999.

[Lam94] Lamport, L., The temporal logic of actions, *ACM Trans. Programming Languages and Systems 16(3):* 872-923, 1994.

[Lew94] Lewin, J., *Differential Games,* Springer, London, 1994.

[Lyg03] Lygeros, J., K.H. Johansson, S.N. Simić, J. Zhang and S.S. Sastry, Dynamical properties of hybrid automata, *IEEE Trans. Automatic Control 48(1):* 2-18, 2003.

[Mos98] Moszkowski, B., Compositional reasoning using interval temporal logic and Tempura, in: *Compositionality: The Significant Difference,* LNCS 1536, pp. 439-464, Springer, Berlin, 1998.

[MPS95] Maler, O., A. Pnueli, and J. Sifakis, On the synthesis of discrete controllers for timed systems, in: *Proc. 12th Symp. Theor. Aspects of Comput. Sci.*, LNCS 900, pp.229-242, Springer, Berlin, 1995.

[Ros98] Roscoe, A. W., *The Theory and Practice of Concurrency,* Prentice Hall, London, 1998.

[RW89] Ramadge, P.J., and W.M. Wonham, The control of discrete-event systems, *Proc. IEEE 77*: 81-98, 1989.

[Si96] Sintzoff, M., Abstract verification of structured dynamical systems, in: *Proc. 3rd Workshop Hybrid Systems*, LNCS 1066, pp.126-137, Springer, Berlin, 1996.

[TB70] Trakhtenbrot, B.A, and Ya. M. Barzdin, *Konechnye Avtomaty (Povedenie i Sintez)*, Nauka, Moscow, 1970. Engl. transl. by D. Louvish, ed. by E. Shamir and L.H. Landweber: *Finite Automata: Behaviour and Synthesis*, North-Holland, Amsterdam, 1973.

[Tho95] Thomas, W., On the synthesis of strategies in infinite games, in *Proc. 12th Symp. Theoret. Aspects Comput. Sci.,* LNCS 900, pp. 1-13, Springer, Berlin, 1995.

[TLS00] Tomlin, C.J., J. Lygeros and S.S. Sastry, A game-theoretic approach to controller design for hybrid systems, *Proc. IEEE 88*(7):949-970, 2000.

[vLS79] van Lamsweerde, A., and M. Sintzoff, Formal derivation of strongly correct concurrent programs, *Acta Informatica 12*: 1-31, 1979.

[Vin00] Vinter, R., *Optimal Control*, Birkhaüser, Boston, 2000.

Incremental Reasoning for Object Oriented Systems

Neelam Soundarajan and Stephen Fridella

Computer and Information Science
Ohio State University
Columbus, OH 43210
neelam@cis.ohio-state.edu and sfridell@emc.com

Abstract. Inheritance and polymorphism are key mechanisms of the object-oriented approach that enable designers to develop systems in an incremental manner. In this paper, we develop techniques for *reasoning incrementally* about the behavior of such systems. A derived class designer will be able, using the proposed approach, to arrive at the richer behavior that polymorphic methods inherited from the base class will exhibit in the derived class, without reanalyzing the code bodies of these methods. The approach is illustrated by applying it to a simple case study.
Keywords and phrases: Incremental design, Incremental reasoning, Behavior of polymorphic methods.

1 Introduction and Motivation

Much of the power of the OO approach derives from the key notions of *inheritance* and *polymorphism*. Given an existing *base class* B, a designer can use inheritance to build a new *derived class* D that extends B. Some of the methods of B are redefined in D while others are inherited unchanged; some methods may be *abstract*, i.e., have no associated definition, in B, and defined in D. Polymorphism[1] ensures that not just the methods redefined in D, but also other methods, these being the *polymorphic methods*, that invoke the redefined methods exhibit enriched behavior even though the polymorphic methods themselves are inherited unchanged from B. Inheritance and polymorphism were two of *Simula*'s [DN66, DMN68] fundamental contributions that have revolutionized software design. But if we are to be able to exploit the full potential of inheritance and polymorphism, we must not only be able to *build* systems incrementally, but also to *reason* about their behavior incrementally. Our goal in this paper is to investigate the problems involved in such incremental reasoning and to develop techniques to address them.

What information about the base class B does the designer of the derived class D need in order to reason incrementally about the behavior of D? Suppose

[1] In this paper, by *polymorphism* we will mean the *subtype polymorphism* of [CW85], implemented using run-time dispatch in standard OO languages.

O. Owe et al. (Eds.): From OO to FM (Dahl Festschrift), LNCS 2635, pp. 302–333, 2004.

$t()$ is a method of B and that it invokes another method $h()$ of B, and suppose $h()$ is redefined in the derived class D. If $t()$ is applied to an object of type D, the $h()$ that will be invoked during this execution of $t()$ will be the one defined in D (rather than the one in B). In a sense, the polymorphic method provides the pattern, or template, of the calls to the methods that are intended to be redefined as needed in the derived class, while the template itself is inherited unchanged. It is for this reason that polymorphic methods are called *template methods* in the design patterns literature [GHJV95], the methods they invoke being called *hook methods*, and we will use this terminology in the rest of the paper. If B includes *polymorphic* methods[2] such as $t()$, the designer of D not only needs to reason about the behavior of the methods she defines or redefines in D, but also about the modified behavior of the polymorphic methods of B resulting from redefinitions of methods that they invoke. One possibility would be for this designer to *reanalyze* the behavior of the body of $t()$ appealing, during this reanalysis, to the modified behavior of the redefined methods. While this would work, it is clearly not an incremental approach. Thus the central question we are interested in is the following:

> What information should we include in the (base-class) specification of the template method so that a derived class designer can, in a sense, "plug-into" this specification, the behaviors of the hook methods as defined in the derived class, to arrive at the enriched behavior that the template method would exhibit (when applied to instances of the derived class), without having to reanalyze the body of the template method?

Note that reanalysis of the template method bodies is not only undesirable, it may even be impossible if, for example, the template method is part of a base class that was purchased from a software vendor who, for proprietary reasons, did not provide access to the source code.

We will see the full details of our answer to this question later, but the key is to include, in its specification, information about which hook methods $t()$ invokes, the order it invokes them in, the arguments passed to the hook methods in these calls, etc. In order to provide this type of information, we will make use of a *trace*, denoted by the symbol τ (or sometimes τ_t), to record the hook method calls that $t()$ makes. The specification of $t()$, in particular its post-condition, will give us information not only about the final values of the member variables when $t()$ finishes but also about the value of τ, i.e., information about the identity of the hook methods $t()$ invoked during its execution, the values of the arguments it passed in these calls, etc. As we will see, the derived class designer can then plug into this specification, the behavior of the redefined hook methods to arrive at the corresponding new behavior of $t()$.

[2] In *Simula* and *C++*, $h()$ must have been flagged as *virtual*, else the $h()$ that is invoked during the execution of $t()$ would be the one defined in B. In languages like *Java* and *Eiffel*, all methods are virtual unless explicitly declared *final*. For concreteness, we occasionally use language-specific terminology but our approach is not language-specific. Note also that we use the terms 'method' and 'function' interchangeably.

There is one important requirement that these redefinitions must satisfy. Suppose that $h()$ is one of the hook methods $t()$ invokes. In arriving at the specification of $t()$ by analyzing its code in the base class, we would have made some assumptions about the effects of the call(s) to $h()$ contained in the body of $t()$. Typically, these would correspond to the behaviors exhibited by $h()$ as defined in the base class and (presumably) specified in the base class specification of $h()$. Unless the redefinition of $h()$ in the derived class satisfies its base class specification, this analysis of $t()$ may no longer be valid, and we would be forced to reanalyze the body of $t()$. Since we want to avoid such reanalysis, we will require the redefinition of $h()$ in the derived class to satisfy its base class specification.

Such a requirement is, in fact, not new to our work. It is the essential idea underlying the work on *behavioral subtyping* [Ame91, LW94, DL95]. Informally, a class A is a behavioral subtype[3] of another class B if the behavior exhibited by objects that are instances of A is in some sense consistent with behaviors allowed by the specification of class B, in other words, if the methods of class A satisfy the specifications of the corresponding methods of B. If A is a behavioral subtype of B, then any reasoning that we may have performed on a piece of code that includes calls to methods of B will continue to be valid if these calls are instead dispatched to the corresponding methods defined in A since in any such reasoning, we could only have appealed to the specifications of the methods in B and the methods defined in A satisfy these specifications. In our case, we want to be sure that whatever conclusions we have arrived at about the behavior of the template method $t()$, on the basis of the base class specifications of the hook method $h()$, continue to be valid in the derived class, so we must require that the derived class definition of $h()$ satisfy its base class specification.

What is new about our work is that, if this requirement is satisfied, then the "plugging-in" process we outlined above will allow us to arrive at the *richer* behavior that $t()$ acquires as a result of the redefinition of $h()$. Thus our work is in a sense a key extension of the behavioral subtyping approach: behavioral subtyping ensures that what we have already concluded (from the analysis of $t()$ in the base class) continues to hold following the redefinition of the hook methods in the derived class; our work allows us to reason about the richer behavior of $t()$ resulting from this redefinition. Since the very *raison d'être* of polymorphism is the ability to enrich the behavior of the polymorphic methods by suitable redefinitions of the hook methods, it is essential that the reasoning system enable us to reason about this enriched behavior. In Section 6, we will consider other related work in some detail.

---

[3] Although from a formal point of view *class* and *type* are distinct notions, in most standard OO languages, as well as in much of standard OO practice, the two notions are identified. Hence in this paper we will use the two terms interchangeably. More importantly, we will only be interested in the notions of *behavioral* subtype/subclass based on the behaviors of the methods of the classes in question, not in syntactic notions of subtype/subclass based on the signatures of the methods.

The main contributions of this paper may be summarized as follows:

– It identifies the key problems involved in specifying precisely the behavior of template methods and hook methods and in arriving at the derived-class behavior of a template method on the basis of its base class specification.
– It develops an incremental reasoning technique to allow the base class designer to specify the behavior of the methods of her class, and to allow the derived class designer to plug-in information about the hook methods redefined in the derived class into the bass-class-specifications of the template methods, to arrive at the derived-class behavior of these methods.
– It illustrates the reasoning technique by applying it to a simple case study.

The rest of the paper is organized as follows: In the next section, we introduce a simple OO language fragment focused on polymorphism. In the third and fourth sections, we develop our incremental reasoning systems for specifying and verifying the behaviors of programs written in this language. The fifth section presents a simple case study to illustrate our reasoning technique. The sixth section summarizes related work. The seventh section reiterates the importance of an incremental reasoning system for dealing with polymorphism, summarizes our approach to such a system, and discusses possible extensions.

2 Language and System Model

The qualification of a method as virtual in *Simula* or *C++*, and the complementary qualification of a method as final in *Java* or *Eiffel*, allow the compiler to determine whether or not run-time dispatching must be used in dealing with that method. For reasoning about the behavior of the methods, a more useful characterization is in terms of *hook* methods and *template* methods. Given that these notions were introduced in order to talk about the designs underlying particular OO systems, it should not be surprising that they are also useful in reasoning about the behavior of such systems. In this section we introduce a simple language notation and model that characterize methods in these terms; in the next two sections we will present our reasoning technique in terms of this model. The (partial) BNF grammar for our simple language appears in Figure 1; ε in these productions denotes the empty string; note also that the symbols "{" and "}" that appear in the productions are terminal symbols (rather than extended BNF symbols indicating repetition of the enclosed constructs).

The following points should be noted:

1. A base class definition specifies the name of the class, the member variables of the class, the constructor function, and the methods of the class. A derived class definition, in addition to the above, also specifies the name of the class it inherits from; note that we consider only single inheritance.
2. We assume that all member variables are *protected*, i.e., accessible to the derived class but not to client code; we also assume that all methods are *public*. Hence there are no keywords such as private or protected.

$$
\begin{aligned}
\langle \mathit{class} \rangle &::= \textsf{class}\ \langle \mathit{id} \rangle\ \{\ \langle \mathit{variables} \rangle\ \langle \mathit{constructor} \rangle\ \langle \mathit{methods} \rangle\ \} \\
&\quad\mid \textsf{class}\ \langle \mathit{id} \rangle\ :\ \langle \mathit{id} \rangle\ \{\ \langle \mathit{variables} \rangle\ \langle \mathit{constructor} \rangle\ \langle \mathit{methods} \rangle\ \} \\
\langle \mathit{variables} \rangle &::= \varepsilon \mid \langle \mathit{variable} \rangle\ \langle \mathit{variables} \rangle \\
\langle \mathit{variable} \rangle &::= \langle \mathit{simple\ type} \rangle\ \langle \mathit{id} \rangle; \\
\langle \mathit{constructor} \rangle &::= \langle \mathit{id} \rangle\ (\langle \mathit{parlist} \rangle)\ \{\langle \mathit{stmts} \rangle\} \\
\langle \mathit{methods} \rangle &::= \varepsilon \mid \langle \mathit{method} \rangle\ \langle \mathit{methods} \rangle \\
\langle \mathit{method} \rangle &::= \langle \mathit{method\ kind} \rangle\ \langle \mathit{id} \rangle\ (\langle \mathit{parlist} \rangle)\ \{\langle \mathit{stmts} \rangle\} \\
\langle \mathit{method\ kind} \rangle &::= \textsf{h-method} \mid \textsf{t-method} \mid \textsf{ht-method} \mid \textsf{nht-method}
\end{aligned}
$$

Fig. 1. (Partial) Grammar for simple OO language

3. Each class has a (single) constructor. The name of the constructor will, as usual, be the same as the name of the class. When an instance of a derived class is constructed, the base class constructor is executed first, then the derived class constructor. Classes do not have destructors.
4. A method may be a *hook method* (h-method), a *template method* (t-method), a *hook-template method* (ht-method), or a *non-hook-template method* (nht-method). Run-time dispatching is done for h-methods and ht-methods but not for t-methods or nht-methods. h-methods and nht-methods may invoke only nht-methods; t-methods and ht-methods may invoke h-methods, ht-methods, and nht-methods.
5. Only h-methods and ht-methods may be redefined in a derived class; t- and nht-methods must be inherited unchanged. When a method is redefined, no changes may be made in the number and types of parameters it expects.
6. All member variables of a class are of simple types such as integer, boolean, etc. So an object will not contain references to other objects. The problem with allowing references to other objects is that this can lead to *aliasing* which presents some well-known problems when reasoning about behavior; since these problems are not directly related to inheritance and polymorphism which is the focus of our work, we feel it is appropriate to eliminate aliasing from the picture.
7. The parameters (other than the self object) to a method are of simple types and are all passed by-value-result. Here again allowing for passing by-reference could lead to aliasing which we wish to avoid.

Our h- and ht-methods are like the *virtual / non-final / non-frozen* methods of *Simula, C++, Java* or *Eiffel* respectively, while the t- and nht-methods are like *non-virtual / final / frozen* methods. *Simula* and *C++* allow non-virtual methods to be redefined in the derived class but such redefinitions have no effect on base class (template) methods that invoke them; we could have similarly allowed our nht-methods to be redefined without this having an effect on the t- and ht-methods that invoke them; the changes in our reasoning technique to deal with this would be straightforward. Alternately, and more importantly, we could have treated *all* methods as ht-methods. While this would be general, it would also make the reasoning task unnecessarily complex since ht-methods are the most difficult to reason about. This is similar to a base class designer flagging appropriate methods as *final*, rather than leaving, in the name of generality, every method open to redefinition in the derived classes. One point of terminology: henceforth, we will use the term '*hook method*' to mean 'h-method or ht-method', since these are the two kinds of methods in our language that can be used to serve the role that hook methods are intended to serve; similarly, we will use '*template method*' to mean 't-method or ht-method'.

Most OO languages allow the hook methods to be *abstract* in the base class; indeed, in *Simula*, a method that is defined in the class cannot be flagged as virtual. For simplicity, we do not allow such methods in our language fragment but our reasoning technique can deal with such methods, as well as with *Java*-type *interfaces* where all the methods are abstract, in a natural manner. One other point worth noting is that a compiler for the language could easily ensure that the conditions on which types of methods may be invoked by a method of a given type are indeed satisfied (or, if not, produce appropriate error messages), and ensure, in the object code, that run-time dispatching is used for the appropriate types of methods; this is no different than a *Simula* or *C++* compiler ensuring that run-time dispatching is used for *virtual* methods but not for non-virtual methods.

We conclude this section with an Account class written in our language notation. This class, in Figure 2, will serve as the base class for our case study later in the paper where we will demonstrate the application of our reasoning technique. Account has a single member variable balance that maintains the current balance in the account; the derived classes we define later will introduce additional variables. The deposit() and withdraw() operations update balance in the expected manner; these are h-methods and will be redefined in the derived class(es) to provide richer behavior. The getInfo() operation returns, as a string, the current balance in the account; note that string() returns the string representation of the value of its (integer) argument. getInfo() is also an h-method and will be redefined in the derived class; in fact, it is via this redefinition that we will be able to see, so to speak, the enriched behaviors of the other operations. It is with an eye toward this redefinition that we have defined getInfo() to return a result of type string (rather than int).

The template method that will invoke these h-methods is processTransSeq(). This method will allow us (i.e., the client code) to process a sequence of transaction requests, each request being for one of deposit, withdraw, or printInfo transactions. processTransSeq() has two string arguments, transs which will contain all the transaction requests, and results via which the method will return the result. processTransSeq() repeatedly reads the next transaction request from transs and processes it. In order to avoid getting involved with issues of string manipulation, we make use of a set of functions (whose definitions we omit) that allow us to extract individual transaction requests and conveniently manipulate them; thus NextTrans(transs) is the first transaction in transs; RestTrans(transs) is the string consisting of all the remaining transactions (beyond the first one); TransName(nextReq), where nextReq is a single transaction request, is the name of the transaction ("deposit", "withdraw", or "printInfo"); and

```
class Account {
    int balance;  // current balance

    Account(int b) { balance := b; }
    h-method deposit(int amt) { balance := balance + amt; }
    h-method withdraw(int amt) { balance := balance − amt; }
    h-method string getInfo() { return string(balance); }
    t-method processTransSeq( string transs, string results) {
        results := ⟨⟩;
        while( transs ≠ ⟨⟩ )
          { nextReq := NextTrans( transs ); transs := RestTrans( transs );
            trans := TransName( nextReq ); amount := Amount( nextReq );
            if( trans == "deposit" ) { deposit( amount ); }
            if( trans == "withdraw" ) { withdraw( amount ); }
            if( trans == "printInfo" ) { results += "<";
                                  results +=getInfo(); results += ">"; } }
    }
}
```

Fig. 2. Class *Account*

Amount(nextReq), is the amount involved in the transaction (0 if the type of transaction is "getInfo")[4].

If the next transaction requested is "deposit" or "withdraw", processTransSeq() invokes the corresponding operation. If the transaction requested is "printInfo", processTransSeq() calls getInfo() and appends the returned result to results (enclosing this inside a pair of angle brackets, "¡" and "¿" to separate this result from the previous result in results); note that "+=" is the string append operator. This means that depending on the derived class design, when this transaction is processed, appropriate information about that particular type of account, as implemented in the (re-)definition of getInfo() in the derived class, will be appended to results. The key reasoning questions are, what information do we include in the base class specification of processTransSeq(), and how, from this specification and the derived class behaviors of the h-methods, can the derived class designer arrive at this richer behavior of processTransSeq(), as exhibited in the value it returns in results? We will see the answers to these questions in the case study section.

3 Reasoning About the Base Class

Consider a base class B. The specification of B will consist of an invariant I_b and specifications for each of its methods. I_b, an assertion over the state, i.e.,

---

[4] Good OO design principles suggest that it would probably make sense to introduce an auxiliary class, Transaction, into which methods such as NextTrans() can be collected but in the interest of space, we will not do so. Note also that we have omitted the declarations of local variables, nextReq, trans, and amount, in processTransSeq().

the member variables of B, will be satisfied at the start and end of execution of each method. Next, consider the various kinds of methods. Suppose $n()$ is an nht-method. Its specification will be of the usual form:

$$\langle pre.n(), post.n()\rangle \tag{1}$$

where the pre-condition $pre.n()$ is an assertion over the state, and the parameters passed to $n()$ at the time that $n()$ starts execution, and the post-condition $post.n()$ is an assertion over the state and the parameters to $n()$ at the time it starts execution and at the time it finishes execution. In the post-condition, we will use the *OCL* [WK99] notation $x@pre$ to refer to the value of the variable x at the time $n()$ starts, and x to refer to its value when $n()$ finishes execution.

The specification of h-methods is similar. The difference between these two types of methods will show up when we consider derived classes in the next section. For nht-methods, we will essentially inherit the specification from the base class since these methods cannot be redefined in the derived class; for h-methods, we will either inherit the base class specification if the method is not redefined, or come up with an appropriate new specification if the method is redefined.

Next consider a t-method $t()$. We will associate two specifications with $t()$. The first, its *functional-* or *f-specification*, will be similar to (1) and will specify the effect of of $t()$ on member variables of B and the parameters of $t()$. The second, its *enrichment-* or *e-specification*, will be for use by the derived class designer and will include information about invocations of hook methods. We will use τ, the *trace* (or *sequence*), to record this information, and the e-specification will give us information about the value of τ:

$$\begin{array}{ll} \textit{F-specification:} & \langle pre.t(), vbpost.t()\rangle \\ \textit{E-specification:} & \langle epre.t(), epost.t()\rangle \end{array} \tag{2}$$

At its start, $t()$ has not yet invoked any h- methods so τ at that point will be the empty sequence ε. $epost.t()$ will give us information about the values of the member variables of B, of $t()$'s parameters, and of course about the value of τ when $t()$ finishes execution. Thus the relation that must hold between the assertions of the f- and e-specifications is as follows:

$$\begin{array}{ll} epre.t() & \equiv (pre.t() \wedge (\tau = \varepsilon)) \\ epost.t() & \Rightarrow post.t() \end{array} \tag{3}$$

What information concerning calls to *hook methods* (i.e., h- and ht- methods) that $t()$ makes should we include in τ? A few examples will help us answer this question. Suppose B consists of just two methods, $t()$ and an h-method $h1()$. Suppose $h1()$, as defined in B, makes no changes to the values of any of the member variables of B. Suppose in a derived class D we introduce a new (integer) variable i and redefine $h1()$ to increment i by 1 (and leave the other member variables, inherited from B, unchanged). If $t()$ is applied to an instance of D, during this execution of $t()$, calls to $h1()$ will be dispatched to the one defined in D, and hence this call to $t()$ will increment i (which is a component of the object

$t()$ is applied to since this object is an instance of D) by an amount equal to the number of times $t()$ invokes $h1()$. In order to enable the derived class designer to arrive at the value that i will be incremented by during such an execution of $t()$ *without reanalyzing the body of* $t()$, the base class specification of $t()$ would therefore have to include information about how many times $t()$ invokes hook methods.

It is easy to see that this alone is not sufficient in general. Suppose in this example that there were *two* h-methods $h1()$ and $h2()$, and that $t()$ invokes each of them several times. Suppose $h1()$ is redefined in D to increment i by 1 as before, and $h2()$ is redefined to increment i by 2. Then, in order to know what effect an execution of $t()$ (applied to an instance of D) will have on i, we need to know how many times $t()$ invokes $h1()$ and how many times it invokes $h2()$, rather than just the combined total of the two. But this is also insufficient in general. Suppose that two variables i, j are introduced in D and that while $h1()$, as before, increments i by 1 each time it is invoked, $h2()$ does not change i but increments j by the current value of i, i.e., the value that i had at the time of this invocation of $h2()$. Then the effect that an execution of $t()$ has on j will depend not only on how many times $h1()$ and $h2()$ are invoked but also on how these invocations are *interleaved*; for example, if $t()$ were to invoke $h1()$ twice and $h2()$ once during its execution, then during this execution the value of j would increase by $i@pre$, or $i@pre+1$, or $i@pre+2$, where as noted earlier $i@pre$ denotes the value of i at the start of this execution of $t()$, depending respectively on whether $t()$ invokes $h2()$ before calling $h1()$, or after the first call to $h1()$, or after the second call to $h1()$.

Hence we need to be able to provide information about the *order* of the calls $t()$ makes to the hook methods. This is still insufficient. Suppose, we revise the example so that $h2()$ (as defined in D) increments j not by i but by $(i + k)$ where k is a member variable of B. Now it is quite possible that $t()$ has changed the value of k before calling $h2()$ and that it will change it further once the call from $h2()$ returns. In this case, to arrive at the effect that $t()$ will have on j without reanalyzing its body, we will need to know what value $t()$ has left in k immediately before the call to $h2()$. In general, we would need to know the entire 'state', i.e., the values of all member variables of B, before each call $t()$ makes to a hook method, and this information will have to be recorded in τ. It turns out that we also need to record the state immediately *following* the return from each call to a hook method; this is because it is possible that the hook method might, according to its specification, assign one of two different values to one of the member variables (of B) and what $t()$ does following the return from the hook method, including what other hook methods it calls, might depend on this value; so in order to be able to relate the values in these variables to what these later calls might do (including, in particular, assigning values to other member variables, some of which might be introduced in the derived class), we need to record in τ the state following each hook method call. Finally, if the hook method receives any additional parameters, we also need to record the values of these arguments and the results returned by the hook method since, as in the case of the values of member variables of B, what $t()$ does following the return will, in general, depend on these results.

To record all this information, we will use the following structure for the sequence τ. Each element of τ will represent one call to a hook method and the corresponding return. As noted earlier, at the start of the execution of $t()$, τ will be the empty sequence ε. Suppose at some point in this execution the current state, i.e., the values of all member variables of B, is σ', and $t()$ invokes an h-method $h()$, the values of the additional arguments passed to $h()$ being $\overline{aa}'$; and suppose that the state when $h()$ returns is σ, and the result values of the additional parameters are $\overline{aa}$. Then this call-return will be recorded in τ as the element:

$$(h,\ \sigma',\ \overline{aa}',\ \sigma,\ \overline{aa}) \tag{4}$$

If $h()$ were an ht- rather than an h-method, we would again record the same information in τ about a call from $t()$ to $h()$. Note that in this case, during its execution, $h()$ may in turn invoke another h-method (or ht-method), call it $g()$. Although this call to $g()$ did arise as a result of the original call that $t()$ made to $h()$, the call to $g()$ will *not* be recorded in the trace of $t()$ (it will, of course, be recorded in the trace of $h()$). If $g()$ were to be redefined in the derived class, the derived class designer would be able, as we will see in detail in the next section, to arrive incrementally at the resulting enriched behavior of $h()$ on the basis of the e-specification of $h()$ (and the information that specification provides about the calls to $g()$ that $h()$ makes), and *then* arrive at the enriched behavior of $t()$ on the basis of the e-specification of $t()$ and the information it provides about the calls that $t()$ makes to $h()$. Thus the enrichment in the behavior of $t()$ arises because of the enrichment in the behavior of $h()$; whether that latter enrichment is due to a redefinition of $h()$ in the derived class or due to a redefinition of an h-method that $h()$ invokes is not relevant when reasoning about the enriched behavior of $t()$. In other words, the functioning of $t()$ depends only on what the call to $h()$ does and what enrichment is done to this behavior of $h()$, not *how* that enrichment is achieved, so we only need record the call to $h()$ in the trace of $t()$, not the calls to h-methods that $h()$ in turn may make.

So much for the structure of τ. In what form should information about τ be included in $epost.t()$, the e-post-condition of $t()$? One extreme approach would be to explicitly list, in $epost.t()$, all the possible values τ could have when $t()$ finishes, i.e., list all the different sequences of hook method calls that $t()$ could have gone through during its execution, and for each, provide complete information about each component of each element of τ. While this would work, doing it naively would generally be far too tedious. A better approach is to define suitable functions, the details of which may depend on the particular application, on τ, and write the specification in terms of these functions; we will see in our case study.

Further, it is usually not necessary to provide complete information about τ. This depends in part upon the kind of enrichments the base class designer expects will be made in the derived classes. If, for example, in the case of the Account class defined in the last section, we do not expect the hook methods to be redefined in such a way as to depend on the value of balance at the time that the hook method is invoked, then there is no need to include information about this in specifying the t-method processTransSeq(). On the flip-side, if the derived class designer *does* redefine a hook method in such a way that its enriched behavior critically depends on the value of balance, she would be unable to reason incrementally about the corresponding enriched behavior of processTransSeq(). We will return to this point later.

How do we show that $t()$ meets its specifications? The main problem has to do with showing that the body of $t()$ meets its e-specification because once we do that, we simply need to check that the relation specified in (3) holds in order to conclude that $t()$ meets its f-specification as well. When reasoning about the body of $t()$, we use standard axioms and rules for dealing with standard statements such as assignment and *if-else*. The one statement for which we need a new rule is call to h-method (or ht-method), to account for recording on τ, information about the call.

R1. h/ht- **Method Call**

$$\frac{\begin{array}{l} p \Rightarrow (I_b \wedge pre.h(\overline{x})[\overline{x} \leftarrow \overline{aa}]) \\ [(\exists\sigma', \overline{aa}').[\, p[\tau \leftarrow abl(\tau),\, \sigma \leftarrow \sigma',\, \overline{aa} \leftarrow \overline{aa}'] \\ \qquad \wedge\, post.h(\overline{x})[\sigma@pre \leftarrow \sigma',\, \overline{x}@pre \leftarrow \overline{aa}',\, \overline{x} \leftarrow \overline{aa}] \wedge I_b \\ \qquad \wedge\, last(\tau) = (h, \sigma', \overline{aa}', \sigma, \overline{aa})\,]\,] \;\Rightarrow\; q \end{array}}{\{\, p \,\}\; h(\overline{aa});\; \{\, q \,\}}$$

$h()$ is the method being called, $\overline{aa}$ being the (additional) arguments for this call. The first antecedent of **R1** requires us to show that if the assertion p which is the pre-condition of the call is satisfied, then I_b, the invariant of B is satisfied; and the pre-condition *pre.h*() of the (f-)specification of the method[5] is satisfied with the actual arguments ($\overline{aa}$) substituting for the formal parameters ($\overline{x}$); "$\leftarrow$" denotes (simultaneous) substitution of all occurrences, in the given assertion, of the variable(s) on the left side of the "$\leftarrow$" by the expression(s) on the right. The second antecedent requires us to show that we have added a new element to τ corresponding to this call and that the state at this point (and the returned values of the arguments) satisfy the post-condition of the call to $h()$. $last(\tau)$, as the name suggests, is the last, i.e. the rightmost, element of τ; $abl(\tau)$ stands for "*all but the last element of* τ" and is the sequence obtained from τ by omitting its last element. In more detail, in this antecedent, σ' denotes the state that existed immediately before the call to $h()$ and $\overline{aa}'$ the values of the arguments at that point; so this antecedent requires us to show that: if the state (and argument values) that existed immediately before the call and the trace, less

[5] If $h()$ is an ht-method, it will have, as we will see shortly, both an f- and an e-specification in the same manner as t-methods. But as far as $t()$ is concerned, only the functional effect of $h()$ is relevant; thus the pre- and post- assertions referred to in the antecedents of **R1** are from $h()$'s f-specification.

its last element, satisfy the assertion that is the pre-condition of the call; and if the post-condition of the f-specification of $h()$ is satisfied with appropriate substitutions for the before- and after-states and argument values; and if the class invariant is satisfied; and if the (newly added) last element of τ consists of the name of the called method (h), the state (σ') immediately before the call, the initial value ($\overline{aa}'$) of the arguments, the state (σ) immediately after the return from h, and the final values of the arguments ($\overline{aa}$); Then it must be the case that the specified post-condition q of this call to $h()$ is also satisfied. If these two antecedents can be shown then, by appealing to the rule, we may derive the specified conclusion.

Although the rule looks rather involved, the complexity is mostly notational. It just captures the fact that the effect of the call to $h()$ is to modify the values of the member variables of B and the arguments passed to $h()$ as specified in the (functional) post-condition of $h()$, and to append an appropriate element to τ to represent the call/return. In practice, in reasoning about the body of $t()$, we encounter such a call we would typically simply write appropriate pre- and post-conditions for the call statement and check semi-formally that what these assertions say about the changes in the values of the member variables of B, the values of the arguments to $h()$, and the value of τ, are consistent with what the f-specification of $h()$ says will be the effect of the method on the members of B and the parameters to $h()$, and with recording this call/return on τ.

The final type of method is the ht-method. Suppose *ht*() is such a method. Its specification will be similar to that of a t-method. In other words, *ht*() will have f- and e-specifications. The former specifies the effect of an execution of *ht*() on the member variables of B and the parameters of *ht*(), and the latter provides information also about the calls that *ht*() makes to hook methods during its execution. The key difference with t-methods will show up when we consider derived classes. For t-methods, we will use the e-specification from the base class and arrive at its enriched behavior (and the corresponding f-specification) by appealing to the richer behavior of the hook methods it invokes. We will do the same also for ht-methods that are inherited unchanged from the base class. But if an ht-method is redefined in the derived class, we will come up with appropriate new f- and e-specifications.

Let us now briefly turn to invariants. In our system, when reasoning about the base class B, we use a standard approach to dealing with invariants. In other words, for each method $f()$, the result we establish for S, the body of $f()$ is:

$$\{ I_b \wedge pre.f() \} \; S \; \{ I_b \wedge post.f() \} \tag{5}$$

where I_b is the invariant for B. Further, when establishing this result, for dealing with calls in S to other methods (either nht-methods or hook methods) of B, we must check that not only is the pre-condition of the method being called satisfied but also the invariant; and, conversely, we may assume, when the method call returns, that not only will the method's post-condition be satisfied but also the invariant. Any functions redefined in a derived class D of B will also have to maintain this invariant (since otherwise, if $f()$ were a t-method and one of the calls in S is dispatched to such a redefined method, the assumption made in establishing (5) that I_b will hold when this call returns will no longer be valid); we will formalize this requirement in the next section. One type of method we have not considered so far is constructors. Clearly, we must check that each constructor $c()$ of B is such that when it finishes execution, I_b is satisfied. The final step in reasoning about B is to ensure that it meets its *abstract specification*, intended for use by clients of B. This can be done in a standard fashion, see for example [Jon90]; inheritance and polymorphism do not add any complexity to these issues, so we will not discuss them further.

We conclude this section with a comment about our trace τ. τ is like an *auxiliary variable* of Owicki and Gries [OG76], but there are some differences. In systems such as those of [OG76], we are allowed, when reasoning about the behavior of a piece of code, to introduce as many auxiliary variables of whatever types as we wish; we also have to introduce suitable assignment statements (into the code whose behavior we are reasoning about) to update the values of the auxiliary variables at appropriate points as we wish. By contrast, in our system, τ is the only additional variable; its structure is fixed, as specified in (4); the updates to τ take place automatically with each call that $t()$ makes to a hook method; this is represented in our system by the rule **R1**. Note also that τ is *not* a member variable of the class; it only records the calls that this method $t()$ makes to h- and ht- methods during one particular execution; thus, τ is like a local variable of $t()$, initialized, as specified in (3), to ε at the start of this execution. Its purpose is not so much to help reason about the behavior of the base class B as to provide more information in the e-specification of $t()$ than can be provided using just the member variables of B. And the purpose of providing this extra information is to enable us to arrive at the richer behavior of $t()$ that results from redefinitions, in a derived class of B, of one or more of the methods that $t()$ invokes, without having to reanalyze the body of $t()$. Thus while Owicki-Gries type auxiliary variables are introduced to help in reasoning about the behavior of the piece of code under consideration, we have introduced τ to help the derived class designer to reason incrementally about the behavior of her derived class.

4 Incremental Reasoning About the Derived Class

Let D be a derived class of B. In our skeletal language, as in most standard OO languages, the designer of D may introduce new member variables in D, define entirely new methods, or redefine hook methods inherited from the base class; nht-methods and t-methods must be inherited unchanged. For methods that are newly defined in D, we use the same approach as in B. From the point of view of *incremental* reasoning, the key question is how to arrive at the richer behavior of inherited template methods without reanalyzing the body of the template method. This question will be the main focus of this section but we start our discussion with the relation between the invariants for B and D and then consider ways to reason about each type of method.

Let I_b, I_d be the invariants for B, D. Since some of the methods will be inherited unchanged from B, and since these methods require I_b to be satisfied before they start execution, we will require the following:

$$I_d \Rightarrow I_b \tag{6}$$

And in order to ensure that each method in D, including the inherited ones, leave I_d satisfied when they finish execution, we will have to impose further conditions on the specifications for the individual methods as we will see below. (6) will be part of the *behavioral subclassing* relation to be defined shortly.

Suppose $n()$ is an nht-method inherited from B. The (concrete) specification of $n()$, as a method of D, will be in terms of the overall state, i.e., the values of the member variables defined in D as well as those inherited from B. For convenience, in our discussion below, we will use σ to denote the overall state, $\sigma \downarrow b$ to denote the portion of the state inherited from B, and $\sigma \downarrow d$ the portion defined in D. Let $\langle pre.B.n(), post.B.n() \rangle$ be the specification of $n()$ in the base class B. Since the method is inherited unchanged by D, execution of $n()$ cannot change the value of any variable introduced in D, i.e., the value of $\sigma \downarrow d$ when $n()$ finishes execution will be the same as when it started. Hence, $\langle pre.D.n(), post.D.n() \rangle$, the specification of $n()$ in D, follows from its base class specification if the following conditions are satisfied:

$$\begin{aligned} &(pre.D.n() \wedge I_d) \;\Rightarrow pre.B.n() \\ &(post.B.n() \wedge I_b \wedge (pre.D.n() \wedge I_d)[\sigma \leftarrow \sigma@pre] \wedge (\sigma \downarrow d = \sigma \downarrow d@pre)) \\ &\qquad\qquad \Rightarrow (post.D.n() \wedge I_d) \end{aligned} \tag{7}$$

If $pre.D.n()$ is satisfied when $n()$ is invoked, the relation between the pre-conditions ensures that $pre.B.n()$ will be satisfied at that point. Hence, given that we have checked (when reasoning about the base class) that the body of $n()$ satisfies its base class specification, the assertion $post.B.n()$ (and I_b) will be satisfied when $n()$ finishes execution. In addition, the clause $(\sigma \downarrow d = \sigma \downarrow d@pre)$ which is essentially an abbreviation for a set of clauses that assert, for each member variable introduced in D, that its value is unchanged from its value at the start of $n()$, will also be satisfied since these variables are unaffected by $n()$. The clause $(pre.D.n() \wedge I_d)[\sigma \leftarrow \sigma@pre]$ asserts that the state, including the values of the variables introduced in D, at the time $n()$ started execution satisfies the (new) pre-condition and invariant. Note that $pre.D.n()$ may include conditions on the values of the variables introduced in D. In that case, the assertion $(\sigma \downarrow d = \sigma \downarrow d@pre)$ will allow us to carry these conditions forward to $post.D.n()$. This may be of help in showing, as required by (7), that I_d will hold at that point.

Next consider $h()$, an h-method. If $h()$ is inherited unchanged, we treat it in the same way as an nht-method. If $h()$ *is* redefined in D, the derived class designer will have to come up with a new specification, $\langle pre.D.h(), post.D.h() \rangle$, and check (or formally verify) that the redefined method satisfies this specification (as well as I_d, as required by (5)). In either case, we also need to impose a requirement of behavioral consistency with the base class specification $\langle pre.B.h(), post.B.h() \rangle$

of $h()$ since otherwise any reasoning that we have done (concerning the behavior template methods that invoke $h()$) on the basis of that specification may no longer be valid.

Definition: The derived class D is a *behavioral subclass* of its base class B if the following conditions are satisfied:

$$I_d \Rightarrow I_b$$

If $h()$ is an h-method or an ht-method, then

$$(pre.B.h() \wedge I_b) \Rightarrow (pre.D.h() \wedge I_d)$$
$$(post.D.h() \wedge I_d) \Rightarrow post.B.h() \tag{8}$$

We require, as part of our reasoning system, that D be a *behavioral subclass*[6] of B.

Consider a call to $h()$ in a t-method, $t()$. In D, this call will be dispatched to the $h()$ defined in D; so when the call returns, $(post.D.h() \wedge I_d)$ will be satisfied and hence, by the relation between post-conditions and invariants required by (8), so will $(post.B.h() \wedge I_b)$ which is what we must have assumed when reasoning about $t()$ in the base class. Thus behavioral subclassing ensures that the reasoning we have performed in the base class about a method that calls $h()$ continues to be valid although $h()$ has been redefined in the derived class. Note also that in order for $post.D.h()$ to be satisfied when $D.h()$ finishes execution, $(pre.D.h() \wedge I_d)$ must have been satisfied at the time of the call to $h()$; the relation required by (8) between the pre-conditions and invariants, given that when reasoning in the base class about the calls in $t()$ to $h()$ we must have checked that $(pre.B.h() \wedge I_b)$ is satisfied immediately prior to each of these calls, ensures this. It is worth noting that (8) imposes severe constraints on the derived class. In particular, the relation that (8) requires between the base class pre-condition & invariant and the derived class pre-condition & invariant means that the derived-class pre-condition of $h()$ cannot impose any requirements on the values of member variables that may be introduced in D. Nevertheless, by using the *@pre* notation to refer to the values of variables at the start of $h()$, we will be able, in $post.D.h()$, to specify how $D.h()$ changes the values of variables introduced in D; and the rule **R2** will allow us to appeal to this information to arrive at the effect that $t()$ has on these variables. In more detail, we will look at each element in the trace τ of $t()$, and add, to the base-class specification of $t()$, the assertion that the states and argument values recorded in this particular element of τ satisfies the derived class post-condition of the h-method invoked. Suppose the kth element of τ is $(h, \sigma 1, \overline{aa}1, \sigma 2, \overline{aa}2)$, then:

a. We can assert $post.D.h()$ with $\sigma 1$ and $\sigma 2$ playing the roles respectively of the state immediately before the call and the state immediately after the call, and $\overline{aa}1$ and $\overline{aa}2$ being the argument values before and after the call.

[6] (8) is very similar to behavioral subtyping [LW93, LW94]; nevertheless we use a different term since behavioral subtyping is a relation that involves the abstract specifications of two classes while ours is a relation between the concrete specifications of a base class and its derived class.

b. We can assert that the D-portion of the state can change only due to calls to h/ht-methods since $t()$ was defined as part of the base class so its code cannot refer to this portion of the state. Thus if σp is the 'final state' of the *previous* element of τ, i.e., is the fourth component of the $(k-1)^{th}$ element of τ, then we must have $(\sigma p \downarrow d = \sigma 1 \downarrow d)$; similarly if σn is the 'initial state' of the *next* element of τ, i.e., is the second component of the $(k+1)^{st}$ element of τ, then $(\sigma 2 \downarrow d = \sigma n \downarrow d)$.

Rule **R2** below formalizes these ideas. The following functions and predicates on traces, trace elements and their components, etc., will be useful in expressing this formalization:

$|\tau|$**:** Length of τ, i.e., number of elements in τ.
$\tau[k]$**:** The kth element of τ.
$\tau[k]$***.hm*:** The identity of the hook method called in the kth element of τ.
$\tau[k]$***.is*:** The initial state, i.e., the state just before this call.
$\tau[k]$***.fs*:** The final state, i.e., the state just after the method returns.
$\tau[k]$***.ia*:** The values of the arguments passed in this call.
$\tau[k]$***.fa*:** The values of the arguments when the method returns.
$\tau \downarrow b$**:** Same as τ except that in each 'state' component of each element of τ, we only retain the base-class portion of the state; similarly $\tau \downarrow d$ is obtained from τ by retaining, in each 'state' component of each element of τ, only the portion of the state introduced in the derived class. Naturally, $\downarrow b$ and $\downarrow d$ operations are applicable only to traces at the derived class level.

ncbc$(\sigma i, \tau, \sigma f)$: *ncbc*() denotes "no change between calls"; i.e., the D-portion of the state does not change between calls to hook methods. σi is the initial state, i.e., the state at the start of $t()$, and σf the final state, i.e., the state at the end of $t()$. More formally:

$$
\begin{aligned}
&ncbc(\sigma i, \tau, \sigma f) \equiv \\
&\quad ((|\tau| = 0) \Rightarrow (\sigma i \downarrow d = \sigma f \downarrow d)) \\
&\quad \wedge (((|\tau| > 0) \Rightarrow ((\sigma i \downarrow d = \tau[1].is \downarrow d) \wedge (\sigma f \downarrow d = \tau[|\tau|].fs \downarrow d) \wedge \\
&\qquad\qquad (\forall j : (1 \le j < |\tau|) :: (\tau[j].fs \downarrow d = \tau[j+1].is \downarrow d))))
\end{aligned}
$$

Since σi is the state that $t()$ starts in, the $\downarrow d$ portion of the state just before the first call recorded in τ will be same as the $\sigma i \downarrow d$ since the portion of $t()$ that precedes this call cannot have modified it. Similarly, the $\downarrow d$ portion of the state when $t()$ finishes execution will be same as the $\downarrow d$ portion of the state immediately after the last call recorded in τ. This explains the first two clauses in the case that $(|\tau| > 0)$. The third clause states that the $\downarrow d$ portion of the 'initial state' recorded in the $(j+1)^{st}$ call is the same as the $\downarrow d$ of the 'final state' recorded in the jth call. If $(|\tau| = 0)$, the $\downarrow d$ portion of the final state when $t()$ finishes is the same as $\downarrow d$ of the state at the start of $t()$ since no hook methods are invoked.

ccds(τ, k): *ccds*() denotes "change (in state) recorded in the kth element of τ is consistent with *d*erived-class *s*pecification (of the hook method)"; i.e., the states and argument values recorded in the kth element of τ is consistent with the f-specification, in the derived class, of the hook method invoked in this element. More formally:

$$ccds(\tau, k) \equiv (post.D.\tau[k].hm()[\overline{xx}@pre \leftarrow \tau[k].ia,\ \sigma@pre \leftarrow \tau[k].is,\ \overline{xx} \leftarrow \tau[k].fa,\ \sigma \leftarrow \tau[k].fs] \wedge I_d[\sigma \leftarrow \tau[k].fs])$$

ccds() asserts that the initial and final values of the arguments and initial and final states recorded in $\tau[k]$ satisfy the conditions that the derived class f-post-condition imposes on the initial and final values of its parameters and the initial and final states when the method begins and ends. *This* is what will allow us to arrive at the richer behavior of $t()$ by appealing to the richer behavior of the redefined $\tau[k].hm$ as expressed in its derived class f-post-condition.

With these preliminaries out of the way, we can present the main rule **R2** that makes it possible to reason incrementally in our system. The rule requires us

R2. Enrichment Rule

$$\frac{\begin{array}{l}(epre.D.t() \wedge I_d) \Rightarrow epre.B.t() \\ {[epost.B.t()[\tau \leftarrow \tau\!\downarrow\! b,\ \sigma \leftarrow \sigma\!\downarrow\! b,\ \sigma@pre \leftarrow \sigma@pre\!\downarrow\! b]} \\ \quad \wedge\ (pre.D.t() \wedge I_d)[\sigma \leftarrow \sigma@pre] \\ \quad \wedge\ ncbc(\sigma@pre, \tau, \sigma) \wedge (\forall k : (1 \leq k \leq |\tau|) :: ccds(\tau, k))] \ \Rightarrow\ (I_d \wedge epost.D.t())\end{array}}{\langle epre.D.t(), epost.D.t()\rangle}$$

to establish the specified antecedents in order to conclude the derived-class e-specification for $t()$. The first antecedent requires us to show that if a state satisfies the derived-class pre-condition of $t()$, it also satisfies the base-class pre-condition. This is needed because when reasoning, in the base class, about what $t()$ does when it starts, we had assumed that the state satisfies the base-class pre-condition; so unless this is true, that reasoning may no longer be valid. In the base class reasoning, we also assumed that the initial state satisfies I_b; this will still be the case because in the derived class we may assume that the state will satisfy I_d at the start of $t()$, and hence, given the requirement of behavioral subclassing, the state will also satisfy I_b.

In the second antecedent, $\sigma@pre$ and σ denote the complete (i.e., both base- and derived-class portions) initial and final states when $t()$ begins and ends execution. Since $epost.B.t()$ refers only to the base class portion of the state, we replace σ and $\sigma@pre$ in $epost.B.t()$ by the $\downarrow b$ portion of these states. Similarly, we replace τ in $epost.B.t()$ by $\tau\!\downarrow\! b$. In practice, these substitutions tend to require no real effort. Thus, for example, suppose x is a member variable of B and that $epost.B.t()$ contains a clause $(x = x@pre + 10)$; since x is a component of both σ and $\sigma\!\downarrow\! b$ (and $x@pre$ a component of $\sigma@pre$ and $\sigma@pre\!\downarrow\! b$), nothing needs to be done, as far as this clause is concerned, to effect the substitutions. We will see this in practice in the case study later in the paper.

Thus this antecedent requires us, given the base class e-post-condition of $t()$, given that the derived class portion of the state doesn't change between calls to hook methods, and given that following each call recorded on τ, the state and argument values satisfy the derived class post-condition of the method called, to show that the derived-class invariant and the derived class e-post-condition of $t()$ are satisfied. As explained earlier, it is the assumption that the state and argument values following calls to the h/ht-methods satisfy the richer derived class specification of these methods, that allows us to arrive at a correspondingly richer post-condition $epost.D.t()$ for $t()$ without having to re-analyze its body.

It maybe useful to summarize our approach for reasoning about the derived class D: We first come up with the invariant I_d for the class, the e-specification and f-specification for each t-method and each ht-method of the class, and the specification for each h-method and each nht-method. Next we check that D is a *behavioral subclass* of B, i.e., the requirements specified in (8) are satisfied. Next, we have to verify that each method satisfies its specification(s). For each method that is newly defined or is redefined in D, we use the same approach as in the base class; for the redefined methods, we also check (or have checked) that the relation, imposed by the behavioural subclassing requirement, between the method's derived class specification and its base class specification. For non-template methods inherited from the base class, as we saw in (7), the specification is the same as in the base class with the addition, in the post-condition of the method, that the method does not change the values of member variables newly introduced in D. For template methods, and this is the focus of our paper, we use the rule **R2** to (arrive at and) justify the richer e-specification for the method, and in turn use this richer e-specification to justify a correspondingly richer f-specification (as required by (3)).

One point is worth stressing: if $h()$ is an ht-method that is redefined in D, the behavioral subclassing requirement has to do with its *f-specification*, not its *e-specification*. This is because, so long as the (functional) behavior of the redefined $h()$ is consistent with its base class f-specification, the reasoning that we have done in the base class about the behavior of any (template) methods that invoke $h()$ will remain valid. The point is that the e-specification for $h()$ in the base class would have allowed us to arrive (using rule **R2**) at its richer behavior if we had inherited $h()$ unchanged but had redefined some of the hook methods it invokes; if instead we redefine $h()$ in D, then its base class e-specification is of no particular relevance in the derived class.

One important question that any axiomatic system has to address is that of soundness and (relative) completeness with respect to the operational model of the programming language/system. Because of space limitations, we will consider this question only briefly. The main question concerns the behavior of template methods since our approach to the other methods is standard. And here, one problem in establishing soundness and completeness of our system is that the trace τ that plays a central role in our axiomatic system is not part of standard operational models of OO languages; as a result, we cannot talk about the validity of our e-specifications with respect to our model.

This may seem an advantage since we would then have to worry only about the f-specifications. But the problem is that in our approach, we first establish the e-specification (with rules **R1**, **R2** being the key ones for dealing with the trace information), and then establish the f-specification by showing that the conditions specified in (3) are satisfied. Hence we cannot establish the validity of an f-specification without first showing the validity of the e-specification that the f-specification is based on. The solution is to introduce traces also into the operational model[7]. As in the axiomatic system, the trace in the model would record calls to and returns from hook methods; each such call-return would record the name of the method called, the argument values and state at the time of the call, and the argument values and state at the time of the return. With this change, it is straightforward to show that results established using our reasoning system in particular using rule **R1**, about a base class are valid in the model.

Results about a derived class, in particular those established using **R2**, are more difficult. One possible approach would be as follows: Consider the proof outline (in the base class) that established the original e-specification of the template method in question. Treat the method as a member of the derived class and develop a new proof outline; this new outline is obtained by adding, to each assertion in the original proof outline, the clauses *ncbc*() and *ccds*() (for all $k < |\tau|$). These clauses must hold at all points in this method (considered as a member of the derived class) for the same reason as before, that is, the member variables introduced in the derived class can change only due to the calls to the hook methods. Thus this new proof outline justifies the enriched e-post-condition that appears in **R2**, and hence shows that any result derived by using that rule[8] must be valid in the model.

So much for soundness. Now consider (relative) completeness. To show completeness, we have to show that the strongest post-condition for any method, i.e., the assertion that is satisfied only by states that can operationally arise when method finishes execution, can be established. Here again the argument is best presented in terms of proof outlines. Consider the base class. For each statement in the method, we simply use the strongest post-condition corresponding to the statement and its pre-condition. Then we can inductively argue that the resulting post-condition is indeed the strongest possible one for the entire method. Consider now a template method and its proof outline in the base class. From this, derive a new proof outline for the method in the derived class by adding the *ncbc*() and *ccds*() (for all $k < |\tau|$) clauses as before to each assertion in the base-class proof outline. Again we can argue inductively that the assertion specified in this proof outline at each point in the method is indeed the strongest possible assertion at that point; and hence that, using **R2**, we will be able to

[7] This is not to suggest that anything is to be gained by introducing traces into actual implementations of OO languages. Our only purpose in introducing traces into the operational model is to bring the model closer to the reasoning system so that soundness and completeness arguments can be more easily developed. When defining a new model in this manner, we must of course ensure that as far as possible values that variables that already exist in the original model are concerned, the new model agrees with the original model.

[8] We have ignored invariants in this argument but they can be added in a straightforward manner.

establish the strongest possible post-condition that applies, in the derived class, to this method.

5 Case Study

The base class for our case study is the Account class defined in Section 2, and we will consider two derived classes of Account. We start with, in Figure 3, the specifications for the constructor and the hook methods of Account. The

$$
\begin{aligned}
&pre.\mathsf{Account(b)} \equiv (\mathsf{b} > 0)\\
&post.\mathsf{Account(b)} \equiv (\mathsf{balance} = b)\\
&pre.\mathsf{Account.deposit(x)} \equiv (\mathsf{x} > 0)\\
&post.\mathsf{Account.deposit(x)} \equiv ((\mathsf{x} = \mathsf{x}@pre) \wedge (\mathsf{balance} = \mathsf{balance@pre} + \mathsf{x}))\\
&pre.\mathsf{Account.withdraw(x)} \equiv (\mathsf{x} > 0)\\
&post.\mathsf{Account.withdraw(x)} \equiv ((\mathsf{x} = \mathsf{x}@pre) \wedge (\mathsf{balance} = \mathsf{balance@pre} - \mathsf{x}))\\
&pre.\mathsf{Account.getInfo()} \equiv (true)\\
&post.\mathsf{Account.getInfo()} \equiv ((\mathsf{balance} = \mathsf{balance@pre}) \wedge (string(\mathsf{balance}) \preceq result)) \qquad (9)
\end{aligned}
$$

Fig. 3. Specification of Account class

specification of the constructor states that the balance in the constructed account is initialized to the given value. The specifications for deposit() and withdraw() tell us that these methods do not change the value of the parameter x, and that they update balance appropriately.

The specification of getInfo() is more interesting. Note first that in this post-condition we use *result* to refer to the value returned by this function [Mey97]. Also we assume that the $string(x)$ represents the string version of x; and "$\preceq$" is the *prefix* relation over strings. Thus this specification tells us that getInfo() leaves balance unchanged, and that the string representation of the balance is a prefix of the *result* returned. The result returned by Account.getInfo() is in fact *equal* to this string, but the specification allows the derived class designer to redefine getInfo() to return additional information beyond the balance in the account (while still satisfying the behavioral subclassing requirement). If our specification instead stated that the result returned by getInfo() was equal to balance, the derived class designer would be prevented, by behavioral subclassing, from implementing such enrichments. By the same token, the specifications of deposit() and withdraw() forbid the redefinition of these methods to, say, impose a transaction fee by deducting an additional amount from the balance. It is straightforward to show that the bodies of the hook methods of the Account class, as defined in Fig. 2, do satisfy the specifications in (9).

Next consider the template method processTransSeq(). It may be useful to briefly summarize the operational behavior of the code, which appears in Figure 2, of this method: The method receives a sequence of transaction requests in its first parameter transs; it extracts each transaction from transs, and invokes the corresponding method; if the transaction is printInfo, it appends to its second parameter results (whose initial value is the empty string) the result returned by the call to getInfo; and terminates after processing all the transactions in transs.

In the e-specification of this method in Fig. 4, we use a number of auxiliary functions and predicates; we start by defining these and then will discuss the specification. In the definitions below, we use *tr* to denote a transaction request and *trs* a sequence of such requests; *ai* will denote a string consisting of account information in the format used by processTrans() for outputting, and *ais* will denote a sequence of such strings. τ, as usual, will denote the trace of hook-method calls:

IsTransReq(*tr*): This predicate is *true* if *tr* is a 'legitimate' transaction request, i.e., specifies a transaction (deposit, withdraw, or printInfo), and if the transaction is deposit or withdraw, specifies a positive amount.

IsTransReqSeq(*trs*): *true* if *trs* is a sequence of legitimate transaction requests.

$|trs|$: The length of, i.e. the number of, requests in *trs*.

$trs[j]$: The jth request in *trs*.

$trs[i:j]$: The subsequence of *trs* from the ith request to the jth.

Trans(*tr*): The operation (deposit, withdraw, or getInfo) involved in this request; note that if the request is for printInfo, the corresponding operation is getInfo().

$trs \backslash \{\text{deposit}\}$: The subsequence of *trs* that includes only those transaction requests for which the transaction involved in the request is deposit; similarly for other transactions.

Amts(*trs*): The sequence consisting of just the *amounts* involved in the transactions in *trs* (the amount in the case of a printInfo request being taken to be 0). We will find it useful to refer to the sequence of amounts involved in, say, just the deposit transactions; this may be written as $Amts(trs \backslash \{\text{deposit}\})$.

$IRNo(trs, k)$: This value is k' if $Trans(trs[k'])$ is getInfo, and $|trs[1:k'] \backslash \{\text{getInfo}\}|$ is k; in other words, $trs[k']$ is a printInfo request and is the kth such request.

AccInfo(*ai*): This predicate is *true* if *ai* is a legitimate account-information string; i.e., it consists of the character "<", followed by the balance in the account, additional information (this will depend on how getInfo() is redefined in the derived class), and finally ">".

AccInfoSeq(*ais*): This predicate is *true* if *ais* is a sequence of legitimate account-information strings.

$ais[k]$: The kth account-information string in *ais*.

Balance(*ai*): The balance information in the account-info string *ai*.

Info(*ai*): The *entire* information, including balance, in the account-info string *ai*. In the case of the base class, this will be identical to *Balance*(*ai*).

We should also note that when discussing our reasoning system in the preceding sections, we did not consider the case of a hook method such as getInfo() returning an explicit *result*. The record, in the trace, of a call to such a method will have to include the result returned by the method. If the kth element of τ records such a call/return, we will use the notation $\tau[k].re$ to refer to the result returned by this call.

In the specification (10), we have numbered some of the lines individually as (10.1), (10.2), etc., for easy reference in the discussion. The pre-condition asserts that the hook method call trace is empty, as is results, and that transs is a legitimate sequence of transaction requests. Let us now consider the e-post-condition.

$$
\begin{array}{ll}
\mathit{epre}.\mathsf{Account.processTransSeq(transs,\ results)} \equiv & (10)\\
\quad [(\tau = \varepsilon) \wedge (\mathsf{results} = \varepsilon) \wedge (\mathit{IsTransReqSeq}(\mathsf{transs}))] & \\
\mathit{epost}.\mathsf{Account.processTransSeq(transs,\ results)} \equiv & \\
\quad [(\mathsf{transs} = \varepsilon) \wedge & (10.1)\\
\quad\ (\mathsf{balance} = (\mathsf{balance}@\mathit{pre} + & \\
\qquad\qquad \sum \mathit{Amts}(\mathsf{transs}@\mathit{pre}\backslash\{\mathsf{deposit}\}) - & \\
\qquad\qquad \sum \mathit{Amts}(\mathsf{transs}@\mathit{pre}\backslash\{\mathsf{withdraw}\}))) \wedge & (10.2)\\
\quad\ (|\tau| = |\mathsf{transs}@\mathit{pre}|) \wedge & \\
\quad\ (\forall k : (1 \le k \le |\tau|) :: (\tau[k].\mathit{hm} = \mathit{Trans}(\mathsf{transs}@\mathit{pre}[k]))) \wedge & (10.3)\\
\quad\ (|\mathsf{results}| = |\mathsf{transs}@\mathit{pre}\backslash\{\mathsf{printInfo}\}|) \wedge \mathit{AccInfoSeq}(\mathsf{results}) \wedge & (10.4)\\
\quad\ (\forall k : (1 \le k \le |\mathsf{results}|) : (k' = \mathit{IRNo}(\mathsf{transs}@\mathit{pre}, k)) :: & \\
\qquad (\mathit{Info}(\mathsf{results}[k]) = \tau[k'].\mathit{re}) \wedge & (10.5)\\
\qquad (\mathit{Balance}(\mathsf{results}[k]) = (\mathsf{balance}@\mathit{pre} + & \\
\qquad\qquad \sum \mathit{Amts}(\mathsf{transs}@\mathit{pre}[1 : k' - 1]\backslash\{\mathsf{deposit}\}) - & \\
\qquad\qquad \sum \mathit{Amts}(\mathsf{transs}@\mathit{pre}[1 : k' - 1]\backslash\{\mathsf{withdraw}\})))) & (10.6)\\
\quad] &
\end{array}
$$

Fig. 4. Specification of Account.processTransSeq()

(10.1) asserts that the value of transs is empty, i.e., when processTransSeq() finishes, all the transaction requests have been processed. (10.2) asserts that the final balance in the account is equal to the starting balance, plus the amounts deposited into the account, less the sum of the amounts withdrawn, in the various transactions. This follows from the fact that the starting balance in the account is balance@*pre*, and from the fact that when processing a deposit/ withdraw/ printInfo transaction, processTransSeq() invokes the deposit()/ withdraw()/ getInfo() method which means, given the specification (9) that the deposit() and withdraw() methods update the balance by the amount deposited or withdrawn and getInfo() leaves the balance unchanged, that the final balance will be as specified in (10.2).

The next few clauses concern the trace; they assert that the length of τ, i.e., the number of hook-method-calls is equal to the number of transactions requested; and that the particular hook method called ($\tau[k].hm$) is the one appropriate for the transaction. Note, however, that no information is provided about the *value* of the argument passed in the hook method calls (in the calls to deposit() and withdraw()). This information could have been provided by including the clause:

$$((\tau[k].\mathit{hm} = \mathsf{deposit}) \vee (\tau[k].\mathit{hm} = \mathsf{withdraw})) \Rightarrow (\tau[k].\mathit{ia} = \mathit{Amts}(\mathsf{transs}@\mathit{pre})[k])$$

This simply asserts that if the hook method whose call is recorded in the kth element of τ is deposit() or withdraw(), the value of the argument passed to the method is the same as the value supplied in the corresponding element of the (initial) sequence of transaction requests. In addition, information about the state (the value of balance) at the time of these calls is also not provided in (10); again, this information could have been provided with a similar clause. The fact that these items of information about these hook method calls are not included means that the base class designer does not expect enrichments that would depend on the values of the arguments passed to the hook methods or on the (base class) state at the time of the calls to the hook methods.

The remaining clauses of (10) give us information about the output that processTransSeq() will produce. (10.4) says that there will be as many elements in the final value of results as the number of printInfo transaction requests, and that each of these elements will be an account-information string. The remaining clauses are concerned with the individual elements of results; since the kth element of results depends upon the portion of transs$@pre$ that precedes the kth printInfo request in transs$@pre$, i.e., on $\mathsf{transs}@pre[1:(IRNo(\mathsf{transs}@pre, k) - 1)]$, we have introduced k' as an abbreviation for $IRNo(\mathsf{transs}@pre, k)$. (10.5) asserts that the information in this element of results is equal to the result returned by the corresponding call to getInfo() recorded in τ; this clause is important since it will allow the derived class designer to establish the enriched behavior of processTransSeq() in the derived class, in particular the enriched output that will result from a redefinition of getInfo(). The final clause (10.6) asserts that the balance information in the elements of results correspond to the actual balance in the account at the time that the information was added to results.

Showing that the body of processTransSeq() satisfies this specification is, of course, more involved than showing that methods like deposit() satisfy their specifications. This is partly due to the fact that we have to reason about the trace and partly due to the complexity of processTransSeq(). Thus, for example, dealing with the loop in processTransSeq() would require us to introduce a suitable invariant (which would be very similar to the e-post-condition). We leave the formal statement of the loop invariant and the derivation of the e-post-condition to the interested reader.

The f-specification of processTransSeq() is easily stated:

$$pre.\mathsf{Account.processTransSeq(transs, results)} \equiv \\ [(\mathsf{results} = \varepsilon) \wedge (IsTransReqSeq(\mathsf{transs}))] \tag{11}$$

$$\begin{aligned}
&post.\mathsf{Account.processTransSeq(transs, results)} \equiv \\
&\quad [(\mathsf{transs} = \varepsilon) \wedge && (11.1)\\
&\quad (|\mathsf{results}| = |\mathsf{transs}@pre\backslash\{\mathsf{printInfo}\}|) \wedge AccInfoSeq(\mathsf{results}) \wedge && (11.2)\\
&\quad (\forall k : (1 \le k \le |\mathsf{results}|) : (k' = IRNo(\mathsf{transs}@pre, k)) :: \\
&\qquad (Balance(\mathsf{results}[k]) = (\mathsf{balance}@pre \\
&\qquad\qquad + \textstyle\sum Amts(\mathsf{transs}@pre[1:k'-1]\backslash\{\mathsf{deposit}\}) \\
&\qquad\qquad - \textstyle\sum Amts(\mathsf{transs}@pre[1:k'-1]\backslash\{\mathsf{withdraw}\}))) \wedge && (11.3)\\
&\quad (\mathsf{balance} = (\mathsf{balance}@pre + \textstyle\sum Amts(\mathsf{transs}@pre\backslash\{\mathsf{deposit}\}) - \\
&\qquad\qquad \textstyle\sum Amts(\mathsf{transs}@pre\backslash\{\mathsf{withdraw}\}))))] && (11.4)
\end{aligned}$$

This states that the balance is appropriately updated corresponding to the transactions specified in transs@pre and the balance values in the results recorded in results represent the balance in the account following the completion of all earlier transactions. It is straightforward to check that the required relation, (2), between the e- and f-specifications is satisfied.

Now consider a derived class. TCAccount in Figure 5 enriches the behavior of the Account class by maintaining a count of the transactions, i.e., the number of deposits and withdrawals made on the account; the count is maintained in the variable tCount. tCount is initialized to 0 in the constructor. deposit() and

```
class TCAccount extends Account {
    protected int tCount;
        // current transaction count
    TCAccount(int b) { tCount := 0; }
    public void deposit(int amt)
        { balance := balance + amt; tCount++;}
    public void withdraw(int amt)
        { balance := balance − amt; tCount++;}
    public string getInfo()
        {res := string(balance); res += "trans count: ";
                res += string(tCount); return(res);}
}
```

Fig. 5. Derived class TCAccount

withdraw() have been redefined to increment tCount in addition to updating balance appropriately. getInfo() has been redefined so that the result it returns contains not only the balance in the account, but also the tCount.

$$\begin{aligned}
&\mathit{pre}.\mathsf{TCAccount(b)} \equiv (\mathsf{b} > 0)\\
&\mathit{post}.\mathsf{TCAccount(b)} \equiv ((\mathsf{balance} = b) \wedge (\mathsf{tCount} = 0))\\
&\mathit{pre}.\mathsf{TCAccount.deposit(x)} \equiv (\mathsf{x} > 0)\\
&\mathit{post}.\mathsf{TCAccount.deposit(x)} \equiv ((\mathsf{x} = \mathsf{x}@\mathit{pre}) \wedge (\mathsf{balance} = \mathsf{balance}@\mathit{pre} + \mathsf{x}) \wedge\\
&\qquad\qquad (\mathsf{tCount} = \mathsf{tCount}@\mathit{pre} + 1))\\
&\mathit{pre}.\mathsf{TCAccount.withdraw(x)} \equiv (\mathsf{x} > 0)\\
&\mathit{post}.\mathsf{TCAccount.withdraw(x)} \equiv ((\mathsf{x} = \mathsf{x}@\mathit{pre}) \wedge (\mathsf{balance} = \mathsf{balance}@\mathit{pre} - \mathsf{x}) \wedge\\
&\qquad\qquad (\mathsf{tCount} = \mathsf{tCount}@\mathit{pre} + 1))\\
&\mathit{pre}.\mathsf{TCAccount.getInfo()} \equiv (\mathit{true})\\
&\mathit{post}.\mathsf{TCAccount.getInfo()} \equiv ((\mathsf{balance} = \mathsf{balance}@\mathit{pre}) \wedge (\mathsf{tCount} = \mathsf{tCount}@\mathit{pre}) \wedge\\
&\qquad (\mathit{result} = (\mathit{string}(\mathsf{balance})\,\hat{}\ \text{"trans count: "}\,\hat{}\ \mathit{string}(\mathsf{tCount}))))
\end{aligned} \tag{12}$$

Fig. 6. Specification of TCAccount class

The specifications for these redefined methods appear in Figure 6. These are similar to those in Figure 3; the only changes are that in the post-conditions of deposit() and withdraw(), we specify how they increment tCount, and in the post-condition of getInfo(), we specify that the result returned consists of the (string representation of the) balance in the account, followed by the string "trans count: ", followed by (the string representation of the) transaction count; note that "^" in the last line of (12) denotes string concatenation. It is easy to check that the methods defined in Figure 5 satisfy these specifications and to check that the specifications in (12) and (9) meet the behavioral subclassing requirements since the pre-conditions in (12) are identical to those in (9) and the post-conditions in (12) imply the corresponding post-conditions in (9)[9].

Let us now turn to the essential point of our reasoning task, that of incrementally arriving at the richer behavior of TCAccount.processTransSeq() due to the richer behavior of the methods it invokes. The key clause in the base class (e-)specification of processTransSeq() that allows such enrichment is (10.5):

$$(\mathit{Info}(\mathsf{results}[k]) = \tau[k'].\mathit{re})$$

First recall, according to the relation between k and k' in (10), that $\tau[k']$ records the kth call to getInfo(). Now, *post.*TCAccount.getInfo() specified in (12) gives us more information about the result returned by this call, in other words about the value of $\tau[k'].re$, than does *post.*Account.getInfo() specified in (9). Specifically, whereas (9) states that the result returned by getInfo() will include the string representation of the balance in the account as a prefix, (12) states what the rest of the result returned by (TCAccount.)getInfo() consists of: the string "trans count:" followed by the string representation of the value of tCount in the account.

What will this value be? According to the specfication (12), TCAccount.-deposit() and TCAccount.withdraw() both increment tCount by 1. So the value that (TCAccount.)getInfo() reports for tCount in the result it returns will depend on the number of calls made so far to these methods. And since these are all hook methods, calls to these methods are all recorded on τ. We first introduce a couple of additional auxiliary functions and predicates which will be of use in stating the richer behavior of processTransSeq():

TCAccInfo(*ai*): This predicate is *true* if *ai* is a legitimate TCAccount-information string; i.e., it consists of "<", the balance in the account, the string "trans count: ", an integer (being the value of the transaction count in the account), and finally, ">".

TCAccInfoSeq(*ais*): This is *true* if *ais* is a sequence of legitimate TCAccount-information strings.

TransCount(*tcai*): The trans count value recorded in the TCAccount-information string *ai*.

The specification of TCAccount.processTransSeq() appears in Figure 7. The pre-condition is the same as in the base class-specification. (13.1) is simply the post-condition from the base class-specification; (13.2) and (13.3) specify the enrichment. (13.2) should be compared with the (second conjunct of) (10.4);

[9] The invariants for both Account and TCAccount are *true*.

$$epre.\mathsf{TCAccount.processTransSeq(transs,\ results)} \equiv \\ [(\tau = \varepsilon) \wedge (\mathsf{results} = \varepsilon) \wedge (\mathit{IsTransReqSeq}(\mathsf{transs}))] \quad (13)$$

$$epost.\mathsf{TCAccount.processTransSeq(transs,\ results)} \equiv$$
$$[\, post.\mathsf{Account.processTransSeq(transs,\ results)} \wedge \quad (13.1)$$
$$\mathit{TCAccInfoSeq}(\mathsf{results}) \wedge \quad (13.2)$$
$$(\forall k : (1 \le k \le |\mathsf{results}|) : (k' = \mathit{IRNo}(\mathsf{transs}@pre, k)) :: \\ (\mathit{TransCount}(\mathsf{results}[k]) = \\ (\mathsf{tCount}@pre + |\mathsf{transs}@pre[1:k'-1]\backslash\{\mathsf{deposit,\ withdraw}\}|)))\quad (13.3)$$
$$]$$

Fig. 7. Specification of TCAccount.processTransSeq()

whereas the latter tells us that results is a sequence of strings each of which consists of "<", followed by the balance in the account, followed (possibly) by some additional information, followed by ">", (13.2) also tells us that this additional information will be the string "trans count:" followed by (the string representation of) the value of tCount in the account at the time this was added to results. And (13.3) tells us that this value will be equal to the value of tCount at the start of TCAccount.processTransSeq(), plus the number of deposit and withdraw transaction requests preceding the printInfo request that led to this TCAccount-information string being added to results.

Let us now see how we can, by using our Enrichment Rule **R2**, establish (13), given the base class e-specification (10) and the derived class behaviors of the hook methods specified in (12). The first antecedent of **R2** is immediate since the e-pre-conditions for the base and derived classes are identical. Now consider the second antecedent. Note first that the various clauses ((10.1) through (10.6)) in *epost*.Account.processTransSeq(transs, results) are such that the substitutions –τ by $\tau \downarrow b$, etc.– specified in the first clause of the left side of this antecedent have no effect since balance is a member of the base class (hence also of the derived class), transs and results are arguments of the method (hence are the same in the base and derived classes), and $\tau[k].hm$ (the identity of the hook method invoked in the kth element of τ) and $\tau[k].re$ (the result returned by this call) are the same in the base and derived classes. Therefore, (13.1) will be satisfied (given the first clause of the left side of the second antecedent of **R2**). (13.2) may be established as follows: From the second clause of (10.4) we know that each element of results is an account-information string; and from (10.5) we know that the information in the kth element of results is the same as the result returned by k^{th} call to getInfo(); (13.2) then follows from what *post*.TCAccount.getInfo() (defined in (12)) tells us about the result returned by TCAccount.getInfo().

Next consider (13.3). Appealing again to (10.5), we can conclude that $\mathit{TransCount}(\mathsf{results}[k])$ is equal to $\mathit{TransCount}(\tau[k'].re)$ where k' is $\mathit{IRNo}(\mathsf{transs}@pre, k)$. The specification (12) of TCAccount.getInfo() tells us that the transaction count in the result returned by this method is the same as the value of tCount at the time the method was called; i.e., equal to the value of tCount in the state $\tau[k'].is$. The clause $ncbc()$ in the left side of the second antecedent of **R2** tells us, given that tCount is introduced in the derived class TCAccount, that the value of this variable as recorded in the "initial state" (the *.is* component) of each element of τ is the same as its value in the "final state" (the *.fs* component) of the previous element; the clause $ccds()$ in the same antecedent tells us that the states as recorded in the *.is* and *.fs* components of each element of τ satisfy the post-condition, specified in (12), of the corresponding hook method. Since, according to (12), TCAccount.deposit() and TCAccount.withdraw() each increment tCount by 1, and TCAccount.getInfo() leaves it unchanged, we can then conclude that the transaction count in the result returned by the call to getInfo() recorded in the k'^{th} element of τ is equal to the value of tCount at the start of processTransSeq() plus the number of calls to deposit()/withdraw() recorded in the first $(k'-1)$ elements of τ. This, combined with (10.3), lets us conclude that (13.3) must be satisfied.

And finally, consider the f-specification of TCAccount.processTransSeq(); we express this in terms of the pre- and post-conditions of the f-specification of Account.processTransSeq(), spelling out only the additional clauses:

$$pre.\mathsf{TCAccount.processTransSeq(transs,\ results)} \equiv \qquad (14)$$
$$pre.\mathsf{Account.processTransSeq(transs,\ results)}$$

$$post.\mathsf{TCAccount.processTransSeq(transs,\ results)} \equiv$$
$$[post.\mathsf{Account.processTransSeq(transs,\ results)} \wedge \qquad (14.1)$$
$$TCAccInfoSeq(\mathsf{results}) \wedge \qquad (14.2)$$
$$(\forall k : (1 \leq k \leq |\mathsf{results}|) : (k' = IRNo(\mathsf{transs}@pre, k)) ::$$
$$(TransCount(\mathsf{results}[k]) =$$
$$(\mathsf{tCount}@pre + |\mathsf{transs}@pre[1:k'-1]\backslash\{\mathsf{deposit,\ withdraw}\}|)))\,] \qquad (14.3)$$

Again it is straightforward to check that the relation (2) holds between the e-specification (13) and the f-specification.

Note that the clause (14.1) follows from behavioral subclassing considerations, given that (12) is consistent with (9) If all we were interested in was to show that TCAccount.processTransSeq() behaves in a way consistent with the (f-)specification of Account.processTransSeq(), we would not need the formalism developed in this paper. But, of course, the whole point of defining the derived class, in particular of redefining the hook methods in the TCAccount class, was to *enrich* the behavior of the template method processTransSeq() as specified in (14.2) and (14.3). And it is this enriched behavior that our formalism allows us to establish. And in establishing this enriched behavior, we did not have to reanalyze the behavior of the code of this method; instead, we plugged in the richer behavior of the derived class hook methods into the e-specification, established during the base-class analysis, of the template method.

We will conclude this section with two remarks. First, suppose we defined a variation of TCAccount in which only *large* transactions, i.e., those in which the amount involved is greater than 5000 are counted. Then we cannot reason about the resulting richer behavior of processTransSeq() on the basis of the specification (10) since that specification does not tell us what argument values processTransSeq() passes to the hook methods it calls. It would have been easy enough to include this information in (10); it is up to the base class designer to anticipate what kinds of enrichments might be implemented in the derived classes and include the appropriate information in the e-specifications. Being too liberal here, that is allowing for all kinds of enrichments, would lead to very complex e-specifications; being too conservative will make it impossible to reason incrementally about enrichments that were not anticipated. This is a trade-off between flexibility of design versus complexity of specs.

Our second observation has to do with the nature of our e-specifications. E-specifications are most conveniently expressed, as in the case of Account.processTransSeq(), by first defining some useful functions on traces that, in a sense, mimic the behavioral pattern exhibited by the template method, and then writing down the e-specification of the method in terms of these functions. For more complex situations, we believe it would be useful to introduce specialized notation for use in writing such specifications, perhaps using constructs similar to those of regular expressions; we plan to investigate such notations in future work.

6 Related Work

A number of authors have addressed questions relating to reasoning about behavioral issues in OO systems. Lamping [Lam93] proposes specifying, for each polymorphic function of a class, the set of virtual functions that it invokes. This will allow a derived class designer to know whether a given polymorphic function might be affected –enriched in our terminology– by redefinitions of specific virtual functions. The idea seems to be that the designer can then go back and study the code of the polymorphic function in the base class to see how it is affected; our goal of course is to try to avoid such reanalysis. Kiczales and Lamping [KL92] propose providing information not just about which virtual functions the polymorphic function will call but also the order in which it will call them. But they don't talk about establishing behavioral specifications or about arriving at the enriched behavior of the polymorphic method in the derived class by plugging in, into the base class specification, information about the behavior of the redefined virtual methods.

Behavioral problems arising from careless use of inheritance have been discussed by a number of authors, see for example [Sak89]. It is, as we noted earlier, to address this problem that the notion of behavioral subtyping was developed; our work extends this since our goal is not just to guarantee that the base-class-level analysis of the template method remains valid in the derived class but also to reason about the richer behavior of the template method in the derived class. We should also note that a class A may be a behavioral subtype of a class B independently of whether or not A is defined as a derived class of B. Dhara and Leavens [DL96] focus on the conditions that will ensure that a derived class will be a behavioral subtype of its base class so there is a natural connection to our work since the primary focus of this paper is the relation between the behaviors of derived and base class. But note that Dhara and Leavens, like other authors who deal with behavioral subtyping, do not address the question of the enriched behavior resulting from the redefinition of methods in the derived class which is our main concern. Stata and Guttag's [SG95] interest is somewhat similar to that of [DL96]. They extend the notion of behavioral subtyping to deal with redefinitions of *groups* of virtual methods in the derived class, but again the question of reasoning about the richer behavior in the derived class is not addressed. Edwards [Edw97] considers the reasoning reuse that may be achieved if the derived class is not necessarily a behavioral subtype of the base class but certain other conditions, such as the invariant for the derived class being the same as that for the base class, are satisfied. But as we just saw, if we want to be able to reason incrementally about the behavior of template methods, behavioral subtyping (or rather behavioral subclassing) is essential.

Abadi and Leino [AL97] propose a logic for reasoning about OO programs expressed in a simple language that they define. They do not have classes in their language; each object, in the logic, 'carries' with it the specifications of its various methods. In addition, the logic takes explicit account of object creation via the *alloc*() function; this allows them to deal with aliasing between objects. But [AL97] does not address the question of reasoning about polymorphic methods; in particular it is not clear that we would be able to reason incrementally about the behavior of the polymorphic method from its specification in the base class (or object); instead, it seems likely that one would have to re-reason about the (body of the) polymorphic method in the context of the new class to arrive at its derived-class behavior.

Buchi and Weck's [BW99] work is closer to our approach. They note that pre- and post-conditions on just the values of member variables are inadequate when dealing with template methods and that one must also make use of traces. They introduce a formalism and a programming language-like notation using which some information about the trace of hook method calls can be specified. Although their use of traces is similar to ours, Buchi and Weck focus only on specifying conditions that the trace must satisfy, not the question of how to use such specifications to arrive at the richer behavior that results from the redefinitions of the hook methods in the application. It is also worth noting that traces have been used extensively [Dah92, Hoa85, MC81] for reasoning about communicating processes. The soundness and completeness arguments we sketched are quite similar to the proofs of soundness and completeness of a trace-based CSP proof system in [SD82].

Keidar *et al.* [KKLS00] present a formal system for arriving at specifications and proofs incrementally. But the kind of inheritance they use is not related to inheritance (of code) from base to derived classes in standard OO languages; rather, their 'inheritance' has to do with starting with the specification for an automaton and arriving at the specification for another automaton that exhibits additional behavior. In particular, [KKLS00] does not deal with incremental reasoning about the behavior of template methods.

Garlan *et al.* [GJND98] develop a temporal-logic based approach to reasoning about *implicit invocation.* Calls to hook methods from template methods can be considered implicit invocations since the actual method invoked cannot be determined from just the body of the template method but also depends on the derived class under consideration. While there are some similarities with our work, a key difference is that whereas we first reason about the base class and then arrive incrementally at the behavior of the derived class, [GJND98] takes a very different approach: Given a system S (consisting of all the methods defined in *all* the classes) and a specification for S, partition S into a number of groups, arrive at a suitable specification for each group, show that each group satisfies its specification, and show that together the specifications of the individual groups imply the original specification of S.

7 Discussion

One of the most important ideas introduced by *Simula* was the notion of polymorphism. Polymorphism allows a derived class designer to enrich the behavior of the template methods of the base class by redefining one or more of the hook methods that the template methods invoke. If the base class has been designed carefully and includes the right hooks and the template methods invoke these at the right points, different derived class designers can achieve different enrichments, appropriate to their particular applications, with relatively little effort; much has been written about the central role that polymorphism plays in building flexible, extensible OO systems see, for example, [Mey97]. The work reported in this paper has been motivated by the belief that the techniques that we use to reason about the behaviors exhibited by such systems must similarly be incremental, in other words, that we must provide suitable characterizations of the behaviors of the base class template methods so that we can arrive at the richer behaviors they exhibit in the derived class by simply plugging-in appropriate information about the redefined hook methods. Although much work has been done in the past few years in developing reasoning systems for dealing with OO systems, most of this work, in particular the work on behavioral subtyping (and subclassing), has focused on ensuring that base class specifications of template methods continue to be satisfied even with the derived class redefinitions of the hook methods. Our main contribution has been to extend this to allow us to reason also about the richer behavior that the template methods exhibit as a result of these redefinitions of the hook methods.

The key component of our approach that makes it possible to reason about this richer behavior without having to reanalyze the code of the template method is what we called the e-specification of a template method. The e-specification gives us information about the trace of hook method calls that the template method in question makes and its relation to the behavior the template method exhibits. Although the e-specification is more complex than the standard (f-) specification that only specifies information about the values of the member variables of the class, it is clear that an incremental reasoning system must include information about the trace of hook method calls since that is the source of the power of polymorphism.

In this paper, we have considered only a single base class and the derived classes that might be defined from it. In a complex OO system, there will of course be many objects that are instances of a variety of classes. Indeed, this corresponds naturally to a distributed system with the individual objects corresponding to the processes of the distributed system. There are of course additional issues to be considered in such a system such as synchronization. It has been observed that this can introduce additional new problems such as the *inheritance anomaly* [MY93]. In future work, we hope to extend our reasoning system to deal with behavioral issues in such systems. The fact that traces which play such a key role in our system also occur naturally when dealing with the behavior of distributed systems [Hoa85, MC81] suggests that such an approach is indeed reasonable.

References

[AL97] M. Abadi and K. Leino. A logic of oo programs. In *Proceedings of TAPSOFT '97*, pages 682–696. Springer-Verlag, 1997.

[Ame91] P. America. Designing an object oriented programming language with behavioral subtyping. In *Foundations of Object-Oriented Languages, REX School/Workshop*, LNCS 489, pages 69–90. Springer-Verlag, 1991.

[BW99] M. Buchi and W. Weck. The greybox approach: when blackbox specifications hide too much. Technical Report TUCS TR No. 297, Turku Centre for Computer Science, 1999. available at http://www.tucs.abo.fi/.

[CW85] L. Cardelli and P. Wegner. On understanding types, data abstraction, and polymorphism. *ACM Computing Surveys*, 1985.

[Dah92] O.J. Dahl. *Verifiable Programming.* Prentice-Hall, 1992.

[DL95] K.K. Dhara and G.T. Leavens. Weak behavioral subtyping for types with mutable objects. In S. Brookes, M. Main, A. Melton, and M. Mislove, editors, *Proc. of 11th Annual Conf. on Math. Found. of Programming*, Elec Notes in Theoretical Computer Sc., pages 269–290. Elsevier, 1995.

[DL96] K.K. Dhara and G.T. Leavens. Forcing behavioral subtyping through specification inheritance. In *Proc. of 18th Int. Conf. on Softw. Eng.*, pages 258–267. IEEE Computer Soc., 1996.

[DMN68] O-J Dahl, B Myhrhaug, and K Nygaard. Simula 67 common base language. Technical Report S-2, Norwegian Computing Center, Oslo, 1968.

[DN66] O.J. Dahl and K. Nygaard. Simula - an algol-based simulation language. *Communications of the ACM*, 9(9):671–678, Sept 1966.

[Edw97] S. Edwards. Representation inheritance: A safe form of 'white box' code inheritance. *IEEE TSE*, 23, 83-92, 1997.

[GHJV95] E. Gamma, R. Helm, R. Johnson, and J. Vlissides. *Design Patterns: Elements of Reusable OO Software.* Addison-Wesley, 1995.

[GJND98] D. Garlan, S. Jha, D. Notkin, and J. Dingel. Reasoning about implicit invocation. In *Proceedings of Foundations of Software Engineering (FSE-6)*, pages 209–221. ACM Press, 1998.

[Hoa85] C.A.R. Hoare. *Communicating Sequential Processes.* Prentice-Hall, 1985.

[Jon90] C. Jones. *Systematic Software Development Using VDM.* Prentice-Hall, 1990.

[KKLS00] I. Keidar, R. Khazan, N. Lynch, and A. Shvartsman. Inheritance-based technique for building simulation proofs incrementally. In M. Harrold, editor, *22nd Int. Conf. of Software Eng.*, pages 478–487. ACM, 2000.

[KL92] G. Kiczales and J. Lamping. Issues in the design and specification of class libraries. In *OOPSLA '92*, pages 435–451, 1992.

[Lam93] J. Lamping. Typing the specialization interface. In *OOPSLA*, pages 201–214, 1993.

[LW93] B. Liskov and J. Wing. A new definition of the subtype relation. In *ECOOP*, 1993.

[LW94] B. Liskov and J. Wing. A behavioral notion of subtyping. *ACM Trans. on Prog. Lang. and Systems*, 16:1811–1841, 1994.

[MC81] J. Misra and K. Chandy. Proofs of networks of processes. *IEEE Trans. on Software Eng.*, 7:417–426, 1981.

[Mey97] B. Meyer. *Object-Oriented Software Construction.* Prentice Hall, 1997.

[MY93] S. Matsuoka and A. Yonezawa. Analysis of inheritance anomaly in oo concurrent languages. In Agha, Wegner, and Yonezawa, editors, *Research directions in concurrent OO programming*, pages 107–150. MIT Press, 1993.

[OG76] S. Owicki and D. Gries. An axiomatic proof technique for parallel programs. *Acta Informatica*, 6(1):319–340, 1976.

[Sak89] M. Sakkinen. Disciplined inheritance. In S. Cook, editor, *Proceedings of ECOOP '89*, pages 39–56. British Computer Workshop Series, 1989.

[SD82] N. Soundarajan and O.-J. Dahl. Partial correctness semantics of CSP. Technical Report 66, Institute of Informatics, Oslo University, 1982.

[SG95] R. Stata and J.V. Guttag. Modular reasoning in the presence of subclassing. In *OOPSLA*, pages 200–214. ACM Press, 1995.

[WK99] J. Warmer and A. Kleppe. *The Object Constraint Langauge.* Addison-Wesley, 1999.

Pure Type Systems in Rewriting Logic: Specifying Typed Higher-Order Languages in a First-Order Logical Framework

Mark-Oliver Stehr[1*] and José Meseguer[2]

[1] Universität Hamburg
Fachbereich Informatik - TGI
22527 Hamburg, Germany
stehr@informatik.uni-hamburg.de
[2] University of Illinois at Urbana-Champaign
Computer Science Department
Urbana, IL 61801, USA
meseguer@cs.uiuc.edu

Dedicated to the memory of Ole-Johan Dahl

Abstract. The logical and operational aspects of *rewriting logic* as a logical framework are tested and illustrated in detail by representing *pure type systems* as object logics. More precisely, we apply *membership equational logic*, the equational sublogic of rewriting logic, to specify pure type systems as they can be found in the literature and also a new variant of pure type systems with explicit names that solves the problems with closure under α-conversion in a very satisfactory way. Furthermore, we use rewriting logic itself to give a formal operational description of type checking, that directly serves as an efficient type checking algorithm. The work reported here is part of a more ambitious project concerned with the development of the *open calculus of constructions*, an equational extension of the calculus of constructions that incorporates rewriting logic as a computational sublanguage.

This paper is a detailed study on the ease and naturalness with which a family of higher-order formal systems, namely *pure type systems (PTSs)* [6,50], can be represented in the first-order logical framework of rewriting logic [36]. PTSs generalize the λ-cube [1], which already contains important calculi like $\lambda\!\!\rightarrow$ [12], the systems F [23,43] and Fω [23], a system λP close to the logical framework LF [24], and their combination, the calculus of constructions CC [16]. PTSs are considered to be of key importance, since their generality and simplicity makes them an ideal basis for representing higher-order logics, either via the propositions-as-types interpretation [21], or via their use as a higher-order logical framework in the spirit of LF [24,20] or Isabelle [39].

* Currently visiting University of Illinois at Urbana-Champaign, Computer Science Department Urbana, IL 61801, USA, e-mail: stehr@cs.uiuc.edu

O. Owe et al. (Eds.): From OO to FM (Dahl Festschrift), LNCS 2635, pp. 334–375, 2004.

Exploiting the fact that *rewriting logic (RWL)* and its *membership equational sublogic (MEL)* [10] have initial and free models, we can define the representation of PTSs as a *parameterized theory* in the framework logic; that is, we define in a single parametric way all the representations for the infinite family of PTSs. Furthermore, the representational versatility of RWL, and of MEL, are also exercised by considering four different representations of PTSs at different levels of abstraction, from a more abstract textbook version in which terms are identified up to α-conversion, to a more concrete version with a calculus of names and explicit substitutions, and with a type checking inference system that can in fact be used as a reasonably efficient implementation of PTSs by executing the representation in the Maude language [13,14].

This case study complements earlier work [31,32], showing that rewriting logic has good properties as a logical framework to represent a wide range of logics, including linear logic, Horn logic with equality, first-order logic, modal logics, sequent-based presentations of logics, and so on. In particular, representations for the λ-calculus, and for binders and quantifiers have already been studied in [32], but this is the first systematic study on the representation of *typed* higher-order systems. One property shared by all the above representations, including all those discussed in this paper, is that what might be called the *representational distance* between the logic being formalized and its rewriting logic representation is virtually zero. That is, both the syntax and the inference system of the object logic are directly and faithfully mirrored by the representation. This is an important advantage both in terms of understandability of the representations, and in making the use of encoding and decoding functions unnecessary in a so-called adequacy proof.

Besides the directness and naturalness with which logics can be represented in a framework logic, another important quality of a logical framework is the *scope* of its applicability; that is, the class of logics for which faithful representations preserving relevant structure can be defined. Typically, we want representations that both preserve and reflect provability; that is, something is a theorem in the original logic if and only if its translation can be proved in the framework's representation of the logic. Such mappings go under different names and differ in their generality; in higher-order logical frameworks representations are typically required to be *adequate* mappings [20], and in the theory of general logics more liberal, namely *conservative* mappings of entailment systems [35], are studied. In this paper, we we further generalize conservative mappings to the notion of a sound and complete full *correspondence of sentences* between two entailment systems. In fact, all the representations of PTSs that we consider are correspondences of this kind. Sound and complete full correspondences are systematically used not only to state the correctness of the representations of PTSs at different levels of abstraction, but also to relate those different levels of abstraction, showing that the more concrete representations correctly implement their more abstract counterparts.

A systematic way of comparing the scopes of two logical frameworks $\mathcal{F}$ and $\mathcal{G}$ is to exhibit a sound and complete full correspondence $\mathcal{F} \rightsquigarrow \mathcal{G}$, representing

$\mathcal{F}$ in $\mathcal{G}$. In view of this quite general concept, it is important to add that the *representational distance*, which we informally define as the complexity of this correspondence, is an important measure of the quality of the representation. Since such correspondences form a category, and therefore compose, this then shows that the scope of $\mathcal{G}$ is *at least as general* as that of $\mathcal{F}$. Since PTSs include the system λP, close to the logical framework LF, and the calculus of constructions CC, the results in this paper indicate that the scope of rewriting logic is at least as general as that of those logics. Furthermore, since there are no adequate mappings from linear logic to LF in the sense of [20], but there is a conservative mapping of logics from linear logic to rewriting logic [32], this seems to indicate that the LF methodology together with its rather restrictive notion of adequate mapping is more specialized than the rewriting logic approach.

In this paper we will be concerned with PTSs as formal systems represented inside informal set theory, or inside another formal system such as rewriting logic or its membership equational sublogic. For formal systems in general, and for PTSs in particular, there is not a single canonical presentation. Instead each presentation is tailored for specific purposes. For example, there are different formulations of PTSs with different sets of rules, but the same sets, or related sets, of derivable sentences. Furthermore, presentations can be more or less abstract, e.g. concerning the treatment of names, or concerning the degree of operationality. It is needless to say that the use of some general terminology is highly desirable in this situation to deal with these issues in a systematic way. To this end, we follow the general logics methodology [35] to use an abstract logical metatheory, which is concerned with formal systems *and* their relationships, together with a particular formal system as a logical framework, namely rewriting logic. Regarding general logics terminology, we furthermore found that the notion of correspondences between sentences that generalizes the idea of maps of entailment systems is a simple a useful tool to structure our results.

In summary, we think that, besides the more technical contributions to PTSs discussed in Section 5, the key contributions of this paper are threefold. First, as already mentioned, the expressiveness of RWL and its MEL sublogic as logical frameworks is tested and demonstrated by showing how a well-known family of typed higher-order logics, that are themselves frequently used for logical framework purposes, are naturally represented. But this brings along with it a second important consequence: our representation maps *suggest fruitful generalizations of PTSs*, in which higher-order reasoning is seamlessly integrated with equational and rewriting logic reasoning. The need for such multiparadigm integrations of equational logic and type theory is clearly recognized by many researchers, because of the restrictive notions of equality and computation in traditional λ-calculi. Specifically, as further explained in Section 5.1, an integration of a typed higher-order λ-calculus with MEL and RWL, namely the *open calculus of constructions (OCC)* [48], has been developed by the first author as a natural extension and generalization of the ideas presented here. It is worth pointing out that the *executability* of the representation maps has made possible the development of a prototype for OCC in Maude which has been used in a wide range of examples concerned with programming, specification and interactive theorem proving [48]. A third and final consideration is that our representation maps have another important advantage: since MEL and RWL theories have *initial models*, theories with initial semantics can be endowed with *inductive reasoning principles*. It is indeed such an initial (or free extension) semantics that is used in all our representations of PTSs. This means that we can not only *simulate* PTSs in MEL or RWL using our representations, but we can also *reason about* the metalogical properties of such systems using induction. Different approaches to metalogical reasoning are touched upon in Section 5.2. These include the use of a higher-order logic such as OCC as a metalogic to reason about formalisms represented in its MEL or RWL sublogic, and the use of a reflective metalogical framework such as RWL, which is discussed at greater length in [4].

1 Preliminaries

1.1 Entailment Systems

In the following sections we are concerned with a variety of different interrelated formal systems that can all be viewed as entailment systems, a notion defined in [35] as a main component of general logics. Since the notion of entailment system is more general than what is needed for the purposes of the present paper, we work with *unary* entailment systems over a fixed signature. A *unary entailment system* $(\mathbf{Sen}, \vdash)$ is a set of *sentences* **Sen**, together with a unary *entailment predicate* $\vdash \subseteq \mathbf{Sen}$.

In [35] maps between sentences are used to relate different logics. Here we introduce a more general notion of morphism, namely a correspondence between sentences of different entailment systems. Let $(\mathbf{Sen}, \vdash)$, $(\mathbf{Sen}', \vdash')$ be unary entailment systems. A *correspondence of sentences* between $(\mathbf{Sen}, \vdash)$ and $(\mathbf{Sen}', \vdash')$ is a relation $\curvearrowright \subseteq \mathbf{Sen} \times \mathbf{Sen}'$. Given such a correspondence $\curvearrowright$, we say that $\curvearrowright$ is *sound* iff for all $\phi \curvearrowright \phi'$, $\vdash' \phi'$ implies $\vdash \phi$. Similarly, we say that $\curvearrowright$ is *complete* iff for all $\phi \curvearrowright \phi'$, $\vdash \phi$ implies $\vdash' \phi'$. Moreover, $\curvearrowright$ is called *total* iff for each $\phi' \in \mathbf{Sen}'$ there is a ϕ such that $\phi \curvearrowright \phi'$. Correspondences compose in the obvious relational way, giving rise to a category **CEnt**. Often a correspondence of sentences $\curvearrowright \subseteq \mathbf{Sen} \times \mathbf{Sen}'$ takes the form of a function $\alpha : \mathbf{Sen} \longrightarrow \mathbf{Sen}'$, but in principle it can also take the form of a function $\alpha : \mathbf{Sen}' \longrightarrow \mathbf{Sen}$ in the opposite direction. Indeed, a *map of entailment systems* $\alpha : \mathbf{Sen}' \longrightarrow \mathbf{Sen}$ in the sense of [35] gives rise to a sound correspondence $\alpha^{-1} \subseteq \mathbf{Sen} \times \mathbf{Sen}'$, and if α is a *conservative* map then α^{-1} is a sound and complete correspondence.

1.2 Rewriting Logic and Membership Equational Logic

A rewrite theory is a triple $\mathcal{R} = (\Sigma, E, R)$, with Σ a signature of function symbols, E a set of equations, and R a set of (possibly conditional) rewrite rules of the form $t \longrightarrow t'$ (with t and t' Σ-terms) which are applied *modulo* the equations E. *Rewriting logic* (RWL) has then a deductive system to infer all possible rewrites provable in a given rewrite theory [36]. Since an equational theory (Σ, E) can be regarded as a rewrite theory $(\Sigma, E, \emptyset)$ with no rules, equational logic is a sublogic of rewriting logic. In fact, rewriting logic is parameterized by the choice of its underlying equational logic, which can be unsorted, many-sorted, and so on.

In this paper, and in the design of the Maude language, we have chosen *membership equational logic* (MEL) [37,11] as the underlying equational logic. Membership equational logic is quite expressive. It has sorts, subsorts, overloading of function symbols, and can express partiality very directly by defining membership in a sort by means of equational conditions. The atomic sentences are equalities $t = t'$ and memberships $t : s$, with s a sort, and general sentences are Horn clauses on the atoms. Both membership equational logic and rewriting logic have initial and free models [36,37]. We denote by $\mathbf{MEL} \subseteq \mathbf{RWL}$ the sublogic inclusion from membership equational logic into rewriting logic.

Logics can be naturally represented as rewrite theories by defining the formulas, or other proof-theoretic structures such as sequents, as elements of appropriate sorts in an abstract data type specified by an equational theory (Σ, E). Then, each inference rule in the logic can be axiomatized as a, possibly conditional, rewrite rule, giving rise to a representation as a rewrite theory (Σ, E, R). Alternatively, we can exploit the rich sort structure of membership equational logic to represent the inference rules of a logic not as rewrite rules, but as Horn clauses H expressing membership in an adequate sort of derivable sentences, leading to a membership equational logic representation of the form $(\Sigma, E \cup H)$. In this paper we will use both forms of representations for different versions of PTSs.

2 Overview and Main Results

In Section 3 we show how the definition of PTSs can be formalized in MEL. The approach we use is not only less specialized than the one used in a higher-order logical framework like LF [24] or Isabelle [39], but it has also more explanatory power, since we explain higher-order calculi in terms of a first-order system with a simpler semantics, and our representations have initial (or, more generally, free extension) models supporting metalogical inductive reasoning about the PTSs thus represented.

In order to make the specification of PTSs more concrete, we introduce in Section 3.5 the notion of *uniform pure type systems (UPTSs)* [46,49,48], that do not abstract from the treatment of names but use CINNI [47,48], a generic the first-order calculus of names and substitutions. UPTSs solve the problem of closure under α-conversion, that has been discussed by Pollack in [40], in a simple and elegant way. Again, a MEL specification of UPTSs is given that directly formalizes the informal definition.

As an intermediate step we employ *optimized UPTSs (OUPTSs)* which are introduced in Section 3.6. OUPTSs have an explicit judgement for well-typed contexts, and can be seen as a refinement of UPTSs towards a more efficient implementation of type checking.

Last but not least, we describe how the meta-operational view of an important class of OUPTSs, namely type checking and type inference, can be expressed as a transition system and can likewise be formalized in rewriting logic. The result of this formalization is an executable specification of *rewriting-based OUPTSs (ROUPTSs)* that is sound w.r.t. the logical specification given before in a very obvious way.

Formally, these different presentations of PTSs are families of unary entailment systems parameterized by *PTS signatures*. We use the notation $\mathbf{PTS}_S$, $\mathbf{UPTS}_S$, $\mathbf{OUPTS}_S$ and $\mathbf{ROUPTS}_S$ to denote the entailment systems of PTSs, UPTSs, OUPTSs, and ROUPTSs, respectively, associated with a PTS signature S.

For appropriate PTS signatures S we obtain a chain of sound and complete total correspondences

$$\mathbf{PTS}_S \curvearrowright \mathbf{UPTS}_S \curvearrowright \mathbf{OUPTS}_S \curvearrowright \mathbf{ROUPTS}_S.$$

Actually, we have two different kinds of connections between the first two entailment systems, leading to two different correspondences of the form $\mathbf{PTS}_S \curvearrowright \mathbf{UPTS}_S$. By composing three correspondences of the form above we finally arrive at a sound and complete total correspondence

$$\mathbf{PTS}_S \curvearrowright \mathbf{ROUPTS}_S$$

which shows the equivalence of the high-level specification of PTSs with the implementation of a type checker.

The deductive system of RWL induces a unary entailment system **RWL** with sentences of the form $\mathcal{R} \vdash \phi$, where $\mathcal{R}$ is a rewrite theory and ϕ is an equation, a membership or a rewrite. In this chapter we abstract from rewrite proofs, so that we use the term rewrite to refer to a sentence of the form $M \to M'$ and we define $\mathcal{R} \vdash M \to M'$ to be derivable iff $\mathcal{R} \vdash P : M \to M'$ is derivable for some rewrite proof P in the deductive system of RWL. Likewise, MEL induces a unary entailment system **MEL** obtained by restricting $\mathcal{R}$ to MEL theories and ϕ to equations or memberships.

The entailment systems $\mathbf{PTS}_S$, $\mathbf{UPTS}_S$, $\mathbf{OUPTS}_S$ and $\mathbf{ROUPTS}_S$ can be easily specified in membership equational logic or in rewriting logic. Specifically, we have the following sound and complete total correspondences:

$$\mathbf{PTS}_S \curvearrowright \mathbf{MEL}$$

$$\mathbf{UPTS}_S \curvearrowright \mathbf{MEL}$$

$$\mathbf{OUPTS}_S \curvearrowright \mathbf{MEL}$$

$$\mathbf{ROUPTS}_S \curvearrowright \mathbf{RWL}$$

In all cases the *representational distance* between the formal system and its representation is practically zero, that is, both the syntax and the inference system of each version of PTSs have direct and faithful representations in the framework logic.

The first correspondence is the representation of PTSs in MEL given in Section 3. Let $\overline{\mathbf{PTS}_S}$ be the MEL specification of $\mathbf{PTS}_S$. Then, for all PTS judgements ϕ of $\mathbf{PTS}_S$ and possible representations ϕ' of ϕ in MEL, the sentence $\overline{\mathbf{PTS}_S} \vdash \phi'$ is derivable in MEL iff the judgement ϕ is derivable in $\mathbf{PTS}_S$. This defines a sound and complete total correspondence of the form $\mathbf{PTS}_S \curvearrowright \mathbf{MEL}$. We are concerned with a correspondence rather than a function, due to the fact that PTSs abstract from names, but in the MEL representation names are part of the description of terms, although by adding appropriate equations an equivalent abstraction can be achieved in MEL at the semantic level.

In the remaining three systems $\mathbf{UPTS}_S$, $\mathbf{OUPTS}_S$, and $\mathbf{ROUPTS}_S$ we do not abstract from names. Hence, the three associated representational correspondences actually take the form of functions, i.e., with each judgement of the type system we can associate a unique sentence in MEL or RWL, respectively. For the presentation of PTSs we follow [52], which can be seen as an informal presentation of the machine-checked formalization [34].

3 The Metalogical View of PTSs

A *PTS signature* is a triple $(\mathcal{S}, \mathcal{A}, \mathcal{R})$ where $\mathcal{S}$ is a set of *sorts*, $\mathcal{A} \subseteq \mathcal{S} \times \mathcal{S}$ is the set of *axioms*, and $\mathcal{R} \subseteq \mathcal{S} \times \mathcal{S} \times \mathcal{S}$ is the set of *rules*. The sorts of a PTS signature are used as types of types and are therefore often referred to as *universes*. We use S to range over PTS signatures, and for the following we fix an arbitrary PTS signature S.

In PTSs there is no a priori distinction between terms and types. *PTS terms* are defined by the following syntax with binders:

$$X \mid (M\ N) \mid [X : A]M \mid \{X : A\}M \mid s$$

Here, and in the following, s ranges over $\mathcal{S}$; M, N, A, B, T range over terms; and X ranges over names. We should add that in $[X : A]M$ and $\{X : A\}M$ the name X is bound in M, and we assume that *α-convertible* terms, i.e. terms that are equal up to renaming of bound variables, are identified.

Formally this identification can be achieved by different means: the definition of PTS terms as equivalence classes modulo α-equivalence, or a representation based on de Bruijn indices are two possibilities. For the following it is important to keep in mind that the choice of particular names for bound variables is part of the informal notation (for readability) but is not reflected in PTS terms.

A *PTS context* is a list of *declarations*, each of the form $X : A$. A declaration $X : A$ *declares* a name X of type A. A context is *simple* if it declares each identifier at most once. In the following, Γ ranges over PTS contexts.

PTS typing judgements are of the form $\Gamma \vdash M : T$, and *derivability*, i.e. the set of *derivable typing judgements*, is defined by the formal system given by the following inference rules:

$$\frac{}{[] \vdash s_1 : s_2} \quad (s_1, s_2) \in \mathcal{A} \tag{Ax}$$

$$\frac{\Gamma \vdash A : s}{\Gamma, X : A \vdash X : A} \quad X \notin \Gamma \tag{Start}$$

$$\frac{\Gamma \vdash M : A \quad \Gamma \vdash B : s}{\Gamma, X : B \vdash M : A} \quad X \notin \Gamma \tag{Weak}$$

$$\frac{\Gamma \vdash A : s_1 \quad \Gamma, X : A \vdash B : s_2}{\Gamma \vdash \{X : A\}B : s_3} \quad (s_1, s_2, s_3) \in \mathcal{R} \tag{Pi}$$

$$\frac{\Gamma \vdash A : s_1 \quad \Gamma, X : A \vdash M : B \quad \Gamma, X : A \vdash B : s_2}{\Gamma \vdash [X : A]M : \{X : A\}B} \quad (s_1, s_2, s_3) \in \mathcal{R} \tag{Lda}$$

$$\frac{\Gamma \vdash M : \{X : A\}B \quad \Gamma \vdash N : A}{\Gamma \vdash (M\ N) : [X{:=}A]B} \tag{App}$$

$$\frac{\Gamma \vdash M : A \quad \Gamma \vdash B : s}{\Gamma \vdash M : B} \quad A \equiv_\beta B \tag{Conv}$$

Here we write $X \notin \Gamma$ iff there is no $X : A \in \Gamma$ for any A, and we denote by $[X := N]M$ the standard (capture-free) substitution of all free occurrences of X in M by N. In the last rule, $\equiv_\beta$ is the usual notion of β-convertibility, which contains α-convertibility (this is trivially satisfied in this presentation). Observe that the side conditions ensure that we can only derive *simple judgements*, i.e. judgements with simple contexts. We say that T is a *type* in the context Γ iff $T \in \mathcal{S}$ or $\Gamma \vdash T : s$ for some $s \in \mathcal{S}$. Furthermore, M is said to be an *element* of type T in the context Γ iff $\Gamma \vdash M : T$, in which case we also say that M is *well-typed* in Γ.

As an example, we can instantiate PTSs by

$$\begin{aligned}
\mathcal{S} &= \{\texttt{Prop}, \texttt{Type}\},\\
\mathcal{A} &= \{(\texttt{Prop}, \texttt{Type})\},\\
\mathcal{R} &= \{(\texttt{Prop}, \texttt{Prop}, \texttt{Prop}),\\
&\quad\ (\texttt{Prop}, \texttt{Type}, \texttt{Type}),\\
&\quad\ (\texttt{Type}, \texttt{Prop}, \texttt{Prop}),\\
&\quad\ (\texttt{Type}, \texttt{Type}, \texttt{Type})\}
\end{aligned}$$

to obtain the calculus of constructions.

This presentation of PTSs is rather abstract for two reasons: firstly, we are working modulo α-conversion, i.e., we identify α-convertible terms, and secondly, we are concerned with an inductive definition of a *set* of derivable judgements, but *not* with an *algorithm* to verify derivability of a given judgement.

Mathematically the abstract presentation has an important benefit: It allows us to reason about PTSs metalogically, without assuming anything about the concrete realization of names. This leads to very general results [1,51] and frees proofs from unnecessary technical details.

Closure under α-conversion is the property that derivability of $\Gamma \vdash M : A$ and $M \equiv_\alpha M'$ implies derivability of $\Gamma \vdash M' : A$. Of course, this property trivially holds for PTSs as presented above, since $\equiv_\alpha$ is the identity. To state a stronger property we extend α-conversion $\equiv_\alpha$ from terms to judgements such that $\Gamma \vdash M : A \equiv_\alpha \Gamma' \vdash M' : A'$ iff $\Gamma' \vdash M' : A'$ and $\Gamma \vdash M : A$ are equal up to consistent renaming of variables. Then we have the following

Lemma 31 (Strong Closure under α-Conversion for PTSs)
Let M, A, M', A' be PTS terms and Γ, Γ' be PTS contexts. If the PTS judgement $\Gamma \vdash M : A$ is derivable in $\mathbf{PTS}_S$ and $\Gamma \vdash M : A \equiv_\alpha \Gamma' \vdash M' : A'$, then $\Gamma' \vdash M' : A'$ is derivable in $\mathbf{PTS}_S$.

Proof Sketch. By induction over derivations of $\Gamma \vdash M : A$. □

The previous Lemma is equivalent to the statement that the following rule is admissible in PTSs:

$$\frac{\Gamma \vdash M : A}{\Gamma' \vdash M' : A'} \quad \text{if } \Gamma \vdash M : A \equiv_\alpha \Gamma' \vdash M' : A' \qquad \text{(Rename)}$$

3.1 PTSs in Membership Equational Logic

In the following specifications, given in Maude syntax, we use the algebraic semantics of MEL for representing PTSs exactly as given above; a more operational version suited for use as an implementation is discussed in Section 4.2.

First, notice that we plan to describe not a single type system but the *infinite family* of PTSs parameterized by PTS signatures which define sorts, axioms and rules. All such PTS signatures can be formalized as models of a single parameter theory that can be specified in Maude as follows:

```
fth PTS-SIG is
sorts Sorts Axioms Axioms? Rules Rules? .
subsort Axioms < Axioms? .
subsort Rules < Rules? .
op (_,_) : Sorts Sorts -> Axioms? .
op (_,_,_) : Sorts Sorts Sorts -> Rules? .
endfth
```

As an example, the PTS signature of CC is given by the following functional module:

```
fmod CC-SIG is

sorts Sorts Axioms Axioms? Rules Rules? .
subsort Axioms < Axioms? .
subsort Rules < Rules? .
op (_,_) : Sorts Sorts -> Axioms? .
op (_,_,_) : Sorts Sorts Sorts -> Rules? .
```

```
op Prop : -> Sorts .
op Type : -> Sorts .

mb (Prop,Type) : Axioms .
mb (Prop,Prop,Prop) : Rules .
mb (Prop,Type,Type) : Rules .
mb (Type,Prop,Prop) : Rules .
mb (Type,Type,Type) : Rules .

endfm
```

PTSs can then be specified as a functional module parameterized by the theory PTS-SIG. Since functional modules have an initial (in this case free) model semantics, this formalization of PTSs is in fact a parameterized inductive definition that captures in a precise model-theoretic way the inductive character of PTS rules.

```
fmod PTS[S :: PTS-SIG] is
```

First we define the sort Trm of terms as an algebraic data type. Notice that we distinguish between a sort of names Qid, that are used in places where a variable is *declared*, and a sort of variables Var, that are used to *refer* to an already declared variable.

```
sorts Var Trm .
subsort Qid < Var .
subsort Var < Trm .
subsort Sorts < Trm .
op __ : Trm Trm -> Trm .
op [_:_]_ : Qid Trm Trm -> Trm .
op {_:_}_ : Qid Trm Trm -> Trm .

vars s s1 s2 s3 : Sorts .
vars X Y Z : Qid .
vars A B M N O P Q R T A' B' M' N' T' : Trm .
```

The usual deterministic version of capture-free substitution can be naturally defined in MEL as demonstrated in [32]. An important point is that we do not want to restrict ourselves to a particular choice of fresh names, since this would make the specification overly concrete. This can be accomplished by leaving unspecified the deterministic function for choosing fresh variables such that the actual function varies with the choice of the model; for details we refer to [32]. Here we only give the signature for set membership, free variables and the substitution function:

```
op _in_ : Qid QidSet -> Bool .
op FV : Trm -> QidSet .
op [_:=_]_ : Qid Trm Trm -> Trm .
```

We can use the substitution operator `[_:=_]_` to semantically identify terms that are α-convertible (we refer to the induced equality as α-equality) by means of the following equations.

```
ceq [X : A] M = [Y : A] ([X := Y] M) if not(Y in FV(M)) .
ceq {X : A} M = {Y : A} ([X := Y] M) if not(Y in FV(M)) .
```

We next define the binary relation of β-convertibility, which is used in the Conv rule of PTSs. The following (conditional) memberships, together with the initiality condition, define β-conversion as the smallest congruence (w.r.t. the term constructors) containing β-reduction.

```
sorts Convertible Convertible? .
subsort Convertible < Convertible? .

op _<->_ : Trm Trm -> Convertible? .

mb  M <-> M : Convertible .

cmb M <-> N : Convertible
    if N <-> M : Convertible .

cmb P <-> R : Convertible if
    P <-> Q : Convertible and Q <-> R : Convertible .

cmb (M N) <-> (M' N') : Convertible if
    M <-> M' : Convertible and N <-> N' : Convertible .

cmb ([X : A] M) <-> ([X : A'] M') : Convertible if
    A <-> A' : Convertible and M <-> M' : Convertible .

cmb ({X : A} B) <-> ({X : A'} B') : Convertible if
    A <-> A' : Convertible and B <-> B' : Convertible .

mb  (([X : A] M) N) <-> ([X := N] M) : Convertible .
```

The judgements of PTSs are of the form $\Gamma \vdash M : A$. We next define the syntax of contexts and judgements. Also, we define the function `_in_` used in the side conditions of some PTS rules.

```
sorts Context Judgement .
op emptyContext : -> Context .
op _:_ : Qid Trm -> Context .
op _,_ : Context Context -> Context [assoc id : emptyContext] .

var G : Context .
```

```
op _|-_:_ : Context Trm Trm -> Judgement .

op _in_ : Qid Context -> Bool .
eq X in emptyContext = false .
eq X in (G,(Y : A)) = (X in G) or (X == Y) .
```

We are now ready to define the inference rules. Semantically, the inference rules define an inductive subset of *derivable judgements*. The derivability predicate is usually implicit in informal reasoning, where $\Gamma \vdash M : A$ refers either to the judgement itself or to the fact that it is derivable.

```
sort Derivable .
subsort Derivable < Judgement .

cmb (emptyContext |- s1 : s2) : Derivable if (s1,s2) : Axioms .

cmb (G,(X : A) |- X : A) : Derivable if
    (G |- A : s) : Derivable /\ not(X in G) .

cmb (G,(X : B) |- M : A) : Derivable if
    (G |- M : A) : Derivable /\
    (G |- B : s) : Derivable /\ not(X in G) .

cmb (G |- {X : A} B : s3) : Derivable if
    (G |- A : s1) : Derivable /\
    (G,(X : A) |- B : s2) : Derivable /\ (s1,s2,s3) : Rules .

cmb (G |- [X : A] M : {X : A} B) : Derivable if
    (G |- A : s1) : Derivable /\
    (G,(X : A) |- M : B) : Derivable /\
    (G,(X : A) |- B : s2) : Derivable /\ (s1,s2,s3) : Rules .

cmb (G |- (M N) : [X := A] B) : Derivable if
    (G |- M : {X : A} B) : Derivable /\
    (G |- N : A) : Derivable .

cmb (G |- M : B) : Derivable if
    (G |- M : A) : Derivable /\
    (G |- B : s) : Derivable /\ A <-> B : Convertible .

endfm
```

In this formalization we have avoided any arbitrary encoding of syntax with binders that would require nontrivial justifications. Also, we have seen that the first-order framework is sufficiently powerful to represent PTSs without making any commitments. In particular, there was no need to change the syntax nor the rules of PTSs to obtain a faithful representation.

3.2 Taking Names Seriously

Although the abstract treatment of names in PTSs leads to a general metatheory that can be used as a high-level theoretical basis for quite different implementations of PTSs, there is a price to pay, in that an abstract view necessarily limits the expressivity of the theory. In the case of PTSs, properties involving names cannot be expressed. Indeed, we often need a more concrete representation with more specialized results to deal, for example, with the implementation of a formal system, or with tools that use the formal system in an essential way. Also in the context of reasoning about a formal system, a more concrete specification that is computationally meaningful can have considerable advantages for the partial automation of metatheoretic proofs in logics with computational sublanguages.

However, as soon as *we take names seriously, i.e., we give up the identification of α-convertible terms*, and interpret the inference rules literally, we encounter at least two problems first discussed in [40] under the title "closure under α-conversion".[3]

The *first problem* is that the set of derivable judgements is not closed under α-conversion. For instance, adapting an example given for $\lambda\!\rightarrow$ in [40], we cannot derive a judgement of the form

$$A : \texttt{Prop}, P : \{Z : A\}\texttt{Prop} \vdash [X : A][X : P\ X]A : \{X : A\}\{X : P\ X\}\texttt{Prop},$$

say in CC, although the α-equivalent version

$$A : \texttt{Prop}, P : \{Z : A\}\texttt{Prop} \vdash [X : A][Y : P\ X]A : \{X : A\}\{Y : P\ X\}\texttt{Prop},$$

where some bound variables are distinct can be derived.

A *second difficulty* pointed out in [40] is that we want to derive

$$A : \texttt{Prop}, P : \{Z : A\}\texttt{Prop} \vdash [X : A][X : P\ X]X : \{X : A\}\{Y : P\ X\}(P\ X),$$

but we should *not* be able to derive

$$A : \texttt{Prop}, P : \{Z : A\}\texttt{Prop} \vdash [X : A][X : P\ X]X : \{X : A\}\{X : P\ X\}(P\ X).$$

However, we cannot derive the first judgement, since the name X in the conclusion of the Lda rule is the same on both sides of the colon.

To tackle the first problem, Pollack proposed a type system $\vdash_{lt}$, a variation of $\lambda\!\rightarrow$. It uses a more liberal notion of context that allows multiple declarations of the same name, the one most recently introduced being visible inside the judgement. Unfortunately, he did not pursue this direction further because of the second difficulty, which appears in the context of PTSs with dependent types but is not present in $\lambda\!\rightarrow$. Concerning $\vdash_{lt}$, he remarks "I don't think we can do the same for PTS."

The solution finally discussed in [40] is the solution employed in the *constructive engine* [25] used in proof assistants such as LEGO [41] and COQ [2]. The

[3] The problem with closure under α-conversion also remains unsolved in [30], where a system with dependent types is presented that does not enjoy this property.

idea is to use a hybrid naming scheme which employs distinct names for *global variables* declared in the context of a judgement, and a de Bruijn representation of terms with bound *local variables.* Clearly, PTSs based on such a hybrid naming scheme are a correct implementation of (abstract) PTSs as described above. More precisely, PTSs using the hybrid naming scheme can be seen as particular models of the MEL specification of PTSs in the sense that the corresponding model is isomorphic to the one given by the appropriately instantiated functional module `PTS`. Nevertheless, an approach which maintains a distinction between global and local variables appears not to be very uniform, complicating formal metatheoretic proofs and type checking. Of course, scaling up Pollack's $\vdash_{lt}$ to PTSs would be much more satisfying, and this is the direction we pursue in the following.

3.3 Indexed Names and Named Indices

We believe that the root of the second difficulty discussed above is that the traditional notion of binding used in logic and in programming reveals an undesirable property, which may be called *accidental hiding*, if the language is refined in the most direct way, i.e., by just giving up identification by α-conversion.

Consider for instance the formula

$$\forall X \,.\, (A \;\wedge\; \forall Y \,.\, (B \Rightarrow \forall X \,.\, C(X)))$$

with distinct names X and Y, where $C(X)$ is a formula that contains X free. Each occurrence of X in $C(X)$ is *captured* by the inner $\forall$ quantifier, so that the outermost $\forall$ quantifier is hidden from the viewpoint of $C(X)$. Indeed there is no way to refer to the outermost $\forall$ quantifier within $C(X)$.

Hence, we are faced with the following problem: a calculus without α-equality is not only less abstract, which is an unavoidable consequence of giving up identification by α-conversion, but also, depending on the (accidental) choice of names, visibility of (bound) variables may be restricted. It is important to emphasize that visibility is not restricted in the original calculus with α-equality, since renaming can be performed *tacitly* at any time.

Clearly, this phenomenon of hiding that occurs in the example above is undesirable[4], because it is not present in the original calculus with α-equality. It is merely an accident caused by giving up identification by α-conversion without adding a compensating flexibility to the language.

This suggests tackling this general problem by migrating to a more flexible syntax, where we express a binding constraint by annotating each name X with an index $i \in \mathbb{N}$, written X_i, that indicates how many X-binders should be skipped before we reach the one that X_i refers to. For instance we write

$$\forall X \,.\, (A \;\wedge\; \forall Y \,.\, (B \Rightarrow \forall X . C(X_0)))$$

to express that X_0 is bound by the inner $\forall$, and

$$\forall X \,.\, (A \;\wedge\; \forall Y \,.\, (B \Rightarrow \forall X . C(X_1)))$$

[4] Of course, in general hiding is important but it is not an issue of binding; it should be treated independently.

meaning that X_1 is bound by the outermost $\forall$. To make the language a conservative extension of the traditional notation, we can identify X and X_0.

In fact, the use of indexed names is equivalent to a representation introduced by Berkling [7,8] in the context of λ-calculus[5] which is why we refer to the notation based on indexed names also as Berkling's notation. As indicated by the example above we use Berkling's representation not (only) for λ-calculus but as the core syntax of CINNI, the *Calculus of Indexed Names and Named Indices* which is generic in the sense that it can be instantiated for a wide range of object languages with different binding constructs. For a detailed treatment of CINNI, its metatheoretic properties, and its relation to other calculi we refer to [47,48].

Obviously, there is some similarity to a notation based on de Bruijn indices [18]. But notice that there is an essential difference: the index m in the occurrence X_m is *not* the number of binders to be skipped; it states that we have to skip m binders for the particular name X, *not* counting binders for other names. Still a formal relationship to de Bruijn's notation can be established: if we restrict ourselves to terms that *contain only a single name* X, then we can replace each X_i by the index i without loss of information and we arrive at de Bruijn's purely indexed notation.[6] In other words, if we restrict the available names to a single one, we obtain de Bruijn's notation as a very special case. In this sense, Berkling's representation can be formally seen as a proper generalization of de Bruijn's notation. Pragmatically, however, the relationship to de Bruijn's syntax plays only a minor role, since a typical user will exploit the dimension of names much more than the dimension of indices. Hence, in practice the notation can be used as a standard named notation, with the additional advantage that accidental hiding and weird renaming[7] are avoided.

The pragmatic advantage of Berkling's notation is that it can be used to reduce the distance between the formal system and its implementation: it can be directly employed by the user who wants to think in terms of names, so that the need for a translation between an internal representation (e.g. using de Bruijn indices) and a user-friendly syntax (e.g. using ordinary names) disappears completely. As far as we know the CINNI substitution calculus is the first calculus of explicit substitutions which combines named and index-based representations and hence provides a link between these two worlds of explicit substitution calculi.

Usually, this translation is not considered to be a problem, and indeed in the case of terms, where all parts are known or accessible, solutions are straightforward. However, it is clear that this gap is not desirable: consider, for example, a tactic-based theorem prover where the user is confronted with an internal representation which reflects the theory only in a very indirect way. More seriously, the translation between internal and external representations becomes unworkable, or at least requires certain restrictions, as soon as we use terms containing

[5] An indexed variable X_i is represented in Berkling's representation as $\#^i X$ where $\#$ is the so-called unbinding operation.

[6] With the slight difference that de Bruijn's indices start at 1 instead of 0.

[7] See the discussion on weird renaming in the next section.

metavariables, holes or placeholders, which are useful for many applications including unification algorithms and representation of incomplete proofs.

3.4 Explicit Substitutions

In the previous section we discussed Berkling's first-order representation for expressions, which contains the conventional named notation as well as de Bruijn's indexed notation as special cases. The most important operation to be performed on such terms represented in this way is capture-free substitution. Therefore, we now present the CINNI substitution calculus, a first-order calculus that can be seen as an (operational) refinement of an external (i.e. metalevel) substitution function such as the one given in [8].

Strictly speaking, CINNI is a family of explicit substitution calculi, parameterized by the syntax (including information about binding) of the language we want to represent. Here we present the instantiation of this substitution calculus for the untyped λ-calculus. λ-terms in CINNI syntax are:

$$X_m \mid (M\ N) \mid [X]M$$

As a motivation for the substitution calculus given below, consider the following example of a β-reduction step in the traditional λ-calculus with distinct names X and Y, again taking names literally, i.e. not presupposing identification by α-conversion:

$$(([X][Y]X)Y) \to [Z]Y$$

Clearly, Z must be a name different from Y to avoid capturing. Unfortunately, there is no canonical choice if all names should be treated as being equal. We call this phenomenon *weird renaming* of bound variables. It is actually a combination of two undesirable effects: (1) names that have been carefully chosen by the user have to be changed, and (2) the enforced choice of a new name collides with the right of names to be treated as equal citizens.

These effects are avoided in the CINNI calculus, when instantiated to the λ-calculus. CINNI is specified by the first-order equational theory given below. Indeed, the only operation assumed on names is equality. CINNI has also an operational semantics viewing equations as rewrite rules. Apart from the two basic kinds of substitutions, namely *simple* substitutions $[X{:=}M]$, and *shift* substitutions $\uparrow_X$, substitutions can be *lifted* using $\Uparrow_X S$, where the variable S ranges over substitutions.

$$
\begin{array}{lcl@{\qquad}lcl}
[X{:=}M]\ X_0 & = & M & \Uparrow_X S\ X_0 & = & X_0 \\
[X{:=}M]\ X_{m+1} & = & X_m & \Uparrow_X S\ X_{m+1} & = & \uparrow_X (S\ X_m) \\
[X{:=}M]\ Y_n & = & Y_n \text{ if } X \neq Y & \Uparrow_X S\ Y_n & = & \uparrow_X (S\ Y_n) \text{ if } X \neq Y
\end{array}
$$

$$
\begin{array}{lcl@{\qquad}lcl}
\uparrow_X X_m & = & X_{m+1} & S\ (MN) & = & (SM)(SN) \\
\uparrow_X Y_n & = & Y_n \text{ if } X \neq Y & S\ ([X]M) & = & [X](\Uparrow_X S\ M)
\end{array}
$$

The CINNI calculus can be instantiated to various object languages with different binding operators to give a more concrete treatment of their associated formal systems. The only equations specific to the syntax of the language are the structural equations. Here, the last two equations in the right column are the structural equations for the λ-calculus. In a similar way, CINNI can be instantiated to other object languages such as Abadi and Cardelli's ς-calculus or Milner's π-calculus [47,48].

Now we can define *β-reduction* by the rule

$$([X]N)M \rightarrow_{\beta} [X{:=}M]N.$$

Notice that weird renaming of bound variables as in the previous example is avoided with the new notion of β-reduction which yields[8]

$$(([X][Y]X_0)Y_0) \rightarrow_{\beta} ([Y]Y_1)$$

As another application of substitution, consider *renaming of a bound variable* X by $\bullet$ as in the following rule of *α-reduction*:

$$([X]N) \rightarrow_{\alpha} ([\bullet][X{:=}\bullet] \uparrow_{\bullet} N) \text{ if } X \neq \bullet$$

where $\bullet$ is an arbitrary but fixed name. Using this rule every CINNI term can be reduced to a nameless *α-normal form* which is essentially its de Bruijn index representation. For terms M,N we use $M \equiv_{\alpha} N$ to denote that M and N are equal up to renaming of bound variables.

Just as Berkling's notation contains de Bruijn's indexed notation as a very special case, the instantiation of CINNI for the λ-calculus reduces to the calculus $\lambda\upsilon$ of explicit substitutions proposed by Pierre Lescanne [27,28,5], but only in the degenerate case where we only use a single name. It is noteworthy that $\lambda\upsilon$ is the smallest known indexed substitution calculus enjoying good theoretic properties like confluence[9] and preservation of strong normalization. It seems that its simplicity is inherited by CINNI although in practice the dimension of names will be much more important than the dimension of indices. Hence, we tend to think of CINNI more as a substitution calculus with names than as one with indices.

3.5 Uniform Pure Type Systems

The application of CINNI to PTSs can be seen as Pollack's $\vdash_{lt}$ scaled up to PTSs. In contrast to the hybrid approach to PTSs adopted in the constructive engine [25] and in the PTS formalization given in [34] based on an idea from [15], both

[8] One might argue that even the change of variable indices constitutes a form of renaming, but an important point is that only references to previously introduced names are affected rather than the binding occurrences themselves.

[9] In fact, we have confluence on terms without metavariables [47,48], but this is sufficient for the approach to type checking/inference presented in this paper, since all metavariables will eventually become instantiated.

distinguishing between global and local variables, we use indexed names *uniformly*. This suggests defining *uniform pure type systems (UPTSs)* by modifying PTSs in three steps:

First, PTS terms are generalized to UPTS terms in the way explained before, i.e., *UPTS terms* are defined by the first-order CINNI syntax:

$$X_m \,|\, (M\ N) \,|\, [X : A]M \,|\, \{X : A\}M \,|\, s$$

As a second step, we adapt the syntax-dependent part of the CINNI calculus to UPTS terms:

$$\begin{aligned} S\ s &= s \\ S\ (MN) &= (SM)(SN) \\ S\ ([X : A]M) &= [X : (S\ A)](\Uparrow_X S\ M) \\ S\ (\{X : A\}M) &= \{X : (S\ A)\}(\Uparrow_X S\ M) \end{aligned}$$

The third and final step is to define the derivable typing judgements. Since we do not want to identify α-convertible terms, this is a fundamental change in the formal system. However, a careful inspection of the typing rules *under the new reading* shows that only minor changes in the rules Start and Weak are needed. The new rules are:

$$\frac{\Gamma \vdash A : s}{\Gamma, X : A \vdash X_0\ : \uparrow_X A} \qquad \text{(Start)}$$

$$\frac{\Gamma \vdash M : A \quad \Gamma \vdash B : s}{\Gamma, X : B \vdash \uparrow_X M\ : \uparrow_X A} \qquad \text{(Weak)}$$

It might appear that the UPTSs we have defined above are a specialization of PTSs, since we have committed ourselves to a particular representation of names. But this is not the full truth, because on the other hand we have described a generalization of PTSs where multiple declarations of the same name are admitted in a well-typed context. Notice that in both rules above we have dropped the side condition $X \notin \Gamma$, which means that we have completely eliminated the need for these side conditions in UPTSs. We would also like to point out, that, in particular, we have not touched the Lda rule: the only place where α-conversion comes into play is in the Conv rule, where $\equiv_\beta$ subsumes α- and β-conversion, just as in the original PTSs.

Finally, we describe how these changes are reflected in the MEL specification, that is how UPTSs can be represented by modifying the previous specification.

First, instead of using names as variables we use indexed names. So we replace `subsort Qid < Var` by

```
op _{_} : Qid Nat -> Var .
```

Second, instead of conventional substitution `[_:=_]_`, we use CINNI for UPTS terms:

```
sort Subst .

op [_:=_] : Qid Trm -> Subst .
op [shift_] : Qid -> Subst .
op [lift__] : Qid Subst -> Subst .
op __ : Subst Trm -> Trm .

var  S : Subst .
vars n m : Nat .

eq  ([X := M] (X{0})) = M .
eq  ([X := M] (X{suc(m)})) = (X{m}) .
ceq ([X := M] (Y{n})) = (Y{n}) if X =/= Y .

eq  ([shift X] (X{m})) = (X{suc(m)}) .
ceq ([shift X] (Y{n})) = (Y{n}) if X =/= Y .

eq  ([lift X S] (X{0})) = (X{0}) .
eq  ([lift X S] (X{suc(m)})) = [shift X] (S (X{m})) .
ceq ([lift X S] (Y{m})) = [shift X] (S (Y{m})) if X =/= Y .

eq  (S s) = s .
eq  (S (M N)) = ((S M) (S N)) .
eq  S ([X : A] M) = [X : (S A)] ([lift X S] M) .
eq  S ({X : A} M) = {X : (S A)} ([lift X S] M) .
```

Third, conversion now explicitly contains α-conversion, something that was implicit in the equality of the previous specification:

```
mb  [X : A] M <->
    [Y : A] ([X := Y{0}] [shift Y] M) : Convertible .

mb  {X : A} M <->
    {Y : A} ([X := Y{0}] [shift Y] M) : Convertible .
```

Finally, the new versions of Start and Weak are:

```
cmb (G,(X : A) |- X{0} : [shift X] A) : Derivable if
    (G |- A : s) : Derivable .

cmb (G,(X : B) |- [shift X] M : [shift X] A) : Derivable if
    (G |- M : A) : Derivable /\
    (G |- B : s) : Derivable .
```

Again, we can see that the representational distance between the mathematical presentation of UPTSs and their MEL specification is practically zero. In particular, the equational nature of the CINNI substitution calculus is directly captured by the MEL specification.

UPTSs are more liberal than PTS, since a derivable judgement $\Gamma \vdash M : A$ may contain multiple declarations of the same name in Γ. However, the set of derivable judgements $\Gamma \vdash M : A$ of PTS can be recovered as the set of derivable UPTS judgements $\Gamma \vdash_1 M : A$ generated by adding the following rule:

$$\frac{\Gamma \vdash M : A}{\Gamma \vdash_1 M : A} \quad \text{if } \Gamma \text{ is simple} \qquad \text{(Simple)}$$

The representation of judgements $\Gamma \vdash_1 M : A$ together with this rule in MEL is straightforward, and we omit it here and in all the following formalizations for the sake of brevity.

To state the following results we proceed as for PTSs: We extend α-conversion $\equiv_\alpha$ from terms to judgements, so that $\Gamma \vdash M : A \equiv_\alpha \Gamma' \vdash M' : A'$ iff $\Gamma' \vdash M' : A'$ and $\Gamma \vdash M : A$ are equal up to consistent renaming of declared *and* bound variables. Then we have the following

Lemma 32 (Strong Closure under α-Conversion for UPTSs)
Let M, A, M', A' be UPTS terms and Γ, Γ' be UPTS contexts. If the UPTS judgement $\Gamma \vdash M : A$ is derivable in $\mathbf{UPTS}_S$ and $\Gamma \vdash M : A \equiv_\alpha \Gamma' \vdash M' : A'$, then $\Gamma' \vdash M' : A'$ is derivable in $\mathbf{UPTS}_S$.

Proof Sketch. By induction over derivations of $\Gamma \vdash M : A$. □

It is noteworthy that a weak form of this lemma using α-conversion on terms instead of judgements, i.e. the special case where $\Gamma = \Gamma'$, cannot be proved directly by induction. The induction would fail for the rules Pi and Lda, since a declared variable X becomes a local variable.

As for PTSs the previous lemma is equivalent to the admissibility of the following rule in UPTSs:

$$\frac{\Gamma \vdash M : A}{\Gamma' \vdash M' : A'} \quad \text{if } \Gamma \vdash M : A \equiv_\alpha \Gamma' \vdash M' : A' \qquad \text{(Rename)}$$

Using the terminology introduced in Section 1.1 for entailment systems, each of the following two propositions establishes a sound and complete total correspondence of the form $\mathbf{PTS}_S \curvearrowright \mathbf{UPTS}_S$, where S is an arbitrary PTS signature.

Proposition 33 (Soundness and Completeness of UPTSs I)
For all PTS terms M,A and PTS contexts Γ, if the PTS judgement $\Gamma \vdash_1 M : A$ is derivable in $\mathbf{UPTS}_S$ then $\Gamma \vdash M : A$ is derivable in $\mathbf{PTS}_S$ and vice versa.[10]

Proof Sketch.

First observe that each PTS rule is a UPTS rule if we restrict ourselves to simple judgements. In particular, the side conditions $X \in \Gamma$ in the PTS rules Start and Weak imply that the shift substitution in the corresponding UPTS rules can be eliminated.

($\Rightarrow$) Given a UPTS derivation of a simple judgement $\Gamma \vdash M : A$, each occurrence of a UPTS inference rule can be replaced as follows: First the original

[10] Here we make use of the convention, introduced in Section 3.3, that ordinary terms (here PTS terms) can be seen as CINNI terms (here UPTS terms).

premises are converted into suitable simple PTS form by virtue of Rename. Then the corresponding inference rule for PTSs is applied (which is also a UPTS rule according to the observation above). Finally, the conclusion in simple PTS form is converted back to the original conclusion in UPTS form, again using Rename. After transforming the entire derivation in this way all intermediate UPTS judgements which are not PTS judgements, i.e. the original premises and original conclusions, can be removed, and the result is still a UPTS derivation. Also, the resulting derivation corresponds to a derivation in PTSs extended by the admissible rule Rename.

($\Leftarrow$) According to the observation above, each application of a PTS rule can be seen as an application of the corresponding UPTS rule. Furthermore, each implicit α-conversion step that is possible in PTSs can be simulated by Rename, which is an admissible rule in UPTSs.

□

In other words, UPTSs are conservative over PTSs. A slightly weaker but more comprehensive correspondence of the form $\mathbf{PTS}_S \curvearrowright \mathbf{UPTS}_S$ can be given modulo renaming of variables:

Proposition 34 (Soundness and Completeness of UPTSs II)
For all UPTS terms M,A, PTS terms M',A', UPTS contexts Γ and simple PTS contexts Γ' with $\Gamma \vdash M : A \equiv_\alpha \Gamma' \vdash M' : A'$, if the UPTS judgement $\Gamma \vdash M : A$ is derivable in $\mathbf{UPTS}_S$ then $\Gamma' \vdash M' : A'$ is derivable in $\mathbf{PTS}_S$ and vice versa.

Proof Sketch.

($\Rightarrow$) Let $\Gamma \vdash M : A$ be derivable in $\mathbf{UPTS}_S$ and let $\Gamma \vdash M : A \equiv_\alpha \Gamma' \vdash M' : A'$. By Proposition 32 (strong α-closure) $\Gamma' \vdash M' : A'$ and therefore $\Gamma' \vdash_1 M' : A'$ are derivable in $\mathbf{UPTS}_S$. So by Proposition 33 $\Gamma' \vdash M' : A'$ is derivable in $\mathbf{PTS}_S$.

($\Leftarrow$) Let $\Gamma' \vdash M' : A'$ be derivable in $\mathbf{PTS}_S$ and let $\Gamma' \vdash M' : A' \equiv_\alpha \Gamma \vdash M : A$. By Proposition 33, $\Gamma' \vdash M' : A'$ is derivable in $\mathbf{UPTS}_S$, and by Proposition 32 (strong α-closure) $\Gamma \vdash M : A$ is derivable in $\mathbf{UPTS}_S$ too.

□

The last proposition implies that, concerning judgements of the form $\Gamma \vdash M : A$, PTSs and UPTSs are equivalent modulo α-conversion. Hence all (metatheoretic) results about PTSs [22] apply to UPTSs after appropriate renaming.

Another consequence of the last proposition is that the new form of judgement $\Gamma \vdash_1 M : A$ is not necessary to ensure soundness, and could therefore be dropped. Sometimes, however, focusing on judgements of the form $\Gamma \vdash_1 M : A$ instead of the more general form $\Gamma \vdash M : A$ is more convenient, e.g. to formulate the weakening/thinning lemma [22,52], since simple contexts can be treated as sets of declarations.

3.6 A Conservative Optimization

The presentations of PTSs and UPTSs given above maintain a good economy in the number of rules and are therefore well-suited for metatheoretic (inductive) reasoning. The judgement $\Gamma \vdash M : A$ implicitly subsumes another judgement $\Gamma \Vdash$, stating that Γ is a well-typed context. Since in practice checking contexts is as important as checking types, we switch to a conservative extension of UPTSs (similar to an optimization for PTSs mentioned in [52]) that is not biased towards any of the two forms of judgement. From a practical point of view, the addition of a separate judgement for well-typed contexts can be seen as an optimization which avoids rechecking contexts in each subderivation. We will refer to this optimized version as *optimized UPTSs (OUPTSs)* and the entailment system will be denoted by **OUPTS**. The only modifications we need are described below. In addition to the *main typing judgement*, which is written now as $\Gamma \Vdash M : A$ (stating that M is an element of the type T in Γ), we use *context typing judgements* of the form $\Gamma \Vdash$ meaning that Γ is a well-typed context, and *relative typing judgements* of the form $\Gamma \vdash M : A$ meaning that M is an element of type A if Γ is well-typed. Furthermore, we add the following rules:

$$\frac{}{[] \Vdash} \qquad \text{(Ctxt1)}$$

$$\frac{\Gamma \Vdash \quad \Gamma \vdash A : s}{\Gamma, X : A \Vdash} \qquad \text{(Ctxt2)}$$

$$\frac{}{\Gamma \vdash X_m : \mathit{lookup}(\Gamma, X_m)} \text{ if } \mathit{lookup}(\Gamma, X_m) \text{ is defined} \qquad \text{(Lookup)}$$

$$\frac{\Gamma \Vdash \quad \Gamma \vdash M : A}{\Gamma \Vdash M : A} \qquad \text{(Main)}$$

where $\mathit{lookup}(\Gamma, X_m)$ is a partial function defined by:

$$\begin{aligned} \mathit{lookup}((\Gamma, X : A), X_0) &= \uparrow_X A \\ \mathit{lookup}((\Gamma, X : A), X_{m+1}) &= \uparrow_X \mathit{lookup}(\Gamma, X_m) \\ \mathit{lookup}((\Gamma, X : A), Y_m) &= \uparrow_X \mathit{lookup}(\Gamma, Y_m) \text{ if } X \neq Y \end{aligned}$$

Then we replace Ax and Simple by:

$$\frac{}{\Gamma \vdash s_1 : s_2} \ (s_1, s_2) \in \mathcal{A} \qquad \text{(Ax)}$$

$$\frac{\Gamma \Vdash M : A}{\Gamma \Vdash_1 M : A} \text{ if no variable is declared in } \Gamma \text{ more than once.} \qquad \text{(Simple)}$$

respectively, and we remove the rules Start and Weak, since they are admissible rules in the new system. The system we have just obtained is similar to the system $\vdash_{vtyp}$, $\vdash_{vcxt}$ presented in [52], but here we are concerned with UPTSs instead of PTSs. Another minor difference is that we make use of an explicit lookup function. As before, we do not need any freshness side conditions thanks to CINNI.

Again, the representation in MEL is quite direct. It nicely illustrates the mixed specification style using equations and memberships, and also the representation of partial functions such as *lookup*.

```
sort Trm? .
subsort Trm < Trm? .

op  lookup : Context Var -> Trm? .
eq  lookup(G,(X : A), X{0}) = [shift X] A .
eq  lookup(G,(X : A), X{suc(m)}) = [shift X] lookup(G,X{m}) .
ceq lookup(G,(X : A), Y{m}) = lookup(G,Y{m}) if (X =/= Y) .

op  _||- : Context -> Judgement .
op  _|-_:_ : Context Trm Trm -> Judgement .
op  _||-_:_ : Context Trm Trm -> Judgement .

mb  (emptyContext ||-) : Derivable .

cmb (G,(X : A) ||-) : Derivable if
    (G ||-) : Derivable /\ (G |- A : s) : Derivable .

cmb (G |- X{m} : lookup(G,X{m})) : Derivable if
    lookup(G,X{m}) : Trm .

cmb (G ||- M : A) : Derivable if
    (G ||-) : Derivable /\ (G |- M : A) : Derivable .

cmb (G |- s1 : s2) : Derivable if (s1,s2) : Axioms .
```

OUPTSs are equivalent to UPTSs, i.e., there is a sound and complete total correspondence of the kind $\mathbf{UPTS}_S \curvearrowright \mathbf{OUPTS}_S$ for arbitrary PTS signatures S, in the following sense:

Proposition 35 (Soundness and Completeness of OUPTSs)
Let M,A be UPTS terms, and let Γ be a UPTS context. If the judgement $\Gamma \Vdash M : A$ ($\Gamma \Vdash_1 M : A$) is derivable in $\mathbf{OUPTS}_S$, then $\Gamma \vdash M : A$ ($\Gamma \vdash_1 M : A$) is derivable in $\mathbf{UPTS}_S$ and vice versa.

Proof Sketch. It is easy to adopt the proof of the similar lemma 23 in [52] to our setting. The main change is that we are using UPTSs instead of PTSs here. A minor point is that we are using an explicit *lookup* function. □

4 The Meta-operational View of PTSs

PTSs can not only be equipped with a logical semantics, e.g. via the proposition-as-types interpretation, but, more fundamentally, PTSs are usually equipped with an operational semantics, defined by an internal notion of functional computation, such as β-reduction. The operational view of PTSs is concerned with their internal notion of computation, but here we are interested in the *meta-operational view*, which deals with the question of how to embed PTSs in a formal system with an operational semantics, so that typical computational tasks like type checking and type inference become possible by exploiting the operational semantics of the metalanguage. In the following we employ for this purpose the efficiently executable sublanguage of rewriting logic that is supported by the Maude engine.

First, we introduce several well-known classes of PTS signatures, giving rise to corresponding PTSs that are practically interesting and enjoy particularly good properties.

Definition 41 A PTS signature S is *decidable* iff: (1) $\mathcal{S}$ is denumerable, (2) $\mathcal{A}$ and $\mathcal{R}$ are decidable, and (3) for all $s_1, s_2 \in \mathcal{S}$ the predicates $\exists s_2' : (s_1, s_2') \in \mathcal{A}$ and $\exists s_3' : (s_1, s_2, s_3') \in \mathcal{R}$ are decidable.

Decidability is a reasonable requirement to ensure that type inference and type checking do not become undecidable because of a too complex PTS signature.

Definition 42 A PTS signature S is *functional* iff (1) $(s_1, s_2) \in \mathcal{A}$ and $(s_1, s_2') \in \mathcal{A}$ implies $s_2 = s_2'$, and (2) $(s_1, s_2, s_3) \in \mathcal{R}$ and $(s_1, s_2, s_3') \in \mathcal{R}$ implies $s_3 = s_3'$.

In functional PTS signatures, the relations $\mathcal{A}$ and $\mathcal{R}$ can be viewed as partial functions $\mathcal{A} : \mathcal{S} \rightsquigarrow \mathcal{S}$ and $\mathcal{R} : \mathcal{S} \times \mathcal{S} \rightsquigarrow \mathcal{S}$. Functionality ensures that every term has a unique type modulo $\equiv_\beta$ [22]. The class of functional PTSs[11] includes, for example, all systems of the λ-cube.

Definition 43 A PTS signature S is *full* iff for all $s_1, s_2 \in \mathcal{S}$ there is an s_3 such that $(s_1, s_2, s_3) \in \mathcal{R}$. A PTS signature S is *semi-full* iff $(s_1, s_2, s_3) \in \mathcal{R}$ implies that for each s_2' there is an s_3' such that $(s_1, s_2', s_3') \in \mathcal{R}$.

Full PTSs allow us to form dependent types $\{X : A\}B$ very liberally, by avoiding those restrictions on the sorts of A and B that are imposed by the side condition $(s_1, s_2, s_3) \in \mathcal{R}$ of the Pi rule. As an example, CC is a full PTS.

Definition 44 Given a PTS signature S, a *top sort* is a sort s such that there is no sort s' with $(s, s') \in \mathcal{A}$. The set of top sorts is denoted by $\mathcal{S}_{\text{top}}$.

To avoid inessential technicalities in our presentation, we will later focus on PTS signatures without top sorts, which introduce some kind of nonuniformity in the set of sorts. Just as $\mathcal{R}$ can be seen as a function $\mathcal{R} : \mathcal{S} \times \mathcal{S} \to \mathcal{S}$ in full PTS signatures, $\mathcal{A}$ can be viewed as a function $\mathcal{A} : \mathcal{S} \to \mathcal{S}$ in functional PTS signatures without top sorts.

Semi-full PTSs have the nice property that we can get rid of the third premise in Lda by replacing it with the following rule:

$$\frac{\Gamma \vdash A : s_1 \quad \Gamma, X : A \vdash M : B}{\Gamma \vdash [X : A]M : \{X : A\}B} \quad (s_1, s_2, s_3) \in \mathcal{R} \text{ and } B \notin \mathcal{S}_{\text{top}} \qquad (\mathsf{Lda'})$$

[11] The attributes for PTS signatures are naturally lifted to the corresponding PTSs.

The premises together with the side conditions in Lda' imply that $\{X : A\}B$ is a type (cf. rule Pi). Indeed, as explained in [52] in the context of PTSs, replacing Lda by Lda' does not change the set of derivable judgements in semi-full UPTSs.

For full UPTSs without top sorts we can completely eliminate the side conditions in the rule Lda', and we obtain Lda" without changing the set of derivable judgements:

$$\frac{\Gamma \vdash A : s \quad \Gamma, X : A \vdash M : B}{\Gamma \vdash [X : A]M : \{X : A\}B} \qquad \text{(Lda")}$$

Our example PTS signature of CC at the beginning of Section 3 has Type as a top sort. However, it is straightforward to extend CC by an infinite universe hierarchy yielding a PTS without top sorts. Our example PTS signature of CC has Type as a top sort. However, it is straightforward to extend CC by an infinite universe hierarchy yielding a PTS without top sorts.

Together with the introduction of UPTSs in the previous section, we have now (following the corresponding arguments for PTSs in [52]) three families of inference systems which only differ in the choice of the rule Lda. For a full PTS signature S without top sorts all of them define the same unary entailment system, which is denoted by $\mathbf{UPTS}_S$.

In the remainder of this paper we will present a standard type checking algorithm for a class of UPTSs using rewriting logic as a formal specification language. In spite of some unsolved theoretical questions such as the expansion postponement problem, efficient algorithms for the important classes of functional PTSs and semi-full PTSs (satisfying appropriate decidability and normalization properties) have been presented in [52]. In order to avoid excessive technical details and to make clear the general way we use rewriting logic to represent type checking algorithms, we restrict ourselves in the following to UPTSs that are decidable, normalizing (w.r.t. β-reduction), functional, full, and without top sorts. The class of UPTSs that are decidable, normalizing, functional and semi-full can be treated along the same lines (using the rule Lda' instead of Lda").

The use of UPTSs instead of PTSs is motivated by our desire to obtain a *formal executable representation* that takes names seriously and makes type checking simpler and more uniform. The approach is different from the constructive engine [25] and its presentation in [40] that employs named global variables and a de Bruijn representation for local variables. It is also different from [15], [52] and the formalization [34] that distinguish between two unrelated sets of global names and local names.

4.1 Uniform PTSs in Membership Equational Logic

The standard way to implement type checking, which goes back to [33] and [25], is to cast the inference rules into an equivalent syntax-directed inductive definition, and to define a type-inference function on the basis of this new system. Formally and technically this could be done in the executable sublanguage of MEL or in any other functional programming language, but the use of MEL is attractive, since it allows us to formulate the logical and operational versions of PTSs in a single uniform language with a simple semantics, which in particular does not presuppose higher-order constructs, but is used to explain them in more elementary terms. Also, data structures and functions of the specification can be directly used in the implementation.

In our setting there is another reason why MEL is more natural than the use of a (higher-order) functional programming language: the equational specification of the calculus of substitutions presented above is naturally equipped with an operational semantics just by viewing the equations as rewrite rules. By contrast, in a functional programming language that is not based on equational rewriting, the substitution calculus has to be *encoded*, which essentially means that a (specialized) rewrite engine for this calculus has to be implemented in the functional language itself and, what is even more cumbersome, this engine has to be explicitly invoked when needed. In this sense, a specification/programming style based on rewriting is more abstract and closer to mathematical practice for applications of this kind than a (higher-order) functional programming approach.

Using the specification of the above substitution calculus, a purely equational executable specification of a type checker for UPTSs with decidable type checking can be written in MEL using standard equational/functional programming techniques. The core of this specification consists of a type-inference function

```
op type : Context Trm -> Trm? .
```

that computes a type for each term which is well-typed in the given context. The function can be defined in a way similar to the one given in [45], but using CINNI, instead of abstracting from the treatment of names.

Thanks to CINNI, freshness conditions are avoided. Therefore, an implementation based on this specification appears to be more elegant than that of the constructive engine with its hybrid treatment of names. As an additional advantage, multiple declarations of the same name are naturally admitted in contexts if we use judgements $\Gamma \Vdash M : A$. However, it is also easy to disallow these more general contexts if desired by implementing simple judgements $\Gamma \Vdash_1 M : A$.

Instead of discussing this purely equational approach in more detail, we present an alternative approach in the following section that exploits features of rewriting logic that are beyond equational and functional languages. Our experience shows that this alternative approach scales up well to more complex type theories, e.g. extensions of UPTSs such as OCC (see Section 5.1) in a more satisfactory way than the purely functional and equational approaches to type checking.

4.2 Uniform PTSs in Rewriting Logic

As shown by an extensive collection of examples in [31,32], rewriting logic can be used as a logical framework that can naturally represent inference systems of different kinds in a logically and operationally satisfying way. In the present section we view a type checker as a particular inference system. In contrast to a (higher-order) functional programming approach that would require us to *encode* the inference system in terms of a type checking function, the rewriting logic approach offers the advantage that inference rules can be expressed directly, namely, as rewrite rules. We will in fact make use of a type inference system expressed as a collection of rewrite rules that transform a conjunction of judgements into a simplified form, in the style of *constraint solving systems.* This yields a rewrite system that is efficiently executable, while still maintaining a close correspondence to the logical specification of UPTSs.

The rewriting logic specification represents *rewriting-based OUPTSs (ROUPTSs)* and is able to perform type checking, i.e. to decide derivability of judgements of the form $\Gamma \Vdash$, $\Gamma \vdash M : A$, and $\Gamma \Vdash M : A$, for the class of decidable, normalizing, functional, full and PTS signatures without top sorts discussed before. As in PTSs, type checking is reduced to type inference, that is, to solving incomplete queries of the form $\Gamma \vdash M$ `->:` ?.

Instead of giving an informal account we directly discuss the formal specification in rewriting logic.

First, we exploit our assumption that the PTS signature is decidable, functional, full and without top sorts, which means that the relations $\mathcal{A}$ and $\mathcal{R}$ can be specified by equationally-defined functions `Axioms` and `Rules`:

```
fth FPTS-SIG is
sort Sorts .
op Axioms : Sorts -> Sorts .
op Rules : Sorts Sorts -> Sorts .
endfth
```

As usual for syntax-directed approaches following the ideas of [33] and [25] we "invert" the inference rules in order to obtain a goal-directed algorithm from the inductive definition. In contrast to a purely equational and functional approach, the rewriting logic specification we aim at has a rewrite transition system as a model, and can therefore be seen as an operational generalization of the equational and functional paradigms. In contrast to [52] and [40], the type-checking algorithm itself receives a direct formal status as a transition system, which is a good basis for reasoning formally about operational properties and especially about its correctness.

The inductive definition of UPTSs can be seen as a static description of a set of judgements that we would like to equip with a dynamic structure. More precisely, a *(static) logical implication*

$$A_1 \ \wedge \ \ldots \ \wedge \ A_n \Rightarrow B$$

can be seen as an *inference rule* or *(dynamic) state transition* refining a goal B into subgoals $A_1, \ldots, A_n$, and can be directly represented as a rewrite rule

$$B \rightarrow A_1 \ \wedge \ \ldots \ \wedge \ A_n$$

in rewriting logic. Each state consists of a finite set of subgoals that remain to be solved.

The static description can be seen as inducing the following invariant that our dynamic system should always satisfy: for each state, the empty set of goals is reachable iff the logical interpretation of the state is true.

Although the inference rules of a formal system typically take the form of Horn clauses that can be operationally refined to rewrite rules, there may be functional and equational parts (e.g. auxiliary functions or substitution calculi) that are more naturally expressed in the MEL fragment. It is this mix of different paradigms that allows us to express the type-checking algorithm in a way that is very close to the logical specification.

We discuss below the rewriting logic specification of the UPTS type checker in some detail. Instead of an equational theory introduced by the `fmod` keyword, the specification takes the form of a rewrite theory, introduced by the `mod` keyword, that has a transition system as its initial semantics:

```
mod PTS[S :: FPTS-SIG] is
```

We reuse most components of the functional module defined before, but in addition to the *typing judgement*

```
op _|-_:_ : Context Trm Trm -> Judgement .
```

we add the following *auxiliary judgements*:

```
op _Sort : Trm -> Judgement .
op (_,_,_)Rule : Trm Trm Trm -> Judgement .
op _=_ : Trm Trm -> Judgement .
op _<->_ : Trm Trm -> Judgement .
op _|-_->:_ : Context Trm Trm -> Judgement .
op _|-(_->:_)(_->:_)->:_ : Context Trm Trm Trm Trm Trm ->
                               Judgement .
```

Recall that, in our setting of PTS signatures without top sorts, T is a type in Γ iff $\Gamma \vdash T : s$. Presupposing that Γ is a well-typed context and A,B are types in Γ, the meaning of the auxiliary judgements is the following: The judgement A `Sort` means that there is an $s \in \mathcal{S}$ such that $A \equiv_\beta s$. The judgement (A, B, s) `Rule` means that there are $s_1, s_2 \in \mathcal{S}$ such that $A \equiv_\beta s_1$, $B \equiv_\beta s_2$ and $(s_1, s_2, s) \in \mathcal{R}$. The judgement A `<->` B just means that $A \equiv_\beta B$. The judgement $\Gamma \vdash M$ `->:` T means that M has an *inferred type* T in Γ. Regarding this refinement of typing judgements we only assume that $\Gamma \vdash M$ `->:` T implies $\Gamma \vdash M : T$, and conversely that $\Gamma \vdash M : T$ implies that $T \equiv_\beta T'$ and $\Gamma \vdash M$ `->:` T' for some T'. Furthermore, the judgement $\Gamma \vdash ((M$ `->:` $S)(N$ `->:` $T))$ `->:` U abbreviates $\Gamma \vdash M$ `->:` S, $\Gamma \vdash N$ `->:` T, and $\Gamma \vdash (M\ N)$ `->:` U. Finally, the judgement $M = N$ just means that M and N are equal terms.

In order to express intermediate goals or queries, like $\Gamma \vdash M$ `->:` ?, that are present in the operational refinement but not in the abstract presentation, we extend terms by explicit metavariables:

```
sort MetaVar .
subsort MetaVar < Trm .
op ? : Qid -> MetaVar .
var MV : MetaVar .
```

In ROUPTSs we use the weak head normal form, calculated by the following function `whnf`, to check if two terms are convertible, and in particular if a term is convertible to the form s or $\{X : A\}M$. We also use sorts `WhNf` and `WhReducible` containing terms in weak head normal form and weak head reducible terms, respectively.

```
sort WhNf WhReducible .
subsort WhNf < Trm .

subsort Sorts < WhNf .
subsort Var < WhNf .
mb  ([X : A] M) : WhNf .
mb  ({X : A} B) : WhNf .
mb  (s N) : WhNf .
mb  (X{m} N) : WhNf .
cmb ((P Q) N) : WhNf if (P Q) : WhNf .
mb  (({X : A} M) N) : WhNf .

subsort WhReducible < Trm .

mb  (([X : A] M) N) : WhReducible .
cmb (M N) : WhReducible if M : WhReducible .

op  whnf : Trm -> Trm? .

ceq whnf(M) = M if M : WhNf .
eq  whnf(([X : A] M) N) = whnf([X := N] M) .
ceq whnf(M N) = whnf(whnf(M) N) if M : WhReducible .
```

A configuration is a conjunctive set of judgements that have to be solved or verified by the type checker. We represent a set of judgements as a list. This allows us to solve goals in a well-defined order, a fact that we exploit later in this section.

```
sort JudgementList .

op emptyJudgementList : -> JudgementList .
subsort Judgement < JudgementList .
op __ : JudgementList JudgementList -> JudgementList
        [assoc id: emptyJudgementList] .

var JS : JudgementList .
```

```
sort Configuration .

op {{_}} : JudgementList -> Configuration .
```

Replacement of metavariables by terms (that is, textual replacement) has the obvious definition, not spelled out here, except for its syntax:

```
op <_:=_>_ : MetaVar Trm Trm -> Trm .
op <_:=_>_ : MetaVar Trm Subst -> Subst .
op <_:=_>_ : MetaVar Trm Context -> Context .
op <_:=_>_ : MetaVar Trm Judgement -> Judgement .
op <_:=_>_ : MetaVar Trm JudgementList -> JudgementList .
```

It is used only in the following *equality elimination rule*, that instantiates a metavariable throughout the entire configuration if it is uniquely determined by an equality:

```
rl [Subst] : {{ (MV = A) JS }} => {{ < MV := A > JS }} .
```

A rule like this is typical of a constraint-based programming approach, and indeed the configuration can be seen as a set of constraints that should be simplified using the subsequent rules [32].

In addition to simplification of constraints by rewrite rules, simplification by equational rewriting also plays a major role in our approach. As an example, the judgement of convertibility between normalizing terms can be checked using **whnf** as follows. In order to avoid redundant reductions we reduce the general problem to a check of convertibility between weak head normal forms (which are treated by the first five rules below). In the case of binders we perform renaming to equalize names.

```
rl  [Conv1] :  {{ (s <-> s) JS }} => {{ JS }} .

rl  [Conv2] :  {{ (X{m} <-> X{m}) JS }} => {{ JS }} .

crl [Conv3] :  {{ ((M N) <-> (M' N')) JS }} =>
               {{ (M <-> M') (N <-> N') JS }}
               if (M N) : WhNf /\ (M' N') : WhNf .

rl  [Conv4] :  {{ ({X : A} T <-> {Y : A'} T') JS }} =>
               {{ (A <-> A')
                  ([X := Y{0}] [shift Y] T <-> T') JS }} .

rl  [Conv5] :  {{ ([X : A] M <-> [Y : A'] M') JS }} =>
               {{ (A <-> A')
                  ([X := Y{0}] [shift Y] M <-> M') JS }} .
```

```
crl [Conv6] :  {{ (M <-> N) JS }} =>
               {{ (whnf(M) <-> N) JS }}
               if M : WhReducible .

crl [Conv7] :  {{ (M <-> N) JS }} =>
               {{ (M <-> whnf(N)) JS }}
               if N : WhReducible .
```

We use two auxiliary judgements to formalize side conditions:

```
rl  [Sort] :   {{ (s Sort) JS }} => {{ JS }} .

rl  [Rule] :   {{ ((s1,s2,MV) Rule) JS }} =>
               {{ (MV = Rules(s1,s2)) JS }} .
```

Each inference rule of OUPTSs gives rise to a rewrite rule obtained by reversing the direction of inference:

```
rl  [Ax] :     {{ (G |- s ->: MV) JS }} =>
               {{ (MV = Axioms(s)) JS }} .

crl [Lookup] : {{ (G |- X{m} ->: MV) JS }} =>
               {{ (MV = lookup(G,X{m})) JS }}
               if lookup(G,X{m}) .

rl  [Pi] :     {{ (G |- {X : A} B ->: MV) JS }} =>
               {{ (G |- A ->: ?(NEW1)) (?(NEW1) Sort)
                  (G,(X : A) |- B ->: ?(NEW2))
                  ((?(NEW1), ?(NEW2), MV) Rule) JS }} .

rl  [Lda] :    {{ (G |- [X : A] M ->: MV) JS }} =>
               {{ (G |- A ->: ?(NEW1)) (?(NEW1) Sort)
                  (G,(X : A) |- M ->: ?(NEW2))
                  (MV = {X : A} ?(NEW2)) JS }} .

rl  [App1] :   {{ (G |- (M N) ->: MV) JS }} =>
               {{ (G |- M ->: ?(NEW1)) (G |- N ->: ?(NEW2))
                  (G |- (M ->: ?(NEW1))(N ->: ?(NEW2)) ->: MV)
                  JS }} .

rl  [App2] :   {{ (G |- (M ->: {X : A} B)(N ->: A') ->: MV)
                  JS }} =>
               {{ (A <-> A') (MV = [X := N] B) JS }} .
```

The terms `?(NEW1)` and `?(NEW2)` above denote fresh metavariables. Hence rewriting has to be controlled by a simple *strategy*, that *constraints* the possible rewrites by instantiating the variables NEW1 and NEW2 only with fresh names each time a rule is applied. Notice that, in contrast to ordinary variables, where names are taken seriously, we abstract from (i.e. we do not care about) metavariable names, since they do not have a formal status inside UPTSs, but belong instead to the metalevel which is partially made explict in the operational refinement.[12]

According to the explanations given before, the new judgements have certain closure properties w.r.t. $\equiv_\beta$. The following simplification rules allow us to work with (partially) normalized judgements in the inference rules:

```
crl [Norm1] :  {{ (T Sort) JS }} =>
               {{ (whnf(T) Sort) JS }}
               if T : WhReducible .

crl [Norm2] :  {{ ((A,B,T) Rule) JS }} =>
               {{ ((whnf(A),B,T) Rule) JS }}
               if A : WhReducible .

crl [Norm3] :  {{ ((A,B,T) Rule) JS }} =>
               {{ ((A,whnf(B),T) Rule) JS }}
               if B : WhReducible .

crl [Norm4] :  {{ (G |- (M ->: A)(N ->: B) ->: T) JS }} =>
               {{ (G |- (M ->: whnf(A))(N ->: B) ->: T) JS }}
               if A : WhReducible .
```

This completes the definition of the *type-inference* system for judgements of the form $\Gamma \vdash M$ `->:` A. *Type checking* is reduced to type inference in the standard way, that is, $\Gamma \vdash M : A$ is verified by first checking if A is a type in Γ, and if this is the case we then check if A and the inferred type of M are convertible. Exploiting the fact that in PTSs without top sorts each type is contained in some sort, this can be specified by the rule

```
rl  [Aux] :    {{ (G |- M : A) JS }} =>
               {{ (G |- A ->: ?(NEW1)) (?(NEW1) Sort)
                  (G |- M ->: ?(NEW2)) (?(NEW2) <-> A) JS }} .
```

This rule can be slightly optimized by using an adaption of Lemma 3 from [42], which allows us to omit the goal `(?(NEW1) Sort)` on the right hand side, since it is implied by the remaining goals.

Finally, we add rules to check the context typing judgement and the main typing judgement:

[12] By a further refinement of the present specification we can obtain a system with takes even metavariables seriously, but this is not necessary for the purposes of this paper.

```
  rl  [Ctxt1] : {{ (emptyContext ||-) JS }} => {{ JS }} .

  rl  [Ctxt2] : {{ (G,(X : A) ||-) JS }} =>
                {{ (G ||-) (G |- A ->: ?(NEW))
                   (?(NEW) Sort) JS }} .

  rl  [Main] :  {{ (G ||- M : A) JS }} =>
                {{ (G ||-) (G |- M : A) JS }} .
endm
```

Again we have omitted the straightforward rule corresponding to Simple, which allows us to check derivability of typing judgements $\Gamma \Vdash_1 M : A$ that disallow multiple occurrences of the same variable in Γ.

To verify a judgement J we start with an initial configuration $\{\{J\}\}$. Either this configuration can be reduced to $\{\{$`emptyJudgementList`$\}\}$, meaning that the judgement has been proved, or the final configuration contains unsolved goals giving an informative indication of an error.

Notice that we have not only used inductive definitions to specify PTSs and UPTSs logically, but that, in addition, the operational version of UPTSs given by the rewrite rules above is an inductive definition of a labeled transition system which gives us a more refined view of the type-checking process.

The most important property of a type checker is soundness, i.e., each judgement that has been verified should be derivable in the type system. In fact the formal system has been defined in such a way that the soundness of each of the rewrite rules above relative to OUPTSs can be verified by straightforward inspection of the rules using the meaning of all auxiliary judgements given earlier.

More precisely, let S range over decidable, normalizing, functional, full PTS signatures without top sorts. We denote by $\mathbf{ROUPTS}_S$ the entailment system in which sentences are rewrites of the form $\{\{JS\}\} \longrightarrow \{\{JS'\}\}$ and such a rewrite is derivable iff it is derivable in the rewrite theory that has been presented above. Then the next proposition gives a sound and complete total correspondence $\mathbf{OUPTS}_S \curvearrowright \mathbf{ROUPTS}_S$.

Proposition 45 (Soundness and Completeness of ROUPTSs)
Let M,A be UPTS terms, let Γ be a UPTS context, and let J be one of the judgements $\Gamma \Vdash$, $\Gamma \Vdash M : A$, or $\Gamma \Vdash_1 M : A$. If the rewrite $\{\{J\}\} \longrightarrow$ $\{\{$`emptyJudgement`
`List`$\}\}$ is derivable in $\mathbf{ROUPTS}_S$, then J is derivable in $\mathbf{OUPTS}_S$ and vice versa.

Proof Sketch. The soundness part follows from the simple observation that for each ROUPTS rewrite rule the right hand side together with its possible condition implies the left hand side under the intended logical interpretation given earlier. The completeness part can be obtained by adapting the inductive proof of Lemma 29 in [52]: Instead of the conventional notion of terms and substitution we have to use CINNI syntax with explicit substitutions, and instead of of PTSs we have to use OUPTSs. □

Executability in the following proposition means that the structural equations are implementable and the remaining equations and membership axioms satisfy the standard variable restriction [13,14]. Since we are interested in completeness of the operational semantics of rewriting logic for the specific goals relevant in our application, we also verify a number of sufficient conditions that are further explained in [37,11,13].

Proposition 46 (Executability of ROUPTSs)
The ROUPTS specification is executable, sort-preserving, equationally confluent, and coherent. Furthermore, the underlying membership equational theory is partially terminating in the sense that all membership, equational, and reduction goals, satisfying the condition that `whnf` is applied only to representations of weak head normalizing UPTS terms, are terminating.

Proof Sketch. Sort-preservation can be easily checked by inspection of each equation. To verify confluence observe that the entire equational specification is orthogonal and has three subspecifications: (1) the specification of explicit substitutions `[_:=_]`, `[shift_]`, `[lift__]`, and their application `__`, (2) the specification of metavariable substitution `<_:=_>_`, (3) the specification of `whnf`, and (4) the specification of `lookup`. Orthogonality of (2) and (4) is obvious, because there are no critical pairs, and orthogonality of (1) and (3) follows from the fact that critical pairs can be eliminated by a simple transformation, because their conditions are unsatisfiable. Furthermore, there are no critical pairs between (1), (2), (3), and (4), so that we can conclude that the membership equational theory is orthogonal and hence confluent. Similarly, coherence of the entire rewrite theory follows from the absence of critical pairs between equations and rules.

Finally, we show partial termination of the membership equational theory, that is termination of all membership and reduction goals under the condition of the proposition. Termination of membership goals M : `WhNf` and M : `WhReducible` follows by structural induction over the terms M. For the remaining termination proof we again exploit orthogonality of our specification, which implies that it is sufficient to prove termination under an innermost reduction strategy [38]. We use the following strategy: Given a reduction goal M or G, we repeat the following two steps as long as applicable: (a) We reduce it to normal form w.r.t. (1) if this form has not been reached yet, and then (b) we select an arbitrary innermost occurrence of `whnf` or `lookup` and apply one the equations from (3) or (4), respectively. Termination of this strategy follows from termination of Step (a), which holds according to the strong normalization property of CINNI proved in [47,48], and from the fact that `whnf` and `lookup` are either eliminated in Step (b) or replaced by corresponding occurrences with smaller measures. For `whnf`(M) the measure is the minimal number of β-reduction steps necessary to reach the weak head normal form from M, and for `lookup`($G, X\{m\}$) the measure is the length of the context G. □

A remarkable property of our specification is that it can be executed efficiently in the sense that we do not need an exhaustive search to verify whether $\{\{J\}\} \longrightarrow \{\{$`emptyJudgementList`$\}\}$ is derivable in $\mathbf{ROUPTS}_S$. Instead, we can use a simple execution strategy, i.e. a strategy without backtracking, and there is no additional restriction on the strategy beyond the freshness requirement for metavariables mentioned before. In fact, this is a consequence of confluence and partial termination of the rewrite part of our specification, which is stated in the following proposition.[13]

Proposition 47 (Confluence and Termination of ROUPTSs)
The ROUPTS specification is rewrite-confluent and partially terminating in the sense that all rewrite goals $\{\{J\}\} \rightarrow ?$, where J is one of the judgements $\Gamma \Vdash$, $\Gamma \Vdash M : A$, or $\Gamma \Vdash_1 M : A$ with UPTS terms M,A and a UPTS context Γ, are terminating.

Proof Sketch. Confluence of rewrite rules follows from an analysis of (conditional) critical pairs. In fact, there is only a single nontrivial critical pair generated by the overlapping rules `Conv6` and `Conv7`. Termination follows from structural induction over terms using the fact that `whnf` is only applied to terms M for which the goals

$$(G \texttt{ ||- }) \; (G \texttt{ |- } M \texttt{ : ?(NEW) }) \; (\texttt{?(NEW) Sort})$$

have been already verified for some context G. As a consequence, M is well-typed in $\mathbf{ROUPTS}_S$, and by the chain of soundness results given in Propositions 45, 35, and 34, we conclude that M is α-equivalent to a well-typed term in $\mathbf{PTS}_S$, and hence strongly normalizing. □

5 Final Remarks

In this paper we have given presentations of PTSs at different levels of abstraction. Moreover, we have discussed very natural representations of these systems in MEL or RWL. Both, abstractions and representations are uniformly captured by the general notion of correspondence between entailment systems. Our treatment is guided by the general logics methodology, which explores the space of formal systems by using a particular formal system, in this case rewriting logic, as a logical framework. Our representations of PTSs range from an abstract textbook representation in membership equational logic to a more refined operational representation for a subclass of PTSs in the executable sublanguage of rewriting logic.

Apart from its methodological aspect concerned with the use of rewriting logic as a logical framework to represent higher-order languages, this paper contains a more technical contribution, namely uniform pure type systems, a new variant of PTSs that provides a solution to the known problem with closure under α-conversion in systems with dependent types. Our solution is inspired by earlier work of Pollack, who first pointed out the difficulty to obtain closure

[13] Confluence modulo renaming of metavariables would be sufficient in practice, but it happens that, due to the deterministic nature of our specification, we have confluence here in the strongest sense.

under α-conversion if names are taken seriously. By instantiating our operational representation of PTSs, our approach directly leads to an executable prototype of the type theory in Maude. In our view the potential of this approach is by no means confined to formal representations and prototyping, but we think that it provides an interesting alternative to the implementation of type theories and typed higher-order logics, which are traditionally conducted using functional programming languages such as ML.

5.1 The Open Calculus of Constructions

We furthermore would like to point out that the techniques presented in this paper have been applied in the development of the *open calculus of constructions* (OCC) [48], an extension of the calculus of constructions that incorporates rewriting logic and its membership equational logic as a computational sublanguage. Although OCC deviates quite considerably from the prevailing, more conservative line of research in the context of the calculus of constructions, it can be seen as a possible realization of the early ideas in [26] on a marriage of these different paradigms.

OCC is a monomorphic type theory with dependent types and universes that is considerably more liberal than the calculus of constructions and several extensions such as the extended calculus of constructions [29] and the calculus of inductive constructions [17], or the calculus of algebraic constructions [9], but it maintains its core feature, which is also shared by all the remaining PTSs, namely that type checking is ultimately based on a notion of computation. Similar to PTSs, OCC is a family of type theories parameterized by a universe hierarchy, but we have imposed the requirement that impredicative universes can only appear at the bottom of this hierarchy. All other universes are predicative and hence form a monomorphic Martin-Löf-style type theory.

Different from the calculus of constructions, OCC is an *open* type theory in the sense that it is based on an *open computational system*, which can be specified by the user within the bounds provided by its logic. The computational system is of similar flexibility as that of membership equational and rewriting logic, which means in particular that restrictive operational properties, such as confluence and normalization, are in general not enforced by syntactic means. Generalizing the operational semantics of membership equational logic and rewriting logic, OCC supports conditional equations, conditional assertions, and conditional rewrite rules together with an operational semantics based on a combination of conditional rewriting modulo structural equations and exhaustive goal-oriented proof search.

Since OCC contains a higher-order equational programming/specification language with dependent types, and simultaneously a higher-order logic with dependent types by virtue of the propositions-as-types interpretation, our approach can be regarded as a marriage between the first-order paradigm of executable specification languages, such as equational and rewriting logic, and the higher-order paradigm, used in functional programming languages and higher-order logic proof assistants. Without excluding alternative models, we have equipped

OCC with a classical set-theoretic semantics, because it best reflects the prevailing practice in mathematics and computer science and also facilitates formal interoperability with many existing classical logic theorem provers.

It is remarkable that in spite of its logical and computational expressiveness, OCC is a rather minimalistic system based on the combination of only two key features: dependent types, and a computational system based on conditional rewriting modulo equations. Therefore, it can also be regarded as a natural higher-order generalization of rewriting logic. A key rationale behind the design of OCC is that an underlying computationally powerful system, like that of MEL and RWL, can increase the degree of automation in theorem proving already at the level of the formal system, rather than delegating the issue of automation entirely to the metalevel by means of tactics. This point is especially important for type theories in the line of PTSs, where type checking does not involve the use of tactics, but is based on the operational semantics of the type theory itself.

Using the techniques developed in this paper we have mapped the higher-order case to the first-order case, and, not surprisingly, we have employed the Maude rewriting engine and its reflective capabilities, to develop an experimental prototype of OCC based on this mapping. The prototype, which can be used as a programming/specification language and as a interactive proof assistant, has been a valuable tool to explore the applications of OCC already in the early phase of its development, and has made possible the study of a wide range of very different examples in various application domains [48]. In summary, our experience indicates that OCC opens a promising new research direction, which we hope will contribute to the long-term goal of a unified language for programming, specification and interactive theorem proving.

5.2 Conclusions

To sum up the main points of this paper, we have shown how a given first-order framework can very naturally and directly express powerful higher-order frameworks and how binders and substitution can be handled in a fully satisfactory way by purely algebraic means. We have also indicated that all this is not only of theoretical interest, but that as a fruit of this study, a proof assistant based on a new framework like OCC that combines the best of higher-order frameworks with the computational flexibility of MEL and RWL has been obtained.

Although we are interested in more complex applications such as OCC and its meta-theoretic properties, in this paper we have focused mainly on PTSs and have emphasized the representational aspects. We believe that choices of formal representation are important in their own right, and a major issue in applying a framework logic like MEL and RWL and in ascertaining the practical value of a logical framework. Apart from the benefit of executability that our last specification of UPTSs enjoys, a formal specification provides the basis for *formal* metatheoretic proofs. Indeed, MEL and RWL together with their initial model semantics provide a very general notion of *equational inductive definitions*, a fact that we exploited for representing several formal systems in this paper. We feel that our work is very much in the spirit of Feferman's first-order approach of finitary inductive systems [19], but by using equational and rewriting logic our approach puts a particular emphasis on executability. In fact, an important benefit of our use of rewriting logic, compared with informal presentations of algorithms by means of (possibly formal) inductive definitions of derivable judgements, is that the algorithms receive a clear formal status as (labeled) transition systems, which is the basis to express and reason about operational properties such as confluence and termination in a formally rigorous way.

The general problem of carrying out metatheoretic proofs, soundness and completeness proofs being typical examples, often involves the development of useful induction principles on the basis of possibly different but related presentations of the formal system. Such induction principles can be formulated either using an *internal approach*, e.g. by using a formal system such as OCC, which contains the framework logic as a sublogic in a suitable sense, or using an *external approach*, such as the one adopted in Twelf [44], where an external first-order logic is added on top of a higher-order logical framework for inductive reasoning about the representations. In a certain sense similar to the latter, but avoiding its hybrid character, one can instead use a *reflective approach* (cf. the approach to reflective metalogical frameworks presented in [3,4]), which introduces induction principles at the metalevel of the representation in a reflective framework such as rewriting logic.

6 Acknowledgements

Support for this work by DARPA and NASA (Contract NAS2-98073), by Office of Naval Research (Contract N00014-96-C-0114), by National Science Foundation Grant (CCR-9633363), and by a DAAD grant in the scope of HSP-III is gratefully acknowledged. We also would like to thank Steven Eker for his help concerning the efficient use of Maude, and furthermore Manuel Clavel, Narciso Martí-Oliet and the anonymous referees of our paper [49] for their useful comments, and, last but not least, Cesar Muñoz for many discussions on calculi of explicit substitutions and on the difficulties caused by α-conversion in type theories with explicit names.

References

1. H. P. Barendregt. Lambda-calculi with types. In S. Abramsky, D. M. Gabbay, and T. S. E. Maibaum, editors, *Background: Computational Structures*, volume 2 of *Handbook of Logic in Computer Science*. Claredon Press, Oxford, 1992.
2. B. Barras, S. Boutin, C. Cornes, J. Courant, Y. Coscoy, D. Delahaye, D. de Rauglaudre, J. C . Filliatre, E. Giménez, H. Herbelin, G. Huet, H. Laulhère, C. Muñoz, C. Murthy, C. Parent-Vigouroux, P. Loiseleur, C. Paulin, A. Saïbi, and B. Werner. The Coq Proof Assistent Reference Manual, Version 6.3.1, Coq Project. Technical report, INRIA, 1999. http://logical.inria.fr/.

3. D. Basin, M. Clavel, and J. Meseguer. Reflective metalogical frameworks. In *LFM'99: Workshop on Logical Frameworks and Meta-languages, Paris, France, September 28, 1999, Proceedings*, 1999. http://plan9.bell-labs.com/who/felty/LFM99/.
4. D. Basin, M. Clavel, and J. Meseguer. Rewriting logic as a metalogical framework. In S. Kapoor and S. Prasad, editors, *Twentieth Conference on the Foundations of Software Technology and Theoretical Computer Science, New Delhi, India, December 13–15, 2000, Proceedings*, volume 1974 of *Lecture Notes in Computer Science*, pages 55–80. Springer-Verlag, 2000.
5. Z. Benaissa, D. Briaud, P. Lescanne, and J. Rouyer-Degli. $\lambda\upsilon$, a calculus of explicit substitutions which preserves strong normalisation. *Journal of Functional Programming*, 6(5):699–722, September 1996.
6. S. Berardi. Towards a mathematical analysis of the Coquand-Huet calculus of constructions and other systems in Barendregt's cube. Technical report, Carnegie Mellon University and Universita di Torino, 1988.
7. K. J. Berkling. A symmetric complement to the lambda-calulus. Interner Bericht ISF-76-7, GMD, St. Augustin, Germany, 1976.
8. K. J. Berkling and E. Fehr. A consistent extension of the lambda-calculus as a base for functional programming languages. *Information and Control*, 55:89–101, 1982.
9. F. Blanqui, J.-P. Jouannaud, and M. Okada. The calculus of algebraic constructions. In *Rewriting Techniques and Applications*, Lecture Notes in Computer Science. Springer-Verlag, 1999.
10. A. Bouhoula, J.-P. Jouannaud, and J. Meseguer. Specification and proof in membership equational logic. In M. Bidoit and M. Dauchet, editors, *TAPSOFT'97: Theory and Practice of Software Development, 7th International Joint Conference CAAP/FASE, Lille, Frace, April 1997, Proceedings*, volume 1214 of *Lecture Notes in Computer Science*. Springer-Verlag, 1997.
11. A. Bouhoula, J.-P. Jouannaud, and J. Meseguer. Specification and proof in membership equational logic. *Theoretical Computer Science*, 236:35–132, 2000.
12. A. Church. A formulation of the simple theory of types. *Journal of Symbolic Logic*, 5(1), 1940.
13. M. Clavel, F. Durán, S. Eker, P. Lincoln, N. Martí-Oliet, J. Meseguer, and J. Quesada. *Maude: Specification and Programming in Rewriting Logic*. SRI International, January 1999. http://maude.csl.sri.com.
14. M. Clavel, F. Durán, S. Eker, P. Lincoln, N. Martí-Oliet, J. Meseguer, and J. Quesada. A tutorial on maude. http://maude.csl.sri.com, March 2000.
15. T. Coquand. An algorithm for testing conversion in type theory. In G. Huet and G. D. Plotkin, editors, *Logical Frameworks*. Cambridge University Press, 1991.
16. T. Coquand and G. Huet. The calculus of constructions. *Information and Computation*, 76(2/3):95–120, 1988.
17. T. Coquand and C. Paulin-Mohring. Inductively defined types. In *COLOG-88, International Conference on Computer Logic, Tallinn, USSR, December 1988, Proceedings*, volume 417 of *Lecture Notes in Computer Science*. Springer-Verlag, 1990.
18. N. G. de Bruijn. Lambda calculus with nameless dummies, a tool for automatic formula manipulation, with application to the Church-Rosser theorem. In *Proceedings Kninkl. Nederl. Akademie van Wetenschappen*, volume 75(5), pages 381–392, 1972.
19. S. Feferman. Finitary inductive systems. In R. Ferro, editor, *Proceedings of Logic Colloquium '88, Padova, Italy, August 1988*, pages 191–220. North-Holland, 1988.

20. P. Gardner. *Representing Logics in Type Theory.* PhD thesis, University of Edinburgh, 1992.
21. H. Geuvers. *Logics and Type Systems.* PhD thesis, University of Nijmegen, 1993.
22. H. Geuvers and M.-J. Nederhof. A modular proof of strong normalization for the calculus of constructions. *Journal of Functional Programming*, 1(2):155–189, April 1991.
23. J. Y. Girard. *Interpretation fonctionelle et elimination des coupures dans l'arithmetique d'ordre superieur.* PhD thesis, Université Paris VII, 1972.
24. R. Harper, F. Honsell, and G. Plotkin. A framework for defining logics. In *Second Annual Symposium on Logic in Computer Science, Ithaca, New York, 22–25 June 1987, Proceedings*, pages 193–204. IEEE, 1987.
25. G. Huet. The constructive engine. In R. Narasimhan, editor, *A Perspective in Theoretical Computer Science.* World Scientific, 1989.
26. J.-P. Jouannaud. Membership equational logic, calculus of inductive constructions, and rewrite logic. In *International Workshop on Rewriting Logic and its Applications Abbaye des Prémontrés at Pont-à-Mousson, France, September 1998, Proceedings*, volume 15 of *Electronic Notes in Theoretical Computer Science.* Elsevier, 1998. http://www.elsevier.nl/locate/entcs/volume15.html.
27. P. Lescanne. From $\lambda\sigma$ to $\lambda\upsilon$, a journey through calculi of explicit substitutions. In Hans Boehm, editor, *Conference Record of POPL'94: 21st ACM SIGPLAN-SIGACT Symposium on Principles of Programming Languages, Portland, Oregon, January 17–21, 1994*, pages 60–69. ACM, 1994.
28. P. Lescanne and J. Rouyer-Degli. The calculus of explicit substitutions $\lambda\upsilon$. Technical Report RR-2222, INRIA-Lorraine, January 1994.
29. Z. Luo. *Computation and Reasoning: A Type Theory for Computer Science.* International Series of Monographs on Computer Science. Oxford University Press, 1994.
30. L. Magnussen. *The Implementation of ALF – A Proof Editor based on Martin-Löf's Monomorphic Type Theory with Explicit Substitutions.* PhD thesis, University of Göteborg, Department of Computer Science, 1994.
31. N. Martí-Oliet and J. Meseguer. General logics and logical frameworks. In D. Gabbay, editor, *What is a Logical System?*, pages 355–392. Oxford University Press, 1994.
32. N. Martí-Oliet and J. Meseguer. Rewriting logic as a logical and semantic framework. In *RWLW'96, First International Workshop on Rewriting Logic and its Applications Asilomar Conference Center, Pacific Grove, CA, USA, September 3-6, 1996, Proceedings*, volume 4 of *Electronic Notes in Theoretical Computer Science.* Elsevier, 1996. http://www.elsevier.nl/locate/entcs/volume4.html. To appear in D. M. Gabbay, F. Guenthner, (eds.), *Handbook of Philosophical Logic* (2nd edition), Kluwer Academic Publishers.
33. P. Martin-Löf. An intuitionistic theory of types. Technical report, University of Stockholm, 1972.
34. J. McKinna and R. Pollack. Pure type systems formalized. In M. Bezem and J. F. Groote, editors, *Typed Lambda Calculi and Applications, International Conference on Typed Lambda Calculi and Applications, TLCA '93, Utrecht, The Netherlands, March 16–18, 1993, Proceedings*, volume 664 of *Lecture Notes in Computer Science.* Springer-Verlag, 1993.
35. J. Meseguer. General logics. In H.-D. Ebbinghaus et al., editors, *Logic Colloquium'87, Granada, Spain, July 1987, Proceedings*, pages 275–329. North-Holland, 1989.

36. J. Meseguer. Conditional rewriting logic as a unified model of concurrency. *Theoretical Computer Science*, 96:73–155, 1992.
37. J. Meseguer. Membership algebra as a logical framework for equational specification. In F. Parisi-Presicce, editor, *Recent Trends in Algebraic Development Techniques, 12th International Workshop, WADT'97, Tarquinia, Italy, June 3–7, 1997, Selected Papers*, volume 1376 of *Lecture Notes in Computer Science*, pages 18 – 61. Springer-Verlag, 1998.
38. M. J. O'Donnell. Computing in systems descibed by equations. In *Fundamentals of Computation Theory, International Conference, Poznań-Kornik, Poland September 19–23, 1977, Proceedings*, volume 58 of *Lecture Notes in Computer Science.* Springer-Verlag, 1977.
39. L. C. Paulson. *Isabelle*, volume 828 of *Lecture Notes in Computer Science.* Springer Verlag, 1994.
40. R. Pollack. Closure under alpha-conversion. In H. Barendregt and T. Nipkow, editors, *Types for Proofs and Programs: International Workshop TYPES'93, Nijmegen, May 1993, Selected Papers*, volume 806 of *Lecture Notes in Computer Science*, pages 313–332. Springer-Verlag, 1993.
41. R. Pollack. *The Theory of LEGO: A Proof Checker for the Extended Calculus of Constructions.* PhD thesis, University of Edinburgh, 1994.
42. R. Pollack. A verified typechecker. In M. Dezani-Ciancaglini and G. D. Plotkin, editors, *Second International Conference on Typed Lambda Calculi and Applications, Edinburgh, UK, April 10–12, 1995*, volume 902 of *Lecture Notes in Computer Science.* Springer-Verlag, 1995.
43. J. Reynolds. Towards a theory of type structure. In *Programming Symposium, Paris*, volume 19 of *Lecture Notes in Computer Science.* Springer-Verlag, 1974.
44. C. Schürmann and F. Pfenning. Automated theorem proving in a simple meta-logic for LF. In C. Kirchner and H. Kirchner, editors, *Automated Deduction - CADE-15, 15th International Conference on Automated Deduction, Lindau, Germany, July 5–10, 1998, Proceedings*, volume 1421 of *Lecture Notes in Artificial Intelligence*, pages 286–300. Springer-Verlag, 1998.
45. P. G. Severi. *Normalization in Lambda Calculus and its relation to Type Inference.* PhD thesis, Eindhoven University of Technology, 1996.
46. M.-O. Stehr. CINNI - A New Calculus of Explicit Substitutions and its Application to Pure Type Systems. Manuscript, CSL, SRI-International, Menlo Park, CA, USA, 1999.
47. M.-O. Stehr. CINNI – A Generic Calculus of Explicit Substitutions and its Application to λ-, σ- and π-calculi. In K. Futatsugi, editor, *The 3rd International Workshop on Rewriting Logic and its Applications Kanazawa City Cultural Hall, Kanzawa Japan, September 18–20, 2000, Proceedings*, volume 36 of *Electronic Notes in Theoretical Computer Science*, pages 71 – 92. Elsevier, 2000. http://www.elsevier.nl/locate/entcs/volume36.html. Extended version at http://www.csl.sri.com/~stehr.
48. M.-O. Stehr. Programming, Specification, and Interactive Theorem Proving — Towards a Unified Language based on Equational Logic, Rewriting Logic, and Type Theory. Doctoral Thesis, Universität Hamburg, Fachbereich Informatik, Germany, 2002. http://www.sub.uni-hamburg.de/disse/810/.
49. M.-O. Stehr and J. Meseguer. Pure type systems in rewriting logic. In *LFM'99: Workshop on Logical Frameworks and Meta-languages, Paris, France, September 28, 1999, Proceedings*, 1999. http://plan9.bell-labs.com/who/felty/LFM99/.
50. J. Terlouw. Een nadere bewijstheoretische analyse van GSTTs. Manuscript, University of Nijmegen, The Netherlands, 1989.

51. L. S. van Benthem Jutting. Typing in pure type systems. *Information and Computation*, 105:30–41, 1993.
52. L. S. van Benthem Jutting, J. McKinna, and R. Pollack. Checking algorithms for pure type systems. In H. Barendregt and T. Nipkow, editors, *Types for Proofs and Programs: International Workshop TYPES'93, Nijmegen, May 1993, Selected Papers*, volume 806 of *Lecture Notes in Computer Science*, pages 19–61. Springer-Verlag, 1993.

Building Optimal Binary Search Trees from Sorted Values in O(N) Time

Jean G. Vaucher, professeur titulaire

Departement d'informatique et de recherche opérationnelle,
Université de Montréal,
C.P. 6128, Succursale Centre-Ville, Montréal, Canada, H3C 3J7
vaucher@iro.umontreal.ca

Abstract. First, we present a simple algorithm which, given a sorted sequence of node values, can build a binary search tree of minimum height in O(N) time. The algorithm works with sequences whose length is, a priori, unknown. Previous algorithms [1–3] required the number of elements to be known in advance. Although the produced trees are of minimum height, they are generally unbalanced. We then show how to convert them into *optimal* trees with a minimum internal path length in O(log N) time. The trees produced, both minimum height and optimal, have characteristic shapes which can easily be predicted from the binary representation of tree size.

Key Words: binary search tree, balanced trees, data structures

1 Introduction

The binary search tree (BST) is a well known data structure: it is a binary tree with the property that the value of any given node is larger than the node values in its left sub-tree and smaller than the values in its right sub-tree. Figure 1 on page 377 shows two such trees. In this figure and in what follows, we assume integer values for the nodes.

The height of the tree is an important factor in the analysis of tree algorithms. In this paper the height, h, is defined to be the number of nodes on the longest path from the root to a leaf. The height of the tree on the left of Figure 1 is 3 and the height of the tree on the right is 4. The tree on the left with all the leaves on the bottom level is said to be perfect. It contains exactly $2^h - 1$ nodes. More generally, the minimum height for a tree containing N nodes is $\lfloor \log_2(N+1) \rfloor$. Conversely, the maximum height is N if the tree has degenerated into a list.

Any modern text on data structures describes the properties of BSTs and gives the basic algorithms to find, add or remove an element. Given random values, the time complexity of these basic operations is O(log n); furthermore, the values from a binary search tree can be output in sorted order in O(n) time by a simple recursive algorithm shown on page 377.

O. Owe et al. (Eds.): From OO to FM (Dahl Festschrift), LNCS 2635, pp. 376–388, 2004.

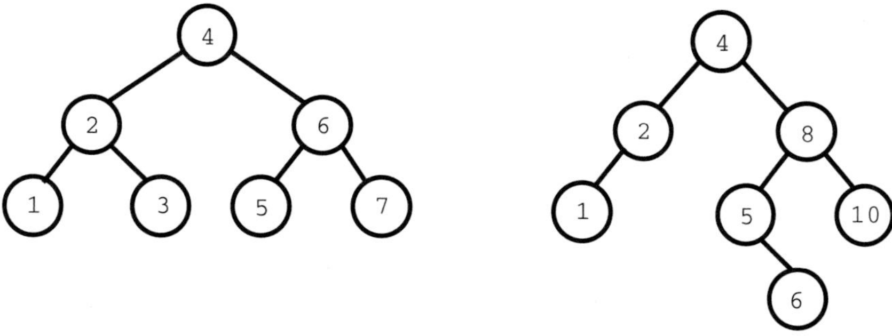

Fig. 1. Binary Search trees

```
class Node {
  vType value;
  Node  left, right;
}

void printTree ( Node p)
{ if p != null then
  { printTree (p.left) ;
    print (p.value) ;
    printTree (p.right) ;
  }
}
```

Now consider the inverse operation, namely: building a tree given a sequence of sorted values such as produced by `printTree`. Of course, this can be accomplished by successive `INSERT` operations but the complexity of this approach is $O(N \log N)$ at best. Actually, if the basic insertion algorithm is used with a sorted set of values, the tree degenerates into a list and the complexity is $O(N^2)$.

In 1976, Wirth [1, p. 195] gave an efficient algorithm to construct a tree of N nodes. The algorithm is recursive: a tree of N nodes is built by reading a node value and doing recursive calls to build two sub-trees of $(N-1)/2$ nodes. The resulting tree is perfectly balanced and the running time is $O(N)$, but the value of N must be known before hand. Wirth was not concerned with node order and the tree was arbitrarily read in *pre-order*. More recently, Carrano [2, p. 480, 3, p. 545], gives a similar algorithm which works with sorted values but again N must be known beforehand. The method is shown below.

```
Node buildTree ( int N )
{   if N = 0 then
        return null ;
    else
```

```
    {   Node  left  := readTree ( N / 2 ) ;
        vType value := nextValue () ;
        Node  right := readTree ( (N-1) / 2 ) ;
        return new Node( value, left, right ) ;
    }
}
```

In what follows, we develop an algorithm which does the same thing as Carrano's but does not require prior knowledge of N. This algorithm is presented in four steps. First, we start with a simple function which works for *perfect* trees such as shown at the left of Figure 1. This function needs a parameter: `h`, the height of the tree. Second we note, that with a test for end of file, the simple function still builds a minimum height tree for any value `h` greater or equal to the correct value. Thirdly, we add a driver routine which builds successively bigger perfect trees until the end of data is reached. This driver function requires no height parameter and works in $O(N)$ time. The tree that is built is of minimum height and supports the usual operations in logarithmic time but it may not have an optimal shape. Finally, we show how to modify the tree to achieve minimum internal path length with $O(\log N)$ *rotation* operations.

The pseudo-code used for the programming examples is based on Java with some Simula (Algol) notation for clarity. The Simula influence can be seen in the use of "`=`" for equality and "`:=`" for assignment and the `if...then...else...` syntax. As in C and Java, we assume that parameters are passed by value and that `return` exits immediately. Finally, in order to make the algorithms match the text and easy to follow, we have used more variables and code than strictly necessary.

2 Reading a Perfect Tree

Given $2^h - 1$ ordered nodes values, the function `readTree1` — shown below — builds a perfect tree of height h. It assumes that the input contains exactly the right number of values and does not check for premature end of data.

```
Node readTree1 ( int h )
{   if h < 1 then
       return null ;
    else
    {   Node  left  := readTree1 ( h-1 ) ;
        vType value := nextValue () ;
        Node  right := readTree1 ( h-1 ) ;
        return new Node( value, left, right ) ;
    }
}
```

3 Handling Premature End of Data

The next version of the input function, `readTree2`, is identical to the first except that we add a test to stop construction when there is no more data to read. We assume that the `end_of_data` test comes before reading and that the test can be repeated without error even after it has returned true. The algorithm still needs the expected tree height, h, as a parameter but it stops creating nodes as soon as the input values are all read.

```
Node readTree2 ( int h )
{   if h < 1 then
       return null ;
    else
    {   Node left   := readTree2 ( h-1 ) ;
        if end_of_data() then return left ;
        vType value := nextValue () ;
        Node  right := readTree2 ( h-1 ) ;
        return new Node( value, left, right ) ;
    }
}
```

As long as the data is not exhausted, all trees returned by `readTree2` will be perfect. Since the algorithm proceeds in order building the left sub-tree before the node, the fact that we are able to read a node value implies that `end_of_data` was not encountered during the construction of the left sub-tree/ it is therefore perfect; but the same cannot be said for right sub-trees.

Figure 2 shows what happens, when the initial value of h is correct or larger than strictly necessary but there are fewer than $2^h - 1$ nodes and `end_of_data` is encountered while building the tree. In the example, there are only 5 node values but the function is called with an expected height $h = 4$. The shaded part shows the virtual perfect tree of height 4 (with 15 nodes) which could have been returned by the read function. When there are fewer nodes, the algorithm traverses this virtual tree in the usual order building nodes with successive input value until the `end_of_data` is reached. Essentially, it fills in the bottom left-hand corner of the virtual tree. In terms of execution time, overestimating the tree height means that we visit the extra virtual nodes between the root and the actual nodes built.

Essentially, the algorithm tries to build successively taller perfect trees until all node values have been read. As long as the initial value of $h \geq \log_2(N+1)$ all nodes will be read and the returned tree will be of minimum height but it may be unbalanced. The left sub-tree of the root — being perfect — contains exactly $2^{h'-1} - 1$ nodes (where h' is the actual height of the tree) but the right sub-tree, which contains the remaining nodes, may contain anywhere from 0 to $2^{h'-1} - 1$ nodes.

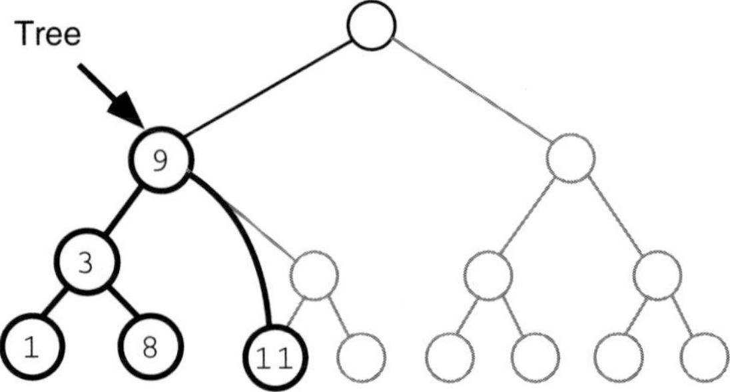

Fig. 2. Tree returned by `readTree2(4)` from values 1, 3, 8, 9 and 11

4 Dispensing with the Estimated Height Parameter

To avoid specifying an initial value for the tree height, h, we use a loop which calls `readTree2` with successively larger values of h to build trees of increasing size until the end of data is reached.

```
Node readMinTree ()
{
    int  h    := 0;
    Node tree := null;
    while not end_of_data() do
    {
        Node  left := tree;
        vType root_value := nextValue () ;
        Node  right := readTree2 ( h ) ;
        tree  := new Node(root_value, left, right ) ;
        h++ ;
    }
    return tree ;
}
```

In the function `tree` is the last tree that was built and its height is `h`. While there are nodes to read, tree is a perfect tree containing exactly $2^h - 1$ nodes. The next larger tree (of height $h + 1$) uses the old tree as its left sub-tree. The next node value is read for the root and we call `readTree2` to build a new right sub-tree of the same height as the left. If data is still not exhausted, the resulting tree is again perfect and we repeat the process until end of data is reached.

Initially, we start with $h = 0$ and an empty tree. When the loop terminates, the tree built by this function has the same shape as described for `readTree2`: minimum height and a full left sub-tree but a right sub-tree containing anywhere from zero to $2^{h-1} - 1$ nodes.

Essentially the algorithm does a recursive traversal of the tree that it builds and its time complexity is $O(N)$.

5 The Shape of Returned Trees

The trees returned by `readMinTree` have a definite characteristic shape. While the left sub-tree of the root is perfect, the right sub-tree contains at most the same number of nodes as the left and generally fewer so the right half of the tree is generally not as deep as the left. The same reasoning applies to right sub-trees, which will either be balanced or skewed to the left. Overall, the tree shape, as shown on page 381, could be characterized as a *staircase*.

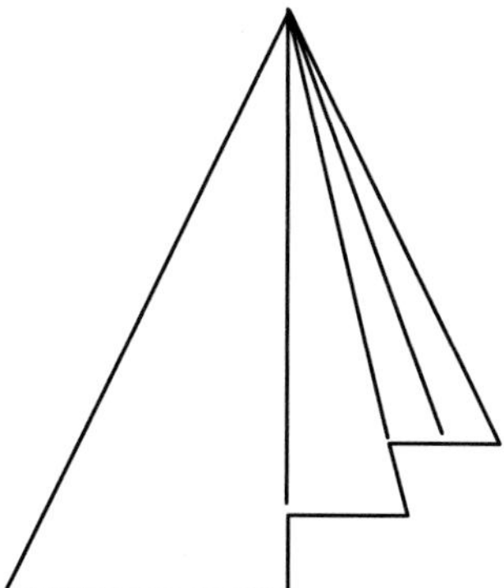

Fig. 3. Characteristic shape of the trees constructed by `readMinTree`

We can get a more precise idea of the tree topology by noting that our tree is composed of a succession of perfect trees that decrease in size as they are built from left to right and we can think of the nodes on the right edge of the tree as a list connecting these perfect trees together. This view will make it easy to determine the shape of the tree from the binary coding of N, the tree size. Consider the perfect tree of height h shown in Figure 4.It contains $2^h - 1$ nodes but, if we add the extra *link* node at the top, the structure accounts for 2^h nodes.

Thus there is a direct correspondence between the perfect trees in our structure and the *ones* in the binary representation of the tree size. For example, consider a tree of 37 nodes: "100101_2" in binary. This corresponds to a tree shown below with 3 linked perfect trees whose sizes correspond to the powers of 2 that add up to 37: $32 + 4 + 1$. The shape is shown in Figure 5.

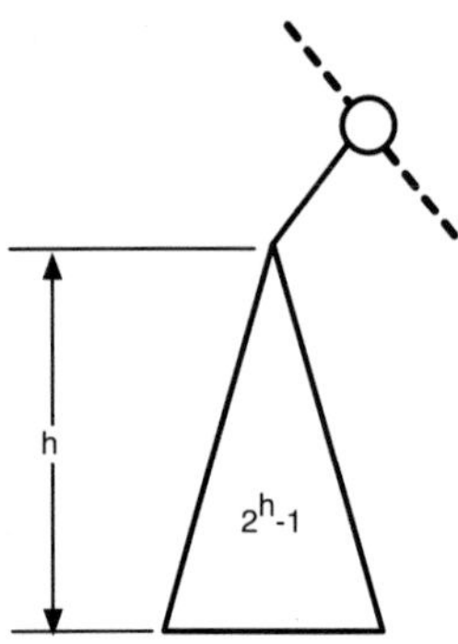

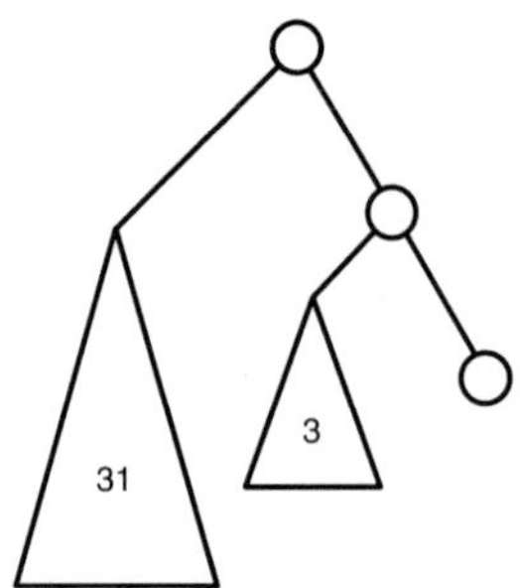

Fig. 4. Perfect tree component

Fig. 5. Staircase of size 37

6 Improving the Tree

The time complexity of traditional search tree algorithms is strongly dependent on the tree height. In the case of our staircase trees, the height is a minimum and equal to $|\log_2(N+1)|$ so that standard operations can be done in $O(\log N)$ time. This height is indicative of worst case operation and compares favorably to balanced AVL trees where the height in the worst case is $1.44\log(N+2)$ [5, p.118].

However, for complexity in the average case, the staircase shape is not optimal. Consider the extreme case when the number of nodes is a power of 2. The tree that we return is shown on the left in Figure 6 on page 382. In such a case, the right sub-tree is empty and all nodes are in a perfect tree on the left. A better disposition of the nodes is shown on the right where all nodes in the left sub-tree have been moved up by one level and the root has been moved to the bottom.

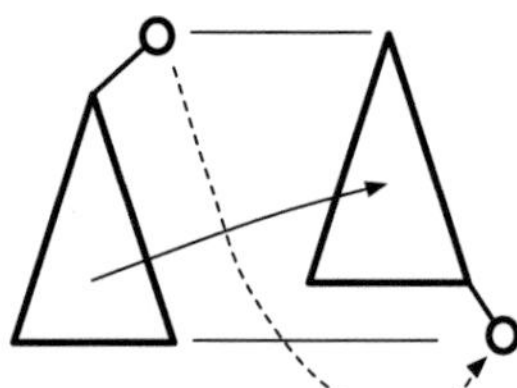

Fig. 6. Optimizing a staircase tree

The tree on the right is an example of an *optimal* search tree: one in which all levels, except possibly for the bottom one, are completely filled. In such a tree, there is no empty slot closer to the root into which a node from the bottom could be moved up and the *total path length*, the sum of the distances between each node and the root, is minimized. Note that the improvement in average path length to be gained from modifying our trees will be marginal — at most one level — as shown in Figure 6. This is because staircase trees are already of minimum height and represent intermediate stages between perfect trees whose heights differ by one.

In what follows, we will show how to modify our staircase tree into an optimal shape in h steps, where h is the tree height. To do this we will use rotations — operations commonly used in AVL trees [4–6] — which move one sub-tree up closer to the root while moving another sub-tree down; all the while keeping the tree height constant. If the number of nodes going up is greater than the number going down, the rotation improves the average path length.

In Figure 7 on page 383, the tree on the left is typical of the staircase trees that we produce. Here X is the root with a perfect sub-tree to its left and a smaller tree (R) to its right. The root Y of the left sub-tree has two equal size (perfect) sub-trees labeled L (left) and M (middle). As a result of a rotation, the old root X and its imperfect right sub-tree R are moved down one level. Y and its sub-tree L move up one level. Y becomes the new root. The middle tree, M, is now tied to X instead of Y, but in terms of distances of its nodes to the (new) root, nothing has changed and it can be thought of as a fixed pivot upon which the other sub-trees balance. Note that the rotation does not change the tree height and it maintains the order between nodes and sub-trees: $L < Y < M < X < R$. The important effect is that L moves up whereas the smaller R moves down.

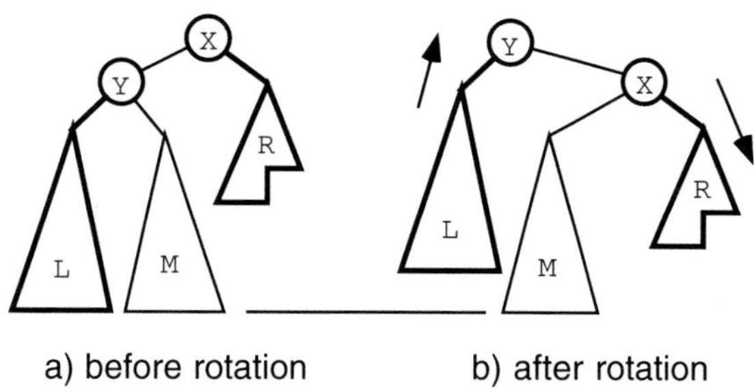

Fig. 7. Effect of a rotation

Another way to consider the effect of the rotations is to note that they modify the tree towards the optimal shape by bringing down the smaller imperfect sub-tree (R) on the right until its bottom layer lines up with the bottom of the tree. One rotation may not be enough. In the example of Figure 7, after the first rotation, R could still move down and we would do further rotations on X. With each rotation, R is attached to a lower point in the main (left) tree. When R

reaches the bottom, we can start applying rotations to R itself with a view of bringing its right half in line with its left. Now for every tree on the right that goes down, a tree on the left must go up but you will note in what follows that the trees that move up (like L) start on the bottom and go up by only one level. Thus these promotions do not destroy the optimal shape.

Knowing N, the number of nodes in the tree[1], we can compute the number of nodes in the various sub-trees and decide if a rotation is warranted:

- nodes in the whole tree: N
- height of the tree: $h = \lceil \log_2(N+1) \rceil$
- height of tree rooted at Y: $hL = h - 1$
- size of tree rooted at $Y : 2^{h-1} - 1$
- size of $R : nR = N - (2^{h-1} - 1) - 1 = N - 2^{h-1}$
- height of R: $hR = \lceil \log_2(nR+1) \rceil$

An example will clarify the situation. In Figure 8 on page 385, we consider the optimization of the staircase tree shown previously. Here, in the initial situation (a), $N = 37$ and $h = 6$, the heights of the trees on the left and right are 5 and 3 respectively. A rotation is warranted and the original root along with the right sub-tree moves down one level as shown in (b) [the arrow always the shows the tree under consideration]. Now, hR remains at 3 but $hL = 4$ and a further rotation brings us to (c). At this point, the right sub-tree is level with the bottom of the tree and further rotation of the original right sub-tree is no longer beneficial.

At this point, we skip the rotation but still go down a level to the right to see if rotations *within* the original right sub-tree could be beneficial. Now we have $N = 5, hL = 2, nR = hR = 1$. A final rotation brings us to (d) where the rightmost leaf being on the bottom, the work is finished. At each step in the optimization process we go down one level, thus the complexity is $O(h) = O(\log N)$.

Going a step further, we can understand the shape of the final tree obtained in (d) above by considering that a perfect tree of the same height would have contained 26 more nodes than our 37-node tree. In an optimal tree, the missing nodes must come from the bottom layer: they are the nodes that would have been leaves below our *promoted* trees. The way we promoted trees was to start with the largest on the left, reducing the size by a factor of two at each step. Therefore, the gaps from right to left in the bottom layer correspond to the binary representation of the missing nodes. In our case: $16+8+2 = 26$ as shown in Figure 9. When comparing figures 8 and 9, remember that the bottom layer of a perfect tree with $2^h - 1$ nodes contains 2^{h-1} nodes and that the (missing) layer below that would contain 2^h nodes.

[1] These should be counted by the input function nextValue and made available in a global variable.

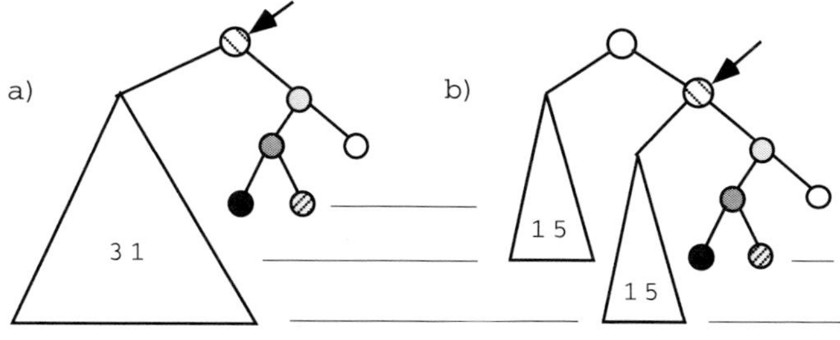

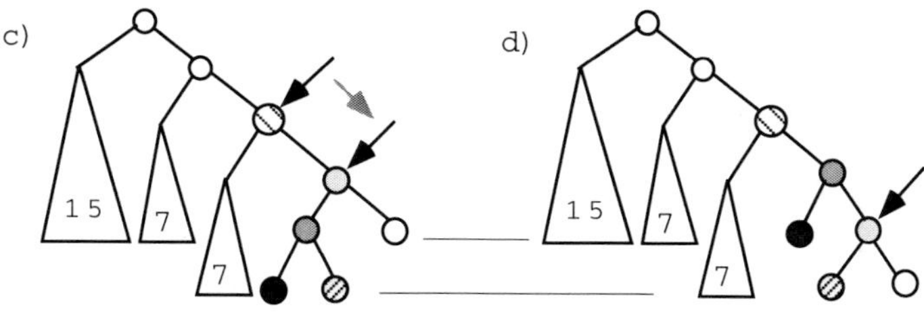

Fig. 8. Optimizing a staircase tree

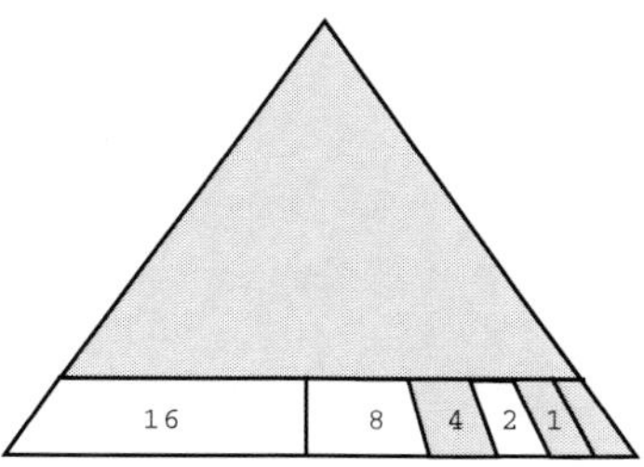

Fig. 9. Layout of an optimized tree

7 The Optimizing Algorithm

The code below implements the technique that we have outlined with a slight improvement. In the example of Figure 8, we showed how a sub-tree several levels above the bottom could be moved down with a sequence of rotations; however, it is more efficient to find the node on the right edge below which the sub-tree will eventually be placed and do a single rotation at that point.

```
1   Node optimize ( Node root, int N, int h )
2     {
3     if N <= 1 then return root;
4
5     int  hL = h-1 ;
6     int  nR = N - 2**(h-1);
7     int  hR = ceiling( log(nR+1));
8
9     Node newRoot = root;
10      if hL > hR then
11      {
12        Node leftTree = newRoot = root.left;
13        hL = hL-1;
14        while hL > hR do
15        {
16          leftTree = leftTree.right;
17          hL = hL-1;
18        }
19        root.left = leftTree.right;
20        leftTree.right = root;
21      }
22      root.right = optimize ( root.right, nR, hR );
23      return newRoot;
24     }
```

The method takes 3 parameters: `root`, a pointer to the root of the staircase tree to be optimized; `N`, the tree size, and `h`, the tree height. It works recursively: on each call, it optimizes a tree by deciding if the right sub-tree should be moved down and if so does the demotion; it then proceeds to optimize the right sub-tree. The algorithm terminates when the tree has shrunk down to a single node (line 3). In the code, we use more significant names, `root` and `leftTree`, to denote the X and Y nodes of Figure 7. Initially (lines 5–6), we compute the size of the right sub-tree, `nR`, as well as the heights of both sub-trees, `hL` and `hR`. `newRoot` represents the root of the optimized tree; it is initialized to `root`, the value that will be returned if no rotation is done. If the right tree is shorter than the left (line 10), then the right tree will be moved down and lines 12–18 determine where it will be inserted. At the same time the value of `newRoot` is changed. The *rotation* to insert the right sub-tree lower in the left Tree is done in lines 19–20. Whether, the right sub-tree has been moved or not, we optimize it (line 22) and return the optimized tree (line 23).

We show below the final version of `readTree` which combines the optimization with the initial tree building to meet the stated objective: constructing an optimal search tree from a sorted set of values.

```
int N;  // number of nodes - incremented by nextValue

Node readTree ()  // final version
{
  int  h    := 0;
  Node tree := null;
  while not end_of_data() do
  {
    Node  left := tree;
    vType root_value := nextValue () ;
    Node  right := readTree2 ( h ) ;
    tree := new Node(root_value, left, right ) ;
    h ++ ;
  }
  return optimize( tree, N, h );
}
```

A Java test version of this algorithm is available on the Internet at the following URL: http://www.iro.umontreal.ca/~vaucher/Pubs/BST.java

8 Conclusions

We have developed a simple algorithm which, given a sorted sequence of node values, can build a balanced binary search tree in $O(N)$ time, without requiring *a priori* knowledge of the number of elements, N. The novel idea is that a minimum height tree can be constructed by trying to build successively deeper perfect trees, using the tree from the last step as the left sub-tree of the new one. It is then a simple — though tricky — matter to reshape the tree with rotations to minimize internal path length. We also showed that the shape of the trees had a simple one-to-one correspondence to the binary representation of the tree size.

This algorithm could also be used to re-balance an arbitrary tree. Given a language with coroutines (like Simula [7]), we could emulate Ole-Johan Dahl's technique from his classic 1972 paper with Tony Hoare [8]: using one coroutine object to recursively traverse the old tree and provide input for another coroutine using our algorithm to build a better tree. With a current language like Java, rebalancing could still be done but would be less elegant.

I met Ole-Johan Dahl along with his colleague Kristen Nygaard in the early 1970s on a visit to Oslo to learn more about Simula. The concern with rigor and clarity as well as innovation evident in their work over the years has been a continuing source of inspiration and I grieve their passing.

9 Acknowledgements

I wish to thank the anonymous referee whose comments contributed to a significant improvement in the original paper. In particular, he prodded me into further reflection into the optimization phase of the algorithm leading to the discovery of the simple relations that determine tree shapes. Finally, the referee's suggestion of using tree height instead of size to control the optimization lead to simplification in both the code and the explanation.

References

1. N. Wirth, Algorithms + data structures=programs. Englewood Cliffs, N.J.: Prentice-Hall, 1976.
2. F. M. Carrano and J. J. Prichard, Data abstraction and problem solving with Java: walls and mirrors, 1st ed. Boston: Addison-Wesley, 2001.
3. F. M. Carrano, P. Helman, and R. Veroff, Data structures and problem solving with Turbo Pascal: walls and mirrors. Redwood City, Calif. ; Don Mills, Ont.: Benjamin/Cummings Pub. Co., 1993.
4. G. M. Adelson-Velskii and E. M. Landis, An Algorithm for the Organization of Information, Soviet Mathematics (translated from Doklady Akademii Nauk, SSSR), vol. 3, pp. 1259-1263, 1962.
5. M. A. Weiss, Data Structures and Algorithm Analysis in Java: Addison-Wesley, 1999.
6. D. E. Knuth, The art of computer programming: Sorting and searching., vol. 3. Reading, Mass.,: Addison-Wesley Pub. Co., 1973.
7. O.-J. Dahl, B. Myhrhaug, and K. Nygaard, SIMULA-67 Common Base Language, Norwegian Computer Centre, Oslo, Norway, Technical Report 1970.
8. O.-J. Dahl and C. A. R. Hoare, Hierarchical Program Structures, in Structured Programming, vol. 8, A.P.I.C. Studies in Data Processing. London: Academic Press, 1972, pp. 175-220.

Author Index

Lecture Notes in Computer Science

For information about Vols. 1–2884

please contact your bookseller or Springer-Verlag

Vol. 3009: F. Bomarius, H. Iida (Eds.), Product Focused Software Process Improvement. XIV, 584 pages. 2004.

Vol. 3005: G.R. Raidl, S. Cagnoni, J. Branke, D.W. Corne, R. Drechsler, Y. Jin, C.G. Johnson, P. Machado, E. Marchiori, F. Rothlauf, G.D. Smith, G. Squillero (Eds.), Applications of Evolutionary Computing. XVII, 562 pages. 2004.

Vol. 3004: J. Gottlieb, G.R. Raidl (Eds.), Evolutionary Computation in Combinatorial Optimization. X, 241 pages. 2004.

Vol. 3003: M. Keijzer, U.-M. O'Reilly, S.M. Lucas, E. Costa, T. Soule (Eds.), Genetic Programming. XI, 410 pages. 2004.

Vol. 2999: E.A. Boiten, J. Derrick, G. Smith (Eds.), Integrated Formal Methods. XI, 541 pages. 2004.

Vol. 2998: Y. Kameyama, P.J. Stuckey (Eds.), Functional and Logic Programming. X, 307 pages. 2004.

Vol. 2997: S. McDonald, J. Tait (Eds.), Advances in Information Retrieval. XIII, 427 pages. 2004.

Vol. 2996: V. Diekert, M. Habib (Eds.), STACS 2004. XVI, 658 pages. 2004.

Vol. 2995: C. Jensen, S. Poslad, T. Dimitrakos (Eds.), Trust Management. XIII, 377 pages. 2004.

Vol. 2994: E. Rahm (Ed.), Data Integration in the Life Sciences. X, 221 pages. 2004. (Subseries LNBI).

Vol. 2993: R. Alur, G.J. Pappas (Eds.), Hybrid Systems: Computation and Control. XII, 674 pages. 2004.

Vol. 2992: E. Bertino, S. Christodoulakis, D. Plexousakis, V. Christophides, M. Koubarakis, K. Böhm, E. Ferrari (Eds.), Advances in Database Technology - EDBT 2004. XVIII, 877 pages. 2004.

Vol. 2991: R. Alt, A. Frommer, R.B. Kearfott, W. Luther (Eds.), Numerical Software with Result Verification. X, 315 pages. 2004.

Vol. 2989: S. Graf, L. Mounier (Eds.), Model Checking Software. X, 309 pages. 2004.

Vol. 2988: K. Jensen, A. Podelski (Eds.), Tools and Algorithms for the Construction and Analysis of Systems. XIV, 608 pages. 2004.

Vol. 2987: I. Walukiewicz (Ed.), Foundations of Software Science and Computation Structures. XIII, 529 pages. 2004.

Vol. 2986: D. Schmidt (Ed.), Programming Languages and Systems. XII, 417 pages. 2004.

Vol. 2985: E. Duesterwald (Ed.), Compiler Construction. X, 313 pages. 2004.

Vol. 2984: M. Wermelinger, T. Margaria-Steffen (Eds.), Fundamental Approaches to Software Engineering. XII, 389 pages. 2004.

Vol. 2983: S. Istrail, M.S. Waterman, A. Clark (Eds.), Computational Methods for SNPs and Haplotype Inference. IX, 153 pages. 2004. (Subseries LNBI).

Vol. 2982: N. Wakamiya, M. Solarski, J. Sterbenz (Eds.), Active Networks. XI, 308 pages. 2004.

Vol. 2981: C. Müller-Schloer, T. Ungerer, B. Bauer (Eds.), Organic and Pervasive Computing – ARCS 2004. XI, 339 pages. 2004.

Vol. 2980: A. Blackwell, K. Marriott, A. Shimojima (Eds.), Diagrammatic Representation and Inference. XV, 448 pages. 2004. (Subseries LNAI).

Vol. 2978: R. Groz, R.M. Hierons (Eds.), Testing of Communicating Systems. XII, 225 pages. 2004.

Vol. 2977: G. Di Marzo Serugendo, A. Karageorgos, O.F. Rana, F. Zambonelli (Eds.), Engineering Self-Organising Systems. X, 299 pages. 2004. (Subseries LNAI).

Vol. 2976: M. Farach-Colton (Ed.), LATIN 2004: Theoretical Informatics. XV, 626 pages. 2004.

Vol. 2973: Y. Lee, J. Li, K.-Y. Whang, D. Lee (Eds.), Database Systems for Advanced Applications. XXIV, 925 pages. 2004.

Vol. 2971: J.I. Lim, D.H. Lee (Eds.), Information Security and Cryptology -ICISC 2003. XI, 458 pages. 2004.

Vol. 2970: F. Fernández Rivera, M. Bubak, A. Gómez Tato, R. Doallo (Eds.), Grid Computing. XI, 328 pages. 2004.

Vol. 2964: T. Okamoto (Ed.), Topics in Cryptology – CT-RSA 2004. XI, 387 pages. 2004.

Vol. 2963: R. Sharp, Higher Level Hardware Synthesis. XVI, 195 pages. 2004.

Vol. 2962: S. Bistarelli, Semirings for Soft Constraint Solving and Programming. XII, 279 pages. 2004.

Vol. 2961: P. Eklund (Ed.), Concept Lattices. IX, 411 pages. 2004. (Subseries LNAI).

Vol. 2960: P.D. Mosses (Ed.), CASL Reference Manual. XVII, 528 pages. 2004.

Vol. 2958: L. Rauchwerger (Ed.), Languages and Compilers for Parallel Computing. XI, 556 pages. 2004.

Vol. 2957: P. Langendoerfer, M. Liu, I. Matta, V. Tsaoussidis (Eds.), Wired/Wireless Internet Communications. XI, 307 pages. 2004.

Vol. 2954: F. Crestani, M. Dunlop, S. Mizzaro (Eds.), Mobile and Ubiquitous Information Access. X, 299 pages. 2004.

Vol. 2953: K. Konrad, Model Generation for Natural Language Interpretation and Analysis. XIII, 166 pages. 2004. (Subseries LNAI).

Vol. 2952: N. Guelfi, E. Astesiano, G. Reggio (Eds.), Scientific Engineering of Distributed Java Applications. X, 157 pages. 2004.

Vol. 2951: M. Naor (Ed.), Theory of Cryptography. XI, 523 pages. 2004.

Vol. 2949: R. De Nicola, G. Ferrari, G. Meredith (Eds.), Coordination Models and Languages. X, 323 pages. 2004.

Vol. 2948: G.L. Mullen, A. Poli, H. Stichtenoth (Eds.), Finite Fields and Applications. VIII, 263 pages. 2004.

Vol. 2947: F. Bao, R. Deng, J. Zhou (Eds.), Public Key Cryptography – PKC 2004. XI, 455 pages. 2004.

Vol. 2946: R. Focardi, R. Gorrieri (Eds.), Foundations of Security Analysis and Design II. VII, 267 pages. 2004.

Vol. 2943: J. Chen, J. Reif (Eds.), DNA Computing. X, 225 pages. 2004.

Vol. 2941: M. Wirsing, A. Knapp, S. Balsamo (Eds.), Radical Innovations of Software and Systems Engineering in the Future. X, 359 pages. 2004.

Vol. 2940: C. Lucena, A. Garcia, A. Romanovsky, J. Castro, P.S. Alencar (Eds.), Software Engineering for Multi-Agent Systems II. XII, 279 pages. 2004.

Vol. 2939: T. Kalker, I.J. Cox, Y.M. Ro (Eds.), Digital Watermarking. XII, 602 pages. 2004.

Vol. 2937: B. Steffen, G. Levi (Eds.), Verification, Model Checking, and Abstract Interpretation. XI, 325 pages. 2004.

Vol. 2934: G. Lindemann, D. Moldt, M. Paolucci (Eds.), Regulated Agent-Based Social Systems. X, 301 pages. 2004. (Subseries LNAI).

Vol. 2930: F. Winkler (Ed.), Automated Deduction in Geometry. VII, 231 pages. 2004. (Subseries LNAI).

Vol. 2926: L. van Elst, V. Dignum, A. Abecker (Eds.), Agent-Mediated Knowledge Management. XI, 428 pages. 2004. (Subseries LNAI).

Vol. 2923: V. Lifschitz, I. Niemelä (Eds.), Logic Programming and Nonmonotonic Reasoning. IX, 365 pages. 2004. (Subseries LNAI).

Vol. 2919: E. Giunchiglia, A. Tacchella (Eds.), Theory and Applications of Satisfiability Testing. XI, 530 pages. 2004.

Vol. 2917: E. Quintarelli, Model-Checking Based Data Retrieval. XVI, 134 pages. 2004.

Vol. 2916: C. Palamidessi (Ed.), Logic Programming. XII, 520 pages. 2003.

Vol. 2915: A. Camurri, G. Volpe (Eds.), Gesture-Based Communication in Human-Computer Interaction. XIII, 558 pages. 2004. (Subseries LNAI).

Vol. 2914: P.K. Pandya, J. Radhakrishnan (Eds.), FST TCS 2003: Foundations of Software Technology and Theoretical Computer Science. XIII, 446 pages. 2003.

Vol. 2913: T.M. Pinkston, V.K. Prasanna (Eds.), High Performance Computing - HiPC 2003. XX, 512 pages. 2003. (Subseries LNAI).

Vol. 2911: T.M.T. Sembok, H.B. Zaman, H. Chen, S.R. Urs, S.H. Myaeng (Eds.), Digital Libraries: Technology and Management of Indigenous Knowledge for Global Access. XX, 703 pages. 2003.

Vol. 2910: M.E. Orlowska, S. Weerawarana, M.M.P. Papazoglou, J. Yang (Eds.), Service-Oriented Computing - ICSOC 2003. XIV, 576 pages. 2003.

Vol. 2909: R. Solis-Oba, K. Jansen (Eds.), Approximation and Online Algorithms. VIII, 269 pages. 2004.

Vol. 2908: K. Chae, M. Yung (Eds.), Information Security Applications. XII, 506 pages. 2004.

Vol. 2907: I. Lirkov, S. Margenov, J. Wasniewski, P. Yalamov (Eds.), Large-Scale Scientific Computing. XI, 490 pages. 2004.

Vol. 2906: T. Ibaraki, N. Katoh, H. Ono (Eds.), Algorithms and Computation. XVII, 748 pages. 2003.

Vol. 2905: A. Sanfeliu, J. Ruiz-Shulcloper (Eds.), Progress in Pattern Recognition, Speech and Image Analysis. XVII, 693 pages. 2003.

Vol. 2904: T. Johansson, S. Maitra (Eds.), Progress in Cryptology - INDOCRYPT 2003. XI, 431 pages. 2003.

Vol. 2903: T.D. Gedeon, L.C.C. Fung (Eds.), AI 2003: Advances in Artificial Intelligence. XVI, 1075 pages. 2003. (Subseries LNAI).

Vol. 2902: F.M. Pires, S.P. Abreu (Eds.), Progress in Artificial Intelligence. XV, 504 pages. 2003. (Subseries LNAI).

Vol. 2901: F. Bry, N. Henze, J. Ma luszyński (Eds.), Principles and Practice of Semantic Web Reasoning. X, 209 pages. 2003.

Vol. 2900: M. Bidoit, P.D. Mosses (Eds.), Casl User Manual. XIII, 240 pages. 2004.

Vol. 2899: G. Ventre, R. Canonico (Eds.), Interactive Multimedia on Next Generation Networks. XIV, 420 pages. 2003.

Vol. 2898: K.G. Paterson (Ed.), Cryptography and Coding. IX, 385 pages. 2003.

Vol. 2897: O. Balet, G. Subsol, P. Torguet (Eds.), Virtual Storytelling. XI, 240 pages. 2003.

Vol. 2896: V.A. Saraswat (Ed.), Advances in Computing Science – ASIAN 2003. VIII, 305 pages. 2003.

Vol. 2895: A. Ohori (Ed.), Programming Languages and Systems. XIII, 427 pages. 2003.

Vol. 2894: C.S. Laih (Ed.), Advances in Cryptology - ASIACRYPT 2003. XIII, 543 pages. 2003.

Vol. 2893: J.-B. Stefani, I. Demeure, D. Hagimont (Eds.), Distributed Applications and Interoperable Systems. XIII, 311 pages. 2003.

Vol. 2892: F. Dau, The Logic System of Concept Graphs with Negation. XI, 213 pages. 2003. (Subseries LNAI).

Vol. 2891: J. Lee, M. Barley (Eds.), Intelligent Agents and Multi-Agent Systems. X, 215 pages. 2003. (Subseries LNAI).

Vol. 2890: M. Broy, A.V. Zamulin (Eds.), Perspectives of System Informatics. XV, 572 pages. 2003.

Vol. 2889: R. Meersman, Z. Tari (Eds.), On The Move to Meaningful Internet Systems 2003: OTM 2003 Workshops. XIX, 1071 pages. 2003.

Vol. 2888: R. Meersman, Z. Tari, D.C. Schmidt (Eds.), On The Move to Meaningful Internet Systems 2003: CoopIS, DOA, and ODBASE. XXI, 1546 pages. 2003.

Vol. 2887: T. Johansson (Ed.), Fast Software Encryption. IX, 397 pages. 2003.

Vol. 2886: I. Nyström, G. Sanniti di Baja, S. Svensson (Eds.), Discrete Geometry for Computer Imagery. XII, 556 pages. 2003.

Vol. 2885: J.S. Dong, J. Woodcock (Eds.), Formal Methods and Software Engineering. XI, 683 pages. 2003.